THE LETTERS OF
Samuel Johnson

'I will be conquered; I will not capitulate.'
—*Life*, November 1784

Sir

I was not sure that I read your figures right, and therefore must trouble you to set down in words how much of my pension I can now call for, and how much will be due to me at Christmas. I am, Sir,

Your most humble servant

Dec. 7. 1784   Sam. Johnson

JOHNSON'S FAILING HAND. HIS LETTER TO
WILLIAM STRAHAN, 7 DECEMBER 1784 (1042.2)

THE LETTERS OF

Samuel Johnson

WITH MRS. THRALE'S GENUINE LETTERS

TO HIM

Collected & Edited by

R. W. CHAPMAN

Sometime Fellow of Magdalen College
Oxford

VOLUME III: 1783—1784

Letters 821.2–1174

OXFORD

AT THE CLARENDON PRESS

Oxford University Press, Walton Street, Oxford OX2 6DP

London New York Toronto
Delhi Bombay Calcutta Madras Karachi
Kuala Lumpur Singapore Hong Kong Tokyo
Nairobi Dar es Salaam Cape Town
Melbourne Auckland

and associated companies in
Beirut Berlin Ibadan Mexico City Nicosia

Oxford is a trade mark of Oxford University Press

Published in the United States
by Oxford University Press, New York

Copyright Oxford University Press 1952

First published 1952
Reprinted 1984

All rights reserved. No part of this publication may be reproduced,
stored in a retrieval system, or transmitted, in any form or by any means,
electronic, mechanical, photocopying, recording, or otherwise, without
the prior permission of Oxford University Press

British Library Cataloguing in Publication Data

Johnson, Samuel, 1709–1784
The letters of Samuel Johnson.
Vol 3: 1783–1784. Letters 821.2–1174
1. Johnson, Samuel, 1709–1784
2. Authors, English – 18th century –
Biography
I. Title   II. Chapman, R. W. (Robert William)
828'.609   PR3533

ISBN 0-19-818538-3

Printed in Great Britain by
Antony Rowe Ltd,
Chippenham

CONTENTS

VOLUME III

1783–1784

CONTENTS

The curve of the extant letters (i.e. all those to which I have given numbers; some are missing, the date of others is uncertain) may be of some interest.

'19	'31	'32	'34	'35	'37	'38	'40	'41	'42	'43	'44	'46	'49	'50	'51
1	2	1	2	3	1	7	1	2	2	6	1	6	2	3	8

'52	'53	'54	'55	'56	'57	'58	'59	'60	'61	'62	'63	'64	'65	'66	'67
6	9	11	28	31	5	10	22	6	3	11	17	7	17	11	16

'68	'69	'70	'71	'72	'73	'74	'75	'76	'77	'78	'79	'80	'81	'82	'83
23	14	27	37	38	67	41	102	73	80	43	69	76	63	128	160

'84
189

LIST OF ILLUSTRATIONS

vii

ABBREVIATIONS

(See also *Authorities*, i. xv)

I. PERSONS

J(ohnson).

J(ames) B(oswell); C(harles) B(urney), F(rances) B(urney); (Francis Barber is Barber or Frank).

B(ennet) L(angton).

L(ucy) P(orter).

F(rances) R(eynolds), J(oshua) R(eynolds).

J(ohn) T(aylor); H(enry) T(hrale); H(ester) L(ynch) T(hrale) or H L P(iozzi); Q = Hester Maria ('Queeny') Thrale.

J(oseph) W(arton), T(homas) W(arton); A(nna) W(illiams).

II. PLACES

A'n = Ashbourn(e). B'm = Birmingham. B'n = Brighthelmston (Brighton). L'd = Lichfield. L'n = London. O'd = Oxford. S'k = Southwark. S'm = Streatham.

III. DATES

'51 = 1751.

IV. BOOKS, PERIODICALS, ETC.

PM = J's *Prayers and Meditations* 1785. Reprint in *JM* (see below).

Account = *Account of the Life of . . . Johnson . . . by himself* 1805.

L = Boswell's Life of J. Undated references are to Hill–Powell (see i. xvi). Dated references are to 1791(–3, –9), and are followed by a bracketed reference to Hill (i.e. Hill–Powell). Hill standing alone = his edition of the *Letters* 1892.

BP = Boswell's *Private Papers* (see i. xvi).

1788 = HLP's *Letters to and from J.* (HLP = her own copy, Lysons = Samuel L's copy, Malone = Edmond M's copy).

Th = *Thraliana*.

JM = Hill's *Johnsonian Miscellanies* 1897.

C = J. L. Clifford's *Hester Lynch Piozzi (Mrs. Thrale)*.

R i (etc.) = Vol. i (etc.) of A. L. Reade's *Johnsonian Gleanings*; Reades = his *Reades of Blackwood Hill*.

E(nglish) *H*(istorical) *R*(eview); *G*(entleman's) *M*(agazine); *M*(odern) *L*(anguage) *N*(otes); *N*(otes and) *Q*(ueries); *R*(eview of) *E*(nglish) *S*(tudies); *T*(imes) *L*(iterary) *S*(upplement).

Rylands 539, etc. = John Rylands Library English MSS.

VOLUME III
1783–84

821.2. W. 8 Jan. '83. John Perkins.

Address: To Mr Perkins.
O. T. Perkins.—

Dear Sir

I am again in distress for coals and desire you to let me have another Chaldron. The last coals which I had were too inflammable, and burned away too fast. If you will be pleased to give orders that what are now to come should be of a more durable kind, or a mixture of two kinds, they will accommodate me better. Be so kind as to send them soon, for I hear, I am quite out.

Jan 8. 1783

I am, Sir, Your humble Servant,
Sam: Johnson

822. F. 10 Jan. '83. John Nichols.

Address: To Mr Nicol.
B.M.—GM Dec. 1784, 893.

Sir   Jan. 10. 1783
I am much obliged by your kind communication of your account of Hinkley. I knew Mr. Carte as one of the Prebendaries of Lichfield, and for some time Surrogate of the Chancellor. Now I will put you in a way of shewing me more kindness. I have been confined by ilness a long time, and sickness and solitude make tedious evenings. Come sometimes, and see, Sir,

Your humble servant,
Sam: Johnson.

822.—Hill suspected that the date 1783 was a mistake for 1784, on the ground that J, though he had long been ill, had not been long 'confined'; he had dined at CB's on 4 Jan. (FB's *Diary* ii. 227). But *Hinckley* was published late in '82, and it is unlikely that N would delay so long in sending J a copy.

I

823. Th. 16 Jan. '83. John Taylor (Ashbourne).

Address: To the Reverend Dr Taylor in Ashbourne Derbyshire.
Postmark (probably): 16 IA.
A. T. Loyd.—*NQ* 6 S. v. 462.

Dear Sir

I have for some time been labouring under very great disorder of Body, and distress of Mind. I wish that in our latter days we may give some comfort to each other. Let us at least not be angry, nor suppose each other angry. We have no time to lose in petulance. I beg you not to take amiss that I trouble you once more about the Colliers. I have but you and Mr Langley to consult, and him I never have consulted, because you dislike him.

I would shew the Lawyers the papers, but that I know not what questions to ask nor can state the case, till I am informed with regard to some particulars.

What do Miss Colliers suppose will be discovered in the writings?

Had Mr Flint a son by their Mother? I think he has.

What had he with their Mother? I think about 200£ a year.

What do they ask from Mr Flint?

What does he offer them? This you have told me, but my memory is not distinct about it, and I know not how to find your letter. Tell me again.

All that has a bad appearance on Flint's part, is his requisition of a discharge from future claims. If they have no claims what is the discharge? Yet this may be only unskilfulness in him.

I think there is no reason to suppose that Mrs Flint's estate could be settled by her father exclusively upon Collier's Children, or that she should be advised at her marriage with Mr Flint to debar herself from providing for her future children whatever they might be, in their due proportions.

Do answer this, and add what it is necessary for me to know, and I hope to trouble you no more about it. When I have your answer I will transact with Mr Flint and Miss Collier; or with as little trouble to you as I can.

You and I have lived on together to the time of sickness

and weakness. We are now beginning another year; May the merciful God protect us both. Let us not neglect our salvation, but help each other forward in our way as well as we can.

I am, Dear Sir Your affectionate,

London Jan. 16, 1783   Sam: Johnson.

824. Th. 16 Jan. '83. George Strahan (Islington).

Sotheby 11 Feb. 1929.—Hill 1892.

Sir

I had very lately a visit from Mr. Strahan our talk was of you, and I am sure he will tell you that I have never been your enemy. What passed is too long to be written, but if you will call on me to-morrow in Bolt court, where I shall be in the afternoon on purpose to receive you, I hope that Peace may be made.

I am Sir, Your most humble servant,

Thursday Jan. 16. 1783   Sam: Johnson.

825. ⟨? Jan. '83⟩. George Strahan (Islington).

Sotheby 11 Feb. 1929.—Hill 1892.

Sir

You seem to suppose that your Father had some influence on my Letter. You are utterly mistaken. He knows nothing of it. My reason for writing was, if I had done any mischief to undo it as far as I could by good counsel. You have done what I wished to be done, and I have nothing more to recommend. Of promises I know nothing, and have nothing to say.

The conference may perhaps as well be forborn, but if must be, it will probably be made by the presence of others shorter and more moderate; and may therefore do less harm, if it does no good.

Debts of kindness there may be, but surely those debts are not very niggardly paid, when nothing is required but to show that they are wanted.

825.—The MS. is mutilated at the top of the first page, so losing its date. It is very doubtful whether, as Hill believed, it is also mutilated at the foot of the same page, i.e. after the second paragraph. The MS. confirms my conjecture 'presence' for 'pressure'.

I flatter myself that by this time peace and content are restored among you, if not, I wish I could recal them.

I am, Sir, Your humble Servant
Sam: Johnson.

825.1. F. 17 Jan. '83. Mrs. Thrale.

Address: To Mrs Thrale.
Rylands.—R. L. *Bull.* Jan. 1932, 39.

Dearest Lady

I lay last night at my new lodging[1] but it is inconvenient, I shall not go above once or twice more. But I had eleven hours sleep in it, and my Breath is easy; Of this relief I see no other cause than my compliance with Dr Pepys's directions. My Life is certainly lightened of great oppression, and, I hope, will be lengthened.

You shall see to morrow, Madam

Your most &c

Jan. 17. 1783   Sam: Johnson

826. M. 20 Jan. '83. Joseph Cradock.

Address: To Mr Cradock.
Sotheby 18 Nov. 1929.—Cradock's *Memoirs* 1828, i. 243.

Jan. 20. 1783

Mr Johnson is very glad of any intelligence, and much obliged by Mr Cradock's favour and attention. The book which he has now sent shall be taken care of, but of a former book mentioned in the note, Mr Johnson has no remembrance, and can hardly think he ever received it, though bad health may possibly have made him negligent.

825.1.—1. For J's difficulty in going upstairs see 835.1. Perhaps Allen or another neighbour had lent him a bedroom on a ground floor; 'go' seems to imply that it was not in his own house.

826.—Cradock explains that the book was a MS. volume containing poems by James I and others, and belonging to Lord Harborough. When J denied knowledge, C applied to Steevens, who said 'That, then, is the book which now lies under his inkstand; it is neatly packed up, and sealed; and I never was able to make out what it was'.

826.1. M. 20 Jan. '83. Joseph Cradock.

Sotheby 18 Nov. 1929.—

Jan. 20. 1783

Mr Johnson who suspected his own memory is glad to find himself clear. The Book will probably be found, and when found shall be carefully laid up, and thankfully returned.

827. Tu. 21 Jan. '83. John Taylor (Ashbourne).

Address: To the Revd Dr Taylor in Ashbourne Derbyshire. *Postmark*: 21 IA.
A. T. Loyd.—*NQ* 6 S. v. 481.

Dear Sir

I am glad that your friends are not among the promoters of equal representation,[1] which I consider as specious in theory but dangerous in experiment, as equitable in itself, but above human wisdom to be equitably adjusted, and which is now proposed only to distress the government.

An equal representation can never form a constitution because it can have no stability, for whether you regulate the representation by numbers or by property, that which is equal today, will be unequal in a week.

To change the constituent parts of Government must be always dangerous, for who can tell where changes will stop. A new representation will want the reverence of antiquity, and the firmness of Establishment. The new senate will be considered as Mushrooms which springing in a day may be blasted in a night.

What will a parliament chosen in any new manner, whether more or less numerous, do which is not done by such parliaments as we have? Will it be less tumultuous if we have more, or less mercenary if we have fewer? There is no danger that the parliament as now chosen should betray any of our important rights, and that is all that we can wish.

If the scheme were more reasonable this is not a time for

827.—1. Hill quotes Walpole, Burke, Gibbon, and Fox, who all, like JT's Whig friends, regarded Pitt's proposals as hazardous.

innovation. I am afraid of a civil war. The business of every wise man seems to be now to keep his ground.

I am very glad you are coming.

Jan. 21, 1783

I am &c.
Sam: Johnson.

827.1. W. 22 Jan. '83. ———.

Harvard.—

Sir

You once gave me hope that you could procure me a large packet sent to me from the East Indies some years ago, which being landed at Lisbon and sent by the packet was charged, as I remember, seven pounds ten shillings, a larger sum than it was convenient for me to pay for intelligence. I have now particular want of it, and if by the great indulgence of your office it be granted me, it will be a high favour to, Sir,

Your most humble servant

Jan. 22. 1783

Sam: Johnson

827.2. *c.* 4 Feb. '83. James Boswell (Edinburgh).

Not traced.—Boswell 1791, ii. 431, extract (Hill iv. 163; overlooked in *Letters*).

I am delighted with your account of your activity at Auchinleck, and wish the old gentleman,[1] whom you have so kindly removed, may live long to promote your prosperity by his prayers. You have now a new character and new duties: think on them, and practise them.

827.1.—We know just what happened, and J's memory as usual served him well. It was on 5 April '76, in JB's presence, that the 'large packet' from Lisbon, charged £7. 10s. 0d., was offered and rejected. 'But upon enquiry afterwards he found that it was a real packet for him, from that very friend in the East-Indies of whom he had been speaking.' *L* iii. 20, 22. The friend was Joseph Fowke (*BP* xi. 227, quoted *L* iii. 471). Whether J recovered the packet JB does not record. The packet might contain the 'letters' of 834; see also 495.

827.2.—'Having given Dr. Johnson a full account of what I was doing at Auchinleck, and particularly mentioned what I knew would please him,—my having brought an old man of eighty-eight from a lonely cottage to a comfortable habitation within my enclosures, where 'he had good neighbours near to him,—I received an answer in February, of which I extract what follows.'

JB's letter of 11 Jan.—a belated answer to 815—is not mentioned in his journal, though he there (5 Jan., written 19 Jan.) mentions his care of the old man (*BP* xv. 144, quoted *L* iv. 508). The date of 827.2 depends on JB's record of its receipt 8 Feb. (*BP* xv. 154). 1. John Colvil (*BP* xv. 144).

Make an impartial estimate of your revenue, and whatever
it is, live upon less. Resolve never to be poor. Frugality is
not only the basis of quiet, but of beneficence. No man can
help others that wants help himself; we must have enough
before we have to spare.

I am glad to find that Mrs. Boswell grows well; and hope
that to keep her well, no care nor caution will be omitted.
May you long live happily together.

When you come hither, pray bring with you Baxter's
Anacreon.[1] I cannot get that edition in London.

828. Tu. 4 Feb. '83. Elizabeth Lawrence (Canterbury).

Address: To Mrs Eliz Laurence in Castle Street Canterbury.
Adam; copy by E. L., Isham.—Boswell 1791, ii. 419 (Hill iv. 144).

Madam

Though the account with which you favoured me in your
last letter could not give the pleasure that I wished, yet I was
glad to receive it, for my affection for my dear friend makes
me desirous of knowing his state, whatever it be.

I beg therefore that you continue to let me know from
time to time all that you observe.

Many fits of severe ilness have for about twelve months
past found my kind Physician often upon my mind. I am
now better, and hope gratitude as well as distress can be a
motive to remembrance.

I am afraid to ask questions, yet I am very desirous to
know what you think of his memory and his judgement, and
whether he is silent for want of words, or by having lost the
power of utterance. Does he grow stronger or weaker? is he
more or less attentive to things about him? Dear Madam
let me know what is to be known; write at leisure and write
at large.

I am, Madam Your most humble servant
Febr. 4. 1783   Sam: Johnson
Bolt court. Fleet street

827.2.—1. See 888, 942, and references in *L* iv. 163. Mr. Reade has pointed out that
it is odd J should forget his own possession, when an undergraduate, of 'Anacreon per
Baxter'. But there were two editions, and Mr. R. suggests that it was the second J
failed to find. Why he should seek it in Cambridge, rather than in Oxford, is another
puzzle. But he might be prompted by recollection of Barnes, the Cambridge professor, who was Baxter's rival as an editor of Anacreon.

828.1. M. 10 Feb. '83. Herbert Croft.

Address: To Mr Crofts.
B.M.—Croker's Boswell 1831, v. 41.

Dear Sir   Febr. 10. 1783
    It was not insensibility of your kindness, I hope, that made me negligent of answering your letter, for which I now return you thanks, and which I consider as a strong proof of your regard.
    I am better, much better, and am now in hope of being gradually well and of being able ⟨to⟩ shew some gratitude for the kindness of my friends. I do not despair of seeing Oxford in the Summer, and, in the mean time, hope now and then to see you here.
                            I am, Dear Sir, Your most obliged
                                                    Sam: Johnson.

828.2. Sa. 15 Feb. '83. ——.

F. N. Pleadwell; a fragment, the subscription only.—

                            Your most humble servant,
Saturday, Febr. 15. 1783   Sam: Johnson

828.3. M. 17 ⟨? Feb. or Mar. '83⟩. Hester Maria Thrale.

Address: To Miss Thrale No 37 Argyle Street. *Postmark* illegible.
Adam.—Hill, *JM* 1897, ii. 451.

Dearest Love
    I am engaged to dinner to morrow, of which I forgot to tell you, but I hope you will favour me with a call early on Wednesday.
                    I am, dearest, Your most humble servant
Monday. 17th   Sam: Johnson
Monday nine in the morning

828.3.—In '83 the 17th was a Monday in Feb., Mar., and Nov. FB fails us here, her Diary being blank for the dates.

829. W. 19 Feb. '83. Joshua Reynolds.

Address: To Sir Joshua Reynolds.

F. W. Hilles.—W. Cotton, *Sir Joshua Reynolds and his Works*, 1856.

Sir

Mr Mason's address[1] to you deserves no great praise it is lax without easiness, and familiar without gayety. Of his Translation I think much more favourably, so far as I have read, which is not a great part, I find him better than exact, he has his authours distinctness and clearness, without his dryness and sterility.

As I suspect you to have lost your Lives,[2] I desire you to accept of these volumes and to keep them somewhere out of harm's way; that you may sometimes remember the writer.

I am, Sir, Your most humble servant

Febr. 19. 1783.   Sam: Johnson

830. Tu. 4 Mar. '83. Joshua Reynolds.

Hodgson 15 Dec. 1917, 92 (not seen); facsimile of p. 1 (to 'page clear') A. M. Broadley, *Chats on Autographs* 1910, 74.—Crabbe's *Poems* 1807, the *Preface*.

Sir

I have sent You back Mr. Crabb's poem which I read with great delight. It is original, vigorous, and elegant.

The alterations which I have made, I do not require him to adopt, for my lines are perhaps not often better ⟨than⟩ his own, but he may take mine and his own together, and perhaps between them produce something better than either.

He is not to think his copy wantonly defaced. A wet

829.—1. The dedication of Mason's translation of Du Fresnoy's *Art of Painting*. J is no doubt thanking JR for a copy.

2. J's suspicion was unjust. The Reynolds family preserved both his set of the *Prefaces* (with this letter, to which they were erroneously thought to pertain) and his set of the 1783 edition. All three are now assembled in Mr. Hilles's collection.

830.—For JR's report of J's praise of *The Village* see C's preface (quoted *L* iv. 509); for JR's letter to C, *L* loc. cit. JR's letter is dated 4 Mar., see facsimile in Broadley, op. cit. 274; Broadley owned also J's letter, but his facsimile does not include the date. If the dates are right—and there is no reason to suspect them—we must suppose that C sent his MS. to J a second time; for JB on 25 Mar. 'read to him [JR] and Miss Palmer a good part of a Poem called *The Village* by a Mr. Crabbe, which had been revised by Dr. Johnson. . . . I got the Poem home with me and copied all the Doctor's fragments.' *BP* xv. 184.

Sponge will wash all the red lines away, and leave the page clear.

His Dedication will be least liked: it were better to contract it into a short sprightly Address.—I do not doubt of Mr. Crabbe's success.

I am, Sir, your most humble servant,
March 4, 1783.   Sam: Johnson.

831. Tu. 4 Mar. '83. William Scott.

Not traced; known to Hill from Christie's Catalogue 5 June 1888; also in Sotheby 4 Feb. 1876.—Extract in both catalogues.

'Asking him to give employment to a young man' for whom I am interested.
He is not without literature, and I hope he will be diligent.

831.1. Sa. 22 (perhaps Su. 23) Mar. '83. Mrs. Thrale.

Address: To Mrs Thrale.
Rylands.—R. L. *Bull.* Jan. 1932, 40.

Dear Madam
I hope you did not take cold with me, and however you took it, I hope it will be soon better. I have already taken all Dr Pepys's pills, which have acted only as opiate, and have not exerted that power in any great degree. Ask his leave that if I find a cathartick necessary I may take it.

I am, I think, recovering. Mr Langton is in town with Lady Rothes. I am invited to meet them to morrow, but will not venture.

I hope, Harriet is well, and all of you.

I am Dear Madam, &c
March 22 (? 23). 1783   Sam: Johnson
Dr Hunter is dying.

831.—Hill, influenced no doubt by the date of this letter, which is the same as that of 830, conjectured that the 'young man' was Crabbe. But 'not without literature' is faint praise; J was much struck with C's literature.

831.2. Su. 30 Mar. '83. Mrs. Thrale.

Address: To Mrs. Thrale.
Rylands.—R. L. *Bull.* Jan. 1932, 40.

Madam

Pray let me know how my dear little Miss[1] does. That is the most pressing question, but as an Episode you may let me know how any of you do.

My *Arthritical* complaints, there's a nice word, rather encrease, but are not yet, as the Scotch say *serious*.[2] I took the poppy last night, and slept so well this morning, as I have not done for some time past. Such a sleep I had as I wish you to have, whenever you are in good humour with

Your humble servant

March 30. 1783   Sam: Johnson

831.3. M. 31 Mar. '83. Mrs. Thrale.

Address: To Mrs Thrale.
Rylands.—R. L. *Bull.* Jan. 1932, 41.

Dear Madam

I hope to hear again that my dear little girl is out of danger. It will now be pleasing to consider that she and her sister[1] have past two of the ambushes of life, and that you may leave them at a distance with less anxiety.

I am willing to think that lightened, as you are, of part of your load,[2] you will bear the rest with less difficulty, and recover your health as you recover your quiet.

My foot is neither better nor worse, the rest of me is rather better.

I am, Madam, Your humble servant,

Bolt court.   Sam: Johnson
March 31. 1783

831.2.—1. Harriet.

2. I cannot explain this. Mr. Wright notes that J may possibly have written 'ferious', which is a Scots dialect form of 'furious'. He notes also that *OED* has no example of 'serious' applied to illness before 1800.

831.3.—1. Harriet and Cecilia.

2. See *Th* 561 (6 and 14 Apr.). She had at last settled Lady Salusbury's claim, and soon retired to Bath to live cheaply. This is the last letter before her departure; he said good-bye to her on 5 Apr., and it is not certain (see 963) that they ever again met. The evidence for this 'crisis' in their lives will be found in *PM* for 5 Apr., *Th*, *L* iv. 164, *BP* xv. 174, C 219–20.

832. Sa. 12 Apr. '83. Joshua Reynolds.

Not traced; copy by JB, Isham.—Boswell 1791, ii. 443 (Hill iv. 201); Northcote, *Reynolds* 1813, 295, perhaps from the original ('which letter I have seen').

Sir

Mr. Lowe considers himself as cut off from all credit and all hope by the rejection of his picture from the exhibition. Upon this work he has exhausted all his powers and suspended all his expectations: and certainly to be refused an opportunity of taking the opinion of the publick is in itself a very great hardship. It is to be condemned without a trial.

If you could procure the revocation of this incapacitating edict you would deliver an unhappy man from great affliction. The council has sometimes reversed its own determination[1] and I hope that by your interposition this luckless picture may be got[2] admitted. I am Sir your most humble servant
April 12 1783.   Sam. Johnson.

833. Sa. 12 Apr. '83. James Barry.

Not traced; copy by JB, Isham.—Boswell 1791, ii. 443 (Hill iv. 202).

Sir

Mr. Lowes exclusion from the Exhibition gives him more trouble than you and the other Gentlemen of the Council could imagine or intend. He considers disgrace and ruin as the inevitable consequence of your determination.

He says that some pictures have been received after rejection and if there be any such precedent I earnestly intreat that you will use your interest in his favour. Of his work I

832.—JB explains, of this and 833, that J 'gave Mr. Lowe the following, of which I was diligent enough, with his permission, to take copies at the next coffee-house'. He adds: 'Such intercession was too powerful to be resisted; and Mr. Lowe's performance was admitted at Somerset Place.' Hill quotes Northcote (*Reynolds* ii. 141): 'it was execrable beyond belief.'

　　1. 'determinations' 1813.

　　2. 'got admitted' is not I think Johnsonian English. I have no doubt that he wrote 'yet'. In 223, where the MS. has 'yet', Hill read 'got'. See also *Journey* 299 (116 in my edition): 'There are tenants below the rank of Tacksmen, who have got smaller tenants under them.'

can say nothing I pretend not to judge of painting and this picture I never saw but I conceive it extremely hard to shut out any man from the possibility of success and therefore I repeat my request that you will propose the reconsideration of Mr. Lowe's case, and if there be any among the Council with whom my name can have any weight be pleased to communicate to them the desire of Sir Your most humble servant, Apr 12, 1783.   Sam. Johnson.

833.1. *c.* 12 Apr. '83. Lucy Porter (Lichfield).

Not traced.—Boswell 1791, ii. 443, extract (Hill iv. 203; overlooked in *Letters*).

It is with no great expectation of amendment that I make every year a journey into the country; but it is pleasant to visit those whose kindness has been often experienced.

833.2. W. 16 Apr. ⟨'83⟩. Thomas Cadell.

Address: To Mr Cadel.
Huntington.—

Mr Johnson begs the favour of Mr Cadel that he will order three sets of lives to be tied up separately with these directions.

To the Honourable Warren Hastings Esq. Governor general of Bengal.

To Sir Robert Chambers.

To Joseph Fowke Esq.

and then let them all be put into one parcel,[1] which Mr Johnson will send for to morrow.

Apr. 16.

833.1.—The date depends on JB, who says J wrote 'about this time' and inserts his quotation between his record of 12 Apr. and his record of 18 Apr.

833.2.—1. The letters to Chambers and Fowke show that the whole was consigned to C for distribution. The parcel no doubt included a letter to Hastings, of which we deplore the loss.

833.2a. Bath. F. 18 and Sa. 19 Apr. ⟨'83⟩. From Mrs. Thrale.

Address: To Dʳ Sam: Johnson Bolt Court Fleet Street London.
Postmark: 21 AP.
R 540.108.—

Good Fryday Night.
My Children, my Income (of course) and my health are coming to an end
Dear Sir—not my Vexations. Harriet is dead, and Ciceley is dying; and Mʳ
Cator writes me word I must'nt sit *philosophically* at Bath, but come to London—(I cannot guess for what) to see them buried I believe.—I am already so
altered that the people here don't know me—my *Philosophy* has not therefore
benefited my Complexion at least—but like Tasso one should learn from it to
bear with *them*. I am sorry for you dear Sir with all the Grief I can spare from
your much distressed Servant

H: L: T.

Sat: Mornᵍ. I have just taken a Vomit, & just received your Letter; I will
set out the first Moment I am able.

833.3. W. 16 Apr. '83. Thomas Lawrence.

Maggs Catalogue 337 (1915) 796 (not seen).—Extract in catalogue.

Since your departure I have often wanted your assistance
as well as your conversation. I have been very ill, but am
now better, and it would be a great comfort added to my
recovery if I could hear that you are better too.
We can now do nothing more than pray for one another.
God bless for Christ's sake.

834. Sa. 19 Apr. '83. Joseph Fowke.

Not traced; copy by Thomas Harwood, *c.* 1820, at Pembroke.—
Rebecca Warner, *Original Letters* 1817, 207.

Dear Sir   *April* 19, 1783.
To shew you that neither length of time, nor distance of
place, withdraws you from my memory, I have sent you a
little present, which will be transmitted by Sir Rob.
Chambers.

833.2a.—It is unfortunate for Mrs. Piozzi's reputation that this undignified outburst
has survived, since we are able to compare it with the revised version (undated, but
containing the words 'This is Good Friday night') published in 1788 (No. 294)—
itself not a dignified letter. See C 220, 301, *Th* 563. I note, however, that the remark
about the funeral is excused by the manners of the age; see on 717.

To your former letters[1] I made no answer, because I had none to make. Of the death of the unfortunate man,[2] I believe Europe thinks as you think; but it was past prevention; and it was not fit for me to move a question in public, which I was not qualified to discuss; as the enquiry could then do no good, and I might have been silenced by a hardy denial of facts, which, if denied, I could not prove.

Since we parted, I have suffered much sickness of body, and perturbation of mind. My mind, if I do not flatter myself, is unimpaired, except that sometimes my memory is less ready; but my body, though by nature very strong, has given way to repeated shocks.

Genua labant, vastos quatit æger anhelitus artus.[3] This line might have been written on purpose for me. You will see, however, that I have not totally forsaken literature. I can apply better to books than I could in some more vigorous parts of my life, at least than I *did*; and I have one more reason for reading; that time has, by taking away my companions, left me less opportunity of conversation.[4] I have led an inactive and careless life; it is time at last to be diligent. There is yet provision to be made for eternity.

Let me know, dear Sir, what you are doing. Are you accumulating gold, or picking up diamonds? Or are you now sated with Indian wealth, and content with what you have? Have you vigour for bustle, or tranquillity for inaction? Whatever you do, I do not suspect you of pillaging or oppressing; and shall rejoice to see you return, with a body unbroken, and a mind uncorrupted.

You and I had hardly any common friends; and, therefore, I have few anecdotes to relate to you. Mr. Levet, who brought us into acquaintance, died suddenly at my house last year, in his seventy-eighth year, or about that age. Mrs. Williams, the blind lady, is still with me, but much broken by a very wearisome and obstinate disease. She is, however, not likely to die; and it would delight me, if you would send

834.—1. See on 495 and 827.1.

2. Warner, followed by Harwood, prints here '(meaning Nundocomar)' in the text. (He is now better known as Nuncomar.) Probably, therefore, Harwood's copy was made from the print of 1817 and has no value.

3. Virgil, *Aen.* v. 432: 'Knees totter, sick panting shakes huge limbs.'

4. Hill collates a number of references for J's reading-habits. See also *L* vi. 208.

her some *petty* token of your remembrance. You may send me one too.

Whether we shall ever meet again in this world, who can tell? Let us, however, wish well to each other. Prayers can pass the line, and the Tropics.

I am, dear Sir, Yours sincerely,[5]
Sam: Johnson.

835. Sa. 19 Apr. '83. The Mercers' Company.

Address (Malone): To the Worshipful Company of the Mercers. Not traced.—Malone's Boswell 1811, iv. 226.

Gentlemen,

At the request of the Reverend Mr. James Compton, who now solicits your votes to be elected Under-Master of St. Paul's School, I testify, with great sincerity, that he is in my opinion, a man of abilities sufficient, and more than sufficient, for the duties of the office for which he is a candidate.

I am, Gentlemen, Your most humble servant,
Bolt-court, Fleet-street, April 19, 1783. Sam: Johnson.

835.1. Sa. 19 Apr. '83. Robert Chambers (Calcutta).

Adam.—

Dear Sir

Of the books which I now send you I sent you the first edition, but it fell by the chance of war into the hands of the French. I sent[1] likewise to Mr. Hastings. Be pleased to have these parcels properly delivered.

Removed as We are with so much land and sea between us, We ought to compensate the difficulty of correspondence by the length[2] of our letters, yet searching my memory, I do not ⟨find⟩ much to communicate. Of all publick transactions you have more exact accounts than I can give; you know our

834.—5. Hill calls the subscription unique; he overlooked 'sincerely yours' 847.

835.1.—1. I have verified that J wrote 'sent' not 'send'. Unless 'sent' is a slip, we must suppose that on the former occasion, as on this, J had sent both sets to C in one consignment. See 834.

2. Mr. Adam printed a photographic facsimile of this letter, which is six pages folio. Except 206 to Barnard, and some of the letters from the Hebrides, it is, I think, the longest extant letter.

foreign miscarriages and our intestine discontents, and do not want to be told that we have now neither power nor peace, neither influence in other nations nor quiet amongst ourselves. The state of the Publick, and the operations of government have little influence upon the private happiness of private men, nor can I pretend that much of the national calamities is felt by me; yet I cannot but suffer some pain when I compare the state of this Kingdom, with that in which we triumphed twenty years ago. I have at least endeavoured to preserve order and support Monarchy.

Having been thus allured to the mention of myself, I shall give you a little of my story. That dreadful ilness[3] which seized me at New inn Hall, left consequences which have I think always hung upon me. I have never since cared much to walk. My mental abilities I do not perceive that it impaired. One great abatement of all miseries was the attention of Mr. Thrale,[4] which from our first acquaintance was never intermitted. I passed far the greater part of many years in his house where I had all the pleasure of riches without the solicitude. He took me into France one year, and into Wales another, and if he had lived would have shown me Italy and perhaps many other countries, but he died in the spring of eighty one, and left me to write his epitaph.[5]

But for much of this time my constitutional maladies persued me. My thoughts were disturbed, my nights were insufferably restless, and by spasms in the breast I was condemned to the torture of sleepyness without the power to sleep. These spasms after enduring them more than twenty years I eased by three powerful remedies, abstinence, opium, and mercury, but after a short time they were succeeded by a strange oppression of another kind which when I lay down disturbed me with a sensation like flatulence or intumescence which I cannot describe. To this supervened a difficulty of respiration, such as sometimes makes it painful to cross a street or climb to my chambers; which I have eased by venisection till the Physician forbids me to bleed, as my legs have begun to swel. Almost all the last year past in a succession of diseases ἐκ κακῶν κακά,[6] and this year till within

835.1.—3. See on 358.   4. C, who knew HLT, would be struck by J's silence.
5. See Index VI.   6. 'Evil upon evil.'

these few days has heaped misery upon me. I have just now a lucid interval.

With these afflictions, I have the common accidents of life to suffer. He that lives long must outlive many, and I am now sometimes to seek for friends of easy conversation and familiar confidence. Mrs. Williams is much worn; Mr. Levet died suddenly in my house about a year ago. Doctor Lawrence is totally disabled by a palsy, and can neither speak nor write. He is removed to Canterbury. Beauclerc died about two years ago and in his last sickness desired to be buried by the side of his Mother. Langton has eight children by Lady Rothes. He lives very little in London, and is by no means at ease. Goldsmith died partly of a fever and partly of anxiety, being immoderately and disgracefully in debt. Dier lost his fortune by dealing in the East India stock, and, I fear, languished into the grave. Boswels father is lately dead, but has left the estate incumbered; Boswel has, I think, five children. He is now paying us his annual visit, he is all that he was, and more. Doctor Scot prospers exceedingly in the commons, but I seldom see him; He is married and has a Daughter.

Jones now Sir William, will give you the present state of the club, which is now very miscellaneous, and very heterogeneous it is therefore without confidence, and without pleasure. I go to it only as to a kind of publick dinner. Reynolds continues to rise in reputation and in riches, but his health has been shaken. Dr. Percy is now Bishop of Dromore, but has I believe lost his only son.[7] Such are the deductions from human happiness.

I have now reached an age which is to expect many diminutions of the good, whatever it be, that life affords; I have lost many friends, I am now either afflicted or threatened by many diseases, but perhaps not with more than are commonly incident to encrease of years, and I am afraid that I bear the weight of time with unseemly, if not with sinful impatience. I hope that God will enable me to correct this as well as my other faults, before he calls me to appear before him.

In return for this history of myself I shall expect some

835.1.—7. P's only, or only surviving, son, 'said to have been a youth of great promise', died at Marseilles this year (*DNB*).

account of you, who by your situation have much more to tell. I hope to hear that the Ladies[8] and the Children are all well, and that your constitution accommodates itself easily to the climate. If you have health, you may study, and if you can study, you will surely not miss the opportunity which place and power give you, beyond what any Englishman qualified by previous knowledge, ever enjoyed before, of enquiring into Asiatick Literature. Buy manuscripts, consult the Scholars of the country, learn the languages, at least select one, and master it. To the Malabarick Books Europe is, I think, yet a Stranger. But my advice comes late; what you purpose to do, you have already begun, but in all your good purposes persevere. Life is short, and you do not intend to pass all your life in India.

How long you will stay, I cannot conjecture. The effects of English Judicature are not believed here to have added any thing to the happiness of the new dominions. Of you, Sir, I rejoice to say that I have heard no evil. There was a trifling charge produced in parliament, but it seems to be forgotten, nor did it appear to imply any thing very blamable. This purity of character you will, I hope continue to retain. One of my last wishes for you, at a gay table was ἀρετήν τε καὶ ὀλβόν.[9] Let me now add in a more serious hour, and in more powerful words—Keep innocency, and take heed to the thing that is right, for that shall bring a Man peace at the last.[10]

I shall think myself favoured by any help that ⟨you⟩ shall give to Mr. Joseph Fowke, or Mr. Lawrence. Fowke was always friendly to me, and Lawrence is the son of a Man, whom I have long placed in the first rank of my friends. Do not let my recommendation be without effect.

Let me now mention an occasion on which you may perhaps do great good without evil to yourself. Langton is much embarrassed by a mortgage made, I think, by his grandfather, and perhaps aggravated by his father. The Creditor calls for his money, and it is in the present general distress very difficult to make a *versura*.[11] If you could let

835.1.—8. C's mother and wife were both with him.
9. ὀλβόν should be ὄλβον: 'virtue and wealth'. Homeric *Hymn* 15.
10. Psalm xxxvii. 38 (Prayer Book version).
11. 'transfer' to a new mortgagee.

him have six thousand pounds upon the security of the same land, you would save him from the necessity of selling part of his Estate under the great disadvantage produced by the present high price of money. This proposal needs give you no pain, for Langton knows nothing of it, and may perhaps have settled his affairs before the answer can be received. As the security is good, you should not take more than four per cent.

Nothing now, I think, remains but that I assure you, as I do, of my kindness, and good wishes, and express my hopes that you do not forget

Your old Friend and humble servant,

Bolt court, Fleetstreet. Apr. 19. 1783   Sam: Johnson.

Mr. Langton, who is just come in,
sends his best respects.
but he knows still nothing.

835.2. W. 23 Apr. '83. ——. ⟨Elizabeth Way.⟩

J. F Roxburgh (see Addenda).

Dear Madam

I have been so long oppressed by illness, that my Friends must forgive many omissions. I am now better, and am desirous of clearing myself from all appearance of incivility and ingratitude by returning thanks for the elegant pocket book, which you have been pleased to send me, and which I shall look and think on with emotions of tenderness. I am, Dear Madam, Your most obliged humble Servant,

Apr: 23. 1783.   Sam: Johnson

836. F. 25 Apr. '83. The Earl of Dartmouth.

Not traced.—Hist. MSS. Commission 1887, *Dartmouth*, xi. App. v. 447.

My Lord   April 25, 1783.

The bearer, Mr. Desmoulins, has persuaded himself that some testimonial from me will be useful to him in his application to your Lordship, and I hope that what I yield merely to his importunity will not be imputed to any vain conceit of my own importance.

He desires indeed nothing to be said but what is true; that

he is not in difficulties by his own fault; that he has a brother and sister in great distress, and that if he should by your Lordship's favour now obtain any little employment, he will, I hope, do the business faithfully, and use the income properly.

I am, my Lord, Your Lordship's most obedient and most humble servant,

Sam: Johnson.

836.1. Sa. 26 Apr. '83. Hester Maria Thrale (Bath).

Address: To Miss Thrale at Bath.
Lansdowne.—Lansdowne, *Johnson and Queeney* 1932, 29.

My dearest Love,   London, April 26, 1783
    You did very kindly in writing to me and I hope you will let me hear of you very often. You have done very wisely in taking a master for arithmetick, a science of which I would not have you soon think that you have enough. It will seem at first difficult, but you will soon find its usefulness so great that you will disregard the difficulty; and the progress will be easier than the beginning. Do not be content with what a single master dictates, but procure books: different authours exhibit the same thing in different views, and what is obscure in one, may be clear in another. When you can readily apply numbers on emergent occasions, you will find yourself to think with so much clearness and certainty that the pleasure of arithmetick will attract you almost as much as the use.

    I am not quite well, but so much better that the sight of me raises wonder. The cough goes and comes, but is not violent, I breathe with tolerable freedom, and the pain in my foot is gone. I may perhaps, with a little caution, have an easy summer. In the winter I shall envy my friend Ramsay's residence.[1]

    The storms of life have for some time beaten hard upon us. I hope, we are all now in port, and glad to find ourselves out of the tumult, *though sails and tackling torn*.[2] Make my compliments.

                    I am, Madam, Your humble servant
                                        Sam: Johnson

836.1.—1. R was in Naples. 2. *Richard III*, iv. iv. 234: 'of sails and tackling reft'. But, as Dr. Pottle points out, J remembered also *P.L.* ii. 1044 'shrouds and tackle torn'.

837. Th. 1 May '83. Mrs. Thrale (Bath).

Address: To Mrs Thrale at Bath. *Postmark*: 1 MA.
Adam.—1788, No. 295.

Dear Madam

I am glad that you went to Streatham, though you could not save the dear, pretty, little girl. I loved her, for She was Thrale's and your's, and by her dear Father's appointment in some sort mine;[1] I love you all, and therefore cannot without regret see the phalanx broken, and reflect that You and my other dear Girls are deprived of one that was born your friend. To such friends every one that has them, has recourse at last, when it is discovered, and discovered it seldom fails to be, that the fortuitous friendships of inclination or vanity are at the mercy of a thousand accidents. But we must still our disquiet with remembring that, where there is no guilt, all is for the best. I am glad to hear that Cecily is so near recovery.

For some days after your departure I was pretty well, but I have begun to languish again, and last night was very tedious and oppressive. I excused myself today from dining with General Paoli, where I love to dine, but I was griped by the talons of necessity.[2]

On Saturday I dined, as is usual, at the opening of the exhibition. Our company was splendid, whether more numerous[3] than at any former time, I know not. Our Tables seem always full. On monday, if I am told truth, were received at the door one hundred and ninety pounds, for the admission of three thousand eight hundred Spectators. Supposing the show open ten hours, and the Spectators staying one with another each an hour, the rooms never had fewer than three hundred and eighty justling each other. Poor Lowe met some discouragement, but I interposed for him, and prevailed.[4]

837.—HLT in 833.2*a* had thanked J for a (lost) letter, reported Harriet's death, and announced her intention of coming to London. J received this letter on 21 Apr., and must have had another before he wrote 837; for in 833.2*a* she had written 'Ciceley is dying'.   1. J was one of the guardians.

2. Not, I think, a quotation. *OED* quotes 'the talons of necessity' from the 113th *Rambler*.

3. 'It was more numerous; 80 (at 8s.) against 57 in 1781.' Leslie and Taylor, *Reynolds*, ii. 397.

4. The picture, 'execrable beyond belief', was hung in an otherwise empty room. Northcote's *Reynolds*, ii. 141 in the 8vo edition.

Mr Barry's exhibition was opened the same day, and a book[5] is published to recommend it, which, if you read it, you will find decorated with some satirical pictures of Sir Joshua and others. I have not escaped.[6] You must however think with some esteem of Barry for the comprehension of his design.

I am, Madam, Your most humble servant

May day 1783 London. Sam: Johnson

838. F. 2 May '83. Joshua Reynolds.

Not traced.—Boswell 1793, iii. 474 (Hill iv. 219).

Dear Sir,
The gentleman who waits on you with this, is Mr. Cruikshanks,[1] who wishes to succeed his friend Dr. Hunter as Professor of Anatomy in the Royal Academy. His qualifications are very generally known, and it adds dignity to the institution that such men[2] are candidates.

I am, Sir, Your most humble servant,

May 2, 1783. Sam. Johnson.

839. Th. 8 May '83. Mrs. Thrale (Bath).

Address: To Mrs Thrale at Bath. *Postmark*: — MA.
Adam.—1788, No. 296.

Dear Madam
I thought your letter long in coming. I suppose it is true

<hr/>

837.—5. *An Account of a Series of Pictures in the Great Room of the Society of Arts*, 1783.
6. The eulogy of J which Hill quotes from B's book cannot be held to imply any censure which J did not 'escape'. But there are two passages which may have provoked J's comment. On p. 13 Barry derides 'those dispensers of fame, the book-makers', as ignorant of his art. The bad pictures they commend are indeed 'made with paint'; and this enables us to 'account for the mistake of many of our short-sighted literati'. The last phrase would naturally be thought to point at J. On p. 74 B describes his picture, 'The Distribution of Premiums in the Society of Arts', in which he portrayed among others Mrs. Montagu and the Duchesses of Devonshire and Rutland. Between the two duchesses he 'placed that venerable sage, Dr. Samuel Johnson, who is pointing out this example of Mrs. Montagu, as a matter well worthy their grace's (*sic*) most serious attention and imitation'. Then follows the passage quoted by Hill. See also *L* iv. 224.

838.—1. Cruikshank. He was not elected. *L* iv. 219.
2. 'Let it be remembered by those who accuse Dr. Johnson of illiberality, that both were *Scotchmen*.' JB.

that I looked but languid at the exhibition, but I have been worse since. The Wednesday[1] of last week, I came home ill from Mr. Jodrels, and after a tedious oppressive impatient night, sent an excuse to General Paoli, and took on thursday, two brisk catharticks, and a dose of calomel. Little things do me no good. At night I was much better.[2] Next day cathartick again, and the third day opium for my cough. I lived without flesh, all the three days. The recovery was more than I expected. I went to church on Sunday quite at ease.

The exhibition prospers so much that Sir Joshua says it will maintain the academy, he estimates the probable amount at three thousand pounds. Steevens is of opinion that Crofts's books will sell for near three times as much as they cost, which however is not more than might be expected.[3]

Favour me with a direction to Musgrave[4] of Ireland, I have a charitable office to propose to him. Is he Knight or Baronet?

My present circle of enjoyment is as narrow for me as the circus[5] for Mrs. Montague. When I first settled in this neighbourhood I had Richardson, and Lawrence, and Mrs Allen[6] at hand, I had Mrs Williams then no bad companion, and Levet for a long time always to be had. If I now go out I must go far for company, and at last come back to two sick and discontented women, who can hardly talk, if they had any thing to say, and whose hatred of each other makes one great exercise of their faculties.

But, with all these evils positive and privative, my health in its present humour promises to mend, and I, in my present humour, promise to take care of it, and, if we both keep our words, we may yet have a brush at the cobwebs in the sky.[7]

839.—1. J wrote 'Last Wednesday' and corrected this above the line to 'The Wednesday of last week'. 1788 prints both.

2. J was at the top of his form on the evening of 1 May, see *L* iv. 217.

3. Here two lines are heavily erased and covered with a piece of paper pasted on. See Addenda, p. 336.

4. Musgrave was an Irishman; it is natural to suppose that the 'charitable office' was that proposed to Windham in 841.

5. The Circus at Bath, close to the Royal Crescent. The houses in both are admirable.

6. Malone in his copy of 1788 corrects this to 'Mr. Allen'. It seems unlikely that J would give him a 'Mr.' denied to Richardson and Lawrence; and see 857: 'Mrs. Allen is dead.' I do not know when she died. Her husband was in '83 still 'at hand'. J therefore meant what he wrote.   7. See on 561.

Let my dear Loves write to me, and do you write often
yourself to,
Dear Madam, Your most obliged and most humble
servant
May 8. 1783 London   Sam: Johnson

839.1. Th. 22 May '83. Hester Maria Thrale (Bath).

Address: To Miss Thrale at Bath.
Lansdowne.—Lansdowne, *Johnson and Queeney* 1932, 31.

My dearest Love,   London, May 22, 1783
    What a terrible accident![1] How easily might it have been
yet more mischievous. I hope my Mistress's hurt is neither
of any danger nor of much pain. It teaches however, what
though every thing teaches, is yet always forgotten, that we
are perpetually within the reach of death.
    I am glad that you have settled your mind to arithmetick,
a species of knowledge perpetually useful, and indubitably
certain. Do not content yourself with your master's lessons,
but buy the books which treat of numbers, such as Cocker's,
Hodder's, and Wingate's Arithmetick, and any other which
every shop or stall will put in your way. Every writer will
shew you something which you did not know, or did not
recollect.
    Last week I was on Monday night at Lady Rothes's con-
versation, it was a heavy night, Mrs. Montague missed. On
Tuesday I was at club, and dined out, I think, two days more.
This week I have been driven to opium and abstinence and
physick, but I have been much visited. I am not much
better for my regimen, but yesterday I dined with Langton,
today I dine with Mr. Whitebread, and tomorrow with Sir
Joseph Banks, I believe I refused an invitation for Saturday.
    Mrs. Desmoulins[2] left us last week, so that I have only one
sick woman to fight or play with instead of two, and there is
more peace in the house.

839.1.—1. Nothing seems to be known of this accident to HLT, which caused her
'hurt' and 'fright', see 843.1.
    2. JB recorded in his journal 17 May: 'Had heard at Miss Burney's that Mrs.
Desmoulins had eloped. Heard that there was an indictment against her.' *BP* xv.
226 (Dr. Pottle's expanded text).

Let me know, my dear Love, how my Mistress goes on, and tell Susy that I shall answer her short letter.[3]

I am writing over the little garden. The poplars, which I have just now watered, grow kindly; they may expect not to be neglected for they came from Streatham.

Crescent illae crescetis amores.[4]

I am, dear Madam, Your most humble servant,

Sam: Johnson

840. Sa. 24 May '83. John Wilkes.

B.M. (the year I think in another hand).—Wilkes *Corresp.* 1805, iv. 321.

Mr Johnson returns thanks to Mr and Miss Wilkes for their kind invitation, but he is engaged for Tuesday to Sir Joshua Reynolds, and for Wednesday to Mr Paradise.
May 24 1783

841. Sa. 31 May '83. William Windham.

Fettercairn.—Boswell 1791, ii. 458 (Hill iv. 227).

Sir

The Bringer of this letter is the Father of Miss Philips a singer who comes to try her voice on the Stage at Dublin.

Mr Philips is one of my old Friends, and, as I am of opinion that neither he nor his daughter will do any thing that can disgrace their benefactors, I take the liberty of entreating you to countenance and protect them so far as may be suitable to your station[1] and character, and shall consider

839.1—3. He answered it in 864.
  4. Virgil, *Ecl.* x. 54. The poet decides to 'cut his love on trees' (meos incidere amores arboribus); 'they will grow, and so, my love, will you'.

840.—See *L* iv. 224 for JB's efforts to arrange this dinner. The party was to be four; 'Nobody but Mr. Boswell should be asked to meet the Dr.' J was compliant, but a day could not be fixed; JB left L'n 30 May. See JB to JW 25 May (Tinker 215).

841.—The original has W's endorsement: 'Dr Johnson recomm^s Philips.—May (Qy. June) 21 ? 1783' (so Prof. Abbott's Catalogue 1588; I myself at one time read it as 'Leg June'). The year also has been doubted, but proved right by Mr. Ketton-Cremer (*TLS* 7 Aug. 1930). June may be right, for a document in K-C's possession shows that W left L'n for Dublin 29 May.
  1. W was in Dublin, Secretary to the Lord-Lieutenant, *L* iv. 521.

myself as obliged by any favourable notice which they shall have the honour of receiving from You.

I am, Sir, your most humble Servant,

London. May 31. 1783. Sam Johnson

841.1. n.d. (? May '83). ⟨William Langley (Ashbourne).⟩

John Grant, Catalogue March 1931 (mutilated).—

Dear Sir

A long continuance of ill health with the evils that attend it, must be allowed as an excuse for many omissions, and you will not therefore much blame me for omitting hitherto those thanks which your honest diligence has deserved. I am compleatly satisfied with what you have done, and written, but could make out no case that I thought could help the girls,[1] if indeed, which dos not very plainly ⟨a line cut out⟩ wish that they should act by any advice of M⟨ine⟩ in opposition to any other. To require that they should give up their contingent claim is certainly a hardship, though that claim as they have a brother and sister is worth very little. You, Sir, have been very friendly.

A new edition of the Lives of the Poets has been lately printed in 4 vol 8vo. I shall send a set to morrow to Mr Davenport, to be transmitted to you, which I desire you to accept from,

Sir, your most humble servant

842. M. 2 June '83. Joshua Reynolds.

Address: To Sir Joshua Reynolds.

Fettercairn.—Boswell 1791, ii. 458 (Hill iv. 227).

Dear Sir

I have sent you some of my God-son's[1] performances of which I do not pretend to form any opinion. When I took

841.1.—Mr. Reade tells me that the date is almost certain; he refers me to *GM* Dec. 1878, 700; where I find a letter from L to J, 19 May '83: 'The favour which you have sent to W. Davenport for me . . . I shall receive with peculiar pleasure. They will be a distinguished ornament in my small collection of books, and confer credit upon me from every person who shall be told that they were a present from Dr. Johnson to his most obdt. and obliged humble servt. W. L.'

1. Collier.

842.—1. Paterson.

the liberty of mentioning him to you, I did not know, what I have been since told, that Mr. Moser had admitted him among the Students of the academy. What more can be done for him I earnestly entreat You to consider, for I am very desirous that he should derive some advantage from my connection with him. If you are inclined to see him I will bring him to wait on You at any time that You shall be pleased to appoint. I am, Sir, Your most humble Servant,

June 2. 1783   Sam: Johnson

843. M. 2 June '83. ———.

Adam; known to Hill from Sotheby's catalogue 27 Nov. 1889, 98.—

Sir
  Please to deliver to the Bearer a set of Ramblers, and put it to the account of

                          Sir, Your humble servant
June 2. 1783   Sam: Johnson

843.1. M. 2 June '83. Hester Maria Thrale (Bath).

Address: To Miss Thrale at Bath.
Lansdowne.—Lansdowne, *Johnson and Queeney* 1932, 33.

My dear Love,   London, June 2, 1783
  In the beginning of your arithmetical studies suffer me to give you one important direction.
  Accustom yourself to make all your figures with critical exactness. In writing a series of language some inattention may be allowed, because one word and one letter explains another, but in numbers every character has its own independent power, which, if by bad delineation it becomes doubtful, cannot be deduced or inferred from any of its concomitants. By a little negligence your own computations will become in a short time unintelligible to yourself. Get an exact copy of all the figures, and do not either for haste or negligence deviate from it.

843.1.—J sometimes practised what he here preaches. He often writes names with extra care, occasionally spacing the letters. His figures are usually unambiguous, but his 5 and 9 are sometimes very similar.

The same attention is to be preserved in words which connexion does not ascertain, such as names and numbers. Very few write their own names in such a manner as that if they stood alone they could be read. I have lately seen letters of which neither those to whom they were sent nor any to whom they have been shewn are able to discover the abode of the writer, though he has spread it widely enough upon paper. This inconvenience is easily avoided by writing all such words in single letters without ligatures, for it is by joining them that they are made obscure, as *Thrale*, T h r a l e. This I mention the rather because you suffer your writing to grow very vagrant and irregular.

I have for some time past been much oppressed, but this ⟨is⟩ a very tolerable day.

I hope my Mistress is recovered from her hurt and her fright.[1] Why do you write so seldom to

Dearest Love, Your most humble servant,

Sam: Johnson

844. W. 4 June '83. Anthony Hamilton.

Not traced.—Croker's Boswell 1835, x. 282.

Reverend Sir   Bolt Court, June 4, 1783.

Be pleased to excuse this application from a stranger in favour of one who has very little ability to speak for herself. The unhappy woman who waits on you with this, has been known to me many years. She is the daughter of a clergyman of Leicestershire, who by an unhappy marriage is reduced to solicit a refuge in the workhouse of your parish, to which she has a claim by her husband's settlement.[1]

Her case admits of little deliberation; she is turned out of her lodging into the street. What my condition allows me to do for her I have already done, and having no friend, she can have recourse only to the parish.

I am, reverend Sir, &c.,

Sam: Johnson.

843.1—1. See 839.1.

844.—1. Hill quotes Blackstone and the *Penny Cyclopaedia* for the law of settlement, which determined a pauper to this or that parish. A wife acquired rights in her husband's parish.

845. Th. 5 June '83. Mrs. Thrale (Bath).

Address: To Mrs Thrale at Bath. *Postmark*: 5 iv.
Adam.—1788, No. 297.

Dear Madam

Why do you write so seldom? I was very glad of your letter, you were used formerly to write more when I know not why you should have had much more to say. Do not please yourself with showing me that you can forget me, who do not forget you.

Mr Desmoulins account of my health rather wants confirmation. But complaints are useless.

I have by the migration of one of my Ladies[1] more peace at home, but I remember an old Savage chief that says of the Romans with great indignation. Ubi solitudinem faciunt, pacem appellant.[2]

M . . .[3] was not Calamity, it was her sister, to whom I am afraid the term is now seriously applicable, for she seems to have fallen some way into obscurity. I am afraid by a palsy.

Whence your pity arises for the thief that has made the hangman idle, I cannot discover. I am sorry indeed for every suicide, but I suppose he would have gone to the gallows without being ⟨la⟩mented.

You will soon see that Miss Hudson, if she finds countenance, and gets scholars, will conquer her vexations. Is not Susy likewise one of her pupils? I owe Susy a Letter, which I purpose to pay next time.

I can tell you of no new thing in town, but Dr Maxwel, whose Lady is by ill health detained with two little babies at Bath.

You give a cheerful account of your way of life, I hope you will settle into tranquillity.

When I can repay you with a narrative of my felicity, you shall see Description.—

       I am Madam, Your most humble servant,
June 5. 1783 London.   Sam: Johnson

845.—1. Mrs. Desmoulins, see 862.
   2. Tacitus, *Agricola* xxx: 'they make a wilderness and call it a peace'.
   3. The erasure is thorough. 'Mrs. Lewis was not Calamity, it was her sister.' HLP.
Mr. Metzdorf, who has checked Mr. Adam's and my reading, thinks that J wrote 'her', not 'his' as in 1788; but it is very like 'his', so we may acquit HLP of faking her text.

846. F. 13 June '83. Mrs. Thrale (Bath).

Sotheby June 1948.—1788, No. 299.

Dear Madam

Yesterday were brought hither two parcels directed *to
Mrs. Thrale to the care of Dr. Johnson.* By what the touch
can discover, they contain something of which cloaths are
made; and I suspect them to be Musgrave's long expected
present.[1] You will order them to be called for, or let me
know whither I shall send them.

Crutchley has had the gout but is abroad again. Seward
called on me yesterday. He is going only for a few weeks first
to Paris, and then to Flanders to contemplate the pictures of
Claude Loraine and he asked me if that was not as good a way
as any of spending time—That time which returns no more,—
of which however a great part seems to be very foolishly
spent, even by the wisest and the best.

That time at least is not lost in which the evils of life are
relieved, and therefore the moments which you bestow on
Miss Hudson, are properly employed. She seems to make an
uncommon impression upon you. What has she done or
suffered out of the common course of things? I love a little
secret history.

Poor Dr. Lawrence and his youngest son died almost on
the same day.[2]

Mrs. Dobson, the Directress of rational conversation,[3] did
not translate Petrarch; but epitomised a very bulky French
life of Petrarch. She translated, I think, the Memoirs of
D'Aubigné.

Your last letter was very pleasing, it expressed ⟨? such⟩[4]
kindness to me, and some degree of placid acquiescence in

846.—1. 'So it was—a beautiful Irish stuff.' HLP.

2. According to *GM* 1783, i. 542, L died 13 June, his son John 15 June. But *GM*
1787, i. 191, a memoir of L, gives 6 June for his death; and Hill quotes corroborative
evidence. The register of St. Margaret's, Canterbury, gives 12 June as the date of
burial. Probably 15 June was an inference; if the author of the first entry in *GM* had
been told that father and son died within two days, he would naturally add two to his
first (erroneous) date. J also was misinformed; for L's second son was not his youngest;
see Index II.

3. For her works see Index III s.vv. D'Aubigné, Petrarch. FB credits her with
'a strong and masculine understanding' (*Diary* i. 346).

4. The word is blotted.

your present mode of life, which is, I think, the best, which is at present within your reach.

My powers and attention have for a long time, been almost wholly employed upon my health, I hope, not wholly without success, but solitude is very tedious.

I am, Madam, Your most humble Servant
London June 13. 1783.   Sam: Johnson

847. Tu. 17 June '83. Edmund Allen.

Not traced.—Hawkins 1787, 556; Boswell 1793, iii. 481 (Hill iv. 228).

Dear Sir,

It hath pleased almighty God this morning to deprive me of the powers of speech; and, as I do not know but that it may be his farther good pleasure to deprive me soon of my senses, I request you will, on the receipt of this note, come to me, and act for me, as the exigencies of my case may require. I am, Sincerely Yours,
June 17, 1783.   S. Johnson.

848. Tu. 17 June '83. John Taylor (Westminster).

Address: To the Reverend Dr Taylor.
A. T. Loyd; copy made for JB, Isham.—Taylor, *A Letter to Samuel Johnson* 1787, 20; Boswell 1791, ii. 458 (Hill iv. 228).

Dear Sir

It has pleased God by a paralytick stroke in the night to deprive me of speech.

I am very desirous of Dr Heberdens assistance as I think my case is not past remedy. Let me see you as soon as it is possible. Bring Dr Heberden with you if you can, but come yourself, at all events. I am glad you are so well, when [when] I am so dreadfully attacked.

I think that by a speedy application of stimulants much

847.—J tells HLT in 850 that in writing this note his 'hand . . . made wrong letters'. As we have not the original we cannot tell how far the text has been mended. I follow Hawkins's text, which was presumably JB's sole source; 1793 has 'It has pleased GOD', and 'Sam. Johnson'; the signature 'S. Johnson' is I think unique. Hawkins does not date the letter.

848.—The slips of the pen are natural. In the postscript (which is not in 1787) 'have' is an afterthought, to which J has failed to accommodate 'make'.

may be done. I question if a vomit vigorous and rough would not rouse the organs of speech to action.

As it is too early to send I will try to recollect what I can that can be suspected to have brought on this dreadful distress.

I have been accustomed to bleed frequently for an asthmatick complaint, but have forborn for some time by Dr Pepys's persuasion, who perceived my legs beginning to swell. I sometimes alleviate a painful, or more properly an oppressive constriction of my chest, by opiates, and have lately taken opium frequently but the last, or two last times in smaller quantities. My largest dose is three grains, and last night I took but two.

You will suggest these things, and they are all that I can call to mind, to Dr Heberden.

I am &c

June. 17. 1783   Sam: Johnson.

Dr Brocklesby will be with me to meet Dr Heberden, and I shall have previously make master of the case as well as I can.

849. W. 18 June '83. Thomas Davies.

Address (Boswell): To Mr. Thomas Davies.
Not traced.—Boswell 1791, ii. 460 (Hill iv. 231).

Dear Sir

I have had, indeed, a very heavy blow; but GOD, who yet spares my life, I humbly hope will spare my understanding, and restore my speech. As I am not at all helpless, I want no particular assistance, but am strongly affected by Mrs. Davies's tenderness; and when I think she can do me good, shall be very glad to call upon her.[1] I had ordered friends to be shut out; but one or two have found the way in; and if you come you shall be admitted: for I know not whom I can see that will bring more amusement on his tongue, or more kindness in his heart. I am, &c.

June 18, 1783.   Sam. Johnson.

849.—1. 'call upon her' means, of course, 'invoke her aid', not 'wait upon her'.

850. Th. 19 June '83. Mrs. Thrale (Bath).

Bergson.—1788, No. 301; a large part in Boswell 1791, ii. 459 (Hill iv. 229).

Dear Madam

I am sitting down in no chearful solitude to write a narrative which would once have affected you with tenderness and sorrow, but which you will perhaps pass over now with the careless glance of frigid indifference. For this diminution of regard however, I know not whether I ought to blame You, who may have reasons which I cannot know, and I do not blame myself who have for a great part of human life done You what good I could, and have never done you evil.

I had been disordered in the usual way, and had been relieved by the usual methods, by opium and catharticks, but had rather lessened my dose of opium.

On Monday the 16. I sat for my picture,[1] and walked a considerable way with little inconvenience. In the afternoon and evening I felt myself light and easy, and began to plan schemes of life. Thus I went to bed, and in a short time waked and sat up as has been long my custom, when I felt a confusion and indistinctness in my head which lasted, I suppose about half a minute; I was alarmed and prayed God, that however he might afflict my body he would spare my understanding. This prayer, that I might try the integrity of my faculties I made in Latin verse.[2] The lines were not very good, but I knew them not to be very good, I made them easily, and concluded myself to be unimpaired in my faculties.

Soon after I perceived that I had suffered a paralytick stroke, and that my Speech was taken from me. I had no pain, and so little dejection in this dreadful state that I wondered at my own apathy, and considered that perhaps death itself when it should come, would excite less horrour than seems now to attend it.

In order to rouse the vocal organs I took two drams. Wine has been celebrated for the production of eloquence; I put

850.—1. To FR, see 876.

2. *Poems* 204. He prays God to spare his mind, 'the only faculty with which I may hope to please thee': 'Summe Pater, quodcunque tuum de corpore Numen | Hoc statuat, precibus Christus adesse velit; | Ingenio parcas, nec sit mihi culpa rogâsse, | Qua solum potero parte, placere tibi.'

myself into violent motion, and, I think, repeated it. But all was vain; I then went to bed, and, strange as it may seem, I think, slept. When I saw light, it was time to contrive what I should do. Though God stopped my speech he left me my hand, I enjoyed a mercy which was not granted to my Dear Friend Laurence,[3] who now perhaps overlooks me as I am writing and rejoices that I have what he wanted. My first note was necessarily to my servant, who came in talking, and could not immediately comprehend why he should read what I put into his hands.

I then wrote a card to Mr Allen, that I might have a discreet friend at hand to act as occasion should require. In penning this note I had some difficulty, my hand, I knew not how nor why, made wrong letters. I then wrote to Dr Taylor to come to me, and bring Dr Heberden, and I sent to Dr Brocklesby, who is my neighbour. My Physicians are very friendly and very disinterested, and give me great hopes, but you may imagine my situation. I have so far recovered my vocal powers, as to repeat the Lord's Prayer with no very imperfect articulation. My memory, I hope, yet remains as it was. But such an attack produces solicitude for the safety of every Faculty.

How this will be received by You I know not, I hope You will sympathise with me, but perhaps

> My Mistress gracious, mild, and good,
> Cries, Is he dumb? 'tis time he shou'd.[4]

But can this be possible, I hope it cannot. I hope that what, when I could speak, I spoke of You, and to You, will be in a sober and serious hour remembred by You, and surely it cannot be remembred but with some degree of kindness. I have loved you with virtuous affection, I have honoured You with sincere Esteem. Let not all our endearment be forgotten, but let me have in this great distress your pity and your prayers. You see I yet turn to You with my complaints as a settled and unalienable friend, do not, do not drive me from You, for I have not deserved either neglect or hatred.

To the Girls, who do not write often, for Susy has written

850.—3. See 802 for L's inability to write.
   4. Swift, *On the Death of Dr. Swift*: '[the queen] so gracious, mild and good | Cries, "is he gone! 'tis time he shou'd".'

only once, and Miss Thrale[5] owes me a letter, I earnestly
recommend as their Guardian and Friend, that They remember their Creator in the days of their Youth.[6]

I suppose you may wish to know how my disease is treated
by the physitians. They put a blister upon my back, and two
from my ear to my throat, one on a side. The blister on the
back has done little, and those on the throat have not risen.
I bullied, and bounced, (it sticks to our last sand[7]) and compelled the apothecary to make his salve according to the
Edinburgh dispensatory, that it might adhere better. I have
two on now of my own prescription. They likewise give me
salt of hartshorn, which I take with no great confidence, but
am satisfied that what can be done is done for me.

O God, give me comfort and confidence in Thee, forgive
my sins, and if it be thy good pleasure, relieve my diseases for
Jesus Christs sake, Amen.

I am almost ashamed of this querulous letter, but now
it is written, let it go.

I am, Madam Your most humble servant
Bolt Court Fleet street June 19. 1783   Sam: Johnson.

851. F. 20 June '83. Mrs. Thrale (Bath).

Address: To Mrs Thrale at Bath. *Postmark*: 20 IV.
C. T. Jeffery.—1788, No. 302.

Dearest Lady[1]

I think to send you for some time a regular diary. You
will forgive the gross images which disease must necessarily
present. Dr Laurence said that medical treatises should be
always in Latin.[2]

The two vesicatories which I procured with so much
trouble did not perform well, for, being applied to the lower
part of the fauces a part always in motion their adhesion was
continually broken. The back, I hear, is very properly flayed.

850.—5. 'He does not call her Queeney' Hill. The implication is not justified;
J not infrequently writes 'Miss Thrale', now she is a young lady.
    6. *Ecclesiastes* xii. 1.   7. Pope, *Knowledge and Characters of Men* 225.

851.—1. 'Dearest Lady' HLP, correcting the 'Dearest Madam' of 1788. This is
I think the only place in which we can be sure that HLP, in annotating her copy,
referred to the original.   2. L's own works were all in Latin.

I have now healing application to the cheeks and have my head covered with one formidable diffusion of Cantharides, from which Dr Heberden assures me that experience promises great effects. He told me likewise that my utterance has been improved since Yesterday, of which however I was less certain. Though doubtless they who see me at interval can best judge.

I never had any distortion of the countenance, but what Dr Brocklesby calld a little prolapsus which went away the second day.

I was this day directed to eat Flesh, and I dined very copiously upon roasted Lamb and boiled pease, I then went to sleep in a chair, and when I waked I found Dr Broaclesby sitting by me, and fell to talking to him in such a manner as made me glad, and, I hope, made me thankful. The Dr fell to repeating Juvenal's tenth[3] satire, but I let him see that the province was mine.

I am to take wine to night, and hope it may do me good.
              I am, Madam, Your humble Servant
London June 20 1783   Sam: Johnson.

852. F. 20 June '83. Mauritius Lowe.

Not traced.—Croker's Boswell 1831, v. 113.

Sir   Friday, June, 20th 1783.
    You know, I suppose, that a sudden illness makes it impracticable to me to wait on Mr. Barry, and the time is short. If it be your opinion that the end can be obtained by writing, I am very willing to write, and, perhaps, it may do as well: it is, at least, all that can be expected at present from,
                    Sir, your most humble servant,
                            Sam: Johnson.

If you would have me write, come to me: I order your admission.

851.—3. 'ninth' 1788, a misreading which has obscured the similarity of a similar incident in Dec. '84, when B in repeating the famous conclusion—'mens sana in corpore sano'—of the same satire made an unmetrical misquotation (*L* iv. 401). We are not to suspect that JB has made an error of date, and that the two incidents were in fact one; for the later occasion ended not in religious talk, but in J's 'discoursing vehemently on the unmetrical effect of such a lapse'.

37

853. Sa. 21 June '83. Mrs. Thrale (Bath).

Address: To Mrs Thrale at Bath. *Postmark*: 21 iv.

Adam.—1788, No. 303.

Dear Madam

I continue my Journal. When I went to Bed last night I found the new covering of my [my] head uneasy, not painful, rather too warm. I had however a comfortable and placid night. My Physicians this morning thought my amendment not inconsiderable, and my friends who visited me said that my look was spritely and cheerful. Nobody has shown more affection than Paradise. Langton and he were with me a long time today. I was almost tired.

When my friends were gone, I took another liberal dinner such as my Physicians recommended and slept after it, but without such evident advantage as was the effect of yesterday's *siesta*. Perhaps the sleep was not quite so sound, for I am harrassed by a very disagreeable operation of the cantharides which I am endeavouring to control by copious dilution.

My disorders are in other respects less than usual, my disease whatever it was seems collected into this one dreadful effect. My Breath is free, the constrictions of the chest are suspended, and my nights pass without oppression.

To day I received a letter of consolation and encouragement from an unknown hand without a name, kindly and piously, though not enthusiastically[1] written.

I had just now from Mr Pepys, a message enquiring in your name after my health, of this I can give no account.[2]

I am Madam, Your most humble servant,

London June 21. 1783   Sam: Johnson

854. M. 23 June '83. Mrs. Thrale (Bath).

Adam.—1788, No. 304.

Dear dear Madam

I thank you for your kind letter, and will continue my

853.—1. Hill is no doubt right in thinking that J uses the word in a bad sense. He defines *enthusiasm* as 'a vain belief of private revelation'.

2. Hill supposes J unable to 'understand why Mr. Pepys who was in London should make such an enquiry in the name of Mrs. Thrale who was in Bath and in constant correspondence with him'. I think J is criticizing her, not P, as guilty of unnecessary finesse.

diary. On the night of the 21st I had very little rest, being kept awake by an effect of the cantharides not indeed formidable, but very irksome and painful. On the 22. The Physicians released me from the salts of hartshorn. The Cantharides continued their persecution, but I was set free from it at night. I had however not much sleep but I hope for more to night. The vesications on my back and face are healing, and only that on my head continues to operate.

My friends tell me that my power of utterance improves daily, and Dr Heberden declares that he hopes to find me almost well to morrow.

Palsies are more common than I thought. I have been visited by four friends who have had each a stroke, and one of them, two.

Your offer,[1] dear Madam, of coming to me is charmingly kind, but I will lay up[2] for future use, and then let it not be considered as obsolete. A time of dereliction may come, when I may have hardly any other friend, but in the present exigency, I cannot name one who has been deficient in activity or attention. What man can do for man, has been done for me.

Write to me very often. I am Madam Your most humble servant

June 23. 1783 London   Sam: Johnson

855. Tu. 24 June '83. Mrs. Thrale (Bath).

Chequers, Bucks.—1788, No. 305.

Dear Madam,

The Journal now like other journals grows very dry, as it is not diversified by operations or events, less and less is done, and, I thank God, less and less is suffered every day. The Physicians seem to think that little more needs to be done.

854.—1. 'A Stroke of the Palsy has robbed Johnson of his Speech I hear, dreadful Event! & I at a Distance—poor Fellow.' *Th* 568. She had the news first from Tom Davies; she was reassured by 'a Letter from himself in his usual Style', i.e. 850. She says nothing in *Th* of going to him: 'I sincerely wish the Continuance of a Health so valuable; but have no Desire that he should come to Bath, as my plan is mere retirement & Oeconomy.'

2. 'lay it up' HLP.

I find that they consulted to-day about sending me to Bath,[1] and thought it needless. Dr Heberden takes leave to morrow.

This day I watered the garden, and did not find the watering pots more heavy than they have hitherto been, and my breath is more free.

Poor dear ——[2] has just been here with a present. If it ever falls in your way to do him good, let him have your favour.

Both Queeny's letter and Yours gave me to day great pleasure. Think as well and as kindly of me as you can, but do not flatter me. Cool reciprocations of esteem are the great comforts of life, hyperbolical praise only corrupts the tongue of one, and the ear of the other.

I am, Dear Madam, Your most humble servant
London. June 24 1783   Sam: Johnson
Your letter has no date.

856. W. 25 June '83. Lucy Porter (Lichfield).

Sotheby 15 April 1929.—Croker's Boswell 1831, v. 112.

Dear Madam
Since the papers have given an account of my ilness, it is proper that I should give my friends some account of it myself.

Very early in the morning of the 16th[1] of this month, I perceived my speech taken from me. When it was light I sat down, and wrote such directions as appeared proper. Dr Heberden and Dr Brocklesby were called. Blisters were applied, and medicines given; before night I began to speak with some freedom, which has been encreasing ever since, so that I now have very ⟨little⟩ impediment in my utterance. Dr Heberden took his leave this morning.

Since I received this stroke I have in other respects been

855.—1. Heberden and Brocklesby had, I suppose, thought of Bath for its waters, not as affording a nurse in HLT.

2. The traces, as reported from Chequers by Mrs. Graham, are what looks like the top of an initial *P* or *R* (but this is doubtful) and the tail of a final *g* or *y*. This rules out HLP's 'Sastres'. Hill thought of Davies, but I do not think there is evidence for 'Davy' (which in earlier days meant Garrick). I have thought of Percy, but why should he be 'poor dear', or in need of 'favour'?

856.—1. A slip for 17th.

better than I was before, and hope yet to have a comfortable Summer. Let me have your prayers.

If writing is not troublesome let me know whether you are pretty well, and how you have passed the Winter and Spring. Make my compliments to all my Friends.

I am, dear Madam, Your most humble servant,
London. June 25. 1783.   Sam: Johnson

857. Sa. 28 June '83. Mrs. Thrale (Bath).

Address: To Mrs. Thrale at Bath. *Postmark*: 28 IV.
Sir Charles Russell.—1788, No. 306.

Dear Madam
Your letter is just such as I desire, and as from you I hope always to deserve.

The black Dog I hope always to resist, and in time to drive though I am deprived of almost all those that used to help me. The neighbourhood is impoverished. I had once Richardson and Laurence in my reach. Mrs Allen is dead. My house has lost Levet, a man who took interest in every thing and therefore was very ready at conversation.[1] Mrs Williams is so weak that ⟨she⟩ can be a companion no longer. When I rise my breakfast is solitary, the black dog waits to share it, from breakfast to dinner he continues barking, except that Dr Brocklesby for a little keeps him at a distance. Dinner with a sick woman you may venture to suppose not much better than solitary. After Dinner what remains but to count the clock, and hope for that sleep which I can scarce expect. Night comes at last, and some hours of restlessness and confusion bring me again to a day of solitude. What shall exclude the black dog from a habitation like this? If I were a little richer I would perhaps take some cheerful Female into the House.

Your Bath news shews me new calamities. I am afraid Mrs. Lewis[2] is left with a numerous family very slenderly supplied. Mrs. Sheward is an old maid, I am afraid, yet sur le pavé.

857.—1. He 'seldom said a word while any company was present'. *L* i. 243.
  2. 'Lewis' and 'Welch' are suppressed in 1788; 'calamities' perhaps glances at 845, 'Mrs. Lewis was not Calamity'.

Welch,[2] if he were well, would be well enough liked, his Daughter has powers and knowledge, but no art of making them agreeable.

I must touch my Journal. Last night fresh flies were put to my head, and hindred me from sleeping. To day I fancy myself incommoded by heat.

I have however watered the garden both yesterday and to day, just as I watered the laurel in the Island.[3]

I am Madam Your most humble servant
London June 28. 1783   Sam: Johnson.

858. M. 30 June '83. Mrs. Thrale (Bath).

Address: To Mrs. Thrale at Bath. *Postmark*: 30 IV.
Owen D. Young (torn, and presumably for that reason lacking the date, which Mrs. Piozzi has added in the original—as 29 June 1783—though not in her print).—1788, No. 307.

Dear Madam

Among those that have enquired after me, Sir Philip[1] is one, and Dr Burney[2] was one of those who came to see me. I have had no reason to complain of indifference or neglect. Dick Burney is come home, five inches taller.

Yesterday in the Evening I went to Church and have been to day to see the great Burning Glass, which does more than was ever done before by transmission of the Rays, but is not equal in power to those which reflect them. It wastes a diamond placed in the focus, but causes no diminution of pure gold. Of two rubies exposed to its action one was made more vivid, the other, paler. To see the glass, I climbed up stairs to the garret, and then up a ladder to the leads, and talked to the artist rather too long, for my voice though clear and distinct for a little while soon tires and falters. The organs of speech are yet very feeble, but will I hope be by

857.—3. For the island in the 'lake or moat' see H. W. Bromhead, *The Heritage of St. Leonard's* 1932, 43.

858.—Though the paper is defective probably nothing is lost but the date. The text suggests that HLP's is wrong by a day. The first page ends 'is not equal', and there seems to be no lacuna; the second ends 'have been very', and if anything is missing it is a whole line; it is more likely that J omitted a word by inadvertence on starting a new page (see on 922), as HLP assumed when she inserted 'sorry'.

1. Jennings Clerk.   2. FB's *Diary* ii. 269 (quoted by Hill).

the mercy of God finally restored, at present like any other
weak limb, they can endure but little labour at once. Would
you not have been very ⟨sorry⟩ for me when I could scarcely
speak?

Fresh Cantharides were this morning applied to my head,
and are to be continued some time longer. If they play me
no treacherous tricks they give me very little pain.

Let me have your kindness and your prayers and think on
me, as on a man who for a very great portion of Your life,
has done You all the good he could, and desires still to be
considered as,

Madam, Your most humble servant

Sam: Johnson.

859. Tu. 1 July '83. Mrs. Thrale (Bath).

Address: To Mrs Thrale at Bath. *Postmark*: 1 IY.
Adam.—1788, No. 308.

Dear Madam

This morning I took the air by a ride to Hampstead, and
this afternoon I dined with the Club.[1] But fresh Cantharides
were this day applied to my Head.

Mr Cator called on me today, and told that he had invited
you back to Streatham, I showed the unfitness of your return
thither, till the neighbourhood should have lost its habits of
depredation,[2] and he seemed to be satisfied. He invited me
very kindly and cordially to try the air of Beckenham,[3] and
pleased me very much by his affectionate attention to Miss
Cecy. There is much good in his character, and much usefulness in his knowledge.

Queeney seems now to have forgotten me.

Of the different appearance of the hills and vallies an
account may perhaps be given, without the supposition of

859.—1. FB hearing from JR that J had dined at the Club, 'called the next morning
to congratulate him, and found him very gay and very good-humoured'. *Diary* ii.
271.

2. Hill quotes from the *GM* statistics of capital sentences for burglary, and from
Walpole some evidence of prevailing 'panic'.

3. J does not seem to have accepted this invitation.

43

any prodigy.[4] If the ⟨? day[5]⟩ had been hot and the Evening was breezy; the exhalations would rise from the low grounds very copiously; and the wind that swept and cleared the hills, would only by its cold condense the vapours of the sheltered vallies.

Murphy is just gone from me; he visits me very kindly, and I have no unkindness to complain of.

I am sorry that Sir Philip's request[6] was not treated with more respect, nor can I imagine what has put them so much out of humour; I hope their business is prosperous.

I hope that I recover by degrees, but my nights are restless, and you will suppose the nervous system to be somewhat enfeebled. I am

Madam Your most humble servant

London. July 1. 1783   Sam: Johnson

860. Th. 3 July '83. Mrs. Thrale (Bath).

Address: To Mrs Thrale at Bath. *Postmark*: 3 IY.
Adam.—1788, No. 309.

Dear Madam

Dr Brocklesby yesterday dismissed the Cantharides, and I can now find a soft place upon my pillow. Last night was cool, and I rested well, and this morning I have been a friend at a poetical difficulty. Here is now a glimpse of daylight again. But how near is the Evening—None can tell, and I will not prognosticate; We all know that from none of us it can be far distant; may none of us know this in vain.

I went, as I took care to boast, on Tuesday, to the Club, and hear that I was thought to have performed as well as usual. I dined on Fish, with the wing of a small Turkey chick, and left roast Beef, Goose, and venison pye untouched.

859.—4. See 869 for the unusual weather of '83. What is here described may, however, be normal; Bath is sometimes in dense fog while the surrounding plateau is bathed in sunshine.

5. J's omission of a word led the compositor of 1788 to misread 'the' as 'she', and consequentially to turn 'hot' into 'out'. Since 'she' must be Queeney, a further corruption, compositor's or editor's, followed: the transference of the sentence 'Queeney . . . forgotten me' to this paragraph.

6. 'Mr. Perkins's gross Ingratitude deserves mentioning . . . he refused to put a poor Fellow into his Brewhouse the other Day, though strongly solicited by Sir Philip Jennings and myself.' *Th* 572. So 'them' means Barclay and Perkins.

I live much on peas, and never had them so good, for so long a time, in any year that I can remember.

When do you go ⟨to⟩ Weymouth?[1] and why do you go? only I suppose to a new place, and the reason is sufficient to those who have no reason to withold them. ——knows well enough how to live on four hundred a year, but whence is she to have it. Had the ⟨Dean⟩ anything of his own unsettled?[2]

I am glad that Mrs Sheward talks of me, and loves me, and have in this still scene of life great comfort in reflecting that I have given very few reason to hate me: I hope scarcely any man has known me closely but to his benefit or cursorily, but to his innocent entertainment. Tell me you that know me best, whether this be true, that according to your answer I may continue my practice, or try to mend it.

Along with your kind letter yesterday, came a one likewise very kind from the Astons at Lichfield, but I do not know whether as the summer is so far advanced[3] I shall travel so far, though I am not without hopes that frequent changes of air may fortify me against the winter, which has been, in modern phrase, of late years very *inimical* to,

Madam Your affectionate humble servant
London July 3. 1783   Sam: Johnson

861. Th. 3 July '83. James Boswell (Edinburgh).

Not traced.—Boswell 1791, ii. 461 (Hill iv. 231).

Dear Sir Your anxiety about my health is very friendly, and very agreeable with your general kindness. I have,

860.—1. They were there by 12 Aug. *Th* 569.

2. Mr. Metzdorf describes the original of this paragraph as 'badly mauled'—by tears as well as by erasures. HLP supplies 'Mrs. Lewis', 'she' (for 'he' of 1788), 'Dean' (i.e. Lewis, Dean of Ossory). Mr. Metzdorf reports that J probably wrote 'she', though the word is hardly legible, and that it seems to have been converted to 'He' by another hand. 'Dean' is consistent with such traces as remain.

3. J, like Trollope a century later, regards August as autumnal.

861.—The *Life* here is silent. There is no journal for June, and in that for August there is a gap between the 7th and 12th. But the Register of letters received and sent comes to the rescue: 'Sent 28 June 1783. Dr. Samuel Johnson, anxious about his being worse, and begging to be relieved (Copy). Received 7 July 1783. Dr. Samuel Johnson, a particular account of the paralytick stroke with which he was affected, and of his recovery. . . . Sent 9 August 1783. Dr. Samuel Johnson, in kind concern about him; inviting him to Auchinleck; that I am dreary (Copy).' The letters of 28 June and 9 Aug. are those mentioned by J in 876.1. See also on 888.

indeed, had a very frightful blow. On the 17th of last month, about three in the morning, as near as I can guess, I perceived myself almost totally deprived of speech. I had no pain. My organs were so obstructed, that I could say *no*, but could scarcely say *yes*. I wrote the necessary directions, for it pleased God to spare my hand, and sent for Dr. Heberden and Dr. Brocklesby. Between the time in which I discovered my own disorder, and that in which I sent for the doctors, I had, I believe, in spite of my surprize and solicitude, a little sleep, and Nature began to renew its operations. They came, and gave the directions which the disease required, and from that time I have been continually improving in articulation. I can now speak, but the nerves are weak, and I cannot continue discourse long; but strength, I hope, will return. The physicians consider me as cured. I was last Sunday at church. On Tuesday I took an airing to Hampstead, and dined with the Club, where Lord Palmerston was proposed, and, against my opinion, was rejected. I design to go next week with Mr. Langton to Rochester, where I purpose to stay about ten days, and then try some other air. I have many kind invitations. Your brother has very frequently enquired after me. Most of my friends have, indeed, been very attentive. Thank dear Lord Hailes for his present.

I hope you found at your return every thing gay and prosperous, and your lady, in particular, quite recovered and confirmed. Pay her my respects. I am, dear Sir, your most humble servant,

London, July 3, 1783.   Sam. Johnson.

862. Sa. 5 July '83. Lucy Porter (Lichfield).

Fettercairn.—Boswell 1791, ii. 461 (Hill iv. 232).

Dear Madam
    The account which You ⟨give⟩ of your health is but melancholy. May it please God to restore You.
    My disease affected my speech, and still continues in some degree to obstruct my utterance, my voice is distinct enough for a while, but the organs being yet[1] weak are quickly weary. But in other respects I am, I think, rather better than I have

862.—1. 'still' 1791.

lately been, and can let You know my state without the help of any other hand.

In the opinion of my friends, and in my own I am gradually mending. The Physicians consider me as cured, and I had leave four days ago to wash the Cantharides from my head. Last tuesday I dined at the Club.

I am going next week into Kent, and purpose to change the air frequently this summer; whether I shall wander so far as Staffordshire I cannot tell. I should be glad to come. Return my thanks to Mrs Cobb, and Mr Pearson and all that have shown attention to me.

Let us, my Dear, pray for one another, and consider our sufferings as notices mercifully given us to prepare ourselves for another state.

I live now but in a melancholy way. My old friend Mr Levett is dead, who lived with me in the house, and was useful and companiable,[2] Mrs Desmoulins is gone away, and Mrs Williams is so much decayed, that she can add little to anothers gratifications. The world passes away, and we are passing with it, but there is, doubtless, another world which will endure for ever; Let us all fit ourselves for it.

I am Dear Madam Your humble Servant
London July 5th 1783   Sam: Johnson

863. Sa. 5 July '83. Mrs. Thrale (Bath).

Address: To Mrs Thrale at Bath. *Postmark*: 5 IY.
Anderson Galleries 7 Jan. 1929.—1788, No. 310.

Dear Madam

That Dr. ⟨Pepys[1]⟩ is offended I am very sorry, but if the same state of things should recur, I could not do better. Dr Brocklesby is, you know, my neighbour and could be ready at call, he had for some time very diligently solicited my Friendship; I depended much upon the skill of Dr Heberden, and him I had seen lately at Brocklesby's. Heberden I could not bear to miss, Brocklesby could not decently be missed, and to call three, had made me ridiculous by the appearance of self importance. Mine was one of those

862.—2. 'companionable' 1791.
863.—1. 'Pepys' HLP, Lysons; the lower tip of the *P* is visible.

47

unhappy cases, in which something must be wrong. I can
only be sorry.

I have now no doctor, but am left to shift for myself, as
opportunity shall serve. I am going next week with ⟨Lang-
ton⟩² to ⟨Rochester⟩, where I expect not to stay long. Eight
children in a small house will probably make a chorus not
very diverting. My purpose is to change the air frequently
this Summer.

Of the imitation of my stile, in a criticism³ on Grays
Churchyard, I forgot to make mention. The authour is,
I believe, utterly unknown, for Mr. Steevens cannot hunt
him out. I know little of it, for though it was sent me, I never
⟨cut⟩ the leaves open. I had a letter with ⟨it⟩ representing it
to me, as my own work; in such an account to the publick,
they (*sic*) may be humour, but to myself it was neither serious
nor comical. I suspect the writer to be wrong headed; as to
the noise which it makes, I have never heard it, and am
inclined to believe that few attacks either of ridicule or invective make much noise, but by the help of those that they
provoke.

I think Queeney's⁴ silence has something either of laziness
or unkindness, and I wish her free from both for both are
very unamiable, and will both increase by indulgence. Susy
is, I believe at a loss for matter. I shall be glad to see pretty
Sophy's Production.

I hope I still continue mending. My organs are yet feeble.
       I am, Madam Your most humble servant
London. July 5. 1783   Sam: Johnson

864. ⟨? July '83⟩. Susannah Thrale (Bath).

Address: (Miss) Susannah Thrale at Bath.
Lansdowne; now mutilated, without date or postmark.—1788, No. 311
(without date, but placed between letters of 5 and 8 July).

Dearest Miss Susy
    When you favoured me with your letter, you seemed to be
in want of materials to fill it, having met with no great

863.—2. 'Langton, Rochester' HLP, Lysons.
    3. 'said to be written by Mr. YOUNG, Professor of Greek, at Glasgow', *L* iv. 392.
FB, who knew Young, ascribes it to him without qualification, *Diary* vi. 194.
    4. Erased in the MS., but restored in 1788.

adventures either of peril or delight, nor done or suffered any thing out of the common course of life.

When you have lived longer and considered more, you will find the common course of life very fertile of observation and reflection. Upon the common course of life must our thoughts and our conversation be generally employed. Our general course of life must denominate us wise or foolish; happy or miserable: if it is well regulated we pass on prosperously and smoothly; as it is neglected we live in embarrassment, perplexity, and uneasiness.

Your time, my Love, passes, I suppose, in Devotion, reading, work, and Company. Of your Devotions, in which I earnestly advise you to be very punctual, you may not perhaps think it proper to give me an account; and of work, unless I understood it better, it will be of no great use to say much, but Books and Company will always supply you with materials for your letters to me, as I shall be always pleased to know what you are reading, and with what you are pleased; and shall take great delight in knowing what impression new modes or new characters make upon you, and to observe with what attention you distinguish the tempers, dispositions, and abilities of your companions.

A letter may be always made out of the books of the morning or talk of the evening, and any letters from you, my dearest, will be welcome to

865. Tu. 8 July '83. Mrs. Thrale (Bath).

Address: To Mrs Thrale at Bath.
Copy by R. B. Adam.—1788, No. 312.

Dear Madam

Time makes great changes of opinion. The Dean of ⟨Ossory⟩ ran perpetually after Charlotte Cotterel in the lifetime of that Lady, to whom he so earnestly desired to be reunited in the grave. I am glad Charlotte is not left in poverty, her disease seems to threaten her with a full share of misery.[1]

865.—1. All the names are erased, but can be certainly read or supplied; 'that Lady' is not Charlotte, but Dean Lewis's first wife (*JM* ii. 408). 'Dean Lewis, Charlotte Cottrell, Mrs. Lewis.' HLP.

Of Miss H⟨udson⟩,[2] whom you charge me with forgetting, I know not why I should much foster the remembrance, for I can do her no good, but I honestly recommend ⟨her⟩ to your pity, for nothing but the opportunity of emptying her bosom with confidence can save her from madness. To know at least one mind so disordered is not with⟨out⟩ its use, it shows the danger of admitting passively the first irruption of irregular imaginations.

Langton and I have talked of passing a little time at Rochester together, till neither knows well how to refuse, though I think he is not eager to take me, and I am not desirous to be taken. His family is numerous, and his house little. I have let him know, for his relief, that I do not mean to burden him more than a week. He is, however, among those who wish me well, and would exert what power he has to do me good.

I think you will do well in going to Weymouth for though it be nothing, it is, at least to the young ones, a new nothing, and they will be able always to tell that they have seen Weymouth.[3] I am for the present willing enough to persuade myself, that a short succession of trifles may contribute to my reestablishment, but hope to return, for it is surely time, to something of importance.

     I am Dear Madam Your most humble servant
London July 8. 1783.   Sam: Johnson.

865.1. Tu. 8 July '83. John Ryland (Cranbrook).

Address: To Mr Ryland in Cranbrook Kent. *Postmark*: 8 IY. C. T. Jeffery.—

Dear Sir

I am gratified to a very high degree with your anxiety for my recovery. Health itself is made more valuable by an intercourse with friends like You. Most of our friends You and I have lost, let us therefore cling close to each other, and cherish our mutual kindness by conversation or letters as the state of life admits.

865.—2. 'Hudson' Lysons, which fits the traces.
   3. Weymouth remained 'nothing' until the king, six years later, made it fashionable by his visit.

My recovery, I think, advances, but its progress is [is] not
quick. My voice has its usual tone, and a stranger in the
beginning of our conversation does not perceive any depravation or obstruction. But the organs of articulation are
weak, and quickly tire. I question if I could read, without
pausing, a single page of a small book. This feebleness however will not, I hope, last very long.

I have some expectation of help from change of air, and
purpose to pass the next week, or ten days with my friend
Langton at Rochester, and afterwards to move to some other
place. I have been favoured with many invitations, and all,
I think, sincere.

Of your retreat I think with pleasure; there is to a busy
man great happiness in an interval of life which he can
spend as he pleases, but it is seldom that the mind is
sufficient for its own amusement, it returns soon with eagerness to external occupations. Do not forget in your hours of
leisure or of hurry, that You have one who wishes you well,
in Sir Your humble servant

London July. 8. 1783   Sam: Johnson

866. F. 11 July '83. ——

Not traced; known to Hill from Puttick and Simpson's Catalogue
16 July 1866, 275, where it is described as 'Note on a card'.

867. Rochester. Tu. 15 July '83. William Strahan.

Address: To William Strahan Esq M.P. London.
F. Bemis.—Hill 1892.

Sir

I have enclosed the receipt; and a Letter to Mrs Williams
which You do me the favour of sending to her.

The house where I am, is very airy, and pleasant, and overlooks the Medway where the channel is very broad, so that I
hardly imagine a habitation more likely to promote health,
nor have I much reason to complain; My general health is
better than it has been for some years. My breath is more
free, and my nights are less disturbed. But my utterance is
still impeded, and my voice soon grows weary with long

sentences. This, I hope, time will remedy. I hope dear Mrs. Strahan continues well.

I am Sir Your humble Servant,

Rochester. July. 15. 1783   Sam: Johnson.

868. Rochester. Tu. 15 July '83. Anna Williams.

Presumably, though not certainly, by J. Not traced; mentioned in 867.—

869. W. 23 July '83. Mrs. Thrale (Bath).

Address: To Mrs Thrale at Bath. *Postmark*: 25 (?) IY.
A. S. W. Rosenbach.—1788, No. 313.

Dear Madam

I have been thirteen days at Rochester and am just now returned. I came back by water in a common boat, twenty miles for a shilling, and when I landed at Billingsgate I carried my budget myself to Cornhil before I could get a coach, and was not much incommoded.

I have had Miss Susy's and Miss Sophy's letters, and ⟨now⟩ I am come home can write and write. While I was with Mr Langton, we took four little journies in a Chaise, and made one little voyage on the Medway with four misses and their maid, but they were very quiet.

I am very well except that my voice soon falters, and I have not slept well, which I imputed to the heat which has been such as I never felt before, for so long time. Three days we had of very great heat about ten years ago. I infer nothing from it but a good Harvest.

Whether this short rustication has done me any good I cannot tell, I certainly am not worse and am very willing to think myself better. Are you better? Sophy gave but a poor account of You. Do not let your mind wear out your body.

I am, Madam, Your most humble servant

London July 23. 1783   Sam: Johnson.

869.—J took boat at Gravesend, see 871. Coaches plied between G and Rochester (Dodsley's *London*, quoted by Hill).

869.1. Th. 24 July '83. Hester Maria Thrale (Bath).

Lansdowne; defective.—Lansdowne, *Johnson and Queeney* 1932, 35.

Dear Madam, London, 24 July 1783
  It is long since I wrote to you, and indeed it is long since I wrote to anybody. Rochester was out of the way, and I sent no letters from that place that could be omitted. The heat was sufficient besides to produce laziness. The thermometer was, as I am told, within four degrees of the greatest heat in Jamaica.
  Your account of your time gives me pleasure. Never lose the habit of reading, nor ever suffer yourself to acquiesce in total vacuity. Encourage in yourself an implacable impatience of doing nothing. He that cannot be idle, and will not be wicked, must be useful and valuable, he must be always improving himself or benefiting others. If you cannot at any particular time reconcile yourself to any thing important, be busy upon trifles. Of trifles the mind grows tired, and turns for its own satisfaction to something better; but if it learns to sooth itself with the opiate of musing idleness, if it can once be content with inactivity, all the time to come is in danger of being lost. And, I believe that life has been so dozed away by many whom Nature had originally qualified not only to be esteemed but admired.
  If ever therefore you catch yourself contentedly and placidly doing nothing, *sors de l'enchantement*,[1] break away from the snare, find your book or your needle, or snatch the broom from the maid.

870. Th. 24 July '83. Sophia Thrale (Bath).

Not traced.—1788, No. 314.

Dearest Miss Sophy London, July 24, 1783.
  By an absence from home, and for one reason and another, I owe a great number of letters, and I assure you that I sit down to write yours first. Why you should think yourself not a favourite, I cannot guess; my favour will, I am afraid, never

869.1.—1. Du Resnel's translation of the opening of Pope's *Essay on Man*: 'Sors de l'enchantement, milord, laisse au vulgaire | Le séduisant espoir d'un bien imaginaire.' For J's familiarity with this version see *L* iv. 496. Perhaps he knew that Q had been reading it.

be worth much; but be its value more or less, you are never likely to lose it, and less likely if you continue your studies with the same diligence as you have begun them.

Your proficience in arithmetick is not only to be commended, but admired. Your master does not, I suppose, come very often, nor stay very long; yet your advance in the science of numbers is greater than is commonly made by those who, for so many weeks as you have been learning, spend six hours a day in the writing school.

Never think, my Sweet, that you have arithmetick enough; when you have exhausted your master, buy books. Nothing amuses more harmlessly than computation, and nothing is oftener applicable to real business or speculative enquiries. A thousand stories which the ignorant tell, and believe, die away at once, when the computist takes them in his gripe. I hope you will cultivate in yourself a disposition to numerical enquiries; they will give you entertainment in solitude by the practice, and reputation in publick by the effect.

If you can borrow *Wilkins's Real Character*,[1] a folio, which the bookseller can perhaps let you have, you will have a very curious calculation, which you are qualified to consider, to shew that Noah's ark was capable of holding all the known animals of the world, with provision for all the time in which the earth was under water. Let me hear from you soon again.

I am, Madam, Your, &c.

871. Th. 24 July '83. John Taylor (Ashbourne).

Address: To the Reverend Dr Taylor in Ashbourne Derbyshire.
Postmark: 24 IY.
A. T. Loyd.—*NQ* 6 S. v. 481.

Dear Sir

When your letter came to me I was with Mr. Langton at Rochester. I was suspicious that you were ill. He that goes away,[1] you know, is to write, and for some time I expected a letter every post.

870.—1. Hill quotes, from W's *Essay towards a Real Character*, 1668, p. 166, part of the 'curious calculation', fortified by diagrams.

871.—1. J had gone away, but for a short time; JT, no doubt, had left Westminster for some months' absence.

My general health is undoubtedly better than before the seizure. Yesterday I came from Gravesend by water, and carried my portmanteau from Billingsgate to Cornhil, before I could get a coach, nor did I find any great inconvenience in doing it.

My voice in the exchange of salutations, or on other little occasions is as it was, but in a continuance of conversation it soon tires. I hope it grows stronger but it does not make very quick advance.

I hope you continue well, or grow every day better, yet the time will come when one of us shall lose the other. May it come upon neither of us unprepared.

I am, dear Sir, Yours affectionately
July 24. 1783   Sam: Johnson.

871.1. Th. 24 July '83. John Ryland (Cranbrook).

Address: To Mr Ryland at Cranbrook Kent. *Postmark*: 24 IY. Adam.—

Dear Sir

For omitting mention of the verses in your first letter I had no particular reason: I did not read them critically, but upon a second view, they seem to me rather to favour solitude too much. Retreat from the world is flight rather than conquest, and in those who have any power of benefiting others, may be consider⟨ed⟩ as a kind of *moral suicide.*[1] I never found any *sweets* in solitude, and it certainly admits not many *virtues*.

In a state of imbecillity retirement is not ⟨only⟩ lawful but decent and proper, and at all times intervals of recess may afford useful opportunities of recollection and such meditation as every Christian ought to practice. But we recollect in order to improve, and meditate for the sake of acting.

I am not yet willing to forsake *towred cities* or to leave *the busy hum of men* quite behind me, but how long I shall be able to sustain my part among them He only knows whose supervision comprises the great drama of the world.

871.1.—1. The underlines in this letter may possibly be R's. I do not suppose 'moral suicide' a quotation; 'sweets', &c., may recall *Comus* 326 'sweet retired solitude'; 'towred cities' and 'busy hum' are *L'Allegro*. See also Index III, s.v. Evelyn.

Of the Latin verses, the first distich was very sweet, the second was less elegant.

Yesterday I returned from Rochester. I came from Gravesend by water. I have been kindly treated, often amused, and hope I am come back rather better than I went. I am warmly invited into Wiltshire,[2] and think to go in the beginning of the next month.

                    I am, Sir, Your most humble servant,
London July 24. 1783   Sam: Johnson

There was not very long ago a Clergyman of great eminence for learning at Cranbroke, whose name was Johnson;[3] enquire what is remembred concerning him.

871.2. Th. 24 July '83. William Bowles (Heale).

Address: To W. Bowles Esq at Heale near Salisbury. *Postmark*: 24 IY. Adam.—

Dear Sir

You will easily believe that the first seizure was alarming. I recollected three that had lost their voices, of whom two continued speechless for life, but I believe, no means were used for their recovery. When the Physicians came they seemed not to consider the attack as very formidable, I feel now no effects from it but in my voice, which I cannot sustain for more than a little time.

When I received your kind letter I was at Rochester with Captain Langton, from whom I returned hither last night, and I flatter myself that I shall be able to obey your generous and friendly invitation.

I hope I am well enough not to give any extraordinary trouble. Will it be convenient that I should bring a servant?[1] I can very well do without one.

Which day I shall come, I cannot yet quite settle you shall therefore have another letter when the time comes nearer.

871.1.—2. By William Bowles.

   3. Presumably John J of Cranbrook, though he had been dead for more than fifty years.

871.2.—1. His usual practice, see references in Index II s.v. Barber. On this occasion he was alone, see 881.

Be pleased to make my most respectful compliments to
your Lady.
I am, Sir, Your most humble servant

London July 24. 1783 Sam: Johnson

872. Sa. 26 July '83. Susannah Thrale (Bath).

Address: To Miss Susannah Thrale at Bath. *Postmark*: 26 IY.
Lansdowne.—1788, No. 315.

Dear Miss Susan

I answer your letter last, because it was received last, and
when I have answered I am out of debt to your house. A
short negligence throws one behind hand, this maxim if you
consider and improve[1] it, will be equivalent to your Parson
and Bird, which is however a very good story, as it shews how
far gluttony may proceed, which where it prevails is I think
more violent and certainly more despicable than avarice
itself.

Gluttony is, I think, less common among women than
among men. Women commonly eat more sparingly, and are
less curious in the choice of meat; but, if once you find a
woman gluttonous, expect from her very little virtue. Her
mind is enslaved to the lowest and grossest temptation.

A friend of mine, who courted a Lady of whom he did not
know much, was advised to see her eat, and if she was volup-
tuous at table to forsake her. He married her however, and
in a few weeks came to his adviser with this exclamation, 'It
is the disturbance of my life to see this woman eat.' She was,
as might be expected, selfish and brutal, and after some years
of discord they parted, and I believe came together no more.

Of men the examples are sufficiently common. I had a
friend[2] of great eminence in the learned and the witty world,
who had hung up some pots on his wall, to furnish nests for
sparrows. The poor sparrows not knowing his character were
seduced by the convenience, and I never ⟨heard⟩ any man
speak of any future enjoyment with such contortions of
delight as he exhibited when he talked of eating the young
ones.

872.—1. The paper is torn, and this word is not certain.
2. 'Isaac Hawkins Browne', HLP.

When you do me the favour to write again, tell me something of your studies, your work, or your amusements.

I am, Madam, Your humble servant
London. July 26. 1783   Sam: Johnson.

872a. Bath. Su. 27 July '83. From Mrs. Thrale.

Tregaskis Catalogue 901 (1925) 756 (not seen).—Extracts in catalogue.

I received your kind letter yesterday, and was very glad to see it, for though I guessed why you were so long in writing, yet we all began to wonder that you never wrote at all; I am not sorry to hear that you have been somewhat incommoded by the heat, as I think you are always better in hot weather than in cold.

'says she has read Johnson's letter to Susan and Sophy, with the advice against laziness; tells him people there have enquired for him' and among the rest, Mrs. Walmesly, who lives on the opposite side of the street.

873 (1). W. 30 July (and 6 Aug., see below) '83. William Cumberland Cruikshank.

Address: To Mr Cruikshank.
Fettercairn.—Boswell 1791, ii. 465, extract (Hill iv. 240).

Sir
Notwithstanding the imaginary diminution of your character,[1] I am going to put myself into your hands.

I have for twenty months had, if I judge rightly a Hydrocele. For twelve months it was totally without pain, and almost without inconvenience, but it has lately encreased so much that the water, if water it be, must be discharged. I beg to see You as soon as You can come, and hope your skill will be able to relieve me.

I am Sir Your most humble Servant,
Bolt court Fleetstreet July 30. 1783   Sam: Johnson

873.1. W. 30 July '83. William Bowles (Heale).

Address: To W. Bowles Esq at Heale near Salisbury. *Postmark*: 30 IY
A. B. Burney.—

Dear Sir
Your invitation is so affectionately pressing, that I think

873 (1).—1. J alludes, I suppose, to the fact that at William Hunter's death in March '83 his 'theatre and museum' in Windmill Street, in which C had been a partner, passed under the control of H's nephew Matthew Baillie; see the *DNB* lives of the three men.

it necessary to tell You the reason of any appearance of delay. To neglect such kindness would be not only incivility but ingratitude.

I will come to You when I can, but I am now delayed by the necessity of suffering a rough chirurgical operation, of which I cannot tell what will ⟨be⟩ the consequence. I need not tell You, dear Sir, that this delay is involuntary. I am Sir Your most obliged and most humble Servant
London July 30. 1783   Sam: Johnson

873.2. M. 4 Aug. '83. William Bowles (Heale).

Address: To W: Bowles Esq at Heal near Salisbury. *Postmark*: 4 AV. Sotheby 30 June 1942.—

Dear Sir
As I sincerely think that You take some interest in my health, I tell You, what I tell very few, that the operation is over with less pain than I feared, and without the benefit which I desired and hoped; I have suffered little, and gained little.

I am ashamed to write so often about a visit, as if I thought my presence or absence of importance. Surely life and experience have taught me better. But convalescence is a very capricious and delusive state. However there will be no more need of poriting,[1] till a note is sent to let You know, when you may expect at Salisbury,
                    Dear Sir Your most humble Servant
London. Aug. 4. 1783   Sam: Johnson

873 (2). W. 6 Aug. (and see above) '83. William Cumberland Cruikshank.

Fettercairn.—Boswell 1791, ii. 465 (Hill iv. 240).

Sir
I beg your acceptance of these volumes[1] as an acknowledgement of the great favours which you have bestowed on, Sir, Your most obliged and most humble Servant,
Boltcourt. Aug: 6. 1783   Sam: Johnson

873.2.—1. This is how I read the word. If I was right, perhaps J intended 'posting', and changed his mind without substituting a *w* for 'writing'. But I am doubtful if 'post' (a letter) was in use so early.

873 (2).—1. A set, as JB tells us, of the *Lives*.

874. See after 879.2.

875. W. 13 Aug. '83. Mrs. Thrale (Weymouth).

Address: To Mrs Thrale at Weymouth. *Postmark*: — AV.
Newton.—1788, No. 316.

Dear Madam
Your letter was brought just as I was complaining that you
had forgotten me.

I am glad that the Ladies find so much novelty at Weymouth. Ovid says that the sea is undelightfully uniform.[1]
They had some expectation of shells, which both by their
form and colour have a claim to human curiosity. Of all the
wonders I have had no account, except that Miss Thrale
seems pleased with your little voyages.

Sophy mentioned a story which her sisters would not suffer
her to tell, because the⟨y⟩ would tell it themselves, but it has
never yet been told me.

Mrs. Ing is, I think, a Baronet's Daughter, of an ancient
house in Staffordshire. Of her husband's father mention is
made in the life of Ambrose Philips.

Of this world in ⟨which⟩ you represent me as delighting
to live, I can say little. Since I came[2] I have only been to
Church, once to Burney's, once to Paradise's, and once to
Reynolds's. With Burney I saw Dr. Rose his new relation,
with whom I have been many years acquainted. If I discovered no reliques of disease I am glad, but Fanny's trade is
Fiction.

I have since partaken of an epidemical disorder, but
common evils produce no dejection.

Paradise's company, I fancy, disappointed him, I remember nobody. With Reynolds was the archbishop of Tuam,[3]
a man coarse of voice, and inelegant of language.

I am now broken with disease, without the alleviation of
familiar friendship, or domestick society; I have no middle
state between clamour and silence, between general conversation and self-tormenting solitude. Levet is dead, and poor

875.—1. *Amores* ii. 11: 'Una est iniusti caerula forma maris', 'one cruel blue'.
    2. 'came home' 1788.
    3. Bourke.

Williams is making haste to dye. I know not if she will ever more come out of her Chamber.

I am now quite alone, but let me turn my thoughts another way.

              I am, Madam, Your most humble servant

London August 13. 1783   Sam: Johnson.

875.1. M. 18 Aug. '83. Frances Reynolds.

Address: To Mrs Reynolds.
A. Houghton.—Croker's Boswell 1831, v. 117.

My dearest Dear

    I wish all that You have heard of my health were true, but be it as it may, if You will be pleased to name the day and hour when You would see me, I will be as punctual as I can. I am, Madam Your most humble Servant

Aug. 18. 1783   Sam: Johnson

876. W. 20 Aug. '83. Mrs. Thrale (Weymouth).

Address: To Mrs Thrale at Weymouth. *Postmark*: 20 AV.
Adam.—1788, No. 317.

Madam

    This has been a day of great emotion. The office of the Communion of the Sick, has been performed in poor Mrs Williams's chamber. She was too weak to rise from her bed, and is therefore to be supposed unlikely to live much longer. She has, I hope, little violent pain, but is wearing out, by torpid inappetence and wearisome decay; but all the powers of her mind are in their full vigour, and when she has spirit enough for conversation, she possesses all the intellectual excellence that she ever had. Surely this is an instance of mercy much to be desired by a parting Soul.

    At home I see almost all my companions dead or dying. At Oxford I have just lost Wheeler the man with whom I most delighted to converse. The sense of my own diseases, and the sight of the world sinking round me, oppresses me perhaps too much. I hope that all these admonitions will not be vain, and that I shall learn to dye as dear Williams is dying, who was very chearful before and after this aweful solemnity, and seems to resign herself with calmness and hope upon eternal Mercy.

I read your last kind letter with great delight, but when I came to *love* and *honour*, what sprung in my Mind?—How lov'd, how honour'd once, avails thee not.[1]

I sat to M[rs] Reynolds yesterday for my picture, perhaps the tenth time, and I sat near three hours, with the patience of *Mortal born to bear*,[2] at last she declared it quite finished and seems to think it fine. I told her it was Johnson's *grimly ghost*.[3] It is to be engraved,[4] and I think, *In glided* &c will be a good inscription.

I am, Madam Your most humble servant,

London Aug. 20 1783   Sam: Johnson

876.1. Sa. 23 Aug. '83. Hester Maria Thrale (Weymouth).

Address: To Miss Thrale at Weymouth.
Lansdowne.—Lansdowne, *Johnson and Queeney* 1932, 37.

My dearest Love,   London, Aug. 23, 1783
The story which Sophy was hindered from telling me, has not yet been told, though I have now expected it a fortnight. Pray let me have it at last with all its circumstances.

My Mistress lately told me of something said in the papers[1] of Boswel and me. I have heard nothing of it, and should be ⟨glad⟩ to know what it was. Cut it out and send it under a cover to Mr. Strahan. There has seldom been so long a time in which I have had so little to do with Boswel, as since he left London. He has written twice and I have written once.[2] I remember no more.

Barry, the painter, has just told me what I delight to tell again, that Ramsay is now walking the streets of Naples in full possession of his locomotive powers.

Poor Mrs. Williams, I am afraid, can expect no such reno-

876.—1. Pope, *To the Memory of an Unfortunate Lady.*
    2. Not traced.
    3. Mallet, *William and Margaret* (in Percy's *Reliques*, iii. 332 in the edition of 1767): ''Twas at the silent solemn hour | When night and morning meet; | In glided Margaret's grimly ghost, | And stood at William's feet.'
    4. For the portrait see *L* iv. 453–4; Dr. Powell does not record any engraving of it.

876.1.—1. Lord Lansdowne failed to find this, and I have been equally unsuccessful.
    2. See on 861.

vation. I have just been to see her, and I doubt she gave perverse answer to my enquiries, because she saw that my tenderness put it in her power to give me pain. This is hateful and despicable, and yet must not be too much hated or despised, for strongly entwisted with human nature is the desire of exercising power, however that power be gained or given. Let us pity it in others, and despise it in ourselves. Write, my dearest, to

Your humble servant
Sam: Johnson

876.2. Su. 24 Aug. '83. Frances Reynolds.

Christie 10 July 1916 (not seen).—Croker's Boswell 1831, v. 118.

Dear Madam   24th August, 1783.
    When your letter came I was so engaged that I could not conveniently write. Whether I shall go to Salisbury I know not, for I have had no answer to my last letter; but I would not have you put off your journey, for all my motions are uncertain. I wish you a happy journey. I am, madam, your humble servant Sam: Johnson.

876.3. M. 25 Aug. '83. William Bowles (Heale).

Address: To W. Bowles Esq at Heale near Salisbury. *Postmark*: 25 AV. Adam.—

Dear Sir
    You are very kind in accepting my apology. I have taken a place for Thursday in a Coach which comes to the white Hart in Stall street,[1] in Salisbury, and hope at last to have the pleasure of sharing your rural amusements.

1 am, Sir Your most humble servant

London Aug. 25.—83   Sam: Johnson

877. Tu. 26 Aug. '83. Mrs. Thrale (Weymouth).

Address: To Mrs Thrale at Weymouth. *Postmark*: 26 AV. Lady Hudson.—1788, No. 318.

Dear Madam
    Things stand with me much as they have done for some

876.3.—1. I am assured that there neither is nor ever was a Stall Street in Salisbury. J was thinking of the White Hart in Stall Street, Bath.

time. Mrs Williams fancies now and then that she grows better, but her vital powers appear to be slowly burning out. No body thinks, however, that she will very soon be quite wasted, and, as she suffers me to be of very little use to her, I have determined to pass some time with Mr Bowles[1] near Salisbury, and have taken a place for Thursday.

Some benefit may be perhaps received from change of air, some from change of company, and some from mere change of place; It is not easy to grow well in a chamber where one has long been sick, and where every thing seen, and every person speaking revives and impresses images of pain. Though it be that no man can run away from himself, he may yet escape from many causes of useless uneasiness. That the *mind is its own place*[2] is the boast of a fallen angel, that had learned to lie. External locality has great effects, at least upon all embodied Beings. I hope this little journey will afford me at least some suspense of melancholy.

You give but an unpleasing account of your performance at Portland. Your scrambling days are then over. I remember when no Miss, and few Masters could have left you behind, or *thrown you out in the persuit of honour*[3] or of curiosity. But *Tempus edax rerum*,[4] and no way has been yet found to draw his teeth.

I am, Dear Madam, Your most humble Servant
London Aug. 26. 1783   Sam: Johnson.

If you write to me, Mr Strahan will send the letters after me.[5]

877a. Weymouth. Tu. 26 Aug. '83. From H. M. Thrale.

Sotheby 10 May 1875, described as a letter from Mrs. Thrale. For the text see Addenda, p. 340. See also 876. 1.

877.—1. An entertaining account of J's journey by a fellow traveller, in the *Monthly Magazine*, is quoted by Croker and by Hill.

2. Milton, *P.L.* i. 254.
3. Addison, *Cato* 1. i ('pursuits').
4. Ovid, *Met.* xv. 234: 'Thy teeth, devouring time' (Dryden).
5. The postscript is omitted in 1788, see on 654.

878. Heale. F. 29 Aug. '83. Richard Brocklesby.

Address: To Dr Brocklesby in London. *Postmark*: 1 SE.
Fettercairn.—Boswell 1791, ii. 462 (Hill iv. 234).

Dear Sir   Heale near Salisbury Aug. 29. 1783.

Without appearing to want a just sense of your kind attention, I cannot omit to give an account of the day which
seemed to appear in some sort perillous. I rose at five, and
went out at six, and having reached Salisbury about nine,[1]
went forward a few miles in my friend's chariot. I was no
more wearied with the journey, though it was a high hung
rough coach, than I should have been forty years ago. The
⟨   ⟩ part I so disposed, that I know not when it has
suffered less.[2] We shall now see what air will do. The
country is all a plain, and the house in which I am, so far as
I can judge from my Window, for I write before I have left
my chamber, is sufficiently pleasant.

Be so kind as to continue your attention to Mrs Williams,
it is great consolation to the well, and still greater to the sick,
that they find themselves not neglected, and I know that
You will be desirous of giving comfort even where You have
no great hope of giving help.

Since I wrote the former part of the letter, I find that by
the course of the post I cannot send it before the thirty first.

I am, Dear Sir, Your obliged humble Servant
Sam: Johnson

879. Heale. W. 3 Sept. '83. John Taylor (Ashbourne).

Address: To the Reverend Dr. Taylor at Ashbourne Derbyshire.
Postmark: 3 SE.
A. T. Loyd.—*NQ* 6 S. v. 481.

Dear Sir

I sat to Opey[1] as long as he desired, and I think the head is
finished, but it ⟨is⟩ not much admired. The rest he is to add
when he comes again to town.

878.—1. That is, 82 miles in some 15 hours; in '76 the journey from Bath to L'n,
106 miles, had taken 20 hours (776).

2. The sentence is erased, doubtless by JB, and the second word (perhaps 'diseased'
or 'swollen' or 'tumid') obliterated.

879.—1. See *L* iv. 455.

I did not understand that you expected me at Ashbourne, and have been for a few days with a Gentleman in Wiltshire. If you write to me at London my letters will be sent, if they should happen to come before I return.

I am, Sir, Your most humble servant,

Heale near Salisbury Sept. 3. 1783   Sam: Johnson.

879.1. Heale. W. 3 Sept. '83. H. M. Thrale (Weymouth).

Address: To Miss Thrale at Weymouth.

Lansdowne.—Lansdowne, *Johnson and Queeney* 1932, 39.

My dear Love,   Heale, near Salisbury, Sept. 3, 1783

Your story[1] is a very pretty story and is very prettily related. I read it to the Gentlemen, and it was agreed that our Consul shewed nothing of the Hero. It is still not very easy to say what he should have done.

I am here in a place which might furnish without any help from fiction the scene of a romance. A good house it is, but rather too modern and too convenient to seize the imagination, but the lawn and the hill, and the thickets, and the water, are almost equal to the fancy of a T r o u b a d o u r.[2] Every thing is done, that I can be supposed to want, for ease or accommodation, but life in a new house is a kind of restraint, both to the guest and to the master, and how long we shall both like it, I cannot tell. You may, I find, write to me from Weymouth or Bath.[3]

I think my general health not impaired. I came from London in one day, in a very rough stage coach, without fatigue. My days pass with ease, for the greater part, but my nights are not quiet.

I cannot hear nor guess what was said of Bozzy[4] and me, if you can recover it send it me, my suspicion is, that Bozz inserted it.[5]

879.1.—1. See 877*a*.

2. The word is spaced in accordance with J's instructions to Q, 843.1.

3. That is, I suppose, J 'found' that his stay at Heale and hers at Weymouth would permit of his receiving a letter at H after she had left W for Bath. But it might be a matter of the 'bye-post'?   4. See on 876.1.

5. See 876.1; and for JB's practice of writing himself up in the newspapers, Pottle's *Literary Career of James Boswell*, 1929, xxiii.

Mrs. Bowles, the Lady of this house, is so taken with your story that she has asked leave to copy it.

My Mistress, I am afraid, forgets me, but if she is got well, she may entertain Mr. Burke and his Brother, who have just past by in their way to Weymouth. I am,

Dearest, Your most humble servant

Sam: Johnson

879.2. Heale. Su. 6 Sept. '83. Joshua Reynolds.

Address: To Sir Joshua Reynolds.
Fettercairn.—

Dear Sir   Heale. Sept. 6. 1783

Your kind attention has done all for me that it could. My Loss[1] is really great. She had been my domestick companion for more than thirty years, and when I come home I shall return to a desolate habitation. I hope all her miseries are past.

Mr Bowles desires me to tell You that he shall take a visit on your return, as a great favour.

Be pleased to assure Mr Burke of my gratitude for his late favour. I am, Sir, Your most humble Servant

Sam: Johnson

I am not well. I wish you a pleasant journey.

874(1). Heale. Tu. 9 Sept. '83 (and see below, 9 Oct.). John Mudge (Plymouth).

Address: To Mr Mudge Surgeon in Plimouth.
Fettercairn.—Boswell 1791, ii. 212 & 466, extracts (Hill iii. 266, iv. 240).

Dear Sir

My conviction of your Skill, and my belief of your friend-

879.2.—For JB's suppression of (parts of) letters to JR see App. E.
    1. By AW's death.

874 (1).—JB printed, s.a. '83, such parts of the letters to Mudge of 9 Sept. and 9 Oct. '83 as concerned the sarcocele, omitting all 'unpleasing technical details'. (He did not date the letters or indicate the division between them, so that Hill was obliged to telescope and misnumber them.) Knowing his own purpose, JB was able to anticipate, and to quote the passage on the soldier's life in an appropriate context, s.a. '78. When J praised the soldier's life he was in general, I suppose, thinking of officers. 'The life of a modern soldier', he had written in *Falkland's Islands*, 'is ill represented by heroick fiction.' His godson, William Mudge, held a commission; he stuck it out, to become a Major-General (*L* i. 378 n. 2).

ship determine me to intreat your opinion and advice. About the latter end of the year –81, I by some accident perceived that my left testicle was much larger than the right. It for some time encreased slowly but without pain or inconvenience, till at last its bulk made it troublesome. In the beginning of this year it a little incommoded my walk, and considering it as a Hydrocele, I, as soon as more formidable disorders gave me leisure intended to discharge the water; But when I showed it to Cruikshank and Pot, they both suspected, and piercing it at my request with a trocar, they found it to be a sarcocele.

This experiment was made about a month ago, since which time the tumour has encreased both in surface and in weight, and by tension of the skin is extremely tender, and impatient of pressure or friction. Its weight is such as to give great pain, when it is not suspended, and its bulk such as the common dress does but ill conceal, nor is there any appearance that its growth will stop. It is so hot, that I am afraid it is in a state of perpetual inflammation.

In this state, I with great earnestness desire You to tell me, what is to be done. Excision is doubtless necessary[;][1] to the case, and I know not any means of palliation. The operation is doubtless painful, but is it dangerous? The pain I hope to endure with decency, but I am loath to put life into much hazard.

Give me, dear Sir, your thoughts upon my case as soon as You can, I shall stay here till I may receive your letter. If You wish to see me, I will come to Plymouth.

My Godson called on me lately. He is weary, and rationally weary of a military life. If You can place him in some other state, I think you may encrease his happiness and secure his virtue. A soldiers time is past in distress and danger, or in idleness and corruption. I am dear Sir Your most humble Servant

Heale near Salisbury Sept. 9. 1783   Sam: Johnson

874 (1).—1. The words 'to the case' were an afterthought; J forgot to delete the semi-colon at the end of the line preceding.

880. Heale. Tu. 9 Sept. '83 ⟨Susannah Thrale⟩ (? Weymouth).

Lansdowne.—1788, No. 320.

Dear Miss

I am glad that you and your sisters have been at Portland.¹ You now can tell what is a quarry, and what is a cliff. Take all opportunities of filling your mind with genuine scenes of nature. Description is always fallacious, at least till you have seen realities, you can not know it to be true. This observation might be extended to Life, but Life cannot be surveyed with the same safety as Nature, and it is better to know vice and folly by report than by experience. A painter, says Sydney,² mingled in the battle, that he might know how to paint it, but his knowledge was useless for some mischievous sword took away his hand. They whose speculation upon characters leads them too far into the world, may ease that nice sense of good and evil, by which characters are to be tried. Acquaint yourself therefore both with the pleasing and the terrible parts of nature, but in life wish to know only the good.

Pray shew Mamma this passage of a letter from Dr. Brocklesby: "Mrs. Williams, from mere inanition, has at length paid the last³ debt to Nature, about 3 o'clock this morning (Sept. 6). She died without a struggle, retaining her faculties intire to the very last, and ⟨as⟩ she expressed it,

880.—This letter is doubtless to Susannah (so 1788). Like the other letters to her it is in bad condition, unlike those to Q (which HLP was not allowed to print). There are no letters to Sophia at Bowood. I have assumed it sent to Weymouth; *Tb* 572 shows them in Bath again by the 11th.

1. 'We go to the Island of Portland tomorrow in a Boat.' *Tb* 20 Aug., 572.

2. *Arcadia*, Book II. I quote the edition of 1627, p. 196: 'That blow astonished quite a poore painter, who stood by with a pike in his hands. This painter was to counterfeit the skirmish between the *Centaures* and *Lapithes*, & had been very desirous to see some notable wounds, to be alle the more lively to expresse them; & this morning . . . the foolish fellow was even delighted to see the effect of blowes. But this last (hapning neere him) so amazed him, that he stood stock still, while *Dorus*, with a turne of his sword, strake off both his hands. And so the painter returned, well skilled in wounds, but with never a hand to performe his skill.' 1788 has 'head' for 'hand'; the same confusion occurred in Goldsmith's *Deserted Village*, where some editions have 'tyrant's head'.

3. 'great' 1788: presumably an improvement by HLP to avoid the repetition of 'last' in 'very last' and 'last summons' below. Perhaps she forgot that she was editing Brocklesby, not J.

having set her house in order, was prepared to leave it at the last summons of Nature."
I do not now say any thing more, than that I am,
My Dearest, Your most humble servant
Sept. 9. 1783   Sam: Johnson.

881. Heale. Tu. 16 Sept. '83. Francis Barber.

Adam.—Croker's Boswell 1848, 739.

Dear Francis   Heale. Sept. 16, 1783.
I rather wonder that you have never written, but that is now not necessary, for I purpose to be with ⟨you⟩ on Thursday before dinner.
As Thursday is my Birthday, I would have a little dinner got, and would have you invite Mrs Desmoulins, Mrs Davis[1] that was about Mrs Williams, and Mr Allen, and Mrs Gardiner.
I am, Your &c.,
Sam: Johnson.

882. Sa. 20 Sept. '83. Charles Burney.

Not traced; collation in Hill's *Boswell* at Pembroke.—Boswell 1791, ii. 465 (Hill iv. 239).

Dear Sir
I came home on the 18th at noon to a very desolate[1] house. You and I have lost our friends,[2] but you have more friends at home. My domestick companion[3] is taken from me. She is much missed, for her acquisitions were many, and her curiosity universal; so that she partook of every conversation. I am not well enough to go much out; and to sit, and eat, or fast alone, is very wearisome. I always mean to send my compliments to all the ladies.
I am Sir your most humble servant
Sept: 20, 1783.   Sam: Johnson

881.—1. Hill is no doubt right in identifying Mrs. Davis with the 'good sort of woman' whom FB found in Bolt Court, again invited to dinner, on 11 Dec. '84 (*Diary* ii. 337).
882.—A copy supplied to Hill adds the subscription and date, which are not in 1791.
    1. So Hill's copy; 'disconsolate' 1791; cf. 884, 886.
    2. CB had just lost Bewley. In April Crisp, FB's 'Daddy', had died.
    3. AW.

886. Sa. 20 Sept. '83. Bennet Langton (Rochester).

Address: To Benet Langton Esq in Rochester Kent. *Postmark*: 20 SE.
Fettercairn.—Boswell 1791, ii. 466, dated 29 Sept. (Hill iv. 240).

Dear Sir

You may very reasonably charge me ⟨with⟩ insensibility of
your kindness, and that of Lady Rothes, since I have suffered
so much time to pass without paying any acknowledgement.
I now at last return my thanks, and why I did it not sooner
I ought to tell you. I went into Wiltshire as soon as I well
could, and was there much employed in palliating my own
malady. Disease produces much selfishness; a man in pain is
looking after ease, and lets most other things go, as chance
shall dispose[1] them. In the mean time I have lost a companion, to whom I have had recourse for domestick amusement for thirty years, and whose variety of knowledge never
was exhausted; and now return to a habitation vacant and
desolate. I carry about a very troublesome and dangerous
complaint, which admits no cure but by the Chirurgical
knife. Let me have your prayers. I am, Sir, Your most
humble Servant
London, Sept. 20. 1783   Sam: Johnson

882.1. Sa. 20 Sept. '83. John Taylor (Ashbourne).

Address: To the Reverend John Taylor in Ashbourne Derbyshire.
Postmark: illegible.
F. B. Vanderhoef.—

Dear Sir

I sent you a letter perhaps improperly short from Heale
in Wiltshire, where I was entertained with great kindness,
but where want of health did not allow ⟨me⟩ to receive, and
perhaps did not enable me to give much pleasure. I went
thither ill and I am afraid came back worse. I have a dreadful
disease which nothing but Mr Pott's knife can remove, and
the operation is not without danger, but I think it more
prudent to venture, than to delay what must probably be
done at last, and will be less safe, as it is procrastinated
longer. I commit myself to eternal and infinite Mercy.

886.—1. 'dispose of' 1791.

I am in other respects better than for some years past, and hope that I shall be able to sustain the operation. Write soon and often to

Sir Your affectionate

London Sept. 20. 1783   Sam: Johnson

883. M. 22 Sept. '83. Mrs. Thrale (Bath).

Sotheby 30 Jan. 1918 (not seen).—1788, No. 321.

Dear Madam   London, Sept. 22, 1783.
Happy are you that have ease and leisure to want intelligence of air-ballons.[1] Their existence is I believe indubitable; but I know not that they can possibly be of any use. The construction is this. The chymical philosophers have discovered a body[2] (which I have forgotten, but will enquire), which, dissolved by an acid, emits a vapour lighter than the atmospherical air. This vapour is caught, among other means, by tying a bladder, compressed upon the bottle in which the dissolution is performed; the vapour rising swells the bladder, and fills it. The bladder is then tied and removed, and another applied, till as much of this light air is collected as is wanted. Then a large spherical case is made, and very large it must be, of the lightest matter that can be found, secured by some method, like that of oiling silk, against all passage of air. Into this are emptied all the bladders of light air, and if there is light air enough it mounts into the clouds, upon the same principle as a bottle filled with water will sink in water, but a bottle filled with æther would float. It rises till it comes to air of equal tenuity with its own, if wind or water does not spoil it on the way. Such, Madam, is an air ballon.

Meteors[3] have been this autumn very often seen, but I have never been in their way.

Poor Williams has I hope seen the end of her afflictions.

883.—1. The subject filled men's minds from this month for about a year. It has its share in J's letters, though by Sept. '84 he was constrained to cry for mercy: 'Do not write about the balloon, whatever else you may think proper to say' (1013). See references in Hill's note here and at *L* iv. 356.

2. See 884.1. The action of sulphuric acid on iron produces hydrogen.

3. Hill quotes Cowper, Crabbe, and the *GM* for the great meteor of 18 Aug. and others. Mrs. Crabbe 'concluded that the end of all things was at hand'.

She acted with prudence and she bore with fortitude. She has left me.

> Thou thy weary task hast done,
> Home art gone, and ta'en thy wages.[4]

Had she had good humour and prompt elocution, her universal curiosity and comprehensive knowledge would have made her the delight of all that knew her. She left her little to your charity school.[5]

The complaint about which you enquire is a sarcocele: I thought it a hydrocele, and heeded it but little. Puncture has detected the mistake: it can be safely suffered no longer. Upon inspection three days ago it was determined *extrema ventura*.[6] If excision should be delayed there is danger of a gangrene. You would not have me for fear of pain perish in putrescence. I shall I hope, with trust in eternal mercy, lay hold of the possibility of life which yet remains. My health is not bad; the gout is now trying at my feet. My appetite and digestion are good, and my sleep better than formerly: I am not dejected, and I am not feeble. There is however danger enough in such operations at seventy-four.

Let me have your prayers and those of the young dear people.

I am, dear Madam, Your, &c.

Write soon and often.

884. M. 22 Sept. '83. Elizabeth Montagu.

Adam.—Croker's Boswell 1831, v. 124.

Madam

That respect which is always due to beneficence makes it

883.—4. Cymbeline iv. ii. 258; 'weary' is a not unlikely misreading of Sh's 'worldly', but is more probably a misquotation.

5. See *L* iv. 246, and for a full account of the school, of which HLT was a manager, Hill's note on this letter. AW had, a few weeks before her death, given the school £200, which Hill suggests was the £200 from her benefit (*L* i. 393), and by her will she left it £157.

6. J, I think, wrote 'tentare', 'to try the extreme' of a surgical operation. The corruption is very easy; in an old errata-list (n.d., but late seventeenth or early eighteenth century) I find 'for Viols read Tryals', and in the errata-list in J's *Journey* is 'for *treason* read *weapon*'. The late H. W. Fowler suggested that 'extrema ventura' might mean 'that the crisis was upon us'; but 'determined' I think naturally describes a decision to do something rather than a forecast.

884.—This letter ended the famous quarrel. J told FB of it, and of Mrs. M's 'very kind answer'. *Diary* ii. 292. See 891.

fit that you should be informed otherwise than by the papers, that on the sixth of this month, died your Pensioner Anna Williams, of whom it may be truly said that she received your bounty with gratitude, and enjoyed it with propriety. You perhaps have still her prayers.

You have, Madam, the satisfaction of having alleviated the sufferings of a Woman of great merit both intellectual and moral. Her curiosity was universal, her knowledge was very extensive, and she sustained forty years of misery with steady fortitude. Thirty years and more she had been my companion, and her death has left me very desolate.

That I have not written sooner, you may impute to absence, to ill health, to any thing rather than want of regard to the Benefactress of my departed Friend.

I am, Madam, Your most humble servant

Sept. 22. 1783 Sam: Johnson

884.1. Tu. 23 Sept. '83. Mrs. Thrale (Bath).

Rylands.—R. L. *Bull.* Jan. 1932, 41.

Madam
You will not much wonder that my own state of body is much in my thoughts, or that since you enquired about it, I should ⟨. . .⟩ what intelligence I obtain.

Having, with all that knew him, a very high opinion of the chirurgical experience and skill of Mr Mudge, I laid my case before him, and inclose his answer, which you may return as you can.

When you have this opinion you will ac— acquit me of impatience or temerity, and perhaps encourage me by your suffrage.

I have written likewise to Dr Heberden, who is now in his retreat at Windsor, and doubt not of his concurrence in the general opinion.

Consider ⟨me⟩ as one that had loved you much, and loved

you long, and let me have your good wishes and your prayers.
Write as often as you can to

> Madam Your most humble servant,

London Sept. 23. 1783   Sam: Johnson

I am told that the *light air*[1] is obtained from iron dissolved
by the vitriolick, or sulphur acid.—But I am not sure.

884.2. Tu. 23 Sept. '83. John Mudge (Plymouth).

Fettercairn.—

Dear Sir

    I thank You for the letter which I received this day. It is
such as I expected clear, judicious, and decisive. I will give
an account of my case as it is at this time. The tension and
inflammation are abated, and the abatement I ascribe first
to a discharge not of *pus* but of *sanies*,[1] and that in no great
quantity from the puncture made a month ago, which till
now appeared externally to be healed, but is lately opened;
and again the gout which has laid hold on both my feet,
seems to have translated the inflammation thither. Of this
you must judge. I can now suspend the tumour without a
defensative. But its weight makes suspension necessary.
I have not nor ever have had the least pain in my back, nor
any other pain but mere soreness, and the tension of the cord
when the cord is too long unsupported.

    Mr Pot and Mr Cruikshank are both of opinion, I think,
that the spermatick cord is yet unaffected; Pot felt it very
accurately.

    I felt very little inconvenience in travelling, though I
came to Salisbury in a rough Stagecoach in one day. I am
Sir your obliged humble Servant,

Boltcourt, Fleetstreet Sept. 23. 1783   Sam: Johnson

If any thing more occurs to you, I desire you to write again.

884.1.—1. See 883.

884.2.—1. Celsus describes *sanies* as 'less crass and glutinous' than pus.

885. W. 24 Sept. '83. John Taylor (Ashbourne).

Address: To the Reverend Dr Taylor in Ashbourne Derbyshire. *Post-mark*: 25 SE.

Adam.—Hill 1892.

Dear Sir,

My case is what you think it, of the worst kind, a Sarcocele. There is I suppose nothing to be done but by the Knife. I have within these four days been violently attacked by the gout, which if ⟨it⟩ should continue in its first ⟨. . .⟩ would retard the other business; but I hope it will abate.

                    I am, Dear Sir, Your humble servant

London Sept. 24. 1783   Sam: Johnson

885.1. W. 24 Sept. '83. William Cumberland Cruikshank.

Address: To Mr Cruikshank.

Fettercairn.—

Sir

The orifice of the puncture discharges so much as, in my opinion, to deserve attention. It has taken away the tension of the integuments, and much abated the general inflammation. I must entreat the favour of a visit this Evening, and wish You would bring with ⟨you⟩ some sticking plaster. I am, Sir, Your obliged humble Servant,

Sept. 24. 1783   Sam. Johnson

886. See above, 20 Sept.

887 (1). W. 24 Sept. (and see below, 11 Oct.) '83. Bennet Langton (Rochester).

Address: To Benet Langton Esq at Rochester. *Postmark*: 24 SE. Fettercairn.—Boswell 1791, ii. 467, extract (Hill iv. 241).

Dear Sir

My case, which you guessed at not amiss, is a Sarcocele; a dreadful disorder which however, I hope, God will not suffer to destroy me. Let me have your prayers. I have consulted Mr Mudge of Plymouth who strongly presses an immediate operation. I expect Dr Heberdens advice to morrow. Make my compliments to your dear Lady, to my Jenny, and to all the little ones.

887 (1). For the reasons of the suppression of (parts of) letters to BL see on 240.1.

The Gout has with⟨in⟩ these four days come upon me with a violence, which I never experienced before. It has made ⟨me⟩ helpless as an infant. It is no great evil in itself but the ⟨ ⟩ delays the Chirurgeon. I am, Sir, Your most &c
London. Sept. 24. 1783   Sam: Johnson

887a. Bath. Th. 25 Sept. '83. From Mrs. Thrale.

Address: To Dr Samuel Johnson.
Harvard.—

Dear Sir—   Bath 25: Sept. 1783.

I return Mr Mudge's Letter, which has given me a juster, but at the same Time a more formidable notion of your Case than I had before. God forbid that I should forbear to encourage you in the sufferance of what seems so very necessary, may that Courage you have always so eminently exerted, be of Use to you now: but I grieve for the sharp Pain my poor dear Mr Johnson must go through.

Who performs the Operation? I love Sharp of the Old Jewry, but my likings are of little Consequence in such serious Matters, and all the people say great Things of Mr Pott. Somebody tells me that you went in a rough Carriage from Salisbury to London, but you probably found any Carriage rough. God give you Strength & Patience, I think the Constitution is equal to all that is required of it.

Mrs Lewis and Mrs Cotterell make the tenderest, and most earnest Enquiries after your Health; and I am sure Mrs Lewis poor Soul! has enough to think on about herself. Every body is solidly, and sincerely concerned for all Danger that may beset, and all real Evil that may befall you but none either are, or ought to be as much concerned as my Daughters or myself: relieve us soon Dear Sir in saying you are *safe*.

after such a Word I can really add no more but that I am most Affectionately Your Obliged Sert.

H: L: T.

888. Tu. 30 Sept. '83. James Boswell (Auchinleck).

Not traced.—Boswell 1791, ii. 467, dated in the text (Hill iv. 241).

You should not make your letters such rarities, when you know, or might know, the uniform state of my health. It is

888.—JB had written to inquire about J's health, and mentioned that 'Baxter's *Anacreon*, which is in the library at Auchinleck, was, I find, collated by my father in 1727, with the MS. belonging to the University of Leyden, and he has made a number of Notes upon it. Would you advise me to publish a new edition of it?' JB does not in *L* date this letter, but it is presumably that recorded in his 'Register': 'Sent 9 August 1783. Dr. Samuel Johnson, in kind concern about him; inviting him to Auchinleck; that I am dreary (Copy).' (Unpublished extract communicated by Dr. Pottle.) See on 861.

very long since I heard from you; and that I have not answered is a very insufficient reason for the silence of a friend. Your *Anacreon*[1] is a very uncommon book; neither London nor Cambridge can supply a copy of that edition. Whether it should be reprinted, you cannot do better than consult Lord Hailes.—Besides my constant and radical disease, I have been for these ten days much harassed with the gout, but that has now remitted. I hope GOD will yet grant me a little longer life, and make me less unfit to appear before him.

888.1. Tu. 30 Sept. '83. Hester Maria Thrale (Bath).

Address: To Miss Thrale at Bath.
Lansdowne.—Lansdowne, *Johnson and Queeney* 1932, 44.

Dear Madam,   London, Sept. 30, 1783
    I am in a state, I think, to be pitied, if pity be a passion ever to come in use. I have a radical disease of a formidable kind and of long continuance, for a great while uneasy, and at last very painful. On Sunday sev'n-night I was seized with the gout, with which in my present state, I did not care to play tricks, and which encreased upon me till I could not without many expedients and repeated efforts raise myself in bed; nor without much pain ⟨and⟩ difficulty by the help of two sticks convey myself to a chair. Dr. Brocklesby allowed large doses of opium which naturally eased the pain. It then withdrew in part from the right foot, but fell furiously on the left. But one foot was a great acquisition. I now walk alone.
    To crown my other comforts a tooth tormented me. I was weary of being diseased from top to bottom; I therefore sent for a Dentist, and pulled it out.
    I am this day not in great pain, nor much dejected. I am not neglected by mankind, but he who lives by himself has many hours of unwelcome solitude, especially when his mind is battered by external evils. These two last years have pressed very hard upon me, and this has yet a severe stroke in store. I pray God for support and deliverance, and think that

888.—1. See on 827.2.

the symptoms are favourable, and hope that you, my dear Love, join your prayers with mine.

Mrs. Cholmondely came to me yesterday, and talked of retiring into Wales. I was not well enough to shew the folly of her scheme, by explaining how she whose whole felicity is conversation, must fall into a state of languor and vacancy, where she found no community of knowledge, could expect no reciprocation of sentiments, nor any mind or manners congenial to her own.

Sheward[1] was with me this morning, just such as Sheward uses to be. I am, Dear Madam,
Your affectionate humble servant,
Sam: Johnson

888.2. Tu. 30 Sept. '83. William Bowles (Heale).

Address: To William Bowles Esq at Heale near Salisbury. *Postmark*: 30 SE.
A. Houghton.—

Dear Sir

The letter which You sent me was from Mudge who has been from home, and was such as might be expected from a very skilful Man. It has raised more hope than fear.

By an unexpected discharge at the puncture, the tension is lessened, the bulk of the tumour diminished, and the inflammation abated, I should have been for some time past almost without pain had not the gout attacked me with great violence. It has been very troublesome for about ten days but has now very much remitted.

Mr Pot has been for some time in Lincolnshire, I expect to see him in a day or two, and then the resolution will be taken, and You shall be informed of the event.

If ever I omit my respects to your Lady you always suppose them intended.

I am Dear Sir, Your obliged humble Servant
London. Sept 30. 1783   Sam. Johnson

888.1.—1. Lord Lansdowne thought 'Sheward' might be a relative of the 'Mrs. Sheward' of 857, 860; but J not seldom names his female acquaintance without prefix, e.g. 'Williams'. It is, I think, impossible to distinguish all references to 'Seward' (William) and 'Sheward', since they may be alternative spellings. 'Sheward' is twice named in *PM*: 6 Apr. ⟨'77⟩ 'I dined with Sheward'; 18 Mar. '82 'I saw Mrs. Lennox and Sheward'; in both places the sex is uncertain.

889. W. 1 Oct. '83. Frances Reynolds.

F. W. Hilles.—Croker's Boswell 1831, v. 128.

Dear Madam
    I am very ill indeed, and to my former illness is superadded the Gout. I am now without shoes and I have lately been almost motionless.
    To my other afflictions is added solitude. Mrs. Williams a companion of thirty years is gone. It is a comfort to me to have you near me.

I am, Madam, Your most &c

Oct 1. 1783 Sam: Johnson.

890. W. 1 Oct. '83. —— Tomkeson.

Address (Croker): To Mr. Tomkeson, in Southampton-Street, Covent Garden.
Not traced.—Croker's Boswell 1831, v. 127.

Sir 1st October, 1783.
    I have known Mr. Lowe very familiarly a great while. I consider him as a man of very clear and vigorous understanding, and conceive his principles to be such that, whatever you transact with him, you have nothing to expect from him unbecoming a gentleman,

I am, sir, Your humble servant,
Sam: Johnson.

890.1. Th. 2 Oct. '83. William Cumberland Cruikshank.

Address: To Mr Cruickshank.
A. T. Loyd.—

Sir
    The critical night is now over. Let me see You as soon as You can, and tell me the success, that I may congratulate or console you.

I am, Sir, Your obliged humble servant

Oct. 2. 1783 Sam: Johnson

My pain and lameness abate, and I am not very uneasy.

890.1. The reference is not to the election of 838, for that was reported in the *GM* for July. It is perhaps to the 'resolution' of 888.2.

890.2. Th. 2 Oct. '83. Frances Reynolds.

Anderson Galleries 30 Nov. 1920 (not seen).—

890.3. Sa. 4 Oct. '83. Robert Chambers. See Addenda.

891. M. 6 Oct. '83. Mrs. Thrale (Bath).

Address: To Mrs Thrale at Bath. *Postmark*: 7 oc.
A. Houghton.—1788, No. 322.

Madam
  When I shall give a good and settled account of my health,
I cannot venture to say, some account I am ready to give,
because I am pleased to find that you desire it.
  I yet sit without shoes with my feet upon a pillow, but my
pain and weakness are much abated; and I am no longer
crawling upon two sticks. To the Gout my mind is reconciled by another letter from Mr. Mudge, in which he
vehemently urges the excision, but tells me that the gout will
secure me from every thing paralytick, if this be true I am
ready to say to the arthritick pains—Deh! venite ogni di,
durate un anno.[1]
  My Physician in ordinary is Dr Brocklesby who comes
almost every day, my Surgeon in Mr Pott's absence is Mr
Cruikshank, the present reader in Dr Hunter's school.
Neither of them however do much more than look and talk.
The general health of my body is as good as you have ever
known it, almost as good as I can remember.
  The carriage which you supposed made rough by my weakness, was the common Salisbury Stage, high hung, and driven
to Salisbury in a day. I was not fatigued.
  Mr Pott has been out of town, but I expect to see him
soon, and will then tell you something of the main affair, of
which there seems now to be a better prospect.
  This afternoon I have given to Mrs Cholmondely, Mrs
Way, Lady Sheffield's relation, Mr Kindersly[2] the Describer
of Indian manners, and another anonymous Lady.

891.—1. Part of a couplet attributed to an *improvvisatore*, which J had thus translated:
'If at your coming princes disappear, | Comets! come every day—and stay a year.'
For the circumstances see *Th* 209 ('venga' for 'venite'), or *Poems* 177.
  2. 'Mr', which is clearly written, is a slip for 'Mrs.', 'Kindersly' a misapprehension
of 'Kinsderley'.

81

As Mrs. Williams received a pension from Mrs. Montague, it was fit to notify her death. The account has brought me a letter not only civil but tender. So I hope, peace is proclaimed.[3]

The state of the Stocks I take to be this. When in the late exigencies, the Ministry gave so high a price for money, all the money that could be disengaged from trade, was lent to the publick. The stocks sunk because nobody bought them. They have not risen since, because the money being already lent out, nobody has money to lay out upon them, till commerce shall by the help of peace bring a new supply. If they cannot rise they will sometimes fall, for their essence seems to be fluctuation, but the present sudden ⟨. . .⟩[4] is occasioned by the report of some new disturbances and demands, which the Irish are machinating.[5] I am,

Madam Your most &c

London. Oct. 6. 1783   Sam: Johnson.

891.1. Th. 7 Oct. '83. William Bowles (Heale).

Address: To William Bowles Esq at Heale near Salisbury. *Postmark*: 7 oc.
Sotheby 30 June 1938.—

Dear Sir

In the account which I now send you, there will be something which your tenderness will dispose you to read with pleasure.

I told you that the tumour had been pierced for experiment. That wound which seemed to close superficially, has since opened, and by a copious ⟨discharge⟩ has so lessened the bulk, and so abated the inflammation of the morbid part, that Mr. Pot who ten days ago seemed to think excision indispensable has now determined to wait the process of Nature.

891.—3. See on 884.
4. Between 'sudden' and 'is occasioned' is a word erased by J, over which he has written 'is'. The word is certainly not 'fall' (1788); it *may* be 'price' or 'prices'. J failed to substitute the word or words he intended.
5. After the passing of the Renunciation Act in '82, which gave the Irish Parliament legislative independence, Flood wanted to proceed to 'simple repeal', that is, a statutory abrogation by the British Parliament of all authority in Irish affairs. Grattan opposed this, and fierce controversy raged in '83.

I have had since I left you, a very sharp fit of the Gout, but it has now remitted, the pain is almost gone and weakness only remains. The tumour now is much less tender, and less cumbrous.

I do not recollect how the five airs[1] were produced by Dr. Saul, be so kind as to tell me, particularly how light air[2] for the flying bubble is generated.

I am now easy, but solitary. My Companion is gone, and at seventy four it is very late to adopt another.

Make my compliments to Mrs. Bowles. I am

Dear Sir Yours most humble Servant

London Oct. 7. 1783.   Sam: Johnson

892. Th. 9 Oct. '83. Mrs. Thrale (Bath).

Rylands: two leaves quarto, without conclusion or date. Adam: two leaves quarto, without opening formula but with conclusion and date. The two sheets were no doubt sent in a franked cover. The second begins 'Two nights ago'.—R. L. *Bull.* Jan. 1932, 42 (and see reprint 1932, 13); 1788, No. 323 (the second part only).

Madam

Many reasons hinder me from believing that opium had any part in my late disorder. I had a long time forborn it. I never used it in any quantity comparable to what is taken by those that habitually indulge themselves with it. It never produces palsies by the utmost excess. My Physicians had so little suspicion of it, though they know my practice, that they made use of it to obviate some effects of the blisters.

891.1.—1. In J's hand one may almost take one's choice between *n* and *v*; but he no doubt wrote 'five airs'. These, Mr. F. Sherwood Taylor tells me, are those which Priestley (*Experiments on Air* 1774) called fixed (carbon dioxide), inflammable (hydrogen), nitrous (oxide of nitrogen), acid (hydrochloric acid), and alkaline (ammonia). Saul remains a problem. He died 1754 and Mr. Taylor cannot find in his book (*Barometer* 1735) anything of the matter. Moreover, before *c.* 1770 no 'airs' were known (other than our atmosphere) except carbon dioxide and hydrogen.

2. Hydrogen for balloons, see 883.

892.—I do not recall another letter to HLT except those from Scotland (which were free), exceeding a sheet. This has no direction and must therefore have been in a cover. It was no doubt franked by Strahan, otherwise it would have borne treble postage. The two halves of the text, now severed by the Atlantic Ocean, were reunited by the acumen of Dr. Powell. HLP presumably rejected the first half as too medical. To the second she gave a date, but no 'Dear Madam' and no indication of lacuna.

It was the paralytick affection which I mentioned sixteen year ago to Dr Laurence, when he allowed my fears to be reasonable. It appeared afterward as an asthma, from which since its invasion of another part I have been almost wholly free, and which in its paroxysms was relieved by opium. The state of the tumour is now changed. When the surgeons visited me, they thought it upon examination a sarcocele, but I was willing to hope something better,[1] and was likewise desirous of knowledge rather than conjecture; I therefore proposed an exploration by puncture; the operation was performed, and the unwelcome opinion was confirmed. The breach made in the integuments closed, but the internal wound never healed. The tumour increased with great encumbrance and very frequent pain, so tender as scarcely to endure any bandage, and so much inflamed as to threaten great mischief.

Such was my misery when I consulted Mr Mudge, and was driven back to town. Mr Pot found the danger not immediate but seemed to think excision unavoidable; but being to take a journey delayed it. While he was away the external wound burst open, and by very frequent effusions the tension is eased, the inflammation abated, and the protuberance so diminished as to incommode me very little, and scarcely to remind me of my disease by any pain.

Mr Pot upon re-examination think⟨s⟩ it best, since Nature has done so much, to look quietly on, and see what it will do more. I proposed another orifice, which I think Mr Cruikshank seems to approve, but Mr Pot thinks not proper. The operation is therefore at least suspended, the tumour is found not scirrous, and therefore not likely to corrupt any other part; and, say⟨s⟩ Pot, one would not carry "fire and sword further than is necessary".

I shall consult Mr Mudge, whose eagerness you know, and of whose judgement I think with great esteem, and enquire whether this new view of the case reconciles him to delay.

I cannot, Madam, yet give an account of settled health, or a cure either perfected or indeed attempted, but I hope, you will be glad to hear that from such a complication of miseries I am now at ease. The Gout, which was for a while very

892.—1. A hydrocele, see 883.

oppressive, is now daily remitting, so that I walk easily enough without shoes between two rooms on the same floor.

I have thus *ended* for the present *joy and woe*[2] and we may now *talk a little like folks of this world*.[3]

——[4] always was a magnifier of herself, but by your description she seems to have improved in her inflations. She was one of ——'s[4] first scholars. She liked him at first, disliked him afterwards, and seems now to have resuscitated her original kindness—sit tibi exemplo.[5]—When you ⟨? write Latin⟩[4] to anybody, but me ⟨take⟩ care to spell it right. *It reflects upon me, as I know of my trade.*[6]

If Mr Shepherd brings me a letter from you, he will have much ado to miss a kind reception, and as my condition is at present he will not be told that I am not at home.

Two nights ago Mr Burke sat with me a long time; he seems much pleased with his Journey.[7] We had both seen Stonehenge[8] this summer for the first time. I told him that the view had enabled me to confute two opinions which have been advanced about it. One that the materials are not natural stones, but an artificial composition hardened by time. This notion is as old as Camden's time, and has this strong argument to support it that stone of that species is nowhere to be found. The other opinion, advanced by Dr Charlton, is that ⟨it⟩ was erected by the Danes.

Mr Bowles made me observe that the transverse stones were fixed on the perpendicular supporters, by a knob formed on the top of the upright stone, which entered into a hollow cut in the crossing stone. This is a proof, that the enormous Edifice was raised by a people who ⟨had⟩ not yet the knowledge of mortar, which cannot be supposed of the

2. Not traced.

3. Prior, 'A Better Answer' (to Chloe Jealous): 'Pr'ythee quit this Caprice; and (as old FALSTAF says) | Let Us e'en talk a little like Folks of This World.'

4. Of the erasures in this paragraph the first and second seem hopeless; of the third I give my conjectural restoration, which is not a mere guess but was suggested by the traces.

5. 'Let her be an example to you'. The appeal produced her 'very kind' letter of 11 Oct. (see 893.1). But see 894. Neither of her letters has survived.

6. Prior, 'Thief and Cordelier': 'It reflects upon Me; as I knew not my Trade.' J no doubt wrote 'knew'; the two words are hardly distinguishable; his 'of' seems to be a slip. The same quotation 636.   7. See 879.1.

8. Hill quotes *Britannia* and Charleton's *Chorea Gigantum*. I abstain from speculation, 'as I know my trade'.

Danes who came hither in ships, and were not ignorant certainly of the arts of life. This proves likewise the stones not to be factitious, for they that could mould such durable masses, could do much more than make mortar, and could have continued the transverse from the upright parts with the same paste.

You have doubtless seen Stonehenge, and if you have not, I should think it a hard task to make an adequate description.

It is, in my opinion to be refered to the earliest habitation of the Island, as a Druidical monument of at least two thousand years, probably the most ancient work of Man upon the Island. Salisbury Cathedral and its Neighbour Stonehenge, are two eminent monuments of art and rudeness, and may show the first essay, and the last perfection in architecture.

I have not yet settled my thoughts about the generation of light air, which I indeed once saw produced,[9] but I was at the height of my great complaint. I have made enquiry and ⟨shall⟩ soon be able to tell you how to fill a ballon.

  I am, Madam, Your most humble servant
London. Oct. 9. 1783   Sam: Johnson

874(2). 9 Oct. '83 (see p. 67). John Mudge (Plymouth).

Fettercairn.—Boswell 1791, ii. 466 (Hill iv. 240).

Dear Sir

By representing the Gout as an antagonist to the palsy, You have said enough to make it welcome. This is not strictly the first fit, but I hope it is as good as the first, for it is the second that ever confined me, and the first was ten years[1] ago, much less fierce and firy than this.

Of the Sarcocele I will try to give a clear account. The bulk, and soreness of the tumour drove me ⟨to⟩ town, where I showed it to Mr Pot, who seemed to think excision necessary, and I saw no reason for any other opinion. He was however to take a journey, and the operation was delayed to his return. In the mean[2] the puncture made experimentally

892.—9. Bowles recorded that J 'whilst he was in Wiltshire, attended some experiments that were made by a physician at Salisbury, on the new kinds of air'. *L* iv. 237.
874(2).—1. In June '76, see 485.
    2. The only example of 'in the mean' in *OED* as late as the eighteenth century, 'time in the mean will be lost', is contextually exceptional. J perhaps omitted 'time' or 'while' after 'mean', which ends a line. See however Index VII.

by the trocar, which though the skin perhaps united, never healed internally, again broke open, and by its discharge reduced the tumour to half its bulk, and by abating the inflammation took away the soreness. I now no longer feel its weight; and the skin of the scrotum which glistened with tension is now lax and corrugated.

Mr Pot, seeing at his return, so great an alteration, thought it proper to suspend all violence, and as Nature has so far favoured us, to wait the process.

This he thinks more reasonable, if I understand him rightly, because the diseased part is totally free from all scirrosity, and he therefore thinks the spermatick cord in no danger. The disorder, he says, is purely local, and indicates no depravity of the constitution.

I have now no pain from the tumour, and very little inconvenience, but I wish it was quite away. The running has now ceased for forty eight hours, and what hope I had, was of its continuance. I shall try if Mr Pot will not open the orifice.

I write thus particularly because, as I trust much to your judgement, I would give a full state of the case. I can scarcely believe that the diseased part will thus cure itself; yet if there be any such hope as the Surgeon thinks, and, as he thinks likewise, no danger in delay, it were madness to demand or solicite the excision.

Write, dear Sir, what you can to inform or encourage me. The operation is not delayed by any fears or objections of mine.

I believe the spermatick cord is uninjured, as well because I find the surgeons of that opinion, as because I never had any dorsal pain, nor any other pain than that of soreness, and of weight, when at its full size, the tumour was sometimes suspended by the cord without support. It is now so much diminished, that the truss is more troublesome than the weight. How long this will be its state I dare not conjecture. You must help me. I am, Sir Your obliged humble Servant,

London. Oct. 9. 1783 Sam: Johnson

887(2). Sa. 11 Oct. (and see above, 24 Sept.) '83. Bennet Langton (Rochester).

Address: To Benet Langton Esq in Rochester. *Postmark*: illegible. Fettercairn.—Boswell 1791, ii. 467, extract (Hill iv. 241).

Dear Sir

Your solicitude for my recovery by the safest means is very kind. My disease is a Sarcocele, a malady very formidable and when it is cured, to be cured commonly only by the excision of the morbid part.

When I was in Wiltshire I spent much of my time in pain, and was at last driven home by my distress. There was for some time little hope but from the knife, but as Mr Pot was to take a journey the operation was delayed, and while he was away, by an unexpected change in the state of the tumour, the necessity of violence is at least suspended, and Mr Pot seems to hope that it may be totally escaped.

In the mean time I have had a very fierce fit of the gout, which however has now remitted, and yesterday I put on my Shoes.

You know, I suppose, that I have lost dear Mr⟨s⟩ Williams who had been my domestick companion for thirty years, and whose death following that of Levet, has now made my house a solitude. She left her little substance to a Charity School.[1] She is, I hope, where there is neither want, nor darkness, nor sorrow.

You will be kind enough to make my compliments to Lady Rothes, and all the young ones. I am, Sir, Your most humble servant,

London Oct. 11. 1783   Sam: Johnson

893. M. 20 Oct. '83. John Taylor (Ashbourne).

Address: To the Reverend Dr Taylor in Ashbourne Derbyshire. *Postmark*: 21 oc. Adam.—Hill 1892.

Sir

Your prohibition to write till the operation is performed is likely, if I observed it, to interrupt our correspondence for a long time.

887(2).—See above, 24 Sept.   1. See on 883.

When Mr Pot and Mr Cruikshank examined the tumid testicle, they thought it a Sarcocele, or flesh swelling, I had flattered myself that it was only a hydrocele or Water swelling. This could be determined with certainty only by puncture, which at my request was made by Mr Pot, and which confirmed their opinion. They advised some palliative, and I went to a Friend in Wiltshire, from whom the bulk and pain of the encreasing tumour drove me home for help. Mr Pot seemed to think that there was no help but from the knife, and only postponed the operation to his return from a journey of a week. In that week the puncture burst open, and by its discharge, abated the inflammation, relaxed the tension, and lessened the tumour by at least half. Mr Pot at his return found so much amendment, that he has left the disease for a time to nature. Mr Cruikshank would cut another orifice, but Mr Pot is not yet willing. In the mean time I have no pain, and little inconvenience.

When all was at the worst I consulted Mudge of Plimouth, a very skilful man, and Dr Heberden who both vehemently pressed the excision, which perhaps would at last be the safer way, but Mr Cruikshank is afraid of it. We must at present sit still.

I have for some weeks past had a sharp fit of the gout, to which I am reconciled by Mr Mudge, who think⟨s⟩ it a security against the palsy; and indeed I recollect none that ever had both. I have now nothing of the gout, but feel a little tender, and ankles somewhat weak. I am in my general health better than for some years past. I am

Sir Your most humble servant

London Oct. 20. 1783   Sam: Johnson

893.1. M. 20 Oct. '83. Hester Maria Thrale (Bath).

Address: To Miss Thrale at Bath.
Lansdowne.—Lansdowne, *Johnson and Queeney* 1932, 43.

My dearest Love,   London, Oct. 20, 1783
    The letter which I received from my Mistress last Monday was very kind, but so short, that I considered it only as a

prelude to a longer, which I have expected from post to post, but having been so often disappointed, begin to fear that the toothach, which at that time contracted her letter, has been succeeded by some more formidable malady. Dear Madam, write immediately and free me from suspense.

Young Mr. Shepherd's commendatory letter dated the 8th of October, was not delivered by him till the 15th. He was therefore in no great haste to pay his visit. He came just at diner time, if I had had any diner time. His unseasonableness did not much affect me, and I entertained him for about an hour as civilly as I could and invited him to tea another day. I have seen no more of him, and do not wonder nor complain that he find stronger attractions in other places, but let him not tell his father, at his return, that he was coldly received.

You may get a Narrative of the loss of the *Grosvenor*[1] India Ship, which I would have you read. You will take the more interest in it, because Sir Robert Chambers whom I think you must remember, and whose ⟨portrait⟩ is in the library, sent in that ship to England his young son for education. He was one of those who staid with the captain, of whom no account has yet been received, and who probably have all perished. Consider the distress of his parents, to whom it ⟨would⟩ be now a comfort to be sure that he is dead.

I go on as I did when I wrote last, in all parts out of pain, but in one, I think, not out of danger. I have no very heavy pressure to sustain, my chief complaint is of sleepless nights, and sleepless without any assignable cause. I am however not neglected. Yesterday I gave tea to Mrs. Siddons,[2] and today Mr. Selwin[3] sent me two partridges. Let me know immediately how is your Mamma.

I am, my dearest, Your most humble Servant,
Sam: Johnson

893.1.—1. Doubtless Alexander Dalrymple's *Account of the Wreck of the Grosvenor* 1783. In the *Memoir* appended to the *Catalogue of Sanskrit MSS. in the possession of the late Sir Robert Chambers*, 1838, Lady C wrote (p. 30) 'The uncertain circumstances of the case left to imagination the most dreadful materials for conjecture.'
2. See *L* iv. 242 for Kemble's account of the visit.
3. Probably not George Augustus S., but the silent banker of *L* iv. 83.

894. Tu. 21 Oct. '83. Mrs. Thrale (Bath).

Not traced.—1788, No. 234.

Dear Madam
   I have formerly heard, what you perhaps have heard too,
that—

> The wheel of life is daily turning round
> And nothing in this world of certainty is found.[1]

When in your letter of the eleventh, you told me that my
two letters had obliged, consoled, and delighted you, I was
much elevated, and longed for a larger answer; but when the
answer of the nineteenth came, I found that the obliging,
consolatory, and delightful paragraphs had made so little
impression, that you want again to be told what those papers
were written to tell you, and of what I can now tell you
nothing new. I am as I was; with no pain and little inconvenience from the great complaint, and feeling nothing from
the gout but a little tenderness and weakness.

   Physiognomy, as it is a Greek word, ought to sound the G:
but the French and Italians, I think, spell it without the G;
and from them perhaps we learned to pronounce it. G, I
think, is sounded in formal, and sunk in familiar language.[2]

   Mr. Pott was with me this morning, and still continues his
disinclination to *fire and sword*. The operation is therefore
still suspended; not without hopes of relief from some easier
and more natural way.

   Mrs. Porter the tragedian, with whom —— spent part of
her[3] earlier life, was so much the favourite of her time, that
she was welcomed on the stage when she trod it by the help
of a stick. She taught her pupils no violent graces; for she
was a woman of very gentle and ladylike manners, though

894.—1. This is probably the last couplet of a Spenserian stanza, and if so is no doubt
quoted from one of the eighteenth-century poems in that metre. It is not (where
I hoped to find it) in *The Castle of Indolence*; it is not in Shenstone's *Schoolmistress*,
nor in Beattie's *Minstrel*.

   2. Walker recognizes only, and *OED* prefers, the pronunciation in which the *g* is
sounded. To-day I think it is commonly silent in what is called standard English.
Walker (I quote the 1806 edition of his *Critical Pronouncing Dictionary*) calls the latter
'a prevailing mispronunciation . . . as if the word was French'.

   3. 'her' HLP ('his' 1788), who fills the blank with 'Mrs. Cottrell'. See Index II for
the connexion between these two ladies.

without much extent of knowledge, or activity of under-standing.

You are now retired, and have nothing to impede self-examination or self-improvement. Endeavour to reform that instability of attention which your last letter has happened to betray. Perhaps it is natural for those that have much within to think little on things without; but whoever lives heedlessly lives but in a mist, perpetually deceived by false appearances of the past, without any certain reliance on recollection. Perhaps this begins to be my state; but I have not done my part very sluggishly, if it now begins.

The hour of solitude is now come, and Williams is gone. But I am not, I hope, improperly dejected. A little I read, and a little I think.

I am, &c.

894.1. Th. 23 Oct. '83. Frances Reynolds.
Address: To Mrs Reynolds.
Adam.—Croker's Boswell 1831, v. 129.

Dear Madam

Instead of having me at your table which cannot, I fear, quickly happen, come, if you can, to dine this day with me. It will give pleasure to a sick friend.

Let me know whether you can come.

I am Madam Yours affectionately

Oct. 23. 1783 Sam: Johnson

894.2. W. 23 Oct. '83 (misdated 1782). William Bowles (Heale).
Address: To William Bowles Esq at Heale near Salisbury. *Postmarks*: 23 and 27 oc (the letter was 'missent to Shaston').
A. Houghton.—

Dear Sir

As I have no reason to doubt of your friendship and tender-ness, I think ⟨you⟩ entitled to an account of my state from time to time.

The Gout has treated me with more severity than any former time, it however never climbed higher than my ankles,

894.2.—The matter of this letter corrects its date. On 23 Oct. '82, moreover, J was at B'n, and a letter posted on that day could not have borne the postmark of the same day

in which it ⟨has⟩ now left a weakness, as well as tenderness in my feet, but when I do not walk or stand too long I have no longer any pain. The puncture by which the tumour discharged itself is now so far healed as to emit nothing. The tumour is so far reduced as to have no pain, or deformity, and very little inconvenience. Nor do I perceive it yet to grow bigger, though of that I am very much afraid.

I had neither pain nor sickness to hinder the enjoyment of Mrs. Bowles's kind present and yours. I called in two friends and dined on it last Sunday. You will both think, I hope, so well of me, as to suppose me thankful.

I still keep the house, except that I have once walked a very little way, and have been twice taken out by my friends in their carriages. I am, Sir

Your most obliged, humble Servant
London. Oct 23, 1782.   Sam: Johnson

895. M. 27 Oct. '83. Mrs. Thrale (Bath).

Sotheby 6 Dec. 1904 (not seen); quotations ('Mrs. Siddons . . . very well') in Quaritch Cat. 253 (1906) 15; and (several) in Anderson Galleries 23 April 1919 (1424/537).—1788, No. 325; Boswell 1791, ii. 467, an extract (Hill iv. 242).

Madam   London, October 27, 1783.

You may be very reasonably weary of sickness; it is neither pleasant to talk nor to hear of it. I hope soon to lose the disgusting topick; for I have now neither pain nor sickness. My ancles are weak, and my feet tender. I have not tried to walk much above a hundred yards, and was glad to come back upon wheels. The Doctor[1] and Mr. Metcalf have taken me out. I sleep uncertainly and unseasonably. This is the sum of my complaint. I have not been so well for two years past. The great malady is neither heard, seen, felt, nor—understood.[2] But I am very solitary.

> Semperque relinqui
> Sola sibi, semper longam incomitata videtur
> Ire viam.[3]

895.—1. Taylor.   2. A parody of Milton?
    3. Virgil, *Aen.* iv. 466: 'She seems alone | To wander in her sleep, through ways unknown, | Guideless and dark.' Dryden.

But I have begun to look among my books, and hope that I am all, whatever that was, which I have ever been.

Mrs. Siddons in her visit to me behaved with great modesty and propriety, and left nothing behind her to be censured or despised. Neither praise nor money, the two great[4] corrupters of mankind, seem to have depraved her. I shall be pleased[5] to ⟨see⟩ her again. Her brother Kemble calls on me, and pleases me very well. Mrs. Siddons and I talked of plays; and she told me her intention of exhibiting this winter the characters of Constance, Catherine, and Isabella in Shakespeare.[6]

I have had this day a letter from Mr. Mudge; who, with all his earnestness for operation, thinks it better to wait the effects of time, and, as he says, to let well alone. To this the patient naturally inclines, though I am afraid of having the knife yet to endure when I can bear it less. Cruikshank was even now in doubt of the event; but Pott, though never eager, had, or discovered, less fear.

If I was a little cross, would it not have made patient Grisel cross to find that you had forgotten the letter that you was answering, but what did I care, if I did not love you? You need not fear that another should get my kindness from you, that kindness which you could not throw away if you tried, you surely cannot lose while you desire to keep it.[7]

I am, Madam, Your, &c.

I have a letter signed S. A. Thrale;[8] I take S. A. to be Miss Sophy: but who is bound to recollect initials? A name should be written, if not fully, yet so that it cannot be mistaken.

896. M. 27 Oct. '83. Frances Reynolds.

Not traced; copy by F. R., Rupert Colomb.—Croker's Boswell 1831, v. 129.

My dearest Dear
I am able enough to write for I have now neither sickness

895.—4. 'great' Anderson Galleries: 'powerful' 1788, perhaps by a whim of HLP's.

5. 'pleased' Quaritch Cat.: 'glad' 1788 (HLP, to avoid repetition?).

6. She played in *King John* in Dec. '83, in *Measure for Measure* in Nov.; I cannot find that she played in *Henry VIII* this winter.

7. In this paragraph I follow the Anderson Galleries punctuation, which being lighter than that of 1788 must be from the original.

8. Not Sophia, but Susannah Arabella.

nor pain; only the Gout has left my ankles somewhat weak.

While the weather favours you and the air does you good, stay in the country when you come home, I hope we shall often see one another, and enjoy that friendship to which no time is likely to put an end on the part of

             Madam Your most humble servant,

London Oct. 27. 1783   Sam: Johnson.

896.1. Tu. 28 Oct. '83. Sarah Wesley.

Sotheby 15 Nov. 1937.—Telford, *Life of Charles Wesley* 1886, 200.

Madam

I will have the first day that You mention, come, my dear, on Saturday next, and, if you can, bring Your Aunt[1] with you, to Your most humble Servant,

Oct. 28. 1783   Sam: Johnson

897. Sa. 1 Nov. '83. Mrs. Thrale (Bath).

Address: To Mrs Thrale at Bath. *Postmark*: 1 NO.
Bergson.—1788, No. 326.

Madam

You will naturally wish to know what was done by the Robbers at the Brewhouse.[1] They climbed by the help of the lamp iron to the covering of the door, and there opening the window, which was never fastened, entered and went down to the parlour, and took the plate off the sideboard, but being in haste and probably without light, they did not take it all. They then unlocked the street door, and locking it again, carried away the key. The whole loss, as Mr. Perkins told me, amounts to near fifty pounds.

Mr. Pott bad me this day take no more care about the tumour. The Gout too is almost well in spite of all the luxury to which my Friends have tempted me by a succession of Pheasants, Partridges, and other delicacies. But Nature has got the better. I hope to walk to Church to morrow.

896.1.—1. Mrs. Hall.

897.—1. Hill quotes *GM* 28 Oct., 1 and 4 Nov., for reports of crimes and executions. 'Villains increase so fast, that a bare recital of their names and atrocious crimes would more than fill our *Magazine*.'

An air ballon has been lately procured by our virtuosi, but it performed very little to their expectation.

The air with ⟨which⟩ these balls are filled is procured by dissol⟨ving⟩² iron filings in the vitriolick (or I suppose sulphureous) acid;³ but the smoke of burnt straw may be used, though its levity is not so great.

If a case could be found at once light and strong, a man might mount with his ball, and go whither the winds would carry him. The case of the ball which came hither was of goldbeaters skin. The cases which have hitherto been used are apparently defective, for the ball⟨s⟩ come to the ground, which they could never do, unless there were some breach made.

How old is the boy that likes Rambler⁴ better than apples and pears?

I shall be glad of Miss Sophy's letter, and will soon write to ? S. A. who since she is not Sophy must be Susy. Methinks it is long since I heard from Queeny.

        I am Madam Your most humble Servant
London. Nov. 1. 1783   Sam: Johnson.

898. M. 10 Nov. '83. Lucy Porter (Lichfield).

Address (Malone): To Mrs Lucy Porter, in Lichfield.
Not traced.—Malone's Boswell 1804, iv. 259.

Dear Madam
    The death of poor Mr. Porter, of which your maid has sent me an account, must have very much surprised you. The death of a friend is almost always unexpected: we do not love to think of it, and therefore are not prepared for its coming. He was, I think, a religious man, and therefore ⟨. . .⟩ that his end was happy.

Death has likewise visited my mournful habitation. Last month¹ died Mrs. Williams, who had been to me for thirty

897.—2. J failed to finish the word ('dissol-' ends a line), and the printer of 1788 read 'iron' as 'ving', to produce 'dissolving filings'.

    3. See on 883. I am informed that burnt straw was actually used.

    4. *Th.* at this date is full of Piozzi and of Sophia's illness. There is no mention of the precocious boy, or even of the robbery.

898.—1. Actually 6 Sept.

years in the place of a sister: her knowledge was great, and her conversation pleasing. I now live in cheerless solitude. My two last years have passed under the pressure of successive diseases. I have lately had the gout with some severity. But I wonderfully escaped the operation which I mentioned, and am upon the whole restored to health beyond my own expectation.

As we daily see our friends die round us, we that are left must cling closer, and, if we can do nothing more, at least pray for one another; and remember, that as others die we must die too, and prepare ourselves diligently for the last great trial.

     I am, Madam, Yours affectionately,

Bolt-court, Fleet-street, Nov. 10, 1783. Sam: Johnson.

898.1. M. 10 Nov. '83. John Taylor (Ashbourne).

Address (Sotheby): To the Reverend Dr. Taylor, in Ashbourne, Derbyshire.
Sotheby 4 Dec. 1916 (not seen); Maggs Catalogue 396 (1920), 2294 A.
—Extract in Maggs catalogue.

What there was in my letter[1] that you could think peevish or unkind, I cannot imagine. When I wrote it, I had nothing in my mind that could dispose me to ill humour, my letter contained as I remember only an account of the process of my distemper.

My health has been in general wonderfully restored. God grant that I may use it well.

I am now enough at ease to enquire after my friends; and wish to know whether you went to Bosworth, and how you bore the journey. . . .

I now live in great and melancholy solitude. But what is best, we do not know.

898.1.—In Sotheby's catalogue this is described as 'The addressed portion of a letter'; that is, no doubt, it consisted of the second leaf, with the direction on what had been p. 4. This may explain JT's failure to give it a number; he numbered 893 and 904 85 and 86; 898.1 was perhaps mislaid, or already a fragment.

 1. JT's numbering of J's letters shows no letter missing between 893 and 904. The letter that JT complained of was, therefore, 893. It was no doubt the peremptory opening paragraph that gave offence.

899. Tu. 11 Nov. '83. Richard Jackson.

No address; 'Richard Jackson Esq' in another hand.
J. D. Hughes (1934).—Hill 1892.

Dear Sir

The Readership[1] of the Temple being vacant, I take the liberty of entreating your Countenance and vote for Mr Hoole a young Clergyman, whom I have known for a great part of his life, and whom I can confidently offer to your notice, as a Man of uncommon parts, and blameless character.

I am, Sir Your most humble Servant
Boltcour⟨t⟩ Fleetstreet Nov. 11. 1783   Sam: Johnson.

900. Th. 13 Nov. '83. Mrs. Thrale (Bath).

Address: To M⟨rs⟩ Thrale at Bath. *Postmark*: 13 no.
Adam.—1788, No. 327.

Dear Madam

Since you have written to me with the attention and tenderness of ancient time your letters give me a great part of the pleasure which a life of solitude admits. You will never bestow any share of your good will on one who deserves better. Those that have loved longest, love best. A sudden blaze of kindness, may by a single blast of coldness be extinguished, but that fondness which length of time has connected with [with] many circumstances and occasions, though it may for a while ⟨be⟩ suppressed by disgust or resentment with or without a cause, is hourly revived by accidental recollection. To those that have lived long together every thing heard and every thing seen recals some pleasure communicated, or some benefit confered, some petty quarrel or some slight endearment. Esteem of great powers or amiable qualities newly discovered may embroider a day or a week, but a friendship of twenty years is interwoven with the texture of life. A friend may be often found and lost, but an *old Friend* never can be found, and Nature has provided that he cannot easily be lost.

899.—1. Hill has a long note on 'all-knowing' Jackson and on the readership, but does not say who was appointed. The sub-Treasurer kindly informed me that William Jeffs, Reader at the Temple Church (that is now the official title), died 4 Nov. '83 and was succeeded 27 Jan. '84 by Haddon Smith. I might have learned this from Sir Frank MacKinnon's edition, 1927, of Lamb's *Old Benchers*.

I have not forgotten the Davenants, though they seem to have forgotten me. I began very early to tell them what they have commonly found to be true. I am sorry to hear of their building. I always have warned those whom I loved, against that mode of ostentatious waste.

You seem to mention Lord Kilmurrey as a stranger. We were at his house in Cheshire, and he one day dined with Sir Lynch. What he tells of the Epigram[1] is not true, but perhaps he dos not know it to be false. Do not you remember how he rejoiced in having *no* park; He could not disoblige his neighbours by sending them *no* venison.

The frequency of death to those who look upon it in the leisure of Arcadia[2] is very dreadful. We all know what it should teach us, let us all be diligent to learn. ⟨Luc⟩y[3] Porter has lost her Brother. But whom I have lost — let me not now remember. Let not your loss be added to the mournful catalogue. Write soon again to

Madam Your most humble servant

London Nov. 13. 1783   Sam: Johnson

901. Tu. 18 Nov. '83. Susannah Thrale (Bath).

Address: To Miss S. A. Thrale at Bath. *Postmark*: 18 NO. Lansdowne.—1788, No. 328; Boswell 1791, ii. 469, extract (Hill iv. 245).

Dear Miss

Here is a whole week, and nothing heard from your house. Baretti[1] said what a wicked house it would be, and a wicked house it is. Of you however I have no complaint to make for I owe you a letter. Still I live here by my own self, and have had of late very bad nights, but then I have had a pig to dinner which Mr. Perkins gave me. Thus life is checquered.[2]

900.—1. In *Th* 575 (23 Oct) HLT quotes a macaronic inscription 'which Lord Killmorey says is written on the Window of a House in the common road to Naples'.

2. Hill remarks that J had quoted Sidney's *Arcadia* in 880. The point of 'the leisure of Arcadia' is not clear to me. But he can hardly have failed to recall the famous 'Et in Arcadia ego' ('I reign even in Arcadia'; the speaker is Death. Often misquoted 'Et ego in'). For George III's knowledge of the phrase—and a fortiori Johnson's?—see *Th* 42.   3. The MS. is torn.

901.—1. 'A hint I gave to Johnson, but he would not take it, because he never thought or could think of Piozzi.' Baretti, quoted by Hill. It is incredible that J should refer to any such 'hint' in a letter to Susannah.

2. See the quotation from Congreve in 262.

I cannot tell you much news because I see nobody that you know. Do you read the Tatlers?[3] They are part of the books which every body should read, because they are the Sources of conversation, therefore make them part of your library. Bickerstaff in the Tatler gives as a specimen of familiar letters, an account of his Cat. I could tell you as good things of Lily the white kitling, who is now at full growth, and very well behaved, but I do not see why we should descend below human Beings, and of one human Being I can tell something that you will like to hear.

A Friend,[4] whose name I will tell when your Mamma has tried to guess it, sent to My Physician to enquire whether this long train of ilness had brought me into any difficulties for want of money, with an invitation to send to him for what occasion required. I shall write this night to thank him, having no need to borrow.

I have seen Mr. Seward[5] since his return only once, he gave no florid account of my Mistress's health. Tell her that I hearken every day after a letter from her, and do not be long before you write yourself to,

My dear, Your most humble servant
Nov[r] 18. 1783   Sam: Johnson.

902. W. 19 Nov. '83. Frances Burney.

Address: To Miss Burney.
H. Murdock.—FB's *Diary* 1842, ii. 283.

Madam
    You have been at home a long time and I have never seen you nor heard from you. Have we quarreled?

901.—3. Hill refers to J's *Life of Addison* ¶ 43, where he quotes Addison's claim (in *Freeholder* 45) that the *Tatler* and *Spectator* 'had a perceptible influence upon the conversation of that time' and adds that this is 'an effect which they can never wholly lose, while they continue to be among the first books by which both sexes are initiated in the elegancies of knowledge'. For the cat, see *Tatler* 112.
    4. W. G. Hamilton, see 905.
    5. For Seward's disapproval of the Piozzi marriage, see *Th* 574, 576, and HLT's letter to FB of 18 Feb. '84, *Diary* ii. 306. As he was consulted in confidence there is no reason to suppose that he enlightened J.
    902.—FB's reply is in *Diary* ii. 283. She pleaded bad weather and invited herself to tea. On J's letter she wrote 'F.B. flew to him instantly and most gratefully.' From her copy of J's letter, evidently written from memory, we learn that the book was 'a volume of the Philosophical Transactions'.

I have sent a book which I have found lately, and imagine to be Dr Burney's. Miss Charlotte will please to examine. Pray write me a direction to Mrs. Chapone,[1] and pray let me sometime have the honour of telling you, how much I am,
Madam, Your most humble servant,
Nov. 19. 1783 Bolt-court   Sam: Johnson.

903. Sa. ——. Frances Burney.

Not traced.—Hill 1892.

Mr. Johnson begs of Miss Burney that she will favour him with a copy of Cecilia to lend a friend.
Saturday.

904. W. 19 Nov. '83. John Taylor (Ashbourne).

Address: To the Reverend Dr Taylor in Ashbourne Derbyshire.
Postmarks: 19 and 20 NO.
Morgan.—Hill 1892.

Dear Sir
You desire me to write often, and I write the same day, and should be sorry to miss any thing that might give you ease or pleasure.

From the fatigue of your journey[1] no harm, I hope, will ensue. Exercise short of great fatigue, must be your great medicine, but painful weariness I would wish you to avoid. You will do well, if you have recourse again to milk, which once restored you beyond expectation, and will now perhaps help you again.

It does not appear from your Doctors prescription that he sees to the bottom of your distemper. What he gives you strikes at no cause, and is only intended for an occasional exciter of the stomach.

Exercise yourself every morning, and when you can catch a momentary appetite, have always something ready. Toast

---

1. See 911.

903.—There is no clue to the date (Hill presumably placed the letter here as a pendant to 902) except the publication of *Cecilia* in the summer of '82. Hill quotes Boswell, Horace Walpole, and Mrs. Barbauld for its popularity. According to Mrs. Barbauld, FB was second only to the balloon as 'the object of public curiosity'.

904.—1. Probably to Bosworth, see 898.1.

and hot wine will be good, or a jelly, or potted meat, or anything that can be eaten without trouble, and dissolves of
itself by warmth and moisture. Let nothing fret you; Care
is all[2] a slow, and may now be to you a quick poison. No
worldly thing but your health is now worth your thought, if
any thing troublesome occurs, drive it away without a parley.
If I were with you, perhaps I might help to keep you easy,
but we are at a great distance.

I do not think that you have so much to hope for from
physick as from regimen. Keep a constant attention to petty
conveniences. Suffer neither heat nor cold in a disagreeable
degree. Beware of costiveness. Take the air every morning,
and very often let me know how you do, and what you eat
or drink and how you rest.

My nights are restless, but my sarcocele gives me no
trouble, and the gout is gone, and my respiration when I am
up is not uneasy.

Let us pray for one another.

I am dear Sir, Yours affectionately,

London Nov. 19. 1783   Sam: Johnson.

905. W. 19 Nov. '83. William Gerard Hamilton.

Fettercairn.—Boswell 1791, ii. 469 (Hill iv. 245).

Dear Sir

Your kind enquiries after my affairs, and your generous
offers have been communicated to me by Dr Brockelsby.
I return thanks with great sincerity, having lived long enough
to know what gratitude is due to such Friendship; and entreat
that my refusal may not be imputed to sullenness or pride.
I am indeed in no want. Sickness is by the generosity of my
Phisicians, of little expence to me. But if any unexpected
exigence should press me, You shall see, dear Sir, how cheerfully I can be obliged to so much liberality.

I am, Sir, Your most obedient and most humble Servant,

Nov. 19. 1783 Boltcourt Fleetstreet   Sam: Johnson

904.—2. J perhaps intended 'always'.
905.—For WGH's inquiries and offers, see 901.

906. Th. 20 Nov. '83. Mrs. Thrale (Bath).

Not traced.—1788, No. 329.

Dear Madam   London, Nov. 20, 1783.

I began to grieve and wonder that I had no letter, but not being much accustomed to fetch in evil by circumspection or anticipation, did not suspect that the omission had so dreadful a cause as the sickness of one of my dears. As her physician thought so well of her when you wrote, I hope she is now out of danger. You do not tell me her disease; and perhaps have not been able yourself fully to understand it. I hope it is not of the cephalick race.

That frigid stillness with which my pretty Sophy melts away, exhibits a temper very incommodious in sickness, and by no means amiable in the tenour of life. Incommunicative taciturnity neither imparts nor invites friendship, but reposes on a stubborn sufficiency self-centered, and neglects the interchange of that social officiousness by which we are habitually endeared to one another. They that mean to make no use of friends, will be at little trouble to gain them; and to be without friendship, is to be without one of the first comforts of our present state. To have no assistance from other minds, in resolving doubts, in appeasing scruples, in balancing deliberations, is a very wretched destitution. If therefore my loves have this silence by temper, do not let them have it by principle; show them that it is a perverse and inordinate disposition, which must be counteracted and reformed. Have I said enough?

Poor Dr. Taylor represents himself as ill; and I am afraid is worse than in the summer. My nights are very bad; but of the sarcocele I have now little but the memory.

I am, Madam, Your, &c.

906.1. Th. 20 Nov. '83. Hester Chapone.

Castle Howard.—

Madam

Though my paper is thus tardy, my compliance was

906.—See *Th* 580. In the entry dated 19 Nov. HLT has no hope: 'my Child, my Sophia will dye: arrested by the hand of God.' It seems unlikely that she wrote to J on that day to complain of Sophy's taciturnity. Perhaps either the entry in *Th*, or J's letter, is misdated.

quicker. Having some way put your letter out of sight, I was forced to ask Miss Burney for your direction. But she knows no more, and You may with great confidence assure Lord Carlisle, that I have never once shewn or mentioned his work,[1] which I return[2] because I did not understand that I have a right to keep it. When it is more freely communicated, I hope not to be forgotten.

I am, Madam, Your most obedient and most humble Servant,   Sam: Johnson
Bolt Court Fleetstreet Nov. 20. 1783

907. Sa. 22 Nov. '83. John Taylor (Ashbourne).

Address: To the Reverend Dr Taylor in Ashbourne Derbyshire.
Postmark: 22 NO.
A. T. Loyd.—*NQ* 6 S. v. 482.

Dear Sir,

You desired me to write often and I now write though I have nothing new to tell you, for I know that in the tediousness of ill health a letter always gives some diversion to the mind, and I am afraid that you live too much in solitude.

I feel the weight of solitude very pressing, after a night of broken and uncomfortable slumber I rise to a solitary breakfast, and sit down in the evening with no companion. Sometimes however I try to read, and hope to read more and more.

You must likewise write to me and tell me how you live, and with what diet. Your Milk[1] kept you so well that I know not why you forsook it, and think it very reasonable to try it again. Do not omit air and gentle exercise.

The Ministry talk of laying violent hands on the East India company,[2] even to the abolition or at least suspension of their charter. I believe corruption and oppression are in

906.1.—1. Carlisle's *The Father's Revenge.* See 911, and *L* iv. 526.
    2. J must, I think, have intended 'returned'; see 759.2.
907.—1. See 747.
    2. Fox's East India Bill, introduced on 18 Nov., was lost. It proposed to transfer the powers of the Company to commissioners to be named, in the first instance, by Parliament. The fall of the coalition ministry soon followed. For J's views on India, see *L* iv. 213.

India at an enormous height, but it has never appeared that they were promoted by the Directors, who, I believe see themselves defrauded, while the country is plundred, but the distance puts their officers out of reach, and I doubt whether the Government in its present state of diminished credit, will do more than give another evidence of its own imbecillity.

You and I however have more urgent cares, than for the East Indian Company. We are old and unhealthy. Let us do what we can to comfort one another.

I am Dear Sir &c

London Nov. 22. 1783   Sam: Johnson

908. Sa. 22 Nov. '83. John Hawkins.

Not traced.—Hawkins, *Life of Johnson* 1787, 561.

Dear Sir,

As Mr. Ryland was talking with me of old friends and past times, we warmed ourselves into a wish, that all who remained of the club should meet and dine at the house which once was Horseman's, in Ivy lane. I have undertaken to solicit you, and therefore desire you to tell on what day next week you can conveniently meet your old friends.

I am, Sir, Your most humble servant,

Bolt court, Nov. 22, 1783.   Sam: Johnson.

909. M. 24 Nov. '83. Mrs. Thrale (Bath).

Address: To Mrs Thrale at Bath. *Postmark*: 24 NO.
Adam.—1788, No. 330.

Dear Madam

The Post came in late today, and I had lost hopes. If the Distress of my dear little Girl keep me anxious, I have much consolation from the maternal and domestick character of your dear letters.

I do not much fear her pretty life, because scarcely any body dies of her disorder, but it is an unpromising entry upon a new period of life, and there is, I suspect, danger lest she

908.—For the Ivy Lane Club, see *L* i. 191; for its reunion, *L* iv. 435, and below, especially 954.

shall have to struggle for some years with a tender, irritable and as it is not very properly called a nervous constitution.[1] But we will hope better, and please ourselves with thinking that nature, or physick, will gain a complete victory, that dear Sophy will quite recover, and that She and her Sisters will love one another one degree more for having felt and excited pity, for having wanted and given help.

I received yesterday from your Physicians[2] a note from which I received no information, they put their heads together to tell me nothing. Be pleased to write punctually yourself, and leave them to their trade. Let me have something every post till my dear Sophy is better.

My nights are often very troublesome, so that I try to sleep in the day. The old convulsions of the chest have a mind to fasten their fangs again upon me. I am afraid that winter will pinch me. But I will struggle with it, and hope to hold out yet against heat and cold. I am, Madam

Your most humble servant

Nov. 24. 1783 London.   Sam: Johnson.

910. Th. 27 Nov. '83. Mrs. Thrale (Bath).

Hyde.—1788, No. 331.

Dear Madam

I had to day another trifling letter from the Physicians. Do not let them fill your mind with terrours which perhaps they have not in their own, neither suffer yourself to sit forming comparisons between Sophy and her dear Father, between whom there can be no other resemblance than that of sickness to sickness. Hystericks and apoplexies have no relation. Hystericks commonly cease at the times when apoplexies attack, and very rarely can be said to shorten life. They are the bugbears of disease of great terrour but little danger.

Mrs. Byron has been with me to day to enquire after Sophy, I sent her away free from the anxiety which she brought with her.

Do however what the Doctors order, they know well

909.—1. J describes the sense 'having weak or diseased nerves' as 'medical cant'.
    2. 'Woodward and Dobson are called.' *Tb* 580.

enough what is to be done. My pretty Sophy will be well, and Bath will ring with the great cure.

Nov. 27. 1783 London   I am, Dear Madam
                              Your most humble Servant
                                        Sam: Johnson

910.1. Th. 27 Nov. '83. Frances Reynolds.

Address: To Mrs Reynolds.
W. T. Spencer (1927); copy by F. R., Rupert Colomb.—Croker's Boswell 1831, v. 135.

Dear Madam
    I beg that you will let me know by this Messenger, whether you will do me the honour of dining with me, and if you will, whether we shall eat our dinner by our own selves, or ask Mrs Desmoulins, I am
                Dearest Dear Your most humble servant
Nov 27. 1783 Bolt Court   Sam: Johnson

911. F. 28 Nov. '83. Hester Chapone.

Castle Howard; copy by JB, Isham.—Boswell 1791, ii. 470, dated 28 Nov. 1783 (Hill iv. 247). The original has no precise date, and JB's copy has no date.

Madam.
    By sending the Tragedy to me a second time I think that a very honourable distinction has been shewn me, and I did not delay the perusal, of which I am now to tell the effect.
    The construction of the play is not completely regular, the stage is too often vacant, and the scene⟨s⟩ are not sufficiently connected. This however would be called by Dryden[1] only a mechanical defect, which takes away little from the power of the poem, and which is seen rather than felt.
    A rigid examiner of the diction might perhaps wish some

911.—See 906.1. JB asked Lord C for a copy, but was shown the original (*BP*, quoted in *L* iv. 246). It does not appear on what ground JB fixed the date as the 28th. His own copy has no date.
    1. Hill quotes from J's Dictionary a passage quoted from Dryden. This is near the beginning of the Preface to *Sylvae* (Malone's *Dryden* iii. 26). D, in reference to Roscommon's 'rules' in his *Essay on Translated Verse*, writes: 'many a fair precept in poetry is like a seeming demonstration in the Mathematicks; very specious in the diagram, but failing in the mechanick operation.' I am not clear that this is the passage J had in mind.

words changed, and some lines more vigorously terminated. But from such petty imperfections what writer was ever free? The general form and force of the dialogue is of more importance. It seems to want that quickness of reciprocation which characterises the English drama, and is not always sufficiently fervid or animated.

Of the sentiments I remember not one that I wished omitted. In the imagery I cannot forbear to distinguish the comparison of joy succeeding grief, to light rushing on the eye accustomed to darkness. It seems to have all that can be desired to make it please. It is new, just, and delightful.

With the characters either as conceived or preserved, I have no fault to find; but was much inclined to congratulate a writer who in defiance of prejudice and Fashion, made the Archbishop a good man, and scorned all thoughtless applause which a vicious Churchman would have brought him.

The catastrophe is affecting. The Father and Daughter both culpable, both wretched, and both penitent, divide between them our pity and our sorrow.

Thus, Madam, I have performed what I did not willingly undertake, and could not decently refuse. The noble Writer will be pleased to remember, that sincere criticism ought to raise no resentment, because judgement is not under the control of will, but involuntary criticism, as it has still less of choice ought ⟨to⟩ be more remote from possibility of offence. I am, Madam, Your most humble Servant,
Nov 1783.   Sam. Johnson

912. Sa. 29 Nov. '83. Mrs. Thrale (Bath).

Adam.—1788, No. 332.

Dear Madam

The life of my dear, sweet, pretty, lovely, delicious Miss Sophy is safe, let us return thanks to the Great Giver of existence, and pray that her continuance amongst us may be a blessing to herself and to those that love her. Multos et felices,[1] my dear Girl.

912.—The printer of 1788, who in general did his work well, broke down in this letter, reading 'suited' as 'devoted' and 'the Muses' as 'Romances'.
   1. 'Many happy' (years, *scil.* annos). She died in 1824.

Now she is recovered, she might write me a little history of her sufferings, and impart her schemes of study and improvement. Life to be worthy of a rational Being must be always in progression; we must always purpose to do more or better than in time past. The Mind is enlarged and elevated by mere purposes, though they end as they begin by airy contemplation. We compare and judge though we do not practice.

She will go back to her arithmetick again, a science which [which] will always delight her more, as by advancing further she discovers more of its use, and a science suited to Sophy's case of mind, for you told in the last winter that she loved metaphysicks more than the Muses. Her choice is certainly as laudable as it is uncommon, but I would have her like what is good in Both.

God bless you and your Children, so says

Dear Madam, Your old friend

London Nov. 29. 1783   Sam: Johnson

913. Sa. 29 Nov. '83. John Taylor (Ashbourne).

Address (Hill): To the Reverend Dr Taylor Ashbourne Derbyshire. Christie 5 June 1888 (not seen).—Hill 1892.

Dear Sir,

Your Doctor's fixed air[1] recommends him but little to my esteem; I like Doxy's prescription better, and your own regimen better than either. By persevering in the use of milk, I doubt not but you will gain health enough to keep your residence, and that[2] we can consult at leisure what may be best for both. This is but at two months distance. If your health or safety could be much promoted by any attention of mine, I would come down, but my own sickliness makes me unwilling to be far from my Physicians, and unless I were sure of some considerable good, such a journey is not to be undertaken. If I come to you, I must go to Lichfield.

While milk agrees with you, do not be persuaded to forsake it. Go to bed, and rise, as Nature dictates, not by rule

913.—1. Hill quotes a review of Priestley's *Observations*, from which it appears that 'fixed air' (CO_2) was used in the treatment of 'putrid' fevers.
2. Perhaps J wrote 'then'.

but according to convenience. Make your mind easy, and
trust God.

My time passes uncomfortably, my nights have been of
late spasmodick without opium and sleepless with it. I hope
that when we meet we shall both be better.

I am, Sir, Your most humble servant,
London, Nov. 29, 1783.   Sam: Johnson.

914. Sa. 29 Nov. '83. Lucy Porter (Lichfield).

Address: To Mrs Lucy Porter in Lichfield. *Postmark*: 29 NO.
Fettercairn.—Boswell 1791, ii. 477 (Hill iv. 256).

Dear Madam
You may perhaps think me negligent that I have not
written to You again[1] upon the loss of your Brother, but
condolences and consolations are such common and such useless things, that the omission of them is no great crime, and
my own diseases occupy my mind and engage my care. My
nights are miserably restless, and my days therefore are heavy.
I try however, to hold up my head as high as I can.

I am sorry that your hearing[2] is impaired, perhaps the
Spring and the [the] Summer may in some degree restore it,
but if not we must submit to the inconveniences of time, as
to the other dispensations of eternal Goodness. Pray for me,
and write to me, or let Mr Pearson write for You.

I am my dear, Your most humble Servant,
London Nov 29. 1783   Sam: Johnson

914.1. M. 1 Dec. '83. Mrs. Thrale (Bath).

Address: To Mrs Thrale at Bath. *Postmark*: 1 DE.
Rylands.—R. L. *Bull.* Jan. 1932, 44.

Dear Madam
If you can be short,[1] I can be as short as you, but though
I had less inclination to write I would not forbear an immediate answer to your letter, which I have just received,
because I think you should lose no time before you go into

914.—1. See 898.   2. 'health' 1791.
914.1.—1. The letter dated, in 1788, 'Nov. 31' (*sic*) '1783' is not short. But it has
every sign of later compilation.

the warm bath, which, in my opinion, promises more help for the whole complication of your disorders, than any thing else. It is at least safe, it can do no sudden mischief, and if any thing forbids its use, you have it wholly in your power. Stay in the bath, each time, till you find some little relaxation, and go in twice a day. I think you will in a week have reason to praise your Physician.[2]

Please to tell all my young Friends, that I love them, and wish them well.

I am, Madam, Your most humble servant

Dec. 1. 1783   Sam: Johnson

915. W. 3 Dec. '83. John Hawkins.

Not traced.—Hawkins, *Life of Johnson* 1787, 563.

Dear Sir

In perambulating Ivy lane,[1] Mr. Ryland found neither our landlord Horseman, nor his successor. The old house is shut up, and he liked not the appearance of any near it; he therefore bespoke our dinner at the Queen's Arms, in St. Paul's church yard, where, at half an hour after three, your company will be desired to-day, by those who remain[2] of our former society.

Your humble servant,

Dec. 3   Sam: Johnson.

915.1. W. 3 Dec. ⟨'83⟩. William Cumberland Cruikshank.

Address: To Mr Cruikshank.
Fettercairn.—

Dr. Johnson earnestly desires to see Mr Cruikshanks as soon as is possible.
Dec. 3

914.1.—2. Meaning himself? But it is not certain that J did not intend 'Physicians'.
915.—1. See 908.
  2. Hawkins in his *Life of Johnson* 563 names the company: J and himself, 'Mr. Ryland, and Mr. Payne of the Bank'.

916. Th. 4 Dec. '83. Joshua Reynolds.

Address: Sir Joshua Reynolds.
Fettercairn.—Boswell 1791, ii. 475 (Hill iv. 253).

Dear Sir
    It is inconvenient to me to come out, I should else have waited on You with an account of ⟨a⟩ little evening club which we ⟨are⟩ establishing in Essex Street in the Strand, and of which You may be sure that[1] You are desired to be one. It will be held at the Essex head now kept by an old Servant of Thrale's. The Company is numerous, and as You will be ⟨? able to⟩ see by the list miscellaneous. The terms are lax, and the expences light. Mr Barry was adopted by Dr Brocklesby who joined with ⟨me⟩ in forming the plan. We meet thrice a week, and he ⟨who⟩ misses, forfeits two-pence.
    If You are willing to become a Member, draw a line under your name. Return the list. We meet for the first time on Monday at eight. I am Sir Your most humble Servant
Dec. 4. 1783   Sam: Johnson

916.1. F. 5 Dec. '83. John Perkins.

O. T. Perkins.—

Mr. Johnson's compliments to Mr. and Mrs Perkins.
    If Mr Perkins is to be at home to day Mr Johnson will wait on him about six to tea, and to do a little business.
Friday. Decem. 5. —83

916.—For the Essex-Head Club see *L* iv. 436 and references in Index V. The 'old servant' was Samuel Greaves (*L* iv. 253; FB calls him 'Samuel, a footman of the late Mr. Thrale'. *Memoirs of Dr. Burney*, ii. 261). Sir Joshua declined the invitation (Hill suggests, because he had quarrelled with Barry), and he, like Hawkins (who had not been invited), wrote disparagingly of the club. But JB (who was elected in '84) names a number of the respectable members, in confutation of this 'misrepresentation'.
    1. 'You may be sure that' *om*. 1791 by homoeoteleuton.

916.2. M. 8 Dec. '83. Frances Reynolds.

F. W. Hilles; copy by F. R., Rupert Colomb.—

Dear Madam
  Be so kind as to dine to Day with Your humble servant
Dec. 8 —83   Sam: Johnson

917. Sa. 13 Dec. '83. Mrs. Thrale (Bath).

Address: To Mrs Thrale at Bath. *Postmark*: 13 DE.
Sir Charles Russell.—1788, No. 334.

Dear Madam
  I think it long since I wrote, and sometimes venture to
hope that you think it long too. The Intermission has been
filled with spasms, opiates, sleepless nights, and heavy days.
These vellications of my breast shorten my breath, whether
they will much shorten my life I know not; but I have been
for some time past very comfortless. My friends however
continue kind, and much notice is taken of me.
  I had two pretty letters from Susy and Sophy to which
I will send answers, for they are two dear girls. You must all
guess again at my Friend.[1]
  I dined about a fortnight ago with three old friends, we
had not met together for thirty years, and one of us thought
the other grown very old. In the thirty years two of our set
have died.[2] Our meeting may be supposed to be somewhat
tender. I boasted that I had passed the day with three
friends, and that no mention had been made among [of] us
of the air ballon, which has taken full possession, with a very
good claim of every philosophical mind and mouth. Do you
not wish for the flying coach?
  Take care of your own health, compose your mind, and
you have yet strength of body to be well.
        I am, Madam Your most humble servant
Dec. 13 1783 London   Sam: Johnson

917.—1. W. G. Hamilton, see 905.   2. See 954.

917.1. Sa. 13 Dec. '83. ⟨Richard Clark⟩.

C. S. Cow (defective).—

Sir

   The Club to which ⟨you⟩ seemed willing to give your name, met last Monday, and Wednesday, and will meet again today at the Essex Head, in Essex Street in the Strand, and your company will be desired as soon as You can conveniently give it us. I am Sir Your most humble Servant
Dec. 13. 1783   Sam: Johnson

918. Sa. 20 Dec. '83. John Taylor (Ashbourne).

Address: To the Reverend Dr Taylor in Ashbourne Derbyshire.
Postmark: 20 DE.
Hist. Soc. of Pennsylvania.—Hill 1892.

Dear Sir

   Perhaps you wonder that I do not write. I am very severely crushed by my old spasm which suffering me to get no sleep in the night, necessarily condemns the day to sluggishness and restlessness. I am indeed exceedingly distressed.

   I think you have chosen well, in taking a later[1] month for yourself, but I was sorry to miss you so long a time. I am indeed heavily loaded with distempers. Sometimes I fancy that exercise would help me, but exercise I know not how to get; sometimes I think that a warmer climate would relieve me, but the removal requires a great deal of money. At present I subsist by opiates, and with them shall try to fight through the winter, and try something efficacious, if life be granted me, in the Spring. The testicle continues well. Write to what comfort you can. We are almost left alone.

                          I am, Sir, Your affectionate &c.
Dec. 20. 1783. London   Sam: Johnson.

917.1.—Though this letter is not addressed the recipient is not in doubt. I owed it, and other letters directed 'To Mr. Clark', to the courtesy of Mr. C. S. Cow.

918.—1. Writing on 29 Nov. (913) J had looked forward to seeing JT within two months.

918.1. Sa. 20 Dec. '83. Hester Maria Thrale (Bath).

Address: To Miss Thrale at Bath
Lansdowne.—Lansdowne, *Johnson and Queeney* 1932, 45.

Dearest Love,   London, Dec. 20, 1783
  My breath was so much obstructed a week ago, that Dr. Brocklesby who came with me to my door,[1] came, as he said, next day to see if I were alive. An opiate however relieved the paroxysm, and the Dr next day, when he saw me so much better made this observation, 'I was afraid last night that your disease was an Hydrops pectoris, but I have reason now to think it only nervous and spasmodick, for if any of the great organs of life were obstructed, you could not obtain so much relief by such slight means in so short a time.' This is so comfortable that I am very willing to think it right.
  But I am very heavily crushed. As I have little sleep in the night, I have little spirit in the day, and though I have for some time before ⟨my⟩ last attack written letters for amusement, I have for several days now shrunk from writing. I have now begun again.
  You are suffering your hand, my Dearest, to grow negligent and indistinct. I found your last letter hard to be read. The name of *Corbets* if I had not known it I should never have disentangled. Names and numbers must always be written plainly. Now I write again, I will take you all round,[2] for I am, with great kindness,
                                    Your humble servant,
                                    Sam: Johnson

919. Tu. 23 Dec. '83. Frances Reynolds.

R. Fletcher (1929).—Croker's Boswell 1831, v. 138.

Dearest Madam
  You shall doubtless be very welcome to Me on Christmas day. I shall not dine alone, but the company will all be

---

918.1.—1. From a meeting, probably, of the Essex-Head Club. See 932.
  2. He wrote to HLT a week later. Letters to the younger girls, if they were written, are lost.

people whom we can stay with or leave. I will expect You at three, if I hear no more. I am this day a little better.

I am, dear Madam, Your most humble Servant,

Dec 23 —83   Sam Johnson

I mean, do not be later than three, for as I am afraid, I shall not be at Church, You cannot come too soon.

920. W. 24 Dec. '83. James Boswell (Auchinleck).

Not traced.—Boswell 1791, ii. 471 (Hill iv. 248).

Dear Sir

Like all other men who have great friends, you begin to feel the pangs of neglected merit, and all the comfort that I can give you is, by telling you that you have probably more pangs to feel, and more neglect to suffer. You have, indeed, begun to complain too soon; and I hope I am the only confidant of your discontent. Your friends have not yet had leisure to gratify personal kindness; they have hitherto been busy in strengthening their ministerial interest. If a vacancy happens in Scotland, give them early intelligence; and as you can serve Government as powerfully as any of your probable competitors, you may make in some sort a warrantable claim.

Of the exaltations and depressions of your mind you

920.—JB's letter is described, without date, in *L*: 'I consulted him on two questions of a very different nature: one, whether the unconstitutional influence exercised by the Peers of Scotland in the election of . . . the Commons . . . ought not to be resisted; the other, What . . . should be done with old horses unable to labour. I gave him some account of my life at Auchinleck; and expressed my satisfaction that the gentlemen of the county had, at two publick meetings, elected me their *Praeses*, or Chairman.' The Register adds nothing except the date, 22 Nov. The journal, though it does not mention the letter, gives useful help. JB records, 21 Nov. ('writing the 25'): 'One of these days I had a serious conversation with the new Lord Advocate. He could make but aukward excuses for my not being appointed Solicitor General; and I plainly saw that Scotland was in the hands of understrapping Managers, of which I wrote to Mr. Burke in strong terms. Erskine however professed much willingness to serve me.' This letter should have reached London on or about 26 Nov., and the first part of J's reply was written almost at once. By 'your friends' he no doubt means especially Burke (see *L* iv. 223), who on the fall of the Shelburne government in Feb. had been reappointed paymaster. Before J resumed his letter, the coalition ministry had been dismissed (18 Dec.).

delight to talk, and I hate to hear. Drive all such fancies from you.

On the day when I received your letter, I think, the foregoing page was written; to which, one disease or another has hindered me from making any additions. I am now a little better. But sickness and solitude press me very heavily. I could bear sickness better, if I were relieved from solitude.

The present dreadful confusion of the publick ought to make you wrap yourself up in your hereditary possessions, which, though less than you may wish, are more than you can want; and in an hour of religious retirement return thanks to God, who has exempted you from any strong temptation to faction, treachery, plunder, and disloyalty.

As your neighbours distinguish you by such honours as they can bestow, content yourself with your station, without neglecting your profession. Your estate and the Courts will find you full employment; and your mind well occupied will be quiet.

The usurpation of the nobility, for they apparently usurp all the influence they gain by fraud,[1] and misrepresentation, I think it certainly lawful, perhaps your duty, to resist. What is not their own they have only by robbery.

Your question about the horses gives me more perplexity. I know not well what advice to give you. I can only recommend a rule which you do not want—give as little pain as you can. I suppose that we have a right to their service while their strength lasts; what we can do with them afterwards I cannot so easily determine. But let us consider. Nobody denies that man has a right first to milk the cow, and to sheer the sheep, and then to kill them for his table. May he not, by parity of reason, first work a horse, and then kill him the easiest way, that he may have the means of another horse, or food for cows and sheep? Man is influenced in both cases by different motives of self-interest. He that rejects the one must reject the other. I am, &c.

London, Dec. 24, 1783.   Sam. Johnson.

A happy and pious Christmas; and many happy years to you, your lady, and children.

920.—1. JB had described them as exercising influence 'by means of fictitious qualifications'.

921. Sa. 27 Dec. '83. Mrs. Thrale (Bath).

Address: To Mrs Thrale at Bath. *Postmark*: 27 DE.
A. J. Scheuer (1933).—1788, No. 335.

Dear Madam
    The wearisome solitude of the long evenings did indeed
suggest to me the convenience of a club in my neighbourhood, but I have been hindered from attending it, by want of
breath. If I can complete the scheme, you shall have the
names and the regulations.
    The time of the year, for I hope the fault is rather in the
weather than in me, has been very hard upon me. The
muscles of my breast are much convulsed. Dr. Heberden
recommends opiates of which I have such horror that I do not
think of them but *in extremis*.[1] I was however driven to them
last night for refuge, and having taken the usual quantity
durst not go to bed for fear of that uneasiness to which a
supine posture exposes me, but rested all night in a chair,
with much relief, and have been to day more warm, active,
and cheerful.
    You have more than once wondered at my complaint of
solitude, when you hear that I am crowded with visits.
Inopem me copia fecit.[2] Visitors are no proper companions
in the chamber of sickness. They come when I could sleep,
or read, they stay till I am weary, they force me to attend,
when my mind calls for relaxation, and to speak when my
powers will hardly actuate my tongue. The amusements and
consolations of languor and depression are conferred by
familiar and domestick companions, which can be visited or
called at will, and can occasionally be quitted or dismissed,
who do not obstruct accommodation by ceremony, or destroy
indolence by awakening effort.
    Such society I had with Levet and Williams, such I had
where—I am never likely to have it more.[3]

921.—1. J said the same to JB in March; *L* iv. 171. The opiates of which he had
'such horror' were, I suppose, a much more drastic dose than it was his habit to take;
he had been taking small doses of opium regularly for many months.
    2. Ovid, *Metam.* iii. 466: 'Plenty has made me poor.'
    3. 'Very true, it was at Streatham Park.' HLP.

I wish, dear Lady, to you and my dear Girls, many a cheerful and pious Christmas.

I am Your most &c

London Dec. 27. 1783   Sam: Johnson.

922. W. 31 Dec. '83. Mrs. Thrale (Bath).

Address: To Mrs Thrale at Bath. *Postmark*: 1 IA.
C. S. Lewis.—1788, No. 336; Boswell 1791, ii. 469, extract (Hill iv.
245).

Dear Madam
    Since You cannot guess, I will tell You that the generous
Man was Gerard Hamilton.[1] ⟨. . .⟩ I returned him a very
thankful and respectful letter.
    Your enquiry about Lady Carlisle I cannot answer, for
I never saw her, unless perhaps without knowing her, at
a conversation.
    Sir Joshua has just been here, and knows nothing of Miss
Bingham, if one of Lord Lucan⟨'s⟩ daughters be meant, the
eldest is now Lady Spencer, the ⟨second[2]⟩ is languishing in
France with a diseased leg, and the third is a child.
    Pray send the letter which you think will divert me, for I
have much need of entertainment; spiritless, infirm, sleepless, and solitary, looking back with sorrow and forward with
terrour. But I will stop.
    Barry of Ireland had a notion that a Man's pulse wore
⟨him⟩ out;[3] my beating breast wears out me. The Physicians
yesterday covered it with a blister, of which the effect
cannot yet be known. Good God, prosper their endeavours!
Heberden is of opinion that while the weather is so oppressive we must palliate.
    In the mean time I am well fed, I have now in the house,
Pheasant, Venison, Turkey, and Ham, all unbought. Attention and respect give pleasure, however late, or however

922.—1. This word is followed by a line and a half, so erased as to be partly illegible.
But Mr. Edgar Lobel, an accomplished palaeographer, read thus: 'Why one of the
young dears should sh . . . guineas . . . I never.'
    2. J omitted 'second' on turning the page, and the printer of 1788 naturally read
his 'the' as 'she'.
    3. Paper torn. See *L* iii. 34.

useless. But they are not useless, when they are late, it is reasonable to rejoice as the day declines, to find that ⟨it⟩ has been spent with the approbation of mankind.

The ministry is again broken, and to any man who extends his thoughts to national considerations the times are dismal and gloomy. But to a sick man what is the publick? The new year is at hand, may God make it happy to Me, to You, to us all, for Jesus Christ's sake. Amen.

   I am, Madam, Your most humble Servant
London Dec. 31. 1783   Sam: Johnson.

923. Sa. 3 Jan. '84. John Taylor (Ashbourne).

Address: To the Reverend Dr. Taylor in Ashbourne Derbyshire.
F. Edwards (1920).—Hill 1892.

Dear Sir

I was intending to write to you, to quarrel with your silence, when waking after a short sleep in my chair, I found your kind letter lying on the table.

Since your Milk has restored you, let it preserve you, do not forsake it again for any length of time. As for me, I know not on which side to turn me, I am irregular in nothing.[1] My breast is now covered with a blister, which is, I believe, to be kept open; it gives no pain, and perhaps has hitherto produced no benefit, for though I have not since its application, suffered any thing from Spasms, I have never been without opium, and therefore know not, which has helped me; nor am I helped much, for in bed I scarce get any sleep; what I have is in a chair. Dr. Heberden tells me that I must be content to support myself by opiates in the winter, and try to get better help in hotter weather.

In Spring I have a desire of trying milk somewhere in the country. My lower parts begin to swell. May we all be received to Mercy.

—— There is likely to be a vacancy soon in [in] Wicher's Almshouses in Chappel street, which it will ⟨be⟩ your Dean's turn to fill up. A poor relation of mine wants a habitation. His name is Heely. I intend to ask Dr. Bell's interest, and if

923.—1. I could not be sure of this word; it is certainly not 'breathing', as might be supposed.

you ⟨think⟩ it proper, wish you would write to the Dean in Heely's favour.[2]

I wish us both a happy year.

                                I am, Sir, Affectionately yours,
Jan. 3, 1784 London   Sam: Johnson.
Write soon, and often.

923.1. Sa. 3 Jan. '84 (misdated '83). William Bowles (Heale).

Address: To W. Bowles Esq at Heale near Salisbury. *Postmark*: 3– (month illegible).
Adam.—

Dear Sir

A dreadful interruption of my health, the effect, in some part at least, of the hard weather, as my Physicians flatter me, and as I am very willing to flatter myself, has hindred me not only from accepting but from acknowledging your kind invitation. My experience of the general course of life at Heal, presents to my Mind a very delightful image of a Heal Christmas, but I have from some time been too ill for pleasure. I have been too troublesome for any house but my own. The state of a sick man is to want much, and enjoy little. Your attention and that of your dear Lady would be fatigued by perpetuity of distress.

My pleasure in my former sickness was to write to my friends, but even this employment has been now less attractive, and even your letter has lain unanswered.

I have not forgotten Dr Talbot's book, when I go up into my study[1] I will try to pick it up, and send it, and anything else that you desire, I shall be glad to do.

The time is, I hope, yet to come when change of air shall be recommended; and if you will then receive me, I know not any air like the air of Heale, a place where the elements and the inhabitants concur to procure health or preserve it.

You live in a very happy region, yet I suppose you have frost and snow, I should like to see their effect upon my little

923.—2. Heeley was appointed to the Almshouse in Chapel Street, Westminster. Hawkins 602.

923.1.—This letter is certainly misdated; J had not seen Heale, or Bowles's children, before his visit in the autumn of '83.

 1. For J's difficulty in going upstairs see 825.1, 835.1 (iii. 17).

friends to whom they are new. I hope they starve their little fingers and feet, and cry, and wonder what it is that ails them. Is your River frozen over? Have you made a Ballon? Your plain would be a good place for mounting. The effects already produced are wonderful, but hitherto of no use, but perhaps use will come hereafter.

I am Sir Your most humble servant

London. Jan: 3. 1783   Sam: Johnson

923.2. M. 5 Jan. '84. John Perkins.

Address: To Mr Perkins.
O. T. Perkins.—

Dear Sir
I have kept the house under great oppression of ilness, for several weeks, and dare not yet ⟨. . .⟩ of going out, as soon as my Physicians allow to go abroad, I will send you word. I am, Sir,

Your obliged humble Servant

Jan 5. —84   Sam: Johnson

Many happy years to you all.

923.3. M. 5 Jan. '84. John Ryland. See Addenda.

924. Tu. 6 Jan. '84. Charles Dilly.

Address: To Mr Dilly Bookseller in the Poultry. *Postmark*: PENYPOST. Fettercairn.—Boswell 1791, ii. 477 (Hill iv. 257).

Sir
There is in the world a set of Books, which used to be sold by the Booksellers on the bridge, and which I must entreat you to procure me. They are called *Burton's Books*, the title of one is, *Admirable Curiosities, Rarities and Wonders in England*. I believe there ⟨are⟩ about 5 or 6 of them they seem very proper to allure backward Readers, be so kind as to get them for me, and send me ⟨them⟩ with the best printed edition of Baxter's call to the unconverted. I am, Sir, Your humble Servant

Jan. 6. 1784 Bolt court   Sam: Johnson

924.—For an account of the houses on London Bridge (until '57) and of the cheap books called Burton's, see *L* iv. 257.

924.1. Su. 11 Jan. '84. John Perkins.

John Grant (1931).—

Mr Johnson's compliments to Mr and Mrs Perkins. Mr Johnson had a sleepless night, but is better to day.
Jan. 11. —84

925. M. 12 Jan. '84. Mrs. Thrale (Bath).

Address: To Mrs Thrale at Bath. *Postmark*: 12 IA.
A. Houghton.—1788, No. 337.

Dear Madam

If, as You observe my former letter was written with trepidation, there is little reason, except the habit of enduring, why this should show more steadiness. I am confined to the house; I do not know that any things grow better; my Physicians direct me to combat the hard weather with opium; I cannot well support its turbulence, and yet cannot forbear it, for its immediate effect is ease; Having kept me waking all the night, it forces sleep upon me in the day, and recompenses a night of tediousness, with a day of uselessness. My legs and my thighs grow very tumid. In the mean time my appetite is good and if my Physicians do not flatter me, death is ⟨not⟩ rushing upon me. But this is in the hand of God.

The first talk of the Sick is commonly of themselves, but if they talk of nothing else, they cannot complain if they are soon left without an audience.

You observe, Madam, that the Ballon engages all Mankind, and it is indeed a wonderful and unexpected addition to human knowledge; but we have a daring projector who disdaining the help of fumes and vapours is making better than Dædalean wings, with which he will master the ballon and its companions, as an Eagle masters a goose. It is very seriously true, that a subscription of eight hundred pounds has been raised, for the wire and workmanship of iron wings;[1] one pair of which and, I think, a tail, are now shown in the haymarket, and they are making another pair at Bir-

925.—1. See 989. Mr. J. E. Hodgson refers me to W. Cooke, *The Air Balloon*, second edition 1783, 34.

mingham. The whole is said to weigh two hundred pounds, no specious preparation for flying, but there are those who expect to see him in the sky. When I can leave the house I will tell you more.

I had the same old friends[2] to dine with me on wednesday, and may say that since I lost sight of you, I have had one pleasant day.

I am Madam, Your most humble Servant,
London. Jan. 12 1784   Sam: Johnson.
Pray send me a direction to Sir —— Musgrave in Ireland.

925.1. W. 14 Jan. '84. William Bowles (Heale).

Address: To W: Bowles Esq at Heale near Salisbury. *Postmark*: 14 1A. Adam.——

Dear Sir
What can be the reason that you do not write to me? A Friends letter is always comfortable, and I, who have now been many weeks confined to the house, have much need of comfort. My nights are sleepless; I sat in a chair till six this morning, to avoid the miseries of bed. My Physicians, who are zealous to help me, can give nothing but opium, with which they fortify me against the violence of the winter. Opium dismisses pain but does not always bring quiet, and never disposes me to sleep, till a long time after it has been taken: Thus I am harrassed between sickness, and a palliative remedy which is still to be repeated, for I need not tell you that opium cures nothing, though by setting the powers of life at ease, I sometimes flatter myself that it may give them time to rectify themselves.

In this state you may suppose I think sometimes of Heale, which I hope to see again when I can enjoy it more. Do not forget me, nor suppose that I can forget you, or your Lady or your young ones. I wish you all many and many happy years, and am

Dear Sir, Your most obedient servant
London. Jan. 14. 1784   Sam: Johnson

925.—2. See 915.

926. W. 21 Jan. '84. Mrs. Thrale (Bath).

Address: To Mrs Thrale at Bath. *Postmark*: 21 IA.
Adam.—1788, No. 338.

Dear Madam.
    Dr Heberden this day favoured me with a visit, and after hearing what I had to tell him of miseries and pains, and comparing my present with my past state, declared me well. That his opinion is erroneous I know with too much certainty, and yet was glad to hear it, as it set extremities at a greater distance; he who is by his physician thought well, is at least not thought[1] in immediate danger. They therefore whose attention to me makes them talk of my health, will, I hope, soon not drop, but lose their subject. But, alas, I had no sleep last night, and sit now panting over my paper. Dabit Deus his quoque finem.[2] I have really hope from Spring, and am ready like Almanzor[3] to bid the Sun *fly swiftly* and *leave weeks and months behind him*. The Sun has looked for five[4] thousand years upon the world to little purpose, if he does not know that a sick man is almost as impatient as a lover.
    Mr Cator gives such an account of Miss Cecy[5] as you and all of us must delight to hear; Cator has a rough, manly, independent understanding, and does not spoil it by complaisance, he never speaks merely to please, and seldom is mistaken in things which he has any right to know. I think well of her for pleasing him, and of him for being pleased; and at the close[6] am delighted to find him delighted with her excellence. Let your Children, dear Madam, be *his* care, and *your* pleasure; close your thoughts upon them, and when sad fancies are excluded, health and peace will return together
                I am, Dear Madam, Your old Friend
Jan. 21. 1784 London   Sam: Johnson

926.—1. The second 'thought' is perhaps an inadvertent repetition.
  2. Virgil, *Aen.* i. 199: 'Even to this God will grant an end.'
  3. At the end of Dryden's *Conquest of Granada*: 'Move swiftly, Sun, and fly a lover's pace; | Leave weeks and months behind thee in thy race.'
  4. HLP, knowing better, prints 'six'.
  5. Cecilia was no doubt staying with the Cators at Beckenham.
  6. The phrase 'at the close' is not in *OED*; it may perhaps be a Gallicism.

927. W. 21 Jan. '84. John Perkins.

Address: To Mr Perkins.
O. T. Perkins.—Boswell 1791, ii. 515 (Hill iv. 257).

Dear Sir
    I was very sorry not to see you, when you were so kind as to call on me, but to disappoint friends and if they are not very good natured, to disoblige them, is one of the evils of Sickness. If You will please to let me know which of the afternoons in this week, I shall be favoured with another visit by you and Mrs Perkins, and the pretty young people I will take all the measures that I can to be pretty[1] well at that time. I am,
                            Dear Sir, Your most humble servant,
Jan. 21. 1784   Sam: Johnson

927.1. F. 23 Jan. '84. John Perkins.

O. T. Perkins.—

    Dr[1] Johnson sends compliments to Mr and Mrs Perkins, and the young Gentlemen, and begs to know when they will favour him with their company.
Jan. 23. [—84 in another hand]

928. Sa. 24 Jan. '84. John Taylor (Ashbourne).

Address: To the Revd Dr Taylor in Ashbourne Derbyshire. *Postmark*: 24 IA.
Huntington Library.—Hill's Boswell 1887, iv. 260.

Dear Sir,
    I am still confined to the house, and one of my amusements is to write letters to my friends, though they being busy in the common scenes of life, are not equally diligent in writing to me.
    Dr Heberden was with me two or three days ago, and told

927.—1. 1791 omits the word, perhaps deliberately, to avoid repetition.
927.1.—1. JB (*L* ii. 332) says that so far as he knew J 'never assumed the title of *Doctor*'. See also *L* iv. 79, 268. In the great majority of his letters in the third person he writes 'Mr. Johnson'. This and 952.1 are the only exceptions of which, having seen the originals, I can be certain; but see 601, and RWC in *Essays on the Eighteenth Century*, Oxford 1945.

me that nothing ailed me, which I was glad to hear though
I know it not to be true. My nights are restless, my breath
is difficult, and my lower parts continue tumid.

The struggle, You see, still continues between the two sets
of ministry: those that are *out* and *in* one can scarce call them,
for who is *out* or *in* is perhaps four times a day a new question.[1] The tumult in government is, I believe, excessive, and
the efforts of each party outrageously violent, with very little
thought on any national interest, at a time when we have all
the world for our enemies, when the King and parliament
have lost even the titular dominion of America, and the real
power of Government every where else. Thus Empires are
broken down when the profits of administration are so great,
that ambition is satisfied with obtaining them, and he that
aspires to greatness needs do nothing more than talk himself
into importance. He has then all the power which danger
and conquest used formerly to give; he can raise a family,
and reward his followers.

Mr Burke has just sent me his speech upon the affairs of
India, a volume of above an hundred pages closely printed.
I will look into it; but my thoughts now seldom travel to
great distances.

I would gladly know when You think to come hither, and
whether this year You will come or no. If my life be continued, I know not well how I shall bestow myself.

I am, Sir, Your affectionate &c

Sam: Johnson.

929. Tu. 27 Jan. '84. Richard Clark.

Address: To Richard Clark Esq.
Fettercairn.—Boswell 1791, ii. 478 (Hill iv. 258).

Dear Sir

You will receive a requisition, according to the rules of the
club, to be at the house as President of the night. This turn

928.—1. The King refused to dismiss Pitt in spite of repeated adverse votes in the
House of Commons.

929.—See *L* iv. 254, 436. If the Club had 24 members as J intended, then since it
met three times a week one does not see why the president's turn should come once
a month. But attendance was irregular, see 1006, and the club may not yet have
received its complement.

comes once a month, and the member is obliged to attend,
or send another in his place. You were enrolled in the club
by my invitation and I ought to introduce You, but as I am
hindered by sickness, Mr. Hoole will very properly supply
my place as introductor, or yours, as President. I hope in
milder weather to be a very constant attendant. I am, Sir,
Your most humble Servant

Jan. 27. –84 Bolt court, Fleetstreet   Sam: Johnson

You ought ⟨to be informed⟩[1] that the forfeits began with
the year, and that every night of nonattendance, incurs the
mulct of three pence, that is nine pence a week.

929.1. Sa. 31 Jan. '84. Hester Maria Thrale (Bath).

Address: To Miss Thrale at Bath.
Lansdowne.—Lansdowne, *Johnson and Queeney* 1932, 46.

Dear Madam,   London, Jan. 31, 1784
    It is indeed a long time since I wrote to Bath. I may ⟨be⟩
allowed to be weary of telling that I am sick, and sick, and
you may well be weary of hearing, but having now kept the
house for seven weeks, and not being likely soon to come out,
I have my want of health much in my mind, and am indeed
very deeply dejected.

    I have however continued my connection with the world
so far as to subscribe to a new ballon which is ⟨to⟩ sustain five
hundredweight, and by which, I suppose, some Americo
Vespucci, for a new Columbus he cannot now be, will bring
us what intelligence he can gather in the clouds. Sure as I
am by reason and by example that there is no great danger
in the expedition, I could not see the earth a mile below me,
without a stronger impression on my brain than I should like
to feel. The King of Prussia taught his soldiers to load
marching, because they would not think of the enemy when
they had something to do. The aerial adventurers have their
globe to ballance, and glass tubes to watch, and therefore
look less often down.

    My friends call on me much oftener than my feebleness

929.—1. 'to be informed' is JB's supplement; the MS. is intact.

allows me to admit them. I am afraid some of them will be angry. This is among the other evils of sickness.

My inability to attend the Essex Head makes the club droop, but if it does ⟨not⟩ languish quite away, I hope my return to it will invigorate and establish it, and then I will transmit to you our number, our names, and our laws.[1]

I am, Dear Madam, Your most humble servant,

Sam: Johnson

929.2. Tu. 3 Feb. '84. William Bowles (Heale).

Address: To W: Bowles Esq at Heale near Salisbury. *Postmark*: 3 FE. Adam.—

Dear Sir

I am still confined to the house, this is the eighth week of my incarceration. I am utterly unable to sustain the violence of the weather. I am willing to be persuaded, and a sick man never wants flatterers, that I am rather oppressed without than weak within, and that I shall find ease and comfort return, when Winter raises the siege.

Confinement I should not much lament, if confinement were my whole restraint. If I could employ my time at will, I could perhaps procure to myself instruction or amusement, but so it is, that my nights passing without sleep, drag days after them of little use. Few states are more uncomfortable, and few more unprofitable than that of drowsiness without sleep.

Opiates, without any encrease of quantity, are still efficacious in quelling any irregular concussions of the body, but I dread their effect upon the mind more than those of wine or distilled spirits.

The encrease of warmth I have tried, and am compelled to practice in all the instances which you so kindly recommended.

I have fits of great dejection and cheerlessness: I take delight in recollecting our evening worship; let me have a place in your devotions.

I subscribed a few days ago to a new ballon,[1] which is to

929.1.—1. For the 'Rules' composed by J see *L* iv. 254.
929.2.—1. For the fate of J's subscription see 997.

carry five hundred weight, and with which some daring
adventurer is expected to mount, and bring down the state
of regions yet unexplored. This power of mounting and
descending is a strange thing, but I am afraid we shall never
be able to give so wide a surface any horizontal direction.
We can ⟨. . .⟩² it. And to make the discoveries which it really
puts in our power, the rise ought to be taken from the
summit of Teneriffe, for so far we know the atmosphere
without its help. The summits of the Alps may be sufficient,
and thither the philosophers of Geneva are not unlikely to
carry it. I wish well to such soaring curiosity.

Be pleased to ⟨make⟩ my compliments to your dear Lady,
to your Father, and to my little friends.—and to all friends.
London Feb. 3. 1784   I am, dear Sir &c Sam: Johnson

929.3. W. 4 Feb. ⟨'84.⟩ John Nichols.

Sotheby 18 Nov. 1929.—

Mr Johnson having been for many ⟨weeks⟩ confined, is
very cheerless, and wishes that when (*sic*) Mr. Nichols would
now and then bestow an hour upon him
Feb. 4

930. F. 6 Feb. '84. William Heberden.

Not traced.—Hill 1892.

Dear Sir

When you favoured me with your last visit, you left me
full of cheerfulness and hope. But my Distemper prevails,
and my hopes sink, and dejection oppresses me. I entreat
you to come again to me and tell me if any hope of amendment remains and by what medicines or methods it may be
promoted. Let me see you, dear Sir, as soon as you can.

I am, Sir, Your most obliged and most humble servant,
Bolt-court, Fleet Street, Feb. 6, 1784.   Sam: Johnson.

929.2.—2. Mr. Metzdorf reads the missing letters as 'n . . row'. The purely conjectural letters are obliterated at the end of a line by the seal. My guess is 'not row'.

930.1. 7 Feb. ⟨? '84⟩. John Nichols.

My note of source mislaid.—

Mr Johnson desires the favour of Mr Nichols company, to meet Mr Allen, at dinner on Monday the 9ᵗʰ. Febr. 7

931. M. 9 Feb. '84. Mrs. Thrale (Bath).

Address: To Mʳˢ Thrale at Bath. *Postmark*: 9 FE. Adam.—1788, No. 339.

Dear Madam

The remission of the cold did not continue long enough to afford me much relief. You are, as I perceive afraid of the opium. I had the same terrour, and admitted its assistance only under the pressure of insupportable distress, as of an auxiliary too powerful and too dangerous. But in this pinching season I cannot live without it, and the quantity which I take is less than it once was.

My Phisicians flatter me, that the season is a great part of my disease, and that when warm weather restores perspiration, this watery disease will evaporate. I am at least, willing to flatter myself.

I have been forced to sit up many nights by an obstinate sleeplessness, which makes the time in bed intolerably tedious, and which continues my drowsing the following day. Besides I can sometimes sleep erect, when I cannot close my eyes in a recumbent posture. I have just bespoke a flannel dress which I can easily slip off and on, as I go into bed, or get out of it. Thus pass my days and nights in morbid wakefulness, in unseasonable sleepiness, in gloomy solitude[1] with unwelcome visitors, or ungrateful exclusions, in variety of wretchedness. But I snatch every lucid interval, and animate myself with such amusements as the time offers.

One thing which I have just heard, you will think to surpass expectation. The Chaplain[2] of the factory at Petersburg

930.1.—Since the 9th of Feb. was a Monday in '84, this letter probably belongs here.
931.—1. A comma here would clarify the sense.
  2. William Tooke. Nichols, *LA* ii. 553, ix. 169. N does not say that T was in England at this period, but does say that he was in Berlin in '83. Perhaps he came to L'n.

relates that the Rambler[3] is now by the command of the
Empress translating into Russian, and has promised when it
is printed to send me a copy.

Grant, O Lord that all who shall read my pages, may
become more obedient to thy Laws, and when the wretched
writer shall appear before Thee, extend thy mercy to him,
for the sake of Jesus Christ. Amen.

I am Madam Your most &c

London. Feb^r 9 1784.   Sam: Johnson

931.1. M. 9 Feb. ('84). Frances Reynolds.

Sotheby 18 Aug. 1941; copy by F. R., Rupert Colomb.—

Dear Madam
I think very well of your dinner, and intend soon to have
something like it. If I could as easily get good nights as good
dinners, I should perhaps soon be well—but I am yet very ill.

I am, Madam, your most, &c.

Feb. 9   Samuel Johnson.

932. W. 11 Feb. '84. James Boswell (Edinburgh).

Not traced.—Boswell 1791, ii. 478 (Hill iv. 259).

Dear Sir
I hear of many inquiries[1] which your kindness has disposed
you to make after me. I have long intended you a long letter,
which perhaps the imagination of its length hindered me
from beginning. I will, therefore, content myself with a
shorter.

Having promoted the institution of a new Club in the
neighbourhood, at the house of an old servant of Thrale's,
I went thither to meet the company, and was seized with a

931.—3. No Russian *Rambler* has been found; confusion with *Rasselas*, of which a
Russian version appeared in '95, is possible. See *L* iv. 277, 529. J, I think, did not
write *Rambler* by inadvertence; the prayer which follows suits his estimate of the
Rambler better than his estimate of *Rasselas*.

932.—JB had written 8 Jan. sending J a copy of his *Letter to the People of Scotland*,
and asking him 'to be liberal enough to make allowance for my differing from you on
two points'—the Middlesex Election and the American War. His journal (17 Jan.)
shows that he also consulted J on a case of conscience, personal and political.

   1. He had written to Reynolds 6 Feb. mentioning his anxiety. This letter would
reach L'n on 10 Feb.

spasmodick asthma so violent, that with difficulty I got to my own house,[2] in which I have been confined eight or nine weeks, and from which I know not when I shall be able to go even to church. The asthma, however, is not the worst. A dropsy gains ground upon me; my legs and thighs are very much swollen with water, which I should be content if I could keep there, but I am afraid that it will soon be higher. My nights are very sleepless and very tedious. And yet I am extremely afraid of dying.

My physicians try to make me hope, that much of my malady is the effect of cold, and that some degree at least of recovery is to be expected from vernal breezes and summer suns. If my life is prolonged to autumn, I should be glad to try a warmer climate; though how to travel with a diseased body, without a companion to conduct me, and with very little money, I do not well see. Ramsay has recovered his limbs in Italy; and Fielding was sent to Lisbon, where, indeed, he died; but he was, I believe, past hope when he went. Think for me what I can do.

I received your pamphlet, and when I write again may perhaps tell you some opinion about it; but you will forgive a man struggling with disease his neglect of disputes, politicks, and pamphlets.[3] Let me have your prayers. My compliments to your lady, and young ones. Ask your physicians[4] about my case: and desire Sir Alexander Dick[5] to write me his opinion. I am, dear Sir, &c.

Feb 11, 1784.   Sam. Johnson.

933. W. 11 Feb. '84. Anthony Hamilton.

Not traced.—Croker's Boswell 1835, x. 283.

Sir   Bolt Court, Feb. 11, 1784.
My physicians endeavour to make me believe that I shall sometime be better qualified to receive visits from men of elegance and civility like yours.

Mrs. Pellè shall wait upon you, and you will judge what

932.—2. The incident was probably that mentioned in 918.1.
  3. J was as good as his word, see 936.
  4. JB applied to four; see *L* iv. 262, 264, 527.
  5. Dick is distinguished from 'your' (i.e. the Edinburgh) physicians as having long ceased to practise.

ANTHONY HAMILTON *W.* 11 *Feb.* '84

will be proper for you to do. I once more return you my
thanks, and am,

Sir, &c.
Sam: Johnson.

933.1. F. 13 Feb. ⟨'84⟩. William Cumberland Cruikshank.

Address: To Mr Cruikshank.
Fettercairn.—

Sir
   I beg that you would send me a large adhesive plaster
spread upon thick leather; it should be about fourteen inches
long, and about eight broad; it is for a defensative for my
breast. The salve I leave to You; perhaps Pix Burgundica
may be as good as any thing. If You are at home let this
messenger bring it, if not, send it to night by any body, and
I will pay him. I am, Sir, Your humble servant
Febr. 13. 1784.   Sam: Johnson

934. Tu. 17 Feb. '84. Mary Rogers (née Prowse).

Rosenbach (1925).—*NQ* 4 S. v. 442.

Madam
   A very dangerous and enervaiting distemper admonishes
me to make my will. One of my cares is for poor Phebe Herne
to whom your worthy Mother left so kind a legacy. When
I am gone who shall pay the rest of her maintenance? I have
not much to leave, but if you, Madam, will be pleased to
undertake it, I can leave you an hundred pounds.[1] But I am
afraid that is hardly an equivalent, for my part has commonly
amounted to twelve pounds or more. The payment to the
house is eight shilling a week, and some cloaths must be had
however few or coarse.
   Be pleased, Madam, to let me know your resolution on my
proposal, and write soon, for the time may be very short.
          I am, Madam, Your most humble servant,
Bolt court, Fleet Street, Feb. 17, 1784   Sam: Johnson

934.—1. The bequest of £100 'to the Reverend Mr. Rogers . . . towards the maintenance of Elizabeth Herne, a lunatick' is in the codicil to J's will dated 9 Dec.
L iv. 403.

934.1. Tu. 17 Feb. '84. Anthony Hamilton.

Not traced.—Croker's Boswell 1835, x. 283.

Sir

 I am so much disordered that I can only say that this is the person[1] whom I recommend to your kindness and favour.

I am, Sir, &c.

Sam. Johnson

934.2. Tu. 17 Feb. '84. William Cumberland Cruikshank.

Address: To Mr Cruikshank in Leicester Fields.
Fettercairn.—

Dear Sir

 An issue is to be made in my thigh, to drain away the water. As you called Mr Pott before I beg You to do the same again, and come as soon as You can together to the Assistance of, Sir, Your most humble Servant

Febr. 17. 1784   Sam: Johnson

935. M. 23 Feb. '84. Lucy Porter (Lichfield).

Address: To Mrs Lucy Porter in Lichfield. *Postmark*: 23 FE.
Fettercairn.—Boswell 1791, ii. 479 (Hill iv. 261).

My dearest Love,

 I have been extremely ill of an Asthma and dropsy, but received by the mercy of God sudden and unexpected relief last thursday by the discharge of twenty pints of water. Whether I shall continue free, or shall fill again, cannot be told. Pray for me.

 Death, my dear, is very dreadful, let us think nothing worth our care but how to prepare for it, what we know amiss in ourselves let us make haste to amend, and put our trust in the mercy of God, and the intercession of our Saviour. I am Dear Madam

Your most humble Servant

Feb. 23. 1784   Sam: Johnson

934.1.—1. Presumably Mrs. Pellé.

935.1. M. 23 Feb. '84. William Bowles (Heale).

Address: To W. Bowles Esq at Heale near Salisbury. *Postmark*:
–3 (or 5) FE.
Adam.—

Dear Sir

I was too well pleased with your name not to send it
immediately to the club; you will have I suppose this night
notice of your reception.

Whether I shall ever see the Club again is yet a doubt. But
I trust in God's mercy, who has already granted me great
relief. Last week I emitted in about twenty hours, full
twenty pints of [of] urine, and the tumour of my body is very
much lessened, but whether water will not gather again, He
only knows by whom we live and move.

My dejection has never been more than was suitable to my
condition. A sinner approaching the grave, is not likely to be
very cheerful.

My present thoughts do not allow me to take pleasure in
the expectation of seeing a mind so pure as yours, exposed
to the contagion of publick life, and contending with the
corrupt, and contaminated atmosphere of the house of
commons. If half of them were like you, I should wish you
among them. Consider well, and God direct you.

       I am, Sir, Your most humble servant
Febr. 23. 1784 London   Sam: Johnson

936. F. 27 Feb. '84. James Boswell (Edinburgh).

Not traced.—Boswell 1791, ii. 480 (Hill iv. 261).

Dear Sir

I have just advanced so far towards recovery as to read a
pamphlet; and you may reasonably suppose that the first
pamphlet which I read was yours. I am very much of your
opinion, and, like you, feel great indignation at the indecency

936.—JB had written again 14 Feb., as appears from the Register. He ignores this
letter (though he had a copy) in the *Life*, perhaps because J ignored it. We may
suppose it to have contained an assurance that he would consult his physicians as
J had asked, and perhaps a repetition of the questions of 8 Jan. See 932. 937 suggests
that the suppressed passage in 936 dealt with 'imaginary evil'.

with which the King is every day treated. Your paper contains very considerable knowledge of history and of the constitution, very properly produced and applied. It will certainly raise your character, though perhaps it may not make you a Minister of State.

*   *   *   *   *   *

I desire you to see Mrs. Stewart once again, and tell her, that in the letter-case was a letter relating to me, for which I will give her, if she is willing to give it me, another guinea. The letter is of consequence only to me.

I am, dear Sir, &c.

London, Feb. 27, 1784.   Sam. Johnson.

937. Tu. 2 Mar. '84. James Boswell (Edinburgh).

Not traced.—Boswell 1791, ii. 481 (Hill iv. 262).

Dear Sir

Presently after I had sent away my last letter, I received your kind medical packet. I am very much obliged both to you and your physicians for your kind attention to my disease. Dr. Gillespie has sent me an excellent *consilium medicum*, all solid practical experimental knowledge. I am at present, in the opinion of my physicians, (Dr. Heberden and Dr. Brocklesby,) as well as my own, going on very hopefully. I have just begun to take vinegar of squills. The powder hurt my stomach so much, that it could not be continued.

Return Sir Alexander Dick my sincere thanks for his kind letter; and bring with you the rhubarb which he so tenderly offers me.

I hope dear Mrs. Boswell is now quite well, and that no evil, either real or imaginary, now disturbs you.

I am, &c.

London, March 2, 1784.   Sam. Johnson.

937.—JB describes his letter as enclosing the opinions of Dick and Gillespie. The Register adds the date, 23 Feb. This should have reached J on 27 Feb., the very day on which he wrote 936. It was not until 7 Mar. that JB wrote to three other physicians.

938. W. 10 Mar. '84. Mrs. Thrale (Bath).

Address: To Mrs Thrale in Bath. *Postmark*: 10 MR.
Lady Hudson.—1788, No. 340.

Madam
  You know I never thought confidence with respect to
futurity any part of the character of a brave, a wise, or a good
man. Bravery has no place where it can avail nothing,
Wisdom impresses strongly the consciousness of those faults,
of which it is itself perhaps an aggravation; and Goodness
always wishing to be better, and imputing every deficience
to criminal negligence, and every fault to voluntary corruption, never dares to suppose the conditions of forgiveness
fulfilled, nor what is wanting in the crime[1] supplied by
Penitence.
  This is the state of the best, but what must be the condition of him whose heart will not suffer him to rank himself
among the best, or among the good, such must be his dread
of the approaching trial, as will leave him little attention to
the opinion of those whom he is leaving for ever, and the
serenity that is not felt, it can be no virtue to feign.
  The sarcocele ran off long ago, at an orifice made for mere
experiment.
  The water passed naturally by God's mercy in a manner
of which Dr Heberden has seen but four examples. The
Chirurgeon[2] has been employ⟨ed⟩[3] to heal some excoriations,
and four out of five are no longer under his care. The
Physicians laid on a blister, and I ordered, by their consent,
a salve, but neither succeeded and neither was very easily
healed.
  I have been confined from the fourteenth of December,

938.—This letter perhaps answers the letter which HLT describes in a letter to FB
of 18 Feb.: 'Johnson is in a sad way, doubtless; yet he may still with care last another
twelvemonth, and every week's existence is gain to him, who, like good Hezekiah,
wearies Heaven with entreaties for life. I wrote him a very serious letter the other
day.' *Diary* ii. 305. This is a strange account of J's letters during his illness. See also
943.
  1. I have left the reading of 1788, 'crime', in the text; but I could not be sure of
the word. I was inclined to believe that J intended 'virtue'. The phrase 'wanting in
the crime' is surprising, though it might be explained by 'deficience' above.
  2. Cruikshank. See *L* iv. 403 (col. 2).
  3. The word is doubtful.

and know not when I shall get out, but I have this day dressed me, as I was dressed in health.

Your kind expressions gave me great pleasure, ⟨do not⟩[4] eject me from your thoughts. Shall we ever exchange confidence by the fireside again?

I hope dear Sophy is better, and intend quickly to pay my debt to Susy.

I am, Madam, Your most humble servant
March 10. 1784 London   Sam: Johnson

939. W. 10 Mar. '84. Lucy Porter (Lichfield).

C. T. Jeffery.—Croker's Boswell 1831, v. 157.

My dearest Love

I will not suppose that it is for want of kindness that You did not answer my last letter, and I therefore write again to tell You, that I have, by Gods great mercy, still continued to grow better. My Asthma is seldom troublesome, and my Dropsy has run itself almost away, in a manner which my Physician says is very uncommon. I have been confined from the fourteen of December, and shall not soon venture abroad, but I have this day dressed myself as I was before my sickness.

If it be inconvenient to You to write, desire Mr Pearson to let me know how You do and how You have passed this long winter. I am now not without hopes that we shall once more see one another.

God bless You. Pray for me.

Make my compliments to Mrs Cobb, and Miss Adey, and to all my friends, particularly to Mr Pearson.

I am My dear Your most humble Servant
Boltcourt, Fleetstreet March 10. 1784   Sam: Johnson

940. Th. 11 Mar. '84. Jane Gastrell and Elizabeth Aston (Lichfield).

Pembroke.—Croker's Boswell 1831, v. 158.

Dear Ladies,

The kind and speedy answer with which you favoured me

---

4. The words 'do not' (1788) are purely conjectural. There is no gap in the MS.

to my last letter, encourages me to hope, that you will be glad to hear again that my recovery advances. My Disorders are an Asthma and Dropsy. The Asthma gives me no great trouble when I am not in motion, and the water of the dropsy has passed away in so happy a manner, by the Goodness of God, as Dr. Heberden declares himself not to have known more than four times in all his practice. I have been confined to the house from December the fourteenth, and shall not venture out till the weather is settled, but I have this day dressed myself as before I became ill. Join with me in returning thanks, and pray for me that the time now granted me, may not be ill spent.

Let me now, dear Ladies, have some account of you. Tell me how [the] you have endured this long and sharp Winter, and give me hopes that we may all meet again with kindness and cheerfulness.

I am Dear Ladies, Your most humble servant,

Sam: Johnson.

March 11, 1784. Boltcourt. Fleetstreet. London.

940.1. M. 15 Mar. ('84). Eva Marie Garrick and Hannah More.

Folger Library.—

Mr Johnson sends his respects to Mrs Garrick and Miss Moor.

He has been confined to the house by diseases from Dec. 13. but is now much better, and hopes to wait on Mrs Garrick in a few weeks, and to tell Miss Moor all that *envy* will sufer him to say of her last poem,[1] which Mrs Reynolds showed him.

March 15

940.1.—1. *The Bas Bleu*, not published until '86, but for its circulation in MS. see 954, and Roberts, *Memoirs of H. M.* 1834, vol. i, s.a. '83–'84. She wrote in April 'I had a very civil note from Johnson about a week since. . . . He tells me he longs to see me, to praise the Bas Bleu as much as envy can praise' (op. cit. i. 319).

941. Tu. 16 Mar. '84. Mrs. Thrale (Bath).

Address: To Mrs Thrale at Bath. *Postmark*: 16 MR.
Adam.—1788, No. 341.

Dear Madam

I am so near to health as a month ago I despaired of being.
The dropsy is almost wholly run away, and the Asthma unless
irritated by cold seldom attacks me. How I shall bear motion
I do not yet know. But though I have little of pain, I am
wonderfully weak. My muscles have almost lost all their
spring, but I hope that warm weather when it comes will
restore me. More than three months have I now been confined. But my deliverance has been very extraordinary.

Of one thing very remarkable I will tell you. For the
Asthma and perhaps other disorders, my Physicians have
advised the frequent use of opiates. I resisted them as much
as I could, and complained that it made me almost delirious.
This Dr Heberden seemed not much to heed, but I was so
weary of it that I tried when I could not wholly omit it, to
diminish the dose, in which contrarily to the know⟨n⟩
custom of the takers of opium, and beyond what it seemed
reasonable to expect, I have so far succeeded, that having
begun with three grains, a large quantity, I now appease the
paroxysm, with a quarter of an ounce of diacodium estimated
as equivalent only to half a grain, and this quantity it is now
eight days since I took.

That I may send to Mrs Lewis, for when I shall venture
out I do not know, you must let me know where she may be
found, which you omitted to tell me.

I hope my dear Sophy will go on recovering. But methinks
Miss Thrale rather neglects me, suppose she should try to
write me a little Latin letter.

Do you however write to me often, and write kindly,
perhaps We may sometime see each other. I am,

Madam, Your most humble servant
London. March 16. 1784   Sam: Johnson

942. Th. 18 Mar. '84. James Boswell (Edinburgh).

Not traced.—Boswell 1791, ii. 482 (Hill iv. 264)

Dear Sir

I am too much pleased with the attention which you and your dear lady show to my welfare, not to be diligent in letting you know the progress which I make towards health. The dropsy, by God's blessing, has now run almost totally away by natural evacuation; and the asthma, if not irritated by cold, gives me little trouble. While I am writing this, I have not any sensation of debility or disease. But I do not yet venture out, having been confined to the house from the thirteenth of December, now a quarter of a year.

When it will be fit for me to travel as far as Auchinleck, I am not able to guess; but such a letter as Mrs. Boswell's might draw any man, not wholly motionless, a great way. Pray tell the dear lady how much her civility and kindness have touched and gratified me.

Our parliamentary tumults have now begun to subside, and the King's authority is in some measure re-established. Mr. Pitt[1] will have great power: but you must remember, that what he has to give must, at least for some time, be given to those who gave, and those who preserve his power. A new minister can sacrifice little to esteem or friendship; he must, till he is settled, think only of extending his interest.

*   *   *   *   *   *

If you come hither through Edinburgh, send for Mrs. Stewart, and give from me another guinea for the letter in the old case, to which I shall not be satisfied with my claim, till she gives it me.

Please to bring with you Baxter's Anacreon;[2] and if you procure heads of *Hector Boece*, the historian, and *Arthur Johnston*, the poet, I will put them in my room, or any other of the fathers of Scottish literature.

942.—JB had written 9 Mar. 'of various particulars, enclosing a letter to him from my Wife'. JB's letter is not in the journal (which was not written until 31 Mar.), nor in the *Life*; but in a footnote to 942 JB mentions his wife's 'very kind letter'.

1. JB's reliance had formerly been rather on Burke; see on 920. But he had no doubt told J that he had written to Pitt, with a copy of his pamphlet, and had received a polite acknowledgement. See *L* iv. 261.

2. See on 827.2.

I wish you an easy and happy journey, and hope I need not tell you that you will be welcome to, dear Sir,
Your most affectionate humble servant,
London, March 18, 1784. Sam. Johnson.

943. Sa. 20 Mar. '84. Mrs. Thrale (Bath).

Address: To Mrs. Thrale at Bath.
F. B. Vanderhoef.—1788, No. 342.

Madam
Your last letter had something of tenderness. The accounts which you have had of my danger and distress were, I suppose, not aggravated. I have been confined ten weeks with an Asthma and Dropsy. But I am now better. God has in his mercy granted me a reprieve, for how much time his mercy must determine.

On the 19th of last Month I evacuated twenty pints of water, and I think I reckon exactly, from that time the tumour[1] has subsided, and I now begin to move with some freedom. You will easily believe that I am still at a great distance from health, but I am as my Chirurgeon expressed it amazingly better. Heberden seems to have great hopes.

Write to me no more about *dying with a grace*.[2] When you feel what I have felt in approaching Eternity—in fear of soon hearing the sentence of which there is no revocation, you will know the folly, my wish is that you may know it sooner. The distance between the grave and the remotest point of human longevity is but a very little, and of that little no part is certain. You know all this, and I thought that I knew it too, but I know it now with a new conviction. May that new conviction not be vain.

I am now cheerful, I hope this approach to recovery is a token of Divine Mercy. My friends continue their kindness. I give a dinner tomorrow.

Pray let me know how my dear Sophy goes on. I still hope that there is in her fits more terrour than danger. But I

943.—1. The reference is, of course, not to the sarcocele, but to the dropsical swelling.
2. See on 938.

hope, however it be, that she will speedily recover. I will take care to pay Miss Susy her letter. God bless you all.

I am Madam, Your most humble Servant
March 20 1784 London   Sam: Johnson

943.1. M. 22 Mar. '84. John Taylor. See Addenda, p. 336.

944. Th. 25 Mar. '84. Susannah Thrale (Bath).

Address: . . . Thrale . . . Bath. *Postmark*: 25 MR. Lansdowne (now mutilated).—1788, No. 343.

My dearest Miss Susy

Since you are resolved to stand it out, and keep *Mum* till you have ⟨heard from me⟩[1], I must at last comply, and indeed compliance costs me now no trouble, but as it irritates a cough, which I got, as you might have done, by standing at an open window, and which has now harassed me many days, and is too strong for diacodium, nor has yet given much way to opium itself. However, having been so long used to so many worse things, I mind it but little. I have not bad nights; and my stomach has never failed me. But when I shall go abroad again, I know not.

With Mr Herschil it will certainly be very right to cultivate an acquaintance, for he can show you in the sky what no man before him has ever seen, by some wonderful improvements which he has made in the telescope. What he has to show is indeed a long way off, and perhaps concerns us but little, but all truth is valuable and all knowledge is pleasing in its first effects, and may be subsequently useful. Of whatever we see we always wish to know⟨, and[2]⟩ congratulate ourselves when we know that of which we perceive another to be ignorant. Take therefore all opportunities of learning that offer themselves, however remote the matter may be from common life or common conversation. Look in Herschel's telescope; go into a chymist's laboratory; if you see a manufacturer at work, remark his operations. By this

944.—The remnants of the MS. comprise (1) From the beginning to 'window and w'; (2) 'With Mr Herschil' to 'that of which'; (3) traces of the last line 'mind will restore her' and of the subscription.

   1. 'heard from me' is a conjectural supplement of 1788.
   2. There is no room for more than ', and'; 1788 prints ';; always'.

activity of attention, you will find in every place diversion and improvement.

Now dear Sophy is got well, what is it that ails my mistress? She complains,[3] and complains, I am afraid, with too much cause; but I know not distinctly what is her disorder. I hope that time and a quiet mind will restore her.

I am, My dearest, Your, &c.,

Sam: Johnson.

945. Sa. 27 Mar.' 84. Bennet Langton (Rochester).

Address: To Benet Langton Esq in Rochester Kent. *Postmark*: 27 MR. Fettercairn.—Boswell 1791, ii. 484 (Hill iv. 267).

Dear Sir

Since You left me, I have continued in my own opinion and in Dr Brocklesby's, to grow better [better] with respect to all my formidable and dangerous distempers, though to a body battered and shaken as mine has lately been, it is to be feared that weak attacks may be sometimes [sometimes] mischievous. I have indeed by standing carelessly at an open window, got a very troublesome cough, which it has been necessary to appease by opium, in larger quantities, than I like to take and I have not found it give way so readily as I expected, its obstinacy however seems at last disposed to submit to the remedy, and I know not, whether I shall then have a right to complain of any morbid sensation. My Asthma is, I am afraid, constitutional, and incurable, but it is only occasional, and unless it be excited by labour or by cold, gives me no molestation, nor does it lay very close siege to life, for Sir John Floyer, whom the physical race consider, as authour of one of the best books upon it, panted on to ninety, as was supposed; and why were we content with supposing a fact so interesting of a Man so conspicuous, because he corrupted, at perhaps seventy or eighty, the register,[1] that he might pass for younger than he was. He was not much less than eighty, when to a man of rank who modestly asked him his age, He answered—Go, look—though he was in general a man of civility and elegance.

3. For HLT's view of her own grave state of health and its causes—Piozzi's absence and the cruel indifference of the world—see *Th* for these months.

945.—1. Dr. Powell has cleared Sir John of the charge. *L* iv. 528.

The ladies I find are at your house all well, except Miss Langton, who will probably soon recover her health, by light suppers. Let her eat at dinner as she will, but not take a full stomach to bed. Pay my sincere respects to the two principal Ladies in your house, and when you write to dear Miss Langton in Lincolnshire let her know that I mean not to break our league of friendship, and that I have a set of lives for her, when I have the means of sending it. I am Sir, Your most humble servant

London. March 27. 1784   Sam: Johnson

946. Tu. 30 Mar. '84. James Boswell (Auchinleck).

Not traced.—Boswell 1791, ii. 483 (Hill iv. 265).

Dear Sir

You could do nothing so proper as to haste back when you found the Parliament dissolved. With the influence which your address must have gained you, it may reasonably be expected that your presence will be of importance, and your activity of effect.

Your solicitude for me gives me that pleasure which every man feels from the kindness of such a friend: and it is with delight I relieve it by telling, that Dr. Brocklesby's account is true, and that I am, by the blessing of God, wonderfully relieved.

You are entering upon a transaction which requires much prudence. You must endeavour to oppose without exasperating; to practise temporary hostility, without producing enemies for life. This is, perhaps, hard to be done; yet it has been done by many, and seems most likely to be effected by opposing merely upon general principles, without descending to personal or particular censures or objections. One thing I must enjoin you, which is seldom observed in the conduct of elections;—I must entreat you to be scrupulous in the use

946.—JB's letter, to which this is an answer, is in *Life* misdated 28 Mar. In JB's Register the date is 26 Mar., and the journal shows (*BP* xvi. 46) that on the 27th he left York for Newcastle. It informed J that JB had been gratified by 'the triumph of monarchical principles over aristocratical influence' in a Yorkshire address to the King; that he had reached York on his way to L'n, but that the dissolution had sent him home again, where he 'had carried an Address to his Majesty by a great majority', and had 'some intention' of standing for the county.

of strong liquors. One night's drunkenness may defeat the labours of forty days well employed. Be firm, but not clamorous; be active, but not malicious; and you may form such an interest, as may not only exalt yourself, but dignify your family.

We are, as you may suppose, all busy here. Mr. Fox resolutely stands for Westminster,[1] and his friends say will carry the election. However that be, he will certainly have a seat. Mr. Hoole has just told me, that the city leans towards the King.

Let me hear, from time to time, how you are employed, and what progress you make.

Make dear Mrs. Boswell, and all the young Boswells, the sincere compliments of, Sir, your affectionate humble servant,

London, March 30, 1784.   Sam. Johnson.

946.1. Tu. 30 Mar. '84. William Adams (Oxford).

Address: To the Reverend Dr Adams at Pembroke College Oxford.
Postmark: 30 MR.
Sir Francis Adams Hyett.—

Sir

In my letter to you of the miscarriage of which I can no⟨t⟩ account, was inclosed a letter from the Prior of the Benedictines, informing me, that the collation of the manuscripts in the King's library at Paris for the use of Dr Edwards is finished, and that of the manuscripts two had never been collated before, and to desire directions how to transmit the papers.

The letter came to me when I was very hard beset with an Ashma and a Dropsy, from both which the Goodness of God has very much relieved me. Of the Dropsy my Physicians seem to think ⟨me⟩ quite recovered, and the Ashma is not very troublesome. I did not however neglect the latter, though my attention has happened to be useless.

1. Fox was elected both for Westminster and for Kirkwall.
946.1.—Edwards's edition 1785 of Xenophon's *Memorabilia* contains 'H. Oweni Praefatio'. Owen states that 'codices Parisienses per totum collati fuerunt' and mentions 'peregrinorum librariorum benignitas'; there is nothing about J's good offices. See 974.

The Prior ought to have an answer. The book being printed, almost all the expence is already incurred, and the addition of so many various readings will of itself make it valuable. Thus we shall complete the desire and preserve the memory of our friend, of a man whom I never found deficient in any offices of civility. The collators must, I suppose, be paid. My Guinea is ready.

You, Sir, must, I think write to Dr Owen to send me the necessary intelligence. I cannot wait on him, having never been beyond the door from the 13th of December. I have however not suffered any sharp pain.

Younger Men die daily about me. I much regret the loss of Dr Wheeler. O God when thou shalt call me, receive me to thy mercy for Jesus Christ's sake.

I have not forgotten the kindness with which Miss Adams invited me to Oxford. I hope to see you in the Summer for a few days. But a sick Man is a very perverse being, he gives much trouble, he receives many favours, yet is never pleased and not often thankful. I will try however when I come to leave both the miseries and vices of disease behind me.

I am, Sir Your most humble Serva⟨nt⟩
London Bolt c⟨ourt⟩ March 30. 1784.   Sam: Johnson

946.2. Su. 4 Apr. '84. Mrs. Lewis.

Now Hyde; for the full text see p. 337.

If you will dine with me name your day, I will invite[1] Mr. Sastres to meet you, and we will be as cheerful as we can together.

947. M. 5 Apr. '84. Ozias Humphry.

Address: To Mr Humphrey in Newman Street Oxford Road. A. Houghton.—Boswell 1791, ii. 486 (Hill iv. 268).

Sir
Mr Hoole has told me with what benevolence You listened to a request which I was almost afraid to make, of

946.2.—This letter is described as 'mentioning Mrs. Thrale (see 941) and speaking of his illness'.

1. I have printed 'invite' for 'write' (Sotheby). In 38 Hill read 'without' as 'instance'; in 468, 1788 printed 'care' for 'love'.

leave to a young Painter[1] to attend you from time to time in your painting room, to see your operations, and receive your instructions.

The young Man has perhaps good parts, but has been without any regular education; He is my Godson, and therefore I interest myself in his progress and success, and shall think myself much favoured, if I receive from You a permission to send him.

My health is, by Gods blessing, much restored, but I am not yet allowed by the Physicians to go abroad, nor indeed do I think myself yet able to endure the weather. I am, Sir, your most humble Servant,

Bolt court, Fleet street Ap. 5. 1784   Sam: Johnson

947.1. M. 5 Apr. '84 (misdated 1748). William Bowles (Heale).

Address: To W. Bowles Esq at Heale near Salisbury. *Postmark*: 6 AP. Adam.—

Dear Sir

My Health appears both to my Physicians and myself to grow in the main every day better and better notwithstanding the unusual length and ruggedness of the winter. I have known Winters that had greater cold than we have felt in this; such as those in which the great rivers and aestuaries have frozen, and in which very deep snows have lain very long upon the ground; but I remember no Winter that has encroached so much upon the Spring, or continued such severity so long beyond the Equinox. Here will be a season lost. The physical, though not the astronomical, summer begins in May, *a Geminis aestas*[1] says Manilius, and Winter yet keeps fast hold of April. But the Sun will prevail at last.

Relating to the club leave the business to me. The basis of our constitution is commodiousness. You may come for sixpence, and stay away for threepence. This week[2] the club does not meet.

947.—1. 'Son of Mr. Samuel Paterson.' JB.

947.1.—1. Man. ii. 266 aestas a Geminis, autumnus Virgine surgit: 'Summer starts from the Twins, autumn from the Virgin.'

2. It was Holy Week.

I am pleased with Collins's project.[3] My friend Sir John Hawkins, a man of very diligent enquiry and very wide intelligence, has been collecting materials for the completion of Walton's lives, of which one is the life of Herbert. I will tell him of the edition intended and he will probably suggest some improvements.

It does not occur to me how I can write a preface to which it can be proper to put my name, and I am not to sink[4] my own value without raising at least proportionally that of the book. This is therefore to be considered.

I am, Dear Sir Your most humble servant,

London Apr. 5. 1748   Sam: Johnson

You will make my compliments to M[rs] Bowles; to your Father who is, I hope, recovered; to your Young people; and to all, and when I leave out services and compliment, you must suppose them.

948. Th. 8 Apr. '84. Bennet Langton (Rochester).

Address: To Benet Langton Esq. in Rochester Kent. *Postmark*: 8 AP. Fettercairn.—Boswell 1791, ii. 485 (Hill iv. 267).

Dear Sir

I am still disturbed by my cough, but what thanks have I not ⟨to⟩ pay, when my cough is the most painful sensation that I feel, and from that I expect hardly to be released, while winter continues to gripe us with so much pertinacity. The year has now advanced eighteen days beyond the equinox, and still there is very little remission of the cold. When warm weather comes, which surely must come at last, I hope it will help both me and your young Lady.

The Man so busy about addresses is neither more nor less than our own Boswel, who had come as far as York towards London, but turned back on the dissolution, and is said now to stand for some place. Whether to wish him success, his best friends hesitate.

Let me have your prayers for the completion of my recovery, I am now better than I ever expected to have been.

947.1—3. The late Dr. F. E. Hutchinson told me that no edition of George Herbert by a Collins was ever published.

4. Mr. Adam printed 'put'; but the reading is certain.

May God add to his mercies the Grace that may enable me to use them according to his Will. My Compliments to all, I am Sir Your most affectionate humble servant

Apr. 8. 1784 London   Sam: Johnson

---

949. Tu. 13 Apr. '84. Ozias Humphry.

Address: To Mr Humphry.
Adam.—Boswell 1791, ii. 487, misdated 10 April (Hill iv. 269).

Sir

The Bearer is my Godson[1] whom I take the liberty of recommending to your kindness, which I hope he will deserve by his respect to your excellence, and his gratitude for your favours. I am,

Sir, Your most humble servant,

Apr. 13. 1784 Bolt court   Sam: Johnson

---

950. M. 12 Apr. '84. John Nichols.

Sotheby 6 Nov. 1951, 399.—*GM* 1788, 49.

Sir

I have sent you inclosed a very curious proposal from Mr. Hawkins, the son of Sir John Hawkins, who, I believe, will take ⟨care⟩ that whatever his son promises shall be performed.

If you are inclined to publish this compilation, the Editor will agree for an Edition on the following terms which I think liberal enough. That you shall print the Book at your own charge. That the sale shall be wholly for your benefit till your expenses be repaid; except that at the time of publication you shall put into the hands of the Editor without price . . . copies for his Friends. That when you have been repaid, the profits arising from the sale of the remaining copies shall be divided equally between You and the Editor. That the Edition shall not comprise fewer than five hundred. I am Sir, Your most humble Servant

Apr. 12, 1784.   Sam: Johnson

949.—1. See 947.

950. The inclosure, sold with the letter, was the proposal, with corrections by J, of *Ignoramus*; see Index II.

951. M. 12 Apr. '84. John Taylor (Ashbourne).

Address: To the Rev^d Dr Taylor in Ashbourne Derbyshire. *Postmark*: 12 AP.

A. T. Loyd.—Taylor, *Letter to Samuel Johnson* 1787; Boswell 1791, ii. 487 (Hill iv. 270).

Dear Sir

What can be the reason that I hear nothing from you? I hope nothing disables you from writing. What I have seen, and what I have felt, gives me reason to fear every thing. Do not omit giving me the comfort of knowing that after all my losses I have yet a friend left.

I want every comfort. My Life is very solitary and very cheerless. Though it has pleased ⟨God⟩ wonderfully to deliver me from the Dropsy, I am yet very weak, and have not passed the door since the 13th of December. I hope for some help from warm weather, which will surely come in time.

I could not have the consent of the Physicians to go to Church yesterday; I therefore received the holy Sacrament at home, in the room where I communicated with dear Mrs Williams a little before her death. O, my Friend, the approach of Death is very dreadful. I am afraid to think on that which I know, I cannot avoid. It is vain to look round and round, for that help which cannot be had. Yet we hope and hope, and fancy that he who has lived to day may live to morrow. But let us learn to derive our hope only from God.

In the mean time, let us be kind to one another. I have no Friend now living but You and Mr Hector that was the friend of my youth. Do not neglect, dear Sir, Yours affectionately,

London Easter Monday April 12 1784   Sam: Johnson

951.1 M. 12 Apr. ⟨'84⟩. Frances Reynolds.

Tregaskis (1925); copy by F. R. (dated Apr. 12. 84), Rupert Colomb.—Croker's Boswell 1831, v. 164.

Dear Madam

I am not yet able to wait on you, but I can do your business commodiously enough. You must send me the copy to

951.1.—For FR's literary efforts see on 738, 958.

show the printer. If you will come to tea this afternoon, we will talk together about it. Pray send me word when then you will come.

I am, Madam, Your most humble servant,
Apr. 12   Sam: Johnson.

952. Tu. 13 Apr. '84. Bennet Langton (Rochester).

Address: To Benet Langton Esq in Rochester Kent. *Postmark*: 13 AP. Fettercairn.—Boswell 1791, ii. 485 (Hill iv. 268).

Dear Sir

I had this evening a note from Lord Portmore, desiring that I would give You an account of my health. You might have had it with less circumduction. I am, by God's Blessing, I think[1], free from all morbid sensation, except a cough, which is only troublesome. But I am still weak, and can have no great hope of strength till the weather shall be softer. The summer, if it be kindly, will, I hope, enable me to support the winter. God, who has so wonderfully restored me, can preserve me in all seasons.

Let me enquire in my turn after the state of your family, great and little. I hope Lady Rothes and Miss Langton are both well. That is a good basis of content. Then how goes George on with his Studies? How does Miss Mary? and how does my own Jenny?[2] I think, I owe Jenny a Letter, which I will take care to pay. In the mean time tell her that I acknowledge the debt.

Be pleased to make my compliments to the Ladies. If Mrs Langton comes to London, she will favour me with a visit, for I am not well enough to go out. I am, Sir, Your most humble servant,
Easter Tuesday Apr. 13. 1784   Sam: Johnson

952.1. Tu. 13 Apr. '84. Earl of Portmore.

Address: The Rt. Hon. Earl of Portmore. Fettercairn.—Boswell 1791, ii. 485 (Hill iv. 268, overlooked in Letters).

Dr[1] Johnson acknowledges with great respect the honour

952.—1. 'believe' 1791—a compositor's inadvertence?
2. His god-daughter. For the payment of his debt see 959.
952.1.—1. For 'Dr.' see on 927.1.

of Lord Portmore's notice. He is better than he was; and will as his Lordship directs, write to Mr. Langton.
Bolt court Fleet street, Apr. 13. 1784

952.2. Tu. 13 Apr. '84. John Perkins.

Address: To Mr Perkins.
O. T. Perkins.—

Dear Sir
    The kindness which ⟨you⟩ and Mrs Perkins, I hope, have for me, will dispose you to hear with pleasure, that, though not yet able to go abroad, I am totally, I think, recovered by God's Blessing from the dropsy, and find all my complaints very much alleviated.
    I have now fifteen pounds due to me, from which must be deducted, what you paid for me of the tax on Servants, and what I owe you for two chaldrons of coals, I think they were two, if they were more deduct the difference.
    I hope that Mr Barclay is recovered from his late disorder, and that Mrs Perkins and yourself, and all your young people are well.

I am Sir Your most humble Servant,

Apr. 13. 1784   Sam: Johnson
You will be pleased to send me what you find due to me any day this week, unless you can be so kind as to call, and bring it.
April 13. 1784 Bolt court.

953. Th. 15 Apr. '84. Mrs. Thrale (Bath).

Address: To Mrs Thrale at Bath. *Postmark*: 15 AP.
Newton.—1788, No. 345.

Dear Madam
    Yesterday I had the pleasure of giving another dinner to the remainder of the old Club.[1] We used to meet weekly about the year fifty, and we were as cheerful as in former

952.2.—HT had acted as J's banker, see on 622; and J's will (*L* iv. 402) shows that he died possessed of 'three hundred pounds in the hands of Mr. Barclay and Mr. Perkins, brewers'. Interest was no doubt paid annually at 5 per cent.
953.—1. See 908, 954.

times; only I could not make quite so much noise, for since the paralytick affliction my voice is sometimes weak.

Metcalf and Crutchley without knowing each other are both members of parliament for Horsham in Sussex. Mr. Cator is chosen for Ipswich.

But a sick man's thoughts soon turn back upon himself. I am still very weak, though my appetite is keen, and my digestion potent, and I gratify myself more at table than ever I did at my own cost before. I have now an inclination to luxury which even your table did not excite, for till now my talk was more about the dishes than my thoughts. I remember you commended me for seeming pleased with my diners, when you had reduced your table; I am able to tell you with great veracity, that I never knew when the reduction began, nor should have known that it was made, had not you told me. I now think and consult to day what I shall eat to morrow. This disease likewise will I hope be cured.[2] For there are other things, how different! which ought to predominate in the mind of such a man as I, but in this world the body will ⟨have⟩ its part; and my hope is that it shall have no more. My hope but not my confidence, I have only the timidity of a Christian to deter me, not the wisdom of a Stoick to secure me.

I hope all my Dears are well. They should not be too nice in requiring letters. If my sweet Queeney writes more Letters like her last,[3] when Franks[4] come in again I will correct them and return them.

I am, Madam, Your most humble servant

Apr. 15. 1784 London   Sam: Johnson.

953a. Bath. Sa. 17 Apr. '84. From Mrs. Thrale.

R 540.109.—

Dear Sir   17: April 1784
    Your comical Account of your own Voracity reached me just as the Salmons came in today, pray accept this very fine one till Pipers and Dorees come in.

953.—2. For J's deliberate indulgence at this time see *L* iv. 330. His description of it as a disease is perhaps more or less jocular; he would hardly, otherwise, have confessed it to Thrale's widow. She so interprets it (953*a*), in spite of the gravity of the context.
    3. It was no doubt in Latin (see 941), which explains its need of correction.
    4. The famine began with the dissolution 25 March and lasted till 18 May.

Eat away my dear Sir & fear no Colours; you will get Strength *by* your Food, and then your Mind will be got Strong too, and you will *scorn* your food—the old Fate of those who help'd in the early Periods of a Struggle, and are thrown away when Struggle subsists no longer. I shall live to be served so myself perhaps, by Puppets who could scarcely have play'd their little parts well, had I not pulled the Strings for them at the beginning of the Evening; but then perhaps I may live on, & see them all thrown into a dirty Basket together when the Show is quite over—& the Managers run out of the Village for fear of Debts.

Your Pupil says She will soon hatch up another Letter at least as good as the last. Be merry dear Sir and make the Club so, I hope 'tis Sam's House for old Acquaintance sake; for tho' Sam was a little spoiled by Indulgence, he was a very active Servant and I think a very honest Man.

I am not well, and I am not happy: my Lawsuit lost, my Money borrowed to pay it with aggravations of Evil very difficult to endure even for me, who am no bad Endurer: yet we read, and walk, and talk, of Cyrus & Scipio

naming the Ancient Heroes round

for of the modern Heroes I have really no Knowledge, but what your Letters bring me; and you live on the *great Mart of Society* as I remember M^r P——'s once called London. Bath does very well for me; Colossal Figures must stand in large Halls, but Miniatures do best over a Chimney in some small Room.

I appeal to my Companions however to tell if I teize them with my Ill humour: Vexations within should teach one to be more watchful over our Words & Actions, lest habitual peevishness the most hateful of all Tempers should take possession of one's Mind: and if I am not merry—*Je m'efforce de l'estre* which is the same Thing to others, & helps to sanctify one's Mirth by making even of *that*, a real Mortification.

You think now all about yourself, continue to do so dear Sir, I know noone better worth thinking on: I am sure you are very kind to your pretty Girls here, in writing to *them* so. They will all three be very lovely young Women indeed   I am ever Your Obedient & faithful Servant

H: L: Thrale

954. M. 19 Apr. '84. Mrs. Thrale (Bath).

Address: To Mrs Thrale at Bath.
F. Leverton Harris.—1788, No. 346.

Dear Madam

I received in the Morning your magnificent Fish, and in the afternoon your apology for not sending it. I have invited the Hooles and Miss Burney[1] to dine upon it to morrow.

954.—1. The company was 'Mr. and Mrs. Hoole and their son, and Mrs. Hall, a very good Methodist, and sister of John Wesley'. FB's *Diary* ii. 310.

The Club[2] which has been lately instituted is at Sam's, and there was I when I was last out of the house. But the people whom I mentioned in my letter are the remnant of a little Club that used to meet in Ivy Lane about three and thirty years ago, out of which we have lost Hawkesworth and Dyer, the rest are yet on this side the grave. Our meetings now are serious and, I think, on all parts tender.

Miss Moore has written a poem called Le Bas blue;[3] which is in my opinion, a very great performance. It wanders about in manuscript, and surely will soon find its way to Bath.

I shall be glad of another Letter from my dear Queeney; the former was not much to be censured.[4] The reckoning between me and Miss Sophy is out of my head. She must write to tell me how it stands.

I am sensible of the ease that your repayment of Mr ⟨Crutchley⟩[5] has given, you felt yourself *génée* by that debt, is there an English word for it?

As you do not [not] now use your books, be pleased to let Mr Cator know that I may borrow what I want. I think at present to take only Calmet,[6] and the Greek Anthology. When I lay sleepless, I used to drive the night along, by turning Greek epigrams into Latin. I know not if I have not turned a hundred.[7]

It is now time to return you thanks for your present.

954.—2. For the Essex-Head Club and Sam Greaves see on 921; for the Ivy-Lane Club and its reunion, see on 908. Hawkins (*Life* 291, 361) says that this club was formed in '49 (which is near enough to J's date in this letter; in 917 he says 'thirty years') and broke up about '56. H names eight members besides themselves: Ryland, Payne, Barker, Salter, Dyer, McGhie, Bathurst, Hawkesworth. Now J twice (917, 954) says all but two (Hawkesworth and Dyer) survived. It is surely unlikely that he overlooked Bathurst. Hill suggests that there were in fact two distinct clubs; and this is perhaps supported by Nichols's statement (*LA* ix. 502) that 'the club' was called 'the Rambler', which is unlikely in '49.

3. Hill quotes from Hannah More's *Memoirs* (i. 319) her account of J's praise and the King's desire for a copy of the poem. See 940.1.   4. For its Latinity, see 953.

5. 'Crutchley' HLP, which is confirmed by the traces (the word is pasted over, and seven asterisks substituted; the initial looks like *C*, and three ascenders show). For her debt to him see *Tb* 551, 561–2, 682, and Hayward (quoted by Hill).

6. Doubtless his Dictionary of the Bible.

7. BL published 98 in the *Works*. See *Poems* 208. J used the edition published by Brodaeus in 1549. He may now have wished to borrow a better or a more legible or a more portable edition. Brodaeus is a finely printed book in folio, but the type is not large. The sale catalogue of J's library does not show him possessed of an *Anthology*; Brodaeus being imposing would hardly be included in the nameless items. Probably BL had it for his editorial purposes.

Since I was sick I know not if I have not had more delicacies sent me, than I had ever seen, till I saw your table.

It was ⟨. . .⟩[8] Dr Heberden's enquiry whether my appetite for food continued. It indeed never failed me; for he considered the cessation of appetite, as the despair of Nature yielding up her power to the force of the disease.

        I am, Madam, Your most humble servant

Apr. 19. 1784 London   Sam: Johnson.

955. W. 21 Apr. '84. Mrs. Thrale (Bath).

Hyde.—1788, No. 347.

Dear Madam

I make haste to send you intelligence which if I do not still flatter myself, you will not receive without some degree of pleasure. After a confinement of one hundred twenty nine days, more than the third part of a year, and no inconsiderable part of human life, I this day returned thanks to God in St. Clement's Church, for my recovery, a recovery in my seventy fifth year from a distemper which few in the vigour of youth are known to surmount; a recovery of which neither myself, my friends, nor my physicians had any hope, for though they flattered me with some continuance of life, they never supposed that I could cease to be dropsical. The Dropsy however, is quite vanished, and the Asthma so much mitigated, that I walked to-day with a more easy respiration than I have known, I think, for perhaps two years past. I hope the Mercy that lengthens my days, will assist me to use them well.

The Hooles, Miss Burney, and Mrs. Hall (Wesly's sister) feasted yesterday with me very cheerfully on your noble salmon. Mr. Allen could not come, and I sent him a piece, and a great tail is still left.

Dr. Brocklesby forbids the club at present, not caring to venture the chillness of the evening but I purpose to shew myself on Saturday at ⟨the⟩ Academy's feast. I cannot publish my return to the world more effectually, for, as the Frenchman says, *tout le monde s'y trouvera.*

For this occasion I ordered some cloaths, and was told by

954.—8. 'Always' 1788.

the taylor, that when he brought me a sick dress,[1] he never expected to make me any thing of any other kind. My recovery is indeed wonderful.

I am, dear Madam, Your most humble servant
London, Apr. 21. 1784   Sam: Johnson

956. M. 26 Apr. '84. Mrs. Thrale (Bath).

Sotheby 30 Jan. 1918 (not seen); signature, etc., H. G. Commin, Catalogue 540 (1936), p. 36.—1788, No. 348.

Madam

On Saturday I shewed myself again to the living world at the Exhibition; much and splendid was the company: but like the Doge of Genoa at Paris,[1] I admired nothing but myself. I went up all the stairs to the pictures without stopping to rest or to breathe,

'In all the madness of superfluous health.'[2]

The Prince of Wales had promised to be there; but when we had waited an hour and half, sent us word that he could not come.

My cough still torments me; but it is only a cough, and much less oppressive than some of former times, but it disturbs my nights.

Mrs. Davenant[3] called to pay me a guinea, but I gave two for you. Whatever reasons you have for frugality, it is not worth while to save a guinea a-year by withdrawing it from a public charity.

I know not whether I told you that my old friend Mrs. Cotterel,[4] now no longer Miss, has called to see me. Mrs. Lewis is not well.

955.—1. See 931.

956.—J dated this letter, as was his habit, at the end. HLP, who no doubt printed it before its mutilation, transferred the date, as was her habit, to the beginning.
    1. See on 329.   2. Pope, *Essay on Man*, iii. 3.
    3. I confess myself puzzled. Why should Mrs. D pay J a guinea unless he were collecting—which seems not very likely—for some 'public charity'? And if that were the case, then why should J 'give' two guineas on HLT's behalf?
    4. I do not know 'Mrs.' C's dates. In those of J's letters to LP, who was six years his junior, of which I know the addresses, his style varies between 'Miss' and 'Mrs.' up to '64, when she was near fifty. Thereafter I have many examples of 'Mrs.', only one (730.2) of 'Miss', and of that one I cannot be sure, for my copyist might easily miss such a point.

Mrs. Davenant says, that you regain your health. That you regain your health is more than a common recovery; because I infer, that you regain your peace of mind. Settle your thoughts and controul your imagination, and think no more of Hesperian felicity.[5] Gather yourself and your children into a little system, in which each may promote the ease, the safety, and the pleasure of the rest.

Mr. Howard called on me a few days ago, and gave ⟨me⟩ the new edition, much enlarged, of his Account of Prisons.[6] He has been to survey the prisons on the continent; and in Spain he tried to penetrate the dungeons of the Inquisition, but his curiosity was very imperfectly gratified. At Madrid they shut him quite out; at Villadolid they shewed him some publick rooms.

While I am writing, the post has brought your kind letter. Do not think with dejection of your own condition; a little patience will probably give you health, it will certainly give you riches, and all the accommodations that riches can procure.

I am, Madam, Your most humble Servant
Apr. 26, 1784. London   Sam: Johnson.

957. M. 26 Apr. '84. Lucy Porter (Lichfield).

Address (Malone): To Mrs Lucy Porter, in Lichfield.
Not traced.—Malone's Boswell 1804, iv. 291.

My Dear
I write to you now, to tell you that I am so far recovered that on the 21st I went to church, to return thanks, after a confinement of more than four long months.

My recovery is such as neither myself nor the physicians at all expected, and is such as that very few examples have been known of the like. Join with me, my dear love, in returning thanks to God.

956.—5. The phrase strongly suggests that J is hinting at Piozzi. For the vexed question, how much he knew or suspected, at various dates, of HLT's wishes or intentions, see *Queeney Letters* 97 (and references there) and especially Lord Lansdowne's careful summing-up, ibid. 124; *Th* 599; FB's *Memoirs of Dr. Burney* ii. 246 (quoted in Hayward, i. 214, in ed. 2); below, 969.1.

6. The edition of '84 is Lot 286 in the sale catalogue of J's library. The purchaser's name is 'Money', which tells us nothing.

Dr. Vyse has been with ⟨me⟩ this evening; he tells me that you likewise have been much disordered, but that you are now better. I hope that we shall sometime have a cheerful interview. In the mean time let us pray for one another.

I am, Madam, Your humble servant,
London, April 26, 1784. Sam: Johnson.

958. F. 30 Apr. '84. Frances Reynolds.

Address: To Mrs Reynolds.
Rupert Colomb.—Croker's Boswell 1831, v. 167.

Dear Madam

Mr. Allen has looked over the papers[1] and thinks that one hundred copies will come to five pounds.

Fifty will cost 4*l*. 10*s*., and five and twenty will cost 4*l*. 5*s*. It seems therefore scarcely worth while to print fewer than a hundred.

Suppose you printed 250 at 6*l*. 10. and without any name tried the sale, which may be secretly done. You would then see the opinion of the publick without hazard, if nobody knows but I. If any body else is in the secret, you shall not have my consent to venture.

I am, Dear Madam, Your most affectionate, and most humble servant,
Bolt court Apr. 30. 1784 Sam: Johnson

958.1. M. 3 May '84. William Bowles (Heale).

Address: To W. Bowles Esq. at Heale near Salisbury. *Postmark*: 3 MA.
Sotheby 30 June 1938.—

Dear Sir

Your attention to me in my acquaintance with you, gives you a right to be told that after a confinement of more than four months I was at Church on the 21st, to present myself before God after my recovery, such a recovery as my Physicians have very rarely seen. I have since been a little abroad, and was again at the Club, a few days ago.

I suppose you had a copy of the Statutes, and therefore

958.—1. This is the work praised by J in 738. But she gave up the idea of printing, at least temporarily, see 961.

know that every Absence forfeits threepence a night. The forfeit is so small that no excuse is ever made. I paid regularly during my long illness. Your forfeits now amount to six shillings, which I purpose to pay for you, and to continue to pay as they rise, for it is better not to suffer those ludicrous expences ever to amount to much at a time.

I am, I think, and so think the Physicians, quite free from the dropsy, and the athsthma, though not cured, troubles me but little. But I am very weak in my limbs, from a false step I do not easily recover. I walked however a few days ago to the picture room in the Academy without stopping to rest or breathe. I hope we shall meet again more cheerfully than we parted.

Be pleased to make my compliments to dear Mrs Bowles, to your Father, and all our friends, and to the young ones, if they yet have any traces[1] of me. When any occasion brings you to town, I will introduce you to the Club.

I am, Dear Sir, Your most humble Servant,
London. May 3. 1784.   Sam: Johnson.

959. M. 10 May '84. Jane Langton (Rochester).

Address (Boswell): To Miss Jane Langton, in Rochester, Kent. Bennet Langton; the letter is framed, and the address is not visible.— Boswell 1791, ii. 488 (Hill iv. 271).

My dearest Miss Jenny

I am sorry that your pretty Letter has been so long without being answered; but when I am not pretty well, I do not always write plain enough for young Ladies.

I am glad, my Dear, to see that you write so well, and hope that you mind your pen, your book, and your needle, for they are all necessary. Your books will give you knowledge, and make you respected, and your needle will find you useful employment when you do not care to read. When you are a little older, I hope you will be very diligent in learning arithmetick; and above all, that through your whole life, you will carefully say your prayers, and read your Bible.

I am, my Dear Your most humble servant,
Bolt court, Fleetstreet. May 10. 1784.   Sam: Johnson.

958.1.—1. An unusual shade of meaning. But *OED* quotes, from a translation 1809 of *Gil Blas*, 'my brain full of curious traces'.

960. Th. 13 May '84. Mrs. Thrale (Bath).

Hyde.—1788, No. 349.

Madam

Now I am broken loose, my friends seem willing enough to see me. On Monday I dined with Paradise; Tuesday, Hoole; Wednesday, Dr Taylor; to day with Jodrel; Friday, Mrs. Garrick; Saturday, Dr Brocklesby. Next Monday, Dilly. But I do not now drive the World about; the World drives or draws me.¹ I am very weak, the old distress of sleeplessness comes again upon me. I have however one very strong basis of Health, an eager appetite, and strong digestion.

Queeney's letter I expected before now. Susy is likewise in debt. I believe I am in debt to Sophy, but the dear Loves ought ⟨not⟩ to be too rigorous.

Dr Taylor has taken St. Margaret's in Westminster vacant by Dr. Wilson's death. How long he will keep it I cannot guess. It is of no great value, and its income consists much of voluntary contributions.

        I am, Madam Your most humble servant

Thursday May 13. 1784 London   Sam: Johnson.

You never date fully.

960.1. Tu. 25 May '84. ——.

No address.
Morgan Library.—

Sir

I have spoken to Mr Davies more than once to settle with Mr Evans, as I rather think I have paid him, the reason why I think it, is inclosed, and I will do just as you would have me, for I am not sure. I am,

        Sir Your most humble servant

May 25. 1784   Sam: Johnson

960.—1. Hill refers to Dryden's *Character of a Good Parson* 31: And forc'd himself to drive; but lov'd to draw.

961. F. 28 May ⟨? '84⟩. Frances Reynolds.

Address: To Mrs Reynolds.
Rupert Colomb; endorsed by F. R. 'Dr Johnson believe in 84'.—
Croker's Boswell 1831, v. 181.

Madam   May 28th
    You do me wrong by imputing my omission to any
captious punctiliousness. I have not yet seen Sir Joshua, and
when I do see him, know not how to serve you. When I spoke
upon your affair to him at Christmas, I received no encouragement to speak again.
    But We shall never do business by letters, We must see
one another.
    I have returned your papers, and am glad that you laid
aside the thought of printing them.[1]
            I am, Madam, Your most humble servant,
                                            Sam: Johnson.

962. M. 31 May '84. Ozias Humphry.

Sotheby 10 May 1875 (not seen); copy made for JB, Isham.—Boswell
1791, ii. 487 (Hill iv. 269).

Sir
    I am very much obliged by your civilities to my god-son,
but must beg of you to add to them the favour of permitting
him to see you paint, that he may know how a picture is
begun, advanced, and completed.
    If he may attend you in a few of your operations, I hope
he will shew that the benefit has been properly conferred,
both by his proficiency and his gratitude. At least I shall
consider you as enlarging your kindness to, Sir, your humble
servant,
May 31, 1784.   Sam. Johnson.

961.—For J's efforts to improve the relations of Sir Joshua and his sister see on 602.
    1. See 958.
962.—See 947.

963. M. 31 May '84. Mrs. Thrale (Bath).

Sir Charles Russell.—1788, No. 350.

Dear Madam

Why you expected me to be better than I am I cannot imagine; I am better than any that saw me in my ilness ever expected to have seen me again. I am however at a great distance from health, very weak and very asthmatick, and troubled with my old nocturnal distresses. So that I am little asleep in the night, and in the day too little awake.

I have one way or other been disappointed hitherto of that change of air from which I think some relief may possibly be obtained; but Boswel and I have settled our resolution to go to Oxford on Thursday. But since I was at Oxford, my convivial friend, Dr Edwards, and my learned friend, Dr Wheeler, are both dead, and my proba⟨bi⟩lities of pleasure are very much diminished. Why, when so many are taken away, have I been yet spared? I hope that I may be fitter to die.

How long we shall stay at Oxford, or what we shall do when we leave it, neither Bozzy nor I have yet settled; he is for his part resolved to remove his family to London, and try his fortune at the English Bar. Let us all wish him success.

Think of me, if You can, with tenderness. ⟨. . .⟩[1]

I am, Madam Your most humble servant
May 31. 1784 London   Sam: Johnson.

963.—Writing at Bath 23 May (29 May, in *Queeney Letters* 64, C 225, seems to be a slip) HLT records (*Tb* 593) 'I have been to London for a Week to visit Fanny Burney, and to talk over my intended—(& I hope—approaching Nuptials) with Mr. Borghi' (a friend of Piozzi). Our knowledge of this visit depends mainly on FB's *Diary*, ii. 314-15. She quotes a note from HLT 'Mortimer Street, Cavendish Square, Tuesday Night, May 1784' (the precise date is not determined, but is unimportant) announcing her arrival. On 17 May FB writes: 'The rest of that week I devoted almost wholly to sweet Mrs. Thrale.' After mentioning two social engagements she goes on: 'But all the rest of my time I gave wholly to dear Mrs. Thrale, who . . . saw nobody else.' Mr. Clifford (225) accepts this. But *Tb* 594 suggests that HLT may have seen Dr. Burney ('We have told all to her Father, and he behaved with the utmost Propriety') and she certainly saw Borghi. Since, therefore, she took *some* risk of being recognized, she may have thought it dangerous to try to keep J in ignorance of her being in town. I am disposed to agree with Miss Balderston (*Tb* 593) that the first sentence of this letter implies a meeting.

1. A line follows, so heavily erased that I could make out nothing.

963.1. M. 31 May '84. William Adams (Oxford).

Adam.—

Sir

 Let me not be thought insensible of your kind invitations, if I have hitherto delayed to accept them. I have been confined to the house one hundred and twenty nine days, and it may be easily supposed that I am yet languid with the debility of so long an ilness, from only part of which I have recovered.

 I hope however, that I have strength yet remaining sufficient to carry me to Oxford, and with Mr. Boswel, my old fellow traveller, I hope to see you on Thursday the 3d of June.

 Our wish is, if it can ⟨be⟩ easily allowed us, to lodge and live in the college.

 A sick Man is a very troublesome visitant. I bring my servant with me, who must be some way or other provided for.

 I return dear Miss Adams my sincere thanks for her two kind visits, and for her imperturbab⟨l⟩e and irresistible tenderness and civility.

I am, Sir, Your most humble servant
Bolt court Fleet street. May 31. 1784   Sam: Johnson

964. Tu. 1 June '84. Joshua Reynolds.

Address: To Sir Joshua Reynolds.
Fettercairn.—Boswell 1791, ii. 495 (Hill iv. 283.)

Dear Sir

 I am ashamed to ask for some relief for a poor man to whom, I hope, I have given what I can be expected to spare. The man importunes me and the blow goes round. I am going to try another air on Thursday.

I am, Sir, Your most &c
June 1. 1784   Sam: Johnson

965. W. 2 June '84. Anthony Hamilton.

Not traced.—Croker's Boswell 1835, x. 283.

Sir   June 2, 1784.
    You do every thing that is liberal and kind. Mrs. Pellè is a bad manager for herself, but I will employ a more skilful agent, one Mrs. Gardiner, who will wait on you and employ Pellè's money to the best advantage. Mrs. Gardiner will wait on you.
    I return you, Sir, sincere thanks for your attention to me. I am ill, but hope to come back better, and to be made better still by your conversation.

I am, Sir, &c.
Sam: Johnson.

965.1. Th. 3 June '84. Hester Maria Thrale (Bath).

Address: To Miss Thrale at Bath.
Lansdowne.—Lansdowne, *Johnson and Queeney* 1932, 48.

My dear Love,   London, June 3, 1784
    I am going to Oxford, and perhaps further, and hear[1] that you are going to Brighthelmston, I hope we shall receive help from our excursions. My nights are very tedious, and my Asthma of late is very troublesome, and as the King has for near a year paid me nothing, I am very poor.
    The Speaking Image,[2] about which you enquire, is a very subtle and wonderful deception. The answer to the question is doubtless made by ventriloquy, or the art of directing the voice in what ⟨way⟩ the speaker wills, but ⟨how⟩ the question is conveyed to the Speaker, wherever he is, has not yet been discovered. The statue is of wax, and incapable of any mechanical operation. Besides, that no mechanism can provide answers to arbitrary questions. No chimes can be set to play any tune that may be called. The artifice is according to all accounts astonishing, yet it will some time ⟨be⟩ resolved into some petty trick.

965.1.—1. Perhaps from FB. For the date and manner of the girls' parting from their mother see *Tb* 598, *Queeney Letters* 137, and below, 969a.
    2. Q had probably heard of it from her mother, see on 963. *The Speaking Figure and the Automaton Chess-Player Exposed*, 1784, has a frontispiece showing how the trick was done by a series of speaking-tubes.

That I love you, and wish you all wise and good and happy,
I hope needs not be told, by
Dearest Love, Your most humble servant
Sam: Johnson

965.2. Oxford. M. 7 June '84. Edmund Allen.

Address: To Mr Allen in Bolt court, Fleet street, London. *Postmark*:
8 IV.
Adam.—Duke of Argyll, *Intimate Society Letters* 1910, ii. 650.

Dear Sir
I came hither on Thursday without the least trouble or
fatigue, but I do not yet perceive any improvement of my
health. My Breath is very much obstructed, my legs are very
soon tired, and my Nights are very restless.
Boswel went back next day, and is not yet returned, Miss
Adams, and Miss Moore are not yet come. How long I shall
stay, or whither I shall go, I cannot yet guess; While I am
away I beg that you will sit for me at the club, and that you
will pay Betsy Barber five shilling a week. I hope I shall by
degrees be better. I am, Sir,
Your most humble servant
Pembroke College, Oxford. June 7. 1784 Sam: Johnson

965.3. Oxford. Tu. 8 June '84. George Nicol.

Address: To Mr Nicol Bookseller in the Strand London. *Postmark*:
9 IV.
Johnson House.—

Sir
You were pleased to promise me that when the great
Voyage¹ should be published, you would send it to me. I am
now at Pembroke College, Oxford, and if you can con-
veniently enclose it in a parcel, or send it any other way,
I shall think the perusal of it a great favour.
I am, Sir, Your most humble servant,
June 8. 1784.   Sam: Johnson

965.3.—1. Cook's last *Voyage*, which was published posthumously in this year.

965.4. Oxford. Tu. 8 June '84. John Taylor (Westminster).

Address: To the Reverend Dr Taylor in Westminster. *Postmark*: 9 IV.
Owen D. Young.—

Dear Sir

I came hither on Thursday without any sense of fatigue
but cannot perceive that change of place does me any good.
I am very weak in my legs, and suspicious that the⟨y⟩ swell
again, but of that I am not sure. My breath is very laborious,
and my nights restless and tedious. I am very kindly treated
here.

Let me know how You go on. In the first place think on
your health. Let nothing vex you, for what is there that
can desire[1] the sacrifice of your quiet? Then tell me what is
your determination about the bill:[2] and when You expect
to be restored to your house in Ashbourne. I am

Sir, Your most humble Servant

Sam: Johnson

Pembroke College, Oxford. June 8. 1784

965.5. Sa. 12 June '84. Mr. and Mrs. Perkins.

Sotheby 21 Jan. 1899 (not seen).—Quoted in catalogue.

Mr. Johnson spent a sleepless night, but is better today.

966. Th. 17 June '84. Mrs. Thrale (Bath).

Sotheby 15 Feb. 1926.—1788, No. 351.

Dear Madam

I returned last night from Oxford, after a fortnight's
abode with Dr. Adams, who treated me as well as I could
expect or wish; and he that contents a sick man, a man whom
it is impossible to please, has surely done his part well. I went
in the common vehicle with very little fatigue, and came
back, I think, with less. My stomach continues good, and
according to your advice, I spare neither asparagus nor pease
and hope to do good execution upon all the summer fruits.
But my nights are bad, very bad; The Asthma attacks me

965.4.—1. I suspect myself of having misread this word, which should perhaps be
'deserve'.
2. I have no clue to this.

often, and the Dropsy is watching an opportunity to return. I hope, I have checked ⟨it⟩, but great caution must be used, and indeed great caution is not a high price for health or ease.

What I shall do next a[1] know not; all my schemes of rural pleasure have been some way or other disappointed. I have now some thought of Lichfield, and Ashbourne. Let me know, dear Madam, your destination.[2]

I am, Madam, Your most humble servant
London June 17, 1784   Sam: Johnson.

967. Sa. 19 June '84. John Taylor (Westminster).

Address: To the Reverend Dr. Taylor.
Hyde.—Hill 1892.

Sir
When we parted last night, I thought worse of your case, than I think since I have thought longer upon it. Your general distemper is, I think, a hectic fever, for which the bark is proper, and which quietness of mind, and gentle exercise, and fresh air may cure. Your present weakness is the effect of such waste of blood, as would weaken a young man in his highest vigour. It might be necessary, but it might sink both your courage and strength.

Dr. Nichols[1] hurt himself extremely in his old age by lavish phlebotomy. Do not bleed again very soon, and when you can delay no longer, be more moderate.

I think you do right in going home, and hope you will have an easy and pleasant Journey.

I am, dear Sir, Yours affectionately,
June 19, 1784. Bolt Court   Sam: Johnson

966.—1. 1788 prints 'I'; 'a' is I suppose a mere slip.
2. It seems idle to conjecture how much lies behind this. It may be no more than that J, knowing HLT to be alone in Bath, may have thought she might think of going elsewhere, e.g. of visiting her daughters.

967.—1. Frank Nicholls, physician to George II. Hill quotes a memoir of him in *GM* 1785, i. 13, from which it appears that he died at 79 from 'an inveterate asthmatic cough'—for which, as J's own case shows, drastic bleeding was orthodox treatment. J was probably acquainted with N, who married a daughter of Dr. Mead, and whose life was written by Lawrence (in Latin, 1780). L does not I think charge N with excessive bleeding; but I note, p. 103, the phrase 'sanguinis missioni repetitae'.

968. W. 23 June '84. John Taylor (Ashbourne).

Address: To the Reverend Dr Taylor in Ashbourne Derbyshire.
Postmarks: 23 and 24 IV.
Huntington Library.—Hill 1892.

Dear Sir

It is now Wednesday Evening. I hope You are lodged easily and safely in Ashbourne. Since we parted I have not been well. I dined on Saturday with Dr Brocklesby, and was taken ill at his house, but went to the club.[1] On Monday I was so uneasy that I staid at home. On Tuesday I dined at the club,[1] but was not well at night, nor am well to day but hope the fit is abating. Boswel has a great mind to draw me to Lichfield, and as I love to travel with him, I have a mind to be drawn if I could hope in any short time to come to your house, for Lichfield will I am afraid, not be a place for long continuance, and, to tell the truth, I am afraid of seeing my self so far from home, as I must return alone.[2]

Sir John Hawkins has just told me that You preached on Sunday with great vigour. You have therefore a great fund of strength left, which I entreat You not to bleed away.

I am, Sir, Yours affectionately
June 23. 1784.   Sam: Johnson.

969. Sa. 26 June '84. Mrs. Thrale (Bath).

Sir Charles Russell.—1788, No. 352.

Dear Madam

This morning I saw Mr Lysons.[1] he is an agreeable young Man, and likely enough to do all that he designs. I received him, as one sent by you has a right to be received, and I hope, he will tell you that he was satisfied, but the initiatory conversation of two strangers is seldom pleasing or instructive

---

968.—1. The first club is the Essex-Head, which met on Saturdays (*L* iv. 275) and two other days a week; the second the Literary (*L* iv. 326).

2. It is not quite clear why the danger of a visit to L'd would be averted by a visit to A'n. A'n however was on a direct road to L'n, which L'd was not. J may also have hoped that JT would in some way facilitate the return.

969.—1. HLT had recorded 13 Jan.: 'I have picked up a Young Man here of very uncommon parts; a Mr Lysons, Nephew to Dr Lysons the Physician.' Then follows a list of his attainments, and later references show that they quickly became intimate (*Th* 586, 592, 594).

to any great degree, and ours was such as other occasions of the same kind produce.

A message came to me yesterday, to tell me that Macbean, after three days of illness, is dead of a suppression of urine. He was one of those who, as Swift says, *stood as a screen between me and death.*[2] He has, I hope, made a good exchange. He was very pious. He was very innocent. He did no ill, and of doing good a continual tenour of distress allowed him few opportunities. He was very highly esteemed in the house.[3]

Write to me, if you can, some words of comfort. My dear Girls seem all to forget me. I am

Madam, Your most humble Servant

June 26. 1784 London Sam: Johnson.

969a. Bath. W. 30 June '84. From Mrs. Thrale.

Address: Doctor Sam: Johnson.
The copy sent to Q, Lansdowne. The circular, Fettercairn.—1788, No. 353; Hayward 1861[2], ii. 238; Lansdowne, *Queeney Letters* 1934, 148. See Addenda, p. 337.

My dear Sir, Bath, 30: June, 1784
The enclosed is a circular Letter which I have sent to all the Guardians, but our Friendship demands somewhat more; it requires that I sh[d] beg your pardon for concealing from you a Connection which you must have heard of by many People, but I suppose never believed. Indeed, my dear Sir, it was concealed only to spare us both needless pain; I could not have borne to reject that Counsel it would have killed me to take; and I only tell it you now,

---

969.—2. *On the Death of Dr. Swift*: 'The Fools, my Juniors by a Year, | Are tortur'd with Suspence and Fear; | Who wisely thought my Age a Screen, | When Death approach't, to stand between.'
  3. Macbean was a poor brother of the Charterhouse.

969a.—The 1788 and Bowood texts are not identical; even in copying documents of such moment, HLT permitted herself to improve. I give the latter version, which its provenance shows to be the copy sent to Q. For the variations see 1788, Hill, or *Queeney Letters*. The most important is the signature H: L: T. to the circular, which does not appear in Hayward. In her collection of 1788 HLP included 969a (but not the circular enclosed); she very properly suppressed J's 'rough' reply 970; she printed his second letter 972, but omitted her own second letter 970.1a, on which see below. Less commendably, she headed 969a 'Mrs. Piozzi to Dr. Johnson', and 972 'to Mrs. Piozzi'; and if the lost original of 969a was unsigned (as both our texts of it are), the intention was to make J believe her already married. The actual dates of the marriage were 23 July (L'n) and 25 July (Bath; C 229). Hill quotes from *Jackson's Oxford Journal* 31 July a notice which begins thus: 'Bath, July 28, Sunday (and not before) was married', &c. The original of 969a is lost; J doubtless destroyed it. HLP kept the original of 970, q.v. See also Addenda.

because all is *irrevocably settled*, & out of your power to prevent. Give me leave however to say that the dread of your disapprobation has given me many an anxious moment, & tho' perhaps the most independent Woman in the World—I feel as if I was acting without a parent's Consent—till you write kindly to your faithful Servt.

I shewed James this Letter & he cried.

Sent this day to Dr Johnson enclos'd in what is written on t'other side the paper.

[*The enclosure.*]

Sir,

As one of the Executors to Mr Thrale's Will, and Guardian to his daughters, I think it my duty to acquaint you that the three eldest left Bath last Fryday for their own house at Brighthelmstone, in company with an aimiable Friend Miss Nicholson, who has some time resided with us here, and in whose Society they may I think find some advantages and certainly no Disgrace: I waited on them myself as far as Salisbury, Wilton &c. and offered my Service to attend them to the Seaside; but they preferred this Lady's Company to mine, having heard that Mr. Piozzi was coming back from Italy, and judging from our past Friendship & continued Correspondence, that his return would be succeeded by our Marriage.

I have the honour to be Sir, Your most humble Servant

H: L: T.

969.1. Th. 1 July '84. Hester Maria Thrale (Brighthelmston).

Address: To Miss Thrale at Brighthelmston Sussex.
Lansdowne.—Lansdowne, *Johnson and Queeney* 1932, 49.

My Dearest,   London, July 1, 1784

I read your letter[1] with anguish and astonishment, such as I never felt before. I had fondly flattered myself that time had produced better thoughts.[2] I can only give you this consolation that, in my opinion, you have hitherto done rightly. You have not left your Mother, but your Mother has left you.

You must now be to your sisters what your Mother ought to have been, and if I can give you any help, I hope never to desert you. I will write to the other Guardians.[3]

969.1.—1. We must deplore the disappearance of this, and of nearly all Q's letters to J. Except for two childish letters of '72 and '77, which J must have left at S'm (*Queeney Letters*, 7, 10), none has been found. See Appendix H.

2. For the question how much J had known or suspected, see the references collected at 956.

3. Cator, Crutchley, and Smith.

I send my kindest respects to your sisters, and exhort them to attend to your counsels, and recommend you all to the care of Him who is the Father of the fatherless.

I am, Dear Madam, Your most humble servant

Sam: Johnson

970. F. 2 July '84. Mrs. Thrale (Bath).

Address: To Mrs Thrale at Bath. *Postmark*: 2 IY.
Adam.—*GM*. Dec. 1784, ii. 893, an 'adumbration'; not in 1788; Hayward's *Piozzi* 1861¹, i. 111, 1861², i. 239.

Madam

If I interpret your letter right, you are ignominiously married, if it is yet undone, let us once talk together. If you have abandoned your children and your religion, God forgive your wickedness; if you have forfeited your Fame, and your country, may your folly do no further mischief.

If the last act is yet to do, I, who have loved you, esteemed you, reverenced you, and served you, I who long thought you the first of human kind, entreat that before your fate is irrevocable, I may once more see you. I was, I once was,

Madam, most truly yours.

July 2. 1784   Sam: Johnson.

I will come down if you permit it.

970.1. Sa. 3 July '84. Hester Maria Thrale (Brighthelmston).

Address: To Miss Thrale at Brighthelmston Sussex.
Lansdowne.—Lansdowne, *Johnson and Queeney* 1932, 51.

Dear Madam,   London, July 3, 1784

In telling you that I sincerely pity you, and that I approve your conduct I tell you only what will be said by all Mankind. What I think of your Mother's conduct I cannot express, but by words which I cannot prevail upon myself to use.

970.—See on 969*a*. Though Hayward states that some words are 'indistinctly written', the text is nowhere in doubt; J wrote 'human kind', not 'womankind'. The *GM* text was described by J as an 'adumbration' (Hawkins 569); I suppose Nichols printed it from memory. See also *L* iv. 339 (where Hill quotes FB's story, *Diary* ii. 328, of J's destruction of HLT's letters; on which see Appendix C), *Th* 599–600, C 227.

Your Guardians, I suppose, have been now with you; I am sorry that I am not with you too. But they have more power to help you than I, and not less inclination. We all compassionate and love you and your sisters, and I hope by our Friendship, and your own Virtue, Prudence, and Piety, you may, though thus unworthily deserted, pass a life of security, Happiness, and honour.

I am, Dearest Love, Your most humble servant

Sam: Johnson

970.1a. Su. 4 July '84. From Mrs. Thrale.

Address: Dr Johnson.
Adam.—Hayward 1861¹, i. 111, 1861², i. 240. Not in 1788.

Sir— 4 July 1784.

I have this Morning received from You so rough a Letter, in reply to one which was both tenderly & respectfully written, that I am forced to desire the conclusion of a Correspondence which I can bear to continue no longer. The Birth of my second Husband is not meaner than that of my first, his sentiments are not meaner, his Profession is not meaner,—and his Superiority in what he professes—acknowledged by all Mankind.—It is want of Fortune then that is *ignominious*, the Character of the Man I have chosen has no other Claim to such an Epithet. The Religion to which he has been always a zealous Adherent, will I hope teach him to forgive Insults he has not deserved—mine will I hope enable me to bear them at once with Dignity & Patience. To hear that I have forfeited my Fame is indeed the greatest Insult I ever yet received, my Fame is as unsullied as Snow, or I should think it unworthy of him who must henceforward protect it.

I write by the Coach the more speedily and effectually to prevent your coming hither.

Perhaps by my Fame (& I hope it is so;) you mean only that Celebrity which is a Consideration of a much lower kind: I care for that only as it may give pleasure to my Husband & his Friends.

Farewell Dear Sir, and accept my best wishes: You have always commanded my Esteem, and long enjoy'd the Fruits of a Friendship never infringed by one harsh Expression on my Part, during twenty Years of familiar Talk. never did I oppose your Will, or controal your Wish: nor can your unmerited Severity itself lessen my Regard—but till you have changed your Opinion of M^r. Piozzi —let us converse no more. God bless you!

970.1a.—This letter, with its lack of signature (for which see on 978a) and its use of the word 'husband', has been suspected of maintaining the implication of her first letter (969a), that she was already married (C 227). If J was deceived, the deception can hardly have lasted; Q's letters must have enlightened him? I note that both 970 and 972 are addressed 'To Mrs. Thrale'.

970.2. Tu. 6 July '84. Hester Maria Thrale (Brighthelmston).

Address: To Miss Thrale at Brighthelmston.
Lansdowne.—Lansdowne, *Johnson and Queeney* 1932, 52.

Dear Madam,   London, July 6, 1784
  Mr. Crutchley[1] gave me an account of your interview, and of the plan which is for the present exigence settled between you and your Friends. But I either misunderstand him or you, for the two accounts seem very different.

If you comply for the time with proposals not very agreeable, you know that any necessity of compliance can be but short. You will soon[2] be mistress of yourself. Do your best; and be not discouraged. Serve God, read, and pray. You have in your hand all that the world considers as materials of happiness. You have riches, youth, and Health, all which I shall delight to see you enjoy. But believe a man whose experience has been long, and who can have no wish to deceive you, and who now tells you that the highest honour, and most constant pleasure this life can afford, must be obtained by passing it with attention fixed upon Eternity. The longest life soon passes away. You that are blooming in all the gayety of youth, will be, before you are aware, as old as he that has now the honour of being
                        Madam Your most humble servant
                                            Sam: Johnson

971. Th. 8 July '84. Joshua Reynolds.

Fettercairn.—Boswell 1791, ii. 534 (Hill iv. 348).

Dear Sir
  I am going, I hope, in a few days to try the air of Derbyshire, but hope to see You before I go. Let me however mention to You what I have much at heart.
  If the Chancellor should continue his attention to Mr. Boswel's request, and confer with You upon the means of

970.2.—1. Lord Lansdowne suggested (*Queeney Letters*, xxviii) that it may have been proposed that C should give asylum in his home at Sunninghill.
  2. She would be twenty-one on 15 Sept. '85.
971.—For JB's 'pious negociation' with Thurlow and JR see *L* iv. 326, 336, 348; and below.

relieving my languid state, I am very desirous to avoid the appearance of asking money upon false pretences.[1] I desire You to represent to his Lordship what as soon as it is suggested he will perceive to be reasonable.

That, if I grow much worse, I shall be afraid to leave my Physicians, to suffer the inconveniences of travel, and pine in the solitude of a foreign country.

That, if I grow much better, of which indeed there is now little appearance, I shall not wish to leave my friends, and my domestick comforts. For I do not travel for pleasure or curiosity. Yet if I should recover curiosity would revive.

In my present State, I am desirous to make a struggle for a little longer life, and hope to obtain some help from a softer climate.

Do for me what you can.

     I am, Dear Sir, Your most humble Servant
Bolt court July 8. 1784   Sam: Johnson

972. Th. 8 July '84. Mrs. Thrale (Bath).

Address: To Mrs Thrale at Bath. *Postmark*: 8 IY.
Sir Charles Russell.—1788, No. 354, headed 'To Mrs. Piozzi'.

Dear Madam

What you have done, however I may lament it, I have no pretence to resent, as it has not been injurious to me. I therefore breathe out one sigh more of tenderness perhaps useless, but at least sincere.

I wish that God may grant you every blessing, that you may be happy in this world for its short continuance, and eternally happy in a better state. and whatever I can contribute to your happiness, I am very ready to repay for that kindness which soothed twenty years of a life radically wretched.

Do not think slightly of the advice which I now presume to offer. Prevail upon Mr. Piozzi to settle in England.[1] You may live here with more dignity than in Italy, and with more security. Your rank will be higher, and your fortune more

971.—1. After 'pretences' are the following words in erasure (doubtless J's own): 'Before I receive the King's bounty to enable me to breath the softer air of the continent.'
972.—1. 'Dr. Johnson's advice corresponded exactly with Mr. Piozzi's intentions.' HLP quoted in Hayward, 1861[2], ii. 56.

under your own eye. I desire not to detail all my reasons; but every argument of prudence and interest is for England, and only some phantoms of imagination seduce you to Italy.

I am afraid, however, that my counsel is vain, yet I have eased my heart by giving it.

When Queen Mary[2] took the resolution of sheltering herself in England, the Archbishop of St. Andrew's attempting to dissuade her, attended on her journey and when they came to the irremeable[3] stream that separated the two kingdoms, walked by her side into the water, in the middle of which he seized her bridle, and with earnestness proportioned to her danger and his own affection, pressed her to return. The Queen went forward.——If the parallel reaches thus far; may it go no further. The tears stand in my eyes.

I am going into Derbyshire, and hope to be followed by your good wishes, for I am with great affection

Your most humble servant,

London July 8. 1784   Sam: Johnson

Any letters that come for me hither, will be sent me.

972.1. Th. 8 July '84. Lucy Porter (Lichfield).

Address: To Mrs Lucy Porter in Lichfield.
Sotheby 15 April 1929.——

Dear Madam
I am coming down to Ashbourne, and, as you may believe shall visit you in my way.

I shall bring a poor, broken, unweildy body, but I shall not trouble you long, for Dr Taylor will in a few days send for me. I hope to find you better than you will find me. I hear that poor Mrs Aston is very ill.

I am Dear Madam Your most humble Servant

London July 8. 1784   Sam: Johnson

972.——2. Hill, having drawn the obvious books blank, found J's story, or one like it, in Adam Blackwood: *Adami Blacvodaei Opera* 1644, 589.
  3. Virgil's 'irremeabilis unda'. *Aen.* vi. 425.

972.2. Sa. 10 July '84. William Bowles (Heale).

Address: To W. Bowles Esq at Heale near Salisbury. *Postmark*: 10 iy.
Adam.—

Dear Sir
 Your kind invitation came two or three days after an
engagement to pay a visit to a friend in Derbyshire, towards
whom I shall, I hope, set out to morrow. When I come back,
your kindness can do again what it has already done, and,
I hope, may be enjoyed, more than I have been yet able to
enjoy it.
 Be pleased in the mean time to accept my thanks, and pay
my respects to your amiable Lady, and your worthy Father,
and all my friends, great and little.
 The Club flourishes; We fill the table. Mr Strahan has
resigned, and My fellow traveller Mr Boswel is put in his
place. This is all the change that has happened in our State.
      I am, Dear Sir, Your most humble servant
Bolt court July 10. 1784   Sam: Johnson

973. Su. 11 July '84. James Boswell (Edinburgh).

Fettercairn.—Boswell 1791, ii. 536, extract, dated 11 June by Boswell
in the context; see 974 (Hill iv. 351).

 I remember, and intreat you to remember, that *virtus est
vitium fugere*;[1] the first approach to riches is security from
poverty. The condition upon which you have my consent to
settle in London is, that your expence never exceeds your
annual income. Fixing this basis of security, you cannot be
hurt, and you may be very much advanced. The loss of your
Scottish business, which is all that you can lose, is not to be
reckoned as any equivalent to the hopes and possibilities that

973.—JB says that 'after repeated reasonings' he had persuaded J to approve his
moving to L'n, 'and even to furnish me with arguments'. He wrote to J accordingly
asking him to put these arguments into writing; 'and I shall extract that part of his
letter to me of June 11'. On 11 June JB was still in L'n. The date of 973 was no
doubt 11 July; JB places it after his account of HLT's intended marriage (iv. 339)
and immediately before the letter to Bagshaw of 12 July. 973 was found at Fettercairn (Abbott, *Catalogue* xvii), but I do not know whether the false date is J's or not.
JB's own letter is not dated in *Life* or journal; but his unpublished Register records
a letter written at L'd 4 July.
  1. Horace, I *Epist.* i. 41; 'to shun vice is a virtue'.

open here upon you. If you succeed, the question of prudence is at an end; every body will think that done right which ends happily; and though your expectations, of which I would not advise you to talk too much, should not be totally answered, you can hardly fail to get friends who will do for you all that your present situation allows you to hope; and if, after a few years, you should return to Scotland, you will return with a mind supplied by various conversation, and many opportunities of enquiry, with much knowledge and materials for reflection and instruction.

974. Su. 11 July '84. William Adams (Oxford).

Morgan Library; misdated 11 June, corrected in another hand to July (the address and postmark are lost).—Croker's Boswell 1831, v. 266.

Dear Sir,

I am going into Staffordshire and Derbyshire in quest of some relief, of which my need is not less than when I was treated at your house with so much tenderness.

I have now received the collations for Xenophon,[1] which I have sent you with the letters that relate to them. I cannot at present take any part in the work; but I would rather pay for a collation of Oppian,[2] than see it neglected; for the Frenchmen act with great liberality. Let us not fall below them.

I know not in what state Dr Edwards left his book. Some of his emendations seemed to me to ⟨be⟩ irrefragably certain, and such therefore as ought not to be lost. His rule was not ⟨to⟩ change the text, and therefore, I suppose he has left notes to be subjoined. As the book is posthumous some account of the Editor ought to be given.

You have now the whole process of the correspondence before you. When the Prior[3] is answered, let some apology be made for me.

974.—1. See 946.1.
    2. Hill consulted Omont of the Bibliothèque Nationale, who suggested that the collation was perhaps wanted for an edition by a Parisian, de Ballu, published in 1786, in which however it was not used. Dr. Paul Maas suggests an explanation. There is no MS. of Oppian in the Bodleian; but there is a late Byzantine MS. (Cod. Canon. Graec. 1) which has been so catalogued and described as to seem like a MS. of Oppian. Perhaps someone looked at it and reported accordingly.
    3. Cowley.

I was forced to devide the collation,[4] but as it is paged, you will easily put every part in its proper place.

Be pleased to convey my respects to Mrs and Miss Adams.

I am Sir Your most humble servant,

London June 11. 1784   Sam: Johnson.

975. M. 12 July '84. Thomas Bagshaw (Bromley).

Address: To yᵉ Revᵈ Mʳ Bagshaw, Rector of Bromley.
Not traced; copy made for JB, Isham.—Boswell 1791, ii. 536 (Hill iv. 351).

Sir

Perhaps you may remember, that in the year 1753,[1] you committed to the ground my dear wife. I now entreat your permission to lay a stone over her; and have sent the inscription, that, if you find it proper, you may signify your allowance.

You will do me a great favour by showing the place where she lies, that the stone may protect her remains.

Mr. Ryland will wait on you for the inscription, and procure it to be engraved. You will easily believe that I shrink from this mournful office. When it is done, if I have strength remaining, I will visit Bromley once again, and pay you part of that respect to which you have a right from, Reverend Sir, your most humble servant,

July 12, 1784.   Sam. Johnson.

976. M. 12 July '84. Bennet Langton (Rochester).

Address: To Benet Langton Esq in Rochester Kent. *Postmark*: 12 IY. Fettercairn.—Boswell 1791, ii. 537 (Hill iv. 352).

Dear Sir

I cannot but think that in my languid and anxious state

974.—4. J perhaps sent the papers in a number of franked packets (the weight of which was no doubt limited by regulation), as he had sent JB a copy of the *Journey* in thirteen such packets. See on 371.

975.—Since Col. Isham's MS. is presumably JB's sole authority, the readings of 1791, 'upon' for 'over' and 'the respect' for 'that respect', must be attributed to the printer.

1. An error for 1752, see on 1032.

I have some reason to complain that I receive from you neither enquiry nor consolation. You know how much I value your friendship, and with what confidence I expect your kindness, if I wanted any act of tenderness that You could perform, at least if you do not know it, I think your ignorance is your own fault. Yet how long is it that I have lived almost in your neighbourhood,[1] without the least notice.

I do not however consider this neglect, as particularly shown to me, I have[2] two of your most valuable friends make the same complaint. But why are all these overlooked, You are not oppressed by sickness, you are not distracted by business, if you are sick you are sick of leisure, and allow yourself to be told that no disease is more to be dreaded or avoided. Rather to do nothing, than do good is the lowest state of a degraded mind. Boileau[3] says to his pupil.

Que les vers ne soient pas vôtre eternel emploi,
Cultivez vos amis.—

That voluntary debility, which modern language is content to term indolence, will, if it is not counteracted by resolution, render in time the strongest faculties lifeless, and turn the flames to the smoke of virtue.

I do not expect nor desire to see You, because I am much pleased to find that Your Mother stays so long with You, and I should think you neither elegant nor grateful if you did not study her gratification. You will pay my respects to both the Ladies, and to all the young people.

I am going northward for a while to try what help the country can give me, but if you write, the letter will come after me.

976.—1. J can hardly have regarded Fleet Street as 'almost in the neighbourhood' of Rochester. Perhaps BL had been staying in, or nearer, L'n. In August, when BL was still at Rochester, J could 'rejoice' in his (intended) 'removal to London'. See 999. Hannah More had written on 8 March that L had 'taken a little lodging in Fleet Street, in order to be near, to devote himself to' J. But Fleet Street was 'in', not 'almost in', J's 'neighbourhood' (Roberts, *Memoirs of H. M.* 1834, i. 310).

2. 'hear' 1791.   3. *Art Poétique* iv. 121.

4. This paragraph is heavily erased, but I was enabled to read it by the courtesy of the Edinburgh police, who made a photographic enlargement. The erasure seems to be J's. One does not see why either he or BL or JB should cancel such a piece of news, unless indeed Wright (whom I have not identified) had 'got a rule' (from his doctor?) forbidding some form of excess. The possibility occurs that J might intend the news for a different correspondent, and erase it on finding that he had put it in the wrong letter. But it is not repeated in any extant letter of this time.

Mr. Wright gets a rule and called on me lately. He looked
well[4]

    I am Sir Your affectionate humble servant
July 12. 1784 London   Sam: Johnson

977. M. 12 July '84. John Ryland.

Address: To Mr Ryland in Muscovy Court Tower hill. *Postmark*:
illegible (penny post).
Adam.—*NQ* 5 S. vii. 381.

Dear Sir
 Mr Payne will pay you fifteen pounds towards the stone
of which you have kindly undertaken the care. The Inscription is in the hands of Mr Bagshaw, who has a right to inspect
it, before he admits it into his Church.
 Be pleased to let the whole be done with privacy, that I
may elude the vigilance of the papers.
 I am going for a while into Derbyshire in hope of help from
the air of the country. I hope your journey has benefited
you. The Club prospers; we meet by ten at a time.
 God send that you and I may enjoy and improve each
other.

   I am, Dear Sir, Your most humble servant,
July 12. 1784   Sam: Johnson

978. Ashbourne. ⟨July '84⟩. John Hawkins.

Not traced.—Hawkins, *Life of Johnson* 1787, 570; Boswell 1791, ii.
528 (Hill iv. 339).

 Poor Thrale![1] I thought that either her virtue or her vice
would have restrained her from such a marriage. She is now
become a subject for her enemies to exult over, and for her
friends, if she has any left, to forget or pity.

978.—1. I do not remember that J elsewhere ever writes 'Thrale' in a letter. But
the lack of ceremony is not necessarily contemptuous; 'Williams', 'Burney', &c., are
quite common in his letters and diaries.

978a. 'Bath' (see note). Th. 15 July '84. From Mrs. Thrale.

Address: Doctor Sam: Johnson Bolt Court Fleet Street London.
Postmarks: 16 IY and BATH.
R 540.110.—Tyson and Guppy, *French Journals* 1932, 24.

15: July 1784.

Not only my good Wishes but my most fervent Prayers for your Health and
Consolation shall for ever attend and follow my dear Mr Johnson; Your last
Letter is sweetly kind, and I thank you for it most sincerely. Have no Fears
for me however; no *real* Fears. My Piozzi will need few Perswasions to settle
in a Country where he has succeeded so well; but he longs to shew me to his
Italian Friends, & he wishes to restore my Health by treating me with a
Journey to many Places I have long wished to see: his disinterested Conduct
towards me in pecuniary Matters, His Delicacy in giving me up all past
Promises when we were separated last Year by great Violence in Argylle
Street, are Pledges of his Affection and Honour: He is a religious Man, a sober
Man, and a Thinking Man—he will not injure me, I am sure he will not, let
nobody injure him in your good Opinion, which he is most solicitous to obtain
& preserve, and the harsh Letter you wrote me at first grieved him to the very
heart. Accept his Esteem my dear Sir, do; and his Promise to treat with long
continued Respect & Tenderness the Friend whom you once honoured with
your Regard and who will never cease to be

My dear Sir Your truly Affectionate and faithful Servt
⟨Signature erased⟩

The Lawyers delay of finishing our Settlements, & the necessity of twenty
six days Residence, has kept us from being married till now. I hope your
Health is mending.

979. Ashbourne. W. 21 July '84. Richard Brocklesby.

Address: To Dr Brocklesby in London. *Postmark*: 24 IY.
Fettercairn.—Boswell 1791, ii. 557, extract dated 20 July (Hill iv.
353).

Dear Sir

The kind attention which You have so long shown to my
health and happiness, makes it as much a debt of gratitude

978a.—It is certain that HLT was in L'n on 15 July, and almost certain that she did
not return to Bath before her (L'n) marriage on the 23rd (C 228). We must suppose
either that HLT postdated the letter before she left Bath, or that she sent it to a
friend there to post, so that it might bear a Bath postmark. (The postmark 16 IY was
affixed in L'n as always.) Clearly she wished to conceal from J that she was in L'n
and still unmarried. The signature is so vigorously erased that no one has yet been
able to read it. 'Had she', Miss Balderston asks, 'signed herself "Piozzi", and later . . .
thought erasure the better part of valour?' (*Th* 600).

as a call of interest, to give you an account of what befals me, when accident removes[1] me from your immediate care.

The journey of the first day was performed with very little sense of fatigue, the second day brought me to Lichfield without much lassitude, but I am afraid that I could not have born such violent agitation for many days together. Tell Dr Heberden that in the coach I read Ciceronianus, which I concluded as I entred Lichfield. My affection and understanding went along with Erasmus, except that once or twice he somewhat unskilfully entangles Cicero's civil or moral, with his rhetorical character.[2]

I staid five days at Lichfield, but, being unable to walk, had no great pleasure, and yesterday (19th) I came hither, where I am to try what air and attention can perform.

Of any improvement in my health I cannot yet please myself with the perception. The water has in these summer months made two invasions, but has run off again with no very formidable tumefaction, either by the efficacy of the Squils, which I have used very diligently, or because it is the course of the distemper, when it is at a certain height, to discharge itself.

The Asthma has no abatement. Opiates stop the fit, so as that I can sit and sometimes lie easy, but they do not now procure me the power of motion; and I am afraid that my general strength of body does not encrease. The weather indeed is not benign; but how low is he sunk whose strength depends upon the weather? I still pass the night almost without sleep.

I am now looking into Floyer,[3] who lived with his asthma to almost his ninetieth year. His book by want of order is obscure, and his asthma, I think, not of the same kind with mine. Something however I may perhaps learn.

My appetite still continues keen enough, and what I con-

979.—1. Malone's conjecture (for 'recovers' 1791) is confirmed by the MS.

2. To make sure of J's meaning would require a close study of Erasmus's lengthy treatise. Mr. H. W. Garrod tells me that though E's main concern is with Cicero's Latinity, he does introduce reflections on the moral tendency of his speeches. This, perhaps, is what J found clumsy.

3. J borrowed the book from the L'd Cathedral Library on 17 July, returning it, as the records show, on 9 Nov. Sir Humphry Rolleston told Dr. Powell that J was right in thinking his asthma not the same as Floyer's (*L* iv. 544). For F's age see *L* iv. 528.

sider as a symptom of radical health, I have a voracious delight in raw summer fruit, of which I was less eager a few years ago.

One of the most troublesome attendants on my Malady is costiveness, which is perhaps caused by the opiates, though I have not for some months taken any thing more potent than diacodium, and of that not more than twice an ounce at a time, and seldom an ounce in twenty four hours; but I can seldom go ⟨ ⟩ the garden without a cathartick. The aloes mixed with the ⟨? Squills⟩[4] even when I exceed the quantity prescribed, has not any effect.

You will be pleased to communicate this account to d⟨ear⟩ Dr Heberden, and if any thing is to be done, let me have your joint opinion.

Now—*abite curæ*[5]—let me enquire after the club. I hope You meet, and do not forget, Dear Sir, Your obliged humble Servant,

Ashbourne, Derbyshire. July 21. 1784   Sam: Johnson

980. Ashbourne. W. 21 July '84. Joshua Reynolds.

Fettercairn.—Boswell 1793, iii. 638 (Hill iv. 366).

Dear Sir

The tenderness with which I am treated by my friends makes it reasonable to suppose that they are desirous to know the state of my health, and a desire so benevolent ought to be gratified.

I came to Lichfield in two days without any painful fatigue, and on Monday came hither where I purpose to stay and try what air and regularity will effect. I cannot yet persuade myself that I have made much progress in recovery. My sleep is little, my breath is very much encumbred, and my legs are very weak. The water has encreased a little, but has again run off. The most distressing symptom is want of sleep. I am, Sir, with great affection Your most humble Servant

Ashbourne, Derbyshire, July 21. 1784   Sam: Johnson

979.—4. The top of an initial S is visible; the paper is torn.
    5. My classical friends have found nothing closer than [Tibullus] iii. vi. 6 ite procul durum curae genus.

981. Ashbourne. M. 26 July '84. James Boswell (Edinburgh).

Not traced.—Boswell 1791, ii. 534, 555 (Hill iv. 348, 378).

'He wrote to me July 26'

I wish your affairs could have permitted a longer and continued exertion of your zeal and kindness. They that have your kindness[1] may want your ardour. In the mean time I am very feeble, and very dejected.

'July 26, he wrote to me from Ashbourne.'

On the 14th I came to Lichfield, and found every body glad to see me. On the 20th, I came hither, and found a house half-built,[2] of very uncomfortable appearance; but my own room has not been altered. That a man worn with diseases, in his seventy-second or third year, should condemn part of his remaining life to pass among ruins and rubbish, and that no inconsiderable part, appears to me very strange. —I know that your kindness makes you impatient to know the state of my health, in which I cannot boast of much improvement. I came through the journey without much inconvenience, but when I attempt self-motion I find my legs weak, and my breath very short; this day I have been much disordered. I have no company; the Doctor is busy in his fields, and goes to bed at nine, and his whole system is so different from mine, that we seem formed for different elements; I have, therefore, all my amusement to seek within myself.

981.—I have I believe shown (*TLS* 2 Mar. 1946, 103) that J wrote three letters to JB from A'n, not as Hill implies two (981, 982). For convenience I number them 981, 982, 982.1, though the last letter is thus slightly out of chronological order. The evidence for the dates is briefly as follows. 981, 26 July, is not in doubt. 982, not dated by JB, must be later than 28 July if the *GM* is right in giving 28 July as the date of Allen's death, and is almost certainly the answer to JB's letter of 3 Aug. (not dated in *Life*, but recorded in JB's unpublished Register); I therefore date it 5 Aug. 982.1, which JB erroneously dates 'two days later, July 28', was written two days later than 982; I therefore date it 7 Aug. JB's mistake was no doubt due to his having quoted 982 without a date; this led him to add his 'two days' to the only date before him, which was 26 July. For JB's letters see on 982, 982.1.

1. For JB's 'pious negociation' with Thurlow see 1007, 1008, and *L* iv. 348.
2. See *L* iv. 548 for JT's building.

982. Ashbourne. (?) *c.* 5 Aug. '84. James Boswell (Edinburgh).

Not traced.—Boswell 1791, ii. 555 (Hill iv. 379). For the date see on 981.

'Having written to him, in bad spirits, a letter filled with dejection and fretfulness, and at the same time expressing anxious apprehensions concerning him, on account of a dream which had disturbed me; his answer was chiefly in terms of reproach, for a supposed charge of' affecting discontent, and indulging the vanity of complaint.

'It, however, proceeded,'

Write to me often, and write like a man. I consider your fidelity and tenderness as a great part of the comforts which are yet left me, and sincerely wish we could be nearer to each other.—********—My dear friend, life is very short and very uncertain; let us spend it as well as we can.—My worthy neighbour, Allen, is dead. Love me as well as you can. Pay my respects to dear Mrs. Boswell.—Nothing ailed me at that time; let your superstition at last have an end.

982.1. Ashbourne. ? *c.* 7 Aug. '84. James Boswell.

Not traced.—Boswell 1791, ii. 555 (Hill iv. 379).
For the date see on 981.

'He two days afterwards, July 28, wrote to me again, giving me an account of his sufferings; after which, he then proceeds:'

Before this letter, you will have had one which I hope you will not take amiss; for it contains only truth, and that truth

982.—JB in the *Life* describes a letter which he does not date. This I identify with the letter described and dated in his unpublished Register: 'Sent 3 August, 1784, Dr. Samuel Johnson, at Ashbourne. A long melancholy letter, quite in misery from my ambitious project of going to the English bar being impracticable, at least for some time. Asking him to come to Auchinleck.' The description of this letter in the *Life* establishes it as the letter answered by 982; J's 'superstition' refers to JB's dream.

982.1.—Of JB's answer to 982 and 982.1 we know only what he tells us in the *Life* (iv. 380): 'Having conjured him not to do me the injustice of charging me with affectation, I was with much regret long silent.' The Journal and the Register both fail us, except that in the latter he notes that from Aug. to Nov. he 'sent a few letters and received several' but failed to enter them. It is to be presumed that he replied promptly, for 982 must have wounded him; J's next letter, 1033, of 3 or 5 Nov., seems to complain of a protracted silence.

kindly intended. *******, *Spartam quam nactus es orna*;[1] make the most and best of your lot, and compare yourself not with the few that are above you, but with the multitudes which are below you. *****. Go steadily forward with lawful business or honest diversions. '*Be* (as Temple[2] says of the Dutchmen) *well when you are not ill, and pleased when you are not angry.*' This may seem but an ill return for your tenderness; but I mean it well, for I love you with great ardour and sincerity. Pay my respects to dear Mrs. Boswell, and teach the young ones to love me.

983. Ashbourne, Sa. 31 July '84, Richard Brocklesby.

Address: To Dr Brocklesby in Norfolk Street Strand.
Fettercairn.—Boswell 1791, ii. 538, extract (Hill iv. 354).

Dear Sir

Not recollecting that Dr Heberden might be at Windsor, I thought your letter long in coming. But, you know, *nocitura petuntur*,[1] the letter which I so much desired tells me that I have lost one of my best and tenderest friends.[2] My comfort is, that he appeared to live like a Man that had always before his eyes the fragility of our present existence, and was therefore, I hope, not unprepared to meet his Judge.

Your attention, dear Sir and that of Dr. Heberden to my health is extremely kind. I am loath to think that I grow worse; and cannot fairly prove even to my own partiality that I grow much better. I have in part of the interval since the great discharge of urine, been much better than I am now. My breath is very short and the Water encroaches and

---

982.1.—1. In a fragment of Euripides' *Telephus* Agamemnon says to Menelaus Σπάρτην ἔλαχες, κείνην κόσμει 'You have got Sparta, rule *her*', i.e. 'Stick to your job'. This is quoted by Cicero (*ad Att.* iv. 6) in the form Σπάρταν ἔλαχες, ταύταν κόσμει. Johnson's Latin is Erasmus, *Adagia*, where *orna* is a mistranslation; κόσμει in the Greek had the sense *rule*, not *adorn*. See references quoted *L* iv. 379.

2. *Observations upon the United Provinces* (*Works* 1720, i. 54): T says of the Spleen 'This is a Disease too refin'd for this Country and People, who are well, when they are not ill; and pleas'd, when they are not troubled'.

983.—1. Juvenal, x. 8: nocitura toga, nocitura petuntur | militia: 'In Wars, and Peace, things hurtful we require' Dryden. J in the *Vanity* paraphrases: 'vengeance listens to the fool's request'.

2. Allen; for the date of his death see on 981.

retires. I yesterday took 80 drops of the vinegar of squils at one dose. I am subject to great dejection, but am willing to impute part of my maladies to the chilness and wetness of the weather.

My great distress arises from want of sleep. In Bed I cannot yet get rest. This morning after having tossed myself almost all night, I had recourse to a chair between five and six. I then slept, though not quite easily, for about three hours.

The business of common life must likewise be attended to. When I left London, I consigned to Mr Allen's care a box of plate, which I now wish to put into your custody, till I come back. This box as I would lodge with you, I have enclosed an order by which You may demand it, and beg that You will take it, as soon as You can.

I am Dear Sir Your most obliged, and most humble Servant   Sam: Johnson
July 31. 1784 Ashbourn

983.1. Ashbourne. Sa. 31 July '84. Lucy Porter (Lichfield).

Address: To Mrs Lucy Porter in Lichfield.
Fettercairn.—

My Dearest Love
When We parted, I left You ill, and was ill myself. I am told that at least I do not grow worse, and hope to hear the same of You if I do not hear better. You have had my prayers and I intreat that I may have yours.

I take the air from time to time in the carriage, and find it pleasant at least. But the pleasures of the sick are not great nor many. But let us thank God for the ease and comfort which he is pleased to grant us. If the Summer grows at last warm, it will bring us some help. Let me know, my dear, how You are, and if writing be troublesome, get Mr Pearson's kind assistance, or that of any other friend. I am Madam Your most humble Servant,
Ashbourne, Derbyshire. July 31 1784   Sam: Johnson
Direct to Ashbourne (Turn at Derby) Make my compliments

983.1.—JB perhaps omitted this letter as repeating a story told in others. But see on 661.1, and App. E.

and return my thanks to Mrs Cobb to whose kindness I have great obligations.

984. Ashbourne. M. 2 Aug. '84. Charles Burney.

Sotheby 30 July 1930.—Boswell 1791, ii. 543, extract (Hill iv. 360).

Dear Sir   Ashbourne Aug: 2. 1784
The Post at this devious town goes out so soon after it comes in that I make haste to tell you, what I hope you did not doubt, that you shall certainly have what my thoughts will supply, in recommendation of your new book.[1] Let me know when it will be wanted. My journey has at least done me no harm, nor can I yet boast of any great good. The weather, you know, has not been very balmy; I am now reduced to think, and am at last content to talk of the weather. Pride must have a fall.

I have lost dear Mr. Allen, and wherever I turn the dead or the dying meet my notice, and force my attention upon misery and mortality. Mrs. Burney's Escape from so much danger, and her ease after so much pain, throws however some radiance of hope upon the gloomy prospect. May her recovery be perfect, and her continuance long.

I struggle hard for life. I take physick, and take air. My friend's chariot is always ready. We have run this morning twenty four miles, and could run forty eight more. *But who can run the race with death?*[2]
I am Dear Sir Your most humble Servant
                                  Sam: Johnson

985. Ashbourne. Th. 5 Aug. '84. Richard Brocklesby.

Address: To Dr Brocklesby in Norfolk Street Strand.
Fettercairn.—Boswell 1791, ii. 538, extract (Hill iv. 354).

Dear Sir
I have just begun to try the tincture of cantharides, and yesterday took eight drops in the morning and ten in the

984.—1. The *Commemoration of Handel*, to which J contributed the dedication to the King. See *L* iv. 544. The evidence of 1004 makes it clear that it was at CB's request that JB suppressed the opening sentences of this letter (his quotation begins at 'the weather') and said nothing of the dedication. See also 998.1, 1000.1.
    2. If the underline is J's, these words must be a quotation. I have not traced it.

evening. I have this morning taken twenty more, and a purge. I do not perceive that my Strength either encreases or diminishes, or that my nights grow better or worse, or my breath easier or straiter. I have sometimes taken of the acet:[1] squill. 120 drops in the day with no sensible effect either upon the stomack or urinary passages. I have now a mind to use the cantharides, and will proceed with caution. My diacodium is almost gone, and I have never been able to get any that seems to admit comparison with Mr Holders. I have taken now and then, indeed pretty frequently, a grain of opium, which being a cheap drug, is every where genuine. When You knew me first I took three grains, but now seldom more at a time than one.

I return you thanks, dear Sir, for your unwearied attention both medical and friendly, and hope to prove the effect of your care by living to acknowledge it. I am, Dear Sir, Your most humble Servant

Ashbourn. Aug. 5. 1784   Sam: Johnson

986. Ashbourne. Sa. 7 Aug. '84. John Hoole.

Not traced.—Boswell 1791, ii. 542, extract (Hill iv. 359).

Since I was here I have two little letters from you, and have not had the gratitude to write. But every man is most free with his best friends, because he does not suppose that they can suspect him of intentional incivility. One reason for my omission is, that being in a place to which you are wholly a stranger, I have no topicks of correspondence. If you had any knowledge of Ashbourne, I could tell you of two Ashbourne men, who, being last week condemned at Derby to be hanged for a robbery, went and hanged themselves in their cell.[1] But this, however it may supply us with talk, is nothing to you. Your kindness, I know, would make you glad to hear some good of me, but I have not much good to tell; if I grow not worse, it is all that I can say. I hope Mrs. Hoole receives more help from her migration. Make her my compliments, and write again to, Dear Sir, your affectionate servant.

985.—1. The pharmacists' term for 'vinegar'.
986.—1. Hill notes that there had been this summer 149 capital sentences.

986.1. Ashbourne. Sa. 7 Aug. '84. William Bowles (Heale).

Sotheby 30 June 1942.—

Dear Sir

I am never long without some proof of your kind attention, and am much obliged by the enquiries which you have
lately made for my convenience and information.[1] What
I shall be able to do in the winter is yet uncertain.

I have been here now about three weeks, and do not
neglect any of the means by which I may hope to grow better.
Neither exercise, diet, nor physick are forgotten, but I
cannot boast of much improvement. I hope, however, that
I am not worse, and not to grow worse, as the weight of time
encreases, is not nothing.

In the mean time I hope, dear Sir, that nothing like sickness or sorrow approaches Heale. That your aimiable Lady,
and lovely children are gay and happy, that my little friend
goes on successfully with his studies, and that the little Lady's
tongue is now as nimble as her feet.

I am Dear Sir Yours most affectionately
Ashbourn, Derbyshire August 7. 1784   Sam: Johnson

987. Ashbourne. Th. 12 Aug. '84. Richard Brocklesby.

Address: To Dr Brocklesby in Norfolk Street Strand London. *Postmark*: 14 AV.
Fettercairn.—Boswell 1791, ii. 538, extract (Hill iv. 354).

Dear Sir

I have not much to say but what is included in a short
wish, O for an efficacious Diuretick!

You may remember that when I left London in my
armamentarium medicum[1] I took by your consent a bottle
of Tincture of Cantharides, which though you seemed to be
a little afraid ⟨of⟩ it, you considered as having great powers
to provoke urine, and such are I believe generally allowed it.
Of this dangerous Medicine you directed me to begin with
five drops.

I had once suffered by my disobedient excess in the use of

986.1.—1. B had already (972.2) invited J to revisit Heale. Perhaps his 'enquiries'
concerned the possibilities of travel abroad.
987.—1. Medicine-chest.

squills, and I considered Cantharides as far more formidable; for a long time I did not venture them, but thinking a powerful medicine necessary, I began the use of them this Month.

August. 4. I took Tinct. Cantharid. in the morning 8 drops, in the evening, 10.

5. In the morning 10 drops, in the evening, 10.

6. I neglected the account.

7. In the day 60 drops, at night 20 more.

8. In the morning, 20. afternoon. 30. Evening 30.

9. In the morning at two doses. 80.

You see, dear Sir, that of this potent and drastick tincture I have taken 80 drops a day, for three days together, and You are expecting to be told the consequence of my temerity, which You suppose to be punished with a strangury, or to be rewarded with a salutary flood of water. But the truth is, a very unpleasing truth, that this acrid and vigorous preparation, this *medicamentum anceps*,[2] has been as impotent as morning dew, and has produced no effect either painful or beneficial. I have therefore for the present left it, and as the water daily seems to encrease shall have recourse to squills, of which I have a box, and hope that, as they are mingled with soap, their virtue is not dried away.

It often comes into my mind that a vomit would give some freedom to my respiration, but I have not lately tried it. Let me know your opinion, and Dr Heberden's, and tell me what emetick I should use. Akensyde speaks much of Ipecacuanha, as relaxing the angustiae pectoris.[3] Have other Physicians found the same effects? Or would You and Dr Heberden have me try it?

Pray be so kind as to have me in your thoughts, and mention my case to others as you have opportunity. I seem to myself neither to gain nor lose strength. I have lately tried Milk but have yet found no advantage, and am afraid of it merely as a liquid. My appetite is still good, which I know is dear Dr Heberden's criterion of the vis vitæ.

I have no great confidence in rural pharmacy, and there⟨fore⟩[4] wish to have all my medicines from Mr Holder.

987.—2. Perilous drug. 3. Stricture of the chest.
4. J left the word unfinished at the foot of a page.

If you have nothing new to order, be pleased to direct a Box of Squil pils, a bottle of Squil vinegar, and a bottle of diacodium to be sent to me at the Rev. Dr Taylor's in Ashbourne, by the Manchester and Ashbourne Coach at the Swan in Lud Lane. It will come quickly to me. They should be sent the day that you receive this.

As we cannot now see each other, do not omit to write, for You cannot think with what warmth of expectation I reckon the hours of a post-day. I am, Dear Sir, Your most humble Servant

Ashbourn. Aug. 12. 1784   Sam: Johnson

988. Ashbourne. Th. 12 Aug. '84.   Humphry Heely.

Address: To Mr Heely No 5 in Pye Street Westminster. *Postmark*: illegible.

Fettercairn.—Boswell 1791, ii. 550 (Hill iv. 371).

Sir

As necessity obliges You to call so soon again upon me, you should at least have told the smallest sum that will supply your present want; You cannot suppose that I have much to spare. Two Guineas is as much as you ought to be behind with your creditor.

If you wait on Mr. Strahan in New-street, Fetter lane, or in his absence on Mr. Andrew Strahan, show this by which they are entreated to advance you two Guineas, and to keep this as a voucher.[1] I am, Sir, Your humble Servant,

Ashbourne Derbyshire. Aug. 12. 1784   Sam. Johnson.

The name is S t r a h a n

988.1. Ashbourne. Th. 12 Aug. '84.   Hester Maria Thrale (Brighthelmston).

Address: To Miss Thrale.

Lansdowne.—Lansdowne, *Johnson and Queeney* 1932, 53.

Dear Madam,   Ashbourn, Derbyshire, August 12, 1784
Your last letter was received by me at this place, and being

988.—JB omitted the postscript, which is pointless unless 'Strahan' is distinctively printed. See Appendix E.
1. H did not fail to cash his 'voucher', which JB had from Andrew Strahan.

so remote from the other Guardians that I could not consult them, I knew not what answer to make.¹ I take it very kindly that you have written again, for I would not have you forget me, nor imagine that I forget you. Our kindness will last, I hope, longer than our lives. Whatever advice I can give you you may always require; for I love you, I loved your father, and I loved your Mother as long as I could.

At present, I have nothing to impress but these two maxims, which I trust you never will dismiss from your mind.

In every purpose, and every action, let it be your first care to please God, that awful and just God before whom you must at last appear, and by whose sentence all Eternity will be determined. Think frequently on that state which shall never have an end.

In matters of human judgement, and prudential consideration, consider the publick voice of general opinion as always worthy of great attention; remember that such practices can very seldom be right, which all the world has concluded to be wrong.

Obey God.   Reverence Fame.

Thus you will go safely through this life, and pass happily to the next.

I am glad that my two other dear Girls are well.

I am dearest Madam, Your most humble servant

Sam: Johnson

989. Ashbourne. 13 Aug. (misdated; perhaps 31 Aug.) '84. John Hoole.

Address: To Mr Hoole in Queens Street, Lincolns Inn London. *Postmark*: — SE.
Adam.—Boswell 1791, ii. 543, extract (Hill iv. 359).

Dear Sir

I thank you for your affectionate letter. I hope we shall both be the better for each other's friendship, and I hope we shall not very quickly be parted. I have a better opinion of myself than I had reason to entertain when I left London.

<hr>

988.1.—1. Q had no doubt consulted J about her proposed visit to Cator. 1003.2 shows that the visit was paid.

My Breath is more free, and my Water is again run off. But my legs are very weak, and my nights generally bad.

Tell Mr Nichols that I shall be glad of his correspondence when his business allows him a little remission, though to wish him less business that I may have more pleasure, would be selfish.

Mr Hastings's Packet I received, but do not know that I have a right to print it, or permit it to be copied. You, Sir, shall see it, if you desire it, when I come to London.

To pay for seats at the Ballon is not very necessary, because in less than a minute they who gaze at a mile's distance will see all that can be seen. About the wings[1] I am of your mind they cannot at all assist it, nor I think regulate its motion.

I am now grown somewhat easier in my body, but my mind is sometimes depressed. I have here hardly any company, and at home poor Williams is gone—but gone, I hope, to Heaven. May We, when we are called, be called to Happiness.

About the club[2] I am in no great pain. The forfeitures go on, and the house, I hear, is improved for our future meetings. I hope we shall meet often, and sit long.

I am, Dear Sir, Your most humble servant

Ashbourn. Aug. 13. 1784   Sam: Johnson

990. Ashbourne. Sa. 14 Aug. '84. Richard Brocklesby.

Address: To Dr Brocklesby in London. *Postmark*: 16 AV. Fettercairn.—Boswell 1791, ii. 539, extract (Hill iv. 354).

Dear Sir

I have hitherto sent you only melancholy letters, You will be glad to hear some better account. Yesterday the asthma perceptibly remitted, and I moved with more ease than I have enjoyed for many weeks. May God continue his mercy.

Of this Remission the immediate cause seemed to be a catharsis and a day's abstinence, but perhaps I have used as much of both often without any benefit. If health encreases and continues, We will not distress our minds with causes.

989.—1. See 925.
    2. JB has written on the original 'At the Essex Head in Essex Street'. He no doubt cancelled this in proof as otiose. The note proves, if proof were needed, that he sent the originals of J's letters to the printer, except some of those to himself.

I doubt not but Mr Holder has sent the bottles for I dare not yet venture to be without my weapons.

This account I would not delay, because I am not a lover of complaints or complainers, and yet I have since we parted, uttered nothing till now but terror and sorrow. Write to me, Dear Sir. I am Your most obliged and most humble Servant Ashbourn. Aug. 14. 1784   Sam: Johnson

991. Ashbourne. Sa. 14 Aug. '84. Thomas Davies.

Not traced.—Boswell 1791, ii. 548 (Hill iv. 365).

The tenderness with which you always treat me, makes me culpable in my own eyes for having omitted to write in so long a separation; I had, indeed, nothing to say that you could wish to hear. All has been hitherto misery accumulated upon misery, disease corroborating disease, till yesterday my asthma was perceptibly and unexpectedly mitigated. I am much comforted with this short relief, and am willing to flatter myself that it may continue and improve. I have at present, such a degree of ease, as not only may admit the comforts, but the duties of life. Make my compliments to Mrs. Davies.—Poor dear Allen, he was a good man.

991.1 Ashbourne. Sa. 14 Aug. '84. Lucy Porter (Lichfield).

Address: To Mrs Porter at Green Hill Lichfield Turn at Derby. A. T. Loyd.—

Dear Madam
        This is the first day when I could give any good account of myself. My Asthma which has harrassed me very much, remitted yesterday in a degree which surprised me, and which I pray God to continue. I have been lately very much dejected, and am still very weak, but am more cheerful.

In this place I have every thing but company, and of company I am in great want. Dr Taylor is at his farm, and I sit at home. Let me hear from you again. And let me hear, if you can, that your[1] are better, Pray for me. I am
        My Dearest Your most humble Servant
August 14. 1784   Sam: Johnson

991.1.—1. *Sic* in MS.

992. Ashbourne. M. 16 Aug. '84. Richard Brocklesby.

Address: To Dr Brocklesby in London. *Postmark*: 18 AV.
Fettercairn.—Boswell 1791, ii. 539, extract (Hill iv. 354).

Dear Sir

Better, I hope, and better. My respiration gets more and more ease and liberty. I went to Church yesterday after a very liberal diner, without any inconvenience. It is indeed no long walk,¹ but I never walked it without difficulty, since I came, before. I have now no care about the vomit, of which the intention was only to overpower the seeming *vis inertiæ* of the pectoral and pulmonary muscles.

I am favoured with a degree of ease that very much delights me, and do not despair of another race upon the Stairs of the Academy.²

If I were however of a humour to see or to show the state of my body on the dark side, I might say,

> Quid te exempta juvat spinis de pluribus una?³

the nights are still sleepless, and the water rises, though it does not rise very fast. Let us however rejoice in all the good that we have. The remission of one disease will enable Nature to combat the rest.

I do not think you chargable with the inefficacy of the Cantharides. You did not originally prescribe them, nor much encourage them, upon my proposal.

The squills I have not neglected. For I have taken more than a hundred drops a day, and one day took two hundred and forty,⁴ which according to the popular equivalence of a drop to a grain is more than half an ounce. I purpose to try the infusion of wood ashes, and indeed to try all the diureticks, and therefore wish for as much intelligence as can be had, of as many as have been found at any time successful. I have now spirit to try any thing.

I thank you, dear Sir, for your attention in ordering the medicines. Your attention to me has never failed. If the virtue of medicines could be enforced by the benevolence of the Prescriber how soon should I be well.

992.—1. It is about 140 yards. 2. See 956, 1022.
    3. Horace, *Epist.* II. ii. 212: 'What good does the removal of one thorn do you, when many are left?'
    4. 7000 grains = 1 lb. av. So 240 grains = 0.55 of an ounce.

Dr Taylor charges me to send his Compliments. I am, dear Sir, Your most humble Servant

Ashbourn. Aug. 16. 1784   Sam: Johnson

992.1. Ashbourne. M. 16 Aug. '84. William Strahan.

Address: To William Strahan Esq.
Not traced.—C. K. Shorter, *Unpublished Letters of S.J.* 1915.

Sir   Ashbourne, Derbyshire August 16, 1784
   If I have been long without writing I have broken no laws of friendship. I have suppressed nothing that my friends could be glad to hear. My time has passed in the toil of perpetual struggle with very oppressive disorder, till I obtained about four days ago an interval of relief. My breath has become more free, and I can therefore move with less encumbrance.
   What has procured this alleviation, or how ⟨? long⟩ I may hope to enjoy it, I cannot tell, but it gives me great comfort, and the delight which I receive I am waiting[1] to communicate to those whose kindness has given me reason to think that they take part in my pains or pleasures. I flatter myself now with coming again to town and being again a member of society.
   I have not now heard for a long time either of your health or that of dear Mrs Strahan. I hope that you are well and that she is better, and that we shall all have a little more enjoyment of each other.
   I am, Sir Your most humble Servant
                                             Sam: Johnson

993. Ashbourne. Th. 19 Aug. '84. Richard Brocklesby.

Address: To Dr Brocklesby in London. *Postmark*: 21 AV.
Fettercairn.—Boswell 1791, ii. 539, extract (Hill iv. 355).

Dear Sir
   The relaxation of the Ashma still continues, yet I do not trust it wholly to itself, but soothe it now and then with an opiate. I not only perform the perpetual act of respiration with less labour, but I can walk with fewer intervals of rest and with greater freedom of motion.
   I never thought well of Dr. James's compounded medi-

992.1.—1. ? 'writing', or 'willing' (cf. 995 'desirous').

cines. His ingredients appeared to me sometimes inefficacious and trifling, and sometimes heterogeneous, and
destructive of each other. This prescription exhibits a composition of about 330 grains, in which there are 4 gr of
Emetick Tartar, and 6 drops of Thebaick tincture. He that
writes thus, surely writes for show. The basis of his Medicine
is the Gum Ammoniacum, which dear Dr Laurence used
to give, but of which I never saw any effect. We will, if
you please let this medicine alone. The Squills have every
suffrage, and in the squills we will rest for the present.

The Water which I consider as *fundi nostri calamitas*,[1] has
made some encroachments, but does not seem just now to
gain ground, my urinary discharges are in the night commonly copious.

I will take my vinegar of squills which has come down safe
with my other medicines, and will be careful to send an
account of any change that may happen. My great distress
is inability to sleep. I am, Dear Sir, your most obliged, and
most humble Servant
Ashbourn. Aug. 19. 1784   Sam: Johnson

994. Ashbourne. Th. 19 Aug. '84. George Nicol.

Address: To Mr (mutilated) Bookseller in the Strand London. *Post-
mark*: illegible.
F. B. Vanderhoef.—Boswell 1791, ii. 547, from a copy by Astle, see
Abbott, *Catalogue* 1600 (Hill iv. 365).

Dear Sir
Since we parted I have been much oppressed by my
Asthma, but it has lately been less laborious. When I sit
I am almost at ease, and I can walk, though yet very little,
with less difficulty for this week past, than before. I hope,
I shall again enjoy my friends, and that you and I shall have
a little more literary conversation.

Where I now am, every thing is very liberally provided for
me but conversation. My friend is sick himself, and the
reciprocation of complaints and groans affords not much of

993.—1. Terence, *Eun.* 1. i. 34. This is no doubt a grim joke; cf. *L* iv. 99: 'the woman
was fundamentally sensible'. Elsewhere J refers only to his legs as swollen; but my
medical friends tell me that the lumbar regions must have been similarly affected.

either pleasure or instruction. What we have not at home this town does not supply, and I shall be glad ⟨of⟩ a little imported intelligence, and hope that you will bestow now and then a little time on the relief and entertainment of, Sir,

Your humble Servant

Ashbourne Derbyshire Aug. 19. 1784   Sam: Johnson

995. Ashbourne. Th. 19 Aug. '84. Joshua Reynolds.

Address: To Sir Joshua Reynolds in London. *Postmark*: 21 AV. Fettercairn.—Boswell 1791, ii. 548, extract (Hill iv. 366).

Dear Sir

Having had since our separation little to say that I[1] could please You or Myself by saying, I have not been lavish of useless letters, but I flatter myself that you will partake of the pleasure with which I can now tell you, that about a week ago, I felt suddenly a sensible remission of my Asthma, and consequently a greater lightness of action and motion.

Of this grateful alleviation I know not the cause, nor dare depend upon its continuance, but while it lasts, I endeavour to enjoy it, and am desirous of communicating, while it lasts, my pleasure to my friends. I am, Dear Sir, Your most humble Servant

Ashbourn. Aug. 19. 1784   Sam: Johnson

Hitherto, dear Sir, I had written before the post, which stays in this town but a little while, brought me your letter.

Mr. Davies seems to have represented my little tendency to recovery in terms too splendid. I am still restless, still weak, still watry, but the asthma is less oppressive.

Poor Ramsay![2] On which side soever I turn, Mortality presents its formidable frown. I left three old friends[3] at Lichfield, when I was last there, and now found them all dead. I no sooner lose sight of dear Allen, than I am told that I shall see him no more. That we must all die, we always

---

995.—JB suppressed the two concluding paragraphs of this letter, no doubt by JR's direction. See App. E.
    1. 1791 omits 'I'.   2. Ramsay had died on 10 Aug.
    3. Mr. Reade himself is unable to identify these people.

knew, I wish I had sooner remembred it. Do not think me intrusive or importunate if I now call, dear Sir, on You to remember it.

That the President of the Academy founded by the King, should be the King's painter[4] is surely very congruous. You say the place ought to fall into your hands *with asking for*, I suppose you meant to write *without asking for*. If you ask for it I believe you will have no refusal, what is to be expected *without* asking, I cannot say.

Your treatment at court has been capricious, inconsistent, and unaccountable. You were always honoured, however, while others were employed. If you are desirous of the place, I see not why You should not ask it. That sullen pride which expects to be solicited to its own advantage, can hardly be justified by the highest degree of human excellence.

996. Ashbourne. *c.* 20 Aug. '84. William Windham.

Fettercairn.—Boswell 1791, ii. 545, dated 'August' (Hill iv. 362).

Dear Sir

The tenderness with which You have been pleased to treat me through my long ilness, neither health nor sickness can, I hope, make me forget; and You are not to suppose that after we parted, You were no longer in my mind. But what can a sick man say, but that he is sick, his thoughts are necessarily concentred in himself, he neither receives nor can give delight; his enquiries are after alleviations of pain, and his efforts are to catch some momentary comfort.

Though I am now in the neighbourhood of the peak, you must expect no account of its wonders, of its hills, its waters, its caverns, or its mines; but I will tell you, Dear Sir, what I hope You will not hear with less satisfaction, that for about a week past my Asthma has been less afflictive.

I am Dear Sir, Your most humble Servant
                     Sam: Johnson
Be pleased to make my compliments to the Burkes.

995.—4. For this dispute see on 1002.
996.—JB omitted the postscript. See Appendix E.

997. Ashbourne. Sa. 21 Aug. '84. Richard Brocklesby.

Address: To Dr Brocklesby in London. *Postmark*: 23 AV.
Fettercairn.—Boswell 1791, ii. 540, extract (Hill iv. 355).

Dear Sir
  My Breath continues still more lax and easy. The history
of this commodious remission you shall now have. Having
been long wearisomely breathless, on thursday the 12th I
took a purge which operated with more violence than is
common. I took no diner at all. I took 240 drops of acet
squill. The Squills seemed to do little. After I had been in
bed some hours I took two grains of opium, and in the
morning, I believe, I slept. When I rise, I find my breath
easier and my limbs lighter. I walked to church, and returned,
with unexpected facility. My breath from that time has
been, though not equal, yet always easier than when we
parted.
  Yesterday, I repeated the experiment of purging without
eating, but in my purge I poured so much of my new
vinegar that after some struggle the stomach rejected it, and
I underwent, in some degree, the operation of an emetick.
I resolved however not to quit my purpose, and when a little
rest had appeased my stomach took another cathartick, and
with very little diner awaited the event. The cathartick
took its natural course, and the squills, though I did not
repeat them, paid me for my sickness, for I think the discharge of urine was encreased, which I am now endeavouring to promote. My Stomach is good, but I have taken no
flesh yesterday or to day.
  The kindness which You show by having me in your
thoughts on all occasions, will I hope allways fill my heart
with gratitude. Be pleased to return my thanks to Sir
George Baker for the consideration which he has bestowed
upon me.
  Is this the Ballon that has been so long expected this
Ballon to which I subscribed, but without payment?[1] It is
pity that Philosophers have been disappointed, and shame
that they have been cheated; But I know not well how to
prevent either. Of this Experiment I have [have] read

997.—1. See 929.2, and J. E. Hodgson, *Aeronautics in Great Britain*, 111–13, 198.

nothing, where was it Exhibited? and who was [was] the man that ran away with so much money?

Continue, dear Sir, to write often and more at a time, for none of your prescriptions operate to their proper uses more certainly than your letters operate as cordials. I am, Dear Sir, Your most humble Servant,
Ashbourn. Aug. 21. 1784   Sam: Johnson

998. Ashbourne. Sa. 21 Aug. '84. Francesco Sastres.

Not traced.—1788, No. 363.

Dear Sir,   Ashbourne, August 21, 1784.

I am glad that a letter has at last reached you; what became of the two former, which were directed to *Mortimer*[1] instead of *Margaret* Street, I have no means of knowing, nor is it worth the while to enquire; they neither enclosed bills, nor contained secrets.

My health was for some time quite at a stand, if it did not rather go backwards; but for a week past it flatters me with appearances of amendment, which I dare yet hardly credit. My breath has been certainly less obstructed for eight days; and yesterday the water seemed to be disposed to a fuller flow. But I get very little sleep; and my legs do not like to carry me.

You were kind in paying my forfeits at the club; it cannot be expected that many should meet in the summer, however they that continue in town should keep up appearances as well as they can. I hope to be again among you.

I wish you had told me distinctly the mistakes in the French words.[2] The French is but a secondary and subordinate part of your design; exactness, however, in all parts is necessary, though complete exactness cannot be attained;

998.—JB, to illustrate the range of J's acquaintance, instances at one extreme 'the brilliant Colonel Forrester of the Guards', Lord Thurlow, and the 'fascinating Lady Craven'; at the other, Levet, 'Mr. Sastres, the Italian master', and 'good Mrs. Gardiner'. Hill describes this mention of S as 'contemptuous', and suggests that JB's motive was 'to punish Mr. Sastres for not letting him publish Johnson's letters'. The juxtaposition is not flattering to S's social or intellectual pretensions; but 'contemptuous' is too strong a word. I do not think JB capable of such petty spite as is suggested; and Hill seems to overlook an obvious explanation, that HLP, to whom S was well known, got in first; she published these letters in 1788.

1. See 778.1. Both streets are close to Cavendish Square.
2. Nothing is known of S's projected dictionary, which was never published.

and the French are so well stocked with dictionaries, that a little attention may easily keep you safe from gross faults; and as you work on, your vigilance will be quickened, and your observation regulated; you will better know your own wants, and learn better whence they may be supplied. Let me know minutely the whole state of your negotiations. Dictionaries are like watches, the worst is better than none, and the best cannot be expected to go quite true.

The weather here is very strange summer weather; and we are here two degrees nearer the north than you. I was I think loath to think a fire necessary in July, till I found one in the servants hall, and thought myself entitled to as much warmth as them.

I wish you would make it a task to yourself to write to me twice a week; a letter is a great relief to,

Dear Sir, Your, &c.

998.1. Ashbourne. M. 23 Aug. '84. Charles Burney.

Address: To Dr Burney in St. Martins Street Leicester Fields London. Sotheby 18 Feb. 1931; endorsed 'From Dr Johnson a fragment Aug[st] 23d. 1784. No. 11'.—

Dear Sir

When I came to think on this, I had quite forgot what we had said to the Queen, and as it was natural to say the same again on the same subject, I was forced to look out for some remote[1] track of thought, which I believe, you will think I have found; but it has given me some trouble and perhaps may not please at last so well. But necessity must be obeyed. . . .

I hope Mrs. Burney is quite recovered, and that my naughty girl is well. I am very poorly, but I think better to day than yesterday. I am Dear Sir Your most humble Servant

August 23. 1784   Sam: Johnson

998.2. M. 23 Aug. '84. ——

Sotheby 10 Nov. 1893, 131, described as about his health.

998.1.—See on 984. 'What we had said to the Queen' refers to the dedication of CB's *History of Music*, which the discovery of this letter first revealed as J's work. Both dedications are printed by Dr. Powell (*L* iv. 544).   1. J intended 'remoter'?

999. Ashbourne. Th. 26 Aug. '84. Bennet Langton (Rochester).

Address: To Benet Langton Esq at Rochester By London. *Postmark*: 28 AV. Fettercairn.—Boswell 1791, ii. 544, dated 25 August (Hill iv. 361).

Dear Sir

The kindness of your last letter, and my omission to answer it, begins to give you even in my opinion a right to recriminate,[1] and to charge me with forgetfulness of the absent. I will therefore delay no longer to give an account of myself, and wish I could relate what would please either myself or my Friend.[2] On July 13. I left London, partly in hope of help from new air and change of place, and partly excited by the sick man's impatience of the present. I got to Lichfield in a stage vehicle, with very little fatigue in two days, and had the consolation[3] to find that since my last visit my three old acquaintance were all dead.

July 20. I went to Ashbourne where I have been till now, the house in which we live is repairing.[4] I live in too much solitude, and am often deeply dejected; I wish we were nearer and rejoice in your removal[5] to London. A friend at once cheerful and serious is a great acquisition. Let us not neglect one another for the little time which Providence allows us to hope.

Of my health I cannot tell you what my wishes persuaded me to expect, that it is much improved by the season or by remedies. I am sleepless; my legs grow weary with a very few steps, and the water breaks its boundaries in some degree. The Asthma, however, has remitted, my breath is still much obstructed, but is more free than it was. Nights of watchfulness produce torpid days, I read very little though I am alone, for I am tempted to supply in the day what I lost in bed.

999.—1. J is thinking of his own complaint, in 976, of BL's silence.

2. 'Friend' should perhaps be 'Friends'; J's final *s* is often vestigial.

3. Malone was perhaps justified in doubting the text, for this kind of irony is rare in J's writing. See however on 578. But M's conjecture, that 'the word *consolation* has been printed by mistake, instead of *mortification*', shows his weakness in textual criticism. For the 'three old acquaintance' see 995.

4. See 981, and *L* iv. 548.

5. See on 976.

This is my history, like all other histories, a narrative of misery. Yet am I so much better than in the beginning of the year,[6] that I ought to be ashamed of complaining. I now sit and write with very little sensibility of pain or weakness. But when I rise, I shall find my legs betraying me.

Of the money which you mentioned I have no immediate need, keep it however for me, unless some exigence requires it. Your papers I will show you certainly when you would see them, but I am a little angry at you for not keeping minutes of your own *acceptum et expensum*,[7] and think a little time might be spared from Aristophanes, for the *res familiares*. Forgive me, for I mean well.

I hope, dear Sir, that You and Lady Rothes, and all the young people, too many to enumerate, are well and happy. God bless you all. I am, dear Sir, Your most humble Servant,

Ashbourn August. 26. 1784   Sam: Johnson

1000. Ashbourne. Th. 26 Aug. '84. Richard Brocklesby.

Address: To Dr. Brocklesby in London. *Postmark*: 28 AV. Fettercairn.—Boswell 1791, ii. 540, extract (Hill iv. 356).

Dear Sir

I suffered You to escape last post[1] without a letter, but You ⟨are⟩ not to expect such indulgence very often, for I write not so much because I have any thing to say, as because, I hope for an answer, and the vacancy of my life here makes a letter of great value.

I ply the Squills hard commonly taking an hundred drops of the vinegar a day, but I am not certain of any sensible effect. The water however does not encrease, and the

999.—6. After 'year' half a line is very heavily erased, apparently by J himself. A photographic enlargement (see on 976) enabled me to read it with virtual certainty as 'there were any hopes this', followed by one short word, blotted in erasing, and not deciphered.

7. 'Receipts and expenditure'; 'res familiares' is domestic economy. J's will (*L* iv. 402) shows a sum of £750 'in the hands of Bennet Langton, Esq.' The present reference is perhaps to some smaller transaction, on which BL, having no record of his own, had to ask J for information. J hints that account-keeping helps people to live within their means.

1000.—1. J's letter to B began this frequency on Th. 12 Aug. Thereafter his letters are dated Sa. 14, M. 16, Th. 19, Sa. 21, Th. 26; so he had spared B on M. 23.

asthma continues in its milder state. My legs are miserably weak, and my nights restless and tedious. but *Spes alit.*[2]

I believe Your intelligence of Dr Taylors return to London, is mistaken. I shall certainly not stay here behind him, but what to do with myself who can tell me?

I have here little company and little amusement, and thus abandoned to the contemplation of my own miseries, I am sometimes gloomy and depressed, this too I resist as I can, and find opium, I think useful, but I seldom take more than one grain. The diacodium has not agreed with me, perhaps its fermentation makes it flatulent.

Is not this strange weather? Winter absorbed the spring, and now autumn is come before we have had summer.

But let not our kindness for each other imitate the inconstancy of the Seasons.

Have You ever known Ol. ter.[3] do any good. It will I know, scent the urine strongly, so will asparagus. If it has ever produced bloody urine, it is a strong proof of its stimulating powers, and would raise hopes; I have no unwillingness to try whatever is recommended by adequate authority. I am, Dear Sir, Your most humble Servant

Aug. 26. 1784   Sam: Johnson

1000.1. Ashbourne. Sa. 28 Aug. '84. Charles Burney.

Morgan Library.—

Dear Sir

You see that I am not a tardy correspondent, though I know not well how to comply with your desire. I have forgotten the series of the paragraphs and if I remembred them it is not easy to knead new matter into a composition.

Of the two additions proposed, relating to the Countenance given to Musick by his name, and, the evidence which he has given of his taste, the first has been expressed

1000.—2. 'I feed on hope.'

3. Oil of terebinth (turpentine). I am told that J's surmise of its properties was just.

1000.1.—This letter is about J's dedication for CB's *Handel*; see 984, 998.1, 1004. For the printed text see *L* iv. 545. J's recollection of his final paragraph was correct. The penultimate paragraph, as printed, follows the wording of this letter with unimportant variations.

in the last paragraph, I think, as if we had foreknown it, so that nothing more can properly be said. The other has more difficulty.

After, *the most elegant of their pleasures* suppose we added something like this. 'But that this pleasure may be truly elegant Science and Nature must assist each other; a quick sensibility of melody [or harmony] is not always originally bestowed, and those who are born with nice susceptibility of modulation, are often ignorant of its principles and must therefore be in a great degree delighted by chance; but when Your Majesty is pleased to be present at Musical performances, the artists may congratulate themselves upon the attention of a judge in whom all requis⟨i⟩tes concur, who hears them not with instinctive emotion, but with rational approbation, and whose praise of Handel is not the effusion of credulity, but the conviction[1] of Science.'

I hope this may serve, or may awaken something in your own thoughts that may do better.

I am, I think, not better, nor worse. I am often very much dejected, and wish for something to make me chearful, to which the letters of my Friends always contribute.

    I am, Dear Sir Your most humble Servant
Ashburn Augst 28. 1784   Sam: Johnson

1000.2. Ashbourne. M. 30 Aug. '84. Richard Brocklesby.

Address: To Dr Brocklesby in London. *Postmark*: 1 SE.
Fettercairn.—

Dear Sir

 Mr Wyndham[1] has called to day, to take up my writing time, however I snatch a moment to tell You that every thing[s] seems to go on better and better. My Water has lately run away, my Man tells me that my legs are grown less; and my breath is much less obstructed. I think the squils have been a very useful medicine. My two last nights have been better. I registred one of them in my medical journal,

---

1000.1.—1. 'conviction' was J's first thought; he added 'dictate' above the line; in the printed text both were rejected in favour of 'emanation'.

1000.2.—1. For W's visit see *L* iv. 544.

nox jucunda,[2] which it is long since I could say of a night before. I am Dear Sir Your most humble Servant
Ashbourn Aug. 30. 1784   Sam: Johnson

1001. Ashbourne. Th. 2 Sept. '84.   Richard Brocklesby.

Fettercairn.—Boswell 1791, ii. 540, extract (Hill iv. 356).

Dear Sir
If nothing is better than when I wrote last, nothing is worse. But I think every thing grows gradually better. By a pertinacious use of the Squils, or by some other cause while I used them, the Flux of water has encreased. My thighs are no longer hard, nor are my legs in any remarkable degree tumid. The Asthma, I think, continues to remit, and my breath passes with more freedom to day than yesterday. I have since the *nox jucunda*, set down *nox felix somno* and *nox placida cum somno*.[1] Such Nights it is long since I have known.

Mr Windham has been here to see me, he came I think, forty miles out of his way, and staid about a day and [and] a half, perhaps I make the time shorter than it was. Such conversation I shall not have again till I come back to the regions of literature and even there Windham is—inter stellas Luna minores.[2]

Your squil pils, are perfect bullets, I commonly divide one into four. They begin now to purge me, which I suppose you intended, and that they produce their effect is to me another token that Nature is recovering its original powers, and the functions returning to their proper state. God continue his mercies, and grant me to use them rightly. I am, dear Sir, Your most obliged and most humble Servant,
Ashbourne. Sept. 2. 1784   Sam: Johnson

1000.2.—2. 'A pleasant night.'
1001.—1. 'A night made happy by sleep'; 'a quiet night, with some sleep'.
   2. Horace, *Odes*, i. 12: 'like the moon among lesser lights.' JB remarks on J's surprising slip, 'stellas' for 'ignes', which makes false metre.

1002. Ashbourne. Th. 2 Sept. '84. Joshua Reynolds.

Fettercairn.—Boswell 1791, ii. 548, extract; 1793, iii. 639 (Hill iv. 366).

Dear Sir

I am glad that a little favour from the court has intercepted your furious purposes. I could not in any case have approved such publick violence of resentment, and should have considered any who encouraged it, as rather seeking sport for themselves, than honour for You. Resentment gratifies him who intended an injury, and pains him unjustly who did not intend it. But all this is now superfluous.

I still continue, by God's Mercy, to mend. My Breath is easier, my nights are quieter, and my legs are less in bulk, and stronger in use. I have however yet a great deal to overcome, before I can yet attain even an old Man's health.

Write, do write to me now and then. We are now old acquaintance, and perhaps few people have lived so much and so long together, with less cause of complaint on either side. The retrospection of this is very pleasant, and I hope we shall never think on each other with less kindness.

I am, Dear Sir, Your affectionate Servant
Ashbourne. Sept. 2. 1784   Sam: Johnson

1003. Ashbourne. Th. 2 Sept. '84. Francesco Sastres.

Not traced.—1788, No. 364.

Dear Sir,   Ashbourne, Sept. 2, 1784.
Your critick seems to me to be an exquisite Frenchman;[1] his remarks are nice; they would at least have escaped me. I wish you better luck with your next specimen; though if such slips as these are to condemn a dictionary,[2] I know not when a dictionary will be made. I cannot yet think that *gour-*

1002.—Part of this letter, from 'I am glad' to 'superfluous', was suppressed in 1791 and restored in 1793; JR died 23 Feb. '92. JR's 'furious purposes' concerned his appointment to succeed Ramsay as Painter to the King; see 995 and *L* iv. 366, 368, for the story. The change in the text shows that JB went back to his source when revising for the second edition. His papers were then still in his L'n house.

1003.—1. That is a good French scholar: a sense recorded in *OED* from the seventeenth and nineteenth centuries.   2. See 998.

mander is wrong; but I have here no means of verifying my opinion.

My health, by the mercy of God, still improves; and I have hope of standing the English winter, and of seeing you, and reading Petrarch at Bolt-court; but let me not flatter myself too much. I am yet weak, but stronger than I was.

I suppose the club is now almost forsaken; but we shall I hope meet again. We have lost poor Allen; a very worthy man, and to me a very kind and officious neighbour.

Of the pieces ascribed by Bembo[3] to Virgil, the *Dirae* (ascribed I think to Valerius Cato), the *Copa* and the *Moretum* are, together with the *Culex* and *Ceiris*,[4] in Scaliger's *Appendix ad Virgilium*. The rest I never heard the name of before.

I am highly pleased with your account of the gentleman and lady with whom you lodge; such characters have sufficient attractions to draw me[5] towards them; you are lucky to light upon them in the casual commerce of life.

Continue, dear Sir, to write to me; and let me hear any thing or nothing, as the chance of the day may be.

I am, Sir, Your, &c.

1003.1. Ashbourne. Th. 2 Sept. '84. John Ryland.

Address: To Mr Ryland.
Major R. J. Nicol.—

Dear Sir

Your jealousy of opium I consider as one more evidence of your kindness, and as it is reasonable, I think the laws of friendship require, that it should be pacified.

When I first began to take opium, my usual dose was three grains, which I found was in the opinion of physicians a great quantity. I know not however that it ever did me harm for I did not take it often; yet that the demands of my constitution might not encrease, I tried to satisfy it with less, and the

---

1003.—3. I have not found this ascription.
   4. Usually spelled 'Ciris'; but it is the Greek κεῖρις.
   5. ? 'one'.

1003.1.—For J's own 'jealousy of opium' see references in Index V, s.v.

event is, that I have sometimes attained my purpose of appeasing spasms or abating chilness by half a grain, sometimes by a grain, and have now perhaps for six Months never taken more than two. My dose at present is one grain, taken not habitually but occasionally, for it is by frequent intermissions that so small a dose can preserve its efficacy. In the last six days I have taken only two grains of opium.

My health is indeed very much improved. My breath which ⟨was⟩ extremely straitened, is now, though far from free, yet much less encumbred, and my thighs which began to swell very formidably, are by discharge of the water again shrunk almost to the size of health. God has been pleased to give me another warning by another reprieve; May he make the warning efficacious. Surely every hour convinces a thinking man how little he does, how little he has done, how little he can do for himself.

You are without female attention, and you have my sympathy, I know the misery of that vacuity in domestick life. The loss of Mrs Williams who had been my inmate for about thirty years is not likely to be repaired, such another cannot easily be found, and I am not now qualified to beat the field of life. She was always at hand for conversation, and in almost all conversation was able to take part.

From the retrospect of life when solitude, leisure, accident, or darkness turn my thoughts upon it, I shrink with multiplicity of horrour. I look forward with less pain. Behind, is wickedness and folly, before, is the hope of repentance, the possibility of amendment, and the final hope of everlasting mercy. In all endeavour of amendments, and in the hope of mercy, let us, for the remaining days whether few or more, support and encourage one another. This is the true use of friendship.

My opinion is that as poor Payne's ilness, was superinduced by too much labour, it will be in a great measure alleviated by rest freely indulged, and properly continued. I should count his death a great loss.

I am, dearest Sir, Your affectionate

Ashbourne. Sept. 2. 1784　　　　　　　　　Sam: Johnson.

1003.2. Ashbourne. Th. 2 Sept. '84. Hester Maria Thrale (Beckenham).

Address: To Miss Thrale at John Cator's Esq.
Lansdowne.—Lansdowne, *Johnson and Queeney* 1932, 55.

Dearest Madam,   Ashbourn, in Derbyshire, Sept. 2, 1784
I am glad that after your storm you have found a port at
Mr. Cator's. You may now make a pause in life, and gather
your scattered thoughts together. I cannot but wish you
would practice, what I recommended in our little pretty
lecture room at Streatham, the registry of your course of
thinking, and accidents of life. It will require little time, for
thoughts or things of frequent occurrence are not worth a
memorial, and the time which it takes it will liberally compensate. If you began to practice it when I recommended it,
you have already derived pleasure from it. If by hurry or
negligence, you should for a time omit it, do not therefore
leave it off, but begin again, and be always careful to set
down dates exactly.

I am, though still at a great distance from health and
vigour, yet much better than when I left London and flatter
myself that I still gain ground of my disorders. As I have
always wished you well, I hope I am sometimes remembered
in your prayers.

I am, Dear Madam, Your most humble servant,
Sam: Johnson

1004. Ashbourne. Sa. 4 Sept. '84. Charles Burney.

Address: To Dr Burney in St Martin's Street, Leicester Fields,
London. *Postmark*: 6 SE.
Miss Blanche Burney.—Boswell 1791, ii. 544, an extract slightly
'edited' (Hill iv. 360). The original has three endorsements: (1) From
Dr Johnson Septr 4th 1784 No. 13; (2) Ashbourne Sept. 4 1784 N° 11;
(3) Fragment of a Letter—The main part not being intelligible.

1004.—The subject is CB's *Handel*, see 984. For the endorsements, see App. G. The
description of the 'main part' as not 'intelligible' is inaccurate, and perhaps disingenuous; the wording is somewhat obscure, but J's general intention is plain enough.
It is clear that CB was determined to conceal J's part in his book. This may strike us
as petty; but Percy and Reynolds behaved in the same way in like case. It was
natural that a writer who had borrowed a pen with which to express his devotion to
his sovereign should not wish the fact to be published, even if it were notorious.
JB was accordingly not allowed to print 1000.1, and was obliged to garble 1004. He

Dear Sir

I have not the least objection to the little insertion[1] in the last paragraph, but am really sorry that there should be any need of recalling our Master's thoughts to his native country.[2] Nothing deserves more compassion than wrong conduct with good meaning; than loss or obloquy suffered by one who as he is conscious only of good intentions, wonders why he loses that kindness which he wishes to preserve, and not knowing his own faults, if as may sometimes happen, nobody will tell him, goes on to offend by his endeavours to please.

Of your *formulas*[3] You may find one in every book dedicated to your patron or his predecessor. I do not like (?) *I have t⟨..⟩en our &c.* Chambers's Dictionary[4] has a dedication, and Dr Hoadley's Play and (?) forty more. I am delighted by finding that You like so well what I have done.

You will do me a real kindness by continuing to write, a postday has now been long a day of recreation.

I am Dear Sir Your most humble Servant
Ashbourne Sept. 4. 1784   Sam: Johnson

1005. Ashbourne. Sa. 4 Sept. '84. William Cumberland Cruikshank.

Address: To Mr Cruikshank.
Fettercairn.—Boswell 1791, ii. 547, extract (Hill iv. 365).

Dear Sir

Do not suppose that I forget You. I hope I shall never be justly accused of forgetting my benefactors. I had till very lately nothing to write but complaints upon complaints of miseries upon miseries, but within this fortnight, I have

omits the first sentence, and the passage from 'Of your' to 'more', both of which are erased in the original. He mends the hole by substituting 'our opinions are the same' (which they were not?) for 'You like so well what I have done'. This discovery, of course, raises the question of the integrity of JB's texts of J's letters; see Appendix E.

1004.—1. I cannot find in the 'last paragraph' of the dedication (*L* iv. 545) anything like the 'insertion' which CB seems to have contemplated.

2. My historical advisers cannot explain this. Perhaps the reference was to some matter of musical patronage.

3. The 'formulas' were perhaps discarded; I do not find in the dedication anything that seems to correspond to what J here deprecates. The words in italic are in erasure, and are doubtful.

4. Chambers dedicated his *Cyclopaedia* 1728 and Hoadley his *The Suspicious Husband* 1747, to the king.

received great relief. My asthma which was exasperated by the smallest effort, and which scarcely permitted me to take twenty quick steps, on a sudden remitted; afterwards the water ran away and my thighs have shrunk almost to their natural size, but what affords me still a greater present comfort, is that my nights are now easy. Of easy nights I have indeed had but, I think, five, but they give me hope of more. Have your lectures any Vacation? If You are released from the necessity of daily study, you may find time for a letter to me.

The medicine to which I owe this help, if I owe it to any medicine is the squil, of which I have taken the vinegar and powder with great diligence, though for a long time without any discoverable effect, but diureticks, you know, are of inconstant and uncertain operation. Of the vinegar I sometimes took more than an hundred drops in the day.

In return for this account of my health, let me have a good account of yours, and of your prosperity in all your undertakings.

I am, Dear Sir Your most humble Servant
Ashbourne Derbyshire Sept. 4. 1784   Sam: Johnson

1006. Ashbourne. Sa. 4 Sept. '84. John Hoole.

Address: To Mr Hoole.
Sotheby 17 Feb. 1930.—Boswell 1791, ii. 543, extract (Hill iv. 360).

Dear Sir

Your Letter was indeed long in coming, but it was very welcome; Our acquaintance has now subsisted long, and our recollection of each other involves a great space, and many little occurences, which melt the thoughts to tenderness. Write to me therefore as frequently as you can.

It has pleased God to grant me a very wonderful recovery. My Water has again run away, my breath is no longer distressfully strait, and I have for a few nights past lain quietly in Bed; when I came hither, I slept much in a chair; but for some days past, having rested in the night, I have been more capable of enjoying the day. This account will, I hope, be welcome to dear Mrs Hoole, and my reverend Friend your

Son, as well as to your self. Make my compliments to them both.

I hear from Dr Brocklesby and Mr Ryland, that the club is not crouded,[1] I hope we shall enliven it when winter brings us together. I am,

Dear Sir, Your most affectionate Servant,

Ashbourn. Sept. 4. 1784   Sam: Johnson

1006.1. Ashbourne. Sa. 4 Sept. '84. ? William Strahan.

Adam.—

Sir

I am pleased that You have been able to adorn the royal library with a Book[1] which I believe to be very rare, for I have not seen it. I have a very good copy, and did not know that it had been printed on two kinds of paper. The Polyglot Bible is undoubtedly the greatest performance of English typography, perhaps of all typography, and therefore ought to appear in its most splendid form among the books of the King of England. I wish you like success in all your researches.

The part of your letter that relates to a[n] writer[2] whom you do not name, has so much tenderness, benevolence, and liberality, in language so unlike the talk of trade, that it must be a flinty bosom that is not softened into gratitude.

It has now pleased God to restore my health to a much better state, than when I parted from London, if my strength

1006.—1. See on 929.

1006.1.—Adam tentatively calls this a letter to F. A. Barnard. Mr. Metzdorf has consulted the complete dossier, and reports that the ultimate provenance is unknown; a former owner or cataloguer had guessed 'the King's Librarian'. The guess was natural, see 206; but I think there are fatal objections: (1) J implies surprise that his correspondent should use 'language unlike the talk of trade'; (2) he implies also intimacy, and I know no evidence that he and B were more than acquainted. The language of the letter seems to point to a bookseller. Mr. Metzdorf finds a note in my hand (with which, to his cost, he is familiar): 'I suggest Wm Strahan.' This I had forgotten; but I made the same guess some twenty years later.

1. Brian Walton's *Biblia Sacra Polyglotta*, 1657, in six volumes folio. This letter reveals J in the unexpected guise of a collector and connoisseur (but see 206). Dr. Claude Jenkins of Christ Church, who made a journey to Lambeth to settle the point, reported that one of two copies there is on paper so much larger and finer that the other 'looks like a dwarf beside it'. According to Lowndes twelve such copies were printed. J left his copy to BL (*L* iv. 403).

2. I suppose J intended 'an authour' and changed his mind. The unnamed writer is himself. His correspondent had urged a new book.

encreases, indeed, if it does not grow less, I shall hope to concert measures with you, and, by your help, to carry on the design to considerable advantage.

In the mean time accept, dear Sir, my sincere thanks for your generous offer, and friendly regard. Event is uncertain and fallacious, but of good intention the merit stands upon a basis that never can be shaken.

Add to your other favours that of writing often to
Sir, Your most humble Servant
Ashbourn. Sept. 4 1784   Sam: Johnson
I trouble you with two letters.[3]

1007. Ashbourne. Th. 9 Sept. '84. Joshua Reynolds.

Address: To Sir Joshua Reynolds in London. *Postmark*: 11 SE.
Adam.—Boswell 1791, ii. 534, 548 (Hill iv. 348, 367).

Dear Sir
I could not answer your letter before this day, because I went on the sixth to Chatsworth and did not come back till the post was gone.

Many words I hope are not necessary between you and me to convince you, what gratitude is excited in my heart, by the Chancellor's Liberality, and your kind offices. I did not indeed expect that what was asked by the Chancellor would have been refused, but since it has, we will not tell that any thing has been asked.

I have enclosed a Letter to the Chancellor, which, when you have read it, you will be pleased to seal with a Head or other general seal,[1] and convey it to him: had I sent it directly to him, I should have seemed to overlook the favour of your intervention.

My last letter told you of my advance in health, which, I think, in the whole still continues. Of the hydropick tumour there is now very little appearance: the Asthma is much less troublesome, and seems to remit something day after day. I do not despair of supporting an English winter.

At Chatsworth I met young Mr Burke, who led me very

1006.1.—3. Strahan was now J's regular franker, and that is further evidence; see above.

1007.—1. JR was to send J's letter with a covering letter, but was to use a non-significant seal; it would then appear that he knew of J's letter but had not read it.

commodiously into conversation with the Duke and
Dutchess. We had a very good morning. The Diner was
publick.² I am, Dear Sir,
              with great affection, Your humble servant
Ashbourne Sept. 9. 1784   Sam: Johnson

1008. Ashbourne. Th. 9 Sept. '84. Lord Thurlow.

Not traced; draft in J's hand, Adam.—*GM* Dec. 1784, 892, from
Reynolds's copy; Hawkins 1787, 571, 'from his own draft now in my
hands'; Boswell 1791, ii. 535, from a draft (Hill iv. 349).

My Lord
    After a long and attentive observation of Mankind, the
generosity of your Lordship's offer,¹ excites in me no less
wonder than gratitude. Bounty, so liberally bestowed if
my condition made it necessary, I should gladly receive,
for to such a Mind who would ⟨not⟩ be proud to own his
obligations? But it has pleased God to restore me such a
measure of health, that if I should now appropriate so much
of a fortune destined to do good² I should not escape from
myself the charge of advancing a false claim. My journey to
the Continent though I once thought it necessary was never
much encouraged by my Physicians, and I was very desirous
that your Lordship be told of it by Sir Joshua Reynolds
as an event very uncertain; for if I grew much better,
I should not be willing, if much worse, I should not be
able, to migrate.

1007.—2. See *L* iv. 367 for the then Duke of Devonshire's letter to Hill on these
dinners at Chatsworth, which were before his recollection. The public dinners at
Wentworth, to which he refers, were kept up within living memory.

1008.—I give the text of the Adam draft, which has many verbal variations from
JB's. For the story of the surreptitious publication of the letter see *L* iv. 349.
    1. Thurlow had asked JR 'to let him [J] know, that on granting a mortgage of his
pension, he should draw on his Lordship to the amount of five or six hundred pounds;
and that his Lordship explained the meaning of the mortgage to be, that he wished
the business to be conducted in such a manner, that Dr. Johnson should appear to be
under the least possible obligation'. *L* iv. 348. J no doubt saw through this tender
artifice; he was aware that the prospective value of his pension was very small. For T's
letter to JR, and for the question whether the King did or did not refuse an application, see *L* iv. 350, 542.
    2. This phrase might, in isolation, be read as referring to J's own 'fortune', which
was 'destined to do good' by maintaining Barber for life (*L* iv. 284). But it is clear
from the tone of the letter that J regarded T's offer as in effect a gift without question
of repayment.

Your Lordship was Solicited without my knowledge, but when I was told that you were pleased to honour me with your patronage, I did not expect to hear of a refusal. Yet as I had little time to form hopes, and have not rioted in imaginary opulence, this cold reception has been scarce a disappointme*n*t; and from your Lordship's kindness I have received a benefit which only Men like You can bestow, I shall live *mihi charior*[3] with a higher opinion of my own merit.

I am.

1009. Ashbourne. Th. 9 Sept. '84. Richard Brocklesby.

Address: To Dr Brocklesby in London. *Postmark*: 11 SE. Fettercairn.—Boswell 1791, ii. 541, extract (Hill iv. 357).

Dear Sir

I have not written to You very lately, because no alteration appeared. Every thing has run smoothly. My Breath grows easy, and the extraneous water is nearly at an end. But my Nights are not so placid and pleasing as they had begun to be. But we will not lose hope.

I now take no squills, lest they should lose their efficacy by custom. I take purges as they are wanted, and living where good milk is easily to be had I now breakfast upon milk.

I think, I gather strength, for having by accident taken lately several false steps, I have never fallen.

Do you know the Duke and Dutchess of Devonshire? and have you ever seen Chatsworth?[1] I was at Chatsworth on Monday: I had indeed seen it twice before, but never when its owner⟨s⟩ were at home, I was very kindly received and honestly pressed to stay, but I told them that a Sick Man is not a fit inmate of a great house. But I hope to go again some time. I am Dear Sir Your most humble Servant

Ashbourn. Sept. 9. 1784   Sam: Johnson

1008.—3. The phrase occurs in Ovid, *Metam.* viii. 405, *Tristia* iv. vi. 46, but with a different application, e.g. in the former passage 'o me mihi carior' is 'dearer to me than myself'. Here it means 'more valuable to myself' (than formerly).

1009.—1. See 1015, and Cavendish in Index II.

1010. Ashbourne. Sa. 11 Sept. '84. Richard Brocklesby.

Address: To Dr Brocklesby in London. *Postmark*: 13 SE.
Fettercairn.—Boswell 1791, ii. 541 (Hill iv. 357).

Dear Sir
   I think nothing grows worse but all rather better except sleep, and that of late has been at its old pranks. Last evening, I felt what I had not known for a long time, an inclination to walk for amusement, I took a short walk, and came back neither breathless nor fatigued. I just now take no physick except now and then a purge.
   This has been a gloomy frigid ungenial Summer, but of late it seems to mend, I hear the heat sometimes mentioned, but I do not feel it.

     Præterea minimus gelido jam in corpore sanguis
     Febre calet solâ.——[1]

I hope however with good help to find means of supporting a winter at home, and to hear and tell at the club, what is doing, and what ought to be doing in the world. I have no company here, and shall naturally come home hungry for conversation.
   To wish You, dear Sir, more leisure would not be kind, but what leisure You have, you must bestow upon me.

     I am, Dear Sir, Your most humble Servant
Ashbourn. Sept. 11. 1784   Sam: Johnson
I took three squil pills last night.

1010.1. Ashbourne. Sa. 11 Sept. '84. Lucy Porter (Lichfield).

Address: To Mrs Lucy Porter in Lichfield. Turn at Derby.
Adam.—

My Dearest
   By great perseverance in the use of medicines, it has pleased God that I am much better. The water is almost all run off, my breath is more free, and my legs grow stronger. My sleep was better for a few nights, but it has not staid with me. I purpose within a fortnight to be again at Lichfield,

1010.—1. Juvenal, x. 217: 'The little blood that creeps within his veins, | Is but just warm'd in a hot fever's pains.' Dryden.

and hope to find you likewise better. The summer has not been kindly, but it seems now to mend, and I hope will at last do us all good.

     I am, Dear Madam, Your humble servant
Ashbourn Sept. 11. 1784   Sam: Johnson

1010.2. Ashbourne. F. 13 Sept. (misdated Aug.) '84. William Bowles (Heale).

Address: To W. Bowles Esq at Heale near Salisbury. *Postmark*: 15 SE. A. B. Burney.—

Dear Sir

     To You the fortunate inhabitants of the South West, a letter from Derbyshire is like a letter from Pontus,[1] but the account which I have to send is not one of the Tristia. I came hither with my Breath so strait, that every motion or effort distressed me; about a month ago the asthma remitted, and has never been very oppressive since. I came hither in some parts tumid with water, which has almost all run off by natural passages.

     I hope You and your dear Lady, and all the youngsters, and all your Friends are well and happy. How soon I can be witness of that happiness I know not. I am now at a great distance, and though I purpose not a much longer stay in this place, where I have wanted no attention yet,[2] as I have more places[3] than one to call at, I fear, that I shall not reach Heale, while any fruit remains on the trees; Therefore eat it, and if Mrs Bowles wishes me my part I shall be satisfied. I am, Dear Sir Your most humble Servant,
Ashbourn. Aug. 13. 1784   Sam: Johnson

1011. Ashbourne. Th. 16 Sept. '84. Richard Brocklesby.

Address: To Dr Brocklesby in London. *Postmark*: 18 SE. Fettercairn.—Boswell 1791, ii. 541, extract (Hill iv. 357).

Dear Sir

     I have now let you alone a long time, having indeed little to say. You charge me somewhat unjustly with luxury. At

1010.2.—1. J is thinking of the poems written by Ovid from his exile in the Black Sea, the *Epistulae ex Ponto* and *Tristia*.
   2. J's punctuation may mislead; 'yet' belongs to what follows.
   3. J visited L'd, B'm, and O'd on his way home.

Chatsworth You should remember, that I have eaten but once, and the Doctor with whom I live, follows a milk diet. I grow no fatter, though my stomach, if it be not disturbed by physick, never fails me.

I now grow weary of Solitude, and think of removing next week to Lichfield, a place of more society, but otherwise of less convenience. When I am settled, I shall write again.

I had last night, many hours of continual sleep, and nothing I think grows worse. My legs still continue very weak. But I hope they likewise, if the water stays away[1] will mend so far as to carry me a little about the town. But we are not to choose. I have already recovered to a wonder.

Of the hot weather that you mention, we have ⟨not⟩ had in Derbyshire very much, and for myself I seldom feel heat, and suppose that my frigidity is the effect of my distemper, a supposition which naturally leads me to hope that a hotter climate may be useful. But I hope to stand another English winter. I am, dear Sir, your most humble Servant
Ashbourn. Sept. 16. 1784   Sam: Johnson

1012. Ashbourne. Th. 16 Sept. '84. Francesco Sastres.

Not traced.—1788, No. 365.

Dear Sir   Ashbourne, Sept. 16, 1784.
    What you have told me of your landlord and his lady at Brompton, has made them such favourites, that I am not sorry to hear how you are turned out of your lodgings, because the good is greater to them than the evil is to you.

    The death of dear Mr. Allen gave me pain. When after some time of absence I visit a town, I find my friends dead;[1] when I leave a place, I am followed with intelligence, that the friend whom I hope to meet at my return is swallowed in the grave. This is a gloomy scene; but let us learn from it to prepare for our own removal. Allen is gone: Sastres and Johnson are hasting after him; may we be both as well prepared!

1011.—1. J would perhaps have added a comma if 'away' had not ended a line.
1012.—1. At L'd, see 995.

I again wish your next specimen success. *Paymistress* can hardly be said without a preface, (it may be expressed by a word perhaps not in use, Pay mistress).[2]

The club is, it seems, totally deserted; but as the forfeits go on, the house does not suffer; and all clubs I suppose are unattended in the summer. We shall I hope meet in winter, and be cheerful.

After this week, do not write to me till you hear again from me, for I know not well where I shall be; I have grown weary of the solitude of this place, and think of removal.

> I am, Sir, Your, &c.

1012.1. Ashbourne. Th. 16 Sept. '84. David Barclay.

Address: To Mr Barclay in Red Lyon Square London (redirected to Youngsbury near Wear Herts). *Postmark*: 20 SE.
A. Houghton.—John Scott, *Critical Essays* 1785, iii.

Sir

As I have made some advances towards recovery, and loved Mr Scot, I am willing to do justice to his memory. You will be pleased to get what account you can of his life, with dates, where they can be had, and when I return, We will contrive how our materials can be best employed.

> I am Your humble Servant

Ashbourn in Derbyshire Sept 16. 1784   Sam: Johnson

1013. Ashbourne. Sa. 18 Sept.' 84. Joshua Reynolds.

Address: To Sir Joshua Reynolds in London. *Postmark*: 20 SE.
Fettercairn (dated 1748).—Boswell 1791, ii. 549 (Hill iv. 368).

Dear Sir

I flattered myself that this week would have given me a letter from You, but none has come. Write to me now and then, but direct your next to Lichfield.

I think, and, I hope, am sure, that I still grow better. I have sometimes good nights. But am still in my legs weak,

1012.—2. The words in parentheses are the 'preface' that J suggests. For S's projected dictionary see 998. *OED* has no quotation for *paymistress* between 1651 and 1886.

1012.1.—The *Account* of Scott's life, prefixed to his *Critical Essays* (p. vii), was by Hoole, though he was not a Quaker as B and S were.

but so much mended that I go to Lichfield in hope of being ⟨able⟩ to pay my visits on foot, for there are no coaches.

I have three letters this day, all about the ballon. I could have been content with one. Do not write about the ballon,[1] whatever else You may think proper to say.

                   I am, Dear Sir, Your most humble Servant
Ashbourn. Sept 18. 1748 (*sic*)   Sam: Johnson

1014. Ashbourne. Sa. 18 Sept. '84. John Ryland.

Address (Hill): To Mr Ryland, Merchant in London.
Goodspeed Cat. 1943 (facsimile).—*NQ* 5 S. vii. 381.

Dear Sir

You are not long without an answer. I had this day in three letters three histories of the Flying Man in the great Ballon. I am glad that we do as well as our neighbours. Lunardi, I find, forgot his barometer[1] and therefore can ⟨...⟩ to what height he ascended.

Direct, if You please, your next letter to Lichfield I am desirous of going thither; I live in dismal solitude and being now a little better and therefore more at leisure for external amusements, I find the hours sometimes heavy, at least for some reason or other I wish for change.

Mr. Wyndham was with me, a day here, and tried to wheedle me to Oxford, and I perhaps may take Oxford in my way home.

                   I am Sir Your most affectionate
Sept. 18. 1784   Sam: Johnson.

1015. Lichfield. W. 29 Sept. '84. Richard Brocklesby.

Address: To Dr. Brocklesby in London. *Postmark*: 1 oc.
Fettercairn.—Boswell 1791, ii. 541, extract (Hill iv. 357).

Dear Sir

On one day I had three letters about the air ballon. Yours

1013.—1. J's impatience at having to read three letters on this subject was soon followed by a revival of curiosity; see 1014, 1015.

1014.—1. Hill quotes Bentham and other authorities for the accident to the barometer and for the sensation caused by the ascent.

was far the best, and has enabled me to impart to my friends in the country an Idea of this species of amusement. In amusement, mere amusement I am afraid it must end, for I do not find that its course can be directed, so as that it should serve any purposes of communication; and it can give no new intelligence of the state of the air at different heights, till they have ascended above the height of mountains, which they seem never likely to do.

I came hither on the 27th. How long I shall stay, I have not determined. My Dropsy is gone, and my Asthma much remitted, but I have felt myself a little declining these two days, or at least to day, but such vicissitudes must be expected. One day may be worse than another; but this last month is far better than the former, if the next should be as much better than this, I shall run about the town on my own legs.

Was it by your means that a paragraph was in the papers, about my visit to Chatsworth?[1] It was like a trick of Boswel's, and I could hardly have suspected any body else. It did indeed no harm, but what was the good?

I have since I left London been troubled with an inconvenience which I never knew in any great degree before. The fæces in the Rectum have concreted to such hardness, that I have been forced three times to dilute them by clysters, the last time there was a necessity of two injections before I was at ease. Think on this and tell me what should be done, for it is not a slight disorder, whether it be estimated by its immediate pain, or remoter consequences. I have made no change in my manner of living, except that I have taken more milk, than I have been used to take. I am, Sir, Your most obliged and most humble Servant,

Lichfield Sept. 29. 1784   Sam: Johnson

1015.—1. See on 1009. We may forgive JB for his suppression of this paragraph, though it is not medical, for J's suspicions seem not to have been justified in this instance. There is no reason to think that J had written to him since the visit to Chatsworth, and he could hardly have heard of it otherwise. I find in *The Public Advertiser* for 22 Sept. this paragraph: 'Within these ten days Dr. Johnson paid a visit to the Duke of Devonshire, at Chatsworth: He was a welcome guest to his Grace and the Duchess, who seemed much pleased with his company, and assured him that his visits would be always welcome to them. The Doctor has now a better prospect of good health than he has had for a long time. All his complaints, if not quite removed, are greatly mitigated: he is now at Litchfield, and is expected in town within a fortnight.'

1016. Lichfield. W. 29 Sept. '84. John Ryland.

Address (*NQ*): To Mr Ryland, Merchant in London.
Christie 5 June 1888; Maggs Catalogue 339 (1915), 1273 (not seen).—
NQ 5 S. vii. 381; extracts in Maggs catalogue, an independent text.
See Addenda, p. 338, for a report of the MS.

Dear Sir,

At my return hither I had the gratification of finding two of my friends,[1] whom I left as I thought, about two months ago, quite broken with years and disease, very much recovered. It is a[2] great pleasure to a sick man to discover that sickness is not always mortal; and to an old man,[3] to see age yet living to greater age. This is, however, whatever Rochefoucault, or Swift[4] may say, though certainly part of the pleasure, yet not all of it. I rejoice in the welfare of those whom I love and who love me, and surely should have the same joy, if I were no longer subject to mortality. As a being subject to so many wants Man has inevitably a strong tendency to self-interest,[5] so I hope as a Being capable of comparing good and evil he finds something to be preferred in good, and is, therefore, capable of benevolence, and supposing the relation[6] of a good and bad man, as to his own interest the same, would rejoice more in the prosperity of the good.

I have for a little while past felt, or imagined some declension in my health. I am still much better than I lately was, but I am a little afraid of the cold weather.

You have not lately told me of Payne, in whom I take a great interest. I think he may by indulgence recover, and that indulgence, since his employers allow it him, he will be very culpable if he denies himself.

I am, dear Sir, Your affectionate humble servant,
Lichfield, Sept. 29, 1784. Sam: Johnson.

1016.—The Maggs catalogue quotes from 'It is a great pleasure' to the end of the paragraph, and gives us a better text than that in *NQ*.
   1. LP and Miss Aston, see 1018.1.
   2. 'a' Maggs, om. *NQ*.
   3. 'and to an old man' Maggs, om. *NQ*; 'to see' is my own correction; the texts have 'so far' or 'so for'.
   4. See on 560.
   5. 'self-interest' Maggs; *NQ* leaves a blank.
   6. 'relation' Maggs; 'volution' *NQ*.

1016.1. Lichfield. Th. 30 Sept. and Sa. 16 Oct. '84. William Strahan.

Address: To William Strahan Esq.
Not traced.—C. K. Shorter, *Unpublished Letters of S.J.* 1915.

Sir   September 30, 1784
    I have now spent the greatest part of the summer in quest of health, which, alas! I cannot boast of having found. I purpose to settle at my own home in a short time. Home has to a sick man a multitude of conveniences, and winter may be passed at London with more amusement and more assistance that at any other place.

    My friends whom I have visited, and those whom I have left, have all contributed as they could to make my life more cheerful. I have had no complaint to make of neglect.
    My living has not been without some expense, though not much, and I shall be glad of two bank notes of ten pounds each as soon as you can.
    Be pleased to make my compliment to dear Mrs. Strahan, whom I hope to find better than I left her. Health and every other real good is sincerely wished you by
                                Sir Your most humble servant
Lichfield, October 16, 1784   Sam: Johnson

1017. Lichfield. Sa. 2 Oct. '84. William Windham.

Fettercairn.—Boswell 1791, ii. 546 (Hill iv. 362).

Dear Sir
    I believe You have been long enough acquainted with the *phaenomena* of Sickness, not to be surprised that a sick man wishes to be where he is not, and where it appears to every body but himself that he might easily be, without having the resolution to remove. I thought Ashbourne a solitary place, but did not come hither till last Monday.
    I have here more company but my health has for this last week not advanced, and in the langour of disease how little can be done. Whither or when I shall make my next remove,

1016.1.—I follow my authority, which seems to have telescoped fragments of two letters. The indications are that the first paragraph only belongs to 30 Sept.

I cannot tell, but entreat You, dear Sir, to let me know from time to time where You may be found, for your residence is a very powerful attractive to, Sir, Your most humble Servant.

Lichfield Oct. 2. 1784   Sam: Johnson

1018. Lichfield. Sa. 2 Oct. '84. Joshua Reynolds.

Address: To Sir Joshua Reynolds in London.
Harvard.—Boswell 1793, iii. 641 (Hill iv. 368).

Dear Sir
    I am always proud of your approbation, and therefore was much pleased that you liked my letter. When you copied it,[1] you invaded the Chancellor's right rather than mine.
    The refusal I did not expect, but I had never thought much about it, for I doubted whether the Chancellor had so much tenderness for me as to ask. He being keeper of the King's conscience ought not to be supposed capable of an improper petition.
    All is not gold that glitters, as we have often been told, and the adage is verified in your place[2] and my favour, but if what happens does not make us richer, we must bid it welcome, if it makes us wiser.
    I do not at present grow better, nor much worse, my hopes however are somewhat abated, and a very great loss is the loss of hope but I struggle on as I can.
              I am Dear Sir Your most humble servant
Lichfield, Oct. 2. 1784   Sam: Johnson

1018.1. Lichfield. Sa. 2 Oct. '84. Eva Marie Garrick.

Address: To Mrs Garrick at the Adelph London. *Postmark*: 4 oc.
Adam.—*Illustrated London News* Dec. 1855.

Madam
    I did not wonder that your heart failed you, when the journey to Lichfield came nearer, and indeed I love you the more for your tenderness and sensibility. I am now at Lichfield a second time, and am returned to it with some improvement of my health, in the two months for which I

1018.—1. See 1007, 1008.   2. See on 1002.

staid away, and have the delight to find both Mrs Aston and
Mrs Porter much mended in the same time. Mr Garrick was
with me lately, and is well. Mr Seward is very lame, but his
daughter flourishes in poetical reputation.¹ What Lichfield
affords more than this I hope to tell when I wait on you in
London.

Please to make my compliments to dear Miss Moore.

I am Madam Your most humble servant

Lichfield. Oct. 2. 1781   Sam: Johnson

1019. Lichfield. M. 4 Oct. '84. John Perkins.

Address: To Mr Perkins in Southwark. *Postmark*: 6 oc.
O. T. Perkins.—Boswell 1793, iii. 634 (Hill iv. 363).

Dear Sir

I cannot but flatter myself that your kindness for me, will
make you glad to know where I am, and in what state.

I have been struggling very hard with my diseases. My
breath has been very much obstructed and the water has
attempted to encroach upon me again. I past the first part
of the summer at Oxford, afterwards I went to Lichfield,
thence to Ashbourn in Derbyshire, and a week ago I returned
to Lichfield.

My breath is now much easier, and the water is in a great
measure run away, so that I hope to see you again before
Winter.

Please to make my compliments to Mrs Perkins, and to
Mr and Mrs Barclay. I am,

Dear Sir Your most humble Servant

Lichfield. Oct. 4. 1784   Sam: Johnson

1020. Lichfield. W. 6 Oct. '84. Richard Brocklesby.

Address: To Dr Brocklesby in London. *Postmark*: 8 oc.
Fettercairn.—Boswell 1791, ii. 542, extract (Hill iv. 358).

Dear Sir

The day on which I received your letter I sent for castor
oil, having just a stoppage in the rectum, but being afraid in

1018.1.—1. The Swan of Lichfield had already published her *Monody on Major
André* and other poetical effusions.

such an exigency to trust too much to a medicine of which I had no experience, I took near an ounce of the oil at night and followed it with another purge in the morning, and all passed without inconvenience.

My dropsy keeps down, my breath is much obstructed, and I do not get strength, nor in any great degree lose it. However I do not advance, and am afraid of winter. Give me what help and what hope You can.

The fate of the balloon[1] I do not much lament[2] to make new balloon⟨s⟩ is to repeat the jest again. We now know a method of mounting into the air, and I think, are not likely to know more. The vehicles can serve no use, till we can guide them, and they can gratify no curiosity till we mount with them to greater heights than we can reach without, till we rise above the tops of the highest mountains, which we have yet not done. We know the state of the air in all its regions to the top of Teneriffe, and therefore learn nothing from those ⟨who⟩ navigate a balloon below the clouds. The first experiment however was bold, and deserved applause and reward. But since it has been performed and its event is known, I had rather now find a medicine that can ease an asthma.

I am, Dear Sir, Your most humble Servant
Lichfield. Oct. 6. 1784   Sam: Johnson

1021. Lichfield. W. 6 Oct. '84. John Ryland.

Address: To Mr Ryland Merchant in London. *Postmark*: 8 oc. Historical Soc. of Pennsylvania.—*Literary Gazette* 8 Dec. 1849.

Dear Sir
    I am glad that so many could yet meet at the club, where I do not yet despair of some cheerful hours. Your account of poor dear Payne makes me uneasy; if his distemper were only the true Sea Scurvey, it is on land easily, and I believe infallibly curable. but I am afraid it is worse, not a vitiation of particular humours, but a debilitation of the whole frame, an effect not of casualty but of time. I wish his recovery, and hope that he wishes, and prays for mine.

1020.—1. By fire, on 20 Sept. See references in *L* iv. 358.
    2. 'lament' ends a page, which would explain the lack of punctuation.

I have for some days, to speak in the lightest and softest language made no advances towards health. My breath is much obstructed, and my limbs are wells[1] of water however I have little cause to complain.

My mind, however, is calmer than in the beginning of the year, and I comfort myself with hopes of every kind, neither despairing of ease in this world, nor of happiness in another.

I shall, I think, not return to town worse than I left it, and unless I gain ground again, not much better. But, God, I humbly hope, will have mercy on me.

    I am, Dear Sir, Your most humble servant,
Lichfield Oct. 6. 1784   Sam: Johnson

1021.1. Lichfield. Su. 10 Oct. '84. William Scott.

Address: To Dr Scot in the Commons London. *Postmark*: 13 (month missing).
Marchioness of Crewe.—

Dear Sir

Considering that the excursion of this Summer was made with your assistance, I cannot think the better of my own attention, for having neglected to give You an account of what has befallen me.

July 13. I left London, very asthmatick, and in some degree, I think, hydropical, and found no help from the air of Staffordshire. I was not however very weak, for I came to Lichfield in two days with little fatigue.

Having languished at Lichfield a few days, I went (July 20) to Ashbourn in Derbyshire, where for some time the asthma harrassed me with great pertinacity, and the Water rose till I dressed myself with difficulty. But in the night between the 12th and 13th of August, after a day of great evacuation by abstinence and purges, by the help of an opiate taken about midnight, the asthma remitted, so that I went to Church with less labour than for some time before;

1021.—1. I could not be quite sure of this word, which implies a rapid aggravation of the dropsy since 1019, written two days earlier. (The dates are ascertained by the postmarks.)

and though the same freedom of respiration has not uniformly continued, and has now for a week been interrupted, yet I have never drawn my breath with that struggle and straitness as before the remission.

The water, by the use, I think, of squils, was in about five weeks driven through the urinary passages and left me in appearance totally free. I remain therefore Asthmatical though not in the extreme. Of the dropsy if it keeps the truce I have little complaint to make. But my limbs are very weak, my legs would not carry me far, if my breath would last, and my breath would not last if my legs would carry me. How I shall pass the winter I know not, but hope to pass part of it with You, and do not despair of a cheerful hour.

I am, Dear Sir, Your most humble Servant
Lichfield Oct. 10. 1784.   Sam: Johnson

1022. Lichfield. W. 13 Oct. '84. William Heberden.

Not traced.—Croker's Boswell 1831, v. 289, extract; Hill 1892, from a copy of the original.

Though I doubt not but Dr. Brocklesby would communicate to you any incident in the variation of my health which appeared either curious or important, yet I think it time to give you some account of myself.

Not long after the first great efflux of the water, I attained as much vigour of limbs and freedom of breath, that without rest or intermission, I went with Dr. Brocklesby to the top of the painters' Academy.[1] This was the greatest degree of health that I have obtained, and this, if it could continue, were perhaps sufficient; but my breath soon failed, and my body grew weak.

At Oxford (in June) I was much distressed by shortness of breath, so much that I never attempted to scale the library:[2] the water gained upon me, but by the use of squills was in a great measure driven away.

In July I went to Lichfield, and performed the journey

1022.—1. See 956.
  2. The Bodleian staircase (still, 1952, its main avenue to knowledge) is of 65 steps—thirteen flights of five.

with very little fatigue in the common vehicle, but found no help from my native air. I then removed to Ashbourn, in Derbyshire, where for some time I was oppressed very heavily by the asthma; and the dropsy had advanced so far, that I could not without great difficulty button me at my knees. Something was now to be done; I took opium as little as I could, for quiet[3] and squills, as much as I could, for help; but in my medical journal,[4] August 10, I find these words, nec opio, nec squillis quidquam sensi[3] effectum. Animus jacet. But I plied the vinegar of squills to an hundred drops a day, and the powder to 4 grains. From the vinegar I am not sure that I ever perceived any consequence.

'Here follow statements of the effect produced by these and other medicines.'

I rose in the morning with my asthma perceptibly mitigated, and walked to Church that day with less struggle than on any day before.

The water about this time ran again away, so that no hydropical tumour[5] has been lately visible. The relaxation of my breath has not continued as it was at first. But neither do I breathe with the same *angustiæ*[6] and distress as before the remission. The summary of my state is this:

I am deprived by weakness and the asthma of the power of walking beyond a very short space.

I draw my breath with difficulty upon the least effort, but not with suffocation or pain.

The dropsy still threatens, but gives way to medicine.

The Summer has passed without giving me any strength.

My appetite is, I think, less keen than it was, but not so abated as that its decline can be observed by any one but myself.

Be pleased to think on me sometimes.

I am, Sir, Your most obliged and most humble servant, Lichfield, Oct. 13, 1784.   Sam: Johnson.

1022.—3. Hill queries the words 'quiet' and 'sensi', presumably as reported doubtful by the copyist; the punctuation might throw unjust suspicion on 'quiet'.

4. 'Neither opium nor squills seemed to do anything. Mind dejected.' J's *Aegri Ephemeris* was in JB's possession; *L* iv. 381. It is now in the Hyde collection.

5. Both Croker and Hill have 'humour'. But J in the letters of this year frequently calls his trouble 'tumour', i.e. tumidity (not quite the modern use).

6. J elsewhere calls it 'straitness'.

1023. Lichfield. Sa. 16 Oct. '84. George Strahan.

Address: To the Rev^d Mr Strahan at Islington London. *Postmark*: 18 oc.
A. Houghton.—Hill 1892 (incomplete, from an auction catalogue; misdated 19 Oct.).

Dear Sir
I have hitherto omitted to give You that account of myself, which the kindness with which You have treated me, gives You a right to expect.

I went away feeble, asthmatical, and dropsical the asthma has remitted for a time, but is now very troublesome, the weakness still continues, but the dropsy has disappeared; and has twice in the Summer yielded to medicine. I hope to return with a body somewhat, however little, relieved and with a mind less dejected.

I hope your dear Lady and dear little ones are all well, and all happy. I love them all.

I am, Dear Sir, Your Most humble Servant
Lichfield Oct 16. 1784   Sam: Johnson

1023.1. Lichfield. Sa. 16 Oct. '84. William Strahan.

See 1016.1.

1024. Lichfield. W. 20 Oct.' 84. William Gerard Hamilton.

Address (mutilated): To Gerard Ha⟨   ⟩ in London. *Postmark*: 22 oc.
Fettercairn.—Boswell 1791, ii. 546 (Hill iv. 363).

Dear Sir
Considering what reason You gave me in the spring,[1] to conclude that You took part in whatever good or evil might befal me, I ought not to have omitted so long the account which I am no⟨w⟩ about to give you.

My diseases are an Asthma and a Dropsy, and, what is less curable, seventy five. Of the dropsy in the beginning of the Summer, or in the Spring, I recovered to a degree which struck

1024.—1. J may have forgotten that H's offer of money was made in Nov. '83; but he may refer to a later act of kindness.

with wonder both me and my Physicians. The Asthma was[2] likewise for a time very much relieved. I went to Oxford where the Asthma was very tyrannical, and the Dropsy began again to threaten me, but seasonable physick stopped the inundation. I then returned to London, and in July took a resolution to visit Staffordshire and Derbyshire where I am yet struggling with my diseases. The Dropsy made another attack, and was not easily ejected, but at last gave way. The asthma suddenly remitted, in bed on the 13th of august, and though now very very[3] oppressive, is, I think, still something gentler than it was before the remission. My limbs are miserably debilitated, and my nights are sleepless and tedious.

When You read this, dear Sir, you are not sorry that I wrote no sooner. I will not prolong my complaints. I hope still to see You *in a happier hour,*[4] to talk over what we have often talked, and perhaps to find new topics of merriment, or new incitements to curiosity. I am, dear Sir, Your most obliged and most humble Servant

Lichfield Oct. 20. 1784   Sam: Johnson

1025. Lichfield. W. 20 Oct. '84. John Paradise.

Address: To — Paradise Esq near the Middlesex Hospital London.
Postmark: 22 oc.
Fettercairn.—Boswell 1791, ii. 547 (Hill iv. 364).

Dear Sir

Though in all my summer's excursion I have given You no account of myself, I hope you think better of me than to imagine it possible for me to forget You, whose kindness to me has been too great and too constant, not to have made its impression on a harder breast than mine.

Silence is not very culpable when nothing pleasing is suppressed. It would have alleviated none of your complaints, to have read my vicissitudes of evil; I have struggled hard

1024.—2. 'now is' 1791; I suppose 'was' was misread 'now' and 'is' added for the sense.
3. The repetition is doubtless inadvertent; he not seldom repeats a small word (e.g. 'the the'), and I do not recall another example of 'very very' used for emphasis. JB, or his printer, thought as I do, and printed one 'very'.
4. Pope, *One Thousand Seven Hundred and Thirty Eight*, i. 29: 'Seen him [Walpole] I have, but in his happier hour | Of Social Pleasure, ill-exchang'd for Pow'r.'

with very formidable and obstinate maladies, and though I cannot talk of health think all praise due to my Creator and Preserver for the continuance of my life. The Dropsy has made two attacks and has given way to medicine, the Asthma is very oppressive but that has likewise once remitted. I am very weak and very sleepless, but it is time to conclude the tale of misery.

I hope, dear Sir, that you grow better, for you have likewise your share of human evil, and that your Lady and the young Charmers are well. I am, Dear Sir, Your affectionate humble Servant

Lichfield, Oct. 20. 1784   Sam: Johnson

1026. Lichfield. W. 20 Oct. '84. John Nichols.

B.M.—Boswell 1791, ii. 549 (Hill iv. 369).

Sir

When you were here, you were pleased, as I am told, to think my absence an inconvenience; I should certainly have been very glad to give so skilful a Lover of Antiquities any information about my native place, of which however I know not much, and have reason to believe that not much is known.

Though I have not given you any amusement, I have received amusement from you. At Ashbourne, where I had very little company, I had the luck to borrow Mr Boyer's Life a book so full of contemporary History, that a literary Man must find some of his old friends. I thought that I could now and then have told you some hints[1] worth your notice, and perhaps we may talk a life over. I hope, we shall be much together, You must now be to me what you were before, and what dear Mr. Allen was besides. He was taken unexpectedly away, but I think he was a very good man.

I have made little progress in recovery. I am very weak, and very sleepless but I live on and hope.

I am, Sir, Your most humble servant

Lichfield. Oct. 20. 1784   Sam: Johnson

1026.—1. Hill thought that the MS. has not 'hints' but 'name'. J's initial *n* is often very like his *h*.

1027. Lichfield. W. 20 Oct. '84. Francesco Sastres.

Not traced.—1788, No. 366.

Sir   Lichfield, October 20, 1784.
    You have abundance of naughty tricks; is this your way of
writing to a poor sick friend twice a week? Post comes after
post, and brings no letter from Mr. Sastres. If you know any
thing, write and tell it; if you know nothing, write and say
that you know nothing.
    What comes of the specimen?[1] If the booksellers want a
specimen, in which a keen critick can spy no faults, they must
wait for another generation. Had not the Crusca[2] faults?
Did not the Academicians of France commit many faults?
It is enough that a dictionary is better than others of the
same kind. A perfect performance of any kind is not to be
expected, and certainly not a perfect dictionary.
    Mrs. Desmoulines never writes, and I know not how things
go on at home; tell me, dear Sir, what you can.
    If Mr. Seward be in town tell me his direction, for I ought
to write to him.
    I am very weak, and have bad nights.
                            I am, dear Sir, Your, &c.

1027.1. Lichfield. W. 20 Oct. '84. John Taylor (Ashbourne).

Address: To the Reverend Dr. Taylor.
A. Houghton.—

Dear Sir
    I can hardly think that the bearer of this comes from you,
for You would surely have written. I am in one of my bad
fits, and having been driven by my Asthma to an opiate last
night, have, I think, never closed my eyes. I should however
have been glad to have heard of your health, and your house,
and whatever belongs to You. I begin now to think of
returning to London, but am in no great haste. I have
attention enough here, and ease, I am afraid, I shall not

1027.—1. See on 998.
    2. *Vocabolario degli Academici de la Crusca*, 1612.

easily find, but I go on hoping and hoping, and trying and trying. I am,

Dear Sir, affectionately yours,

Lichfield Oct. 20. 1784   Sam: Johnson

1027.2. Lichfield. W. 20 Oct. '84. Richard Brocklesby.

Address: To Dr Brocklesby in London. *Postmark*: 22 oc. Fettercairn.—

Dear Sir
    I should continue my frequency of letters, if I had any thing pleasing to communicate, but the plain truth is that I have rather gone backwards these three weeks. I sometimes fancy that I eat too much, though I have no suppers, and am now trying to live more sparingly. My nights are wretched, and though opiates still the asthma, they give no sleep.
    The oil of castor I have tried, and it seems particularly fitted for our intention. It has no great power of stimulation, but seems to mingle itself with the matter in the intestines, and by hindering its concretion, to facilitate its ejection. Perhaps it does something by lubricating the passage.
    My limbs are very weak, my breath is very short, and the water begins to threaten, and I have begun to oppose by squil pills, which I think have prevailed over it twice this Summer. I purpose to ply them diligently and have great hope of success, though I am sometimes very much dejected. I am Dear Sir, Your most humble Servant
Lichfield. Oct. 20. 1784   Sam: Johnson

1028. Lichfield. Sa. 23 Oct. '84. John Taylor (Ashbourne).

Address: To the Reverend Dr Taylor in Ashbourn Derbyshire. Maggs (1926), defective.—Morrison Catalogue 1885, ii. 343.

Dear Sir,
    Coming down from a very restless night I found your letter which made me a little angry. You tell me that recovery is in

1028.—Endorsed by JT: 'This is the last letter. My answer, which were the words of advice he gave to Mr. Thrale the day he dyed, he resented extremely from me.' JT noted also 'No. 102 last letter' (not 108 as Hill stated, Preface p. viii) and 'Some person has torn off the bottom'. For J's advice to HT on the peril of overeating see *Tb* 488; for J's 'quarrel, if quarrel it might be called' with JT for advising him 'in his

my power. This indeed I should be glad to hear, if I could once believe it. But you mean to charge me with neglecting or opposing my own health. Tell me therefore what I do that hurts me, and what I neglect that would help me. Tell it as soon as you can. ⟨one line lost⟩. I would do it the sooner for your desire, and I hope to do it now in no long time, but shall hardly do it here. I hope soon to be at London. Answer the first part of this letter immediately.

I am, dear Sir, Your most humble servant,
Lichfield, Oct. 23, 1784.   Sam: Johnson.

1029. Lichfield. M. 25 Oct. '84. Richard Brocklesby.

Address: To Dr Brocklesby in London. *Postmark*: 27 oc. Fettercairn.—Boswell 1791, ii. 542, extract (Hill iv. 358).

Dear Sir
You write to me with a zeal that animates, and a tenderness that melts me. I am not afraid either of a journey to London or a residence in it. I came down with little fatigue, and I am now not weaker. In the smoky atmosphere I was delivered from the dropsy, which I consider as the original and radical disease. The town is my element, there are my friends, there are my books to which I have not yet bidden farewell, and there are my amusements. Sir Joshua told me long ago that my vocation was to publick life,[1] and I hope still to keep my station, till God shall bid me *Go in peace*.[2]

I have not much to add of medical observation. I believe some vigorous pill must be contrived to counteract the costiveness which opiate⟨s⟩ now certainly produce, and to which it is too troublesome to oppose a regular purge. If You can order such a pill send me the prescription next post.

own unaltered phrase', see HLP's *Letters*, ii. 381 (quoted by Hill). If JT really wrote 'such eating is little better than Suicide', 'resentment' was inevitable. But HLP adds that the quarrel was short-lived; the old friends met again in London.

1029.—1. If JR's opinion were quoted in isolation, it would naturally be taken to mean that he, like others of J's contemporaries, deplored J's failure to fulfil his 'vocation' by becoming a great lawyer or a great statesman (*L* i. 134). But the context shows that 'publick life' here means virtually 'London life': that J was not fitted for rural solitude. Streatham had been a compromise; when that ended, or was interrupted, J's life when health permitted, and especially in his *annus mirabilis*, 1780, had been that of a 'man about town'.

2. St. Mark, v. 34.

I now take the squils without the addition of aloes from which I never found other effect, than that it made the pill more bulky and more nauseous, but if it be of any use I will add it again. I am Sir Your most obliged and most humble Servant

Lichfield. Oct. 25. 1784   Sam: Johnson

1029.1.   Lichfield.   M. 25 Oct. '84.   John Perkins.

Address: To Mr Perkins.
O. T. Perkins.—

Dear Sir
The experience which I have often had of your kindness is now bringing another trouble upon you. I beg that you will be pleased to employ some proper agent to do for me what this summons, which I have this day received, requires.

I am little better, and I flatter myself little worse, than when I left London. Please to make my compliments to Mrs Perkins, and to all my friends about the Brewhouse. I hope soon to see you all again. I am, Dear Sir,
                    Your most humble Servant
Lichfield Oct. 25. 1784   Sam: Johnson

1029.2.   Lichfield.   Sa. 30 Oct. '84.   John Ryland.

Address: To Mr Ryland Merchant in London. *Postmark*: — NO. Adam.—

Dear Sir
I have slackened in my diligence of correspondence certainly not by ingratitude or less delight to hear from my friends, and as little would I have it imputed to idleness, or amusement[1] of any other kind. The truth is that I care not much to think on my own state. I have for some time past grown worse, the water makes slow advances, and my breath though not so much obstructed as in some former periods of my disorder, is very short. I am not however heartless. The water has, since its first great effusion, invaded me twice, and twice has retreated.

Accept my sincere thanks for your care in laying down the stone;[2] what you and young Mr Ryland have done, I doubt

---

1029.2.—1. See Index VII.   2. At Bromley, see 975, 977.

not of finding well done, if ever I can make my mind firm
enough to visit it.

I am now contriving to return, and hope to be yet no
disgrace to our monthly meeting.[3] When I shall be with you,
as my resolution is not very steady, and as chance must have
some part in the opportunity, I cannot tell. Do not omit to
write, for your letters are a great part of my comfort. I am,

Dear Sir, Your most humble servant
Lichfield Oct. 30. 1784   Sam: Johnson
Pray write.

1030. Lichfield. M. 1 Nov. '84. Charles Burney.

Address (see 1030.1): To Dr Burney in St. Martin's Street Leicester
Fields London. *Postmark*: 3 NO.
Not traced.—Boswell 1791, ii. 544 (Hill iv. 361).

Our correspondence paused for want of topicks. I had said
what I had to say on the matter proposed to my consideration;[1] and nothing remained but to tell you, that I waked or
slept; that I was more or less sick. I drew my thoughts in
upon myself, and supposed yours employed upon your book.
—That your book has been delayed I am glad, since you have
gained an opportunity of being more exact.—Of the caution
necessary in adjusting narratives there is no end. Some tell
what they do not know, that they may not seem ignorant,
and others from mere indifference about truth. All truth is
not, indeed, of equal importance; but, if little violations are
allowed, every violation will in time be thought little; and
a writer should keep himself vigilantly on his guard against
the first temptations to negligence or supineness.—I had
ceased to write, because respecting you I had no more to say,
and respecting myself could say little good. I cannot boast
of advancement, and in cases of convalescence it may be
said, with few exceptions, *non progredi, est regredi.* I hope
I may be excepted.—My great difficulty was with my sweet
Fanny, who, by her artifice of inserting her letter in yours,

1029.2.—3. This can hardly describe the Essex-Head Club, which met thrice a week,
unless J is referring obscurely to his turn as chairman, which *was* monthly (see 929).
The revival of the old Ivy-Lane Club (908) seems to have become a monthly fixture.
See 1032.

1030.—1. See on 984.

had given me a precept of frugality[2] which I was not at liberty to neglect; and I knew[3] not who were in town under whose cover I could send my letter. I rejoice to hear that you are all so well, and have a delight particularly sympathetic in the recovery of Mrs. Burney.

1030.1. Lichfield. M. 1 Nov. '84. Frances Burney.

Address: To Miss Burney. (See 1030; the letter was written on p. 3 of 1030, p. 4 of which bore the postal address, &c.) Morgan Library.—

Dear Madam
    My heart has reproached me with my ingratitude to you, and my vanity has been mortified with the fear of being thought to want a due sense of the honour conferred on me by such a correspondence. I am obliged to Dr Burney for the opportunity that he has given me of surmounting all difficulties.
    Yet now I am enabled to write, what can I say? only one melancholy truth, that I am very ill, and another more chearful, but, I hope, equally sincere, that I wish You, dear Madam, to be better. I am now scheming to come home, but the schemes of the sick are dilatory, and then You must try what comfort vou can give, to, Dear Madam,
                    Your most humble servant
Nov. 1. 1784   Sam: Johnson

1031. Lichfield. M. 1 Nov. '84. Francesco Sastres.

Not traced.—1788, No. 367.

Dear Sir   Lichfield, Nov. 1, 1784.
    I beg you to continue the frequency of your letters; every letter is a cordial; but you must not wonder that I do not

1030.—2. For FB's 'artifice' see 1030.1, which no doubt imitates it; i.e. her letter was on the same sheet as her father's.
    3. 1791 has 'know'; J's *e*, when tied to a preceding letter, is hardly distinguishable from his *o*. He means that he could not think of any member of parliament whom he could ask to forward a letter. This seems an excess of 'frugality', unless he had papers to enclose; 1030 cost CB fivepence.

1030.1.—Endorsed by FB: 'Written on half a letter to Dr. Burney, from Litchfield —only the month previous to his Death—which took place the 14 (*sic*) of the following December, 1784.'

answer with exact punctuality. You may always have something to tell: you live among the various orders of mankind, and may make a letter from the exploits, sometimes of the philosopher, and sometimes of the pickpocket.[1] You see some ballons succeed and some miscarry, and a thousand strange and a thousand foolish things. But I see nothing; I must make my letter from what I feel, and what I feel will[2] so little delight, that I cannot love to talk of it.

I am certainly not[3] to come to town, but do not omit to write; for I know not when I shall come, and the loss of a letter is not much.

I am, dear Sir, Your, &c.,
Sam: Johnson.

1032. See after 1033.

1033. Lichfield. W. 3 Nov.' 84. James Boswell (Edinburgh).

Not traced.—Boswell 1791, ii. 556 (Hill iv. 380). The letter is dated 5 Nov. in 1793, which Hill inadvertently followed (see note).

Dear Sir

I have this summer sometimes amended and sometimes relapsed, but upon the whole, have lost ground very much. My legs are extremely weak, and my breath very short, and the water is now encreasing upon me. In this uncomfortable state your letters used to relieve; what is the reason that I have them no longer?[1] Are you sick, or are you sullen? Whatever be the reason, if it be less than necessity, drive it away, and of the short life that we have, make the best use

1031.—1. Hill quotes *GM* 1784, 228: balloon-gazing was a good opportunity, and on one occasion 'some noblemen and gentlemen lost their watches and many their purses'.

2. 'will' Lysons: 'with' 1788.

3. Doubtless a slip; unless indeed J wrote 'certainly soon'.

1033.—Dr. Pottle suggests to me that the date of receipt of this letter (11 Nov.) rather favours 5 Nov. as the date of writing. But he agrees that the change made in 1793 is unlikely to have been made by reference to the original. He tells me that JB's 'Book of Company' shows him dining and sleeping at Auchinleck on 10 Nov., and his journal (*BP* xvi. 51) shows him sleeping in Edinburgh on 11 Nov. The session began 12 Nov. If J directed to Edinburgh and the letter was not forwarded, JB might well record 11 Nov. as the day of receipt.

1. For the probable date of JB's last letter, and for his own account of his long silence, see on 981.

for yourself and for your friends ✱✱✱✱✱✱2 I am sometimes afraid that your omission to write has some real cause, and shall be glad to know that you are not sick, and that nothing ill has befallen dear Mrs. Boswell, or any of your family. I am, Sir, your, &c.

Lichfield, Nov. 3, 1784.   Sam. Johnson.

1032. Lichfield. Th. 4 Nov. '84. John Ryland.

Address: To Mr Ryland Merchant in London. *Postmark*: 8 NO. Adam.—*Athenæum* 1848, 958.

Dear Sir

I have just received a letter in which you tell me that you love to hear from me, and I value such a declaration too much to neglect it. To have a friend, and a friend like you, may be numbered among the first felicities of life; at a time when weakness either of body or mind loses the pride and the confidence of self-sufficiency, and looks round for that help which perhaps human kindness cannot give, and which we yet are willing to expect from one another.

I am, at this time very much dejected. The water grows fast upon me, but it has invaded me twice in this last half year, and has been twice expelled, it will I hope give way to the same remedies. My Breath is tolerably easy, and since the remission of asthma about two months ago, have¹ never been so strait and so much obstructed as it once was.

I took this day a very uncommon dose of squills, but hitherto without effect, but I will continue their use very diligently. Let me have your prayers.

I am now preparing myself for my return, and do not

1033.—2. JB describes the suppressed passage: '. . . he still persevered in arraigning me as before.' In the *Life* he continues thus: 'I, however, wrote to him two as kind letters as I could; the last of which came too late to be read by him.' The journal tells us more; on 12 Nov. (immediately after the receipt of 1033) 'callous by reiteration of misery . . . I wrote a short letter to him in a kind of despair. My valuable spouse made me keep it.' *BP*, xvi. 57. Finally JB's unpublished Register gives us the date of the first of the two letters that *were* sent: 'Sent 19 November 1784. Dr. Samuel Johnson, of my sad illness.' The date of the second, and last, letter is unknown; if it reached L'n before J's death on 13 Dec., JB might learn from Barber that it came too late to be read.

1032.—1. 'have' here and 'the' below show the writer's infirmity.

despair of some more monthly meetings.[2] To hear that dear Payne is better gives me great delight.

I saw the draught of the stone. I am afraid the date is wrong. I think it should be 52.[3] We will have it rectified. You say nothing of the cost but that you have paid it. My intention was the[1] Mr Payne should have put into your hands fifteen pounds which he received for me at Midsummer. If he has not done it, I will order you the money, which is in his hands.

Shall I ever be able to bear the sight of this stone? In your company, I hope, I shall. You will not wonder that I write no more. God bless you for Christs sake.

I am Dear Sir Your most humble servant
Lichfield Nov. 4. 1784   Sam: Johnson

1033.1. Lichfield. Sa. 6 Nov. '84. Richard Brocklesby.

Address: To Dr Brocklesby in London. *Postmark*: 8 no. Fettercairn.—

Dear Sir

Nothing now goes well, except that my Asthma is not oppressive to the degree that I have sometimes suffered. The water encreases almost visibly and the squills which I get here are utterly inefficacious. My Spirits are extremely low. Yet I have recovered from a worse state. I have supported myself with opiates till they have made me comatous. I have disobeyed Dr Heberden, and taken Squills in too great a quantity for my Stomach. My Stomach at least is less vigorous, and the Squills I have taken in great quantities.

I am endeavouring to make haste to town. Do not write any more hither. I am Dear Sir Your most humble Servant
Lichfield Nov. 6. 1784   Sam: Johnson

1034. Lichfield. Su. 7 Nov. '84. John Hawkins.

Not traced.—Hawkins, *Life of Johnson* 1787, 575, an extract.

I am relapsing into the dropsy very fast, and shall make such haste to town that it will be useless to write to me; but

1032.—2. See 1029.2.
3. The error was J's own, see 975; see also *L* i. 241.

when I come, let me have the benefit of your advice, and the
consolation of your company.

Nov. 7, 1784.

1035. Lichfield. *c.* 10 Nov. '84. Jane Gastrell and Elizabeth
Aston (Lichfield).

Pembroke.—Hill 1892.

Mr. Johnson sends his compliments to the Ladies at Stowhill, of whom he would have taken a more formal leave, but
that he was willing to spare a ceremony, which he hopes
would have been no pleasure to them, and would have been
painful to himself.

1036. W. 17 Nov. '84. Charles Burney.

Address: To Dr Burney in St Martins Street Leicester Fields.
Not traced; facsimile in Hill's Boswell 1887, iv. 377.—Boswell 1791,
ii. 554 (Hill iv. 377). See App. G.

Mr Johnson who came home last night, sends his respects
to dear Doctor Burney, and all the dear Burneys little and
great.

Nov. 17

1036.1. W. 17 Nov. ⟨'84⟩. Francesco Sastres.

Maggs Catalogue 286 (1912), 1709, 'to Mr. Saltres' (not seen).—
Quoted in catalogue.

Mr. Johnson is glad to inform Mr. Sastres that he came
home last night.

1037. W. 17 Nov. '84. Edmund Hector (Birmingham).

Address: To Mr. Hector in Birmingham. *Postmark*: 17 NO.
Fettercairn.—Boswell 1791, ii. 554 (Hill iv. 378).

Dear Sir

I did not reach Oxford until friday morning, and then I
sent Francis to see the Ballon fly, but could not go myself.[1]

1037.—1. *L* iv. 548.

I staid at Oxford till Tuesday, and then came in the common vehicle easily to London. I am as I was, and having seen Dr. Brocklesby, am to ply the squils. But whatever be their efficacy, this world must soon pass away. Let us think seriously on our duty.

I send my kindest respects to dear Mrs Careless. Let me have the prayers of both. We have all lived long, and must soon part. God have mercy on us for the Sake of our Lord Jesus Christ. Amen.

I am Dear Sir Your most humble Servant
London. Nov. 17. 1784   Sam: Johnson

1037.1. Sa. 27 Nov. '84. (?) John Hollyer.

Frederick Hollyer (defective).—

Sir

I desire Y⟨. . .⟩ know, what Children of our ⟨. . .⟩ are now living, what are their name⟨. . .⟩ is their condition. Be pleased to make ⟨. . .⟩ possible haste. I am, Sir, Your most humble Servant
Bolt court, Fleetstreet, Nov. 27. 1784   Sam: Johnson

1038. ⟨*c.* 17 Nov. '84⟩. Thomas Cadell.

Address: To Mr Cadel.
A. Houghton.—Known to Hill only from an auction catalogue.

Sir

I desire you will make up a parcel of the following Books,

1037.1.—See R ix. 71. Mr. Reade conjectures that J's inquiries concerned the children of his cousin Thomas J, who are named in the codicil to his will, dated 9 Dec., though not in the will itself, which is dated 8 Dec. The spaces make it possible to fill three of the four lacunae with virtual certainty: (1) 'You will let me'; (3) 'names and what'; (4) 'all'. The second chasm cannot be filled on this kind of evidence.

1038.—The approximate date and the intention of this letter are settled by a letter from Adams to Scott, J's executor, 8 Feb. 1785, in the Adam collection: 'We have recd. a most agreeable Token of our Friend Dr. Johnson's Regard for his College in a Present of his Books and of his Publications of every kind, which he sent us a little while before his Death.' Was it the Dictionary or the periodicals that Adams was unwilling to regard as 'Books'? The second *Rambler* was perhaps a personal gift. The only books, now in the College Library, inscribed as presentation copies, are the *Journey* and Vols. 1–3 (out of four) of the 1784 *Rambler* (*L* i. 527).

and send them to Oxford directed to Dr Adams at Pembroke College

Johnson's Dictionary Fol.

— — 8vo

— Rambler 2 Sets

— Idler

Political tracts

Hebrides

Rasselas

Lives of the Poets.

Irene a tragedy

(if it can be easily got at

Dodsley's else leave it

out)

and please to let me know the whole of my debt to You. I am, Sir, Your most humble Servant Sam: Johnson

1039. M. 29 Nov. '84. William Vyse.

Address: To the Reverend Dr Vyse in Lambeth.

Howell Ll. Davies.—Malone's Boswell 1804, iv. 437.

Sir

I am desirous to know whether Charles Scrimshaw of Woodsease (I think,) in your father's neighbourhood, be now living, what is his condition, and where he may be found. If you can conveniently make any enquiry about him, and can do it without delay, it will be an act of great kindness to me, he being very nearly related to me. I beg to pardon this trouble.

I am, Sir, Your most humble servant,

Bolt court, Fleet street Nov. 29. 1784   Sam: Johnson.

1039.1. M. 29 Nov. '84. William Strahan.

Address: To William Strahan Esq.

Not traced.—C. K. Shorter, *Unpublished Letters of S.J.* 1915.

Dear Sir   November 29, 1784

I am very weak. When I am a little better I will beg your

1039.—The motive of this letter was the same as that of 1037.1, but the result was different; J told Vyse that 'he was disappointed in the inquiries he had made after his relations' (Malone). See also R ix. 112.

The following notes are written on the letter in an unknown hand, which is probably Vyse's: 'Old Mr. Boothby of Tooley married to his 2d wife a sister of Charles Scrimshaw, by whom he had issue a son Captain Schrimshaw Boothby who is dead without issue, and a daughter who married a Beaumont of Leicester, whether living and has issue uncertain. Mr. Broomfield of Leake married his sister. She died a widow without children and after the death of her husband lived near Congleton.'

company; in the meantime, I beg you to inform me in two lines, when you shall have received my pension to Michaelmas, how much will be coming to me.

I am, Sir, Your most humble Servant

Sam: Johnson

1039.2. M. 29 Nov. '84. ⟨Bennet Langton⟩.

Sotheby 25 Nov. 1929.—

Dear Sir

I earnestly beg the favour of seeing you this afternoon, do not be hasty to leave me, for I have much to say, I am, Dear Sir,

Your most &c.,

November 29, 1784.   Sam: Johnson

1040. Th. 2 Dec. '84. Richard Greene (Lichfield).

Address (Boswell): To Mr. Green, Apothecary, at Lichfield. Not traced; copy made for JB, Isham.—*GM* April 1785, 288, extract; Boswell 1791, ii. 566 (Hill iv. 393).

Dear Sir

I have enclosed the epitaph[1] for my Father, Mother, and Brother, to be all engraved on the large size, and laid in the Middle Isle in St. Michael's Church, which I request the Clergyman and the Church-wardens to permit.

The first care must be to find the exact place of interment, that the stone may protect the bodies. Then let the stone be deep, massy, and hard, and do not let the difference of ten pounds or more defeat our purpose.

I have enclosed ten pounds, and Mrs. Porter will pay you ten more, which I gave her for the same purpose. What more

1039.2.—For BL's attention to J in his last days see *L* iv. 406, 414. One of their subjects of conversation was no doubt the publication of J's Latin poems, see *Poems*, xviii. A pencil note on the original, 'To Mr. Langton', is confirmed by Hoole's 'Narrative' of Johnson's last days; Hoole records that Langton was 'with him on business' on the evening of 29 Nov. *JM* ii. 152.

1040.—JB's copy (presumably by Greene) includes this: 'To Mrs. Porter. Madam, be pleased to pay to Mr Greene ten pounds Sam. Johnson. £10 = 0 = 0. Decem. 2ᵈ 1784.'

1. It is printed in the *Works*, and in *L* iv. 393, q.v. for the fate of the stone, which is doubtful.

is wanted shall be sent, and I beg that all possible haste may be made, for I wish to have it done while I am yet alive. Let me know, dear Sir, that you receive this.

I am, Sir, your most humble servant,

Decem 2ᵈ 1784.　　　　　　　　　　　　Sam. Johnson.

1041. Th. 2 Dec. '84. Lucy Porter (Lichfield).

Fettercairn.—Boswell 1791, ii. 566, extract (Hill iv. 394).

Dear Madam

I am very ill, and desire your prayers. I have sent Mr Green the epitaph, and a power to call on You for ten pounds.

I laid this summer a stone over Tetty in the chapel of Bromley in Kent. The Inscription is in Latin of which this is the English.

Here lie the remains of Elizabeth, descended from the ancient house of Jarvis at Peatling in Leicestershire; a Woman of beauty, elegance, ingenuity, and piety. Her first Husband was Henry Porter; her second, Samuel Johnson, who having loved her much, and lamented her long, laid this stone upon her.

She died in March. 1752.

That this is done, I thought it fit that You should know; what care will be taken of us, who can tell? May God pardon and bless us, for Jesus Christs sake. Amen.

I am, Madam, Your most humble Servant

Dec. 2. 1784　　　　　　　　　　　　Sam: Johnson.

1042. M. 6 Dec. '84. John Nichols.

Address: To Mr Nicholls.
B.M.—*GM* Dec. 1784, ii. 892.

The late learned Mr. Swinton of Oxford having one Day remarked that one Man, meaning I suppose no Man but himself, could assign all the Parts of the ancient universal History to their proper Authors. At the Request of Sir Robt Chambers or of myself gave the Account which I now transmit to you in his own Hand, being willing that of so great a

1041.—For J's translation of the epitaph JB substitutes: [Here a translation].

252

Work the history should be known and that each Writer should receive his due Proportion of Praise from Posterity.

I recommend to you to preserve this Scrap of literary Intelligence in Mr. Swinton's own Hand, or to deposit it in the Museum, that the Veracity of this Account may never be doubted.

I am Sir Your most humble servant,

Dec. 6th 1784   Sam: Johnson

Mr. S——n.

The History of the Carthaginians. Numidians. Mauritanians. Gætulians. Garamantes. Melano Gætulians. Nigritae. Cyrenaica. Marmarica. The Regio Syrtica. Turks, Tartars, and Moguls. Indians. Chinese.

The History of the Peopling of America.

Dissertation on the independency of the Arabs.

The Cosmogony, and a small part of the history immediately following. By Mr. Sale.

To the Birth of Abraham. Chiefly by Mr. Shelvock.

History of the Jews, Gauls, and Spaniards. By Mr. Psalmanazar.

Xenophon's Retreat. By the same.

History of the Persians, and the Constantinopolitan Empire. By Dr. Campbell.

History of the Romans. By Mr. Bower.

1042.1. Tu. 7 Dec. '84. William Strahan.

Owen D. Young.—C. K. Shorter, *Unpublished Letters of S.J.* 1915.

Sir

I was not sure that I read your figures right, and therefore must trouble You to set down in words how much of my pension I can call for now, and how much will be due to me at Christmas. I am, Sir, Your most humble servant

Dec. 7. 1784   Sam: Johnson

1042.2. F. 10 Dec. '84. William Strahan.

Address: To William Strahan, Esq.

Not traced.—C. K. Shorter, *Unpublished Letters of S.J.* 1915.

Sir   Bolt Court, December 10, 1784.

I am very unwilling to take the pains of writing, and therefore make use of another hand to desire that I may have whatever portion of my pension[1] you can spare me with prudence and propriety.

I am Sir your humble Servant

Sam: Johnson

1043a. 20 Sept. n.y. Margaret Penelope Strahan.

Address: To Mrs Strahan.
Yale.—Hill 1892.

Dear Madam
 When You kindly invited me to dine with ⟨You⟩ to morrow, I had forgotten that I had myself invited a friend to dine with me. I will therefore wait on you any other day. I am, Madam, Your most humble Servant

Sept. 20   Sam: Johnson

1043b. 29 Nov. n.y. ——.

A. B. Burney.—Hill 1892.

Dear Sir
 I have seen your proof as I told you, and seen I think only one word that I wished to alter.
 Be pleased to make my compliments to the Ladies at your house. I am

Sir Your most humble Servant

Nov. 29   Sam: Johnson

1042.2.—1. Hill (*Letters* ii. 433) prints J's receipt for £75, 'one quarter's pension', dated 13 Dec.

1043a.—I place this and the following letter here because Hill numbered them. For other unplaced letters see below.

1043b.—This letter was sold at Sotheby's; the cataloguer assumed it to be to Strahan. A pencil note by an unknown hand ascribes it to '1755'.

LETTERS UNDATED OR INCOMPLETELY DATED, AND NOT PLACED

I begin this series with the arbitrary number 1101, thinking that some consulters of the edition may find it convenient to remember that any letter numbered 11.. is unplaced.

Letters to Mrs. Thrale are followed by letters to other correspondents in alphabetical order. Those to named correspondents are numbered from 1120, those to unnamed persons from 1170.

LETTERS TO MRS. THRALE

1101. 4 Feb. n.y. Mrs. Thrale.

Sotheby 30 Jan. 1918 (not seen).—Abstract in catalogue.

'About Dr. Worthington, Mr. Hoole, and other friends, and a meeting at the Club.'

1102. 8 Mar. n.y. Mrs. Thrale.

Sotheby 4 June 1882 (not seen).—Abstract in catalogue.

'Mentions Baretti, Wetherel and others.'

1103. 27 March n.y. Mrs. Thrale.

Sotheby 30 Jan. 1918 (not seen).—Quotation in catalogue.

You have now been at court, your presentation was delayed too long. What you intend to do at all it is wise to resolve on doing quickly. *Fugit irrevocabile tempus.*[1]

1103a. From Mrs. Thrale.

Address: Dr. Johnson Fleet Street.
R 539.12.—

Dear Sir
    Mrs Nesbitt desired me to give you the enclosed, so I send it according to her desire. Yesterday I went to Court for the first Time as you know: the Ceremony was trifling, but I am glad it's over; one is now upon the footing

---

1103.—Neither this letter nor 1103a has been dated. There is no official record of 'presentations'; there may be lists in the daily newspapers.
    1. Virgil, *Georgics*, iii. 284.

one wishes to be—and in a manner free of the Drawing Room, I confess I am pleased at having been there. Queeney has caught a slight Cold with her London Expedition, but I find we are to make another Cruize next week, & you are to meet us at Mr Paradice's where the Improvisatore is engaged to divert us. Farewell! and get better Nights and lose no tittle of your kindness for your most faithful

humble Servant H L T.

1104. 21 May n.y. Mrs. Thrale.

Adam.—

Madam

I have now got more books for Mr Thrale than can be carried in the coach, and, I think, he may better send a cart than we can get one, because he may send with it baskets or sacks for the smaller volumes. We have of all sizes more than four hundred. If I could know when the cart would come I would take care to have somebody in the way. But perhaps there is no haste; yet I now care not how soon they are gone. Please to send me word that you are pretty well, at least tell me how you are.
                                                    I am Madam, Your most obedient
May 21.   Sam: Johnson

1105. Saturday. Mrs. Thrale.

Sotheby 30 Jan. 1918 (not seen).—Quotation in catalogue.

I long to come to that place which my dear friends allow me to call HOME.

1106. n.d. Mrs. Thrale.

Cecil Tildesley.—

Mr Johnson will wait for dear Mrs Thrale tomorrow and shall be to the last degree unwilling to do anything which she shall forbid. He will go with her to Streatham, for he longs to be again with so much kindness, and prudence.

1107. Tuesday. Mrs. Thrale.

Adam.—

Mr Johnson is much obliged by Mrs Thrales enquiry.

He came home on Saturday. He is still very much disordered, but would have come to Streatham if Mrs Thrale had called. Quo me vertam, nescio.[1] Tuesday.

1108. n.d. Mrs. Thrale.

Rosenbach Co. (1925).—

Vous me chargiez hier, Madame, de tant de pain, que je n'en pouvois prendre qu'une partie, il en reste assez pour ce jour.

1109. n.d. Mrs. Thrale.

Sir Charles Russell.—

Qu'il vous plaise, Madame, de m'envoyer le son[1] que vous trouvez bon que je prenne; il pourra venir a l'aide de ma medicine. Pour vous, mon illustre maîtresse, il faut toutefois conserver vôtre gaietè, et esperer tout le meilleur.

1110. n.d. Mrs. Thrale.

Sir Robert Hudson (defective).—

. . . bleeding, and Physick, and . . . , and innumerable Miseries. There are many Ups and Downs in the world, and my dearest Mistress, I ⟨have?⟩ been down, and up, and down again. When you are up again, keep up.

1111. n.d. Mrs. Thrale.

Sotheby 30 Jan. 1918 (not seen).—Abstract in catalogue.

'Mentioning Steevens and Shebeare.'

1111a. n.d. From Mrs. Thrale.

R 539.32.—

When I am taking leave of my Family tho' for so short a Time, I must likewise take leave—I feel I must—of him who next to my Family is most dear to me. On this Day we set out, and as I could not go to Town conveniently either yesterday or on Saturday last because of the Coach &c. *My* Clerk Mr Perkins

1107.—1. Literally, 'I know not whither to turn me'. The reference need not be to change of place.

1109.—1. Dr. Onions tells me that the medical use of decoction of bran goes back to antiquity.

1110.—This letter is badly defaced, as well as mutilated; but I think I have read most of it.

came down hither on Sunday purposely to tell *me* that all went well before I left Streatham. But tho' the Man had nothing but good to say, my Master looked very black upon him indeed, & not very white upon me, though when I urge him to tell the Cause of his Ill humour, he alledges some trifle which I know to have nothing to do with it. Upon the whole I am glad we are going from that about which we shall never agree. In regard Esteem & Affectionate Gratitude to you for that Friendship which is the greater honour to us both, we most heartily agree, & I am particularly

Dear Sir Your most faithful Servant H: L: Thrale.

My Master always sees your Letters to me.

LETTERS TO OTHER CORRESPONDENTS

1120. n.d. James Boswell (London).

Not traced.—Boswell 1791, i. 454 (ii. 307, overlooked by Hill in *Letters*).

Mr. Johnson does not see why Mr. Boswell should suppose a Scotchman less acceptable than any other man. He will be at the Mitre.

1121. 31 May n.y. Thomas Cadell.

Address: To Mr Cadel Bookseller.

Adam.—

Mr Johnson desir⟨es⟩ Mr Cadel to send him
Duty of Man 8vo
Nelson on the Festivals 8vo
they must be handsomely bound being for a present.

May. 31.

1122. n.d. Thomas Cadell.

Adam.—

Sir,

I shall be glad to see you and Mr Nicol on tuesday morning.

1120.—'I have deposited in the British Museum, amongst other pieces of his writing, the following note in answer to one from me, asking if he could meet me at dinner at the Mitre, though a friend of mine, a Scotchman, was to be there' JB. The MS. is not in the Museum, see *L* ii. 297. JB gives the story s.a. '75, but does not date it. Dr. Pottle suggests the date 3 Apr. '76 (*L* iii. 8), when the Solicitor-General for Scotland was JB's other guest.

1121.—I failed to connect this letter with 609, which seems to place it in '78.

1122.—The reference is, I think, to the revised edition of the *Lives*, 1783, for which the booksellers made J a present of £100.

Be pleased to return my respectful thanks to the proprietors, to whom I wish that success in all their undertakings which such liberality deserves. I am Sir, Your very humble Servant

Sam. Johnson

1123. n.d. Thomas Cadell.

A. H. Hallam Murray.—

Mr Johnson desires Mr Cadel to send him, if he has it, Xenophon de Rebus Graecorum, the Scotch Edition.

1124. n.d. Thomas Davies.

Not traced.—Boswell 1791, ii. 460 (Hill iv. 231, overlooked in *Letters*).

Come, come, dear Davies, I am always sorry when we quarrel; send me word that we are friends.

1125. n.d. James Elphinston (Edinburgh).

Not traced.—Quotation in Elphinston, *Forty Years' Corresp.* 1791, i. 34.

'In one letter (among many now lost) he said . . .'

My health seems to be returning; and with health of mind and body a man may supply or bear the remainder of his wants.

1126. Thursday. William and Elizabeth Franklin.

Address: Governor Franklin, Norton Street.
Not traced.—Quaritch Catalogue 438 (1930), 585; 'reputed to be written by Francis Barber from Dr. Johnson's dictation'.

Dr Johnson presents best compliments to Governor and Mrs Franklin, & intends himself the honor of waiting upon them tomorrow (friday) at five o'Clock, as obligingly invited: —He could not sooner owne it in his power, 'till he had excused himself from a prior engagement, on which account he hopes not to be taxed with inattention. Thursday afternoon.

1125.—The quotation is in a footnote to 29.
1126.—If J had used his own hand he would probably have written 'his best compliments'; 'owne' is not very like his spelling.

1127. n.d. David Garrick.

Sotheby 3 Dec. 1856, 1151 (not seen).—

'An interesting letter to Garrick, n.d.'

1127.1. David Garrick.

Sotheby 5 May 1900 (not seen).—

Mr Johnson has been so hindered that he could wait on Mr. Garrick only once (last Friday in the afternoon) he will call as soon as he can. Mr. Johnson begs to have the plays back, if they are done with.

1128. 20 Jan. n.y. John Hawkesworth.

Sir Owen Morshead.—

Dear Sir

You may by chance remember that I once mentioned in your grove[1] the fitness of an epitome of Chambers Dictionary, which you said you would some time undertake. This gives you a right of refusing it to another, but if you have now, as I suppose you have, laid aside all such thoughts, I would transfer it to a gentleman now out of business. Pray send me word.

But send me word with more care of the health of dear Mrs Hawkesworth. She is negligent of herself, and by consequence of you and me. I shall never love her when she is sick because she gets sick by her own fault

    I am Dear Sir Your most affectionate

Jan. 20.   Sam: Johnson

1129. Thursday. John Hoole.

Tregaskis (1925).—

Mr Johnson has heard from Mr Barrington, and has seen

1127.1.—The plays were presumably Shakespeare's, see 168.

1128.—The subject of the letter is no doubt the same as that of 453. It appears from Nichols, *LI* iv. 801, that Calder originally proposed to 'abridge' the dictionary. Since the contract for the work was dated 29 Oct. '73 (op. cit. iv. 805) this letter probably belongs to that year.

1128.—1. At Bromley.

1129.—I was inclined to place this letter in '83 and to suppose it concerned with the Essex-Head Club, of which Hoole and Barrington were members. No Jackson is

Mr Jackson, and begs to see Mr Hoole as soon as he can.
Thursday afternoon.

1130. n.d. John Hoole.

Dobell (1937).—

Mr Johnson returns thanks to Mr and Mrs Hoole for their
kind attention and enquiries.

1131. n.d. John Hoole.

Address (catalogue): To Mr. Hoole in Queen's Street.
Sotheby catalogue 12 Apr. 1875, 653. Extracts in catalogue.

'Thanks him for his affectionate letter, and hopes'

we shall both be the better for each other's friendship. . . .
I am now grown somewhat easier in my body, but my mind
is sometimes depressed.

'He touchingly mentions the death of poor Williams' ('poor Williams' is no
doubt a quotation) 'who'

is gone I hope to Heaven. May we when we are called, be
called to happiness.

1132. n.d. (?) George Johnstone.

Not traced.—Described in *Parl. Hist.* xvii. 1105, quoted by Hill
L i. 304.

In a Debate on the Copyright Bill on May 16, 1774, Governor Johnstone
said:—'It had been urged . . . that Dr. Johnson had received an after gratification from the booksellers who employed him to compile his Dictionary; . . . he
had in his hand a letter from Dr. Johnson, which he read, in which the doctor
denied the assertion, but declared that his employers fulfilled their bargain,
and that he was satisfied.'

recorded as a member; he might decline the invitation. But Dr. Powell convincingly
suggests that Jackson is 'the omniscient', and that the letter is about the Readership
of the Temple, see 899. All the clues now fit, for Barrington was a Bencher of the
Inner Temple. The date will still be '83.
1132.—It is only a guess that this letter was a letter to Johnstone.

1133. 9 Oct. n.y. Griffith Jones.

Not traced.—*Whitehall Evening Post* 10–12 July 1798.

Sir

You are accustomed to consider Advertisements & to observe what still has most effect upon the Public. I shall think it a favour if you will be pleased to take the trouble of *digging twelve lines of common sense out of this strange scribble*, and insert it three times in the Daily Advertiser at the expense of, Sir Your humble servant

Oct. 9   Sam. Johnson

Please to return me the paper.

1134. 14 June n.y. Thomas Lawrence.

Address: To Dr Laurence.
A. Houghton.—

Dear Sir

I have enclosed some account of your Son, with which, upon the whole, I think you will be pleased, otherwise I should not wish to be the reporter.

The Lady's Letter you must not show, as it contains secret history. I am, Sir, Your most obliged and most humble Servant,

June 14.   Sam: Johnson

1135. n.d. Andrew Millar.

Anderson Galleries, 12 Jan. 1932 (not seen).—Description in catalogue.

'A note in third person on small slip, asking for a copy of The Elements of Criticism.'

1133.—This letter was contributed by Jones's son Stephen. As the year is not given, I have not searched the files of *The Daily Advertiser* for 'twelve lines of common sense'. Perhaps someone can guess on whose behalf J was paying for this advertisement. The editor of *The Whitehall Post* adds that the elder Jones, 'at that time Editor of the Daily Advertiser', lived in Bolt Court.

1134.—My guess is that 'your Son' is the 'young adventurer' of 367, who went to seek his fortune in India, and that J's enclosures were letters from Sir Robert Chambers and his wife.

1136. n.d. 〈? Sir John〉 Miller.

University of Texas (draft).—

Sir
    The kind attention which you pay to my requests encourages me to repeat them; and the activity with which you have solicited the affair makes me hope for success. I therefore trouble you once again.

From the answer which you gave me, that the Riding Master's office must not be made a sinecure, and from Lord Mansfield's doubt of the sufficiency of the fund, I collect that both You and He consider the intended riding house, as a School endowed with a salary, which will require a large sum for its foundation, and may be afterwards neglected.

This is not what either the Heads of the Colleges which have been consulted, intend, nor what Mr Carter or his friends have ever desired. His petition is that he may 〈be〉 enabled to profess horsemanship in Oxford, at such prices and under such regulations as shall be fixed by the Magistrates of the University.

This proposal has been made and been approved, nor is any thing wanting to the completion of the Scheme but a proper building. Of the building requisite this estimate has been given by one that is willing to undertake it.

For the Ridinghouse—	450–0–0	
the stable	125–0–0	
A house for the Master	300–0–0	

The sum required, you see, Sir, is not very large, and yet it is sufficient. The Master will have the means of exercising his art, and his success will be the effect of his own abilities and behaviour.

Lady Miller, I believe, will forgive me, if I exhort her upon this occasion to add her solicitation to that of Sir
Yr

1136.—The subject of this letter is the affair of Carter. It was perhaps written for Thrale. The Thrales were acquainted with the celebrated Lady Miller of Batheaston at about the appropriate date (*Tb* 229). I do not know why those Millers should be interested in Carter; but I have not found a better candidate. For J's acquaintance with M. see Campbell's diary for 5 April '75 (ed. Clifford 1948, 72).

1137. Thursday. Hannah More.

Folger Library.—

Mr Johnson will wait on Miss Moore to morrow, about seven in the evening. Thursday

1138. Friday. Hannah More.

Address: To Miss Moore.
John Grant, Catalogue March 1931.—

Madam
I will wait on Mrs Garrick and you on friday, it was by mere forgetfulness, not inadvertence, that I made an improper appointment before. I am Madam Your most humble servant
Friday   Sam: Johnson

1139. n.d. Hannah More.

Edward Howard, Manchester, Catalogue 114 (1897).—Abstract in catalogue.

'Mentions Mr. Boswell, General Paoli, Mrs. Garrick.'

1140. n.d. ⟨John Mudge.⟩

Not traced.—Boswell 1791, ii. 212, an extract (Hill iii. 266, overlooked in 1892). I find, too late for excision, that this is a mare's nest; see iii. 68.

'I have, in my large and various collections of his writings, a letter to an eminent friend, in which he expresses himself thus:'

My god-son called on me lately. He is weary, and rationally weary, of a military life. If you can place him in some other state, I think you may increase his happiness, and secure his virtue. A soldier's time is passed in distress and danger, or in idleness and corruption.

1140.—This fragment raises two problems: who was the 'eminent friend', and who the godson. Dr. Powell remarked that 'eminent friend' usually means Burke (L ii. 222 n. 4, iii. 519). There are difficulties in making this identification here: (1) if JB had possessed a letter from J to Burke he would have printed it complete, and with flourish of trumpets; unless indeed Burke forbade; (2) there seems to be no evidence that JB ever applied to Burke, as he did to many, for letters, and there is evidence that some of Burke's papers were destroyed at his death—not very many letters to him have, I believe, survived; possibly JB did not ask, knowing it useless. Dr. Powell is now satisfied that J's eminent friend was John Mudge, brother of

1141. Friday. John Nichols.

British Museum.—

Mr Johnson is going to tea, and begs the favour of Mr Nicol's company. Friday afternoon

1142. n.d. John Nichols.

F. W. Hilles.—

Mr Johnson wishes that Mr Nichol could favour him for one hour with the Drummer, and Steele's original preface.

1143. n.d. John Nichols.

Dobell (1937).—

Mr Nicol is desire⟨d⟩ to procure the dates of Pope's Works upon the Dunciads. Mr Reed can probably supply them.

1144. n.d. The Earl of Orrery.

Adam.—

My Lord
It is, I believe, impossible for those who have the honour of your Lordship's regard to be indifferent to any thing to

Thomas M and father, '62, of a godson of J's; see 146 and 874 (iii. 67). Since the child had had time to grow 'weary of a military life', this letter may be supposed not earlier than '82.

So far as is known J had only two other godsons, the sons of Samuel Paterson and Mauritius Lowe (*L* iii. 519). The elder Lowe was a painter, and the younger Paterson hoped to become a painter.

1142.—On the verso, in a hand not J's, which as I have not seen it I may presume to be N's, is this note: 'last Sheet of Vol. 4—Sheet I i of Vol. 5 and last Sheet—last Sheet of Vol. 6.' I think I can show the relevance of one of these entries to the text of the letter. The only reference to *The Drummer* in the index to Hill's edition of the *Lives* is at the end of the Life of Addison. 'His humour . . . as Steele observes, is peculiar to himself.' This is from Steele's dedication to *The Drummer*: 'He was above all men in that talent we call humour' (I quote Bohn's 'Works' v, 1856, 151). Now in J's original *Prefaces* in ten volumes, 1779–81, the Life of Addison is in vol. v (1781). The quotation from Steele is not indeed in sheet I i of this volume, nor is it in the last sheet. But it *is* in the last sheet of the Life of Addison, K 6 recto p. 155. Perhaps then we may conclude that J made a last-minute addition at this point.

1143. 'Works' may be thought obscure. I suppose the reference is to P's successive revisions and additions.

1144.—This letter is endorsed: (1) in ink, 'Mr Saml Johnson'; (2) in pencil, 'to Lord Orrery given me by Lady Cook'; this is followed by initials which Mr. Metzdorf cannot read with certainty; they might be 'CB', but the hand is not Burney's. Mr.

which You are pleased to direct their Attention. I could not forbear this morning to review what had been said concerning Virgil's Creteus, and as I think the best way of examining a Conjecture, is to disentangle its Complication, and consider in single Propositions, I have taken the Liberty to lay down a few facts, and postulates, of which your Lordship will be pleased to consider the ultimate Result.

1 It is known that Virgil in his Eneid interwove the History of Rome, partly by Anticipation, and perhaps partly by allusion.

2 It is probable that he descended to the commemoration of facts not historical, and of private friendship. *Genus unde tibi Romane Cluenti*, shows that he took opportunities of gratifying single families.

3 It has been believed from very early times that Homer celebrated his Friends however mean and obscure such as *Tichius* the Currier and why should not Virgil be supposed to imitate his morals as well as his Poetry.

4 Such Allusions, as they are necessarily made to slight peculiarities or casual Circumstances, such as may fall in naturally with the main tenour of the Poem, must be often unintelligible to Posterity and always obscure. Thus Popes Satire on Dennis

> 'Tis well, might Critics—
> But *Appius* reddens at each word you speak.

This was clear enough for a few years after the publication of Dennis's Tragedy of *Appius* and Virginia, but is already impenetrably dark to the greater number of Readers, who are equally strangers to the real and fictitious Name.

5 If therefore evidence can be produced as may barely turn the Balance by a small weight of probability, more is not to be required, and this Probability is obtained in cases like that before us, if there be any characteristic annexed to a particular personage in a Poem which could mark out to

---

Metzdorf thinks it is 'Cook'; one hopes, of course, that it is 'Cork', Lord Orrery's other title. J's ingenious conjecture breaks down. No doubt he found Creteus in an edition of Virgil. But the true spelling is Cretheus, and Cretheus (a minor person in the *Odyssey*) has nothing to do with Crete. Atterbury identified Iapis, Aeneas' physician (*Aen*. xii. 391), with Antonius Musa, said to have cured Augustus. For the classical allusions in this letter see Index III A.

those of the Poets time, a resemblance to some one whom that Poet might be supposed willing to commemorate.

6. We are then to suppose—that Virgil was generally understood to mean real Persons by fictitious names—and that he was generally known to be the Friend of Horace.—It then remains only to be examined whether there be any circumstances in the Character of Cret⟨eus⟩ which might determine the Romans of Augustus's time to apply to Horace rather than to any other Poet.

7 When an Eminent Man is already pointed out by his Profession, when we are prepared to expect the mention of him by knowing his alliance with the Writer, any slight additional allusion to his Works is sufficient to appropriate a passage to him, which might otherwise be indifferently applied to others.

8 Virgil introduces a Poet—thus far the passage is unlimited—He strongly expresses the species of his Poetry—*numeros intendere nervis*—This confines the attention, at least leads it, to the Lyric Poets, who at Rome were always few, and of whom Horace, the chief, would naturally recur.

9 Thus far it appears that Creteus may be Horace, rather Horace than any other—if there be any allusion to the works of Horace which might still more plainly point him out, will it not follow, not only that he *may* but that he *must* be meant.

10 This allusion may be perceived in the Resemblance of *amicum Cretea Musis*, to *Musis Amicus*—*in mare Creticum*—*Musis Amicus* denominates a Poet, *Creteus Musis amicus*, points out the Poet who throws his Cares *in mare Creticum*.

11 It is luckily demonstrable that this Ode was written before we can believe it likely that Virgil had composed the ninth book of the Eneid, because it makes mention of *Tiridates's*, escape to Rome, *quid Tiridatem terreat*—which happened in the year urbis conditae,   and to which Virgil is supposed to allude in the seventh Book which he was then composing.

—Seu tendere ad Indos &c.

Augustus being suspected of intending to war upon the Parthians at the instigation of Tiridates.

12 To conjectures of this fanciful and capricious kind it cannot be expected that there should be no objection. The chief difficulty which can retard the reception of this arises from the last line—semper Equos atq—the poems of Horace being always either gay or moral rather than heroic. to this it may be answered

1 That introducing his Poet among heroes he was obliged to make him sing Songs of War.

2 That Horace has given many specimens of his abilities for Martial Subjects.

3 That Mecænas called upon Horace to write upon the Roman Wars, and that Virgil might naturally second the demand of their common patron.

4 That this is in the whole proposed only as a Conjecture a slight and uncertain Conjecture, but if the last line had given us fuller evidence, it would have almost reached to certainty.

Thus, My Lord, I have detailed the evidence as it appears to me, and really think it not less strong than that which Atterbury has offered for Iapis. But I am in less concern what your Lordship will think of the positions, than how You will judge of his (*sic*) precipitant officiousness of

My Lord, Your Lordship's most obliged and most humble servant

Fryday morning.   Sam: Johnson

1145. n.d. Thomas Percy.

Address: To the Reverend Dr Percy.
E. H. W. Meyerstein.—Hill, *JM*. ii. 441.

Sir

I have sent you home a parcel of books, and do not know that I now retain any except Gongora and Araucana. If you can spare Amadis please to return it to, Sir, Your most humble,

                                                Sam: Johnson

1145.—For J's and Percy's interest in Spanish poetry see *L* i. 49, *JM* i. 192 (J's translating Lope de Vega). Percy would be interested in Gongora's ballads. *La Araucana* is a military epic by the sixteenth-century poet Ercilla. *Amadis* is presumably *Amadis of Gaul*, a Spanish or Portuguese romance, written (as we know it) by Garcia de Montalvo in the fifteenth century.

1146. 24 Jan. n.y. John Perkins.

Address: To Mr Perkins.

O. T. Perkins.—

Dear Sir   Jan 24.

I am sorry for You all, and shall hope soon to see You all well, when You come, allow yourselves time for talk and tea, else I shall be discontented.

I am, dear Sir Your most humble Servant

Sam: Johnson

My compliments to Mrs Perkins

1147. n.d. John Perkins.

Address: To Mr Perkins.

O. T. Perkins.—

Sir

I have sent a receipt for the interest.[1] I have a draught of 200£ upon the house when shall I bring it? I am

Sir Your most humble Servant

Sam: Johnson

1148. 3 Feb. n.y. John Perkins.

O. T. Perkins.—

Mr Johnson expected Master Perkins's[1] yesterday, and supposes there was some mistake in the message. He begs the favour of seeing them to day, or as soon as is convenient to them.

Febr. 3.

1149. n.d. Frances Reynolds.

R. Colomb.—Hill, *JM*. ii. 455.

Dear Madam

This is my letter which at least I like better than yours. But take your choice, and if you like mine alter any thing that you think not ladylike.

1147.—1. On his money in the hands of Barclay and Perkins (*L* iv. 402).

1148.—1. The use of *'s* for a plural is very common, though I have read somewhere an eighteenth-century condemnation of the practice. For the whole phrase cf. 'Miss Colliers' in 793.

1149.—For J's attempts to reconcile JR and FR see 961.

I shall call at about one.

Dear Brother

I know that complainers are never welcome yet you must allow me to complain of your unkindness, because it lies heavy at my heart, and because I am not conscious that I ever deserved it. I have not perhaps been always careful enough to please but you can charge me, and I can charge myself, with no offence which a Brother may not forgive.

If you ask me what I suffer from you, I can answer that I suffer too much in the loss of your notice; but to that is added the neglect of the world which is the consequence of yours.

If you ask what will satisfy me, I shall be satisfied with such a degree of attention when I visit you, as may set me above the contempt of your servants, with your calling now and then at my lodgings, and with your inviting me from time to time with such parties as I may properly appear in. This is not much for a Sister who has at least done you no harm, and this I hope you will promise by your answer to this letter; for a refusal will give me more pain than you can desire or intend to inflict.
                                                    I am &c.

1150. n.d. Frances Reynolds.

Address: To Mrs Reynolds.
Society of Antiquaries ('Dr Johnson believe in March 83').—

Dear Madam

I have not been at Mrs Thrales since I saw You, and therefore have not the papers. I am going to day.

For saturday I have engaged company. Please to let it alone to the saturday following, or some other day. I am Madam Your most &c
                                                    Sam: Johnson

1151. n.d. Frances Reynolds.

Address: To Mrs Reynolds
R. Colomb.—

Mr Johnson will wait ⟨on⟩ dear Miss Reynolds in about two hours. Bolt court, 2 in the afternoon.

1152. 14 Aug. n.y. Joshua Reynolds.

F. W. Hilles.—

Mr Johnson hopes that Sir Joshua Reynolds will do this little book the honour of reading it, and that he will then return it. Aug. 14

1153. 25 Apr. n.y. Francesco Sastres.

Address: Apr. 26. morning To Mr Sastres at Mr —— Bookseller in Mortimer Street Oxford Road. *Postmark*: (penny post) illegible. Huntington.—

Sir

I am very much displeased with myself for my negligence on Monday. I had totally forgotten my engagement to You and Mr ⟨   ⟩ for which I desire you to make my apology to Mr ⟨   ⟩,[1] and tell him that if he will give me leave to repay his visit, I will take the first opportunity of waiting on him.

I am Sir, Your most humble Servant
April 25.   Sam: Johnson

1154. n.d. Anna Maria Smart (Dublin).

Not traced.—Smart's *Poems* 1791, i. xxi; Boswell 1799, iv. 377, extract (iv. 358, overlooked by Hill in *Letters*).

Madam

To enumerate the causes that have hindered me from answering your letter would be of no use; be assured that disrespect had no part in the delay. I have been always glad to hear of you, and have not neglected to enquire after you. I am not surprised to hear that you are not much delighted with Ireland. To one that has passed so many years in the pleasures and opulence of London, there are few places that

1153.—1. The name is ruthlessly erased. For J's mistake—he should have written Margaret Street—see 998, which suggests that this letter belongs to '84. But see 778.1; I am guilty of duplication.

1154.—The text is suspicious in some minutiae. J probably wrote 'conveniencies', 'splendour', 'I wish it were in my power', and 'do not use me'.

can give much delight; but we can never unite all conveniences in any sphere; and must only consider which has
the most good in the whole, or more properly which has the
least evil. You have gone at the worst time; the splendor
of Dublin is only to be seen in a parliament winter; and even
then matters will be but little mended. I think, Madam, you
may look upon your expedition as a proper preparation to the
voyage which we have often talked of. Dublin, though a
place much worse than London, is not so bad as Iceland.[1]
You will now be hardened to all from the sight of poverty,
and will be qualified to lead us forward, when we shrink at
rueful spectacles of smoaky cottages and ragged inhabitants.
One advantage is also to be gained from the sight of poor
countries; we learn to know the comforts of our own. I wish,
however, it was in my power to make Ireland please you
better; and whatever is in my power you may always command. I shall be glad to hear from you the history of your
management; whether you have a house or a shop,[2] and
what companions you have found; let me know every good
and every evil that befalls you. I must insist that you don't
use me as I have used you, for we must not copy the faults
of our friends: for my part I intend to amend mine, and for
the future to tell you more frequently that I am, &c.

Sam. Johnson

1155. Thursday (no month or year). John Taylor.

Sotheby 31 March 1875 (not seen).

1156. n.d. John Taylor.

'Sale catalogue of Major Ross, 6 June 1888' (not seen).—Description
in catalogue.

'Knows not what to think of his affair with Mr. Broderie. Advises him to
write again.'

1154.—1. For 'talk of his going to Iceland' see L i. 242, iii. 455.
2. This need not mean that J supposed Mrs. S possibly a shopkeeper. People of
fashion (e.g. BL) often lodged over a shop.
1156.—I can make nothing of 'Broderie'; possibly J wrote 'Broderic' i.e. Brodrick;
but I know of no Brodrick connected with JT.

1157. n.d. ⟨? Thomas⟩ Warton.

Address (defective): Rev^d . . . Warton.
Morgan Library (date perhaps removed).—

Dear Sir
    I wish you had given me notice a little sooner before I had parcelled out the day, but I will come to you if I can, and I believe I can. I am Dear Sir &c   Sam: Johnson

1157.1. Monday. Thomas Warton (Oxford).

Address: to the Rev^d Mr Warton.
Trinity College.—

Sir
    I beg the favour of you when you sued for your books not to let the table be forgotten. Make my compliments to your Brother and do not forget
                                    Your affectionate
Monday Night   Sam: Johnson

1158. Wed. (no month or year). ⟨? Charles Wesley⟩.
Note of source mislaid.

Sir
    I beg that you, and Mrs. and Miss Wesley, will dine with your brother and Mrs. Hall, at my house in Bolt Court, Fleet Street, to-morrow. That I have not sent sooner, if you knew the disordered state of my health, you could easily forgive me. I am, Sir, your most humble servant,
Wednesday   Sam: Johnson

1157.—I conjecture that this note was to Thomas Warton and was written at O'd. But it might be to either brother when in L'n.

1157.1—This document was found in the Warton papers late in 1951. A pencil note by John Wilson, President of Trinity 1850–66, connects it with 'Kettell Hall' and J's 'first visit to Oxford in 1754'.

LETTERS TO UNNAMED CORRESPONDENTS

1170. Friday.

Rosenbach Co. (1925).—

I have not yet seen the Doctor, but will have his help to morrow, for I have no news to write at which my friends can rejoice.
Fryday night.

1171. 19 Aug. n.y. ———.

A. P. Trotter.—

Mr Johnson is this day engaged to the Bishop of Dromore. To refuse invitations from great friends is very vexatious. Do not think it perverseness in, dear Madam,
Aug. 19.

1172. n.d. ———.

A. B. Burney (defective).—

only help, for she¹ would see no physical man. Mrs Gastrel is brisk and merry. Since I was at Lichfield last time three of my old acquaintances are dead. This is frightful.

1173. Ashbourne. W. 21 July '84. ———.

See 1172.

Madam,

Your most humble Servant

Ashbourne, July 21. 1784   Sam: Johnson

1174. n.d. ———.

Morgan Library.—

My eye tells me that he will work no longer.

1172.—This fragment and the next are pasted to the covers of a copy of the sixth edition of the Dictionary, one in each volume. There is no other evidence to suppose them parts of the same letter, and I do not think of any woman to whom, in July '84, I would report on Miss Aston's illness. The first piece must, however, belong to the summer or autumn of '84, for the 'three acquaintances' are clearly the 'three friends' of 995.

1. 'she' is Mrs. Gastrell's sister, Elizabeth Aston.

APPENDIXES

Note. These appendixes were completed before the transference of the Boswell papers (Malahide and Fettercairn) to Yale and of the Johnson MSS. (Adam and Fettercairn) to the Hyde collection.

APPENDIX B

THE JOHNSON–BOSWELL CORRESPONDENCE

1. For the decision to exclude JB's letters to J from this edition, which includes HLT's, I had three reasons. (1) They are readily accessible to any probable reader of this book. (2) Of their total content only a fraction is strictly relevant. JB. wrote to J 24 June '74 (*L* ii. 279) 'Neither can I prevail with you to *answer* my letters, though you honour me with *returns*'. Again, 29 Sept. '77 (*L* iii. 209) 'I have observed, that unless upon very serious occasions, your letters to me are not *answers* to those which I write'. (3) The saving in space is substantial, though I have had to quote freely in my notes.

2. Since, however, the evidence for their correspondence is complicated, and in part not readily accessible, it seemed worth while to offer a conspectus in the form of a calendar.

3. *J's letters to JB*. With three exceptions (355, 550.1, 973) these have not been found. Following the usual practice of the age, JB as a rule sent the originals of J's letters to the printer.[1] Accordingly, in the copy for the *Life*, the printer is directed to 'take in' J's letters and other documents in their places. But when the manuscript of the *Life* was found at Malahide, it contained no letters. The inference is that when the manuscript came back to him, JB took out the letters and kept them apart. That is why, though Professor Abbott found at Fettercairn 120 of J's letters printed in the *Life* (only one, alas, of those to JB), he found no other part of the copy.

It was JB's practice to record in his journals and registers the date of the receipt of J's letters. That record is for various reasons incomplete. But JB nowhere records the receipt of a letter that is not recorded in the *Life*. I inferred (in *RES* xviii. 71, July 1942, 323) that he kept all J's letters and printed them all in whole or in part in the *Life*. (This does not hold of the 'cards or notes' in the third person mentioned in *L* ii. 332.)

JB did not print *all* of all J's letters. He frequently indicates lacunae. Whether he shows omission wherever he omits, we cannot know unless the originals are recovered. But I am confident that there is no deliberate concealment of a suppression.

For the integrity of JB's text of J's letters in general, see Appendix E. In one case (378) a suppressed passage is supplied by JB's journal; in

---

[1] On some of them JB wrote the footnotes that were printed in the *Life*. The latest find at Malahide, however, includes some *copies* of letters from J to JB. See below, p. 277.

another (185) a sentence suppressed in the manuscript of the *Life* is supplied by JB's copy.

When the interval between J's dates and JB's record of receipt is not four days, which it should be for London–Edinburgh letters, one or both dates *may* be wrong. But usually there is a more innocent explanation. Thus 515, dated 3 May '77, is recorded as received 9 May. Since 3 May was a Saturday, it is likely that this letter was posted on Monday 5 May.

4. *JB's letters to J.* The evidence is more intricate. JB recovered most of the originals[1] in '84, and it was his usual practice—not uncommon in his day—to make copies at the time of writing (*L* ii. 2). With a few exceptions (see '72, '77, '79, '82) both originals and copies have disappeared. We have, however, a great deal of information: (1) The *Life* includes many quotations or descriptions. (2) The published journals add not a few picturesque details. (3) Dr. Pottle has sent me extracts from JB's unpublished rough notes, and from the unpublished 'Register of letters written and received', covering, with gaps, Aug. '82–Oct. '90. (4) The Fettercairn journals (Abbott, 1361–2) are still in part unpublished. These are the journals for '62–3 and for Mar.–May '78. (5) The Fettercairn Register (in two quarto volumes, with some loose leaves inserted) is of two kinds. From June '69 to the end of '75 only the correspondents' names and the dates are recorded. Thereafter, to the end of the Register (Aug. '82) JB has almost always added a summary of the contents of each letter. The Register was not always kept up; for '80 and '81 it is fragmentary. In other years there are indications of failure in frequent entries out of place ('ommitted', &c.), and unrevealed lacunae that can be inferred. Thus J's letter 457, 24 Feb. '76, is not recorded; this is explained by the fact that the *Received* column contains no entries between 27 Feb. and 4 Mar. I indicate these assumed lacunae by the note 'Register fails'.

In 1948 I owed to Col. Isham's generosity photostats or collations of a number of copies of J's letters, made by or for JB (and in the latter case sometimes corrected by JB). These came from the latest find at Malahide. They include copies of seven letters from J to JB: 163, 181, 185, 222, 435, 475, 575. It is clear that JB sent to the printer sometimes the originals of J's letters to himself, sometimes copies of them. On the same piece of paper which contains a copy of 435 (not in JB's hand, but corrected by him) he has written these directions:

'Take in his of 27 August, leaving out last line page first . . . to the end of the paragraph.'
'Take in his of 30 August.'
'These two 27 and 30 August are attached to this leaf.'

[1] 'He kept the greater part of mine very carefully.' *L* ii. 2.

From this it appears that the originals of 431 (a passage omitted) and 432.1 (doubtless complete) were sent to the printer, whereas 435 was copied (a passage omitted). Why JB copied *any* of those letters is not clear to me. In general he sent the originals of J's letters to the printer if he could. His exception to this practice, in the case of J's letters to himself, might be due to veneration for the august documents; but then why not copy them all? or it might be due to reluctance to submit suppressed passages to the printer's eye.

The results of this discovery are disappointing; only in one letter (185) do we acquire the text of a sentence not printed in the *Life*.

5. In the calendar following I start from JB's letters, because in general J did not write unless he had a letter to 'answer'. It should be presumed, unless a place is named, that the letters were written from Edinburgh to London (or Southwark or Streatham) and vice versa. On the left, accordingly, I give:

1. References to *Life* if a letter is there mentioned.
2. Date of time and (except as above) place.
3. A note of any salient description in *Life* or journals, &c. (with reference to *BP*, &c.); and a note whether a letter purports to be complete in *Life*, or not.
4. Information from the Registers.

The information on the right, for J's letters, is similar; but, since the letters are printed in full, is briefer. The date in brackets is that of the receipt of the letter, if recorded by JB, and is followed by a reference to *BP* or a register. (The normal course of post between London and Edinburgh was four days. See above, p. 277.)

JB TO J	J TO JB
1763	1763
i. 473. Autumn. Utrecht.	163 = i. 473. Th. 8 Dec. To Utrecht.
The Life describes two letters. The Utrecht journal was lost in JB's lifetime.	(Wed. 14 Dec.; JB wrote an unpublished memorandum 15 Dec.: 'You was indeed a great man yesterday. You received letters from Lord Auchinleck, Mr. Samuel Johnson, Sir David Dalrymple.') A copy is in Col. Isham's collection; see i. 428.
JB's unpublished memoranda for autumn '63 contain several self-admonitions about letters to J. On 6 Oct. he wrote to himself 'This letter to Mr. Johnson is a terrible affair. Don't take any more time to it. But either send him a short substantial one, or copy out the large one; 'tis natural tho' rude. He will like it, & you can correct your copy & make it very pretty; for there are fine, strong, lively passages in it.	

Copy out today the first business
you do. Then lay the copy by, not
to be looked at for a long time, &
seal the letter comfortable, & send it
off. You'll never have such a task
again.' This was no doubt the second
of the two letters above.

i. 475. Tu. 20 Dec. The Hague.

JB in *L* gives an undated extract from
'one of my letters'. This we can
identify from his unpublished
memoranda: 20 Dec. 'Yesterday
you . . . wrote . . . a noble letter to
Mr. Johnson.' 21 Dec. 'Yesterday
you . . . wrote your letter cleverly to
Mr. Johnson.' But see below, 1764.

1764

? Mar.

JB's unpublished memoranda: 5 Mar.
'finish Johnson's letter'. 2 Apr. 'Get
Japix'. The reference to Japix may
suggest that the fragment above
(*L* i. 475) belongs in fact to '64, or
that JB finished it in '63 but delayed
sending it. But JB may have wanted
a second copy of the book for his
own use.

Th. 9 Aug. Brunswick.

'I sent forth my Imagination to the
Inner Temple' *BP* iii. 49. Not in
Life.

? Aug.

JB's unpublished memoranda 10–21
Aug. frequently exhort him to
write: 21 Aug. 'This day finish lett.
to Johnson.' But there is no proof
that any letter was sent.

iii. 122. Su. 30 Sept. (but sent 23 June
'77). From Wittenberg.

Complete in *Life*. JB in an unpublished memorandum 1 Oct.
writes 'Yesterday . . . was in true
solemn humour, kneeled, & lay at
length on the tomb of Melancthon
& wrote to Mr. Samuel Johnson.'
In his published journal (*BP* iii.
109): 'I shall not send it till I see if
he gives a favourable Answer to my
two last.'

1765

ii. 2. Nov. Corte.
Quoted in *Life*. Not in *BP*. J replied in 181.

1766

ii. 20. Summer.
JB quotes the first of two letters and mentions the second. Neither availed to 'move his indolence'; but when JB sent J a copy of his legal thesis, J replied in 185. There is no journal for this period.

ii. 22. Th. 6 Nov. Auchinleck.
Incomplete in *Life*. No journal.

1766

181 = ii. 3. Tu. 14 Jan. To Paris (21 Jan., vii. 60). JB's copy is in the Isham collection; see i. 428.

185 = ii. 20. Th. 21 Aug. Incomplete. JB's copy in the Isham collection restores the suppressed sentence; see my text, and i. 428.

1768

ii. 58. Tu. 26 Apr. London to Oxford.
Incomplete in *Life*, not mentioned in journal.

1768

200 = ii. 58. W. 23 (? F. 25) May. From Oxford.
Forwarded to JB in London from Edinburgh (vii. 169). (JB notes, *L* ii. 46, that this was J's first letter since 185).

1769

(JB's Register begins in June)

Tu. 5 Sept. Oxford to Brighthelmstone.
Not in *Life*. Recorded in journal, *BP* viii. 93, and in Register (6 Sept.). In an unpublished memorandum, 5 Sept.: 'Write Mr. Johnson from Oxford'. The wording of *L* ii. 68, 'having informed him that I was going to be married in a few months' may seem to suggest an earlier unrecorded letter. JB was married 25 Nov. He wrote to some of his friends, announcing the event, about the middle of August. But there is no letter to J in the Register before that of 5 (or 6) Sept.

Th. 14 Sept., Register. Not in *Life*. Presumably from London to Brighton, for J does not seem to have returned to London much before 30 Sept. (See *L* ii. 71–3, and letter 223, where note 'now'.) JB's letter may have been a mere notification of his impatience to meet J.

1769

222 = ii. 70. Sa. 9 Sept. Brighton to London.
(11 Sept., viii. 106 and Register.) JB's copy is in the Isham collection; see i. 429.

ii. **107.** F. 27 Oct. London, 'a note'.
Quoted in *Life*. No journal. Not in
Register.

ii. **110.** W. 8 or Th. 9 Nov. London to
Streatham.
Described in *Life*. No journal. Not in
Register.

1770

[ii. **116.** 'During this year there was a
total cessation of all correspondence
. . . merely from procrastination.']

1771

ii. **139.** Th. 18 Apr.
Incomplete in *Life*. No journal.
Noted in Register.

ii. **141.** Sa. 27 July.
Complete in *Life*. No journal. Noted
in Register.

ii. **142.** Oct.
Described in *Life*. No journal.
17 Oct., Register.

1772

ii. **144.** Tu. 3 Mar.
Incomplete in Life. Holograph copy
in Adam Collection (Tinker 111).
Register fails.

ii. **201.** Summer.
'I renewed my solicitations that Dr.
Johnson would this year accomplish
his long-intended visit in Scotland.'
This seems to describe a letter,
rather than a parting injunction by
JB before he left London early in
May. J's 276 reads like a prompt
reply. No journal. The Register
records a letter of 16 July.

ii. **203.** Tu. 25 Dec.
Incomplete in *Life*. No journal.
26 Dec., Register. This is no doubt
the 'kind letter' answered in 295.

1773

? Mar. J to HLT 25 Mar. (304): 'Did
not I tell you that I thought, I had

225 = ii. **110.** Th. 9 Nov. Streatham
to London.
(No journal. Register fails after
8 Nov.)

1771

250 = ii. **140** Th. 20 June. (24 June,
Register.)

1772

274 = ii. **145.** Su. 15 Mar. (ix. 20,
Register fails.)

276 = ii. **201.** M. 31 Aug. Incomplete.
(4 Sept., Register.)

1773

295 = ii. **204.** W. 24 Feb. (3 Mar.,
Register. Belated?)

written to Boswel? he has answered my letter.' J's letter was no doubt 295. JB does not mention his (which no doubt announced his coming to London; he arrived 2 Apr.) in *Life* or in journal. Not in Register.

ii. 264. Sa. 29 May.

Described in *Life*. No journal. This is no doubt the '1 June' of Register.

ii. 265. Late July.

Described in *Life*; JB wrote that the Court rose 12 Aug. The journal May–Aug., a small fragment, is unpublished. This is no doubt the '29 July' of Register. J replied in 315.

ii. 269. Th. 2 Dec.

Incomplete in *Life*. No journal. Noted in Register.

ii. 270. Sa. 18 Dec.

Incomplete in *Life*. No journal. 20 Dec., Register.

313 = ii. 264. M. 5 July. (10 July, Register.)

314 = ii. 265. Tu. 3 Aug. (7 Aug., Register.)

315 = ii. 266. Tu. 3 Aug. (7 Aug., Register.)

317 = ii. 266. W. 11 Aug. Newcastle. (13 Aug., Register.)

319 = ii. 266. Sa. 14 Aug. In Edinburgh.

340 = ii. 268. Sa. 27 Nov. (1 Dec., Register.)

1774

? late Feb. or 1 Mar.

J in 348 asks JB to 'return my thanks to Dr. Webster' for his 'informations'. This suggests that W had not written direct to J, and that we must assume an unrecorded letter from JB.

ii. 275. Sa. 5 Mar.

Described in *Life*. Noted in Register. The journal here is a fragment, not published. J replied in 352.

ii. 278. Th. 12 May.

Presumably complete in *Life* as to text, but without subscription. Not in journal. 13 May, Register.

? May or June.

J in 357 writes 'Of your second daughter you certainly gave the account yourself, though you have forgotten it'. Euphemia was born 20 May. This suggests an unrecorded letter from JB between those of 12 May and 24 June.

1774

343 = ii. 271. Sa. 29 Jan. (4 Feb., Register (29 Jan. = Sat.).)

344 = ii. 272. M. 7 Feb. (14 Feb., Register, ? belated.)

348 = ii. 274. Sa. 5 Mar. (9 Mar., Register.)

352 = ii. 276. *circa* 19 Mar. (23 Mar., Register.)

354 = ii. 277. Tu. 10 May. (14 May, Register.)

ii. 279. M. 24 or Tu. 25 June.

Presumably complete in *Life* as to text, but again no subscription. Not in journal. The change of date in *Life*, from 25 June (1791) to 24 June (1793) may be mere accident. The letter is presumably that dated 27 June in the Register.

ii. 283. Tu. 30 Aug.

Incomplete in *Life*. Not in journal. Presumably the '3 Sept.' of Register; the letter was a long one. The sentence quoted by JB in a note, *L* ii. 285 (his appeal to J to interpose in favour of John Reid) belongs either to this letter or to an unrecorded letter. J replied belatedly in 360.

ii. 284. F. 16 Sept. Incomplete in *Life*. In his journal 19 Jan. '75 (*BP* x. 86) JB notes that he had promised J that he 'would not let a soul see it [an early copy of the *Journey*] till Mr. Strahan's cargo was arrived'. This promise was probably part of this letter, or of a later letter; for in his letter of 19 Jan. '75 he writes 'I really did ask the favour twice'. The Register is blank between 12 and 22 Sept.

ii. 288. ? Late Sept. or Oct.

JB says here that he had told J of Col's death (25 Sept.) before he received 362. This suggests an unrecorded letter. This, or a later letter, is that quoted by JB at ii. 288, n. 2. Not in Register.

1775

ii. 290. Th. 19 Jan.

Incomplete in *Life*. Recorded in journal, *BP* x. 86, and in Register.

ii. 293. F. 27 Jan. ii. **295.** Th. 2 Feb. ii. **308.** Sa. 18 Feb.

Incomplete in *Life*. Not in journal. But 19 Jan. JB had noted 'My register of *Letters Written and Received* makes it unnecessary' (*BP* x. 86). All three dates are confirmed by the Register.

355. F. 27 May. Not in *Life* or Register. See note.

356 = ii. **278.** Tu. 21 June. (25 June, ix. 28 and Register.)

357 = ii. **279.** M. 4 July. (9 July, ix. 138 and Register.)

360 = ii. **284.** Sa. 1 Oct. (5 Oct., x. 13 and Register.)

362 = ii. **287.** Th. 27 Oct. (4 Nov., Register, ? belated.)

363 = ii. **288.** Sa. 26 Nov. (30 Nov., Register.)

1775

371 = ii. **290.** Sa. 14 Jan. (18 Jan., x. 85 and Register.)

374 = ii. **292.** Sa. 21 Jan. (25 Jan., x. 88 and Register.)

375 = ii. **294.** Sa. 28 Jan. (1 Feb., Register.)

378 = ii. **296.** Tu. 7 Feb. (11 Feb., x. 95 and Register.)

380 = ii. **309.** Sa. 25 Feb. (1 Mar., Register.)

iii. 122. Sa. 22 Apr., not sent until June '77.

Wilton. Complete in *Life*. Not in journal. The covering letter, dated 9 June 1777, in *Life* iii. 116, is a very long one; it is the '12 June' of the Register for '77.

ii. 380.

Extracts from three letters, n.d. Not in JB's short 'Review of my Life during the Summer Session 1775', *BP* x. 227. The Register records letters of 2 and 11 June, 26 July (these are no doubt the 'three letters' written 'after my return to Scotland' late in May), 22 Aug., 6 and 23 Sept. The last three are not in *Life* or journal.

ii. 386. Tu 24 Oct.

Complete in *Life*. Not in journal. 26 Oct., Register.

ii. 406. Tu. 5 Dec.

Complete in *Life*. Not in journal. Noted in Register.

ii. 410. M. 18 Dec.

Quoted in *Life*. Journal 18 Dec.: 'I wrote to him this evening and to Mr. Thrale in case of his being ill.' *BP* ix. 42. Noted in Register.

1776

From this point the Register gives summaries.

Tu. 2–Th. 4 Jan. Journal: 'In the afternoon (2 Jan.) I wrote a long, serious, and earnest letter to Dr. Johnson upon the subject of the settlement of our Estate . . . I resolved to write a Postscript still stronger.' 'I wrote [4 Jan.] a Postscript to my Letter.' 4 Jan. he notes that the letter and Postscript 'made three gilt sheets' *BP* xi. 56–7, 60, 61. Merely mentioned in *Life* (ii. 415), where he records 'wrote at full length'; he preferred to give a fresh (and doubtless briefer) 'state of the question' (ii. 413). 5 Jan., Register.

ii. 422. Th. 4 Jan. 'My Wife wrote also.' J refers to her letter in 457.

398 = ii. 379. Sa. 27 May. (31 May Register.)

431 = ii. 381. Sa. 27 Aug. Incomplete. (Register fails.)

432.1 = ii. 384. W. 30 Aug. (5 Sept., Register.)

435 = ii. 384. Th. 14 Sept. Incomplete. (18 Sept., Register.) JB's copy is in the Isham collection; my collator noted no variant.

438 = ii. 387. Th. 16 Nov. (25 Nov., Register; but the entries preceding and following are both 20 Nov., so 25 is no doubt a slip.)

446 = ii. 411. Sa. 23 Dec. (27 Dec., x. 50 and Register.)

1776

447 = ii. 412. W. 10 Jan. (16 Jan., xi. 73 and Register.)

448 = ii. 415. M. 15 Jan. (20 Jan., xi. 75 and Register.)

ii. 419. Tu. 30 Jan.
Mentioned in *Life* and in journal, *BP* xi. 83. Noted in Register.

ii. 422. Tu. 20 Feb.
Quoted in *Life* and described in journal, *BP* xi. 102. Noted in Register.

ii. 423. Th. 29 Feb.
Described in *Life* (where the date 20 Feb. is a slip, or more probably a misprint) and in journal, *BP* xi. 108. Register fails.

Sa. 9 Mar. Journal: 'I wrote to him begging that he might not be from London when I arrived' *BP* xi. 118. Not in *Life*. If the date 9 Mar. is correct, J could not have had this letter when he wrote 462 on 12 Mar.; but it is not necessary to suppose 462 an answer to this; he might refer to JB's of 29 Feb. Register again fails.

W. 10 Apr. Journal: 'I had called at Dr. Johnson's with a letter to defend myself against his severity. He was gone. I found him at Mr. Thrale's, where we were to dine' *BP* xi. 233. Not in *Life*. Perhaps the letter was not delivered; the journal, which might have enlightened us, is defective. Not in Register.

iii. 44. Sa. 20 Apr.
JB mentions that he wrote from London to J at Bath and received 475 in reply. Not in journal; but there is a gap 24–27 Apr.; by 28 Apr. JB was at Bath. Noted in Register.

W. 24 Apr. Register: 'Dr. Samuel Johnson that I had searched for the law-cases, and had not found them.'

iii. 86. Tu 25 June.
Incomplete in *Life*. Described in journal, *BP* xii. 12. Noted in Register.

iii. 89. Th. 18 July.
Incomplete in *Life*, not in journal. Noted in Register.

iii. 91. F. 30 Aug.
Incomplete in *Life*, mentioned in journal, *BP* xii. 35. (31 Aug., Register.)

450 = ii. 416. Sa. 3 Feb. (7 Feb., xi. 91 and Register.)

452 = ii. 419. F. 9 Feb. (12 Feb., xi. 96 and Register.)

454 = ii. 420. Th. 15 Feb. (19 Feb., xi. 101; Register fails.)

457 = ii. 422. Sa. 24 Feb. (28 Feb., xi. 107; Register fails.) Incomplete.

458 = ii. 423. Tu. 5 Mar. (9 Mar., xi. 118 and Register.)

462 = ii. 424. Tu. 12 Mar. Forwarded from Edinburgh. (19 Mar., Register.)

475 = iii. 44. Apr. Bath to London. (23 Apr., Register.) JB's copy is in the Isham collection; my collator noted no variant.

481 = iii. 85. Th. 16 May. To Mrs. Boswell. (xi. 291.)

493 = iii. 86. Tu. 2 July. Incomplete. (7 July, Register (7 July = Sun.).)

494 = iii. 88. Sa. 6 July. Incomplete. (11 July, Register.)

JB recording the receipt, 20 Nov., of 502, writes: 'Received a kind letter from Dr. Johnson, which consoled me, as I had not heard from him for near three months.' Since the interval between 494 and 502 exceeds four months, there may possibly have been a lost letter between them. It is more likely that JB's memory misled him.

iii. 92. M. 21 Oct.

Described in *Life.* Journal: 'I sat up rather late tonight (20 Oct.) from a kind of whim, or local attention, that I would write to Dr. Johnson and General Oglethorpe *from Auchinleck*', *BP* xii. 66. This may be the letter dated (? wrongly) 28 Oct., but not summarized, in Register.

iii. 94. Sa. 16 Nov.

Described in *Life.* Not in journal, except that JB 'wrote letters to different friends on my wife's delivery' *BP* xii. 82. Noted in Register.

502 = iii. 93. Sa. 16 Nov. (20 Nov., xii. 83 and Register.) Incomplete.

505 = iii. 94. Sa. 21 Dec. (25 Dec., xii. 105 and Register.)

1777

iii. 101. F. 14 Feb. Incomplete in *Life.*

The concluding leaf, there omitted, was found at Malahide. It no doubt survived because it had been detached. JB omitted it from the *Life* not because he had mislaid it— for he does print the subscription— but presumably because it was in part too personal. *BP* xii. 241. The letter as a whole is recorded in journal as 'finished' 17 Feb., *BP* xii. 133. 17 Feb., 'date 14th', Register.

iii. 105. M. 24 Feb.

Incomplete in *Life.* Mentioned in journal, *BP* xii. 136. Noted in Register. The summary shows the nature of the passage omitted from the Life: 'More of Sir Allan's Cause —wishing to be *settled* whether I should try my fortune in England or continue to practise at the Scotch bar, and several other topicks (copy).'

iii. 106. F. 4 Apr.

Incomplete in *Life.* Not in journal. Noted in Register.

iii. 107. Th. 24 Apr. Glasgow.

Complete in *Life.* Mentioned in journal, *BP* xii. 183, and in Register.

1777

507 = iii. 104. Tu. 18 Feb. (22 Feb., xii. 135 and Register.) Incomplete.

510 = iii. 105. Tu. 11 Mar. (18 Mar., Register. ? belated.) Incomplete.

515 = iii. 108. Sa. 3 May. (9 May, Register (3 May = Sat.).) Incomplete.

iii. 116. M. 9 June.

Incomplete in *Life*. Mentioned in journal for 7 June, *BP* xii. 196. The letter is long, and was perhaps finished 9 June or later, for the date in Register is 12 June.

iii. 120. M. 23 June.

Described in *Life*. Not in journal. Noted in Register.

iii. 126. Tu. 15 July.

Incomplete in *Life*. Not in journal. Noted in Register.

iii. 129. M. 28 July.

Incomplete in *Life*. In his journal JB records that he wrote 28 and again 29 July about his Ashbourne visit. *BP* xii. 211. The Register expands JB's summary, in the *Life*, of the parts not there quoted: 'Anxious about my Wife's bad health. That am somewhat embarrassed as to the time of our meeting as my Chief Mr. Bosville is coming to Scotland and I must attend him at Auchinleck in August. Hoping that Dr. Johnson may stay at Ashbourne till the end of September. But if he cannot I will come to him at all events.'

iii. 131.

Described in *Life* without date. This summary covers both the letters of 12 Aug. recorded in journal, *BP* xii. 216. The summaries in the Register show that the two letters, of which one was directed to Streatham, the other to Ashbourne, were to the same effect, and are to be identified with the undated letter of *Life* iii. 131. Dr. Powell was I think mistaken in dating it 29 July, which moreover disturbs the sequence, since J's of 4 Aug. immediately precedes.

Sa. 6 Sept. Not mentioned in *Life*. Recorded in journal, 5 Sept., *BP* xii. 223. Perhaps merely about the date of his visit to Ashbourne. Not in Register.

522 = iii. 124. Tu. 24 June. (Register 10 July. Seward no doubt delivered the letter in person.)

524 = iii. 120. Sa. 28 June. (2 July, Register.)

528 = iii. 127. Tu. 22 July. (Mon. 27 July, Register.)

529 = iii. 129. Tu. 22 July. To Mrs. Boswell. (See above.)

534 = iii. 130. M. 4 Aug. Oxford. (9 Aug., Register.)

540 = iii. 131. Sa. 30 Aug. Ashbourne. (3 Sept., Register (30 Aug. = Sat.).)

541 = iii. 131. M. 1 Sept. Ashbourne. (7 Sept., Register.)

iii. **132.** Tu. 9 Sept.

Incomplete in *Life*. Not in journal. Noted in Register.

iii. **209.** M. 29 Sept.

Incomplete in *Life*. Mentioned in journal, *BP* xiii. 67. Noted in Register as 'of 30 Sept.' but as sent 3 Oct.

iii. **211.** Sa. 29 Nov.

Incomplete in *Life*. Mentioned in journal, *BP* xiii. 78, and in Register.

1778

iii. **212.**

Described in *Life* as written 'about this time', that is about the date of the preceding, 29 Nov. Not in journal, but 19 Jan. he notes 'afternoon writing letters'. Since the letter gave an 'account of the decision of the *Negro cause*' on 15 Jan. '78 (Morison, *Dict. of Decisions* 14545), it was written between 15 and 20 Jan. (J replied in 568). Not in Register.

iii. **215.** Th. 8 Jan.

Incomplete in *Life*. Not in journal. 9 Jan., Register.

iii. **219.** Th. 26 Feb.

Incomplete in *Life*. Not in journal. 27 Feb., Register. The summary supplies the gist of the passage omitted in *Life*: 'proposing to be up in London for Douglas's Cause. Begging to know by return of post if he approves &c. &c.'

iii. **220.** Sa. 28 Feb.

Complete in *Life*. Mentioned in journal, *BP* xiii. 91, and in Register.

iii. **221.** Th. 12 Mar.

Complete in *Life*. Not in journal or Register; JB set out for London 13 Mar.

iii. **277.** Apr. London.

Complete in *Life*, without date. For the journal see column 2. 18 Apr., Register.

iii. **359.** 25 May. Thorpe.

Described in *Life*. Not in journal. 26 May, Register.

544 = iii. **135.** Th. 11 Sept. Ashbourne. (Register fails.)

550.1. Tu. 23 Sept. Not in *Life*. A note, when they were both at Ashbourne.

565 = iii. **210.** Tu. 25 Nov. (29 Nov., xiii. 78 and Register.)

567 = iii. **214.** Sa. 27 Dec. (31 Dec., Register.)

1778

568 = iii. **215.** Sa. 24 Jan. (28 Jan., xiii. 89 and Register.)

575 = iii. **277.** Th. 25 Apr. London. (23 Apr., Register.) JB's copy is in the Isham collection; my collator noted no variant.

[JB to J, iii. 277. The journal for Apr. '78 has many references to this letter and to 575.]

JB TO J

iii. 359. Th. 18 June.

Incomplete in *Life*. Not in journal, nor in Register.

iii. 366. Tu. 18 Aug., F. 18 Sept., F. 6 Nov.

Described in *Life*. There is no journal for 18 Aug., and for the other two dates the journal is silent. The Register records only two letters of this period, 18 Aug. 'of my late dreary dejection and of a variety of things [copy]' and 14 Nov. 'uneasy at not having heard from him &c. &c. [copy]'. These summaries are less full than the summary (of three letters) in *Life*, and do not correspond to its order. The discrepancy in the date of the last letter would be explained if we assumed that it was sent not on 6 Nov. but on Mon. 16 Nov., having been written 14 Nov. That would give J just time to write his reply 21 Nov., which reads as if written very soon after the receipt of JB's last.

1779

iii. 371. W. 22 Jan.

Described in *Life*. Mentioned in journal under 21 Jan., *BP* xiii. 194. Noted in Register (where the summary adds to that in *Life*).

iii. 371. Tu. 2 Feb.

Complete in *Life*. Mentioned in journal, *BP* xiii. 198, and in Register.

iii. 372. Tu. 23 Feb.

Described in *Life*. No journal. Noted in Register, where the summary shows that JB complained that this was his third letter since J's last (i.e. 593), and announced his coming to London in March. (J's failure to notice this in 607 is due, no doubt, to his writing in some anger and in haste.)

iii. 391. M. 26 Apr. London.

Complete in *Life*. No journal. Not in Register.

J TO JB

578 = iii. 362. F. 3 July. (8 July, Register.)

593 = iii. 368. Sa. 21 Nov. (25 Nov., Register.) Incomplete.

1779

607 = iii. 372. Sa. 13 Mar. JB arrived in London 16 Mar. J's letter is referred to in journal for that date, *BP* xiii. 210. It was returned from Edinburgh and received 22 Mar., Register.

610 = iii. 391. M. 26 Apr. To JB in London. (Register fails.)

Th. 29 Apr.

Not mentioned in *Life*, and there is a gap in the journal. But the letter is in the Malahide papers, in copy or draft, *BP* xiii. 310.

iii. 395. Sa. 17 July.

Complete in *Life*. Mentioned in journal, *BP* xiii. 270. 19 July, Register.

iii. 396. Th. 22 July.

Described in *Life*. Mentioned in journal under 19 July, *BP* xiii. 271. The letter was 'a pretty long one', and was no doubt finished 22 July. Register fails.

iii. 399. M. 20 Sept.

Described in *Life*, where JB quotes an 'added' passage. Not in the journal; but the complete text is in the Malahide papers, *BP* xiii. 312, though not the 'addition', which must have been a separate sheet. Register fails.

iii. 400. Th. 30 Sept. Leeds.

The journal of this Jaunt is lost. Noted in Register.

iii. 411. F. 22 Oct. Chester.

Complete in *Life*. No journal. 23 Oct., Register.

iii. 415. Su. 7 Nov. Carlisle.

Complete in *Life*. No journal. Noted in Register.

iii. 418. M. 22 Nov.

Described in *Life*. The original is in the possession of Prof. C. B. Tinker. J's letter 649 shows that he sent this letter to Lucy Porter. Thus it was missing from his collection, and was never returned to JB. Not in journal. 23 Nov., Register.

iii. 418. Tu. 21 Dec.

Described in *Life* together with the preceding. Not in journal. 23 Dec. 'date 21', Register.

626 = iii. 395. Tu. 13 July. (17 July, xiii. 270. Not in Register.)

628 = iii. 396. Th. 9 Sept. (13 Sept., xiii. 286. Register fails.)

639 = iii. 413. W. 27 Oct. To Chester. (30 Oct., Register.)

646 = iii. 416. Sa. 13 Nov. (19 Nov., xiv. 272; 20 Nov., Register.)

1780

iii. 418. Sa. 1 Jan. and M. 13 Mar. Described together in *Life*. Not in journal. Noted in Register.

iii. 433. Sa. 29 Apr. Complete in *Life*. Not in journal. Noted in Register.

iii. 424. W. 2 May. Described in *Life*, and in journal, *BP* xiv. 75. Noted in Register.

iii. 438. Th. 24 Aug., W. 6 Sept., Su. 1 Oct. Quoted together in *Life*. Mentioned in journal 24 Aug., *BP* xiv. 104, not under the later dates; but see the next entry, where I give also the evidence of the Register.

Th. 5 Oct. Not in *Life*. In his journal 5 Oct. JB writes 'I again wrote to Dr. Johnson to meet me at York' *BP* xiv. 128. As JB wrote the entry from 1–5 Oct. on 14 Oct., it is likely that the letters of '1 Oct.' and '5 Oct.' were the same. 1 Oct. was a Sunday. The quotation in *Life* mentions a 'third' letter, not a fourth. The Register records the letters of 24 Aug. and 6 Sept.; it has no entries for Oct.

1781

iv. 71. Feb. Described in *Life* as about Liberty and Necessity; J replied in 715. Not in journal; but JB there records, 17 Feb., that his melancholy was brought on by reading determinist philosophy; and a gap of eight pages follows. 17 Feb., Register (no summary).

iv. 136. Autumn–Winter. The *Life* describes two letters; the second, respecting Mrs. Boswell's alarming illness, must have been very late Dec. or 1 Jan., since J replied at once 5 Jan. (756). Not in journal (which is missing for 17–18 Dec.); this is the letter of Register dated 31 Dec. (no summary). The earlier letter is that dated 'Sept.' (no day) in Register (again no summary).

1780

The Register for 1780 is very faulty in respect of letters received.

655 = iii. 420. Sa. 8 Apr. (12 Apr., xiv. 62–3. Register fails.)

701 = iii. 435. M. 21 Aug. (4 Sept., forwarded to Auchinleck, xiv. 110. Register fails.)

708 = iii. 441. Tu. 17 Oct. (Register fails.)

1781

The Register for 1781 is on separate sheets and is a mere fragment.

715 = iv. 71. W. 14 Mar. (JB arrived in London 19 Mar. Not in Register.)

iv. 148. Before 19 Mar.

The *Life* describes several, probably three, letters of 'different dates', all answered in 775. Not in journal, which is incomplete for this period. *PM* records the receipt of a letter from JB on 23 Mar. The Register records two letters before 775: 25 Feb. 'that my Wife is better—affraid I shall not have a good reason for being in London this spring. Will he meet me in Cumberland &c. (copy)'; and 18 Mar. 'to the same effect' (as in a letter to Burke of the same date 'wishing for employment in London') 'as to my coming up to London at present (copy)'. J in 775 deals with Mrs. B's health, JB's proposals for a meeting, *Deformities*, and JB's hopes of employment in London.

iv. 151. F. 28 May.

Not described in *Life* except as in J's reply 3 June (785) written on the day of receipt. Not in journal, which for 16 May–9 June is only 'the bones of my life', *BP* xv. 82. For the Register see below.

iv. 153. Tu. 13 Aug.

Again not in *Life* except as acknowledged ('your kind letter') in J's (*not* 'immediate') reply 24 Aug. (801). Not in journal. The Register records three letters of the period: '30 May [date 28] in most sincere concern for his illness [copy]'; '27 June of my Wife's spitting of blood—If she shall recover, purposing to meet him in London next autumn &c &c [copy]'; '13 August uneasy at having no answer to my last letter. My Wife much better. I am now ready to meet him when and where he pleases. But beg to hear from him without delay [copy]'. J's 785 is an answer to JB's of 30 May, written on the day of receipt. It is surprising that JB did not quote or even describe a letter

756 = iv. 136. Sa. 5 Jan. (9 Jan., xv. 54 and Register.)

775 = iv. 148. Th. 28 Mar. (1 Apr., xv. 72. Register fails.)

785 = iv. 151. M. 3 June. (8 June, forwarded to Valleyfield, xv. 84. Register fails.)

801 = iv. 153. Sa. 24 Aug. (Register fails.)

The Fettercairn Register ends here and the Malahide Register begins.

803 = iv. 154. Sa. 7 Sept.

805 = iv. 155. Sa. 21 Sept. (27 Sept. at Auchinleck, xv. 125.) Incomplete. Dated in J's diary (Bodleian).

815 = iv. 156. Sa. 7 Dec. (11 Dec., xv. 138. Register fails.) Incomplete.

804 = iv. 156. Sa. 7 Dec. (Misdated Sept.) To Mrs. Boswell. See xv. 244.

which J commended for its 'earnestness and tenderness'. J's 801 answers
JB's of 13 Aug. It is surprising that
he did not answer JB's alarming
letter of 27 June, or even, in 801,
refer to it; it is possible that he did
not receive it.

iv. 153. F. 30 Aug. Auchinleck.

Described in *Life*; JB wrote to report
his father's death. Not in journal;
but JB there records that he was
'up all night . . . writing letters in
a giddy state', *BP* xv. 121. J replied
7 Sept. (803) 'I received your letters
[*sic*, if the text is sound] only this
morning.' For the Register see
below. In J's diary for '82 (Bodleian)
he seems (it is hard to read) to have
written, 7 Sept., 'Letter (sing.) from
Boswel. I wrote to Boswel'.

iv. 155. JB mentions, but does not date,
his 'next letter', to which J replies in
805, 21 Sept. The letter which it
answered was no doubt written
c. 15 Sept. *Life* iv. 155 mentions also
Mrs. B's letter, for which see note on
805 (ii. 506). The Malahide Register
(which begins after Lord A's death and
is headed 'Post Successionem') has no
letters to J for Aug. or Sept.

Tu. 1 Oct. Auchinleck.

Not in *Life* or journal, but the com-
plete text is in *BP* xv. 248, and in
Register it is noted as sent 3 Oct.
See note on 805.

A gap follows: 815 complains of JB's
silence.

1783

iv. 163. Su. 11 Jan. Auchinleck.

Register: 'Sent 14 (date 11) January
1783, Dr. Samuel Johnson, giving
him an Account of my "Winter's
Walk" at Auchinleck'. Described in
Life. Not in journal. J replied in
827.1.

Sa. 28 June.

Register: 'Sent 28 June 1783 Dr.
Samuel Johnson, anxious about his

1783

827.1 = **iv. 163.** *circa* 4 Feb. (8 Feb.,
xv. 154.) Incomplete.

861 = **iv. 231.** Th. 3 July. (7 July,
Register.)

J wrote to Q 23 Aug. that since he and
JB parted (29 May) 'he has written
twice and I have written once': i.e.
JB's of 28 June and 9 Aug., and
861.

being worse, and begging to be relieved.' JB had had the news from his brother. Not in *Life* or journal.

iv. 241. Sa. 9 Aug. Auchinleck.

Register: 'Sent 9 August 1783. Dr. Samuel Johnson, in kind concern about him; inviting him to Auchinleck; that I am dreary.' Described (presumably) in *Life*. Not in journal.

iv. 248. Sa. 18 Oct. Auchinleck.

Described in journal, *BP* xvi. 8. Register: 'Sent 19 October 1783. Dr. Samuel Johnson, of my bad spirits this Autumn, & sudden relief. Affectionate inquiries about him. Why should I not venture in London?'

iv. 248. 22 Nov.

Described in *Life*. Not in journal (which however, 21 Nov., throws light on his political aspirations). Register: 'Sent 22 November 1783. Dr. Samuel Johnson, as to Peers interfering in County Elections, & what is to be done with old horses, &c. &c.'

888 = iv. 241. Tu. 30 Sept. (10 Oct., forwarded to Auchinleck, xvi. 7.) Incomplete.

920 = iv. 248. W. 24 Dec. (31 Dec., delayed by frost, xvi. 18.)

1784

iv. 258. Th. 8 Jan.

Incomplete in *Life*. Not in journal of this date, but referred to, 17 Jan., *BP* xvi. 24. In Register.

Sa. 14 Feb.

Not in *Life* or journal. Register: 'Sent 14 Feb. 1784. Dr. Samuel Johnson (copy)'. If JB made this copy, we cannot account for the silence of the *Life* by supposing that he did not recover the original.

iv. 262. M. 23 Feb.

Described in *Life* (without date) and in Register; not in journal.

iv. 264. Tu. 9 Mar.

Register: 'Sent 9 March 1784. Dr. Samuel Johnson, of various particulars, enclosing a letter to him from my Wife.' JB's letter is not in *Life*,

1784

932 = iv. 259. W. 11 Feb. (15 Feb., Register.)

936 = iv. 261. F. 27 Feb. (2 Mar., Register.) Incomplete.

937 = iv. 262. Tu. 2 Mar. (6 Mar., Register.)

942 = iv. 264. Th. 18 Mar.

but in a footnote to 942 he mentions his wife's 'very kind letter'. Not in journal, which JB did not write up until 31 Mar.

iv. 265. F. 26 Mar. York.

Described in *Life*, where it is misdated 28 Mar. Not in journal (which shows, *BP* xvi. 46, that JB returned to Newcastle 27). Register: 'Sent 26 Mar. 1784. Dr. Samuel Johnson, of my being stopt on my way to him, &c., &c.'

? F. 30 Apr.

Register: 'Dr. Samuel Johnson from Lichfield.' The entry in the register is undated, but is followed by an entry of a letter to Dilly from Lichfield: 'I am soon to be in London.' On 27 Apr. JB was at Douglas Mill on his way to London (see the Malahide Catalogue, No. 206). If the journey was made in the same time as that of '85, he was in Lichfield 30 Apr. He reached London 5 May (*Life* iv. 271). I owe all this to Dr. Pottle. Not in *Life* or journal.

iv. 351. Su. 4 July. Lichfield.

Register: 'Sent 4 July 1784. Dr. Samuel Johnson, from Lichfield, of various particulars.' The 'various particulars' are in the *Life* (where JB accepts the false date 11 June for J's reply, see 973). No journal.

iv. 379. ? Late July, 'a letter filled with dejection and fretfulness'.

Not in journal or Register. J replied in 982. He perhaps received JB's after writing 981 on 26 July.

iv. 379. Tu. 3 Aug. To Ashbourne.

Described in *Life*, without date, as 'a letter filled with dejection'. Not in journal. Register, 3 Aug. See my note on 982.

iv. 380. ? mid-Aug. See note on 982.1.

iv. 380. 12 Nov., 19 Nov., and (?) early Dec.

In the *Life* JB writes: 'I . . . wrote to

946 = iv. 265. Tu. 30 Mar.

973 = iv. 351. Su. 11 July, misdated June. Original at Fettercairn (Abbott, p. xvii). Incomplete.

981 = iv. 348, 378–9. M. 26 July. Ashbourne. Incomplete.

982 = iv. 379. ? *c.* 5 Aug. Ashbourne. Incomplete (not in Register).

982.1 = iv. 379. *c.* 7 Aug. Ashbourne. Incomplete. For the dates of 982 and 982.1 see my notes.

1033 = iv. 380. W. 3 Nov. or F. 5 Nov. Lichfield. (11 Nov., xvi. 57.) Incomplete.

him two as kind letters as I could;
the last of which came too late to be
read by him'—which may, but need
not, mean 'after his death' 13 Dec.
(JB might learn from Barber that
his letter was not opened.) Journal:
On 12 Nov., 'callous by reiteration
of misery', JB 'wrote a short letter
to him in a kind of despair. My
valuable spouse made me keep it',
BP xvi. 57. Register: 'Sent 19
November 1784. Dr. Samuel Johnson, of my sad illness.' The journal
fails after 28 Dec., and the register,
though it seems to be complete for
Dec., records no second letter. The
first of the 'two' is doubtless *not* that
of 12 Nov., which was presumably
never sent.

Undated

ii. 307. n.d. See J's 1120.

Undated

1120 = ii. 307. See my note for a conjectural date.

APPENDIX C

THE JOHNSON-THRALE CORRESPONDENCE

THE extant letters begin in '65 and end with the rupture of July '84. The writers are on the one side J, whose letters comprise a few to HT, a large number to HLT, 33 to Q, and a few to her sisters Susan and Sophy; on the other HLT almost alone, for with the exception of two childish efforts from Q none of the girls' letters has survived.

Since, throughout the period, J was normally a member of the Thrale household in S'k, S'm, or L'n, the chief occasions of the correspondence are his absences in the Midlands or in Scotland, or theirs (her's) at Bath or B'n. The circumstances explain why, for instance, we have so many of J's letters to HLT for '73 and '75, when J was in Scotland or spent a long summer at L'd and A'n, and for '81–'83, when HLT was for the most part at Bath or B'n. In '74 on the other hand, when the Welsh tour kept them together, we have only two letters.

The use of franks has a result which I have not seen remarked, but which may be of some importance for this and other correspondences. While HT was alive and a member of Parliament, J's letters to HLT were ordinarily directed 'To Henry Thrale Esq.' Now since a letter so directed might in fact be intended for HT, it follows that he would more naturally open, and perhaps read, a letter than would a husband open a letter addressed to his wife. It was I think impracticable to address a letter 'To Mrs. Thrale' in care of HT; such a letter would not be delivered free? At least I have seen no letter so addressed. The same sort of thing holds of her letters to J, which the law required HT to address wholly in his own hand. She might indeed present them to him ready folded and sealed. The evidence suggests (see 561.1a) that in fact HT often read the letters, with his wife's approval, at least her acquiescence.

'Do you keep my letters?' J asked her in '75 (428). In '73 (330) he writes to HT 'I hope my mistress keeps all my very long letters'. The evidence positive and negative suggests that she was a faithful repository. Doubtless many notes of no lasting interest, from, for example, Bolt Court to S'm, were discarded. But it looks as if most of his letters, deserving the name, have survived. There are about 400 of them, of which about 350 are to HLT. On the other hand, it is clear that many of hers to him have perished. We have over 100; perhaps as many are lost. Now the letters show that he was the better correspondent; perhaps he wrote two letters for her one. If so, we should expect his total to be about 400. But these guesses are hardly worth recording.

J's letters to Q were, by '88, in that determined young woman's control, and unlike her sisters she declined to permit their publication. Nothing was known of them until their publication in 1932. There are thirty-three of them, from '71 to Sept. '84; not a few are lost.

In *NQ* 185.5, 28 Aug. 1943, I asked the question, Did J destroy HLT's letters? The only positive evidence is Fanny Burney's story of her interview with him on 25 Nov. '84: 'If I meet with one of her letters, I burn it instantly; I have burnt all I can find' (*Diary* 28 Nov.; ii. 328 in 1842). Hill, who was justly suspicious of the letters which Mrs. Piozzi in '88 published as Mrs. Thrale's, remarks on one of them (10 June '80) that of a letter written in great alarm and at 3 o'clock in the morning it is hardly credible that she kept a copy. He does not, I think, start the question of her having recovered the originals. We now know (C 297) that J's executors returned to her all they found. In my article in *NQ* I suggest that their dates may be significant. Whereas we have twenty-four of her letters for '73, seventeen for '75, and eleven for '80, for the two years '82 and '83 we have only seven in all. Now in those two years she and J were for the most part separated, and though there was gradual estrangement she wrote to him frequently. It looks as if he *did* destroy all he found, but was not angry enough, or not diligent enough, to probe far below the surface of his papers.

When, in his last days, he decreed a general destruction of his papers, we can hardly suppose that the preservation of her letters was accidental. We know, I think, of no other letters that survived, except his own to his wife—of which Frank confessed the later destruction—and Hill Boothby's to himself, published in 1805; she too was a woman to whom he had been deeply attached.[1] The tenderness which spared HLT's letters might conceivably lead J to destroy, as we must assume he did destroy, her daughter's; for Q's letters after the rupture must have seemed to him like an accusation.

HLT's letters to J fall into three classes: (1) A miscellaneous group from various sources: 506.2*a*, 553*a*, 662*a*, 872*a*, 887*a*, 969*a*, 970.1*a*. (2) The John Rylands Library at Manchester in 1931 acquired over one hundred originals. These I publish for the first time. (3) The Rylands Library at the same time acquired the manuscripts of the letters printed in '88. But these, with very few exceptions, are not originals, and the originals which they reproduced, or on which they

---

[1] We know that J had had these letters bound (*Account of the Life of Johnson,* 1805). It is likely enough that the volume was taken for a printed book and included (without description) in the sale of his library.

were based, are to seek.[1] (For an exception of a different kind, where we have two versions, see on 833.2a.) Now copies may be exact copies. But why should she copy? It was not the practice of the age, and she sent J's letters to the printer, though she prized them, and though her editorial labours on them, doubtless less laborious than transcription, were none the less severe. It is, I think, abundantly clear what happened. She began with the intention of sending her originals to the printer, *mutatis mutandis*. But as she warmed to her work she very soon found that the amount of editing she was impelled to practise was beyond what could be effected by interlineation.

The published letters of '88 differ widely from any originals they can be supposed to represent; they are far longer, and far more literary, than her genuine letters, and they have for the most part little relation to J's letters, and not much to J. I have not printed them. But they contain genuine elements, of which I make use in my commentary.

'My chief labour has been spent on the two volumes of correspondence published by Mrs. Piozzi.' So wrote Hill in 1892. His difficulties arose partly from the nature of J's letters to HLT, which are much more allusive than his letters to others, partly from Mrs. Piozzi's editing of them. Hill did admirable work in supplying or correcting dates and in detecting Mrs. Piozzi's occasional misplacements. But his materials were scanty indeed when compared with the mass of documents that confronts his successor. For the text he had to make the best use he could of the edition of 1788, in which many names are suppressed or reduced to an initial. For corroboration he had little except Mrs. Thrale's own published letters, which he rightly distrusted, and Baretti's notes in his copy (in the British Museum), which are far less reliable. I have been able virtually to neglect these sources, since better sources were open to me. Of the originals of the letters printed in 1788 I have seen about six-sevenths, with my own eyes or the eyes of scholars whom I could trust. These have cleared up many obscurities of 1788, and revealed not a few passages which HLP did not publish. But they have greatly increased my editorial task. Mrs. Piozzi sent the originals to the printer;[2] and that was fortunate, for a good compositor is more accurate than most copyists;

[1] For the physical character of these MSS. see C 299–301.

[2] An exception is the letters from Scotland. Some of these are so blotted as to be hardly legible. The evidence that she made copies seems decisive: the conclusions are, for the most part, intact in the extant originals, not condensed (as usually elsewhere) to 'Your, &c.'; no compositors' marks have been found in the originals; in one, 326, we should expect such marks if it had been in a printer's hand, since it forms the end of one sheet, and the beginning of another, in 1788. The point is of some interest; the copies may have been made for J's use in writing his *Journey*; if so, we may suppose that he would correct errors of transcription. The text of these letters, considering the state of some of the MSS., is surprisingly pure.

there are many misreadings, but the text is on the whole faithful. On the other hand she was not content to make her suppressions and omissions by working on the proofs, or by light erasures on the manuscripts. She was clearly afraid of leakage, and determined to conceal many words, and not a few passages, from the printers themselves. She did not cut the paper,[1] since that would have affected both sides of the leaf. But she had several methods; erasure with a pen, varying in thoroughness; 'salts of lemon';[2] pieces of paper pasted over the word or words to be concealed.

For the restoration of the text, when an original is missing, or when HLP had done her work too well, and for the explanation of some other obscurities, we now have two important witnesses: the copy which belonged to Samuel Lysons, who helped HLP with the book, and her own copy. Lysons's notes were made with the originals before him, or at least when they were fresh in his memory. His copy, moreover, includes proofs of a few letters which HLP at one time intended to include but later withdrew. The notes in her own copy were made at various times between 1803 and 1812 or 1813 and, as appears, almost without reference to the MSS. Her memory not seldom failed her, and some of her guesses are even bad; but the notes are numerous, and on the whole are valuable.

In dealing with this editorial problem I have followed a rule, though I have not observed it with rigid consistency. When a name can be read, with certainty or virtual certainty, from the MS. I have restored it without any marks in the text, and have in general ignored the restoration in my notes. HLP's initials and blanks are numerous, and often the disguise was merely formal; 'B——i' for 'Baretti' was never meant to deceive. These editorial suppressions, moreover, while they are of interest to a student of Mrs. Piozzi's mind, have nothing to do with Johnson's, though they are a part of the history of the text. I have, however, given a note where a suppression had some intrinsic interest. When a restoration depends on external evidence or on the context (a name is sometimes disguised in one place and left open in another) I have used brackets in the text and given the supplement in the notes as well. Finally, when a restoration is purely conjectural I have printed the text of 1788, adding a note.

In the way of corroborative evidence Hill had little except Fanny Burney's diaries, Mrs. Piozzi's own *Anecdotes* of 1786, and the often tantalizing scraps published by Hayward in his *Autobiography . . . of Mrs. Piozzi.* Fanny Burney is still important to an editor; the two other sources we can now almost ignore, for we have a complete and authoritative edition of *Thraliana* itself, and Mr. J. L. Clifford in his

---

[1] Except that of 408.1.   [2] C 298.

Life of HLP has drawn also on her 'Children's Book' and other unpublished diaries and letters.

Mrs. Piozzi's selection from her store was judicious; the letters she omitted are with two exceptions of little importance. The exceptions are 307.1, an enigmatic letter in French, and 970, J's first angry outburst on hearing of her second marriage. She did right, I think, to suppress both. In editing J's letters she allowed herself to make certain omissions more important than the suppressions, total or partial, of proper names which I have discussed. Most of the passages omitted concern details of sickness, childbirth, or domestic finance; some of them might have given pain or offence. There is here nothing for complaint. HLP, however, unlike JB, did not declare her omissions by dots or otherwise, so that when the original is missing we cannot be sure of the integrity of the text. All her omissions of any consequence are, I believe, recorded in my notes. Outstanding examples are the omission, in 408, of a passage in praise of JB, effected by mutilation of another letter, and the mysterious, but almost certainly unscrupulous, suppression of a date from 235.

My tentative conclusion is that we are entitled to suspect Mrs. Piozzi, as an editor of J, as often as anything appears to be intrinsically suspect, but need not go out of our way, as Hill did, to convict her of forgery. She was, I think, indifferent honest.

The table following gives the number of letters for each year (1) from HLT to J; (*a*) not published by HLP, (*b*) published by her in 1788; (2) from J to HLT.

	HLT *to* J					HLT *to* J			
	a	*b*	*Total*	J *to* HLT		*a*	*b*	*Total*	J *to* HLT
1765	..	..	..	2	1775	15	2	17	45
1766	..	..	..	..	1776	8	1	9	18
1767	..	..	..	4	1777	18	2	20	32
1768	..	..	..	12	1778	9	1	10	7
1769	..	..	..	5	1779	7	1	8	27
1770	1	1	2	10	1780	7	4	11	29
1771	4	..	4	16	1781	5	1	6	22
1772	5	..	5	15	1782	..	2	2	32
1773	18	6	24	36	1783	1	4	5	39
1774	2	..	2	2	1784	3	2	5	16

For a discussion of the quality of the text of 1788 see p. 323 below.

APPENDIX D

JOHNSON'S LETTERS TO TAYLOR

JOHN Taylor was a slow, exact, tenacious man: tenacious of his habits, his rights, his property; tenacious, too, of his friendships. How he and Johnson kept it up, across a wide gulf of temperament, is known to readers of Boswell, and is very familiar to readers of Johnson's letters. We owe to JT's fidelity the preservation of these letters, which begin in '32 and end in Oct. '84. The list below shows wide gaps of time in the early years: we have nothing between '32 and '42, nothing between '42 and '52. I have suggested[1] the probability that not many letters were lost by JT. In this I rely first on his character, next on his confession to JB that he *had* lost one letter (41), that which J wrote on the day of Mrs. J's death,[2] and lastly on his careful (though not quite impeccable) numeration of those he had preserved.

The antecedent probability that this numeration was made after the long series had been closed by J's death is enhanced by other evidence. In '87 JT included in his *Letter to Samuel Johnson, LL.D., on the Subject of a Future State* three of J's letters to him (42, 848, 951). That he at one time contemplated a fuller publication of these letters is, I think, proved by the erasure, in some of the originals, of passages thought too intimate for publication. See 17, 98, 106, 277, 461, 516. These erasures were not designed to make the MSS. unreadable; they look like a direction to a copyist or printer.

The subsequent history of the MSS., the dispersal of which began at least as early as 1861, is of little interest except to an editor or a collector. I have discussed it in *RES* xv. 57, Jan. 1939. The interest of the list that follows is hardly less limited. I print it because it gives us a close approximation to the total of the letters that were kept by JT but have not since been traced, and to their dates. It is very likely that they are somewhere extant. In addition to some fifteen letters entirely untraced there are four of which the text is not available for verification. These are 14.1, 378.1, 773, 898.1.

I give JT's number in brackets where it is inferential, and indicate the lack of one (two, &c.) letters by a gap of one (two, &c.) lines.

[1] Introductory Note, i.

[2] JT must have lost also the letter to which he replied on 1 Dec. '60 (Commins's catalogue 127 (1946), 2).

		JT
2	27 July 32	1
14.1	2 Jan. 42	[2]
17	10 Aug. ,,	3
[41	17 Mar. 52	Lost by JT]
42	18 ,, ,,	4
68	11 Apr. 55	[5]
98	31 July 56	6
106	18 Nov. ,,	7
156	13 Aug. 63	8
157	18 ,, ,,	9
158	25 ,, ,,	10
159	3 Sept. ,,	11
161	29 ,, ,,	12
165	22 May 64	13
171	15 July 65	14
175	1 Oct. ,,	15
223	5 Oct. 69	16
231	2 July 70	[17]
275	17 Apr. 72	[18]
275.1	15 Aug. ,,	[19]
277	31 ,, ,,	20
278	6 Oct. ,,	21
278.2	13 ,, ,,	22
279.1	19 ,, ,,	23
291.1	12 Dec. ,,	,,[1]
296	27 Feb. 73	24
303.1	20 Mar. ,,	[25]
312	22 June ,,	26
316	5 Aug. ,,	27
342	15 Jan. 74	28
360.1	20 Oct. ,,	30
369	22 Dec. ,,	[31]
372	14 Jan. 75	[32]
378.1	9 Feb. ,,	[33]
384.4	23 Mar. ,,	34
387	8 Apr. ,,	35
387.2	13 ,, ,,	36
398.1	27 May ,,	[37]
440	16 Nov. ,,	38
449	15 Jan. 76	41
455	17 Feb. ,,	42

		JT
461	7 Mar. 76	43
464	23 ,, ,,	44
469	4 Apr. ,,	45
473	13 ,, ,,	46
475.1	29 ,, ,,	47
492	23 June ,,	48
506.2	23 Jan. 77	51
516	3 May ,,	52
519	19 ,, ,,	53
660	20 Apr. '78';	misdated, see below2
605.1	9 Mar. 79	56
614.1	4 May ,,	57
627	3 Aug. ,,	59
635	19 Oct. ,,	60
[660	20 Apr. 80	see above]
676	6 June ,,	61
729.1	12 May 81	62
739.1	24 Sept. ,,	63
766.1	2 Mar. 82	64
767.1	14 Mar. ,,	[65]
773	22 ,, ,,	[66]
791.1	13 June ,,	[67]
793	8 July ,,	68
795	22 ,, ,,	69
797	3 Aug. ,,	70
798	12 ,, ,,	No number
799	17 ,, ,,	[71]3
806	21 Sept. ,,	[72]
807	3 Oct. ,,	73
815.1	7 Dec. ,,	75
816	9 ,, ,,	[76]
821	31 ,, ,,	77
823	16 Jan. 83	78
827	21 ,, ,,	79
848	17 June ,,	80
871	24 July ,,	81
879	3 Sept. ,,	82
882.1	20 ,, ,,	83

---

1 If Hill's note of this letter is correct, JT must have failed to number it.

2 Presumably JT when he numbered the letters was deceived by J's false date and called this 54 or 55.

3 J in his diary (Bodleian) 26 Aug. records 'Wrote to Miss Lawrence Mrs. Hervy Taylor'. Of these letters the first is 802, the second and third are lost. The numbering seems to show that JT did not keep his.

		JT				JT
885	24 Sept. 83 ⎱	[84]¹	943.1	22 Mar. 84	[94]
893	20 Oct. „ ⎰		951	12 Apr. „	95
898.1	10 Nov. „	85	965.4	8 June „	96
904	19 „ „	86	967	19 „ „	[97]
		2	968	23 „ „	98
907	22 „ „	88			
913	29 „ „	[? 89]³			
918	20 Dec. „	No number?⁴	1027.1	20 Oct. „	101
			1028	23 „ „	102
923	3 Jan. 84		1155	Thursday n.y.	—
928	24 „ „	93			

¹ Here we must assume that JT overlooked one of two letters.

² It is very unlikely that J wrote a letter between those of 19 and 22 Nov. JT's mistake?

³ Again it is unlikely that J wrote a letter between those of 22 and 29 Nov. 913 is therefore probably 89.

⁴ My evidence is not conclusive.

When, by Col. Isham's generosity, I received photostats or collations of copies of J's letters, made by or for JB, and found at Malahide, I was surprised to find that JB had copies not only of 848, on which he has noted 'see Taylor's *printed* Letters', but also of 156, a very intimate letter on JT's dispute with his wife, the publication of which he can hardly have contemplated. The copy is in Malone's hand. However he came by it, JB had no authority to publish it, and it is not in the *Life*.

THE TEXT AND ITS SOURCES

I. General

The notes following have been compiled 'in usum editorum'. I borrow Housman's phrase with a different implication. If I hint a criticism of editors of texts similar to this, it is directed not to congenital incapacity but to an erroneous assumption common to most of them. My lists disclose, moreover, the gradual progress of my own enlightenment.

Everyone has heard that ancient and medieval scribes fell into error, and it is common knowledge that up to a certain date printers were likewise fallible. But for the period that may be called modern, in which proofs were normally corrected by the author, the tacit assumption has been made that the print is right, or that if it is wrong it is idle, or imprudent, or even indecent to attempt its correction. Though the collation of extant MSS., especially in prose, seldom fails to reveal errors made by the printer and not detected by the author, a superstitious reverence for the printed word persists, and attempts at conjectural emendation are often received with apathy or impatience, sometimes with resentment.[1] Even the editors of letters[2] have too often forgotten that they are dealing with texts that, since they are posthumous, depend on the accuracy of a printer with, in most cases, some degree of editorial supervision. This latter safeguard can seldom be implicitly trusted, for it is abundantly clear that before the present century very few editors thought it their duty to compare their proofs with the originals.

[1] See the late Gavin Bone's article, in *RES* Oct. 1941, on my attempts to emend the text of *Phineas Redux*. In a friendly correspondence that accompanied this controversy Bone admitted that my original essay in Trollopian criticism had 'annoyed' him, though its guesses (many of which the holographs confirmed) were, I believe, without any taint of Bentleian arrogance.

[2] Including, I believe, virtually all editors of the *Life*.

I give below my reasons for the belief that Boswell's text of the letters is not infallible, and that Mrs. Piozzi's is seriously faulty. Scepticism, it is clear, is more amply justified in regard to the rest of our unverified texts, which depend on more occasional editors, copyists, or printers. With the exception of Boswell himself, of John Nichols, and perhaps of Malone,[1] I know of no editor whom we can trust to have been familiar with Johnson's hand and to have read it with critical diligence. Hill himself, when he edited the letters, had had no very frequent opportunities of making himself familiar with the hand.[2] Examples of corruption that, in this third or residual section of the letters, are proved by the MSS. will be found in my notes. Outstanding examples from the first and second are collected below, §§ II 4 and III.

II. The Texts of 1791 and 1793

§ 1. *Boswell's Sources; his Credibility*

A substantial part of Johnson's letters still depends on a printed source. Of our authorities in this class Boswell is the most important. He is also, apart from Nichols and some modern scholars, incomparably the best. He was necessarily innocent of the rigours of modern editorial method, and judged by the standards of his own time he was not an exact scholar; not on the plane of Percy or Dalrymple or Nichols. How far his native wit and conscience served him, how much he owed to Malone's collaboration, can only be conjectured. Even without Malone's help, which was certainly of very great value, I am confident that he would have deserved from posterity the commendation he received from Johnson,[3] as 'a faithful chronicler'.

But not even Boswell and Malone compared their proofs, word for word, with the originals. Many years ago I printed for the first time[4] a note by Boswell on the revised proofs of the *Life* which, I think, makes this probable. In letter 177 the reader[5] had queried the word 'exist'. Boswell replies: 'There is no wonder that a word in Dr. Johnson's hand-writing should be mistaken. But I wonder that I did not perceive the mistake from the sense. The word, I find, is *assist*.' The words 'from the sense' seem to imply that Boswell thought he

[1] I say perhaps, because M was not in any precise sense an editor of J's letters.
[2] Later he republished *PM* from the originals.
[3] In letter 329.
[4] In *Johnson and Boswell Revised*, 1928, 43.
[5] The corrector, good Mr. Selfe (for whom see *Johnson and Boswell Revised*, 22–34); he worked on the second proofs. The MS. was presumably returned with the first proof; if so, Selfe had no opportunity of collation. To this day the 'reader's' work is gravely vitiated by his lack of access to the author's MS.

should have done enough if he had read the proof with a wakeful eye, and was not bound to collate it with the MS.

But such indirect evidence is now of only historical interest. The discovery of the letters preserved at Fettercairn, which I have been privileged to collate, demonstrates Boswell's fallibility. The list given below, p. 320, includes, I believe, all verbal corruptions of any significance. The total of ascertained error is very small in relation to the whole. The text is in the main sound; and since Johnson's hand lends itself to misreading, it does credit to Baldwin the printer. Boswell himself, if he did not collate verbatim, was doubtless familiar with the text of the letters; either he had read them recently for the first time, or if they were to himself—or to Chesterfield, or Macpherson—had read them many times. How far the printer misread the MSS. and was corrected by Boswell cannot be determined; this would be done on the first proofs, of which only a small fragment survives.

But the absolute sum of error in the Fettercairn texts justifies a cautious scepticism in estimating the texts which we still cannot collate. We must first, however, distinguish, as best we can, between the texts of which Boswell saw the originals and those for which he himself relied on copies. He does not always draw the distinction for us; he tends to use ambiguous expressions like 'communicated'. When he makes an acknowledgement, not explicitly of a copy, it may be presumed that he had the originals. He makes none, if I am not mistaken, in respect of the letters to LP, BL, JR, or Brocklesby, all of which were found at Fettercairn, or of those to Perkins, which it is known he borrowed and returned.[1] The same is true of texts which he took from printed sources, e.g. from the magazines. When he does make an acknowledgement, he sometimes tells us that he had the original, sometimes that he had a copy. See below, the alphabetical list.

It remains to inquire how far Boswell edited his texts either by omission or by alteration. In the matter of omissions his practice seems to be impeccable; I find no evidence that he ever presented as complete a text which he had in fact abridged.[2] (For his omissions from the letters to himself see App. B.) He, of course, filled such lacunae as were due to mutilation of a MS. (see, e.g., 771) or to Johnson's inadvertences. Of editorial 'improvements' I find little trace. Possible examples are in 116 ('death' for 'end', to avoid a jingle); 117 ('well' for 'publickly', an unaccountable change ?); 135 'equal' for 'proportionate' —as unaccountable); 182 ('first appearance' for 'appearance', a

---

[1] But see below, p. 330.

[2] He sometimes, e.g. 673, 771, silently omits an unimportant postscript. HLP did the same thing.

justifiable change; 'respects' for 'compliments', which may be merely a compositor's synonym). The only letter of Johnson's that Boswell can plausibly be suspected to have garbled is 1004. But he was almost certainly innocent; see Appendix G.

The text of Johnson's letters to Boswell himself calls for separate consideration because of their intrinsic interest and of their special place in Boswell's regard. He regarded them, no doubt, as entitled to his peculiar veneration and therefore to the most scrupulous textual fidelity. On the other hand he probably had them almost by heart, and their very familiarity might induce carelessness in reading proofs. Only three of these letters are known to have survived. Of these two (355 and 550.1) are very brief and unimportant, and since they are not in the *Life* do not concern us. The third is 973. This was found at Fettercairn (Abbott, *Catalogue* xvii); but it was found apart from the other Boswell papers, and may have come from a different source. I regret my inability to say anything about the passages that Boswell omitted.

But I am not wholly without a clue. My inference from the error in 177 (see p. 306) is perhaps confirmed by the evidence of 803, where two false readings of 1791 are corrected in 1793. Of these one is significant only of Boswell's inadvertence; the printer had read Johnson's 'Coriatachin' as 'Coriatachat'; Boswell corrected in 1793 to 'Corrichatachin' (see note). The other correction is somewhat disconcerting. The reading of 1791, 'its sorrows', is nonsense; Boswell substituted in 1793 'it grows'; I suggest in my note that the change was probably made without reference to the MS., and may be erroneous.

Other discrepancies between 1791 and 1793 are very small matters, and do not require us to assume editorial intervention. An exception, indeed, is 1002, where JR's death allowed Boswell to restore a passage which he had suppressed in 1791, doubtless on JR's instructions. But that was a case of addition, not of correction. See my note.

Another palpable error of 1791 is in 541, where Johnson is strangely made to advise Boswell to refer a decision to, *inter alia*, 'wine'. The error is in a poetical quotation, so that the true reading, 'time', is not in doubt. The mistake is clearly not Johnson's, but Boswell's printer's. Another error, virtually certain, is in 578, where Malone's correction of 'without asserting Stoicism' is confirmed by Johnson's note on *Henry V*, III. v. 40, where the correction 'affected' for 'asserted' (1765) is clearly necessary.

We need not doubt that the text of Johnson's letters to Boswell is good; by the standard of comparable texts of that date it is probably very good indeed. But we are not to regard it as impeccable, or as beyond the reach of criticism. I have offered conjectures, for the most part tentative, or have suggested doubts, in my notes on 295, 344, 447, 655. A fuller discussion is in *TLS* 25 Feb. (p. 128) and 4 March (p. 140) 1939.

So far, then, the ultimate authorities for Boswell's text are: (1) Boswell himself; (2) Nichols, for letters to Cave and Birch and a few others; the extant originals show him at least as reliable as Boswell; (3) Tom Warton, for the letters to him; his blunders, though significant in general, do not directly concern us, since we have the originals. There remains a number of letters, Boswell's sources for which are not always known, since he sometimes makes no acknowledgement, and his acknowledgements when made are not always explicit. It is therefore perhaps worth while to give the evidence, which I do in the alphabetical order of Johnson's correspondents. I have formed the impression that letters which are not known, and are not likely, to have been returned to their owners were printed from copies (unless they were already in print). The relevance of this for textual criticism is, of course, that copies made by unpractised hands are likely to contain misreadings.

This appendix had been long drafted when in 1948 I received, by Colonel Isham's generosity, photostats or collations of a number of copies of J's letters to JB and others, made by or for JB and recently found at Malahide. (This discovery confirms the impression reported in my last paragraph.) In so far as these documents are copies of J's letters to JB, they are dealt with in Appendix B. See, alternatively, the Addenda to Vol. I, pp. 427–9, and especially the notes on 185 (where a suppressed sentence is restored to us) and 222 (which raises the question of 'editing'). Copies of letters to other correspondents are discussed in § 2 below, under the heads Cave, Elphinston, Levett. A typical example of JB's minor changes, deliberate or inadvertent, is 598, where his copy, in his own hand, normalizes J's 'remembred' and promotes his 'God' to 'GOD'.

II. § 2. *Alphabetical List of Some of Johnson's Correspondents; Sources of the Letters*

I should perhaps apologize for having intercalated notes on the latest Malahide finds by way of postscripts. My excuse is that this form of statement exhibits the process of trial and (sometimes) error, which does not lack edification.

ADAMS. Tinker 227, 234 (21 Jan. and 22 Dec. '85). In the first JB asks for 'communications' and specifies letters. In the second he repeats his request for letters: 'You mentioned to me that they are chiefly recommendations of visitors to your University.' Though JB got 'good packets' from A

(*BP* xvi. 72, 21 Jan. '84), he got no letters. Since we have five (of which one only, 484, is a letter recommending a visitor) but none in the *Life*, we may infer (1) that A was reluctant (like, e.g., Percy); (2) that he had letters now lost.

ALLEN, EDMUND. A and his wife both died before J, and JB had perhaps no later access to A's papers. He prints only one letter, 847, and that without acknowledgement. But the lack of acknowledgement may be due to the fact that the letter was an addition of 1793. This seems to rule out the hypothesis that he got it from A in L'n in '84. On the other hand if he copied it from Hawkins's *Life*, it is difficult to account for the discrepancies in the texts.

ASTLE. JB prints 737 without acknowledgement, though he had thanked A for letters to Cave, q.v. We know that A gave him a copy of the letter to Nicol, q.v. Presumably, therefore, 737 was from A's copy. This conjecture was confirmed by the discovery at Malahide of a copy, presumably by A; the footnote (printed in 1791) is in the same hand as the text. JB's hand does not appear; the correction of 'Diligence or Opportunity in both' to 'or both' (1791) was presumably conjectural.

BAGSHAW. JB owed 307 and 975 to copies by John Loveday. These were found at Malahide and are now in Col. Isham's collection.

BANKS. The text of 272 depends on a copy by JR.

BARETTI. JB prints 138, 142, 147 without acknowledgement, but with a note that they had been 'communicated' to the *European Magazine*, which was doubtless his source. We know from *L* ii. 24 that in '66 JB had already seen 138; and if Baretti showed him one he probably showed him all. But if JB had made copies he must have said so. The text seems to be good; but we must reckon with the possibility that Baretti made copies for the *EM*.

BARNARD, F. A. JB had seen 206 (*L* ii. 33) but B would not let him print it.

BARRY. JB copied 833 (and 832 to JR, q.v.) while in the hands of Mauritius Lowe, pursuing him for that purpose to 'the next coffee-house'. *L* iv. 201.

BEATTIE. JB prints 700 without acknowledgement. The presence of a footnote by Beattie suggests that Beattie sent a copy. It would be like him not to risk the original.—This conjecture was confirmed by the discovery at Malahide of Beattie's copy; Beattie's note is added on the MS. by JB, who no doubt copied it from a covering letter.

BIRCH. Though JB noted that J's correspondence with B 'proves that he had no mean opinion of him' (*L* i. 160), he printed three only of the ten letters published in *GM* Jan. 1785. The reason was that most of the letters are mere requests for the loan of books.

BOND. See White.

BOOTHBY. JB printed 80 from 1788.

BOSWELL. See Appendix B.

BROCKLESBY. JB's journal for 29 June '85 (*BP* xvi. 103) records that B 'brought me sixteen letters'. Writing to Malone 29 Jan. '91 (Tinker 292) he reports that he has 'twenty to Dr. Brocklesby, most of which will furnish only extracts'. Of the twenty found at Fettercairn JB printed parts of seventeen. The letters to Cruikshank and Mudge are in like case.

THE LETTERS IN THE *LIFE*

Burney, Charles. JB's journal 3 Nov. '87 (*BP* xvii. 52) records that CB 'gave' him 'some letters'. It is clear from 1004 that CB in fact supplied nine letters. For details see Appendix G.

Bute. JB had copies of 143 and 145. These are in Col. Isham's collection. JB has added headings and footnotes on the MS.

Cave. JB records, *BP* xviii. 11, that on 18 Dec. '89 C's great-niece showed him J's 'original letters' to C. But he could not have taken copies on such a visit, and he doubtless knew that most of the letters were already in print in *GM*. That is his source except for 15 and 16, which he owed to Astle. His note, 'I am obliged to Mr. Astle for his ready permission to copy the two following letters', *ought* to mean that he copied them himself; but since he says of 16 that it has 'no date, nor signature' it is probable that Astle sent him a copy, imperfect in those respects.

PS. Since this was written I have seen photostats of 15 and 16. These are of copies—of 15 by Astle, corrected by JB, of 16 by JB. We have the originals of both. The copies supply evidence of JB's diligence (in his instruction to himself, on 15, to 'read his handwriting better') and of his carelessness (in failing to look at the verso of 16 and so thinking that it lacked signature and date).

I have also a photostat of 23 to 'Mr. Urban', partly in JB's hand. See i. 428.

Chambers. JB had 54 in Warton's copy. C was in India when the *Life* was in preparation, and JB (who disliked him) presumably made no application.

Chapone. JB had 911 from Lord Carlisle. He asked for 'the favour of a copy' (*L* iv. 246), but Lord C did better, sending his chaplain with the original (*BP* xviii. 15).

Chesterfield. We know from *L* that C did not immediately destroy 61, but characteristically showed it to his friends. It may have survived; but the likely earls whom I have importuned know nothing of it.

Davies. JB printed 849, 991, 1124, without acknowledgement. D no doubt lent them and had them back, as we should expect from his dog-like devotion.

Dilly. Though JB had and retained the original of 924, he printed 625 from D's copy.

Dodd. When J and JB met at A'n in Sept. '77, J told him a good deal. But he did not tell him all. He had acted in the matter with unusual secrecy, and (inordinately) kept copies of his own letters. JB printed 523 from 'the copy' (evidently J's own copy; see *L* iii. 148) and 521 from a source not named.

Drummond. JB printed 184 (*L* ii. 26, v. 370), and presumably therefore 189 and 193, from 'the original in my possession'. Possession is not necessarily ownership;[1] the originals were not found at Fettercairn, and I am tempted to think that JB in fact printed from copies. 184 is a long letter, and he might employ an amanuensis. This suspicion was later confirmed when a copy of 184, made for JB and corrected by him, was found at Malahide. JB's chief corrections are 'rigorously' for 'religiously', 'reformed' for 'reformers', and 'traduction' for (I think) 'tradition'. He has not corrected 'propogate' (a quite common error) or 'geneology', but those words are

[1] 'Mr. M'Lean of Corneck possesses the two ends of Col which belong to the Duke of Argyll.' Boswell's *Hebrides*, 6 Oct. There however the word is technical.

311

correctly spelled in 1791. In the penultimate paragraph, where 1791 has 'grossness' my photostat is ambiguous; it looks as if the copyist had left a blank space. Finally JB reduced the conclusion to 'Sir &c.'; but 1791 restores the full formula. 189 has not been found.

EDWARDS. JB prints 589 to E and 588 to Wheeler without acknowledgement. Both E and W died before J. The letters are letters introducing CB. The possibility occurs that CB may have retained them. But they do not seem to have come on the market as the other Burney letters have. See Appendix G.

ELPHINSTON. The problem of J's letters to E is complex, but not so as to excuse a careless blunder in my note on 24 (i. 30, see also i. 428).

We have four letters: 24, 29, 30, 580. All four are in Shaw's *Memoirs* 1785 and in Vol. XIV 1788 of the *Works*. In Shaw they appear thus: 24 (pp. 166-7), 29 (pp. 91-4), 30 (pp. 96-100), 580 (pp. 168-70). In XIV thus: 24 (pp. 503-4), 30 (pp. 505-6), 29 (pp. 507-8), 580 (pp. 518-19). JB printed only 29 and 30. That he printed them in that, erroneous, order does not prove that he followed Shaw rather than XIV, for E's own copies (see note on 29) are in the wrong order. On what ground the editor of XIV corrected this mistake I do not know; but see my note on 29 (i. 39). But JB's overlooking 24 and 580 would more naturally result from use of Shaw than from use of XIV, where the letters are less widely dispersed. That JB used a second source in addition to E's copies I have shown at i. 428. This may explain why his text is less accurate than is usual.

FARMER. Though the original of 227 was found at Fettercairn, JB no doubt intended to return it (cf. 19 to Levett; see below, or i. 427). He accordingly made a copy, which was found at Malahide. As in other cases he reduced the conclusion to 'Sir &c.'

FOTHERGILL. A note by TW tells us that JB printed 385 from a copy by F.

GARRICK. Of the eight letters to G and his wife not one is in the *Life*. JB nowhere, I believe, refers to G as J's correspondent. I know no evidence that he applied to the widow, but it is possible that he applied and was repulsed.

GOLDSMITH. Our single black pearl, 305, remained unknown to JB.

GREENE. JB prints 1040 without acknowledgement. He may have had it from J. B. Pearson; or it might be in the 'good packet' of 'materials' that he had from Anna Seward (*BP* xvi. 72).

HAMILTON, W. G. JB records (*BP* xvi. 195) that on 15 June '86 he dined with H, who promised him two letters. After this it is perhaps surprising to learn, *L* iv. 245, that JB 'applied to Mr. Hamilton by a common friend'. But all 's well that ends well.

HASTINGS. JB borrowed and returned the three letters, 353, 367, 712. Copies of 353 and 367, in a clerkly hand, were found at Malahide. That JB collated his copies is shown by the addition in his hand of the word 'trace' in 353, which the copyist had omitted. He failed to detect the copyist's misreading, in the same sentence, of 'remains' as 'wonders'. See also i. 429.

HEELY. JB's acknowledgement of 988 as 'obligingly communicated' by Andrew Strahan (whose father had the letter 'as a voucher') might suggest a copy. In fact the letter was given to him, or lent and not returned; it was at Fettercairn.

HOOLE. JB's journal 8 Apr. '88 (*BP* xvii. 91): 'Mr. Hoole ... gave me some letters.' This shows that JB's 'gave' is not to be understood strictly. The originals were not at Fettercairn; but JB had them, sent them to the printer (a footnote to 989 is written on the MS.), and must have returned them, for 366, 989, 1006 (not 986) have been found. Hoole, like Davies (q.v.), was not the man to part with such treasures.

HUDDESFORD. 63 is unusual in bearing its own pedigree. A note on the MS. states that it was sent under cover to TW (see 64), was bequeathed by Malone (whose ownership is not explained) to James Boswell the younger, and was sold at his death in 1825 and again in 1831, when the writer of the note bought it. JB had a copy by TW, now in the Isham collection.

HUMPHRY. On 5 Jan. '90 (*BP* xviii. 15) JB 'visited Mr. Humphrey'. It may have been then that he either copied 947, 949, 962, or borrowed them; if the latter, they were returned. There is no acknowledgement except the footnote detailing the ancient glories of the Humphrys.

HUSSEY. JB's letter to H, 15 Oct. '87 (Tinker 246), shows that JB copied and returned 598. His copy is now in Col. Isham's collection.

JENKINSON (afterwards Lord Hawkesbury, later Earl of Liverpool) assured JB that J's letter, 520, about Dodd, never reached him. We may conclude that JB printed from J's own copy (see above, Dodd).

JOHNSON, W. S. See below, White.

KEARSLEY. JB prints 782 without acknowledgement, doubtless from K's *Beauties of Johnson* 1781.

LANGTON, BENNET. All except one (1039.2) of our letters were at Fettercairn. The fact that the letter to BL's daughter Jane (959) was (and still is) at Langton is evidence that the letters to BL himself were given, not lent, to JB. They were given, however, with restrictions; 240.1 is endorsed by JB 'not to be printed', 491.1, 506.3, 526.1, 581.1 were also suppressed, and the two letters numbered 887 were given in extract.

BL, not a tidy man, found the letters at various times, and some of them, including all the earliest, came too late to be placed, even in 1793, where they are printed together in an appendix. When Malone arranged JB's materials for the edition of 1799 he did no more than put the letters in their places. That is why the earliest of all (70) appears without preamble, whereas the first letter to CB, which in 1799 (and all later editions) is on almost the same page, is introduced with a flourish of trumpets.

Our thirty-two letters cover the thirty years '55–'84. Of these thirty, we have letters of eighteen; and no one year has more than three except '84, which has six. This suggests that few, if any, letters were lost.

LAWRENCE, CHARLES. JB took 704 from the *European Magazine*.

LAWRENCE, THOMAS and ELIZABETH. JB prints four letters to TL (377, 650, 757, 779.1) and extracts from three to his daughter (794, 802, 828). The only acknowledgement, I believe, is that at *L* iv. 143: 'I have been favoured by Miss Lawrence with one of these letters' (those to her father in Latin) 'as a specimen.' 362.1 was in Col. Isham's collection, but *not* from Malahide or Fettercairn.

PS. This question is partly settled by recent discoveries at Malahide.

Col. Isham has sent me photostats of Elizabeth L's letter to JB enclosing copies of 377, 650, 779.1, 794, 802, and 828 (all in *L*), as well as of 770.1 ('Nugae anapaesticae'), which JB did not print (reserving it for his edition of J's poems?); the same sheets contain extracts from letters to EL herself (*L* iv. 144). Evidently the sheet containing 757 is missing from the Malahide MS.

650. JB's departures from his text seem to be editorial. His change of 'I have bled once' to 'I have been bled once' was ill judged.

802. EL's copy has, I think, 'or his mind' not 'in his mind' (1791); it is 'or' in the original.

LEVETT OF LICHFIELD. In Col. Isham's collection is a copy, corrected by JB, of 19. The original was at Fettercairn. The copyist read *remit* as *write*— a common type of error; but JB made the necessary correction.

LEVET, ROBERT. JB prints (1793) 359, 436, 437, 500; he acknowledges these at *L* iii. 92: 'I am indebted to my old acquaintance Mr. Nathaniel Thomas' —whether for originals or copies does not appear.

MACPHERSON. JB prints 373 from his own copy, dictated by J. He would hardly suspect that the original had, surprisingly, survived.

MALONE. JB had 764, 766, from his friend and collaborator; they were perhaps copied in M's own house. (M regarded transcription as normal, though he must have known that it was not JB's normal practice; see on 541).

METCALFE. JB prints 806.1 without acknowledgement.

MONTAGUE. I find no evidence that JB applied to this great lady, though he had dined with her.

MUDGE. M writing to JB 13 Nov. '87 (Abbott, *Catalogue* 611) enclosed 'the only three letters he still has of many written'; he had lost the rest in moving house. These are 874 (2 letters), 884.2. See below, p. 319.

NICHOLS. We have thirty-four letters—most of them scraps—between '78 and '84. Nearly all are now B.M., and almost as many were published by N in *GM*, most of these in Jan. 1785. JB printed (from *GM*) 580.1, 597, 603, 611 (all these in a footnote at iv. 36), 810, 812, 1026. (JB's journal for 21 Dec. '89, *BP* xviii. 12, merely records a visit to N for 'little Johnsonian particulars'.) JB's fourth volume (i.e. the second half of the second volume of 1791) shows some signs of haste as well as of fear of excessive bulk, and his selection from the notes about the *Lives* is less judicious than usual.

Short as they are, these letters are incomparable for their glimpses of J at work. We have nothing like their wealth of information for the Dictionary, or the *Rambler*, or Shakespeare, or even the *Journey*.

NICOL. JB prints 994 without acknowledgement; but we know from Prof. Abbott (*Catalogue* 1600) that he had a copy from Astle.

NOLLEKENS. JB had two letters, 505.2 and 539.1. I am at a loss to explain his failure to use these, which are about Goldsmith's epitaph and N's 'head' of J.

O'CONOR. JB prints 107, 517, from copies by Joseph Cooper Walker of Dublin. Another copy of 107 by JCW is in the Adam collection.

PARADISE. JB prints 1025 (from the original) with no acknowledgement other than a footnote in praise of P.

PERCY. JB was much indebted to his friend for materials, and must have hoped for letters, though his own to P (Tinker 228, 241, 247, 272, 274) mention only 'anecdotes', 'materials', 'information'. We must suppose that P, an anfractuous man, was unwilling.

In a letter quoted by Tinker (p. 394) P condemned JB for 'violating the primary law of civil society in publishing a man's unreserved correspondence and unguarded conversation'.

PERKINS. Hill rashly complained (*Letters* i. xi) that neither JB nor he was permitted to publish entire a correspondence which would have told the world 'what was the part that Johnson took in founding the new firm of Barclay and Perkins'. In fact JB had almost all the known letters, and returned them; in a covering letter, which I have seen, he apologized for having defaced one of them by adding to it a footnote for the printer. That he printed only five (361, 730, 796, 927, 1019) is easily explained: the chief subjects of the letters are small money-matters, 'chaldrons' of coal, and the Perkins children.

PORTER. LP died in '86, and her representative (later her executor) J. B. Pearson was able to find only twelve letters for JB; these were at Fettercairn; JB printed also 833.1, from an unknown source. He suppressed two letters, 661.1 and 983.1. The former is undated; JB thought, wrongly, that it was of '84. The second is of July '84, a point in the *Life* at which he felt himself embarrassed by the bulk of his materials; see on Nichols.

Pearson wrote to JB 2 Apr. '84 (Abbott, *Catalogue* 668) asking for the return of the letters. JB replied 7 Apr. (Sotheby 19 Mar. 1930, 617); he would return them when his book was published, or sooner 'if Mrs. Porter be impatient'. He omitted to do so; see on J. Warton.

We have in all forty-nine letters: one of '49, one or more for almost every year from '59 to the end. It is unlikely that many letters later than '59 are lost.

PORTMORE. JB prints 952.1 from the original. He perhaps had it from BL, who was intimate with Lord P.

REYNOLDS, FRANCES. JB deplores (*L* i. 486) the 'too nice delicacy' that prevented his publishing J's 'many letters which I have seen'.

REYNOLDS, JOSHUA. We have twenty-five letters, but only six before '81. The history of the MSS. shows that they were not methodically filed, and the gaps between '64 and '71 and between '76 and '81 may suggest losses. Most of our letters are in the *Life*, and of these most were found at Fettercairn, enclosed in a wrapper on which JB had at two dates (perhaps three) noted its contents.

I print JB's list, or lists, from Prof. Abbott's *Catalogue* (p. 251), adding my own numbers and the year of publication:

Fourteen letters from Dr. Johnson to Sir Joshua Reynolds.

1. Aug. 19, 1764 = 166 (1791).
2. July 17, 1771 = 261 (1791).
3. Feb. 27, 1772 = 271 (1791).
4. June 2, 1783 = 842 (1791).
5. Sept. 6, X1783 = 879.2.
6. Dec. 4, 1783 = 916 (1791).
7. June 1, 1784 = 964 (1791).
8. July 6, 1784 = 971 (1791).

   9. July 21, 1784 = 980 (1793). See No. 19 below.
  10. Aug. 19, X1784 = 995 (1791).
  11. Sept. 2, X1784 = 1002 (1791, part only; the rest 1793).
  12. Sept. 9, 1784 = 1007 (1791); Adam collection.
  13. Sept. 18, 1784 = 1013 (1791).
  14. Oct. 2, 1784 = 1018 (1793); Harvard.
also 15. one Nov. 1782 = 813 (1791).
and the following additional:
  16. May 6 (*sic* for 16), 1776 = 480 (1793).
  17. Aug. 3, 1776 = 496 (1793).
  18. June 22, 1776 = 491 (1793).
  19. July 21, 1784 = ? see No. 9 above.
This list presents us with a number of problems.

    1. The list purports to contain nineteen letters; but No. 19 duplicates No. 9.

    2. The number of letters actually found at Fettercairn was not nineteen but sixteen. Now No. 12 is in the Adam collection, No. 14 is at Harvard. If we suppose that No. 9/19 is merely an accidental duplication, the whole list is accounted for. But

    3. There is other evidence. *Bibliotheca Boswelliana* 1825, the sale catalogue of the library of JB the younger, contains (lot 3169) three letters to JR: two about J's pension, and a third not described. The two are clearly Nos. 12 and 14, which JB the younger doubtless retained when his father's MSS. were sent to him for inspection. What was the third? A letter sold in so famous a sale is not very likely to have disappeared since; now the only letter known to be extant, that is not in the Fettercairn list, is 733 (New York Public Library); so there is a presumption that 733 is the third letter sold in 1825. On the other hand we know from the *Life* that 733 was found by Malone, one of JR's executors, after his death; and it would be like Malone to send JB a copy; if so, the original would not come into the hands of JB the younger—unless, indeed, Malone gave or bequeathed it to him, as well he might. See Huddesford above, p. 313.

    4. JB describes Nos. 16–19 as 'additional'. But since No. 15 was not one of the original 'Fourteen', it too must have been acquired later.

    Again, if we assume that the letter of 21 July '84 is really No. 19 not No. 9, it will be seen that the original fourteen were all printed in 1791 except No. 5 (not printed at all) and No. 14, and that the whole of the second ('additional') series was printed in 1793 except the first, No. 15. I am tempted to believe that No. 9 is a ghost and that therefore No. 15 was really 14. But the obstinate No. 14 still mars the symmetry by belonging to the 1793 class.

    5. If No. 9 is not a ghost it hides either a lost letter (Prof. Abbott suggests a letter of 12 July) or one of the letters printed in the *Life* but not in the list and not found at Fettercairn: these are 716, 733, 832, and 838. 716 is undated, which might cause confusion. For 733 see (3) above. 832 was given to Lowe by J for delivery to JR, and JB shot it on the wing (see Barry above); it is not unlikely that L, after waiting on JR, took the letter away again. If JB had only a copy, he would not, I think, have listed it; the Fetter-

cairn collection includes no copies of J's letters. 838, like 733, is a 1793 letter, which makes them both unlikely candidates.

PS. JB's copies of 832 and 833 (to Barry) were found at Malahide and are in Col. Isham's collection.

6. What, finally, is the meaning of JB's symbol X? As affixed to Nos. 5 and 10 it should be a reminder that JR had (as I presume) forbidden the publication of 879.2, I suppose because of the allusion to Burke's 'late favour' (JB would not have scrupled?), and of part of 995, which dealt with JR's quarrel with the Court. What is its meaning for No. 11 (1002)? 1002 deals, in part, with the same forbidden subject as 995; in the end, however, JB allowed himself (JR had died in '92) to print the letter entire, including the reference to JR's 'furious purposes'.

The brief entry in JB's journal for 13 July '87 (*BP* xvii. 39) records 'Letters to Sir Josh, etc., from Frank'; F, I suppose, acted as a messenger.

It remains to consider the few letters that are not in the *Life*. 819 is untraced; it was probably overlooked, or excluded by JR as trivial. 829 remained with the *Lives* which it accompanied. 830 was no doubt given to Crabbe, who later published it.

RICHARDSON. JB strangely omitted 94, which is in *GM* 1788.

RYLAND. JB seems not to have applied to R, though he knew him as a member of the Essex Head Club, and of him as J's intimate in '52 (*L* i. 242).

SASTRES. JB had been forestalled by HLP, and was always reluctant to borrow from that tainted source.

SHARP. JB printed 526, wrongly describing it as a letter to Dilly. See my note for a conjectural explanation.

SIMPSON. 134 is unusual in that it is in both 1788 and 1791. The explanation is that both HLP and JB had copies from Mary Adey.

SMART, MRS. A sentence from 1154 is quoted in 1799. The source was the 1791 edition of Smart's poems.

STAUNTON. JB had 140 'by the solicitation of' William Seward. This was a copy, now in Col. Isham's collection. JB's hand does not appear.

STEEVENS. JB had the originals of 345, 346, 347. He printed also 508, from a source unknown. As the letter concerned a project of 'assistance to a female relation of Dr. Goldsmith', S may have handed it on to another philanthropist.

STRAHAN, GEORGE. Any application JB may have made to GS would no doubt be refused. To none of his intimate correspondents does J write more critically. The later letters concern the quarrel between father and son; even the earlier, which are mainly on G's studies, contain strictures on his disposition. Of our eleven letters the first six belong to '63–'65, the rest to '82–'84. Once S was settled in or near L'n, J would have little occasion to write to him, except the emergent occasion of the quarrel.

STRAHAN, WILLIAM and MARY. We have thirty-three letters to S and three to his wife: seven of the '50s, one of the '60s, eleven of the '70s, fifteen of the '80s, two n.d. It is surprising that JB printed so few of the letters. He was intimate with S; S sent him 'a copy in his own hand-writing' of his long letter recommending J for a seat in parliament (*L* ii. 137). Yet JB printed only three letters and part of a fourth. 505.1 was at Fettercairn; JB quotes one sentence.

579 (see below) was not at Fettercairn. The reason is that this letter was not the original but a copy, forming part of a letter (4 Jan. '79) from S to JB; probably, therefore, when the MS. of the *Life* came back from the printer, this document was not placed with the holograph letters. JB printed also, from the originals found at Fettercairn, two letters to Mrs. S, 728 and 759. The explanation of this paucity may be found in S's state; on 1 June '85 JB breakfasted with him; 'He seemed quite failed. Gave me a LITTLE about Dr. Johnson, and promised to look out some of his letters and notes' (*BP* xvi. 97). S died in that year; JB was in communication with his son Andrew, to whom he acknowledges the letter to Heely, q.v. above.

PS. Since this was written I have had a photostat of 579 from the Isham collection. JB has marked the part of S's letter that he intended to print.

A number of the letters belonged to the late Clement Shorter, who had parted with them before my work began; I have had therefore to rely (not without misgiving) on his privately printed *Unpublished Letters of Dr. Samuel Johnson* 1915, except for 1042.1, which I have seen.

THRALE. See Appendix C.

THURLOW. For the source of 1008 see my note.

VYSE. JB printed 527; if from the original, it was returned.

WARTON, J. In the wrapper in which 46 and 239 were found at Fettercairn JB had written: 'These to be kept for Dr. Warton'. But on 22 Mar. '87 he was 'searching for Dr. Johnson's letters to Dr. Warton, which I feared were lost'. He failed to return them; see on Porter.

WARTON, T. See above, p. 309.

WETHERELL. JB made his own copy of 463, by W's leave. This was found at Malahide and is in Col. Isham's collection. See ii. 528. I note here that JB failed to detect a misreading by the compositor, 'interrupted' for 'intercepted' (ii. 114).

WHEELER. See Edwards.

WHITE. JB 11 June '92 wrote to James Abercrombie of Philadelphia (Tinker 310) thanking him for 'the packet with which your spontaneous kindness has been pleased to honour me'. A's covering letter was not found at Fettercairn, though a later letter from him was. The packet contained 'two letters from Dr. Johnson to American gentlemen'. These were the letters of 4 Mar. '73 to Bond and White, 297 and 298. Since neither was at Fettercairn, and 298 is in the Adam collection, I infer that Abercrombie sent copies. Both letters were printed in 1793. JB noting the last sentence of 298, which indicated that J had sent a third letter to White to be forwarded, asked A to 'procure a copy'. He did not receive it, but the original (299) is now at Columbia University.

WILKES. JB sent 840 to Wilkes with his letter of 25 May '83 (Tinker 215). No doubt he kept a copy.

Unidentified Correspondents.

132.1 is described by JB in an unusual way: he writes of J's '59 'excursion to Oxford, of which the following short characteristical notice, in his own words, is preserved'. Then follows '× × × is now making tea for me', &c. We are not told where or by whom the fragment was preserved, or why the name is suppressed.

136.2 was seen at Oxford *circa* 1843, and may yet survive.

141 was printed by JB from a copy furnished by Farmer, but not in his hand. Being a copy this document did not get into the Fettercairn file of J's autographs; it was found at Malahide.

781 was printed by JB from *GM* Feb. 1786, i. 93. The clergyman at Bath to whom it was addressed has recently been identified.

MUDGE. See above, p. 314. 1140 was printed by JB from the original 'in my large . . . collection'. It is a very short extract, and no doubt JB copied it into the MS. of the *Life* instead of directing the printer, as usual, to 'take in' a separate document. This might explain the disappearance of the original. JB did not name M as the recipient.

II. § 3

I add a consolidated list of places I have noted, in JB's letters and journals, that refer to his sources. I include both people to whom he applied and J's correspondents who were the subject of his applications; the two classes are not identical.

ABERCROMBIE. Tinker 310 (11 June '92). See above, White. Tinker 317 (28 July '93); J's lost letter to Jonathan Odell.

ADAMS. Tinker 227 (21 Jan. '85), 234 (22 Dec. '85). *BP* xvi. 72 (21 Jan. '85), 'good packets of materials'. See above, Adams.

BARBER. Tinker 244, 249, 250, 251 (June '87–Apr. '88). These letters call on B to help JB to force Hawkins to surrender books and papers which were B's property. JB makes no reference to letters. He may not have noticed that H had not printed all he had, or he may have despaired of success. *BP* xvi. 148 (22 Dec. '85); B had 'burnt some letters from Dr. Johnson to Mrs. Johnson'. xvii. 96 (19 Apr. '88).

BEATTIE. Tinker 245. Prof. Tinker took this from M. Forbes, *Beattie and his Friends*, 1904, 233. This passage, whether quoted from a letter from JB or from Beattie's diaries, shows that JB applied to Beattie for 'any letters he had received from Johnson'. Tinker 253 ('88), JB thanks B for 'some contributions'. See Beattie above.

BROCKLESBY. *BP* xvi. 103 (29 June '85), Tinker 292 (29 Jan. '91). See Brocklesby above.

BURNEY, CHARLES. *BP* xvii. 52 (3 Nov. '87); B 'gave me some letters'. See Burney above and Appendix G.

CARLISLE. *BP* xviii. 15 (2 Jan. '90). See Carlisle above.

CAVE. *BP* xviii. 11 (18 Dec. '89). See Cave above.

CHESTERFIELD. *BP* xvi. 109, 110 (10 and 12 July '85); 'Jephthson's recollection' of J's letter; 'Got Letter' from BL. See Chesterfield above.

HAMILTON, W. G. *BP* xvi. 195 (14 June '94); H promised two letters. See Hamilton above.

HASTINGS. Tinker 286 (4 Dec. '90). JB tells Malone that he has received, from H, J's three 'long and admirable' letters.

HAWKINS. *BP* xvi. 84 (7 May '85), xvii. 16 (20 Mar. '87), 96 (19 Apr. '88); see Barber in this list.

HECTOR. *BP* xvi. 72 (21 Jan. '85); 'good packets of materials'.

HOOLE. *BP* xvii. 91 (8 Apr. '88); H gave him 'some letters'.

HUMPHRY. *BP* xviii. 15 (5 Jan. 90); 'Visited Mr. Humphrey'. See Humphry above.

HUSSEY. Tinker 246 (15 Oct. '87), returning J's letter after copying it.

JOHNSON, ELIZABETH. See Barber in this list.

NICHOLS. *BP* xviii. 12 (21 Dec. '89). A visit to N. See Nichols above.

PERCY. Tinker 228 (20 Mar. '85), 241 (12 July '86). See Percy above.

SEWARD, ANNA. *BP* xvi. 72 (21 Jan. '72), 'good packets of materials'.

WALKER, J. C. Tinker 231 (1 July '85); W's offer to collect letters in Dublin. See O'Conor above.

WARTON, J. *BP* xvii. 18 (22 Mar. '87); 'searching' for J's letters, 'which I feared were lost'. See Warton above.

II. § 4. *Corruptions*

19. obliged to 1791 : obliged by *orig.*

30. useful and wise; innocent Shaw's *Memoirs* : useful, wise, and innocent 1791. See note.

46. readily 1791 : easily *orig.*

53–73. JB printed the letters to T. Warton from copies made by W and found at Fettercairn. These I have not collated, so it remains open whether a departure from the holograph is a misreading by, or of, W.

53. my disrespect 1791 : any disrespect *orig.*
libraries at Oxford 1791 : Libraries of Oxford *orig.*
a fortnight 1791 : about a fortnight *orig.*

54. The paragraphs beginning The Answer and If Mr Warton are transposed in 1791.

55. not been 1791 : not yet been *orig.*

56. shall send 1791 : should send *orig.*
at your hand 1791 : in your hand *orig.*
may yet recover 1791 : might yet recover *orig.*
again 1791 : soon again *orig.*
direction 1791 : certain direction *orig.*

58. on the shore 1791 : upon the shore *orig.*
resist 1791 : eat me *orig.*
if Polypheme comes, have at his eye 1791 : if Polypheme comes to me, have at his eyes *orig.*
skill and strength 1791 : skill or strength *orig.*

59. return 1791 : return you *orig.*
parks, and 1791 : parks to *orig.*

60. affair 1791 : little affair *orig.*
yet which 1791 : which yet *orig.*
not you 1791 : not yet *orig.*
of which I am glad *om.* 1791.

65. are to subscribe 1791 : have subscribed *orig.*
think much 1791 : much think *orig.*

71. beg you will never 1791 : beg that you never will *orig.*

73. will not willingly 1791 : will not *orig.*

70. carry 1793 : hurry *orig.*

109. shall certainly 1791 : will certainly *orig.*

110. imagined 1793 : imaged *orig.*

112. received 1791 : yet received *orig.*

114. acceptable 1791 : acceptable to me *orig.*
As you 1791 : You *orig.*
115. glad 1791 : very glad *orig.*
116. terrours 1793 : horrours *orig.*
death 1793 : end *orig.* The change seems deliberate.
117. well 1793 : publickly *orig.* See my note.
134. miscarried 1791 : married 1788. This and other discrepancies may be due to the existence of two independent copies of the original.
135. equal 1793 : proportionate *orig.*
curing 1793 : recovery *orig.*
182. the loss 1793 : less *orig.*
first appearance 1793 : appearance *orig.* An editorial change.
respects 1793: compliments *orig.* See note.
207. come 1791 : come soon *orig.*
238. failings 1791 : of my failings *orig.*
271. send 1791 : seal *orig.*
272. perpetua 1791 : perpetui JR's copy and *Europ. Mag.* See notes for variants between these two texts.
436. for 1791 : see, Hill (a certain correction).
444. do 1791 : do you *orig.*
480. willing 1793 : willing enough *orig.*
521. most 1791 : must *orig.*
673. second 1791 : forward *orig.*
711.2. crossed (*bis*) 1791 : erased *orig.*
728. suffer 1791 : must suffer *orig.*
truly be 1791 : be truly *orig.*
go to 1791 : to go to *orig.*
732. disencumbered of 1791 : disencumbred from *orig.*
759. deserted 1791 : dejected *orig.*
765. had been 1791 : had been to me *orig.*

768. but little 1791 : little *orig.*
770. could 1791 : could possibly *orig.*
time 1791 : time when *orig.*
mournful 1791 : very mournful *orig.*
796. I am 1793 : for I am *orig.*
842. since been 1791 : been since *orig.*
862. still 1791 : yet *orig.*
companionable 1791 : companiable *orig.*
882. disconsolate 1791 : desolate *orig.*
886. dispose of them 1791 : dispose them *orig.*
914. health 1791 : hearing *orig.*
916. You may be sure that *om.* 1791.
947. a regular 1791 : any regular *orig.*
952. believe 1791 : think *orig.*
975. upon her 1791: over her JB's copy.
the respect 1791 : that respect JB's copy.
990. remitted, perceptibly remitted 1791 : perceptibly remitted *orig.*
992. fifty 1791 : forty *orig.*
995. could 1791 : I could *orig.*
999. are all dead 1791 : were all dead *orig.*
1001. Paraphrasing part of the third para. JB himself misread *recovering* as *returning*, but the printer corrected him. On the other hand the printer misread JB's *token* as *taken.*
1004. For the editing of this letter see note.
1009. before 1791 : twice before *orig.*
1010. back again 1791 : back *orig.*
1024. now is 1791 : was *orig.*
1029. am now 1791 : I am now *orig.*
1030. know 1791 : knew *orig.*

II. § 5. *Boswell's Omissions*

JB's omissions of or from letters (to correspondents other than himself, for which see Appendix B) are for the most part readily explicable. I attempt a classification.

(*a*) Omissions dictated by owners. I refer, of course, not to correspondents who denied all access (as F. A. Barnard, Fanny Burney, Percy, Frances Reynolds, George Strahan, Taylor) but to those who gave restricted permission. See in § 3 above Langton, J. Reynolds, Charles Burney.

(*b*) Letters or passages omitted as trivial. See in § 3 Birch, Nichols, Perkins, W. Strahan (505.1).

(*c*) Omitted as unpleasant. JB suppressed many (parts of) letters to Brocklesby, Cruikshank, and Mudge in which J detailed the symptoms of his illness of '84.

(*d*) Overlaps with (*c*). Towards the end of his second volume JB was afraid of excessive bulk. This explains his drastic abridgement of the medical letters and his abridgement of the numerous other letters, not medical, of '84. See also Porter in § 3.

(*e*) Oversights, culpable or venial. See in § 3 Elphinston, Nollekens, Richardson.

(*f*) JB's attitude to Mrs. Piozzi and to 1788 is a special problem. That he was not much restrained by any respect for copyright is suggested by his borrowings from 1788. That he was not restrained by any respect for HLP's feelings is shown by his printing her own letter 662*a* from the MS. in his possession. But whatever his motive, his use of 1788 was sparing. He quotes freely from 663, excusing himself by saying that 662*a* 'is of value as a key to Johnson's answer, which she has printed by itself' (i.e. without 662*a*). This is perhaps disingenuous? His real motive was not to furnish a commentary to HLP's collection of J's letters, but to throw ridicule on herself?

JB quotes also 677, having no other letter descriptive of the Gordon Riots; 850, as the fullest account of J's paralytic stroke; 895, for Mrs. Siddons's sake; and 901 and 922, to pay a compliment to W. G. Hamilton.

HLP had included in 1788 letters to Hill Boothby and to Sastres. JB ignores the latter and prints one only of the former, for the good reason he gives: that the other letters to HB do not show J at his best.

III. The Text of 1788

I have elsewhere[1] discussed at length the question of Mrs. Thrale's preservation of Johnson's letters and Mrs. Piozzi's treatment of them. Many brief notes from London to Southwark or Streatham have no doubt perished; but it seems likely that she had kept almost all his full-dress letters,[2] and on the whole unlikely that she ever destroyed any of them. Her collection has been, in the course of years, very widely dispersed; I have been favoured by fortune, and have seen most of them. But for some 50 letters the text of 1788 remains the sole authority. It is therefore still of some importance to estimate the quality of that text; my list of ascertained errors shows that while not seriously corrupt it is far from infallible.

Such questions of sources as I have discussed for 1791 hardly arise for 1788, most of which was certainly printed direct from the originals.[3]

The edition of 1788 is happily for the most part superseded. It remains, however, our best criterion of the quality of the text of Johnson's letters, *as a whole*, of which the MSS. have not been found. That the verification of the proofs by Mrs. Piozzi and/or Lysons was perfunctory is shown by their overlooking some gross errors. 1788 is thus a rather unsophisticated sample of the transmission of a Johnsonian text by a good printer and his 'corrector of the press'.

I have not thought it necessary to burden my notes with all the errors of 1788 that have been disclosed by the MSS. I have elsewhere (*TLS* 25 Feb., 4 Mar. 1939) attempted an analysis of the proved corruptions in the editions of Johnson's letters and have given a description (empirical rather than scientific, for I am no graphologist) of his hand. I add here a liberal selection from the errors of 1788. This will indicate the extent of the corruptions, which make it abundantly clear that an editor is not merely entitled, but is bound, to scan with a sceptical eye those letters for which we still depend on the evidence of 1788 or on similar sources.

Errors of 1788

1788	Original	1788	Original
172. dismiss	discharge[4]	205. could	would
190. at	in	306. benevolence	what benevo-
proposed	purposed		lence

[1] *RES* xxii. 85, Jan. 1946, 17.

[2] An exception is his second, 173, the loss of which she deplored.

[3] 134 to Simpson was from a copy. The text of the letters from the Hebrides is surprisingly good in view of the illegibility of some of them (notably 327, 329). It is, I think, certain that she sent her copies of these to the printer, not the originals, and likely that Johnson corrected most of the errors due to the state of the MSS. See on 321; to my note there I add that no trace of printers' marks has been found in any of the originals; 329 occupies, in 1788, part of two sheets, and we should expect to find a mark at the point of division.   [4] See errata in vol. i.

1788	*Original*	*1788*	*Original*
318. wanting of cu-riosity	unworthy of cu-riosity	666. next	now
320. once been	been once	672. save	secure
321. disputed	differed	679. omits by ho-moeoteleuton	and you and Burney . . . frighted
322. larger (? editorial)	bigger		
327. fine rooms	fire rooms	702. true	real
337. wilderness	wild recess	interrupted	intermitted
416. seem or ever	from violence	725. agues	Agnes
419. prating	pretty	743. saving	having
423. move (editorial?)	turn	747. are soon to be	are to be soon
427. put	send	854. tiresome	irksome
429. ratify	rectify	civility	activity
settling	sorting	858. the rubies	two rubies
468. qualification	gratification	859. If she had been out	If the ⟨day?⟩ had been hot
care	love		
479. here	where	860. where	whence
483. More	More news	875. sun	sea
549. resolution	reputation	876. left	lost
550. Ham	Ilam	891. foot	feet
553. Ham	Ilam	897. dissolving filings	dissol-⟨ving⟩/ iron filings
554. unspelled	huspelled		
rocks	rucks	will	ball
591. an ounce	half an ounce	912. discerns	discovers
609. might	must	devoted to Sophy's ease	suited to Sophy's case
me	us	romances	the Muses
623. funny	? sunny (see note)	917. here ever	however
		922. she is languish-ing	the ⟨second⟩ is languishing
633. less	long		
636. knew	know	938. few	four
637. you	few	cure	care
644. one	me (?)	953. determine	deter me
657. still	skill		

IV. MISCELLANEOUS

To avoid overlap I have attempted in this Appendix to combine my notes on the texts and on their sources; the validity of a text varies with the nature of its source. But the investigation of sources suggests other questions of interest: notably those of our losses and of the possibility of finds in the future. I have discussed some of these questions in the foregoing sections and in Appendixes B and C; in this I gather up some loose ends. Like the rest of this Appendix, these remarks are mainly *in usum editorum*. The history of Johnson's letters is of uncommon complexity, and the evidence for them of uncommon variety. Editors in similar fields may perhaps learn something from my successes and failures.

ASTON, ELIZ., AND GASTRELL. Miss A was paralytic, and died in '85; Mrs. G died in '91; Boswell, though he was acquainted with the ladies, seems to have made no direct application; and he got no letters to them from Pearson or Anna Seward. Mrs. Piozzi in 1814 noted in her commonplace book 'the *high* price given by the Rev: Henry White for 15 letters to Mrs Aston & Mrs. Gastrel'. Seventeen letters are known; but of these two (434 and 769) are lost. The fifteen that survive are no doubt White's. They range from '67 to '84, but of these four are of '77 and five of '79; perhaps some earlier letters are lost.

BEAUCLERK. The sole survivor, 147.1, is a fragment remembered by BL. It is unlikely that Johnson wrote to him often, but he might write when Beauclerk was out of town. There is no evidence that Boswell applied to Lady Diana.

THE BURKES. The only letters known to have survived are two to Edmund (229.2 (see i. 442) and 610.1) and 437.1 to his wife. Percival Stockdale, who had perhaps no adequate motive for lying, claimed to have seen a letter to Edmund; see 598.1. In view of Boswell's intimacy with Burke, with whom he was in correspondence between '80 and '91, it would be odd if he had made no application. He may have failed to record a letter or a conversation. That few letters from Johnson have survived need not mean that few were written.

DESMOULINS. 430 is the only known surviving letter to any of Johnson's female pensioners. See Williams, below.

JOHNSON, SARAH. No letters from Johnson to his mother have been found except four written in her last illness. These were no doubt kept with the letters of the same month to Lucy Porter, q.v. below.

PORTER, LUCY. We have forty-nine letters; one of '49, one or more for almost every year from '59 to the end. I think it unlikely that many letters later than '59 are lost. It is possible that when Lucy moved to her new home she did not take many with her, except those to herself and his mother (q.v. above) written in '59. For the twelve letters printed by Boswell see above, p. 315.

SAVAGE. Johnson must surely have written to his 'Thales' in his retreat. But nothing has been found.

WILLIAMS. Though AW was blind, Johnson wrote to her; see 553, 868. Since she died in his house, her papers may have perished with Johnson's own.

APPENDIX F

THE LETTERS IN THEIR MATERIAL ASPECTS, FRANKS, DATES, ETC.

THE notes prefixed to each letter are not complete in respect of their physical qualities; that is partly because, even for letters of which the originals have been seen, my information was imperfect.

Postage was paid by the recipient; it varied with distance, and was (in relation to the value of money) a serious matter. Except in the area covered by the L'n 'penny post', it was fourpence or sixpence for even a moderate distance. Moreover, two sheets were charged double. It followed that letters, if paid for, seldom exceeded a single sheet. That is the reason of 'my paper reminds me to conclude', and similar formulae.

The great majority of J's letters consisted of a single quarto sheet of two leaves, the fourth page carrying the address or 'direction' as it was oftener called.

If that page was used for text also, space had to be left for the direction and the seal. If the second leaf, pp. 3–4, was otherwise blank, it was apt to be removed later; paper was costly, and the 'backs of letters' were often put to other uses. The lack of any address, therefore, normally means that this has happened; but it may mean that the letter, being delivered by hand or franked, was enclosed in a separate cover. This was seldom J's practice; his letters to HLT, almost always delivered free, are, if extant and complete, almost always found to be directed on p. 4.

In using the evidence of the postmark it is important to remember that, in England, the date-stamp was affixed in London only. Thus if a letter from L'n to L'd is dated 1 January, the postmark will normally be 1 January; if a letter from L'd to L'n is dated 1 January, the postmark will normally be 3 January. The great majority of J's letters went from, through, or to L'n; but Gray's letters from Cambridge to Durham have no date-stamp. The other postmark, e.g. LITCHFIELD, occurs irregularly; I have not in general recorded its presence or absence; we almost always know where J was when he wrote.

In J's time the date-stamp gave the day and month (IA, FE, MR, AP, MA, IV, IY, AV, SE, OC, NO, DE) only; the year was added at the end of the century. I do not recall a case in which the date is even probably wrong. The stamps, though small, were good, but were often badly inked or carelessly impressed. Moreover, the stamp often coincides with a fold, and if a letter has been kept unfolded (as it should be, lest the edges fray) can be read only by refolding so that the original state is restored.

The penny post, which was very frequent, had two date-stamps, of which one gives the hour.

The post was quicker than might be supposed; the regular course of post between L'n and L'd was two days, between L'n and Edinburgh four. There are more complaints of total failure than of delay; the B'n posts in particular seem to have had a bad reputation. There were no Sunday posts in the pre-railway age.

The most interesting posts for our purpose are those between L'n (in which term I include S'm and S'k) and Edinburgh, O'd, L'd, A'n, Bath, B'n. The Edinburgh mail was very regular; see Appendix B, p. 277. There was a daily (i.e. six-day) post between L'n and O'd; but J complained in '75 (382) that it was hardly possible at O'd to answer a letter on the day of its receipt. At Bath (I think throughout the period of most of our letters) the post left for L'n every week-night except Friday, and came in from L'n every week-morning except Tuesday. Bath compared favourably with B'n; see 718, and other letters written when the Thrales were there, for complaints of letters lost or delayed. In '50 the post left L'n for L'd and A'n on Tuesday, Thursday, and Saturday; the return post left on the alternate days. But there was a six-day post between L'n and B'm, and the by-post[1] would probably operate between B'm and L'd. In '58 a six-day post was instituted to Derby (within easy reach of A'n), and in '70 the same was done for L'd. (Information from the G.P.O.) However that might affect the situation, up to '81 J's letters to LP and JT are nearly all dated Tuesday, Thursday, or Saturday. It is characteristic that he hardly ever brought himself to write (except to HLT) before post-day.

Franks. During the life of a Parliament, members were entitled to receive letters without charge, and to frank their own letters or those of others. They were required to write the whole direction. Fraud was common, and HT used a device of which I have seen other examples:[2] he wrote 'Hfreethrale' as one word. So long as HT sat for S'k, J's letters to all members of that family were addressed to him. Many of his letters to others were franked by HT; and he sometimes in writing to him or to HLT enclosed another letter to be franked and posted. J was not a beggar of franks; he sometimes had his letters franked by Strahan; one is franked by AW's patron Sir John Phillips.

The sending of anything at all bulky by post was impracticable.

[1] The by-post is mentioned 407.1, 427.
[2] JB's Lord Pembroke wrote P: Embroke (Abbott, Fettercairn Catalogue, p. 106). I have seen a letter of '56 franked FrAyeelesford.

J sent JB the sheets of his *Journey* 'in thirteen franks'. That was an emergent occasion. There are frequent references to 'carriers'; and J sometimes offers to send a book or the like to a correspondent if the latter will tell him the method. Mrs. Boswell's present of orange marmalade, and the famous box in which J packed his Scottish collections, were sent by sea.

Dates. In the matter of dating J was in general as scrupulous as he wished HLT to be; but he does not often give the day of the week. Incomplete dating is not uncommon, and erroneous dating is common enough to call for vigilance. This is of two kinds:

1. Before the Act of 1751, the year was variously regarded as beginning on 1 Jan. and on 25 March. In careful, especially printed, documents a date between the two termini was written or printed, e.g., 25 Jan. 1740/1 or 174$\frac{0}{1}$. But in less formal documents the same writer might alternate between 25 Jan. 1740 and 25 Jan. 1741. The ambiguity persisted in people's minds for some years after the Act. Thus two of J's letters to L'd, in early '59, are dated '58.

2. Positive error. A false day of the month is unusual; 166 and 807 are examples; in 989 J seems to have put 13 for 31 August, since the postmark is September. In three letters, 402, 619, 788, he puts July for June. In 627.1 he puts '77 for '79, in 660 and 660.1 '78 for '80.

On the question of Old and New Style I write with trepidation, being constitutionally feeble in all such matters. J's use of O.S. before '52 is perhaps not in need of certification; but I have verified the only complete date of the period, 'Thursday Septr. 29th 1743' (18), with a perpetual calendar, and of the dates to which I have supplied the day of the week I have verified some from *Rambler* or *Adventurer*. J. noted in his diary (*PM*): 'Jan. 1, 1753, N.S. which I shall use for the future'. JB tells us (*L* i. 234) that Mrs. Johnson died 'on the 17th of March, O.S.', and that 'the next day' he wrote 42 to JT, which is dated 'March 18'. Our next full date is 'Tuesday 25 March 1755', which is N.S.

The late Sir Frank Mackinnon persuaded himself and sought to persuade me that Johnson 'hardly ever' wrote a letter on a Sunday. He pointed to a number of letters, purporting to be written on a Sunday, of which in his view the date must or may be suspected, e.g. 166, 224, 255, 256, 644, 664. The evidence is too strong for my lamented friend. There are too many letters to permit us to believe that they are all, or nearly all, falsely dated; and I note that in *GM* 1809, 1116, Elphinston refers to a lost letter from J as 'last Sunday's'. It is, on the other hand, clear that J seldom wrote on a Sunday; the maximum is under two per cent. of the whole. Of those that were written on a Sunday, moreover, several had a charitable purpose (e.g. 521, 521.1, 525, 624) and more were written on matters, or in circumstances, of urgency (e.g. 788.1, 973, 974, 1034). See also note on 32.1. HLT dated 505.3*a*, 575*a*, 703*a*, 742*a* 'Sunday'.

Addresses. It will be seen that, outside London, no elaborate direction was needed to find a person of distinction. It was well known that Mrs. Thrale was at Bath or B'n, and we do not learn the name of lodgings from the letters. In London, of course, more detail was needed; but though some houses were numbered, numbers seldom appear in our addresses; HLT wrote to 'Johnson's Court Fleet Street' (393*a*) or 'Bolt Court, Fleet Street' (482*a*).

I note the abbreviation 'Derbys', which is, I think, obsolete, unlike 'Yorks' or 'Lancs'.

For aspects of J's letters which are formal, but not physical—his salutations and subscriptions, his (rare) use of the third person, and so on—I may refer to my article in *Essays on the Eighteenth Century* (Oxford 1945).

APPENDIX G

LETTERS TO THE BURNEYS

I. Charles Burney

CB's endorsement of 1036 shows that only a small part of J's letters had been kept; these were either of exceptional importance or belonged to the last years; we have four between '55 and '65, twelve between '78 and '84. Of the sixteen letters, nine are in the *Life* (JB, however, was not allowed to print the whole of 1004). JB's journal for 3 Nov. '87 (*BP* xvii. 52) records only that CB 'gave me some letters'. The word is not to be taken strictly; see above, p. 313, Hoole. In the list below I give such information as I have: (1) CB's number, if known to me; (2) whether in *Life* or not. At some time after J's death—probably at the time of JB's application—CB gave numbers to the letters he had found.

- 67. (Not seen.) In *Life*.
- 112. ?—In *Life*.
- 113. 3* (1). I have a facsimile of the first page only; the symbol * may refer to a note on another page. In *Life*.
- 177. ?—In *Life*.
- 589.1. 5.—In *Life*.
- 620.1. ?—the MS. is partly obscured by a frame.
- 661. (Not seen.) Seen by Hill.
- 689.1. 7.—In *Life*.
- 767.4. 8.— In *Life*.
- 882. ?—In *Life*.
- 984. ?—In *Life*.
- 998.1. 11.
- 1000.1. No number.
- 1004. 11 and 13. In *Life*.
- 1030. The part addressed to FB (1030.1) is numbered 8. In *Life*.
- 1036. 13 and 15. In *Life*. 1036 is endorsed (1) 'Dr Johnson's last rembrance (*sic*) 17 Novr 1784 No 13'; (2) 'Dr Johnson's last remembrance! Novr 17th. 1784. No 15'; (3) 'NB. The *Numbering* is by what is *preserved*; not by what were *received*' (with other notes). Sixteen letters to CB are now known, of which nine were supplied to Boswell. Doubtless many letters are lost in the long gap between the precious documents of the early years and those which in 1784 were still recent.

It will be seen that (except for 620.1 and 661, for which only one number is available) the numbering is consecutive (the higher numbers being right for 1004 and 1036) and indicates that we have all the letters CB found.

II. Frances Burney

The letters to FB, like those to CB, were numbered, less methodically:

736.	(Not seen.)
787.4.	3.
902.	No endorsement.
903.	5.
1030.1.	8.

So we seem to miss three letters. For the well-known story of JB's application for letters, and FB's refusal, see *Diary* v. 167.

III

We have also one letter,

792.2, to James Burney.

Postscript. Since these appendixes were set up Dr. and Mrs. Pottle have examined the relevant parts of the MS. of the *Life* found at Malahide in 1946. These make it almost certain that JB had only copies of the letters in CB's possession (including 588 and 589) and that the copies were made by CB. This is important, because it acquits JB of having tampered with the text of 1004.

APPENDIX H

LETTERS TO JOHNSON

WE know from the *Life* (i. 108) that J in his last days destroyed almost all his private papers. Letters to him survived either because they had previously passed out of his keeping or because they were deliberately or inadvertently excepted from the general destruction. I deal with the three classes in order.

I

JB had recovered his letters from J. See Appendix B. Two letters from Q (287*a*, 539*a*) were found with J's to her. He no doubt took them to S'k or S'm to show them to HLT and left them there.

II

A large number of HLT's letters were found by J's executors and returned to her. Hill Boothby's letters also survived. There is a strong temptation to think that J found himself unable to destroy these memorials of two women to whom he had been deeply attached.[1] But the survival of Miss Boothby's letters may have been accidental. They were published in 1805 with J's *Account* of his early years. The editor, Richard Wright, acquired them from Frank Barber's widow; he states that J 'numbered them, wrote the dates upon them, and had them bound together in one volume'. J or Frank, who presumably helped in the work, may have failed to recognize such a volume as containing manuscript.

I think that the preservation of HLT's letters was probably deliberate. That he had destroyed some of her letters at the time of the rupture was asserted by Fanny Burney (*Diary* ii. 328); and her story seems to be borne out by the paucity of the surviving letters of the years '82 to '84. Earlier letters might escape by accident, if, e.g., they were together in a drawer. But that does not seem very likely. See Appendix C.

III

Some letters from other correspondents are extant or are known to have survived J's lifetime. These may in general be presumed accidental survivors of the holocaust; but it is always possible, sometimes virtually certain, that there had been earlier leakage; some letters can be traced to a Piozzian source.

[1] He burst into tears when he found he had destroyed letters from his mother. *L* iv. 405.

I have made no systematic search for letters to J. The known facts made it unlikely that such a search would be productive. I add, however, a list of those that have come to my notice. Letters from HLT and Q, and from JB, are excluded; for the former see the text and Appendix C, for the latter Appendix B. Persons to whom J is known to have written are distinguished, as in Index II, by capitals. All letters now in the Rylands Library or at Bachycraig, and others as indicated, are from a Piozzian source.

ARGYLL, Duke of. 29 Oct. '73. *L* v. 363.

Aston, Mary (?). HLP in 1788, ii. 383 (quoted *L* iii. 341, n. 1): 'Nobody has ever mentioned what became of Miss Aston's letters, though he once told me himself, they should be the last letters he would destroy.' The nature of J's statement as reported seems to identify 'Miss Aston' with the lovely 'Molly'. I find it difficult to believe in such a correspondence. Miss A would hardly write letters to J in their youth, and there is no evidence that he revisited Lichfield (which might renew the acquaintance) before her death in '65. If my doubts are just, J must have meant the letters of Molly's sister, 'Mrs' Elizabeth Aston.

Bathurst, Richard. 13 Jan. and 18 Mar. '57. Croker's Boswell 1831, i. 230, from Harwood's *Lichfield* 1806, 451. H owned these letters, which J had perhaps sent to L'd.

Bellamy, George Anne. 11 May '83. *L* iv. 244.

BIRCH, THOMAS. 3 Apr. '55. *L* i. 285. Original in B.M.

BOOTHBY, HILL. '53 and later. J's *Account* of his early years, 1805. See above, p. 332.

BRIGHT, HENRY. 31 Mar. '70. Now Hyde, from a Piozzian source. 24 Mar. '71. Wright, *Unpublished Letters to and from Dr. Johnson* 1932, 24. Original in Rylands Library.

BROCKLESBY, RICHARD. 6 Sept. '83. Quoted in 880.

BURNEY, CHARLES. 16 Feb. '55. FB's *Memoirs* of CB, i. 119. Sotheby 16 Feb. 1926, 403.
14 Apr. '55. *Memoirs* i. 122.
28 Mar. '57. *Memoirs* i. 124.

BURNEY, FRANCES. Brighton, Oct. or Nov. '79. See on 642.
Brighton 16 Nov. ('79). Unpublished original from a Piozzian source.
19 Nov. '83. See on 902.

Burton, John. n.d. Wright, op. cit. 29. Original in Rylands Library.

CALDER, JOHN. 10 Feb. '76. Nichols, *L* iv. 811. Tregaskis Catalogue 453 (1935), 37.

CAVE, EDWARD. 2 Dec. '34. *L* i. 92.

Chamier, Anthony. 17 June '77. *L* iii. 491. 23 Aug. '79. Quoted 627.1.

CONGREVE, RICHARD. '55. See on 75.2.

Corbett, —. (? 26) July '32. R v. 80-1.

Coxeter, Thomas. 23 Apr. '71. *NQ* 12 Apr. 1941, from a Piozzian source.

CROFT, HERBERT. Sept. '80 and Sept. '82. J's Life of Young, §§ 2, 153.

DAVIES, THOMAS. 18 June ⟨? '74⟩. Wright, op. cit, 27. Original in Rylands Library.

Dick, Sir Alexander. 17 Feb. '77. *L* iii. 102.

    n.d. Sotheby 22 Jan. 1907, 740, from a Piozzian source.

DODD, WILLIAM. 25 June '77. *L* iii. 147.

Dodington, George Bubb. n.d. (? *c.* '52). Hawkins 1787, 329.

Elibank, Lord. 21 Aug. '73. *L* v. 182.

ELPHINSTON, JAMES. All in E's *Correspondence* 1791–4.

    4 Oct. '50. i. 31.   28 July '78. ii. 247.

    26 Mar. '52. i. 36.   30 Mar. '84. iii. 110.

    22 Feb. '59. i. 69.

Faulkner, George. See on 51.1.

Ford, Phoebe. 17 May '80. Salt Library, Stafford. R iv. 47.

GARRICK, DAVID. 31 May '65. *Garrick Correspondence*, i. 186. Quoted by Hill on 168. 22 Dec. ('71; the year is determined by J's letter 269 of 12 Dec.). See *Poems* 154. Sotheby, March 1922, 588.

Glasse, Samuel. 2 Oct. '71. Sotheby 6 Dec. 1904, 347, from a Piozzian source. (Maggs Catalogue 773 (1948) 98: 'reproaching Dr. Johnson for . . . accusing Glasse of Methodism'.)

HASTINGS, WARREN. 7 Aug. '75. Gleig's *Hastings*, ii. 17.

HAWKINS, SIR JOHN. 1 Dec. '84. *L* iv. 406.

Herne, Phoebe. 16 June '77. Original in Rylands Library.

Hervey, Thomas. n.d. *L* ii. 32.

JENKINSON, CHARLES. 25 Oct. '65. *L* i. 520. Original in B.M.

Langley, William. Originals in Bodleian. 21 Mar. '74. 14 Feb. '83. 24 Feb. '83. 19 May '83.

LANGTON, BENNET. 10 June '71. Sotheby 14 Dec. 1901, 220, from a Piozzian source.

    Mar. '82. R. B. Adam Catalogue.

Lennox, Charlotte. 17 June '77. Sotheby 22 Jan. 1907, 741, from a Piozzian source.

    29 May ('78). Wright, op. cit. 27. Original in Rylands Library.

    Monday ('78). Wright, op. cit. 28. Original in Rylands Library.

LOWTH, ROBERT. (*c.* July '80). See on 686.1.

McLEOD of Raasay. *c.* Dec. '75. See 446.

MACPHERSON, JAMES. (Jan. '75). Hawkins 1787, 490, thus describes the letter to which J replied in 373: 'Mr. James Macpherson . . . in a letter . . . threatened him with corporal chastisement.' See also *L* ii. 511–13.

Mitchell, W. n.d. Sotheby 17 June 1842, 225. 'A curious letter to Johnson from W. Mitchell, respecting the sum of two pounds, which he states "your wife stands indebted to me, ever since Agust (*sic* in catalogue) 12th, 1749".'

ORRERY, Lord. See 42.1.

PATTEN, THOMAS. 4 Sept. '81. *GM* Apr. 1819, i. 293.

PERCY, THOMAS. 15 Nov. '83. Sotheby 11–13 Dec. 1902.

    n.d. Sotheby 24 (1831).

PORTER, LUCY. 15 Apr. '80. *TLS* 28 Aug. 1937, from a Piozzian source. Now in the possession of Dr. J. L. Clifford.

Pratt, Samuel Jackson. 6 Apr. '69. Wright, op. cit. 17. Original in Rylands Library.

    16 Aug. '69. J. L. Clifford in *Bull. of the John Rylands Library* xx. 2,

LETTERS TO JOHNSON

July–Aug. 1936. Original in Rylands Library.

n.d. Sotheby 22 Jan. 1907, 740, from a Piozzian source.

Prouse: *see* Rogers.

RICHARDSON, SAMUEL. This is not a letter, but it is too amusing to omit. It is an envelope addressed by SR to 'Mr Johnson Dec. 26. 1757 By Mr Allan of Oxfd' and returned by SJ addressed 'To Mr. Richardson in Salisbury Court'. F. C. Butters to *The Times*, letter dated 7 July 1941.

REYNOLDS, FRANCES. Monday ⟨presumably 29 July '71⟩. This letter concerns 'the debt at Oxford', which is clearly that described in 264.1. I copied it many years ago by the courtesy of Mr. Rupert Colomb. I then noted that he had several other letters from FR to J, but recorded no particulars.

21 June '76. Croker's Boswell 1831, iii. 446.

REYNOLDS, JOSHUA. 17 Dec. ⟨'77⟩. F. W. Hilles, *Letters of Sir Joshua Reynolds* 1929, 57.

⟨23 Dec. '80⟩. Hilles, op. cit. 75.

ROGERS, MARY. Feb. 84. Hill 1892, ii. 379 (note on 934).

RYLAND, JOHN. Nov. '84. A draft written on the original of 1032. A photostat is in my possession.

ST. ALBYN, LANCELOT. 4 May '82. *GM* 1786, i. 93.

SCOTT, WILLIAM. Wednesday ⟨'75⟩. Clifford, op. cit. 6. Original in Rylands Library.

STEEVENS, GEORGE. 27 Oct. '80. Original in Morgan Library.

STRAHAN, GEORGE. 5 Apr. '71. Sotheby, 14 Dec. 1901, 228, from a Piozzian source.

STRAHAN, WILLIAM. ⟨'71⟩. Sotheby, 14 Dec. 1901, 228, from a Piozzian source.

22 July '75, perhaps a letter to J. Wright, op. cit. 30. Original in Rylands Library.

TAYLOR, JOHN. 1 Dec. '60. Endorsed by J; 'Dr. Taylor, Desires my assistance in changing his Preferments.' Hodgson 11 July 1946, 23.

Thompson, John. 21 Feb. '82. See on 760.

THRALE, HENRY. See 729.2.

THURLOW, Lord. 24 Oct. '80. *L* iii. 441.

WARTON, JOSEPH. Dec. '54. See 56. 27 Jan. '78, 'relative to admitting Richard Burney, Dr. Burney's Youngest son, on the Foundation of Winchester College'. Original at Winchester College.

Welch, Anne. Naples, 27 May '77. Unpublished original in the possession of J. L. Clifford; from a Piozzian source.

WETHERELL, NATHAN. 12 Mar. '76 and n.d. Sotheby 22 Jan. 1907, 740, from a Piozzian source.

Whittell, Thomas. 26 Aug. '78. See on 578.1.

WINDHAM, WILLIAM. 6 Oct. '84. *Windham Papers* 1913, i. 64. Original in B.M.

Anonymous.

'Anti-Ossian' n.d. (? *c*. '81). Shaw's *Memoirs of* . . . *Johnson* 1785, 159. 'A letter of consolation.' See 853.

839, n. 3. The pasted strip has been removed by experts of the Houghton Library at Harvard, and the hidden piece partly read:

M . . . . I know, but whom did Sir Joshua offend, and what did he do or think that could so much displease?

879.2, 874(1), 874(2). I note that these letters have no postmarks, which indicates that they were sent under cover. JR's letter of 18 Sept. to his niece (*Letters* ed. Hilles) shows that he and the Burkes were at Saltram together on that date. Saltram is almost in Plymouth. Perhaps these letters were directed to Burke.

883.1. M. 22 Sept. '83. William Bowles (Heale).

Address: To William Bowles Esq. at Heale near Salisbury.
Postmark illegible.

Hyde.——

Dear Sir

You insisted with great kindness upon knowing the result of the consultation upon my disease. Mr Pot inspected the tumour on Saturday, and thought excision necessary. The operation is intended to be in the beginning of next week. Mr Pot being this week called into Lincolnshire.

I am otherwise well, except that the Gout has a slight inclination to be troublesome. I believe it will be no fit, and, if it be, it is wholly unconnected with the great complaint.

You may suppose that I am not without anxiety, but I hope, God will grant a happy Issue. Let me have your prayers.

Hoole, I think, is well. I know not whom else I have seen of your acquaintance. You will easily believe that I go little out, but my friends do not neglect me.

Be please⟨d⟩ to pay my respects to your dear Lady. I have now little milk, and little fruit. Do not let the young ones quite forget me. I am, Sir, Your affectionate &c.

London Sept. 22. 1783   Sam: Johnson

923.3. M. 5 Jan. '84. John Ryland.

Sotheby 12 June 1876, 109.

Described in catalogue as an invitation to R to bring young R and Payne to eat a hare.

943.1. M. 22 Mar. '84. John Taylor.

Sotheby 5 Apr. 1894, 152, 29 Feb. 1896, 405.

Extract in Catalogue.

The physicians pertinaciously told me that I was not very near death, yet they did not think I ever should recover, but imagined my soul would for some time more or less inhabit an unweeldy bloated, half drowned body.

946.2. (Hyde).
Dear Madam,

That you had left Bath, and were gone gone (*sic*) to town, I had heard from Mrs. Thrale; but she did not tell me where I might find you.

I hope you do not think that I have forgotten, or can forget Miss Charlotte Cotterel. But as we are both ill, the first visit might be paid by him or her who goes first abroad. I have been confined here for more than a quarter of a year, and my Physicians this day have forbidden me to go out for some time to come.

If you can dine with me, name your day. I will invite Mr. Sastres to meet you, and we will be as cheerful as we can, together, and as soon as I can, I will come to you.

I am, Madam, Your most humble Servant,

Sam: Johnson
Apr. 4. 1784

To M^{rs}. Lewis.   Bolt Court, Fleet Street

954.1. Hannah More wrote to her sister, April '84: 'I had a very civil note from Johnson about a week since. . . . He tells me he longs to see me, to praise the Bas Bleu as much as envy can praise;—there's for you!' (*Memoirs*, ed. William Roberts, 1834, i. 319).

969a. In addition to the documents cited on p. 172, the Hyde collection contains the copy retained by HLT of both her letter to J and the circular enclosed. The texts are as follows:

Sent this Day To D^r. Johnson inclosed in what is written on the other side of the Paper.

My Dear Sir—

The enclosed is a circular Letter which I have sent to all the Guardians, but our Friendship demands somewhat more; it requires that I should beg your pardon for concealing from you a Connection which you must have heard of by many, but I suppose never believed. indeed my dear Sir it was concealed only to spare us both needless Pain: I could not have borne to reject that Counsel it would have killed me to take, and I only tell it you now, because all is *irrevocably settled*, and out of your power to prevent. Give me leave however to say that the dread of your Disapprobation has given me many an anxious Moment; and though the most independent Woman in the World perhaps, I feel as if I was acting without a parent's Consent—till you write kindly to your Faithful Servant. Bath 30: June.

I shewed M^r. James this Letter, & he cried.

[The enclosure.]

Sir—

As one of the Executors to M^r. Thrale's Will, & Guardian to his Daughters, I think it my duty to acquaint you that the three eldest left Bath last Fryday for their own house at Brighthelmston, in Company with an amiable Friend Miss Nicholson, who has sometime resided with us here, and in whose Society they may I think find some Advantages, & certainly no Disgrace. I waited on them to Salisbury, Wilton &c. and offered to attend them to the Sea-side; but they prefer'd this Lady's Company to mine, having heard that M^r. Piozzi is coming back from Italy, & judging perhaps by our past Friendship & continued Correspondence, that his Return would be succeeded by our Marriage.

I have the honour to be Sir Your Obedient Servant
Hester: L: Thrale.
Bath June 30: 1784.

1016. I now have a photostat, courteously communicated by the executors of the late Victor McCutcheon of New York City. It confirms my text in all essentials; but in line 4 for 'a great' read 'great'.

JOHNSON'S LETTERS TO MRS. WAY

The good offices of Prof. Clifford and the courtesy of Major R. H. Way and Mr. J. F. Roxburgh have enabled me, at a very late stage, to add one to the roll of Johnson's correspondents and to show his intimacy with an acquaintance of whom nothing more was hitherto known than that they were acquainted. His letters to Mrs. Way (for whom see Index II) have been preserved among the family papers; one of them Major Way gave to Mr. Roxburgh. This was 835.2 (see iii. 20), a duplicate of which made its way to Sotheby's, in the sale of 17 Dec. 1928. That it is a letter to Elizabeth Way, Major Way's information has satisfied me. I have numbered the letters—as best I could. It was not practicable to distribute them.

After 779.3. Sa. 4 May '82. Elizabeth Way.

Dear Madam

I am compelled by a very frequent and violent cough, with an oppressive and distresful difficulty of breathing to delay the pleasure which I promised myself from your company and that of Lady Sheffield. I am indeed very much disordered, as I have been for several days, but for a time I

338

expected to grow speedily well, and was not in haste to send you notice. I am, Dear Madam, Your most humble servant,
May 4.—82   Sam: Johnson

779.5. M. 6 May '82. Elizabeth Way.

Mr Johnson is truly sensible of dear Mrs Way's kindness. He hopes that he is now better, but he is still very much disordered.
May 6.—82

790.1. Oxford. W. 12 June '82. Elizabeth Way.
Address: To Mrs Way at the Southsea House London. *Postmark*: I-IV.

Dear Madam
I am much indebted to You for your attention to my health, which is not yet as I wish it. I cannot perceive that I have yet had any other advantage from change of place but the amusement of the journey, and of new company, and believe that my stay here will not be very long. I shall try however for a few days what advantage I can find, and when I return shall perhaps have the gratification of seeing You better. I am, dear Madam, Your most humble Servant
Oxford. June 12. 1782   Sam: Johnson

After 1037. Tu. 23 Nov. '84. Elizabeth Way.

Dr Johnson is very ill, but returns his thanks with great sense of Mrs Way's kindness, and with true wishes for her happiness.
Nov. 23 1784

1157.2. July (10th added in another hand). Elizabeth Way.
Address: South Sea House.

Mr Johnson returns his sincere thanks to dear Mrs Way for her kind enquiries.
July

877a. Weymouth. Tu. 26 Aug. '83. From H. M. Thrale.
Address: To Dr Johnson, Bolt Court, Fleet Street.
Photostat, Hyde Collection.—

Dear Sir
The Story we have so long talked of, ought to have been told at Bath, I believe, as it was there my Mother heard it, from Mrs Cotterell, who said she

339

knew it to be true. The English Consul at Aleppo, took Delight in planting and forming his Gardens in the English Fashion which was so new and surprizing to the Inhabitants of the Place that they were continually begging his Leave to see them, amongst the rest, the Bashaw who had frequently seen them himself, often hinted to Mr Masters, (the Consul,) that his Harem were particularly desirous of seeing them, Mr Masters thinking such Visitors would bring him nothing but Trouble and Inconvenience, excused himself, as long as he decently could but at last being obliged to comply, he went from his House early in the Morning, having provided an elegant Entertainment for them, and leaving none but Women Servants to attend them. He returned late at Night, and found all had gone well, that they were gone, and seemed much pleased with his Behaviour, so he retired to his Room, and went to Bed, where he had not long been, before his Closet Door was opened, and a Woman came out, who immediately threw herself upon her knees before him, told him she was one of the Bashaw's Wives, that she had concealed herself there, with the hopes of escaping from him, and trusted to his Mercy not to discover her, but Mr Masters more sollicitous for his own Safety, than that of the Lady, got up, and ran out of the Room, fastening the Door after him, and sent to the Bashaw instantly to let him know what had happened; proper Persons were soon sent by the Bashaw to take her and she was the next Day thrown over the Bridge by his Order. Mr Masters thought it prudent not to stay any longer at the Place, lest Suspicions might be entertained, so he got his Dismission and is now in England. This is the story and a very long one I think, it is however exactly as I heard it related.

I am Dear Sir
your most obedient Servant

H: M: Thrale

Weymouth
August 26: 1783.

INDEXES

These are:

I believe that the merits of this separation will be found to exceed its obvious defects.

I. In this index I have tried to collect what Johnson in his letters tells us about himself. Since his frequent illnesses and persistent ill health form the sombre background of his correspondence, I have indexed only salient comments. References to diseases and remedies will be found in Index V s.v. Health.

II. In this index I give some biographical information, and refer the student to other authorities, notably to the *DNB* and to the *Life*, i.e. to Dr. Powell's index. I have tried to assemble the references in an intelligible form, and much is here collected that readers might expect to find in the commentary. J's correspondents are distinguished by CAPITALS, and within the article for any correspondent letters to that correspondent are distinguished by **heavy type**.

The Thrales, who bulk large for nearly twenty years of the correspondence, offer a special problem. I have assumed that any student of J's *Thraliana* will peruse the letters to and from them, and have indexed those letters lightly; references to Thrales in letters to other correspondents are given more liberally. Mrs. Thrale's letters to J are included in my text only as commentary on his to her, and they are not indexed.

III. This index gives the evidence of the letters for J's reading. Since, however, many of the books he read were by authors who are mentioned in the letters in other capacities, all references to authors to whom he was personally known are given together in Index II, and are in III only by cross-reference.

IV. The significance of places named in the letters is often indicated by the addition of the name or names of persons who lived in those places. Places known to have been visited by J are distinguished by CAPITALS.

V. Subjects. See my note, p. 450.

VI. Johnson's Works—a chronological list.

VII. Johnson's English. This is a selection of words and uses that struck me as obsolete, or possibly obscure, or otherwise remarkable.

ABBREVIATIONS

(See also *Authorities*, i. xv)

I. PERSONS

J(ohnson).

J(ames) B(oswell); C(harles) B(urney), F(rances) B(urney); (Francis Barber is Barber or Frank).

B(ennet) L(angton).

L(ucy) P(orter).

Q = Hester Maria ('Queeny') Thrale.

F(rances) R(eynolds), J(oshua) R(eynolds).

J(ohn) T(aylor); H(enry) T(hrale); H(ester) L(ynch) T(hrale) or H L P(iozzi); Q = 'Queeny' Thrale.

J(oseph) W(arton), T(homas) W(arton); A(nna) W(illiams).

II. PLACES

A'n = Ashbourn(e). B'm = Birmingham. B'n = Brighthelmston (Brighton). L'd = Lichfield. L'n = London. O'd = Oxford. S'k = Southwark. S'm = Streatham.

III. DATES

'51 = 1751.

IV. BOOKS, PERIODICALS, ETC.

PM = J's *Prayers and Meditations* 1785. Reprint in *JM* (see below).

Account = *Account of the Life of . . . Johnson . . . by himself* 1805.

L = Boswell's Life of J. Undated references are to Hill–Powell (see i. xvi). Dated references are to 1791(–3, –9), and are followed by a bracketed reference to Hill (i.e. Hill–Powell). Hill standing alone = his edition of the *Letters* 1892.

BP = Boswell's *Private Papers* (see i. xvi).

1788 = HLP's *Letters to and from J*. (HLP = her own copy, Lysons = Samuel L's copy, Malone = Edmond M's copy).

Th = *Thraliana*.

JM = Hill's *Johnsonian Miscellanies* 1897.

C = J. L. Clifford's *Hester Lynch Piozzi* (*Mrs. Thrale*).

R i (etc) = Vol. i (etc.) of A. L. Reade's *Johnsonian Gleanings*; *Reades* = his *Reades of Blackwood Hill*.

E(nglish) H(istorical) R(eview); G(entleman's) M(agazine); M(odern) L(anguage) N(otes); N(otes and) Q(ueries); R(eview of) E(nglish) S(tudies); T(imes) L(iterary) S(upplement).

Rylands 539, etc. = John Rylands Literary English MSS.

SAMUEL JOHNSON

J's experience of life in general is most conveniently indexed under the several heads of Persons (Index II), Authors (III), Places (IV), Subjects (V), and his own Works (VI). But it would be hard to collect from these lists the evidence of the letters, which though not bulky is of great interest, for his own life and character. I have in this index tried to classify what may be called the autobiographical elements in the letters, under the heads of Books, Character, Charities, Conversation, Correspondence, Domesticity, The Fashionable World, Friends and Acquaintances, Godchildren, Habitations, Health and Spirits, Hobbies, Languages, Livelihood, Loneliness, Personal Appearance, Politics, Quarrels, Reading and Writing, Religion, University Honours. For his appreciation of natural sights and sounds see Nature in Index V. For his travels see i. xxi and Travel in Index V.

JOHNSON, SAMUEL, 18 Sept. 1709 N.s.—13 Dec. 1784, elder son (his y. b. Nathaniel '12–'37) of Michael Johnson, 1656–'31, bookseller at Lichfield, and Sarah Ford, 1669–(? 21 or 22) Jan. '59 (L i. 514). Educated Lichfield '16, Stourbridge '25, Pembroke College, Oxford '28–'29; m. 9 July '35 o.s., Elizabeth Porter (*née* Jervis) 1688–17 Mar. '52, o.s., widow '34 of Henry Porter; M.A. Oxon. Feb. '55 (55, 56, 59, 62, 63); LL.D. Trinity Coll. Dublin '65 (178); 'LL.D.' Oxon. '75 (385, 386, 387.1). For a full chronology see L vi, Johnson.

BOOKS. For J's reading *see* READING AND WRITING below, and Index III. For his undergraduate library see 3.1. To his later collections the letters hardly refer. He mentions (1006.1) his 'good copy' of the *Biblia Polyglotta* of 1657. For his borrowings see the letters to Birch and e.g. 44 (Millar, Mrs. Strahan), 186 (Garrick), 345 (Steevens), 551 (Streatham), 611 (Nichols), 1145 (Percy). 'I was bred a bookseller' 609; a borrowed book 'too fine for a Scholar's talons' 583; cf. 347 'I wish he were not so fine'.

CHARACTER.

(1) *Self-examination.* ('51 or '52) 'I go wrong in opposition to conviction' 29, cf. 96; ('53) 'I ought to do many things which I do not' 46; ('54) 'too apt to be negligent' 53, cf. 70; ('56) 'a pang for every moment that any human being has by my peevishness or obstinacy spent in uneasiness' 106; ('60) 'intended to do great things which I have not done' 135; ('61) 'have hitherto lived without the concurrence of my own judgement' 138; ('67) a visit to L'd 'recals . . . years in which I purposed what . . . I have not done' 190; ('68) 'this little Dog does nothing' 197; ('73) 'corroded with vain and idle discontent' 296; 'a life of which I do not like the review' 306; 'threescore and four years in which little has been done . . . a life diversified by misery' 326 (356); ('76) 'I have not practised all this prudence myself' 502; ('77) sixty-eight years have 'run away' almost 'without account, without use, and without memorial' 542, 'to lament the past is vain' 548; 'Life has . . . fallen . . . very short of my early expectation' 555; ('80) 'would I recal plans of life which I never brought into practice? . . . Is it reasonable to wish for suggestions of shame?' 686; 'any good of myself I am not very easy to believe' 699; ('81) 'To what I have done I do not despair of adding something' 746; 'I have through my whole progress of authorship honestly endeavoured to teach the right,

though I have not been sufficiently diligent to practise it' 748; ('82) 'you (JB) would have . . . perhaps found me peevish' 785; ('83) 'I have not done my part very sluggishly, if it now begins' ('it' is 'to live heedlessly in a mist') 894; ('84) 'From the retrospect of life . . . I shrink with multiplicity of horrour. . . . I look forward with less pain' 1003.1.

(2) *Self-portraiture*: I remark that J hardly mentions his mental powers except his memory; on his genius and learning he is silent. ('50) 'I read them' (letters describing a death) 'with tears' 30; ('55) 'a retired and uncourtly Scholar' 61, 'vir umbraticus' 63; ('62) 'the journey of a wit to his own town '(L'd) 142; ('64) his 'kindness' in sending presents to LP 164; ('72) 'I think it impossible that I should have suffered such a total obliteration, from my mind, of any thing which was ever there' 292; ('74) 'a bad manager in a croud' 361; ('75) 'I fret at your (HLT) for-getfulness as I do at my own' 432; ('77) 'Why should you suspect me of forgetting lilly lolly?' 553; ('77) 'Our ramble in the islands hangs upon my imagination' 528; ('80) 'my *genius* is always in extremes, . . . very noisy, or very silent . . .' 686 (not wholly serious); 'the civillest creature in nature' 703.1 (to Queeney); 'unskilful in Biblical criticism' 707; ('81) 'As I have not the decrepitude I have not the callous-ness of old age' 718; 'It almost enrages me to be suspected of forgetting . . .' 745, cf. ('82) his forgetting a poem of his own 782.2; ('83) suspected his memory unjustly 826.1; 'sometimes my memory is less ready' 834; 'I am afraid that I bear the weight of time with unseemly . . . impatience' 835.1 (18); 'I love a little secret history' 846; has benefited or entertained all who knew him 860; his life 'has been spent with the approbation of mankind' 922; ('84) 'till now my talk was more about the dishes than my thoughts' 953; 'if I should recover, curiosity would revive' 971; 'The town is my element . . . Sir Joshua told me long ago, that my vocation was to publick life, and I hope still to keep my station' 1029 (society, not politics).

CHARITIES (personal or vicarious). 133 (Mrs. Ogle), 193, 207.1 (Heely), 211.1, 264.1 (anonymous), 228, 229 (Tom Johnson), 393, 394 (Peyton, Macbean), 527 (De Groot), 637 (J's poor neighbours in Bolt Court), 733 (JR's 'splendid benefac-tion', see note); 577, 705 (Lowe); 934 (Herne).

CONVERSATION. Talking for victory: 321 (345, Lord Monboddo); 'the Ladies . . . said . . . *there is no rising unless somebody will cry fire*' 669.

CORRESPONDENCE. See my general remarks i. xvii. Apologies for silence are frequent; for his 'parsimony of writing' see especially 98, 138, 163, 181; 'there are very few writers of more punctuality' (483) is exceptional, since it is to HLT. Lack of subject is sometimes pleaded in letters from L'd and A'n; 'here sit poor I, with nothing but my own solitary individuality' 425. There is in the letters them-selves no indication that he ever contemplated their publication after his death; but his interest in them is shown by his willingness (428) to reread them, and by his hope (330) that HLT kept them. His reluctance to write letters is shown in e.g. 98, 'I never did exchange letters regularly but with dear Miss Boothby'. The exception is his correspondence with HLT: 'our letters will pass and repass like shuttlecocks' (561.1). His eagerness to receive letters is shown by complaints to e.g. Hector, JB, BL, HLT of their silence; see especially 108 ('I tear open a letter with great eagerness'), 129 (asking LP to write once a week), 308 (reading HLT's twice), and the letters of summer and autumn '84 *passim*. Note also 583 'prattle upon paper'; 559 'if our correspondence were printed'.

As few letters to J have survived (see Appendix H) we learn little of his corre-spondents' opinions of his letters. JB's and HLT's contain much, occasionally ful-some, flattery, and JT endorsed 106 'the best Letter in the World'.

For J's epistolary style see READING AND WRITING. For letters of condo-lence see e.g. 30 and 580 (Elphinston), 183 (Peregrine Langton), 202 (Kitty

CORRESPONDENCE

Chambers), 437.1 (Jane Burke's father), 466 and 717 (Harry Thrale and his father), 601 (Garrick). For his occasional mis-dating see Letters in Index V.

Some Elements in J's Letters. Humour, Irony, &c. Humour abounds, especially in letters to HLT; I note especially 659 'Though I am going to dine with Lady Craven, I am' &c. Irony is rare. I note 329 (366) Romish superstition contrasted with 'the active zeal of Protestant devotion'; 423 Baretti's 'elegance' in forwarding a letter without a cover; 578 Aberdeen 'not much nearer' BL's 'navigation'; 677 'the good Protestants' (rioters); 999 'consolation' in the death of acquaintances.

DOMESTICITY. For J's household *see* FRIENDS X (1), and for domestic discord, e.g. 591, 633, 646, 647. Dinners at home (*L* ii. 215, and other references in *L* vi s.v. Johnson, *Dinners*): 754.1 the Wesleys; 881 a birthday party, 919 Christmas Day; 946.2 Mrs. Lewis and Sastres; 953 'the remainder of the old Club'.

THE FASHIONABLE WORLD. *See* FRIENDS X (11) and for his dining out, &c. some of the names in that list: ('82) 'the world willing enough to caress me' 771.

FRIENDS AND ACQUAINTANCES. His tenacity of friendship finds frequent expression in the letters. He often insists, especially to Hector and JT, that nothing can make up for the friends of one's youth; see e.g. 108, 303.1, 541, 729.1.

I attempt a classification, by reference to Index II, of the Johnsonian circles. This is in part topographical; the last class (mainly London) is divided according to the callings of its members. There is of course much overlapping. Capitals indicate CORRESPONDENTS.

I. J's *Family and Relations*

See Collier, FORD, Harrison, HEELY, Herne, HOLLYER, Hunter, JOHNSON, PORTER, Scrimshaw.

II. *The Midlands*

See Addenbroke (L'd), Adey (L'd), ASTON (L'd), Bailey (L'd), Boylston (? B'm), Brodhurst (? L'd), Chambers (C., L'd), Cobb (L'd), CONGREVE (L'd), CORBET, Dale (A'n), [Darwin? (L'd)], Dixie (Bosworth), Doxy (L'd), Dyott (A'n), Eld, Falconer (L'd), GARRICK (DAVID and Peter, L'd), Gell (A'n), GREENE (L'd), HECTOR (B'm), Hervey (L'd), HICKMAN (Stourbridge), Hinckley (L'd), Hodgson (A'n), Howard (C., L'd), Jackson (Harry, L'd), Kennedy (A'n), LANGLEY (A'n), LEVET (J. and T., L'd), Littleton, Lloyd (B'm), Longden (A'n), Mousley (A'n), Newton (A., L'd), Norton (? B'm), Pearson (L'd), Perks (B'm), Pratt (L'd), Proby (L'd), Prujean (L'd), Rann (Coventry), REPINGTON, Roebuck (B'm), Scarsdale, Sedgwick (L'd), Seward (A. and T., L'd), SIMPSON (J., L'd), Smith (Lady, L'd), Swinfen (L'd and B'm), TAYLOR (J., A'n, and Taylor of B'm), Turton (L'd), VYSE (L'd), Walmsley (L'd), Warren (B'm), Whitby (L'd).

III. *Oxford*

See ADAMS, APPERLEY, BENTHAM, BRIGHT, CHAMBERS, Colson, EDWARDS, FISHER, FOTHERGILL, Griffith, HORNE, HUDDESFORD, Jones (Mary and William), King, Maurice, Parker, Prince, SCOTT (W.), Spicer, Swinton, Tyrwhitt, Vansittart, WARTON (T.), WETHERELL, WHEELER, Wise.

IV. *Cambridge*

See FARMER.

V. *Bath, Bristol, and the West*

See Barret, Bowles, Catcott, Dobson, Guest, Harrington (H.), Hinchliffe, Johnson (William), MILLER, Morison, Tolcher, Woodward.

VI. *Ireland*

See Andrews, Campbell, Grierson, JESSOP, LELAND, Madden, Maxwell, O'CONOR.

JOHNSON

VI. *Scotland*

(Feb. '73) 'My northern friends have never been unkind' 295.

See ARGYLE, BEATTIE, Blacklock, Blair, Boyd, Colquhoun, Dick, DRUMMOND (W.), Eglinton, ELIBANK, ELPHINSTON, Fraser, Gordon (T.), Hailes, Janes, Loudon, Macaulay, Macdonald, Mackinnon, Maclaurin, Maclean, MACLEOD (of Macleod) and other McLeods, MACPHERSON (J.), Macquarry, Macqueen, Monboddo, Ord (R.), Oughton, Ritter, Robertson, Shaw (W.), Sinclair, Smollett, Watson, Webster.

VIII. *America*

('73) 'I set a high value on my American friends' 297.

See BOND, FRANKLIN, JOHNSON (W. S.), JOHNSTONE, Lee, WHITE.

IX. *The Streatham Circle*

See BARCLAY, Bridge, Brooke, Carter, Cator, Clerke (P. J.), Colebrook, Cotton, Crutchley, Davenant, Dobson, Evans, Hotham, Jackson (Humphrey), Keep, Lade, Lester, Lisgow, Lysons, Manucci, Mawbey, MILLER, Mills, Musgrave, Myddleton, Nesbitt, OWEN (M.), PENNICK, Pepys (W. W.), PERKINS, Piozzi, Pitches, Plumbe, Polhill, Pool, Robson, SALUSBURY, Scrase, Seward or Sheward (Mrs.), Shelley, Smith (Henry, Mrs.), Streatfield, Thomas (Dr.), THRALE, Whitbread.

X. *London and General*

(1) *The Household*: see BARBER, Carmichael, DESMOULINS, LEVET (R.), Williams. 'If I were a little richer I would perhaps take some cheerful Female into the House' (June '83) 857.

(2) *J's Intimates*: see ALLEN (E.), BARETTI, Bathurst, BEAUCLERK, BOOTHBY, BOSWELL, BURKE, BURNEY, CARTER, CHAMBERS (Robert), COTTRELL, FOWKE, GARRICK (D.), GOLDSMITH, Gwynn, HAMILTON (W. G.), HAWKESWORTH, HAWKINS, LANGTON, LAWRENCE, Murphy, NICHOLS, PARADISE, PERCY, Ramsay, REYNOLDS, RICHARDSON, RYLAND, Savage, STRAHAN (W. and his wife), TAYLOR, THRALE, the WARTONS.

(3) *The Clergy (see also Literature)*: see BAGSHAW, Bell, Blair, Crane, Derby, DODD, HAMILTON (Anthony), Markham, Maxwell, Mayo, Newton (T.), PATTEN, PERCY, Porteus, Tooke, VYSE, Warburton, the WESLEYS, WILSON (of Westminster), Worthington.

(4) *Literature and Learning*: see ASTLE, BARETTI, BARNARD (F. A.), BEATTIE, BIRCH, Blair, BOYLE, Browne (I. H.), Bryant, CALDER, Cambridge, Carlisle, Carte, CARTER, CHAPONE, CHESTERFIELD, Collins (W.), Coxeter, CRADOCK, CROFT, Cumberland, Delap, DOUGLAS, Dunbar, ELPHINSTON, FARMER, GOLDSMITH, Graham, GRANGER, Harris, HAWKESWORTH, HAWKINS, Howard (J.), HUGGINS, Huntingford, HUSSEY, JONES (G.), Kelly, Kennedy, Lennox, Lucas, LYE, Macbean, MACPHERSON (J.), MALONE, Marsigli, Martinelli, Melmoth, Moore, MORE, Murphy, NICHOLS, Oldys, Parr, PERCY, Peyton, Reed, RICHARDSON, Robertson, Rose, Savage, SCOTT (J.), Shaw, Smart, Solander, Spence, STEEVENS, STOCKDALE, STRAHAN (G.), Stuart, Twiss, Walker, Warburton, the WARTONS, Watson, WESTON, WILSON (of Clitheroe), Wraxall, Young.

(5) *The Booktrade*: see ALLEN (A.), Baskerville, CADELL, CAVE, DAVIES (T.), DILLY, DODSLEY, FAULKNER, HAMILTON (ARCHIBALD), HENRY, Hitch, Johnston, JONES (G.), KEARSLEY, Knapton, LONGMAN, MILLAR, NEWBERY, NICOL, Nurse, PATERSON, Payne, RIVINGTON, Roberts, STRAHAN (W.), Thomas, TONSON, Vaillant.

(6) *The Stage*: see Abington, Chetwood, COLMAN, Fletewood, Foote, GARRICK, Kemble, Porter (M.), Powell, Sheridan, Siddons.

(7) *Physicians* : see Baker, BROCKLESBY, Bromfield, Butter, CRUIKSHANK, HEBERDEN, Holder, HUNTER, James, JEBB, LAWRENCE, Lewis, MUDGE, Pepys (L.), Pott, Sharp (S.), STAUNTON, Turton.

(8) *Artists*: see BARRY, Hogarth, HUMPHRY, LOWE, NOLLEKENS, OPIE, Ramsay, REYNOLDS.

CORRESPONDENCE

(9) *Clubmates*: these are members of the 'Literary' Club unless I indicate that a man was only or also a member of the Ivy-Lane or Essex-Head. BANKS, BARNARD (T.), Barrington (Essex-Head), BARRY (Essex-Head), BOSWELL, BOWLES (Essex-Head), BROCKLESBY (Essex-Head), Bunbury, BURKE, CHAMBERS (Robert), Chamier, Charlemont, CLARK (R. (Essex-Head)), COLMAN, Dunning, Dyer (also Ivy-Lane), Elliot, Fordyce (G.), Fox, Gibbon, GOLDSMITH, HAWKESWORTH (Ivy-Lane), HAWKINS (also Ivy-Lane), HOOLE (Essex-Head), Jodrell (Essex-Head), Jones (W.), LANGTON, MACARTNEY, MALONE, NICHOLS (Essex-Head), Nugent, Palmerston, PARADISE (Essex-Head), Payne (Ivy-Lane), PERCY, REYNOLDS, RYLAND (Ivy-Lane and Essex-Head), SASTRES (Essex-Head), SCOTT (W. (also Essex-Head)), Seward (W. (Essex-Head)), Shipley, STEEVENS (also Essex-Head), Vesey, WINDHAM (also Essex-Head).

(10) *Politicians*: see BURKE, BUTE, Chamier, HAMILTON (W. G.), JENKINSON, Lewis (E.), North, THURLOW, Wedderburn, WILKES.

(11) *The World of Fashion*: see Bingham, Boufflers, Buller, Byron, Carlisle, Cavendish, Charlemont, CHESTERFIELD, Cholmondely, Craven, Edgcumbe, Elliot, Fitzherbert, Fitzmaurice, George III, GALWAY, Greville, HORNECK, Jefferies, LYTTELTON, Middleton, Monckton, MONTAGUE, Ord (W.), Palmer, Sheffield, SOUTHWELL, Vesey, WAY.

(12) *Protégés*: Angel, Coxeter, Davenport, Davis, De Groot, LOWE, Ogle, Otway, Paterson, Pellé, Stockdale.

(13) *Roman Catholics*: see Brewer, COMPTON, Cowley, Strickland, Wilks.

(14) *Miscellaneous*: see Akerman, Barnard (E.), Boswell (T. D.), Bruce, CUMINS, Fordyce (Miss), Gardiner, Gordon (A.), Harding (C.), HASTINGS, JACKSON (R.), METCALFE, Oglethorpe, Paoli, PAUL, Philipps, Phillips, PROWSE, ROLT, Rose, SASTRES, Selwyn, Sharp (W. and Miss), Smalbrooke, Strickland, Tolcher, Villette, WELCH.

GODCHILDREN. *See in* Index II Langton, Mudge, Paterson, (?) Perkins (739.2), Thrale (Lucy); and for Mauritius Lowe's son and daughter, *L* iv. 403.

HABITATIONS OR ADDRESSES. (For a complete list see *Life* iii. 534, and for his travels see my Contents, i. xxi.) ('31–'35) Lichfield 1, 2, 3.1; (? '31) Market Bosworth 1.1; ('34) Birmingham 3; ('35) Great Haywood 3.2; Edial (?) 3.3; ('37) Greenwich 4; ('38) Castle Street 5, 6; ('40) Lichfield 12; ('41) Durham Yard, Strand 14; ('43) Gray's Inn 19; (? '46 or '52) Golden Anchor, Holborn 21, 23.1; ('49–'57) Goff or Gough Square 25, 28, 67, 69, 87, 94, 112; 'the garret in Gough Square' 176; ('59) 'I have left off housekeeping' 117 (9 Jan.); move to Staple Inn 130 (23 Mar.); Gray's Inn 132.3 (9 Nov.), 133 (17 Dec.); ('61–'65) Inner Temple Lane 137, 144.1, 145, 171 (*L* i. 350); ('65–'76) No. 7 Johnson's Court 174.1, 175, &c.; 'my new study' 182 (*L* ii. 427); ('75, 16 Nov.) 'a ship . . . without an anchor', in reference to his travels in Scotland, Wales, France; ('76–'84) 'No 8 Bolt Court, Fleet Street (not Johnson's Court)' 469 (4 Apr.); his garden there 692, 855, 857.

HEALTH AND SPIRITS. J's persistent ill health and frequent illnesses form the sombre background of his letters. I have listed only salient passages. Some references to specific ailments and to remedies will be found in Index V, s.v. Health. For J's physicians *see above*, Friends X. 7. (? '46) 'I am very ill' 22; ('51 or '52) 'I am often, very often, ill' 29; ('54) 'often near his (Collins) state' 57; ('55) 'afraid of my Lungs' 77, 78; 'weakness and misery' 78; 'who have thought much on Medicine' 79; ('56) 'From that kind of melancholy indisposition which I had . . . at Birmingham, I have never been free' 103; ('67) 'ill health . . . has crusted me into inactivity' 190.1; 'my old melancholy' 191.1; ('68) inability to help friends in 'exigencies . . . has been commonly' J's state 199; 'for a long time very poorly' 202, 'miserably disordered' 203.1; ('70) rheumatism 227.1, 228; see s.a. '74; imputes 'failings to want of health' 238; ('71) rheumatism, lumbago 255, 257; ('72) better than for

347

many years 275.1; a prey to morbid fancies ('something, which I know to be nothing') preventing sleep 277; ('73) ten weeks cough and six weeks fever, 'near fainting' 296; for 'the secret' (HLP) see on 307.1; never quite well in Scotland, 320, 326 (p. 353), 329 (p. 373); ('74) 'I have never recovered from the last dreadful illness' (? that of '70) 358, cf. 835.1; ('76) 'a very poor creeper upon the earth' 487; ('77) self-bleeding 506; ('78) sleeplessness 593; ('79) gout 630; health 'improved very perceptibly' 640.1, 643; ('80) 'as well as people of my age commonly are' 656, cf. 684; 18 Sept. 'concludes another of my wretched years' 703; better, for over a year, 'than for many years before' 708, cf. 674; ('81, Nov.) 'visibly disordered', loses his superiority to weather 746, cf. 984; ('82) '. . . pectus tentatur, ita ut . . . somnus prorsus pellatur' 756.2; 'my health has been, from my twentieth year, such as has seldom afforded me a single day of ease' 772; 'the terrour that had seized me' 792; (31 Dec.) 'a very sickly and melancholy year' 821; ('83) account of the last ten years 835.1 (17); (17 June) the 'paralytick stroke' 847, &c.; (Sept.) the sarcocele 882.1, &c.; 'in other respects better than for some years' 882.1, cf. 891, 893, contrast 'these two last years have proved very hard upon me' 888.1; 'I shall I hope lay hold of the possibility of life which yet remains' 885, 'I hope God will yet grant me a little longer life' 888; ('84) asthma and dropsy; (21 Apr.) 'returned thanks . . . for my recovery' after 'a confinement of one hundred twenty-nine days' 955, see also 923.1, 925, 935, 945, 946.1; 'trepidation' of handwriting 925; climbed the Academy stairs 'in all the madness of superfluous health' 956; (31 May) 'very weak and very asthmatic' 963; 'twenty years of a life radically wretched' 972; 'content to talk of the weather. Pride must have a fall' 984; letters July–Nov. from L'd and A'n are largely to Brocklesby and other physicians detailing symptoms; he came home 16 Nov. to die; failing eyesight 1042.1; the last letter (1042.2) dated 10 Dec.; he died 13 Dec.

HOBBIES. *See also* BOOKS. Chymistry 259, 264; Print-collecting 634 (*and see* Montague in Index II); Gardening (Bolt Court) 839.1 (poplars), 855; 857; Cats 901 'Lily the white kitling'; Riding 539 ('77, B'n); Swimming 132.1 ('59, O'd).

LANGUAGES. See the same heading in Index V.

(1) *Greek*. For the 'Epigram to Eliza' see 7, for the 'tetrastick' on Goldsmith 358; Greek phrases 835.1 (17, 19).

(2) *Latin*. For letters in Latin see 63, 385, and s.v. Lawrence in Index II; For occasional use of Latin phrases, certainly or probably not quotations, see e.g. 2 'e carcere exire', 10 ('impransus'), 64, 151, 170, 259, 310, 642; J corrects JB's Latin 185; J's prayer in Latin verse, composed when paralysed 850.

(3) *French*. For letters in French see 213, 248, 307.1, 400; 'I will try to speak a little French' (Calais, Sept. '75) 436. For occasional French phrases 79, 93, 258, 311, 419, 423, 539, 779.5, 857, 954, 955.

(4) *Italian*. 4, 116.1, 891.

(5) *Spanish*. 'learning Spanish of Mr. Baretti' 304.1.

LIVELIHOOD. For J's literary earnings *see also* Index VI. ('31) 'I am yet unemploy'd' 1; ('32) he leaves Sir W. Dixie and applies for 'a Vacancy at Ashburne' 2; ('34) Proposals (for Politian) 2.1; application to Cave 3; ('35) 'going to keep a private boarding-school' 3.2; ('38) 'very disadvantageous circumstances' 5; Cave's 'present' 6; ('43) asks Cave for 'another Guinea tonight' 15; his debt to Levetts of L'd, q.v. in Index II; ('44) his wife's property 20; ('51) asks Newbery for £2, 32, for a guinea 33, 34; (n.y.) to Strahan, 'the point is to get two Guineas' 38; (? '52) 'I have sold a property' for £100, 40, 42.2; ('53) 'my servant' 45; ('56) 'under an arrest', borrows six guineas from Richardson 94; ('58) borrows £40 from Tonson 112.1; ('59) 'not much richer' 117; sends 12 guineas to his mother 118, £20 to LP 125; ('62) his pension 143, 144, 145; *see also* 152; ('63) offers to help LP 150; ('66) 'unwilling to sell' the L'd house 180, cost of repairs 187; debt (?) of £100 to

Garrick 186; ('70) property in L'd (?) 228, 229; ('72 and later) dealings with W. Strahan, q.v. in Index II; ('77) 'my money has not held out so well as it used to do' 528; ('78) £100 for a friend, advanced by Strahan 589.2; ('82) borrows £30 from Barclay and Perkins 738.1, 739.2; ('84) 'the King has for near a year paid me nothing' 965.1; asks Strahan 'how much will be coming' 1039.1; asks him (10 Dec.) for 'whatever portion of my pension you can spare' 1042.2.

LONELINESS. There is in the letters so little *complaint*—of poverty, or even of ill health and low spirits—that the confessions of loneliness are the more impressive. *See in* Index II Allen, E., Levet, R., Richardson, Williams. ('49) 'my recluse kind of life' 24; ('54) 'a kind of solitary wanderer in the wild of life' (since his wife's death) 56; ('56) 'none but you (H. Boothby) on whom my heart reposes' 80; 'almost single in the world' 106; ('59) 'my grief (his mother's death) makes me afraid to be alone' 126.1; 'very solitary and comfortless' 127; 'very desolate' 129; 'a man unconnected is at home everywhere . . . (or) no where' 134; ('61) goes to the theatre 'only to escape from myself' 138; ('64) JR almost his only friend 166; ('76) Happiness of brother and sister surviving; 'I have nobody to whom I can talk of my first years' 460; ('79) 'I live here in stark solitude' 642; ('81) misses the 'consanguineous unanimity' of family life 749; ('83) 'self-tormenting solitude' 875; 'a very desolate house' 882; 'unwelcome solitude' 888.1, cf. 891.1, 898.1; 'I rise to a solitary breakfast, and sit down in the evening with no companion' 907; ('84) 'abandoned to the contemplation of my own miseries' 1000, cf. 1003.1.

PERSONAL APPEARANCE, HABITS, ETC.

Portraits (L iv. 447). ('71) By JR (L iv. 421) admired at L'd; 'Every man has a lurking wish to appear considerable in his native place' 261; ('77–'78) Head by Nollekens; cast sent to LP 564; generally condemned 572; By JR 583, 586; ('79) 'a little print' 605; ('80) By FR 682; 'my print' 657; ('83) By FR, 'Johnson's grimly ghost' 876; by Opie 879.

Eyesight. 311 ('the seeing eye'), 311.1, 312.

Food and Drink. There are hardly any mentions of either except in references to dieting or to presents of food. Wine is mentioned 78, 82.

Clothes. ('73) 'a great coat' (a sign of 'infirmity') 296; ('75) 'best black cloaths' (mourning) at the Thrales' 393, 395–7, 'Mr. Thrale's direction' 551.

Habits. ('55) shaved by a barber 75.1; ('66, '75) early rising 182 ('about eight') 183, chapel at six 399; ('68) riding 209.1; ('71) less 'lounging and untidy' (LP) than last year 255; ('73, '75) 'I run pretty well' 318; 'ran a race' 437.

POLITICS. For J's political tracts see Index VI. For references to public events see Politics in Index V. For J's indifference see ('56) 'unconcerned about the marches and countermarches in America' 98.1, and references in Index VII s.v. *publick*.

('59) 'clapped . . . at Dr. King's speech' 132.1 (see note); ('66–'67) 'the late embargo' 187.1 (see note), 'East Indian affairs' 187.2, 187.3; cannot leave L'n 'during the Session' 180; ('73) 'I do not much wish well to discoveries' 299 (i.e. by explorers); ('75) 'I am again gotten into politicks' 384.4; ('76) 'a man who has had the honour of vindicating his Majesty's Government' 472.

QUARRELS. J's rather numerous altercations, due to native pugnacity and the manners of the age, were nearly always short-lived. See 247, 263 (Miss Langton), 401 (Colson), 575 (Percy), 579 (W. Strahan), 891 (Mrs. Montagu), 1124 (Davies). An exception is 215 (see note); if J and TW ever had a quarrel, there is no sign of reconciliation.

READING AND WRITING. *See* Indexes III, Authors, and VI, J's Works. General references to his own habits are infrequent, apart from confessions of procrastination in e.g. revising the Dictionary or composing the *Lives*. For marginalia see 79; for his reading of authors' MSS., 106.1, 501, 748 ('persecuted').

For help or advice to individual authors see in Index II Blair, Burney (C.),

Calder, Carlisle, Chambers, Collins (J.), Edwards, Garrick, Greville (F.), Grierson, Hailes, Hawkesworth, Hoole, Horne, Kelly, Lucas, Lye, More (H.), O'Conor, Percy, Reynolds (F.), Richardson, Robertson, Sastres, Shaw (W.), Warton (J. and T.), Watson, Wilson (of Clitheroe).

'I have much curiosity after the Manners . . . of the Middle Ages, but . . .' 737; 'I have . . . honestly endeavoured to teach the right' 748; reading promoted by solitude ('83) 834 (see note); 'I have been a friend at a poetical difficulty' 860; 'I have begun to look among my books' (Oct '83, proof of convalescence) 895.

Johnson's Style, see also CORRESPONDENCE. Though not a few of the letters might be extracts from his *Rambler*, most are in his middle style, between his formal and his oral manner. Outstanding examples of the first class are the letters to Chesterfield (61) and to Drummond (184). He is at his most colloquial and allusive in the letters to HLT, especially perhaps in those of '75, a happy year, and of the *annus mirabilis* '80.

A striking example of J's (? Latinizing) inversion is the opening sentence of 87; Of his power of packing a sentence, 'If Crutchly did nothing for life but add weight to its burden, and darkness to its gloom, he is kindest to those from whom he is furthest' 748.

I note his addiction, perhaps unconscious, to the figure called chiasmus, e.g. 'imagination of love and greatness . . . hopes of preferment and bridal raptures' 147.

RELIGION. *See also* RELIGION and DEATH in Index V. I give here some references for J's personal religion and religious observance. Many letters contain pious ejaculations. His belief in immortality, and in the need to prepare for death, appears regularly in his remarks on the deaths of friends. He often asks his correspondents for their prayers: see, e.g. 42 (JT), 78 (Boothby), 120 (his mother), 202 (LP), 205 (HLT), 523 (Dodd), 929.2 (Bowles), 940 (Gastrell and Aston), 1003.2 (Q).

('55) 'I cannot receive my religion from any human hand' 79; 'calamities often sent to produce good purposes' 78; ('56) has no 'right to condemn' Cave for neglect of 'the positive duties of religion' 87; ('59) 'she is happy' (his mother's death) 125, cf. ('68) 'one Protector who can never be lost but by our own fault' 202; ('72) unwilling to dine out on Easter Eve 275; ('73) crossed from Raasay to Skye 'though it was Sunday' 329 (366) (for Sunday letter-writing see App. F); ('84) 'I am extremely afraid of dying' 932; 'the approach of death is very dreadful'; Easter communion 'at home' 951; 'I have only the timidity of a Christian . . . not the wisdom of a Stoick' 953; 'may God pardon and bless us, for Jesus Christ's sake' (2 Dec.) 1041.

UNIVERSITY HONOURS. I remark the absence of any allusion to his undergraduate days. ('54, '55) J thanks TW and Wise for their 'kind design', i.e. his M.A. degree 55, 56, 59, 62; his letter to the Vice-Chancellor 63, 64, 65; ('65) his Dublin doctorate 178; ('75) his Oxford doctorate: 'praises in the diploma' 386.

PERSONS

I give no list of Johnson's Correspondents; but they are distinguished in this index by CAPITALS. In each article dealing with a correspondent, letters to that correspondent are similarly distinguished by **heavy figures**.

References are to the numbers of the letters; in indexing J's few long letters I add a page-number in brackets, e.g. 329(371). Users of the book will soon come to know that e.g. 329 is in the first volume. Occasional references to pages *only* are preceded by the volume-number.

If any person is in the *Dict. of Nat. Biography* or is in the index to Boswell (ed. Hill–Powell), *Thraliana*, Fanny Burney's Diaries, or Mr. Reade's *Gleanings*, that is indicated (*DNB, L, Th,* FB's *Diaries,* R i, &c.).

A student of any of J's intimacies will naturally turn first to his letters to the person concerned. For that reason facts and opinions about AB in letters to AB are more lightly indexed than facts and opinions about AB in letters to others.

To lighten the burden of my commentary, I have in general noted there only such persons as are ambiguously or obscurely named, and have not always given cross-references. Instead I have collected the references to any person in this index in chronological order, with a note of the year, e.g. ('81), before each reference or group of references for that year. A valid reason, I believe, for this method is that the persons are for the most part either famous or, for the general reader, negligible. I hope that many of my articles will be found informing, and even readable, and will recompense the labour of turning from the text to another page or another volume.

As J's academic associations were almost exclusively Oxonian, I have judged it permissible to write (even!) 'Trinity College', without further identification.

Abbess, —, ? housekeeper at S'm.—('80) 'Mrs. Abbess gave me some mushrooms' 669.

Aberdeen, Provost of: see Jopp.

Abington, Frances, '37–1815, actress. (*DNB, L*).—('75) 'I had I know not how much kiss of Mrs. Abington' 390.

ADAMS, WILLIAM, '06–'89, Scholar of Pembroke Coll. '20, Fellow '23, Master '75; D.D. '56; m. '42 Sarah Hunt (d. '85); their d. Sarah, '46–1804 (*DNB, L,* R v).— ('54) J introduces to Richardson 'Mr. Adams under whom I had the honour to perform exercises at Oxford . . . his confutation of Hume on Miracles' 51.1 (*An Essay in Answer to Mr. Hume's Essay on Miracles* '52); ('76, '77) J sends A a letter by 'a learned Benedictine' from Paris 484; 'Father Wilkes . . . took Oxford in his way. I recommended

him to Dr. Adams' 551; ('78) J's letter (? to A, see note) pleading for Gwynn 570; ('81) J dines with A 741; ('82) J dines with A and meets Hannah More 789, 790, 791, 'Dr. Edwards has invited Miss Adams and Miss More' to dinner 792; ('84) Miss A's invitation to Oxford 946.1, J thanks her for visits, invites himself to stay at Pembroke (bringing JB) 963.1, J writes from Pembroke that 'Miss Adams and Miss Moore are not yet come' 965.2, 'a fortnight's abode with Dr. Adams' 966, thanks for visit, messages to Mrs. and Miss A 974, orders copies of his principal works to be sent to A 1038.

Addenbroke, John, c. 1690–'76, of St. Catharine's Coll., Cambridge; Dean of Lichfield '45 (*L*).— ('71) 'as well in mind and body as his younger neighbours' 267; ('74) 'the Dean did me a kindness about forty years ago' 364.

Adeys of L'd: Felicia (Hammond), '12–'78, widow '63 of Joseph A., town-clerk of L'd; their d. Mary, '42–1830. *See also* Cobb (*L*, R vi, viii).—mentioned frequently in letters to LP, occasionally in letters to HLT from L'd.

Akerman, Richard, *c*. '22–'92, Keeper of Newgate (*L* iii. 431).—('80) A's part in the Gordon Riots 677.

Alexander, Thomas, Chymist, 108 Long Acre (*Directory* '90) (*Tb*).—('73) 'your transaction with A' 300, 301, 301.3.

Alexander the Great 585.1.

Alfred the Great: Astle's 'notes on Alfred' 737.

ALLEN, CHARLES, *c*. '30–'95, Vicar of St. Nicholas, Rochester, '65.—('80) J recommends Shaw to A **711.1**.

ALLEN, EDMUND, '26–28 July '84, s. of Thomas A, Rector of Kettering; printer; J's 'landlord and next neighbour in Bolt-court, for whom he had much kindness' (JB); m. — (*L*).—('57) J consults 'Mr. Allen' (i.e. Edmund?), 'about some literary business for an inhabitant of Oxford' 111; ('65) J recommends A to Lye as a good printer and a Northamptonshire man 174; ('75) J recommends A to JR and to Davies for a place **407.1, 408.2**; ('77) J employs A as go-between in the Dodd affair **519.3**, 521, **521.1**; ('78) J asks Cadell to employ A 569; ('81) J pays A rent 740, proposes 'a row and a dinner' **751**; ('82) mentioned 819.1; ('83) J misses Mrs. A 839, 857; J sends for A to 'act for me' when paralysed **847**, 850; J asks A to dine on his birthday 881; ('84) J asks Nichols to dine to meet A 930.1; A estimates for printing 958; J at O'd asks A to 'sit for me at the club' (Essex Head) **965.2**; J leaves plate in A's care 983; his death: 'one of my best and tenderest friends' 983, 984, 991, 995, 'a very kind and officious neighbour' 1003, 1012, 1026.

Allen (? Hollyer, b. '30), of Magdalen Hall (*L*).—('58) a stock of receipts for Shakespeare 'deposited with Mr. Allen of Magdalen Hall' 114.

Althorpe: *see* Bingham.

Andrews, Francis, — — '74, Provost of Trinity Coll., Dublin (*L*).—('65) 178.

Angel, George, a boy at Christ's Hospital.—('78) 574.1; ('81) 741a.

Anne, 'fine Mrs.', LP's maid.—('78) 538.

ANONYMOUS CORRESPONDENTS not identified.—('34) One to whom J sent Proposals **2.1**; ('43) 'a friend' **17.1**; ('56) **99.1**; ('62) 'a Lady' who asked J to solicit the abp. of Canterbury for her son **141**; ('69, '70, '71) J's travelling companion from L'n to L'd 220, **230.1**, 248.1; perhaps the same as the companion of ('61) 179, see next article; ('71) a lady **270.1**; ('72) a friend **274.3**; ('73) — **304.2**; ('78) a correspondent at O'd (? Adams) to whom J pleaded for Gwynn 570; ('82) **784**, a business letter.

Anonymous Persons, other than correspondents, not identified: (? '46 or '52) a 'Gentleman' who helped J in the Levett affair 22; ('54) the 'learned Swede' who gave J a Finnick Dictionary 55; ('55) 'a Gentleman desirous of giving his assistance' in the *Universal History* 58.1; a 'young Gentleman' to be employed to copy Bodleian MSS. 75; an Oxford barber 75.1; J's neighbour lately dead 78; ('56) 'another Doctor' (of medicine) 82; 'the Child' employed as a messenger 86; a 'Gentleman' conversant with Tickets 89; an unnamed poet 106.1; ('60) a 'celebrated Mathematician of Italy' 134.1; a 'Chirurgeon at Coventry' 135; J's 'only remaining friend' at L'd 142; ('61–'62) J's companion to L'd 179 (see the preceding article s.a. '69); ('62) the Abbot with whom Baretti quarrelled 142, his capricious patron (the same?) 147; a clergyman's widow in Devonshire 146; ('63) 'a very ingenious Gentleman', on whose behalf J sent a question to Chambers at O'd 148.1; it is just possible that the ingenious gentleman was Lord Harborough (q.v.), who franked this letter; ('63, '70) JT's housekeeper at A'n 161, 230.1; ('64) G. Strahan's tutor at O'd 167; ('67) the 'Ladies' at New Inn Hall 191.1; ('68) 'the poor maid' (a servant of the Thrales?) 195, 197; ('71) J's barber, and another, at L'd 253; J's 'old acquaintance' at L'd who 'had had a matter of four wives' 256; 'a Gentleman reading philosophical lectures at A'n 259; one of J's schoolfellows at L'd 260; 'young Mr. —' of Pembroke College 264.1 (later identified, see i. 431); ('72) 'the poor Clerk' (? at S'k or S'm) 286.1; ('73) 'a Highland Lady': the story is not in JB's journal, but the lady was probably Florence 'Rorie' Macdonald (*Tour* ed. Pottle and Bennett 116) 326 (356); ('74) 'a lady' who 'has a law-suit', whom J recommends to JB 354, 355; ('75) 'the Duke' who sent the Thrales venison 426; ('77) a maid 528; J's barber at L'd 535; ('79) FR's 'German friend' 624, perhaps the same as 'a lady whom she has lately known' 640; J's 'poor neighbours' in Bolt Court 637, 640, 641; 'a very furious fellow writing . . . against the life of Milton' 637; ('80) 'a Lady has sent me a Vial' 672; HT's doctor at Bath, presumably Moysey, q.v., 675; '—'s case' (? Owen, q.v.) 684; 'a decayed gentlewoman' civilized a parish 704; ('81) 'a very learned and ingenious Clergyman' who had never heard of Hammond on the Psalms 739; 'a medical man who only saw me at church' at L'd, and 'sent some pills' 746, 748; an anonymous author at L'd, possibly Darwin, q.v., 748; ('82) 'Lady Frances not at home' 779.2; ('83) A versifier 860; 'a friend' and his gluttonous wife 872; 'the boy that likes Rambler better than apples' 897; ('July 7. 1771', but the date is doubtful) an old L'd acquaintance 256 (see note).

Anson: George Anson, Baron A, 1697–'62 (*DNB*).—Z. Williams's letters to A, Appendix A, i. 432, 436.

APPERLEY, THOMAS, matric. Oriel College (commensalis) '66.— ('68) 198.

ARGYLE: John Campbell, '20–1806, 5th D '70; m. '69 Elizabeth (*c.* '33–'90), d. of John Gunning and widow of the 6th D of Hamilton (*DNB, L*).—('73) 'the Duke kept us yesterday' (at Inveraray) 334; J thanks him for the

loan of a horse; the Duchess's 'little commission' 335; 'we dined with the Duke and Dutchess' 336; ('77) 'we met the Duke and Dutchess of Argyle' (changing horses at A'n, which is on the Carlisle road) 552; (June '80) 'we frighten one another with seventy thousand Scots to come hither with the Dukes of Gordon and Argyle, and eat us' 679.

Ashburton: *see* Dunning.

ASTLE, THOMAS, '35–1803; F.S.A. '63, F.R.S. '66, Keeper of the Tower Records '83 (*DNB, L*, Nichols *LA* iii. 202). His brother Rev. Daniel A, '43–1826 (*L*).—('81) J commends TA's 'notes on Alfred' (*The Will of King Alfred* 1788) 737. JB was indebted to DA for copies, or loan, of 15, 16, and 737; see i. 427.

ASTONS of Lichfield: ELIZABETH ASTON, '08–'85, 3rd d. of Sir Thomas A, 3rd Bt; of Stowe Hill, L'd (usually 'Mrs. Aston'); JANE GASTRELL, '10–'91, 5th d. of Sir Thomas A, widow '72 of Rev. Francis G; of Stowe House (for this later distinction in the names of the houses see R v. 251. J seems always to write 'Gastrel').— (*L*, R v and vi; *see also* Hervey, Walmesley, Prujean).

Letters to: most are to EA, whom J addresses as 'Dear Madam' or 'Dearest Madam'; 566 to G; 776, 940, 1035, to the two jointly. (Hill includes in his numeration two lost letters, 434 and 769.) ('67) J deprecates A's solitude 194; ('69) J sends A a corn-mill 221; ('70) A mentioned 232; ('71) A mentioned 252, 260; ('72) A 'says she is somehow akin to the Cottons' 289, mentioned 289.2; ('75) A mentioned 381, 408; 'I go every day to Stowhill' 405; 'the Ladies on the Hill offer me a lodging' 426, advise a chaise 429; G mentioned 433; ('76) A mentioned 464.1; her remark on Harry Thrale's death, 'such a death is the next to translation', 465; Mrs. G. asks JB to dine 465.1; ('77) A's paralysis; besides the letters to her, and 566 to G, there are frequent mentions in letters from L'd to HLT; A 'one of the friends

whom I value most' **509**; her health
511; he deplores her 'resolute inactivity' **563**, urges the pursuit of health
as a duty **546, 566**; G (who 'wraps her
head in a towel' and condemns the
fashion in head-gear **539**) is also frequent in these letters; ('79) J rejoices
in A's recovery **599**, sends her oysters
604 and 'little books' (i.e. Vols. 1–4 of
his *Lives*) **613**; her chaise **616**; mentioned 616.1, **620**; no 'violence of faction' at Stow Hill **638**; 'the hill between Mrs. Gastrel's house and yours'
643; ('80) A mentioned **686**; ('81) A,
'for three years a paralytick crawler'
746, is frequent in letters to HLT
from L'd; 'Mrs. Gastrel is brisk and
lively' **743**; ('82) J thanks his 'Dearest
Ladies' for inquiries **776**; ('83) mentioned **860**; ('84) J writes to both
ladies **940** and (a valedictory) **1035**;
mentions 972.1, 1016, 1018.1, (n.d.,
1172.

Aston, Hon. and ('43) Rev. Henry Hervey, 4th s. of 1st E of Bristol, '01–'48;
m. '30 Catherine, e. d. of Sir Thomas
Aston; in '44 he assumed the name
of A on his wife's inheriting the
estate (*L*, R vi, viii).—(v.y.) A's connexion with the Levett mortgage 21,
32.1, **40** (and see note on 19).

Atterbury, Francis, 1662–'32 (*DNB, L*).
—('43) 'extracted' from the *State
Trials* 16.

Auchinleck, Lord: see Boswell, Alexander.

Augustus Frederick, Elector of Saxony
585.1.

Bagot, Walter Wagstaffe, '02–20 Jan.
'68, Bt '12; M.P. for Univ. of Oxford
'62–'68.—('68) 201.

BAGSHAW, THOMAS, c. '11–'87,
chaplain of Bromley Coll., Kent, '35
(*L*).—('73) B's notes on the Dictionary
307; ('84) J asks B, who had 'in the
year 1753... committed to the ground
my dear wife', for 'permission to lay a
stone upon her' **975**; 'the Inscription
is in the hands of Mr. Bagshaw' **977**.

Bailey or Bayley, Hester, ——'85, of Lichfield.—('82) 'my old friend, Hetty
Bailey' **768** (R iv. 105).

Bajazet 585.1.

Baker, George, '22–1809, Bt '76, physician (*DNB, L*).—('84) B's 'consideration' for J **997**.

Baker, Mrs., 'of the theatre', Edinburgh
(*L*).—('67) 193.

Ballard: perhaps Percy B, prebendary of
Westminster '58.—('53 or '55) 68.

BANKS, JOSEPH, '43–1820; F.R.S.
'66, P.R.S. '78; Bt '81; explorer;
member of the Club 11 Dec. '78
(*DNB, L*).—('72) J's inscription for
B's goat 271, **272**; ('73) Monboddo
deplores B's failure to discover 'long-
tailed Men' 321 (344); coupled with
Phipps **338**; ('78) B 'will be a very
honourable accession' to the Club **587**,
'we talk of electing Banks' **593**; ('80)
B 'had not gained much by circum-
navigating the world' 707.1; ('83)
J dines with B 839.1.

BARBER, FRANCIS, d. 1801; J's negro
servant. 'Given' (132.3) to J by
Richard Bathurst, prob. '52. Accompanied J on most of his visits (not to
Scotland) from '63, and is frequently
mentioned (esp. in letters to HLT
from L'd and A'n) usually as 'Francis',
often 'Frank'. He m. c. '76 Elizabeth
—, (?) '56–1816, and had issue (*L,
R ii*).

Selected references: ('55) 'my servant', presumably FB (?) **76**; (? '56)
'my Boy is run away' 100 (see note); ('59)
J applies to a Lord of the Admiralty
for his discharge 132.3; ('68–'70) J's
letters to B at Bishop's Stortford 207,
238, 241; ('71) thought by LP 'much
improved' 255; ('76) his wife 'Betsy'
498.1, 500; ('77) denies 'trusting some
other hand to the post office' 543; 'tells
sternly that it is past two o'clock' 545;
('78) 'wants to read' *Evelina* 591; ('79)
his intelligent observation 629; ('81)
J anxious about the colour of his child
750; ('83) J instructs him about a
dinner **881**; ('84) asks Allen to 'pay
Betsy Barber five shilling a week'
965.2; (n.d.) a letter reputedly written
by him to J's dictation 1126.

BARCLAY, DAVID, '28–1809, of
Youngsbury, Herts., half-uncle of
Robert, c. '40–1828 (*L, Th*).—All refer-
ences are to RB except 1012.1. ('81—

negotiation for the sale of the brewery) interview with 'Mr. B' 729.3, J sends Perkins 'good wishes for the Prosperity of you and your Partner' 730, tells P that B's 'interest . . . requires your concurrence' 735; ('82) mentioned 779.4; ('84) mentioned 952.2; J writes to DB about a Life of John Scott 1012.1; 'Mr. and Mrs.' B mentioned 1019.

BARETTI, JOSEPH (Giuseppe Marc' Antonio), '19–'89; teacher of languages; intimate with J soon after coming to London '51 (L i. 302); member of the Thrale household '73–'76 (DNB, L, Th, C).—B is addressed as 'Sir', but in the text of the letters J twice calls him 'my Baretti'. ('54) B's relations with Huggins and Croker 53.1, 53.2 (i. 442); mentioned (to Chambers) 54; ('55) J asks T. Warton to lend B Crescembeni 58; mentioned (to Charlotte Cottrell) 74; ('58) J introduces B to T. Warton and Chambers at Oxford 115, 115.1; ('61, '62) Letters to B at Milan 138, 142, 147; 'your friends here expect such a book of travels as has not been often seen' 138; ('68) his Italian Library (1757) quoted 206 (217); ('70) His Journey from London to Genoa (1770); 'I know not whether the world has ever seen such travels before' 236; ('73) his 'furious quarrel' with Davies 295; 'I have been learning Spanish of Mr. Baretti' 304.1; ('74) teaches Queeney Italian 360.1; ('75) his book not sold out 384.2; B and Queeney 'plague and darling' 401; his hen 408; J sends a letter from Mrs. Chambers for B's amusement 418 (she had been 'his pupil' 423); his 'fair captives' 420; HLT must forgive his rudeness 'the rather, because of his misbehaviour . . . he learned part of me' 420; she is reconciled to him 423; in Paris, 'a fine fellow, and speaks French . . . quite as well as English' 437, 439; ('76) B reports from Bath on Queeney's health 466, mentioned 476, helps J entertain Benedictines 483.1, his book reviewed 485; J writes to JB 'Baretti went away from Thrale's in some whimsical fit of

disgust, or ill nature, without taking any leave'; he had translated JR's Discourses into Italian for 25 guineas, and HT had given him 100 guineas in the spring 505; ('78) B's 'musical scheme' (Carmen Seculare) told to Burney 592 (see note); ('79) B's 'golden dream (Carmen) now but silver' 606; dines with J 645; ('83) J writes to Susannah Thrale, 'Baretti said what a wicked house it would be' 901 (see note); (n.d.) mention in a lost letter 1102.

Barker, —: perhaps one of several members of the B family who were stewards to the Dukes of Devonshire (information from the late Dr. Ernest Sadler). — ('81) 'Mr. Barker, who must know the family' (of Cavendish) 739.1.

Barnard, Edward, '17–'81; D.D. Cantab. '64; Provost of Eton '64 (DNB, L).— ('80) at Mrs. Vesey's 'there was Dr. Barnard of Eaton, and we made a noise all the evening'; 'Dr. Bernard' (sic) speaks of Evelina 'with great commendation' 657.

BARNARD, FREDERICK AUGUSTA, '43–1830; F.R.S., F.S.A.; Librarian to George III; 'he was presumed to be a natural son of Frederick Prince of Wales' (GM, L).—('68) J's advice to B when about to go abroad to collect books for the royal library 203.1, 206; ('79) B fails to learn the King's opinion of J's Lives 606; ('81) J sends B his Lives for the King 730.1.

BARNARD, THOMAS, '28–1806; M.A. Cantab. '49; Dean of Londonderry '69, Bp of Killaloe '80; member of the Club '75. (DNB, L).— ('77) J's charade on B 506.1.

Barrett, William, '33–'89, surgeon of Bristol (DNB, L).— ('76) B's 'declaration against Chatterton's productions' 483, 'Catcot has been convinced by Barret' 485.

Barrington, Hon. Daines, '27–1800; member '83 of the Essex-Head Club (DNB, L).—(? '83) his letter to J 1129.

BARRY, JAMES, '41–1806, Professor of Painting in the R. Academy '82 (DNB, L).—('83) J asks B to reconsider 'Mr. Lowe's exclusion from the Exhibition' 833; 'Mr. Barry's exhibition' and his book 837 (see note); J tells Lowe he is too ill 'to wait on Mr. Barry' 852; mentioned 876.1; 'adopted by Dr. Brocklesby' as a member of the Essex-Head Club 916.

Baskerville, John, '06–'75, printer of B'm (*DNB, L*).—('55) 'Mr. Baskevill called on me . . . his printing house . . . will I think be something considerable' 69; ('69) J gives B's *Virgil* to Trinity 215.

Bathurst, Richard, — –'62; B.M. Peterhouse Cambridge '45. For his letter to J in '57 *see* Croker 1831, i. 230 (*DNB, L*, R ii).—('53) B contributes to *Adventurer* (?) 46; J proposes to Strahan a book to be compiled by B 47; ('59) 'a Friend whom I much respect' 132.3; ('62) 'went physician to the army, and died at the Havannah' 147, 'vix Priamus tanti' 147.1.

Beatniffe, Richard, — – '92, Recorder of Hull.—J's request for information about R. Levet 760 (see note).

Beatoun, David, 1494–1546, Cardinal Archbp of St. Andrews (*DNB, L*).—321 (343).

BEATTIE, JAMES, '35–1803, Professor of philosophy in Marischal Coll., Aberdeen, '60; m. '67 Mary Dunn; D.C.L. Oxon '73 (*DNB, L*).—('71) J introduces B to the Thrales 268.1; ('72) B's regard for JB, 'his lady puts him out of my head' 274; his *Essay on Truth* (1770) 'every day more liked' 276; ('73) J's 'testimony to his merit' 295; 'caressed, and invited, and treated, and liked, and flattered by the great' 313; J's regret that he and JB shall not find B at Aberdeen 314, 317; his financial 'difficulties' 316.1; his pension 337 (385); ('75) B 'lives grand at the Archbishop's' 395 (see note); ('76) 'Miss Reynolds has a mind to send the Epitaph (Goldsmith's) to Dr. Beattie' 491; ('77) J introduces W. Seward to B 524; ('80) failure to correspond 700; ('81) 'an opportunity of making it up with Beattie' 729.4.

BEAUCLERK, TOPHAM, ('Beau'), '39–'80, g.s. of 1st D of St. Albans; of Great Russell St.; m. '68 Lady Diana (Spencer), '34–1808, e. d. of 2nd D of Marlborough, divorced wife '68 of 2nd Vt Bolingbroke; original member of the Club (*DNB, L*).—('60) mentioned (to BL) 135; ('62) J asks Baretti (at Milan) to show civilities to B 142; but B 'stopped at Paris' 147; Bathurst's death 147.1; ('73) B's life in danger, 'Lady Di. nurses him with very great assiduity' 374; talks of going to Bath 398; ('77) still very ill 507; tells a story against J 565; ('79) his alleged gambling losses and flight 642, 645, 645.1, 646; ('80) his death: 'his wit and his folly', &c.; his mother (Lady Sydney B), wife and children (cf. 835.1); his library offered to the Russian ambassador 655; ('83) 'desired to be buried by the side of his Mother' 835.1 (18).

Bedford: John Russell, '10–'71, 4th D of (*DNB*).—Lewis Paul's letter to B, Appendix A, i. 441.

Bell, William, '31–1816, D.D. '67, Prebendary of Westminster '65 (*DNB, L*).—(n.y.) J asks Garrick to 'reserve four places' for B 169; ('80) J dines with B 662; ('84) 'I intend to ask Dr. Bell's interest' (to get Heely into an almshouse) 923.

Bellamy, George Anne, '31 (?)–'88, actress (*DNB, L*).— ('59) 'left nothing to be desired' in Dodsley's *Cleone* 117.

BENTHAM, EDWARD, '07–'76; D.D. Oxon. '49, Canon of Christ Church '54, Reg. Prof. of Divinity '63 (*DNB, L*).—('75) J acknowledges B's 'testimony in my favour' 387.1 (see note).

Bentley, Richard, — –'86, D.D. Cantab. '50, Rector of Nailstone, Leicestershire; acquaintance of JT.—('72) 'I wish we could borrow of Dr. Bentley the Preces in usum Sarum' 277.

Berenger, Richard, — –'82 (*DNB, L,Tb*). —('75) 417 (identification doubtful).

Bewly, William, — –Sept. '83, surgeon of Massingham, Norfolk (*L*, FB's *Early Diary*).—('81) J sends *Lives* to FB for 'the gentleman whose name I do not know' 736; ('83) CB's loss 882.

Binghams: Sir Charles B, — –1814, 1st B LUCAN '76, 1st E of L '95; of Charles Street, Berkeley Square; member of the Club '82; m. '60 Margaret Smith; 1 s. 3 dd.: Lavinia, m. 6 Mar.

'81 Vt Althorpe '58–1834 (later 2nd E Spencer), Margaret, Anne (*DNB*, *L*).—('77) 'Be civil to Lord — (HLP's erasure), he seems to be a good kind of man' 556; ('78) 'Monday, Lord Lucan . . . Sunday Lady Lucan' 576; ('79) 'Lord and Lady Lucan sent to enquire' 632; 'yesterday came Lady Lucan, and Miss Bingham' 636; 'bespoken by Lady Lucan' 637; 'I dined at —'s (*sic* 1788, original not seen), and found them well pleased with their Italian journey. He took his Lady and son, and their daughters' 641; mentioned 644; 'dined at Mr. Vesey's with Lord Lucan. . . . After dinner came in Lady Lucan and her three daughters, who seem all pretty people' 645.1; ('80) 'you must do a great deal more before I leave you for Lucan or Montague' 659; 'at night with Lady Lucan' 662; dines with Lord L 664, 665; 'Lady Lucan says, she hears Queeney is wonderfully accomplished' 666, 672; ('81) J writes to Lord L congratulations on his daughter's engagement **712.1** (but see note); ('82) J meets 'Althrop' at the Club 817.1; ('83) Lord L and his daughters mentioned 922.

BIRCH, THOMAS, '05–'66; D.D. Lambeth '53; secretary to the Royal Society '52–'65 (*DNB*, *L*. See also Thurloe, Index III.)—('43) J asks B for information **18**; ('50) submits to B a MS. reputed Sir W. Raleigh's **28** (see note); ('52–'54) J asks B to lend books **43, 45, 50**; ('55) J sends B parts of his Dictionary 'for your Inspection' **66**;' asks him to lend Wood's *Athenae* **76**; ('56) asks him to help in AW's benefit **85**; returns a borrowed book and sends his *Life of Browne* **95**; sends him receipts for *Shakespeare*; can he lend 'any of the contemporaries or Ancestors of Shakespeare?' **97**.

Blacklock, Thomas, '21–'91, D.D. Aberdeen '67 (*DNB*, *L*).—('73) J in Edinburgh meets 'Dr. Blacklock the blind poet' 320.

Blackstone, Sir William, '23–'80. (*DNB*, *L*).—('66) J asks Chambers to get B's opinion on 'the late embargo' 187.1.

Blair, Hugh, '18–1800, D.D., Minister of the High Church, Edinburgh, '58–1800, Prof. of Rhetoric '62 (*DNB*, *L*). —('73) 'a very pleasing man' 348; ('75) 'deceived' by Macpherson 378 (see note); ('76) his first sermon; 'to say it is good, is to say too little' 505.1; ('77) 'if they are all like the first . . . they are *sermones aurei*' 507, J asks JB to thank Blair 'for his sermons' 515; 'now universally commended . . . but I had the honour of first finding . . . his excellencies' (*Sermons by Hugh Blair D.D.*, printed for Strahan and Cadell 1777) 565.

Bolton: *see* Boulton.

Bolingbroke: Marie Claire 1675–'50; m. 1700 Henry St. John Vt B (*L* iii. 324). —Her witticism on Pope 712.1 (see note).

BOND, PHINEAS, '49–1815, of Philadelphia; admitted Middle Temple '71; Consul-General for the Middle and Southern States '86.—('73) J entrusts him with a packet for America **297**.

BOOTHBY, HILL, '08–'56, sister of Sir Brooke B, 5th Bt, of Ashbourne Hall, Derbyshire; *see* Fitzherbert (J addresses her as 'Dearest Madam', 'Dearest Dear', 'My Sweet Angel'). (*Th*, Hill's *Letters* i. 45, *L*, R vi). Letters to: (? '53) **49.3**; ('55) **78, 79, 80**; ('56) **81, 82, 84**; ('56) 'I never did exchange letters regularly but with dear Miss Boothby' **98**.

Bosville, Godfrey, '17–'84, of Thorpe Gunthwaite, Yorks.; believed by JB to be kin to the Boswells (*L* iii. 541).— ('77) JB's 'project disconcerted' by 'a visit from a relation of Yorkshire, whom he mentions as the head of his clan' 533.

Boswell, Alexander, '07–'82, of Auchinleck in Ayrshire; lord of session, styled Lord Auchinleck, '54; m. (1) Euphemia Erskine, '18–'66; their three sons included James and (Thomas) David, qq.v.; (2) '69 Elizabeth Boswell of Balmuto, — –'99 (*DNB*, *L*). —*Passim* in letters to JB; ('66) 'your father's liberality' 181; ('73) 'I shall be expected to pass a few days at Lord Auchinleck's' 330, 331.1, 333, 337; to have a copy of the *Journey* 371; ('75) JB's present to 'his Mother in law' 395; ('76) JB's dispute with Lord A about entail 448; 'a fig for my father and his new wife' 478; JB reconciled to his father 502, 505; 'your new mother . . . treat her with respect' 505; ('78) 'you seem . . . to be gaining ground at Auchinleck' 593; ('79) 'please him as much as you can' 646; ('80) 708; ('82) 'your father's death . . . his general life had been pious', 'a kind though not a fond father' 803; ('83) his death and will 835.1 (18).

BOSWELL, JAMES.

(Always *Boswel*, though B himself wrote *Boswell*. He is addressed as 'My dear Boswel' 200, 378, and (in the body of the letter) 163; 494, 715 (in the body of these letters) as 'my dear Bozzy'; but usually as '(My) dear Sir'. He is named to others as 'Bozzy', 529, 631, 633, 963, as 'Bos' or 'Bozz' 331, 393, 679.1.)

'40–'95, e. s. of Alexander B., q.v.: m. '69 Margaret Montgomerie, q.v.; their children Veronica, '73–'95, Euphemia, '74–1837, Alexander, '75–1822, 1st Bt. 1821, David, '76–'77, James, '72–1822, Elizabeth, '80–1814, are often mentioned in letters to JB. Of James's Court, Edinburgh (*L* v. 22, 463), and

from '82 of Auchinleck, Ayrshire. (*DNB, L, Th*)

Letters to: I have I believe proved (*RES* xviii. 71, July 1942, 323) that B kept all J's letters and that he printed them all, in whole or in part, in the *Life* (except for those notes in the third person which he mentions, *L* ii. 322). Their varying frequency is therefore significant of the fluctuations of the friendship. In the list following the figure in brackets gives the total for each year. ('63: 1) 163; ('66: 2) 181, 185; ('68: 1) 200; ('69: 2) 222, 225; ('71: 1) 250; ('72: 2) 274, 276; ('73: 5: J and B spent three months together) 295, 313, 317, 319, 340; ('74: 11) 343, 344, 348, 352, 354, 355, 356, 357, 360, 362, 363; ('75: 11) 371, 374, 375, 378, 380, 398, 431, 432.1, 435, 438, 446; ('76: 14) 447, 448, 450, 452, 454, 457, 458, 462, 475, 481, 493, 494, 502, 505; ('77: 14) 507, 510, 515, 522, 524, 528, 529, 534, 540, 541, 544, 550.1, 565, 567; ('78: 4) 568, 576, 578, 593; ('79: 6) 607, 610, 626, 628, 639, 646; ('80: 3) 655, 701, 708; ('81: 1) 715; ('82: 7) 756, 775, 785, 801, 803, 805, 815; ('83: 3) 827.1, 861, 920; ('84: 9) 932, 936, 937, 942, 946, 973, 981, 982, 1033. The following B indicates, by asterisks or otherwise, that he has not given in full (the originals of 355, 550.1, 973 only are known to survive): 185, 276, 431, 435, 457, 493, 494, 502, 507, 510, 515, 593, 805, 815, 827.1, 888, 936, 973, 981, 982, 1033. For extant copies made by or for JB see i. 427, ii. 528–9.

1. Events in B's life

('66) J had seen him off at Harwich for his European tour 181; 'the profession you have chosen' 185; ('69) 'I am glad that you are going to be married' 222; ('71–'77) the Scottish Tour of 1773 and others projected: ('71) 'I hope the time will come when we may try our powers both with cliffs and water' 250; ('72) 'I . . . have not given up the western voyage' 274; regret at missing 'a journey so pregnant with pleasing expectations' 276; ('73) 'the survey of a Caledonian loch' 313; see also the letters from Scotland '73 and J's letters to B '73–'75 *passim*; ('77) 'delight in talking over the Hebridean Journey' 541; ('77) B 'shrinks from the Baltic expedition . . . wants to see Wales' 545; ('73) election to the Club 305; ('75) B 'has entered himself at the Temple, and I joined in his bond '390; ('82) J's advice to B on succeeding his father 803, 807; ('82–'83) B's encumbered inheritance 807, 835.1 (18); ('84) B's political activities 920, 946, 948; his project of moving to London 973.

2. *B's virtues and amiable qualities*

('66) his 'wise and noble curiosity' in visiting Corsica 181; ('72) generally popular 274; 'while I am writing I expect to hear him come in, with his noisy benevolence' 274.2; ('73) 'an active lively fellow' 316; 'his troublesome kindness' 326 (356); 'his good humour and perpetual cheerfulness. He has better faculties, than I had imagined, more justness of discernment, and more fecundity of images' 337 (387); ('74) 'I have endeavoured to do you some justice in the first paragraph' (of the *Journey*) 356; ('75) 'I love you as a kind man, I value you as a worthy man, and hope in time to reverence you as a man of exemplary piety' 431; 'write often, and tell me all your honest heart' 432.1; ('77) 'very brisk and lively' 547; 'his usual vivacity' 548; 'gay and good humoured in his usual way' 551; ('78) 'I have heard you mentioned as *a man whom every body likes*' 578; ('79) J introduces B to John Wesley; 'worthy and religious men should be acquainted' 612; ('83) 'he is all that he was, and more' 835.1 (18).

3. *B's vices and weaknesses*

(*a*) *his instability*: ('63) J's dissertation on B's ambition of versatile genius without application 163; ('66) 'do not . . . enchain your volatility by vows' 185; ('71) 'caprice' 250; ('77) 'it is a pity he has not a better bottom' 545; ('78) 'in his *old lunes*' 581.1.

(*b*) *his melancholy, or (as J thought) affectation of melancholy*: ('71) work and marriage admit 'neither melancholy nor caprice' 250; ('75) 'the black

fumes which rise in your mind' 431; ('78) 'I am very sorry that your melancholy should return' 458; 'these black fits'; read Cheyne, 'but do not let him teach you a foolish notion that melancholy is a proof of acuteness' 493; 'if you are really oppressed with . . . involuntary melancholy, you are to be pitied rather than reproached' 494; ('77) B's distrust of J's friendship 'is a mode of melancholy which . . . it is foolish to indulge' 544; ('79) 'the *black dog* that worries you' 639; ('80) 'you are always complaining of melancholy, and I conclude . . . that you are fond of it' 655; ('81) 'hypocrisy of misery . . . affectation of distress' 715; ('84) 'of the exaltations and depressions of your mind you delight to talk, and I hate to hear' 920; 'I hope . . . that no evil, either real or imaginary, now disturbs you' 937; 'affecting discontent, and indulging the vanity of complaint' 982.

(*c*) *other 'intellectual excesses' (J's words* 646) *or moral weaknesses*: ('73) B's letter anticipating the delights of the tour; 'he that forms expectations like yours, must be disappointed' 315; 'disturbed' by a Highland superstition 329 (369); calls a gust a tempest 331; afraid of a rough sea 332 (381); ('74) exaggerated notion of 'local sanctity' 352; ('75) 'I write . . . lest in some of your freaks and humours you should fancy yourself neglected' 435; 'morbid suspicions' that J's silence meant a diminution of regard 446, cf. ('77) 'do not fancy that an intermission of writing is a decay of kindness' 544; ('76) tendency to scruples 454, 'let me warn you very earnestly against scruples' 458; B's omission to open boxes of books sent him by J; 'I am . . . very angry that you manage yourself so ill' 493; ('77) B's letter had 'a strain of cowardly caution' 565; ('78) 'restrain your imagination' and do not think that happiness is possible only in London 578; ('79) J urges B 'neither to exalt your pleasures, nor aggravate your vexations, beyond their real . . . state' 646.

(d) *B's love of publication*: ('75) 'Your love of publication is offensive and disgusting, and will end, if it be not reformed, in a general distrust' **378** (not printed in *L*); ('84) his suspected 'trick' in sending to a newspaper a paragraph about J's visit to Chatsworth **1015** (not printed in *L*).

(e) *B's extravagance*: ('82) 'Poverty ... is so great an evil ... do not borrow' **775**; 'do not accustom yourself to consider debts only as an inconvenience; you will find it a calamity' **785**; 'let it be your first care not to be in any man's debt' **803**; 'whatever you have, spend less' **815**; ('83) 'resolve never to be poor' **827.2**.

(f) *B's intemperance*: ('84) 'one night's drunkenness may defeat the labour of forty days' (electioneering) **946**.

4. *J's love for B*

('66) 'Nothing has lessened either the esteem or love with which I dismissed you at Harwich' **181**; ('72) 'my kindness for you' **274**; ('73) 'I love you too well to be careless when you are serious' **352**; ('75) 'I hold you ... "in my heart of heart" ' **431**; 'my regard for you ... is become part of my mind' **435**; 'I consider your friendship as a possession, which I intend to hold till you take it from me' **446**; ('77) 'your kindness is one of the pleasures of my life' **507**; 'everything that belongs to you, belongs ... to' (me) **524**; 'I set a very high value upon your friendship, and count your kindness as one of the chief felicities of my life' **544**; ('78) 'I very highly esteem and very cordially love you. I hope to tell you this at the beginning of every year' **568**; ('80) 'I love you so much, that I would be glad to love all that love you' **708**.

5. *B's relation and conduct to J*

('68) B publishes J's 'letters' (in fact an extract from one letter) to him (in *Corsica*) **200**; ('74–'75) B helps J in his *Journey*: B sends him pamphlets **357**; 'your notes of remembrance added to your Names' **360**; 'I have mentioned all that you recommended' **363, 374**, 'let me know if any mistake is com-

mitted' **371**; ('76) 'Why do you talk of neglect?' **475**; ('78) 'You always seem to call for tenderness' **568**; ('82) 'the earnestness and tenderness of your letter' **785**.

6. *B's failure to write*

('79) J asks Dilly for news of B **625**; 'Is it a fit of humour, that has disposed you to try who can hold out longest ?' **626**; 'are you playing the same trick again ?' **628**; ('80) 'one of your fits of taciturnity' **701**; ('82) 'at your long silence I am rather angry '**815**; ('83) 'seldom ... so long a time in which I have had so little to do with Boswel ... He has written twice and I ... once' **876.1**; 'you should not make your letters such rarities' **888**; ('84) 'are you sick, or are you sullen?' **1033**.

7. *J's help in B's law cases and advice on legal problems*

('72) 'the ejection which you come hither to oppose' (of a severe schoolmaster; an appeal in the Lords) **274, 276**; 'sorry that you lost your cause of Intromission' **295**; ('75) 'a case ... in which I have no facts but what are against us' **375** (Dr. Memis's grievance at being styled 'Doctor of Medicine') J consults Lawrence **377**, 'a very slender cause of prosecution' **378, 505**; 'feudal inheritance': B's 'wrangling' with his wife on female inheritance ended by the birth of a son **446** ('76) B's dispute with his father on this question **448, 450, 452, 454, 458**; ('77 B engaged to prosecute a schoolmaster **567**.

8. *B's Works, published or projected*

('66) J's 'reception of your Thesis (*Disputatio Juridica ... de Supellectili Legata ...* 1766); J's criticism of B' Latin **185**; 'As to your *History of Cor sica*, you have no materials' **185**; ('68 'I wish you would empty your head of Corsica' **200**; 'your History is like othe histories, but your Journal is in a ver high degree curious and delightful' **22** (*An Account of Corsica, the Journal a Tour to that Island ...* 1768); ('7 B's projected 'character of Bruce' **43** ('80) perhaps the only evidence fur nished by the letters of B's intentio to be J's biographer (apart from references to his journals, see § 9) is J's undertaking to give him a copy of the letter to Chesterfield **655**; ('83) B projects a new edition of Baxter's Anacreon **888**; ('84) 'I received your pamphlet' **932** (*A Letter to the People of Scotland, on the Present State of the Nation* 1783), 'it will certainly raise your character, though perhaps it may not make you a Minister of State' **936**; 'the influence which your address must have gained you' ('a loyal Adress to the King from our County' *BP* xvi. 39) **946**.

9. *B's Journals*
('66) 'the pleasure which I promise myself from your journals' (of B's life abroad) **181**; for the journals of 1773 and 1777 see § 10a.

10. *B's relations with HLT*
(The evidence of J's letters is mainly in those to HLT; I therefore give here, though it involves some repetition, all the passages, in those letters, which mention B, noting in each case whether (1) the passage was printed by HLP in 1788, (2) the letter was printed in 1788 but the reference to B is known, the original having been seen, to have been 'edited', (3) the letter was not printed in 1788.)

(*a*) *References to B in J's letters to HLT*: ('73: all in 1788, without any editing (so far as the extant originals make this certain) except that, in these as in other letters, B's name is sometimes suppressed, a disguise which deceived no one): mentioned **304**; in Edinburgh **320**; at St. Andrews and Aberbrothick **321**; angry with Aberdeen professors **322**; gives the Macraes tobacco, his 'troublesome kindness', 'provided for' with rum and sugar, 'reposed in Linen like a Gentleman' **326**; impatient of delay in Skye **328**; expedition with Macleod, 'disturbed' by a Highland superstition, 'writes a regular journal . . . a faithful Chronicler' **329** (365, 369, 370); calls a gust a tempest **331**; afraid of spectres, dislikes a rough sea **332**; Mrs. B 'in a proper degree inferior to her husband',

B's 'perpetual cheerfulness . . . better faculties than I had imagined', B's thought of collecting stories of Sir Alex. Macdonald 'and making a novel of his life' **337** (385, 387); ('75) entered at the Temple **390** (in 1788); mentioned **393** (in 1788); his journal read by HLT, 'is it not a merry piece?' **395** (in 1788); 'I omitted to enquire, how you were entertained by Boswell's Journal. One would think the man had been hired to be a spy upon me' **405** (*sic* 1788, original not traced); 'Boswel's narrative is very natural, and therefore very entertaining. . . . He is a very fine fellow' **408** (the paragraph suppressed in 1788); 'I am glad you have read Boswel's journal' **415** (the words 'Boswel's journal' erased in the MS., but restored 1788); 'I am glad that you read Boswel's journal' **423** (in 1788); ('76) B will go to Oxford with J **463**.1 (letter not in 1788); 'Mr. Thrale sent me a letter from Mr. Boswel' (condolence on Harry's death) **466** (in 1788); B has been promised 'a place, and then a fig for my father and his new wife' **478** (in 1788, B's name suppressed); B 'paid another visit, I think, to *Mrs. Rudd*, before he went home *to his own Deary*. He carries with him two or three good resolutions; I hope they will not mould upon the road' **482** (in 1788; but HLP generously suppressed the words which I have italicized); ('77: all in 1788, without interference except **547** and **553**): B 'makes a huge bustle about all his . . . motions **533**; mentioned **542**, **543**; B 'shrinks from the Baltic expedition' **545**; B 'seems to be very brisk and lively, and laughs a little at —' (object of B's mirth suppressed in 1788, original not seen) **547**; 'his usual vivacity' **548**; 'gay and good humoured' **551**; 'kept his journal very diligently . . . I should be glad to see what he says of —' **553** (the end of the sentence suppressed in 1788 and not legible in original); ('79) B's observation of HT's health **630** (in 1788); B came, 'and much talk we had' **631** (in 1788); B 'never saw me so well' **633** (in 1788);

'I have had a letter for —, which I have inclosed' (*sic* 1788, original not legible; J perhaps intended 'from Boswel') 640; ('84) 'Bozzy . . . is . . . resolved to . . . try his fortune at the English Bar. Let us all wish him success' 963 (in 1788).

(*b*) *Other references*: ('69) J is 'ordered by the lady of this house' to invite B to S'm 225; ('72) 'Mrs. Thrale loves you' 274; ('73) 'you continue to stand very high in the favour of Mrs. Thrale' 295; ('75) 'Mrs. Thrale was so entertained with your *Journal*, that she almost read herself blind. She has a great regard for you' 431; 'your friends are all well at Streatham' 435; 'Mr. Thrale . . . wishes to see you' 446.

11. *Miscellaneous*

('72) J recommends study of 'the antiquities of the feudal establishment' 276; ('74) J introduces a lady who 'has a law-suit' 354, 355; asks B for hints, from Scottish lawyers or himself, for *Taxation no Tyranny* 374; ('75) B on Ossian; see Macpherson, James; B takes from London 'a present for his Mother in law' 395; ('76) mentioned 463.1; his letter of condolence to HT 466; mentioned 469; 'some great men have promised to obtain him a place, and then a fig for my father and his new wife' 478; 'he has led a wild life. . . . Pray take care of him, and tame him' 481 (to Mrs. B); reconciliation to his father, see Alexander B; ('77) B's 'old room' in J's house 507; B considered by William Shaw 'as a great encourager of ingenious men' 510; B's speech: Veronica's 'Mamma has not much Scotch, and you have yourself very little' 510; rents his uncle's country house 524, 528, 534; at A'n with J, letters from there *passim*; ('78) reconciles J and Percy 575; ('79) 'Why should you take such delight to make a bustle?' 607, cf. 533; J introduces B to John Wesley 612; B's triumphal visits to L'd and Chester 639, 643; J sends him 'a petition from Lucy Porter' 646; ('80) B's letter to T. Warton 667; ('81) B on 'Liberty and Necessity' 715; 'I . . . have laid up for

you a load of copy (for the *Lives*), all out of order, so that it will amuse you a long time to set it right' 715; ('83) B at Auchinleck 827.2; a newspaper report 'of Boswel and me' 876.1, 'my suspicion is, that Bozz inserted it' 879.1; ('84) B's 'many inquiries' about J's health 932; 'very much obliged both to you and your physicians' 937; B's political aspirations 946; with J at Oxford 963, 963.1; 'has a great mind to draw me to Lichfield' 968; his application to Thurlow on J's behalf 971; at the Essex-Head Club 972.2; (n.d.) mentioned 1139.

BOSWELL, MARGARET (*née* Montgomerie) '38–'89, m. '69 James B, q.v. —('72) 'you tell me nothing of your lady' 274; ('73) 'Mrs. Boswel had warned us that we should *catch something*' 326 (358); 'she is in a proper degree inferior to her husband' 337 (385); 'I know Mrs. Boswell wished me well to go' 340; ('74) 'I do not love her the less for wishing me away' 343, cf. 348, B's duty to her; 'she permitted you to ramble last year, you must permit her now to keep you at home' 352 ('75) 'I suppose she is now just beginning to forgive me' 380, and see below 'teach Veronica to love me. Bid her not mind Mamma' 398; 'she knows in her heart that she does not love me' 431, 438, 446; ('76) 447, 450; her letter to J 457, his reply 481; 'my hope that she is reconciled' 462; ('77) 'I love her very well' 507; 'I shall taste her marmalade cautiously . . ., *Timeo Danaos*' 515, 'your jar of marmalade . . . I received it as . . . a proof of reconciliation' 529, 533; 'Mrs. Boswell' illness . . . a more serious distress' 534. 'Boswel . . . says, his Wife does not love me quite well yet, though we have made a formal peace' 553; 'my dear enemy' 565; ('78) J invites B to bring his wife to London; 'I will retire from my apartments, for her accommodation' 568; her health 593; ('79) J will send *Lives* and *Poets* 'to dear Mrs Boswel' 607; ('80) 'I love your naughty lady'; he will send his *Lives* to complete her set 701, 714; 'I have love very ready for Mrs. Boswell' 708; ('82) 'in losing her you would lose your anchor' 756; her invitation to J to visit Auchinleck; her health **804**; 'let nothing be omitted that can preserve Mrs. Boswell ... she is the prop and stay of your life' 805; 'if his Wife lives I think he will be prudent' 807; ('84) 'the attention which you and your dear lady show to my welfare' 942.

Boswell, Thomas David, '48–1826, y. s. of Alexander B, Lord Auchinleck (*L*). —('80) 'a Spanish merchant, whom the war has driven from ... Valencia ... a very agreeable man, and speaks no Scotch' 684; 'I take a great liking to your brother 708; ('83) 'your brother has very frequently enquired after me' 861.

BOUFFLERS Marie-Charlotte-Hyppolyte de Camps de Saujon, '24– *c.* 1800, m. '46 Édouard Comte (later Marquis) de Boufflers-Rouverel (*L*).— ('71) **248** (in French).

Boulton (Bolton), Matthew, '28–1809, engineer, of B'm (*DNB*, *L*).—('76) J 'sent Mr. Boswel with Hector to Bolton's' 464.1.

Bourke, Joseph Deane, '36–'94, Abp. of Tuam '82, 3rd E of Mayo '92 (*L*).— ('83) 'a man coarse of voice, and inelegant of language' 875.

Bowen, J., bookseller in Brighton.—('79) J's sorrow 'for poor Thomas ... It is hard that he should be overwhelmed by a newcomer' 633; B's share in 'Johnson's Poets' 636, 637.

Bowker, —, of Northampton, a partner of Touchet, for whom Lewis Paul, q.v., worked (*Life of S. Crompton*, 1859, 265).—('56) 104.

BOWLES, WILLIAM, '55–1826, of Heale House, Wilts.; s. of Rev. William B, '16–'88, Canon of Salisbury; m. '79 Dinah, d. of Sir Thomas Frankland, Bart. (*L* iv. 235). Member of the Essex-Head Club.—('80) J dines with B 662; ('83) J hopes to 'obey your generous and friendly invitation' **871.2**, **873.1**, **873.2**; 'I have taken a place for Thursday' 877; Heale 'might furnish . . . the scene of a romance'

879.1; B asks JR to visit him 879.2; 'entertained with great kindness' 882.1; J reports on his illness **803.1**, **888.2**, **891.1**; B's remarks on Stonehenge 892; 'I went to a Friend in Wiltshire' 893; 'Mrs. Bowles's kind present' **894.2**; ('84) J too ill to go to Heale **923.1**; 'Do not forget me, nor suppose that I can forget you, or your Lady or your young ones' **925.1**; 'make my compliments to ... your Father' (who had presumably made Heale over to his son; he d. at Woodford, Wilts.) **929.2**; B's election to the Essex-Head Club; his political ambitions; 'if half of them were like you, I should wish you among them' (in the House of Commons) **935.1**; 'Collins's project'; suggestion that J should write a preface' **947.1**; 'when any occasion brings you to town, I will introduce you to the Club' **958.1**; B's invitation to revisit Heale **972.2**; J's good wishes **986.1**; 'I fear that I shall not reach Heale, while any fruit remains on the trees' **1010.2**.

Bowyer, William, 1697–'77, printer (*DNB*, *L*). *See* Nichols.—('82) 'a passage in the Life of Bowyer' 798.1.

Boyds: James B, who later took the name of Hay, '26–'78; 15th E. of Errol '58 (succeeding his great-aunt); m. (2) '62 Isabella Carr, '42–1808; his y. b. Charles Boyd, '28–'82 (*L*).—('73) J's visit to Slaines 322, 323.

BOYLE, JOHN, '07–'62, 5th E ('31) of Orrery and 5th E (3 Dec. '53) of Corke; Christ Church, D.C.L. Oxon. '43 (*DNB*, *L*).—('51) J has given him 'so much trouble about my Book'; his praise of Charlotte Lennox's book (see Lennox) 36; ('52) his *Remarks on . . . Swift* 1752, his patronage of C. Lennox, **42.1**; (? '53) 'My Lord Corke did me the favour to leave his name' 49.1; ('54) 'My Lord Corke is desirous to see Mr. Falkner's letter to me' 51.1; (n.d.) the letter **1144**, to 'My Lord', on Virgil's Creteus, is probably to Lord O.

Boylston (not Brylston as in Hill), George, (?) of B'm, an early acquaintance of J. ('65) 179.

Bradley, James, 1693–'62, Astronomer

Royal '42; his nephew and assistant John B (*DNB*); Z. Williams's correspondence with them, Appendix A, i. 432–4.

Brewer, Father: *see* Wilkes, Father.

Brewse, John, Major '72, — *-c*. '85 (*L* v. 509).—('73) 'The Major of Artillery . . . showed us' the fortifications of Fort George 323.

Bridge, Edward (—), agent for the Salusbury estate in Flintshire (*Tb*).—('72) mentioned 280; ('73) 'I wish Bridge success in his new Mine' 337 (388).

BRIGHT, HENRY, '24–1803; presumably the HB who matric. Trinity Coll. '43, M.A. New Coll. '61; Master of Abingdon School, Berks. (*Tb*).—('62) J asks B if he will take George Strahan as a pupil 144.1, B's 'unscholarlike' reply 144.2; ('63) mentioned 148, 160; ('70) will B take another and more troublesome pupil? (Ralph Plumbe) 226; 'Mr. Alderman Plumbe will bring his son' 226.2; ('75) J at Oxford 'supped with Mr. Bright' 401.

BROCKLESBY (Broaclesby 851), RICHARD, '22–'97; M.D. Leyden '45, F.R.S.; one of J's regular physicians after his loss of Lawrence; of Norfolk Street, Strand (in '78, and still there '88); member of the Essex-Head Club (*DNB*, *L*).—*Letters to*: ('83) 878; ('84) 979, 983, 985, 987, 990, 992, 993, 997, 1000, 1000.2, 1001, 1009, 1010, 1011, 1015, 1020, 1027.2, 1029, 1033.1 (JB printed extracts only, except 1029); ('83) 'I sent to Dr. Brocklesby, who is my neighbour' 850; 'the Dr fell to repeating Juvenal's tenth satire' 851; mentioned 856; his visits keep 'the black dog at a distance' 857; mentioned 860, 861, 863; B sends news of AW's death 880; 'my physician in ordinary' 891; mentioned 905; 'joined with me in forming the plan' of the Essex-Head Club 916; 'Dr Brocklesby who came with me to my door, came, as he said, next day to see if I were alive' 918.1; ('84) mentioned 937, 945, 946; 'forbids the club' 955; J dines with B 960, 968; 'your

attention . . . and that of Dr. Heberden, to my health, is extremely kind' 983; 'if the virtue of medicines could be enforced by the benevolence of the prescriber, how soon should I be well' 992; mentioned 1006; 'you charge me somewhat unjustly with luxury' 1011; B's letter about the balloon 'far the best' 1015; mentioned 1022; 'you write . . . with a zeal that animates, and a tenderness that melts me' 1029; mentioned 1037.

Broderie (?) 1156.

Brodhurst: probably Walter Broadhurst, watchmaker of Breadmarket Street, L'd (R iii. 136).—('79) 'I saw my old friend Brodhurst . . . the play fellow of my infancy' 616.

Broglio, '18–1804.—('42) 17.

Bromfield, Robert, '22–'86, L.R.C.P. in '78, later F.R.S.; of Gerrard St. (*Tb*). —('71) attended Mrs. Salusbury 255, 258; ('79) attended HT 617.

Brooke, Francis, attorney of Town Malling, Kent (visited by J and the Thrales '68; C 75).—('77) 'His house is one of my favourite places' 538.

Browne, Isaac Hawkins, '05–'60 (*DNB*, *L*, *Tb*).—'a friend', his learning, wit, and gluttony 872.

Brownes (?) 702 (see note).

Browne, Mrs, a Methodist at Bath (*Tb* 568).—('80) on business and solitude 657.

Bruce, James, '30–'94, explorer (*DNB*, *L*).—('75) 'I was to dine with Mr. Bruce, and hear of Abissinia' 386.

Bruce, Robert, 1274–1329. 321 ('the Bruces'), 438.

Bruce, a widow at St. Andrews. 321.

Bryant, Jacob, '15–1804 (*DNB*, *L* v. 458). —('77) J dines with B 505.3.

Buller: Sir Francis B, '46–1800, Bt '90, m. Susannah Yarde, '40–1810 (*L*).—('80) 'one Mrs. B— (*sic* 1788, original not seen), a travelled lady' 663.

Bunbury, Henry William, '50–1811, caricaturist; m. '91 Catherine Horneck, q.v. A member of the Club '74 (*DNB*, *L*).—('74) added to the Club 348; ('80) his wife 681.

Burkes: BURKE, EDMUND, '29–'97; m. '56 JANE (q.v.) d. of J's friend

Christopher Nugent (who d. 12 Oct. '75); M.P. Wendover Dec. '65; original member '64 of the Club. His b. Richard, '33– (not known). His e. (and only surviving) s. Richard, '58–'94; member of the Club '82 (*DNB*, *L*).—('66) less frequent at Club since he took to politics; 'a great man by nature, and is expected soon to attain civil greatness' 182; J sends B Cowley's Latin works **229.2** (see i. 442); ('70) J's application to B on HT's behalf 240, mentioned **240.1**; ('77) 'all the Burkes' at JR's 512; (? '78) J recommends Stockdale to B **598.1**; ('79) J asks B to help the Vicar of Coventry **610.1**; J asks FR to buy him a print of B 634; ('80) J and B talking in company, 'there is no rising unless somebody will cry fire' 669; ('81) 'young Burke has just been with me' at Oxford 741; ('82) 'Fox has resigned, Burke's dismission is expected' (8 July) 793; the family 'computed to have lost by this revolution' £12,000 a year 795; 'a very crowded Club' (10 Dec.) including 'Bourk' **817.1**; ('83) 'Mr. Burke and his Brother' on their way to Weymouth **879.1**; J's 'gratitude for his late favour' **879.2**; 'Mr. Burke sat with me' and discussed Stonehenge 892; ('84) B 'has sent me his speech upon the affairs of India' (the speech of 1 Dec. '83) 928; 'at Chatsworth I met young Mr. Burke' 1007.

BURKE, JANE, wife of Edmund B, q.v.—(Oct. '75) on her father's death **437.1**.

Burnet(t): *see* Monboddo.

Burneys: CHARLES BURNEY, '26–1814, Mus.Doc. Oxon. '69; of King's Lynn '52–'60, Poland St. '60–'71, Queen's Square '71–'75, St. Martin's St. '75–'89; member of the Club '84; m. (1) '49 Esther Sleepe, ——'61; their children included JAMES, '50–1821, Captain R.N. '82; FRANCES, 13 June '52–1840; Susan, '55–1800; Charlotte Anne, '59– —; (2) '61 Elizabeth, c. '28–'96, widow of Stephen Allen of King's Lynn; she had by her first husband 2 dd., of whom the elder, Maria, m. '77 — Rishton; EB's chil-

dren by C.B. included Richard Thomas, '68–1808 (*DNB*, *L*, *Th*, FB's *Diaries*; see App. G).

Letters to CB: ('55) 67; ('57) 112; ('58) 113; ('65) 177; ('78) 589.1; ('79) 620.1; (? '80) 661; ('82) 767.4; ('83) 882; ('84) 984, 998.1, 1000.1, 1004, 1030, 1036.

Letters to FB: ('81) 736; ('83) 902; ('82 or '83) 903; ('84) 1030.1.

Letter to JB: ('82) 792.2.

1. *Mentions of CB and of the family in general*: ('55) B's inquiries about J's Dictionary; 'your friendship thus voluntarily offered' 67; ('57) B's praise of the Dictionary and interest in J's *Shakespeare*; 'your Lady' 112; ('58) J sends him 'a bundle of proposals' for *Shakespeare* 113; ('65) B's agreement with J's criticism of Shakespeare 177; ('73) J borrows B's 'Musical Journey' from S'm (? *Present State of Music in Germany* 1773) 294; ('77) 'so have at you all at Dr. Burney's to morrow' 512; 'I wish you well; B—y and all' (HLP's erasure; CB was at B'n with the Thrales) 552; mentioned 556; Mrs. B's 'calamity' (elopement of her d. Maria Allen), her step-daughters' 'consolations' 557, their 'triumph' and CB's satisfaction 560; ('78) B and Mrs. B robbed by highwaymen 583; 'I call now and then on the Burneys, where you (HLT) are at the top of mortality' 585; J introduces B, 'engaged in a History of Musick', to Wheeler at Oxford 588, to Edwards at Oxford 589, 'Mr. Warton can help you' **589.1**, Mrs. B's health **589.1**, his ill luck in finding the Bodleian closed, help at Oxford with Arabic and Welsh 591, 'Burney is to bring me' to B'n 591, 'Burney and I have settled it' 592, B on Baretti's 'musical scheme' (*Carmen Seculare*) 592; ('79) B at S'm when HT had a stroke **620.1**; B's discoveries at Cambridge, 'his Book must be a Porter's load' (the *History of Music*, vol. i, 4°, 1776; vol. 2, 1782) 636, J has 'seen some more sheets' of it 641; 'you (HLT) can write often enough to Dr. Burney' 642; ('80) B 'has given fifty seven lessons this week' 658, **660.1**;

'To Dr. Burney — or any Burney' **661**; 'Sunday at Dr. Burney's' **662**; mentioned **685**; Mrs. B's illness, 'at Burney Hall a little complaint makes a mighty bustle' **686.2**; 'Dr. Burney and Fanny and Sophy are gone to be happy with Mr. Crisp, and Mrs. Burney and Susan are left at home' **703.1**; ('82) J shortens B's 'long apology' **767.4** (see note); ('83) 'Dr. Burney came to see me' **858**, mentioned **875**; ('84) Mrs. B's recovery **984, 998.1**, **1030**; dedication by J to B's *Account of the Musical Performances . . . in Commemoration of Handel* 1785: 'I had quite forgot what we had said to the Queen' (i.e. in J's dedication for B's *History of Music*, vol. i, 1776) and have therefore rewritten that part **998.1**; J discusses B's criticisms and suggestions **1000.1, 1004**; the book delayed for correction (it contains many cancels) **1030**; 'Mr. Johnson who came home last night (16 Nov.), sends his respects to dear Doctor Burney, and all the dear Burneys little and great' **1036**.
2. *Specific mentions of FB* ('Miss Burney' **541.1**, **679**; usually 'Burney', sometimes 'Fanny'): ('77) 'Miss Burney and Master Wesley' (a duet) **541.1**; ('78) she visits J **586**; 'Madam Frances' **589.1**; Frank Barber wants to read *Evelina* (*Evelina, or the history of a young lady's entrance into the world*, published 1778) **591**; ('79) 'I begin now to let loose my mind after Queeney and Burney' **621**; 'the young ones (Q and FB) are very good in minding their book' **636**; 'I thought the two young things were to write' (him letters) **641**; FB's 'silly short note' added to Q's **642**; 'does Burney dance?'; her quarrel with Cumberland, **644**; *Evelina* praised; 'do not tell this to Burney for it will please her' **645.1**; 'tell Burney that now she is a good girl, I can love her again' **648**; ('80) mentioned **654**; *Evelina* praised by Lawrence and Barnard; yet 'she no more minds me than if I were a Brangton' **657**; 'Fanny tells me good news of you' (HLT) **658**; J owes her a

letter **660.1**; 'my two dear girls' **664**; 'Mr. Thrale well, Queeney good, — pleasing and welcome' (the name erased by HLP may be FB's) **669**; mentioned **677, 679, 681, 684**; J asks Nichols 'to save the proof sheets of Pope' for a Lady (FB) **697**; FB 'gone to be happy with Mr. Crisp' **703.1**; ('81) J sends her Vols. 5–10 of his *Prefaces* 'to be sent after the former to the gentleman whose name (Bewley, q.v.) I do not know' **736**; FB leaves S'm **743**; *Evelina* not heard of at L'd **747**; J asks FB to 'engage' a young man to James B. **787.4**; ('82) 'talk of Cecilia' (*Cecilia, or memoirs of an heiress*, 1782) **817.1**; ('83) 'Fanny's trade is Fiction' **875**; her silence, 'have we quarreled?' **902**; asks her for a *Cecilia* 'to lend a friend' (date uncertain) **903**; ('84) she dines with J **954, 955**; 'my naughty girl' **998.1**; her 'precept of frugality' **1030**; 'my heart has reproached me with my ingratitude' **1030.1**.
3. *Specific mentions of JB*: ('80) 'I have seen Captain Burney and his cargo' **707.1**; ('81) the ship 'which carries the fate of Burney' **749**; 'I do not like poor Burney's vicarious captainship' **752**; ('82) J recommends Mara as a servant **787.4**; J congratulates him on his 'fine ship', and introduces Mara **792.2**.
4. *Specific mentions of others*: ('80) Mrs. B. and Susan **703.1**; ('83) 'Dick Burney is come home, five inches taller' **858**; 'Miss Charlotte' to examine a book thought her father's **902**.

Butter, William, '26–1805, M.D., physician, of Derby and L'n (*DNB, L*).— ('72) 'You (JT) tell me nothing of . . . Dr. Butter who seems to be a very rational Man' **277, 312**; ('79, '81) JT consults B **605.1, 729.1**.

Byrkes (Berk), Robert **318**.

Byron (Biron), John, '23–'86, Rear-Admiral; 'Foul-weather Jack'; m. '48 Sophia Trevannion, — –'90; defeated by the French off Grenada 6 July '79, and never again employed. Their d. Augusta (*DNB, L, Tb*).—('78) 'Of Mrs. Byron I have no remembrance' **586**; 'Miss Biron, and, I suppose, Mrs.

Biron, is gone' 592; ('79) 'Mrs. Byron . . . puts me out of your head' 641; 'poor Mrs. B—' (J's dash) I am glad that she runs to you . . . for shelter. . . . Her husband is well enough spoken of' 644; 'you shall not hide Mrs (HLP's erasure) from me . . . I can bear a feeler as well as you' 645 (see note); 'It is well that she has yet power to feel' 647; ('80) 'Poor B—'s (HLP's erasure) tenderness is very affecting' 659; ('81) 'she has the courage becoming an admiral's lady' 748; ('82) 'I visited Mesdames . . . Biron' 782.1; ('83) 'Mrs. Byron has been with me' 910.

CADELL (Cadel), THOMAS, '42–1802, bookseller; successor '67 to Andrew Millar; printer to the R. Academy '78 (*DNB*, *L*).—('71) J's order for binding 270; ('75) C publisher of a book by Baretti 384.2; ('76) J names C as typical of the 'primary agent in London', the highest rank in the trade 463; J recommends a proposal by Stockdale, perhaps to C, 497.1; ('78) J asks C to employ Allen for R. Academy printing 569; J returns proofs of *Lives* 584; 'my old reckoning with Mr. Cadell' (for the *Journey*) 589.2; ('79) J complains of ill treatment in the matter of author's copies of the *Lives* 609; ('81) *Political Tracts* 'left without bargain to your (Strahan's) liberality and Mr. Cadel's' 713; J asks C to pay Dilly for sets of *Lives* 714; ('83) J asks C to send copies of *Lives* 833.2; ('84) to send his works to Adams 1038; (n.d.) J asks C to send him books 1121, 1123; to thank 'the proprietors' of the *Lives* 1122.

Caesar, Julius 585.1.

CALDER, JOHN, '33–1815, D.D., of Aberdeen (*DNB*, *L*).—(? '73) J asks Hawkesworth if 'a gentleman now out of business' (no doubt C) may undertake 'an epitome of Chambers Dictionary' 1128; ('76) C's abortive editorship of Chambers's *Cyclopaedia*; his quarrel with Archibald Hamilton and Strahan 453, **456**.

CALDWELL, SIR JAMES, of 675 is no doubt the 'Sir James C—, a

bawling old man' of FB's *Diary* for 31 May '80 (1842, i. 369), who is no doubt Sir James Caldwell, '22–'84, 3rd Bt, of Castle C., Ireland (*L*).—('67) J's account to him of his conversation with the King **187.4** (i. 431).

Calvert, Mrs, inmate or neighbour of Edward Lye, q.v.—('65) 174, 174.1.

Cambridge, Richard Owen, '17–1802, writer (*DNB*, *L*).—('82) 'I have . . . seen . . . Cambridge' 819.1.

Campbell, —, of Auchnaba, purchaser '77 of Mac Quarry's estates (*L* iii. 133). —('77) 528.

Campbell, —, 'the Duke of Argyle's factor in Tyr-yi' (*L* v. 312).—332.

Campbell, Rev. Thomas, '33–'95 (*DNB*, *L*, J. L. Clifford, Life of C. in his edition of his *Diary* 1947).—('77) J's conversation with C on Irish antiquities 517.

Canterbury, Archbp of: see Cornwallis.

Car: ('42) 'Mr. Car's affair' 17.

Car(e)less: see Hector.

Carlisle: Frederick Howard, '48–1825, 5th E '58 of C; m. '70 Lady Margaret Leveson-Gower (*DNB*, *L*).—('83) J's letters to Hester Chapone about C's tragedy *The Father's Revenge* 1783: 906.1, praise and blame 911; 'your (HLT) enquiry about Lady Carlisle I cannot answer' 922.

Carmichael, 'Poll', a 'young woman' in '73 (*L* ii. 215), inmate of J's house (*L*).—('73) her lawsuit 292.1, 293.1; ('74) 'Miss Carmichael's cause' 343.1; ('78) 'Mrs. Williams . . . scolds, but Poll does not much flinch' 590, 'Poll loves none of them' 591.

Carte, Samuel, 1653–'40, Prebendary of L'd 1682 (*DNB*).—('83) 'I knew Mr. Carte' 822.

CARTER, 'Mrs.' ELIZABETH ('Eliza'), '17–1806, scholar and writer (*DNB*, *L*).—('38) J's 'Greek Epigram to Eliza' 7; her translation of Crousaz's 'Examen' (*An Examination of Mr. Pope's Essay on Man. Translated from the French of M. Crousaz*, 1739) 10; ('56) J asks her to help AW's benefit; 'poor dear Cave I owed him much, for to him I owe that I have known you' **87**; ('77) mentioned 539; ('80) mentioned

675; ('82) 'Mrs. Carter's Miss Sharpe' 778.

Carter, —, riding-master (*Tb*, *L*).— (Dec. '74–Mar. '76) J's efforts to 'establish Mr. Carter, the riding Master of Oxford' (402), *passim* in letters to HLT and HT; also in letters to John Douglas, 459, 461.1, see note on 379; and to Miller 1136; his d. Laura 386.1, 395 (*Tb* 118); his sons 368, 369, 384.2 (*Tb* 117).

Carteret, John, 1690–'63, 2nd Baron C 1695, 1st E Granville '44 (*DNB*, *L*).— ('42) 'the address of Carteret' in negotiating a peace 17.

Carwarthen (or -urthen, MS. not clear). (21 Dec. '62) Mentioned 146 (I learn from Prof. Hilles that JR's engagement book 21 Dec. records an appointment —at 6 p.m., therefore not with a sitter —'Miss Carwardine'). Probably Penelope C (*DNB*).

Castiglione, Prince Gonzaga di (*L* iii. 411).—('77) 'My mistress has added to her conquests the Prince of Castiglione' 513.

Catcott (-ot), George Symes, '29–1802, pewterer, of Bristol (*L*).—('76) 'Catcot has been convinced by Barret' (that the Rowley Poems were Chatterton's) 485.

Catherine II, '29–'96, Empress of Russia (*L*).—('84) 'The Rambler is now by command of the Empress translating into Russian' 931.

Cator, John, '30–1806, of Beckenham, Kent, and the Adelphi (*L*, *Tb*).—('75) 'You (HLT) . . . have very judiciously chosen Cator' (as a trustee) 423; ('77) 'you go to Mr. Cator's, and you are so happy' 537; (7 Apr.–2 July '81) *passim* in letters on management and sale of the brewery (C was one of HT's executors); ('82) C and Lady Salusbury's claim on HLT 817.1, 817.4; ('83) 'Mr. Cator . . . told that he had invited you back to Streatham'; invited J to Beckenham 859; ('84) 'Cator . . . never speaks merely to please' 926; mentioned 954; 'I am glad that after your storm you (Q) have found a port at Mr. Cator's' 1003.2.

Caulfield, Miss, doubtless a relation of Lord Charlemont (q.v.): 508.

CAVE, EDWARD, 1691–'54, bookseller; proprietor of *The Gentleman's Magazine* (*DNB*, *L*).—('34–'42 or '43) J's letters to C (3–11, 15, 16) are addressed to him as bookseller, and as publisher of *The Gentleman's Magazine* and of J's *London*; ('41) C's connexion with the affair of Lewis Paul, q.v., 13; ('43) J asks Birch to send books to C for his use 18; J's letter to 'Mr. Urban' 23; ('51 or '52) C printed translations of the *Rambler* mottoes in the *GM* 29; ('56) 'Poor dear Cave' 87.

CAVE, Richard and William (1695–'57). —('56) J's letters to Lewis Paul (q.v.) seem to distinguish 'Mr. Cave', who is probably William, y. b. of Edward C, from 'young Mr. Cave', i.e. Richard, Edward's nephew (see on 104). See also Henry, David, who after EC's death conducted the *GM* with RC. (? '56) J's letter 'To Mr. Cave' (? whether RC or WC) 89.

Cavendishes: William, 1698–'55, 3rd D of Devonshire '29; Lord Lieutenant of Ireland '37–'45; of Devonshire House, Piccadilly, and Chatsworth, Derbyshire; William, '48–1811, 5th D '64; m. '74 Georgiana, '57–1806, d. of 1st E Spencer (the beautiful Duchess); his uncles: Lord Richard C, d. '81, Lord George-Augustus Henry, '54– —, Lord George Henry Compton (*DNB*, *L*).—('42) 'the time of the Duke's government' (in Ireland); JT's hopes of preferment from him 17; ('77) JT's acquaintance is 'with the Lord Cavendishes, he barely knows the young Duke and Dutchess' 518; J asks JT for his interest, 'that she (HLT) may have a ticket of admission to . . . Devonshire House' 519; ('78) 'the Duchess is a good Duchess for courting you' (HLT) 585; ('81) JT and the Duke and his uncle 739.1; ('82) 'Mrs. Sheridan refused to sing, at the Duchess of Devonshire's request, a song to the Prince of Wales' 779; 'the Cavendishes were expected to be left out' (of the new government, July) 793, 795; ('84) J's visit to Chatsworth 1007, 1009.

Chambers, Catherine ('Kitty'), '08–

3 Nov. '67, of L'd; with J's mother there and after her death with LP (*L, Reades* 242).—(Jan.–Aug '59) *passim* in letters to LP at the time of Mrs. J's death; ('61) 'Pray give my love to Kitty 137; ('62) 'Be so kind as to tell Kitty' (the news of his pension) 144; ('63) her 'use of the house', J's payment to her for board, 153, 154; ('64) mentioned 164; ('66) 'loath that Kitty should leave the house, till I had seen it once more' 180; her illness 187; ('67) J consults Lawrence about her disease 189.2, 189.3 ('Mrs. Chambers'); 'poor Kitty has done what we have all to do, and Lucy has the world to begin anew' 194.

CHAMBERS, RICHARD, b. of Robert C, q.v.—**793.1.**

CHAMBERS, ROBERT, '37–1803, of Lincoln Coll.; M.A., B.C.L., Vinerian scholar '58, Fellow of Univ. Coll. '61, Vinerian Prof. '66, Prin. of New Inn Hall '66–1803; of 6 King's Bench Walk, Inner Temple, '64–'73; member of the Club '68; Judge of the Supreme Court of Bengal '74, Kt. '77; m. 8 Mar. '74 Fanny, *c.* '58–1839, o.d. of Joseph Wilton the sculptor (*DNB, L*).—('54) C has left L'n **54**; ('55) his 'company and kindness' at O'd **74.1, 75.1**; ('56) his 'Life' and other contributions (? to the *Lit. Magazine*) **98.1**; ('58) J exerts his 'little interest' with F. Wise and others in support of C's candidature for the Vinerian schol. **113.1, 114.1, 115.1**; sends him receipts for his *Shakespeare* 114; ('60) J recommends an Italian scholar to C **134.1**; mentioned 135; J asks him about Sir J. Philipps **136.1**; ('62) C goes circuit 142; J employs C about G. Strahan **144.2**; ('63) J asks C about T. Warter **148.1**; ('66) J asks C about Blackstone **187.1**; urges C to work in L'n on his lectures (see note), asks him about India **187.2**; ('67) India, C's 'old business' **187.3**; J contemplates visiting C at O'd **191.1**; ('68) J visits C at N.I.H. **194.1**, C's kindness 204; Weston's 'regal plan' **203.1**; 'Chambers has no heart' **211.1**; ('69) 'our affairs' 214; ('70) J and C at O'd **227.1, 227.2**; ('71)

J declines invitation to N.I.H. **246.1**; ('72) J unable to visit C **274.2**; C's 'advertisement', J asks for beds at N.I.H. **289.1**; ('73) C retained as counsel for Poll Carmichael 292.1, 293.1 (but see 343.1); 'going a Judge to Bengal', will be J's companion to Newcastle 313, 316; finds a monument at Doncaster 318; letter from Dunvegan **324.1**; India, 'many opportunities of profitable wickedness' **329.1**, J anxious to see him before he leaves **331.1**, will visit him at O'd **340.1**; ('74) his 'exquisitely beautiful' wife, his 'lawyer's tongue' 348, takes a present for Hastings 353, 'I pray God to bless you' **353.1**, 'Chambers is gone far' 358; ('75) 'a letter from Mrs. Chambers of Calcutta', C 'does not now flatter himself that he shall do much good' 413; J sends it to HLT to amuse Baretti (Mrs. C had been his pupil) 418, B sends it to Miss Williams 423; ('79) 'your long letter and Lady Chambers's pretty journal' **640.1**; ('82) J writes to C's b. Richard: 'I think the danger over' (of C's recall by Parliament) 793.1; C 'slipped this session through the fingers of revocation' 795 (see '83); ('83) J asks Cadell to send C his *Lives* 833.2; C's life in India, his unique opportunity of 'enquiring into Asiatick Literature', 'a trifling charge' against him 'in parliament' (see '82), J suggests a loan to BL **835.1**; AW's death **890.3**; C's young son lost with the '*Grosvenor*' India Ship'; C's portrait in the library at S'm 893.1; ('84) C or J had asked Swinton about the authors of the *Universal History* 1042; (n.d.) 1134 (a guess, see note).

Chamier, Anthony, '25–'80, M.P.; Under-Secretary of State '75; original member of the Club (*DNB, L*).—('70) C's return from France 240.1; ('75) J consults him about 'Mr. Lawrence's conduct' (*see* Lawrence, Thomas) 375.1; ('77) tells J there is no hope of a reprieve for Dodd 524; ('79) tells J about the French and Spanish fleets 627.1.

Chaplin of Lincolnshire: doubtless Charles C of Blankney, '59– —, who succeeded his father John '64.—('77) 'a Cow has just been sold to Mr. Chapplin a great breeder in Lincolnshire for one hundred and thirty pounds' 541.1, 557.

CHAPONE, HESTER, née Mulso, '27–1801, essayist; m. '60 John C, who d. '61; of Dean St., Soho (*DNB*, *L*).—('53) probably a contributor to *Adventurer* 46; ('80) J warns HLT against the 'crime' which caused a quarrel between Miss Mulso and Richardson 659; ('82–'83) J's letters to C about Carlisle's (q.v.) tragedy 759.2, 906.1, 911; ('83) J asks FB for C's direction 902.

Charlemont: James Caulfeild, '28–'99, 4th Vt C '34, 1st E of C '63; Irish politician; member of the Club (*DNB*, *L*).—His account of 'the pedigree of Bingham' 712.1 (but see note).

Charles XII 585.1.

Charles Edward, Prince (*L*).—('73) 326 (360), 327 (362), 329 (367).

Charlotte, Queen: see George III.

Chester, Bp of: see Markham.

CHESTERFIELD: Philip Dormer Stanhope, 1694–'73, 4th E of C (*DNB*, *L*).—('42) Rumour of his appointment to Ireland 17; ('55) J's letter to C **61**, 655.

Chetwood, William Rufus, — –'66, prompter at Drury Lane '22–'40 (*DNB*).—('40) C 'is desirous of bargaining for the copy' of *Irene* 12.

Cholmondeley, Hon. Mrs.; Mary, y. s. of 'Peg' Woffington, *c*. '29–1811; m. '46 Robert C, s. of the 3rd Earl C; Cholmondeley, George James, '52–1830, their son (*L* iv. 345, Croker 1831, ii. 472, *Tb*, incorrectly).—('77) 'Cholmondely's story shocks me, if it be true' 558; ('80) J told Mrs. C 'that nobody in the world could judge like her of the merit of a critick' 687; ('82) 'I visited Mesdames . . . Cholmondely' 782.1; ('83) 'Mrs. Cholmondely came to me yesterday' 888.1; 'this afternoon I have given to Mrs. Cholmondely . . .' 891.

Clanranald: chief of the clan in '75 (*L* ii. 309).—('75) 380.

Clapp, Mary, — –'81, widow '67 of

Joseph C, headmaster of Bishop's Stortford School '64–'67; see Barber, Francis (*L*, R ii).—('68–'71) mentioned 207, 238, 241, 269.1.

Clare: Robert Nugent '02–'88, took the name of Craggs '57; Vt Clare '66, E Nugent '76; of 11 North Parade, Bath, &c. (*DNB*, *L*).—('71) 'Goldsmith is at Bath, with Lord Clare' 246.

Clarendon: see Hyde.

CLARK, RICHARD, '39–1831, attorney; Lord Mayor of L'n '84; member of the Essex-Head Club (*DNB*, *L*).—('73) J asks Hawkins to recommend Poll Carmichael's case to C 292.1, J thanks C for undertaking it 293.1; ('74) Chambers transfers it to Murphy 343.1; ('78) C invites J and BL to dine 574.1, see also Angel; J asks C for information about the City Laureates 578.1; ('82) J recommends Collet, q.v., 815.2; ('83) J summons C to the Club 917.1; ('84) 'You were enrolled in the Club by my invitation' **929**.

Claude Lorraine 846.

Clerk(e): Philip Jennings (properly Jennings-C), *c*. '22–'88: of Oriel Coll.; '74 succeeded his maternal uncle, Sir Talbot C of Launde Abbey, Leicestershire, was created Bt, and took the name of Clerke; M.P. '68 for Totnes; of Cavendish Square and Duddlestone Hall, Salop (*L*, *Tb*).—('79) 'I hope Sir Philip . . . comforts you' 617; 'has not yet called' 636; 'never called upon me, though he promised' 642; ('80) C's bill rejected by the Lords 659; 'the honour of a visit from Sir Philip Clerk' 666; ('83) 'enquired after me' 858; 'Sir Philip's request' 859 (see note).

Cobb: Mary Hammond, '18–'93, widow of Thomas C; of the Friary, L'd. See Adey (*L*, R vi, viii).—('68–'84) Often mentioned in letters to LP and from L'd to HLT.

Colebrook, George, '29–1809, '61 2nd Bt; '69 and '71, Chairman of Directors of the East India Co. (*L*, *Tb*).—('71) J asks HT to ask C to procure the discharge of Coxeter 245.

Collet, —. ('82) J asks R. Clark 'to favour . . . Collet, in his petition for the place of Tollgatherer on the Bridge' 815.2.

Collier, Arthur, '07–'77, of Doctors' Commons; friend of HLT's youth (*Tb*).—('78) 'Dr. Collier's Epitaph' 583 (see my note, which I now think may be wrong).

Collier, George, '38–'95, R.N.; Kt '75, Vice-Admiral '94 (*DNB*).—(*c.* '64) acquaintance of FR 162.

Collier, Mary, '33–(?) '76, d. of John Dunn, d. '57, of Wolseley, Staffs., q.v.; m. (1) Thomas Collier, d. '65; their dd. Mary, b. '54, and Sophia, b. '60; (2) '66 Thomas Flint, q.v. For the complicated story of the Collier–Flint dispute see the skilful and patient investigation in R ix, or for a brief outline L v. 581. J regarded the girls as his cousins. For the case drawn up on their behalf (? '83) see facsimile of the MS. (found at Malahide 1946) in *Dr. Johnson and the Misses Collier* privately printed Yale Un. Press 1949. —('82) 'the girls' 766.1; 'the Children are my near relations' 791.1; 'Miss Colliers' (i.e. Misses Collier) 793; 795, 797, 806; 'my cousin Colliers' 815.1; 816; ('83) 823; (n.d., *c.* May '83) 'the girls', their 'brother and sister' (i.e. Thomas and Martha Flint, q.v.) 841.1.

Collins, John, '41–'97 (*DNB*).—('84) his 'project' of an edition of 'Herbert' 947.1 (see note).

Collins, William, '21–'59, poet (*DNB*, *L*).—('54) C's madness: 'I knew him . . . full of hopes and full of projects, versed in many languages, high in fancy, and strong in retention' 51; ('55) 'Poor dear Collins—would a letter give him any pleasure?' 55; J. Warton sends J 'some account of poor Collins' 56; 'I have often been near his state' 57; ('56) 'I wrote him a letter which he never answered' 96; ('75) the Foulis edition of the Poems 1771, 398.

COLMAN, GEORGE, the elder, '32–'94, manager of Covent Garden Theatre '67–'74; member of the Club '68 (*DNB*, *L*).—('61) C's comedy *The Jealous Wife* (Drury Lane, 12 Feb.) 138; ('67) J 'glad to find my poetical civilities superseded by a voluntary performance' 190.1 (see note); ('69) J writes about AW's benefit 212; ('73)

C 'predicts ill success' to *She Stoops to Conquer* 298; 'distressed with abuse about this play' 304; ('77) buys Foote's patent 505; ('80) J writes (probably to C) about 'Mr. Walpole's Tragedy' 650.1.

Colquhoun ('Cohune'), James (*né* Grant), '14–'86, 1st Bt of Luss; 'young C' is no doubt his 3rd s. Ludovic, '57 (*L*).—('73) 'Sir James Cohune, who lives upon the banks of Loch Lomond'; 'Young Cohune'; 336.

Colson or Coulson, John, '19–'88, of University Coll.; Rector of Checkendon, Oxon., '79 (*L*).—('70) 'I did not go out . . . and can therefore give no account of Mr. Coulson' 227.2; ('75) 'Mr. Colson is well, and still willing to keep me' 399; 'such is the uncertainty of all human things, that Mr. C— (*sic* 1788) has quarrelled with me' 401; mentioned 432; ('77) 'Mr. Coulson is here, and well' 533.

Columbus 929.1.

Colvill, John (*L*).—('83) 'the old gentleman' 827.2.

Combe, J—, presumably of Abingdon School 228.1.

COMPTON, JAMES, —; librarian to the Benedictines in Paris; converted to Anglicanism, and came to L'n (see L iv. 504) (*L*, *Tb* 706).—('82) J sends C a letter from Vyse 808; J writes to C about his book (which seems not to have been published); 'go to Mr. Davies . . . He will tell you . . . to what Bookseller you should apply' 811.1; 'I have . . . seen . . . Compton' 819.1; ('83) J recommends C as 'Under-Master of St. Paul's School' 835.

CONGREVES: Charles Walter C, *c.* '08–'77, Archdeacon of Armagh '38; J's schoolfellow; Rev. RICHARD C, his y. b., '14–'82; M.A. Christ Church '36 (*L*, *R* iii).—('35) J sends compliments to RC at Christ Church 3.1; J tells RC he is 'going to . . . keep a private boarding-school' 3.2; ('55) J thanks RC for offering to pay an old debt (to J's mother); 'where is your brother Charles?' 75.2; ('74) 'Charles Congreve is here . . . sunk into . . sordid self-indulgence' 369; ('75) mentioned

372; 'confesses a bottle a day' 387;
'I . . . called on Congreve' 390; ('76)
'our schoolfellow Charles Congreve
. . . very dull, very valetudinary, and
very recluse' 460, 'answered everything
with monosyllables' 461; ('81) 'I have
lately heard that Charles Congreve is
dead' 729.1.
Cooper: probably Sir Grey C, Bt, d.
1801, M.P. and Treasury official
(*DNB*, *L*).—('75) J causes a copy of
Taxation No Tyranny to be sent 'to
Mr. Cooper' 382 (see note).
Coote, Eyre, '26–'83; Kt '71, Lt.-
General '77 (*DNB*, *L*).—('73) 'We
dined with the Governor Sir Eyre
Coote' (at Fort George) 323 (349).
Corbet, Andrew, '09–'41, of Shropshire,
J's schoolfellow (*L*, R v. 81; identification doubtful).—('32) C informs J of
'a Vacancy at Ashbourne' 2.
Corke: see Boyle.
Cornbury: see Hyde.
Cornwallis, Frederick, '13–'83, Archbp
of Canterbury '68–'83 (*DNB*, *L*).—
('77) J recommends De Groot to C's
charity 527; ('81) C receives Macbean's
oath on admission to the Charterhouse
720.
Costollo (? -ello), an Irish lawyer, perhaps named 778.1, see note.
Cottons:
  Lynch Salusbury C, c. '05–14 Aug. '75;
  4th Bt '48 of Combermere, Cheshire,
  and Lleweney, Denbighshire; m. c.
  '38 Elizabeth Abigail Cotton, '13–
  4 Jan. '77.
  Robert Salusbury C, c. '39–1809, 5th
  Bt '75, e. s. of the above; m. '67
  Frances Stapleton, — –1825; M.P.
  and soldier.
  Sidney Arabella C, — –'81, HLT's
  maternal aunt; of Bath. Elizabeth
  Aston, — –'95, m. Rowland Cotton
  (ultimately Admiral), — –'94; of
  Bath. Mrs. Cotton was cousin to Miss
  Elizabeth Aston of L'd (R v. 242; see
  662a) (*DNB*, *L*, *Th*).—*See also* Davenant. ('72) Eliz. Aston claims to be
  'somehow akin to the Cottons' 289;
  ('75) 'Poor Sir Lynch! . . . It is sad to
  give . . . no pleasure but by dying' 427;
  ('76) SAC mentioned (?), 479 (see

note); SAC mentioned (?) 550 (see
note on 479), 554, 555; 'You will see
the Shellys, and perhaps hear something about the Cottons' 553; ('78) 'Sir
Robert Cotton . . . is not the greatest
man that has inhabited a tent' 585.1;
('80 to HLT at Bath) 'my compliments
to . . . Mrs. Cotton' 654, 'pleased . . .
that Mrs. Cotton thinks me worth a
frame' 657, 'you must . . . try to make
a Wit of her' 658; ('83) 'Lord Kilmurrey . . . one day dined with Sir
Lynch' (in '74) 900.
COTTRELL (always -erel): FRANCES
and CHARLOTTE (Mrs. Lewis), dd.
of Admiral Charles C (d. '54); John
Lewis, c. '15–28 June '83, Dean of
Ossory '55, m. (1) Catherine Villiers,
d. '56, (2) Charlotte C (*GM*, *L*, *Th*
579 n. 4. The identifications are often
conjectural restorations of HLP's erasures; see the notes).—('55) Since the
y. s. was still unmarried, 'Miss C'
should be Frances, not Charlotte as I
had assumed; this is supported by the
reference to Mrs. Porter, see below;
74; ('62) 'Miss C clings to Mrs. Porter';
Charlotte's marriage and children 142,
147; ('83) the two sisters; Mrs. Lewis's
family and income; Dean L's two
wives 845, 857, 860, 865, 894; ('84)
Mrs. L in L'n 941, J asks her to dinner
946.2, 'Mrs.' C (an old maid) and Mrs.
L 956.
Cowley, Father: see Wilkes, Father.
Coxeter, Thomas, 1689–'47, a literary
friend of J (*DNB*, *L*); his children
Thomas, Elizabeth.—('71) J asks HT
to use influence to get the younger C
discharged from the E. India Co.'s
service 245; ('76) J asks Percy to get
him admitted to the Middlesex Hospital 503, 504; to secure the D of
Northumberland's charity for Elizabeth 504.1.
Crabbe, George, '54–1832 (*DNB*, *L*).—
('83) J's letter to JR commending,
with 'alterations', *The Village* 830.
CRADOCK, JOSEPH, '42–1826, writer
(*DNB*, *L*).—('83) C lends J books 826,
826.1 (see note).
Craggs, James, the elder, 1657–'21, Post-
master-General; the younger, 1686–

'21; Secretary of State (*DNB, L*).—
('43) 'I am at a loss for the Lives and
Characters of . . . the two Craggs' 18.
Cranbourne (-burne), Lady: James
Cecil, '48–1823, E of Salisbury, styled
Vt Cranbourne till '80; m. (2) '73
Lady Emily Mary Hill, '51–1835.—
('80) J meets Lady Cranburne 669.
Crane, Edward, 1696–'77, of King's Coll.,
Cambridge; LL.D. '28; Prebendary
of Westminster '48–'77 (*Tb*).—('76)
'Dr. Crane enquired after you' 483.
Craven: Elizabeth Berkeley, '50–1828,
playwright; m. (1) '67 William 6th
Baron Craven; (2) '91 the Margrave
of Anspach (*DNB, L*).—('80) J dines
with her 659, 665; meets her at Miss
Monckton's 669; 'poor Stockdale . . .
having thrown away Lord Craven's
patronage' 687.
Crisp, Samuel, '08–Apr. '83, of Chessing-
ton; FB's 'Daddy Crisp' (FB's *Early
Diary, L*).—('80) 'Dr. Burney and
Fanny . . . are gone to be happy with
Mr. Crisp' 703.1; ('83) CB's loss 882.
Croft (Crofts), George, '47–1809, servi-
tor of University Coll. '62; M.A. '69
(*DNB*).—('68) supported by J for an
Oriel fellowship 198 (see note).
CROFT (Crofts), Rev. HERBERT, '51–
1816, 5th Bt '97; of University Coll.
'71; writer (*DNB, L*).—('80) 'I think,
I have got a life of Dr. Young' 690, 'I
shall have Young's life given me' 691
(the *Life* is by C); 'written by a friend
of his son' (Frederick Young) 711.2;
('83) J answers a letter from C 828.1;
the sale of C's books 839.
Croker, Temple Henry, ? '30–? '90.—
('54) C concerned with Huggins (q.v.)
in translating Ariosto 53.1, 53.2 (i.
442).
Cromwell (-wel), Oliver, 1599–1658. 321.
Crosse: a mistake for George Croft, q.v.
Crow, Mrs., the Johnsons' landlady.—
('40) in Castle Street, Cavendish
Square. 12.
CRUIKSHANK   (-s),   WILLIAM
CUMBERLAND, '45 (?)– 1800, surgeon (*DNB, L*; for the year of his birth
see Hill on 891). *See* Hunter.—('83)
J recommends him for the professor-
ship of anatomy in the R. Academy

838; (July '83–Feb. '84, letters about
J's sarcocele) 873, 885.1, 890.1, 891,
892, 893, 895, 915.1, 933.1, 934.2;
('84) J's letter from A'n 1005.
Crutchley (Crichley), Jeremiah, '45–
1805, M.P., of Sunninghill, Berks.; one
of HT's executors (*L, Tb*).—('81)
Perkins 'frights Mr. Crichley' 721,
729.3 (?); 'the iron resolution' of Cator
and C. not to admit Perkins to partnership 735; 'if C—y (*sic* 1788, original not seen) did nothing for life but
add weight to its burden, and darkness
to its gloom, he is kindest to those
from whom he is furthest' 748; ('83)
C in Paris 'to contemplate the pictures
of Claude Loraine' 846; ('84) elected
M.P. for Horsham 953; HLP repays
C's loan 954; his interview with Q
970.2.
Cumberland, Richard, '32–1811, playwright (*DNB, L, Tb*).—('76) '*past
compute* to use the phrase of Cumberland' 468; ('79) 'Mr. Cumberland is a
Million'; 'what makes Cumberland
hate Burney?' 636; Charlotte Lennox
accuses C 'of making a party against
her play' 640 (see note); 'Mr. Cumberland puts me out of your head' 641;
'I had heard . . . that — (*sic* 1788, original not seen) had lost . . . ten thousand' 642, 'I thought Cumberland had
told you his loss' 645, 'Cumberland's
distresses' 645.1; 'I would have Burney
dance with Cumberland' 644; ('82)
C's 'third night . . . put into his own
pocket five pounds' 779.
CUMINS (or Cumming), THOMAS, of
Clerkenwell, — –'74 (*DNB, L* v. 496,
Tb).—('74) J's letter of advice 354.1.
Cummins.—('81) 'Cummins's claim' 745
(see note).
Cumyns (Cumins, Cummins), Elizabeth,
née Thornton, schoolmistress in Kensington Square (*Tb*).—('75) Laura
Carter's 'Mistress' 386.1; 'does Betsy
a little exaggerate?' 395; ('80) 'the
girl that Mrs. Cumins rejected' 684;
('81) Miss Seward has heard of Susan
Thrale 'from Mrs. Cummins' 745.
Curtius 681.
Cuxon, —, and Garlick, persons somehow
associated with Lewis Paul, q.v.—105.

D—. ('75) 642; perhaps Delap, q.v.

Dale, Mrs., of Ashbourne; no doubt Mrs. D, *c.* 1694–'83, m. of Robert D, '49–1835, who '75 m. Catherine, d. of Richard Dyott (q.v.) (*L* v. 581).—('75) 'Mrs. Dale . . . at fourscore has recovered' 418.

Dalrymple: *see* Hailes.

Darby: *see* Derby.

Darius 585.1.

Darnley: Henry Stewart, 1545–67, husband of Queen Mary of Scotland 320.

Dartmouth: William Legge, '31–1801, 2nd E '50 of D; Lord Privy Seal '75 (*DNB*, *L*).—('77) 'Let Lord Dartmouth have it' (Dodd's sermon) 521.1.

Darwin, Erasmus, '31–1802, of L'd (*DNB*, *L*).—('81) D is possibly the 'anonymous authour' at L'd 748 (see note).

Davenant: Hester Cotton, *c.* '48–1822, y. d. of Sir Lynch C, q.v.; m. '74 Corbet D'Avenant (*Tb*).—('75) 'If you go with Mrs. D— (HLP's erasure), do not forget me' 407; ('78) 'is it true that Mrs. Davenant is enceinte?' 586; ('83) 'I have not forgotten the Davenants' 900; ('84) 'Mrs. Davenant called to pay me a guinea' 956.

Davenport, William, — –'92 (*L*, R ix).— ('74) J asks Strahan to take D as apprentice 368; ('75) I have placed young Davenport in the greatest printing house in London' 387; 'I hope poor Davenport will do' 387.2; ('83) J sends Langley the *Lives* by D 841.1.

DAVIES, THOMAS, '12 (?)–'85, author and bookseller; of Russell St., Covent Garden; m. *c.* '52 — Yarrow, d. of an actor at York (Malcolm's *Granger* 1805, 69) (*L*).—('67) perhaps amanuensis of 187.4; ('73) 'Baretti and Davies have had a furious quarrel' 295; ('75) J dines with D 386.1; J recommends D to Allen 408.2; ('77) mentioned 543; 'you (HLT) fall to writing about me to Tom Davies' 562; ('78) mentioned 569; 'poor Davies, the bankrupt bookseller'; Mrs. Montague's charity 573, 574; ('80) his 'great success as an authour (of *Memoirs of Garrick* 1780), generated by the corruption of a bookseller' 700; ('82) mentioned 791; J

sends Compton to D for advice 811.1; ('83) 'Mrs. Davies's tenderness' 849; ('84) mentioned 960.1; 'the tenderness with which you always treat me' 991; mentioned 995; (n.d.) 'come, dear Davies, I am always sorry when we quarrel' 1124.

Davis: ('83) 'Mrs Davis that was about Mrs Williams' 881 (note) (*L*).—('67) perhaps amanuensis of 187.4.

Decii 681.

De Groot, Isaac, *c.* 1694–79 (*L* iii. 125). —('77) J's efforts to get De G admitted to the Charterhouse 525; 'let it not be said that in any lettered country a nephew of Grotius asked a charity and was refused' 527, 531, 531.1.

Delap, John, '25–1812, D.D.; of Lewes, Sussex; playwright (*DNB*, *L*, *Tb*).— ('75) D's 'simplicity should be forgiven for his benevolence' 416; ('79) 'a rival' to Cumberland 636; Delap is perhaps the D— of 642.

Denmark, Queen of: Caroline Matilda, '51–11 May '75, y. s. of George III; m. '66 Christian VII of Denmark.— ('75) mourning for her 393, 395.

Derby (Darby) John, — –'78, Rector of Southfleet, Kent (*L*).—('78) 'My two clerical friends Darby and Worthington' 585.

DESMOULINS: Elizabeth, '16– —, d. of Dr. Swynfen, q.v.; m. — Desmoulins (*L*, R iii. 55).—('75) J sends her a message for Garrick 430; ('77–'83) frequent in letters to HLT, many of which (e.g. 586, 591) describe her feuds with J's other inmates. Among other references: ('80) J asks Vyse to recommend her to the Archbp. as matron of the Chartreux 711; ('83) 'Mrs Desmoulins left us last week . . . there is more peace in the house' 839.1; ('84) 'Mrs Desmoulins never writes . . . tell me . . . what you can' 1027.

Desmoulins, John, s. of the above.— ('78) 'Young Desmoulins is taken in *an undersomething* of Drury Lane' 585, 'five and twenty shillings a week' 592.

Desmoulins, Mr., recommended ('83) by J to Lord Dartmouth 826; mentioned 845; may be the above, or possibly a brother or uncle of the above.

D'Estaigne, Charles-Hector, Comte, '29-'94, French admiral.—('79) D and Macartney 645.1.

Devonshire: see Cavendish.

Dicey, —; mentioned in connexion with Paul 99.

Dick, Alexander, '03-'85, Bt '46 of Prestonfield, Edinburgh; physician (*DNB, L*).—('77) 'the only Scotsman liberal enough not to be angry that I could not find trees, where trees were not' 528; ('84) J asks JB to get D's opinion on his case 932; asks JB to thank D for his letter 937.

DILLY brothers, booksellers in the Poultry: Edward '32-'79, CHARLES '39–1807 (*DNB, L*).—('73) J 'dined at a dissenting Bookseller's' 306.2; see on 393; ('75) J dines with D 386; D supplies J with 'the transcript of the Stone at Genoa' 385.1, 387.3; ('76) 'Mr. Dilly' named by J as typical of the 'wholesale bookseller' 463; 'I dined in the poultry' with 'grave aldermen' (Wilkes and others) 479; ('79) J asks CD for news of JB 625; ('81) CD mentioned 714; J writes to him 737.1; ('84) J asks CD to get him 'Burton's Books' 924; dines with him 960.

Dixie or Dixey, Sir Woolstan, *c*. '01-'67, 4th Bt, of Bosworth; 'an abandoned brutal rascal' (*L*, R v).—('32) 'my leaving Sir (MS. torn, Woolstan's It) was really e Carcere exire' 2.

Dixie, Willoughby, '42-1802, nephew of the above (R vi).—('82) 'the refusal of Mr. Dixie' of JT's proposal of an exchange of livings 797.

Dobson, Susannah, — -'95, w. of Matthew D, HLT's physician in Bath; author of *Life of Petrarch collected from Mémoires pour la Vie de Petrarch* 1775 (*DNB, Tb*).—('83) 'Mrs. Dobson, the directress of rational conversation' 846; her husband 909.

DODD, WILLIAM (often Dod), 'the unfortunate divine', '29-'77, LL.D. '66; hanged for forgery (*DNB, L*, R.W.C., *Papers by Johnson and Dodd* 1926).—('77) *passim* in letters 19 May–1 Sept. (For *The Convict's Address* and other pieces by J *see* Chapman-Hazen.) Note especially: J urges D to write 'the

history of his own depravation. . . . The history of his own mind, if not written by himself, cannot be written' 519.3; 'of his behaviour in prison an account will be published' 524 (see note); injunctions to secrecy: 'Tell nobody' **521**, LP not told 535; J's advice how to meet death **523**; 'surely the voice of the publick, when it calls so loudly, and calls only for mercy, ought to be heard' 524; ('78) 'I never said with Dr. Dodd that *I love to prattle upon paper*' 583.

DODSLEY, ROBERT ('Doddy'), bookseller, '03-'64 (*DNB, L*).—For his concern in J's publications see Index VI. ('38) 6, 7, 8; ('46) agreement for Dictionary **23.2**, J sends D a receipt **23.3**; (? '51) 39; ('54) his wife's death 56; ('55) his 'recommendation' of J for Dictionary 67; 'gone to visit the Dutch' 72; ('59) D's quarrel with Garrick; first night of his *Cleone*; 'Doddy, you know, is my patron' 117; ('60) D's 'moderately good' offer to Percy for the *Reliques* 134.2; (? '65) about Shakespeare **179.1**.

Doge of Genoa 329 (370), 956.

DOUGLAS, JOHN, '21-1807, of Balliol Coll., D.D. '58, Bp of Salisbury '91; a Clarendon Trustee (*DNB, L*).— ('76) J's letters to him on behalf of Carter the riding-master, q.v., **459, 461.1**; his letter on the Clarendon Press 463.

Douglas, Margaret, d. '74, w. of Archibald, 1st Duke of D, 1694-'61 (*DNB, L*).—('73) 'an old Lady who talks broad Scotch with a paralytick voice' 320.

Doxy: Docksey, Merrial, d. of Thomas D of Snelston, Derby; m. 13 Jan. '80 at L'd James Susannah Patton, '53–1812, of Clatto, Fife, and the Priory, Lichfield (*L* iii. 536).—('79) J asks JB to find out about her suitor 646.

Doxy, —, a physician.—('83) 913.

Drake, Sir Francis, 1540?-1596.—236.

Drummond, Robert Hay, '11-'76; M.A. Christ Church '35, Archbp. of York '61; a Clarendon Trustee (*DNB, L*).— ('75) applications to him on behalf of Carter (q.v.) 386, 399, 402.

DRUMMOND, WILLIAM, 'Old Mr.

Drummond', '09–'74, of Callendar, Perthshire, and bookseller in Edinburgh; his son Alexander, d. '82 (*L*).— ('58) J advises D on the education of his son **116.**1; ('66–'67) on the controversy about the proposed Gaelic Bible; mention of D's son; inquiry about Mrs. Heeley **184, 189, 193**; ('73) ' I shall direct Mr. Drummond Bookseller at Ossian's Head, to take care of my letters' 318, 324; ('76) 'Dr. Drummond, I see, is superseded. His father would have grieved' 494 (see note).

Dunbar, James, — –'98, of King's Coll., Aberdeen, LL.D. (*DNB, L*).—('80) 'Dr. Dunbar of Aberdeen' 685; (to JB) 'the bearer of this is Dr. Dunbar, of Aberdeen, who has written . . . a very ingenious book' (*Essays on the History of Mankind* 1780) 701.

Dunn, John, d. '57; *see* Collier.—('82) his will 807.

Dunning, John, '31–'83; Solicitor-General '68–'70; 1st B Ashburton '82; member of the Club '77 (*DNB, L*).—('76) consulted by JT 449; ('77) 'Mr. Dunning, the great lawyer, is one of our members' 528; ('82) consulted by HLT: 'the writing of which Lord Ashburton required the perusal' 817.1, 817.4, 818.1.

Dury, Alexander, — –'58, Major-General; m. an aunt of B. Langton; killed in action near St. Cas in France (*L*).—('58) 'your mind is now full of the fate of Dury' 116.

Dyer, Samuel, '25–'72, classical scholar; of London, but educated Leyden; member '49 of the Ivy-Lane Club, and original member of the Club (*DNB, L*).—('66) 'Dyer is constant at the Club' 182; ('79) J asks FR to buy him a print of D 634; ('83) D's speculation; 'languished into the grave' 835.1; J recalls his old friend 917, 954.

Dyott (Diot), Richard, '23–'87, of Freeford Hall near Lichfield; m. *c.* '50 Catherine Herrick, '24–1810 (*L* v. 581).—('75) 'I saw Mrs. Diot at church' (A'n) 414; 'to the Diots I yet owe a visit' 418; ('77) 'I am going to dine with Mr. Dyot' 545.

Edgcumbe, Emma (*née* Gilbert), m. '61 George E, '21–'95, 3rd Baron E '61 and 1st E of Mount Edgecumbe '89 (*DNB*, FB's *Early Diary*).—('79) her comment on *Evelina*; 'do not tell this to Burney for it will please her' 645.1.

EDWARDS, EDWARD, *c.* '26–'83, of Jesus Coll.; Rector of Besselsleigh, Berks.; D.D. '56; Vice-Principal '62–'83 (*L*).—('78) J asks E to help Burney in the Bodleian, and asks 'what comes of Xenophon?' **589**; ('82) 'Dr. Edwards has gone out of his own rooms for my reception' 789; E 'invited some men from Exeter College' 790; 'invited Miss Adams and Miss More' 792; ('84) J procures the collation of MSS. in Paris for E's use; 'a man whom I never found deficient in any offices of civility' 946.1; 'my convivial friend' 963; J praises his emendations in Xenophon (*Memorabilia*, Oxford 1785) 974.

EGELSHAM, WELLS, fl. '50–'86 (Plomer, *Dict. of . . . Printers* 1932); printer of *The General Advertiser*.— ('50) **27.**

Eglinton: Archibald Montgomerie, '26–'96, 11th E of E '69; Lt.-General '77; his mother, Susannah (Kennedy), 1688–'80, m. '09 the 9th E (*DNB, L*). —('73) 'We paid a visit to the Countess of Eglinton, a Lady who for many years, gave the laws of Elegance to Scotland' 337; ('77) William Shaw's request, through J, 'to Lord Eglintoune, that he may be appointed Chaplain to one of the new-raised regiments' 567.

Eld: probably Francis, 1691–'60, of Seighford Hall, Stafford.—('42) 'Eld is only neglected not forgotten' 17 (to JT).

ELIBANK: Patrick Murray, '03–'78, 5th Baron E (*DNB, L*).—('71) 'I see but little of Lord Elibank . . . perhaps by my own fault' 250; ('73) J hopes to visit E in Scotland **325**; ('74) 'remind Lord Elibank of his promise to give me all his works' 348.

Elliot: Edward Eliot, '27–1804, M.P.; '84 cr. Baron Eliot; member of the Club '82 (*DNB. L*).—('79) J meets 'Mr. Elliot of Cornwall' at JR's 637;

('80) mentioned, in a letter written for HT, as 'long my friend' 706.1.

Ellis, Rev. William, —, headmaster from '70 of Bishop's Stortford Grammar School; see Barber (L, R ii).—('70) 238, 241.

ELPHINSTON, JAMES, '21–1809, schoolmaster and translator (DNB, L). —('49) J thanks E for kindness 24; ('50) on E's mother's death; E's letters to Mrs. Strahan 30; ('51 or '52) E's translations of the Rambler mottoes 29; ('58) J's 'old intimacy' 116.1; ('67) I believe him to be prosperous' 189; ('73) J puts 'young Otway to school with Mr. Elphinston' 304; ('78) E's wife's death; 'a loss, such as yours, lacerates the mind' 580; (n.d.) a letter to E 1125.

Errol: see Boyd.

Evans, James, — –c. '86, Rector of St. Saviour's and '77 of St. Olave's, Southwark (L iii. 537, Tb).—('73) J quotes E's phrase 'your friend and servant' 310; ('76) mentioned 477; ('80) 'Mr. E— and Mr. P— (sic 1788; Evans and Perkins); their criticism of HLT's letter to the electors of S'k 662, 666; visits J 686.2.

Evans, —.—('84) J's debt to a man of this name 960.1.

Evans, —, Apothecary of Knightsbridge (Tb 118).—('75) 384.2.

Eyles 301.3.

Falconer, James, '37–1809, D.D., of Lichfield (R i).—('82) His visit to J 776.

FARMER, RICHARD, '35–'97, Master '75 of Emmanuel Coll., Cambridge (DNB, L).—('70) J asks F to help Steevens with Shakespeare 227; J's 'plunder of your pamphlet' (Essay on the Learning of Shakespeare 1767, 2 editions); 'I hope amongst us all Shakespeare will be better understood' 244; ('72) F's alleged loan of a pamphlet 292; ('77, '80) J asks F for information about Cambridge poets 530, 673; ('82) J too ill to meet F and Malone 764.

FAULKNER, GEORGE, 1699 (?)–'75, bookseller of Dublin (DNB, L).—('42) F's edition of Thurloe 17; ('54) 'Mr.

Falkner's letter to me' 51.1; ('57) his 'favour' to J 107; ('67) 'honest George' and AW 187.4; ('75) J introduces Twiss to Leland and F 390, 392 (lost).

Fielding, Henry, '07–'54 (DNB, L).— ('84) 'sent to Lisbon' 932.

Fielding, John, — –'80, the blind magistrate; Kt '61; of Bow Street (DNB, L).—('80) the rioters 'pulled down Fielding's house' 677.

FISHER (or Fy-), PHILIP, c. '50–1842, Fellow '72 of University Coll., Master of the Charterhouse (L).—('75) J asks F 'to give the Earse books with the proper message to the librarian' 403.1 (see note).

Fitzherbert, William, '12–'72, of Tissington, Derbyshire widowed '53; his distant relation Hill Boothby, q.v., was in charge of his motherless children (L, R vi, Tb).—('55–'56) offers J wine 78; 'my dear little Miss' (presumably F's child) 79, 81; ('61) 'a member of the new Parliament' 138 (133).

FITZMAURICE: William Petty (Fitzmaurice), '37–1805, Prime Minister '82–'83; 2nd E of Shelburne '53; m. (2) his cousin Anne Fitzmaurice, who '80 died at Lleweney, Denbighshire, 'at an advanced age' (GEC); their children included Thomas, '42–'93, who '77 m. Mary, afterwards in her own right Countess of Orkney, and had a son 2 Oct. '78; he bought Lleweney from the Cottons, q.v., in '80 (DNB, L, Tb).—('78) J congratulates TF on the birth of his son; 'with Lady Shelburn I once had the honour of conversing' 596; ('80) 'I dined . . . with Mr. Fitzmaurice, who almost made me promise to pass part of the Summer at Llewenney' 664; (July '82) 'Shelburne speaks of him (Burke) in private with great malignity'; his hostility to Chambers 795; (Sept. '82) 'Of the probability of Shelburne's continuance I can make no judgment' 806.

FLETCHER, GEORGE, c. '30–1800, R. of Cubley (L).—(? '80) J's inquiries about his own family 711.3.

Fletcher, Mrs. — (L).—793.

Fletewood, Charles, — –'47, patentee of

Drury Lane, R vi (L).—('40) His promise that *Irene* 'shall be the first next season' 12.

Fleury, Cardinal, 1653–'43.—('42) 17.

FLINT, LOUISE MATHER, 'a *very* young lady' (HLP) in '69; d. 1821 (Hill, *Letters*).—('69) J's letter to her in French 213.

Flint, Thomas, '24–'87, Taylor's clerk; m. (2) '66 Mary Collier, q.v.; their d. Martha, b. '67, and s. Thomas, b. '69; m. (3) '83 Dorothy Tunnicliffe (L, R ix).—('63) 'you (JT) may less disgracefully be governed by your Lady than by Mr. Flint' 159; ('75) 'Mr. Flint's little girl' 419; ('77) 'my cousin Mr. Flint's wife' 541.1 (see Collier); ('82) JT's doubts of F's 'veracity' 766.1, 791.1, 806, 807, 816; ('83) 'had Mr. Flint a son by their (the Colliers') Mother?' 823; (? '83) F's children 841.1.

Foote, Samuel, '20–'77, actor (DNB, L). —('76) Colman's purchase of F's patent 505; ('77) F's life should be written, 'at least . . . a Footeana' 561.

Ford, Cornelius, J's grandfather, 1632–'09, of The Haunch, King's Norton, Birmingham; his children included Joseph, 1662–'21, Nathanael, 1676–'29, and Sarah, 1669–'59, J's mother (L, R iii).—('75) J asks Hector to apply 'to the Rector of *Kingsnorton* . . . for the date of the Christenings of the . . . children of Cornelius Ford, who formerly lived at the *Haunch* in his parish'; J names, of his 'eight' children, Joseph ('born, I believe, about 1660'), Nathanael, and Sarah, 'who was my Mother' 384.3.

Ford, Cornelius, 1694–'31, 'Parson Ford', J's cousin (L, R iii. 144).—('71) J's regret that he cannot go to Hagley to 'recall the images of sixteen, and review my conversations with poor Ford' 257 (see note).

Ford, Elizabeth (Betty): see Heely.

FORD, SAMUEL, '17–'93, J's cousin; of Trinity Coll., O'd, '36, and Emmanuel, Cambridge, '38; Rector of Brampton Abbotts near Ross, '42 (L, R iii. 44).— ('35) J's letter of advice 3.3.

Fordyce, Alexander, — –'89, banker

(DNB).—('72) 'the failure of Fordice, who has drawn upon him a larger ruin than any former Bankrupt' 275.1.

Fordyce, Miss, later wife of — a relative of Alexander F, q.v.—J meets her at Durham 318.

Fordyce, George, '36–1802, M.D., F.R.S.; member of the Club '74 (DNB, L).—('74) his election to the Club 348.

Forster, Mrs., schoolmistress at Tottenham Green.—('74) 354.1.

Foster, Elizabeth, 1688?–'54, Milton's granddaughter (L).—('50) 27.

FOTHERGILL, THOMAS, '16–'96, D.D. '62; Provost of Queen's '62, Vice-Chancellor '72–'75; 'un esprit foible' 419 (L).—(Mar.–July '75) J's letter to F thanking the University for his doctorate 385; *passim* in letters to HLT about Carter, q.v., about books given to the Bodleian 403.1.

Foulis, Robert, '07–'76, and his b. Andrew, '12–'75, printers in Glasgow (DNB, L).—('75) 398.

FOWKE, FRANCIS and his f. JOSEPH '22–1806 (L iii. 471).—('76) J's letter to FF about the trial and sentence of 'my dear friend Joseph Fowke' (for conspiring with Nuncomar against Barwell) 495; ('79) J is glad that Chambers has 'thought it proper to show some countenance to Mr. Joseph Fowke' 640.1; ('83) J asks Cadell to send F his *Lives* 833.2; J's letter to JF; execution of Nuncomar 834 (see note on 827.1); J asks Chambers to befriend JF 835.1 (19).

Fowler, Rev. Robert, of Magdalene Coll., Cambridge; headmaster '67–'69 of Bishop's Stortford Grammar School; see Barber (L, R ii).—('68) 207.

Fox, Charles James, '49–1806; member of the Club '74 (DNB, L).—('74) his election to the Club 348; ('82) F's resignation 793; F at 'a very crouded Club' 817.1; (Mar. '84) 'Mr Fox resolutely stands for Westminster' 946.

FRANKLIN, WILLIAM, —, Governor of New Jersey; m. (2) Elizabeth —. WF was in England '57–'63 and in '78 (Dict. Amer. Biog.).—(n.d.) J accepts their invitation 1126.

Fraser, Alexander, — -'94, of Strichen; his neighbour Dr. F (*L* v. 500).—('73) J and JB dine with 'a Country Gentleman (AF) who has ... the remains of a Druid's Temple' 323 (348); 'I was owned ... by one who had seen me at a Philosophical Lecture' 326 (354).

Frederick the Great '12–'86 (*L*).—('42) 17; ('84) 929.1.

Gale, —: not identified.—('80) 'Gale and Smith never came' 707.1.

GALWAY, Mrs.—('55) J sends her an almanack 57.1 (see i. 430).

Gardiner, Anne, *c*. '16–'89, 'wife of a tallow-chandler on Snow-hill, not in the learned way, but a worthy good woman' (JB) (*L*).—('75) 'I forgot ... to send Mrs. Gardiner's card' (to HLT) 390; ('77) J dines with her 505.3, 506; ('80) '— (*sic* 1788; Lady Lade) called ... at Mrs. Gardiner's, to see how she escaped' (Gordon riots) 679; ('83) dines with J on his birthday 881; ('84) 'a more skilful agent' for Mrs. Pellé 965.

Garlick, —: see Cuxon.

GARRICK, DAVID, '17–20 Jan. '79; m. '49 EVA MARIE VIOLETTI, '24–1822; of 5 Adelphi Terrace from '72; member of the Club '73; his brother Peter, '10–'95 (*DNB*, *L*).—('40) 'David wrote to me ... on the affair of Irene' 12; ('43) 'I never see Garrick' 17.1; ('50) G to speak J's *Prologue* to *Comus* and to perform in his own *Lethe, or, Esop in the Shades* (1745, '49) 27; ('56) G gives AW a benefit 85; ('59) 'David and Doddy have had a new quarrel' 117; ('65) J asks G to inspect 'such plays (of Shakespeare) as you would see' 168; ('66) J's debt (?) to G 186; ('71) J sends G criticisms and suggestions on his epitaph for Hogarth 269; (? *c*. '72) J asks G for places for Bell of Westminster 169; ('73) 'Mr. G— has ... sent his brother to me with a confutation of Mr. M—' (HLP's erasures) 303.2; 'Murphy is preparing a whole pamphlet against Garrick' 304; ('75) J tells G that he has no letters of Hawkesworth's fit for publication 430; ('78) Nollekens' bust of J condemned by

Mrs. G 572; J intercedes with G for M. Lowe 577; ('79) G's death: condolence to Mrs G 600.1, 601; 'futurity is uncertain, poor David had doubtless many futurities in his head' 604; ('81) G's legatees at L'd 'Very angry that they receive nothing' 744; ('82) J to dine with Mrs. G 778, 779, but illness prevented him 779.2; G's 'funeral expences are yet unpaid, though the Undertaker is broken' 779; ('84) J dines with Mrs G 960; 'I did not wonder that your heart failed you, when the journey to Lichfield came nearer' 1018.1; (n.d.) J's untraced letter to G 1127; J asks G to return 'the plays' 1127.1; J to wait on Mrs G and H. More 1138, Mrs. G mentioned 1139.

Garrick, Peter, '10–'95, e. b. of David G; wine-merchant of Lichfield (*L*, R iii).—('73) 'Mr. G— has just now sent his brother to me with a confutation of Mr. M—' 303.2; ('76) G shows JB 'the City' (L'd) 464.1; ('77, '79, '81) mentioned 537, 616, 744; ('84) visits J at L'd 1018.1.

Gastrell: see Aston.

Gawler, —, of Putney.—('80) J and Lawrence dine with G 687.

Gell, Philip, *c*. '23–'95, of Hopton Hall, Derbyshire; m. 11 May '74 Dorothy Milnes '58–1808 (*L*).—('75) G 'rejoicing at fifty-seven (*sic*, erroneously) for the birth of an heir male' 418.

George II, 1683–'60 (*L*).—('61) 'We were so weary of our old King, that we are much pleased with his successor' 138.

George III, 4 June '38–1820; acceded '60; m. '61 Charlotte Sophia of Mecklenburg-Strelitz, '44–1818 (*L*; see also George II, George IV).—('61) 'The young man is hitherto blameless ... he has been long in the hands of the Scots' 138; his coronation 139; ('62) J's pension: 'the favours which his Majesty has ... been induced to intend for me' 143; J tells LP that the King had empowered Bute 'to do something for me' 144; ('67) J's conversation; his literary and political information 187.4; ('68) J writes to Weston of

Greene', '16–'93, apothecary and antiquary of Lichfield; often spelled *Green*, but his bookplate has *Greene* (*DNB, L*).—('68) mentioned 209.1; ('70) 'Mr. Grene the Apothecary has found a book which tells who paid levies in our parish' 233; ('71) 'Mr. Green's curiosities' 267; ('73) 'I . . . lent Mr. Greene the axe and lance' 296; ('75) 'has got a cast of Shakespeare' 406; a lost letter making an appointment **412**; came to A'n 'and having nothing to say, said nothing' 418; ('76) JB visits G 464.1; his relationship to Wood (q.v.) 483, cf. 614.1; ('77) mentioned 535, 'Green's Museum' 537; ('79) 'comes home loaded with curiosities' 613, 'loaded with Sir Ashton Levers Superfluities' 614.1, 'much enriched by Mr. Lever' 616.1; mentioned 616; ('84) J sends G 'the epitaph, for my Father, Mother, and Brother' **1040**; 'I have sent Mr. Green the Epitaph' 1041.

GRENVILLE, GEORGE, '12–'70, M.P.; Chancellor of the Exchequer April '63 (*DNB, L*).—('63) J's letter about the payment of his pension **152**.

Greville, —, physician of Gloucester.—('71) 'Dr. Grevil of Glocester' 258.

Greville, Richard Fulke, *c.* '17–*c.* 1806, of Wilbury, Wilts.; m. '48 Frances Macartney, — –'89 (authoress of *A Prayer for Indifference*) (*L* iv. 535, FB's *Diaries*, *Tb*, Yale Walpole xi. 47, Greville Memoirs ed. Fulford, ii. 318).—('56) J's criticism of G's *Maxims* (1756) 93; ('78) 'Mrs. Greville that downs my Mistress' 586; ('80) J meets G at the Burneys' 662.

Grierson, George Abraham, *c.* '28–'55, King's Printer in Dublin (*DNB, L*).—('66) 183.1 (see note).

Griffith, Thomas, *c.* '24– —, of Pembroke Coll.; D.D. '72.—('71) 264.1, 264.2, 265.

Guest, Mary Jane, *c.* '64–*c.* 1816; performed in London '83; m. — Miles (*L*, FB's *Diary*).—('80) 'encourage, as you can, the musical girl' (to HLT at Bath) 663.

Guild, —. 702 (see note).

Gwynn (Gwin), John, — –'86, architect, of Shrewsbury; designer of Magdalen Bridge and other buildings at Oxford (*DNB, L*).—('76) 'Gwin neglected to get places in the coach' (for O'd) 463.1; ('77) 'his work was finished so ill that he has been condemned to pay three hundred pounds for damages' 533; ('78) J's letter pleading G's cause 570.

Hailes (Hail 353.2): Dalrymple, Sir David, '26–'92, 3rd Bt '51 of Hailes, E. Lothian; judge of the Court of Session as Lord H. '66 (*DNB, L*).—('74) J tells Horne that 'Lord Hail . . . appears to have the same design' as Horne of editing Walton's *Lives* 353.2; tells JB that Horne has resigned in H's favour 357; sorry H will not do it 360; ('74–'79) H's *Annals of Scotland* (1776, continued 1779): J's commendation of the book and work on the MS. *passim* in letters to JB; note esp. 'a new mode of history' 431; ('75) 'Is Lord Hailes on our side?' (about Ossian) 374; J's verses on Inchkenneth not to be shown by JB 'except to Lord Hailes, whom I love better than any man whom I know so little' 374; the *Journey*: 'I shall long to know what Lord Hailes says of it. Lend it him privately' 375; his wish that J should write 'a character of Bruce' 438; ('76) J advises JB to consult H, as a lawyer and a Christian, about female inheritance 448, 450, 452, his 'aversion from entails' 452, 454, shaken by J's arguments 458; mentioned 462; ('77) J asks JB what H thinks of 'the negro's cause' 528; ('78) H 'on the side of liberty' in 'the negro's cause' 568; J compares H and Percy 575; ('79) *Lives* for H 607 (714, 815); his 'description of Dryden' 628; ('82) 'Thank dear Lord Hailes for his present' 861; J advises JB to consult H whether to reprint Baxter's *Anacreon* 888.

Halifax: George Montagu Dunk, '16–'71, 2nd E of H (*DNB*).—Z. Williams's letter to him, Appendix A, i. 433.

Hall, Mrs.: *see* Wesley.

HAMILTON, ANTHONY, '38–'74, of Corpus Christi Coll., Cambridge, D.D. '75, Vicar of St. Martin's in the

Fields '76.—('83) J's application for a poor woman 844 (Mrs. Pellé?); ('84) 'Mrs. Pellé shall wait upon you' 933; 'this is the person whom I recommend' 934.1; 'Mrs. Pellé is a bad manager for herself' 965.

HAMILTON, ARCHIBALD, '20–'93, printer in Fleet Street (*L* ii. 226).— (? '53) Macbean's wager with H on progress of Dictionary 44 (see note on the identification, which may be doubted); ('76) H's quarrel with Calder (q.v.) 453, 456.

HAMILTON, WILLIAM GERARD, 'Single-speech H', '29–'96, of Oriel Coll.; M.P. (*DNB, L*).—('75, '80) J dines with H 386, 660.1, 662; [('81) 'Gerard . . . like Pope is *un politique aux choux et aux raves* 712.1, but see note]; ('83) H offers J money: 'a Friend, whose name I will tell when your Mamma has tried to guess it' 901; 'your generous offers' 905; 'you must all guess again at my Friend' 917; 'the generous Man was Gerard Hamilton' 922; ('84) 'I hope still to see you *in a happier hour*' 1024.

HAMILTON, —.—('82) 774 (see note).

Hannah —, maidservant of JT.—('63) 156, 159, 161.

Harborough: Bennet Sherard, '09–'70, 3rd E of H '50.—148.1; Lord H franked this letter, and might possibly be the 'ingenious gentleman' in whose interest it was written; but I have no other evidence that J was acquainted with him.

Harcourt: Simon H, '14–'77, 1st Earl H '49 (*DNB*).—('77) his death by drowning 550.

Harding(e), Caleb, c. 1700–'75, physician (R iii. 130).—('75) 'Poor Caleb Harding is dead. . . . How few dos the Man who has lived sixty years now know of the friends of his youth' 455.

Hardinge, George, '43–1816, writer (*DNB, L*).—('80) 'Mr. Walpole's Tragedy, which was stolen from Mr. Hardinge' 650.1.

Hardy, Charles, '16 (?)–'80; Kt '55; Admiral '70; Governor of Greenwich '71; M.P. Portsmouth '74 (*DNB*), commander of the Channel Fleet '79

(*DNB*).—('74) 'Hardy has no mind to serve us' 362.1 (see note for the identification, which is conjectural); (24 Aug. '79) 'the French fleet within sight of Plymouth . . . the English fleet under Hardy is much inferiour . . . in number' 627.1.

HARDY, SAMUEL, of Emmanuel Coll. Cambridge '20–'93, Afternoon Lecturer at Enfield, Middlesex; author of *The Scripture-Account of the Nature . . . of the Holy Eucharist* 1784.—('80) J's criticism of H's book 707.

Harley, Thomas, '30–1804, M.P., Lord Mayor of London '67–'68 (*DNB, Th* 117).—('74) 'I beg your (JT's) interest with Mr. Harley' to get a boy into 'the Bluecoat Hospital' 369.

HARRINGTON: Caroline Fitzroy, '22–'84; m. '46 the 2nd E of H (*DNB, L*). —('77) J's letter to her on behalf of Dodd 522.1 (see note).

Harrington, Henry, '27–1816, physician of Bath (*L, Th*).—('76) 'your Woodwards and your Harringtons' 479; 'Woodward . . . is gone to Bristol. . . . You have now only Harington' 483; ('80) 'Do you see Dr. Woodward or Dr. Harrington?' 657.

Harris, James, 'Hermes Harris', '09–'80, writer; of Wadham Coll.; of Salisbury; M.P. for Christchurch '61; m. '45 Elizabeth Clarke (*DNB, L*, FB's *Early Diary*).—('77) 'the Harris's' at JR's 512; ('80) 'Mr. Harris' at the Burneys 662.

Harrison, Cornelius, 1700–'48, g. s. of Cornelius Ford, 1632–'09, q.v.; Fellow of Pembroke Coll., Cambridge; Perpetual Curate of Darlington (*L*, R iii). —('73) 'Cornelius Harrison a Cousin German of mine . . . the only one of my relations who ever rose in fortune above penury or in character above neglect' 318 (339).

Hastie, John, *fl.* '72, JB's schoolmaster client (*L*).—('72) 276.

HASTINGS, WARREN, '32–1818 (*DNB, L*).—('74) J's letter sent by 'my friend Mr. Chambers'; J recalls H's visit 353; J sends H his *Journey*, recommends Chauncy Lawrence 367; ('76) J cannot prepare Joseph Fowke's 'narrative for the press', since 'I live in a reciprocation of civilities with Mr. Hastings' 495; ('81) J recommends Hoole's Ariosto to H's patronage; 'it is a new thing . . . for a Governor of Bengal to patronise Learning' 712; ('83) J asks Cadell to send H his *Lives* 833.2, 835.1 (16); ('84 to Hoole) 'Mr. Hastings's Packet I received' 989.

HAWKESWORTH, JOHN, '15–'73; LL.D. Lambeth '56; m. Mary Brown of Bromley, Kent, — –'96. (Monument in Bromley Church, destroyed in the Six Years War, quoted in *History of Bromley* 1929.) (*DNB, L*).— ('53–'54) H's *Adventurer* 46, 51; ('56) J hopes to visit H (at Bromley?) 'to see the spring and Mrs. Hawkesworth' 93; ('67) H a friend of Caldwell 187.4; (? '73) See 1128 below; ('75) J tells Garrick about his correspondence with H 430; ('76–'77) J writes to Ryland of Bromley about H's works: a play (commended by HLT) 498; sends R a 'selection' 501; details, with advice to Mrs H about publication, 514; ('77) J asks HLT to lend H's *Voyages* 536; ('80) J asks Nichols to lend 'Swifts works with Dr. Hawkesworths life' 696; ('83–'84) H a member of the Ivy-lane Club 917, 954; (n.d.) J asks H about an epitome of Chambers's Dictionary and about Mrs. H's health 1128.

HAWKINS, JOHN, '19–'89, attorney and writer; Kt '72; member '49 of the Ivy-Lane Club and an original member of the Club; m. '53 Sidney Storer; their s. John Sidney H, '58–1842, antiquary (*DNB, L*).—('66) 'Hawkins is remiss' (at Club) 182; ('73) J asks H to recommend Poll Carmichael's cause to R. Clark (his successor in business); 'compliments to Lady Hawkins' 292.1, 293.1; ('74) H's 'late edition of the Angler, very diligently collected, and very elegantly composed' (Izaak Walton, *The Compleat Angler*, ed. JH 1760) 353.2 (see note); ('82) H lends J volumes of his *History of Music* (1776) for Lawrence 767.2, 767.5 (J's praise of it); ('83) J's proposal that 'all that remained of the club' meet and dine in Ivy-Lane 908; the dinner arranged 915; ('84) 'Sir John Hawkins, a man of very diligent enquiry and very wide intelligence', his 'materials for the completion of Walton's lives' (not published) 947.1; J sends Nichols 'a very curious proposal' by young H (his edition 1787 of Ruggle's *Ignoramus*; Nichols, *LA* ix. 35) 950; H's praise of JT's sermon 968; J on HLT's marriage 978; 'let me have the benefit of your advice, and the consolation of your company' 1034.

Hay, John, one of J's Highland guides (*L* v. 131) 323 (350).

HAY, GEORGE, '15–'78; of St. John's College; D.C.L. '42; Kt '73; Lord of Admiralty '56–'65 (*DNB, L*, R ii. 12–13).—('59) J applies to him for release of Barber 132.3 (see note); ('68) rejected by the electors of Oxford University 201.

Hay-Drummond: *see* Drummond.

Heartwell, —, of Lichfield (a Hartwell family of L'd is mentioned in R iv).— ('70) 235.

'Head, Mr', a nickname.—644 (see note).

HEBERDEN, WILLIAM, '10–1801, physician, 'ultimus Romanorum'; M.D. '39; Fellow of St. John's Coll., Cambridge '49; F.R.S. '49; of Pall Mall (Hill on 850); one of J's regular physicians after he lost Lawrence (*DNB, L*).—('73) J advises JT to 'write your case to . . . Heberden' 312; ('79) H's talk to JT 'rather prudential than medical' 605.1; H attends HT 618, 620, 621, 627, 629; ('82) H attends Lawrence 782.1; (June–July '83) J's paralytic stroke: *passim* in letters of this period ('Heberden I could not bear to miss' 863); (Sept.–Oct. '83) J's sarcocele: *passim* in letters of this period ('now in his retreat at Windsor' 884.1); (Dec. '83–Aug. '84) J's dropsy and breathlessness: *passim* in letters of this period ('recommends opiates' 921, 'declared me well' 926, 'my Distemper prevails' 930, 'the water passed naturally . . . in a manner of which Dr. Heberden has seen but four examples' 938; 'tell Dr. Heberden, that in the coach I read *Ciceronianus*' 979; 'my appetite is still good, which I know is dear Dr. Heberden's criterion of the *vis vitae*' 987); (Oct.–Nov. '84) J at A'n reports his state **1022**; 'I have disobeyed Dr. Heberden' **1033.1**.

HECTOR, EDMUND, '08–'94, surgeon in Birmingham; his sister Ann, '11–'88, widow '57 of Rev. Walter Careless or Carless (*L*, R iii).—(? '31 or '32) J's 'lost' letter to H quoted by H **1.1**; ('55) J recalls 'evenings at Warrens and the Swan, sends H 'Books', i.e. the Dictionary **69**; 'so long a cessation of correspondence' must not recur, hopes to visit B'm **71.1**; ('56) J tells H of his *Shakespeare* **103**, **105.1**; ('57) J begs for letters **108**; ('65) *Shakespeare*; 'many of my hopes disappointed' but still hopes for B'm **179**; ('67) H's present of a teaboard, his wife's illness **193.1**; ('70) J spent a day at B'm with H 'and his sister, an old Love' **235**; ('72) J's visit to B'm in Dec. **290**, **291**, **296**; ('73) H's carrot-poultice **301.2**; ('74) mentioned **369**; ('75) H's and Mrs. C's present of china to HLT **376.1**, **384.3**; J visits B'm, 'but Hector had company in his house' and could not give him a bed **404**; H's compliance 'with all my requests', his health **441**; ('76) 'dear Mrs. Careless' **460**; J's visit to B'm **464.1**; ('77) J's visit to B'm **535**; ('78) H's visit to L'n **591**; ('81) J's visit to B'm **742**, H's 'prognostick' **742**, **749**; ('82) J writes of their friendship **772**; ('84) Taylor and H the only friends of his youth left **951**; 'we have all lived long, and must soon part' **1037**.

Hector, a dog **750**.

HEELY, HUMPHRY, '14–(?) '97; m. Elizabeth, '12–'68, d. of J's uncle Samuel Ford (*L*, R viii).—('67) J asks Drummond to inquire about 'the wife of Mr. Heely, who had lately some office in your theatre'; 'I am willing to go to ten pounds' **193**; ('68) 'Mr. Heely . . . is come . . . from Scotland very poor, his wife, my cousin died on the road' **207.1**; ('75) 'He seems to have a genius for an alehouse' **370**; ('76) 'has yet got no employment' **463.1**; ('84) J tries to get H into

Wicher's Almshouses **923**; 'you cannot suppose that I have much to spare. Two guineas . . .' **988**.

Henry, David, '10–'92. *See* Cave and Paul (*L*).—('56) 'too wise to do ill without interest' **102**, **104**.

Hereford, Dean of: *see* Wetherell.

Herne, Elizabeth, d. '92; a lunatic; J's first cousin once removed; *see* Prowse (*L*).—('80) 'the unhappy girl' **693**; 'the unfortunate woman . . . is, in her way, well . . . Of her cure there is no hope' **710**; ('84) J's legacy for her maintenance **934**.

Herschel, William, '38–1822, astronomer; K.H. 1816 (*DNB*).—('84 to S. A. Thrale) 'With Mr. Herschil it will certainly be very right to cultivate an acquaintance' **944**.

HERTFORD: Francis Seymour-Conway, '18–'94, 1st E of H '50; Lord Chamberlain '66–'82 (*DNB*, *L*).—('76) J's application for rooms in Hampton Court **472**.

Hervey, Catherine or Katherine, e. d. of Sir Thomas Aston, 3rd Bt; m. '30 Rev. Henry H, '01–'48, 4th s. of Bishop of Bristol. *See* Aston (*L*, R v, vi).—('71) J's letter 'from Mrs. Hervey' **263**; ('77) 'Mrs. Hervey blind' **557**; ('79) 'Mrs. Hervey has just sent to me to dine with her' **613**; ('80) 'blind Mrs. Hervey has sent me a peremptory summons to dine' **703.1**.

HICKMAN, GREGORY, 1688–'48, of Stourbridge, Worcestershire; half-b. of Cornelius Ford, q.v. (*L*, R, *Reades* and iii).—('31) J's letter of thanks **1**.

Hinchliffe, John, '31–'94, Master of Trinity Coll., Cambridge, '68–'88; Bp of Peterborough '69–'94 (*DNB*, *L*, *Tb*).—('80) 'We were at the Bishop of St. Asaph's, a Bishop little better than *your* (HLT) Bishop' **669**; 'you think to run me down with the Bishop' **675**.

Hinckley, Mrs.: presumably Blanche H, — –'72, widow of Thomas H of L'd (R iv. 178), or Mary, *née* Bayley, '18–'88, widow '68 of Richard H (R vii. 165).—('67) J sends her his compliments **194**.

Hitch: perhaps Charles H, — –'64, Bookseller in Paternoster Row, one of the publishers of the Dictionary. *See* Paul (*L*).—('56) 91, 92.

Hoare's Bank 557.

Hodgson, Brian, *c.* '09–'84, of the Old Hall Inn, Buxton, and of Ashbourne; f.-in-law of Beilby Porteous, q.v. (*L*). —('81) 'the Bishop of Chester is here (A'n) now with his Father in law' 747.

Hogarth, William, 1697–'64, painter (*DNB, L*).—('71) J's epitaph 269.

Holder, (?) Robert, — —'97, apothecary, of Norfolk St., Strand (*L, The New Rambler* Jan. 1944, 16).—('82) H attends Levet 757, 'imperetur nuncio Holderum ad me deducere' 779.1; ('84) H sends drugs to J at A'n 985, 987, 990.

Holderness: Robert D'Arcy, '18–'78, 4th E of H (*DNB, L*).—('76) his part in a 'Revolution in the Prince's household' 492.

HOLLYER, JOHN, *fl.* '41–'84; of Coventry; J's cousin (R ix. 71).—('74) J asks H's advice about 'our Cousin Thomas Johnson' 365; ('84) J writes (presumably to H) about the children of Mr. (presumably Thomas Johnson; MS. torn) 1037.1.

HOOLE, JOHN, translator, '27–1803; of Great Queen St. ('85); in the service of the E. India Co. — —'85; member of the Essex-Head Club; m. '57 Susannah Smith of Bishop's Stortford; their son, Rev. Samuel H, *c.* '58–1839 (*DNB, L*).— ('67) dines with J and Caldwell 187.4; ('73) J dines with H 304.1; ('74) J commends his *Cleonice, Princess of Bithynia* (Covent Garden 2 March '75; published 1775) 366; ('75) H's *Cleonice* 376.2, 380.1; J dines with H 386; ('76) Mrs. H's illness 500.1; ('78) J dines with H 576; ('80) J meets H at the Burneys' 685; ('81) J writes to Hastings commending H's *Tasso* (1763) and asking Hastings to 'promote his proposals' for *Ariosto* (1783) 712; ('82) J dines with H 778, 779; mentioned 819.1; ('83) J recommends young H for the Readership of the Temple 899; ('84) Essex-Head Club 929, 989, 1006; mentioned 946; H and Ozias Humphry 947; 'the Hooles' dine with J 954, 955; J dines with H

960; 'every man is most free with his best friends' 986; 'dear Mrs. Hoole, and my reverend friend your Son' 1006; (n.d.) mentioned 1101; J on his health, on death, 1129, 1130, 1131.

Hopkins, Benjamin, — —'79, elected Chamberlain of the City '76, defeating Wilkes 492.

HORNE, GEORGE, '30–'92, of University College; President of Magdalen '68–'90, Vice-Chancellor '76–'80, Bp of Norwich '90 (*DNB, L*).—('74) J's letter about Walton's Lives 353.2; 'Dr. Horne . . . wrote to me . . . that he proposed to reprint *Walton's Lives*, and desired me to contribute' 357.

HORNECK: Mrs. H, —, widow (before '69) of Capt. Kane H; 2 dd.: Catherine, '50–'98, m. '71 Henry William Bunbury, '50–1811 (q.v.); Mary, '53–1840, m. '78 Col. Francis Edward Gwyn (*DNB, L*, Forster's *Goldsmith*). —('70) J sends Mrs. H good wishes for their journey to Paris 229.1; its disappointments 240.1; ('75) 'I am glad . . . you have seen the Hornecks, because that is a publick theme' 415; ('77) 'Mrs. Horneck and Miss' 512; ('80) 'Mrs. Horneck, and Mrs. Bunbury, and other illustrious names' 681; 'at Mrs. Horneck's' 686.2; ('81) 'you may give the books to Mrs. Horneck' 734; Mrs. H mentioned 782.1.

Horseman, keeper '49 of a tavern in Ivy Lane.—('83) 908, 915.

Hotham, Richard, — —'99, Kt '69, M.P. '80 for Southwark; hatter of Serle St., Lincoln's Inn (*L, New Rambler*, 13 July 1948, p. 18).—('80) 'Mr. Polhil . . . has refused to join with Hotham' 666; (15 June) 'among the heroes of the Borough . . . rides that renowned . . . Knight, Sir Richard Hotham . . . Hotham the Hatmaker' 681.

Howard, Charles, '07–'71, lawyer of Lichfield; probably J's schoolfellow (*L*, R iv).—('59) 'Mr. Howard will advise you' (LP) 126; J sends LP a *Rasselas* 'for Mr. Howard' 131; ('63) J advises JT to 'consult our old friend Mr. Howard' 157, 159.

Howard, John, '26 (?)–'90, prison-reformer (*DNB*).—('84) 'Mr. Howard called on me . . . and gave the new edition . . . of his Account of Prisons' (*The State of the Prisons of England and Wales* 1784, the third edition, including the results of H's observations abroad) 956.

HUDDESFORD, GEORGE, 1699–'76, D.D. '37, President of Trinity Coll. '31, Vice-Chancellor '53–'56 (*L*).—('55) to T Warton: 'I have enclosed a letter to the Vice chancellor' (about J's M.A.) 62, 64; J's letter of thanks in Latin 63, 65; ('57) J introduces Marsigli to H (in a lost letter) 109.

Hudson, —, 'the Embroideress' of Bath (*Tb*).—('83) 'Miss Hudson, if she . . . gets scholars, will conquer her vexations' 845; 'the moments which you bestow on Miss H— (*sic* 1788, original not seen) are properly employed' 846, 865.

HUGGINS, WILLIAM, 1696–'61, translator of Ariosto; Fellow '22 of Magdalen Coll.; of Headley Park, Farnham (*DNB*, *L* iv. 473).—('54) relations with J, Baretti, and Croker 53.1, 53.2 (i. 442); ('62) H called Baretti's 'enemy' 147.

HUMPHRY, OZIAS, '42–1810, painter (*DNB*, *L*).—('84) J asks H to let his godson Paterson 'see your operations, and receive your instructions' **947, 949, 962.**

Hunter: Lucy Porter, 1690 (?)–'68, widow '41 of John H; aunt of LP (*L*, *R* iii).—('59) J sends LP a *Rasselas* 'for your aunt Hunter, who was with my poor dear mother when she died' 131; ('68) to LP; 'You have had a very great loss' 202.

HUNTER, WILLIAM, '18–30 Mar. '83, anatomist; the Queen's physician '64; F.R.S. '67; Professor of Anatomy, R. Academy, '68; founded an anatomical school and museum '70 (*DNB*, *L*).—('74) J sends his *Journey* to H for the King and himself **369.1**, 369.2; ('82) 'the present state of the court. Dr. Hunter whom I take to have very good intelligence has just left me . . .' 793; ('83) J introduces to JR 'Mr. Cruikshanks, who wishes to succeed his friend Dr. Hunter as Professor of

Anatomy in the Royal Academy' 838; 'Mr. Cruikshank, the present reader in Dr. Hunter's school' 891.

Huntingford, George Isaac, '48–1832, Warden of Winchester '89 (*DNB*).— H honours J with Greek Epigrams 668.

HUSSEY, Rev. JOHN, '51–'99; of Hertford Coll.; Chaplain to the Factory at Aleppo (*L*).—('78) J's gift of books **598.**

Hutton, James, '15–'95, Moravian (*DNB*, *L*, *Tb*, FB's *Early Diary*).— ('80) H's praise of FB 679.

Hyde, Henry, '10–'53, styled Vt Cornbury, e. s. of 4th E of Clarendon, whom he predeceased; 1st Baron H '50 (*DNB*, *L*).—('76) his bequest to the University 461.1, 463.

Impey, Elijah, '32–1809, Kt '74; Chief Justice of Bengal '74 (*DNB*).—('82) Chambers 'is, by the recal of Impey, now chief Justice' 793.1.

Inge (Ing), Henrietta, — –'90, d. of Sir John Wrottesly, Bt, and widow '53 of Theodore William I of Thorpe, Staffs.; of 37 Welbeck Street.—('83) 875.

Jack, a cowman at S'm.—329 (374).

Jackson, Cyril, '46–1819, sub-preceptor to the elder sons of George III '71–'76; Dean of Christ Church '83 (*DNB*). —('76) 'Revolution in the Prince's household . . . the quarrel began between Lord Holderness, and Jackson' 492.

Jackson, Harry, of L'd or B'm, — –'77 (*L*, *R* iii).—('67) 'Harry Jackson visited me several times. He seems to be in great indigence' 193.1; ('76) No friends of J's youth left at L'd 'but Harry Jackson and Sedgwick' 455; 'a letter from Harry Jackson who says nothing, and yet seems to have something which he wishes to say' 460; ('77) His death 535, 536, 537, 541.

Jackson, Humphry, 'the Imposter' (*Tb*).—('73) 'We will at least keep him (HT) out of J—ck—n's (*sic* 1788) copper' 303.

JACKSON, RICHARD, d. '87, 'the Omniscient' (*DNB*, *L*).—('83) J recommends young Hoole to RJ for the Readership of the Temple **899**; mentioned 1129.

James, Robert, '05–'76, of L'd, St. John's Coll. O'd, M.D. Cantab. (*DNB, L*).— ('41) RJ and Paul (q.v.) 13; 'the Doctor . . . hints his intentions somewhat obscurely' 14 (and cf. **91**); ('56) 'another Doctor'—possibly James 82; 'will not pay Miss (AW) for three box tickets which he took. It is a strange fellow' 91; ('73) 'Dr. James called on me last night, deep, I think, in wine'; his opinion on Mrs. Salusbury's case 300; ('84) 'I never thought well of Dr. James's compounded medicines' 993.

James V of Scotland, 1512–1542.—329 (367).

Janes or Jeans, John, *c.* '24–1804, of Aberdeen (*L*).— ('73) 'at Macdonald's I was claimed by a Naturalist' (in the *Journey* 'Janes the fossilist') 326 (354).

JEBB, RICHARD, '29–'87, physician; F.R.S.; Bt '78 (*DNB, Tb*).—('80) 'Jebb shall scold him (HT) into regularity' 663; (Feb.–June '82) his attentions to J *passim* in letters to HLT; J's letter of thanks, **789.1**; (J is probably the 'Doctor' of 787.1).

Jefferies, Elizabeth, — –1802.—('75) 'I had . . . very good looks from Miss Jefferies the maid of Honour' 390.

JENKINSON, CHARLES, '27–1808, 1st E of Liverpool '96 (*DNB, L*).— ('65) 'You will find all your papers carefully preserved' **178.2**; ('68) CJ, a nominee of Government, defeated at Oxford 201; ('77) J's plea for Dodd **520**.

Jennings-Clerke: see Clerke.

JESSOP, Rev. WILLIAM, of Lismore. —('66) J's letter to WJ about Grierson, q.v., **183.1**.

Jodrell (-el), Richard Paul, '45–1831, F.R.S., M.P., scholar and playwright, of 21 Portland Place; a member of the Essex-Head Club (*DNB, L*).— ('80) J dines with RPJ 654; ('83) 'I came home ill from Mr. Jodrel's' 839; ('84) J dines with RPJ 960.

JOHNSON, ELIZABETH, J's wife (She is 'Dearest Tetty' in **12**, 'Tetty' in 1041 to LP; elsewhere 'my wife' and (once) 'Mrs. Johnson'): Elizabeth Jervis, 1689–17 Mar. '52 (o.s.), m. (1) '15 Harry Porter, mercer of Birmingham, 1691–'34 (for their children see Porter); (2) 9 July '35 Samuel Johnson (*L*, R vi).—('40) J's letter to her from L'd **12**; ('42) her illness 14.1; ('44) 'Mrs. Johnson . . . was her first husband's executrix' 20; ('49) 'Your poor Mamma' 25 (to LP); (18 Mar. '52) J asks JT for 'your Company and your Instruction. . . . My Distress is great' 42 and see 41; ('54) J hopes Dodsley, who has lost his wife, 'will not suffer so much as I yet suffer for the loss of mine . . . a kind of solitary wanderer in the wild of life' 56; ('55) 'till I am solitary and cannot impart it' (Chesterfield's patronage) 61; ('64) J sends LP some books 'which were your poor dear Mamma's' 164; ('71) 'the boy (Coxeter) was a favourite with my wife' 245; ('81) 'No death since that of my Wife has ever oppressed me like this' (HT's) 717; ('84) J's directions about her grave at Bromley 975, 1029.2, 1032, 1041.

Johnson, John, 1662–'25, of Cranbrook, 'a very able writer in controversial divinity' (*DNB*).—('83) J asks Ryland for information 871.1 (see note).

Johnson, Michael: *see also* Johnson, Sarah.—('44) J thanks Levett for 'a long series of kindness to my Father and myself' 20.

Johnson, Nathaniel, '12–'37, Samuel's y. b., is not named in the letters, but is probably identified by Mr. Reade (R vi. 60, x. 125), with the 'near relation' of 693, 710 (*L*).—('84) His grave at L'd 1040.

Johnson, Samuel. See Index I.

Johnson, Samuel, son of William J, q.v.

JOHNSON, SARAH, J's mother: Sarah Ford, *y. d.* of Cornelius F, q.v., 1669–Jan. '59, m. '06 Michael J, 1656–'31, bookseller of Lichfield; 2 ss., Samuel, and Nathaniel, q.v. (*L*, R).

Letters to: ('19) 0, ('59) 118, 120, 121, 123—('19) J's letter from B'm 0; ('40) J to his wife: 'my Mother sends her service' 12; ('43) 'my dear mother' 19; ('49) J to LP: 'my mother, whose death is one of the few calamities on which I think with Terrour' 25; (? '51) J sends her money to pay a debt 32.1; ('52) J's wife's death: 'what mourning I should buy for my Mother' 42; J asks John Levett for time to pay a debt 'for the sake of my Mother' 42.2; ('55) J had empowered her to give receipts for the Dictionary 69; hopes to visit 'a Mother more than eighty years old, who has counted the days to the publication of my book, in hopes of seeing me' 70; 'I fully persuade myself that I shall pass some of the winter months with my mother' 75.2; ('56–'57) proposals and receipts for *Shakespeare* to be had from her 103, 105.1, 108; ('59) *passim* in letters to her and to LP (q.v.), Jan.–June; ('84) J 2 Dec. sends Greene 'the Epitaph for my Father, Mother, and Brother, to be engraved . . . and laid in the middle aisle in St. Michael's church' 1040.

JOHNSON, THOMAS, J's cousin, '03–'79, of Coventry; m., and had 3 children (*L*, R iv, ix).—('69) at Coventry 'I did not send for my Cousin Tom, but I design to make him some amends' 220; ('70) 'my nearest relation . . . now old and in great want' 228, 'I hope to help Tom: some other way' 229; ('74) J consults Hollyer (q.v.) about their common relation; J's charities to him; 'the impropriety of his management' 365; ('77) J's 'token of reconciliation' 565.1; ('79) 'at Coventry . . . I saw Tom Johnson who had hardly life to know that I was with him. I hear he is since dead' 616; (Nov '84) J asks John Hollyer, in a defective letter, 'what children of our . . . are now living'; doubtless TJ was indicated in the lacuna 1037.1.

Johnson, William, y. s. of Samuel J (——'46); Vicar of Torrington, Devon; m. Elizabeth, e. s. of Sir Joshua Reynolds.—('62) 'Mr. Johnson's school'; his scheme about salmon; 'Mr. Johnson's widow' is presumably the widow (*née* Skinner) of Samuel J, William J's mother (information from

F. W. Hilles) 146; WJ's son Samuel is no doubt the young man of 264.1; see i. 431.

JOHNSON,Rev.WILLIAM SAMUEL, '27–1819, of Connecticut; M.A. Oxon. '56, D.C.L. '66; President '87 of Columbia Coll., New York (*Dict. Amer. Biog.*).—('73) 'there is scarce any man whose acquaintance I have more desired to cultivate than yours' 299.

Johnston, William, *fl.* '48–'73, bookseller (*L*).—('59) His offer for *Rasselas* 124; ('72) J asks Paterson to recommend certain projects 'to Mr. Johnson or any other Bookseller' 274.1.

JOHNSTONE, GEORGE, '30–'87, 'Governor J'; gov. of W. Florida '65 (*DNB, L*).— (before May '74) Johnson's lost letter to him about payment for the Dictionary 1132.

JONES, GRIFFITH, '22–'86, Editor of the Daily Advertiser (*DNB*).—(n.y.) 'You are accustomed to consider Advertisements' 1133.

Jones, Mary, ——, of Oxford, 'the Chantress', s. of Rev. River J, Chanter of Christ Church (*L*).—'Professors (Tom Warton) forget their friends. I will certainly complain to Miss Jones' 109.

Jones, William, '46–'94, lawyer and orientalist; Fellow '66 of University Coll.; member '73 of the Club; Kt '83 (*DNB, L*).—('73) 'that your favourite language is not neglected will appear from the book' sent to Hastings (Jones's *Grammar of the Persian Language* 1771) 353; ('80) 'Scot and Jones both offer themselves to represent the University' 666, 'Jones and Scot oppose each other' 675; ('83) 'Jones, now Sir William, will give you the present state of the club' 835.1 (18).

Jones, ——, Captain of the ship Shrewsbury.—('71) 245.

Jones, ——, a shoemaker.—('80) 707.1.

Jopp, James, *fl.* '73, Lord Provost of Aberdeen (*L*).—('73) 'I had the honour of attending the Lord Provost' 322.

Kam, a dog.—741b, 750.

KEARSL(E)Y, GEORGE, *fl.* '58–'97, Bookseller (*L*).—('81) J condemns K's 'last proposal' 740; ('82) J asks K to call and 'bring with him the last edition of what he has honoured with the name of Beauties' (*see* Index VI) 782.

Keep, —, an elector of S'k.—294.

Kelly, Hugh, '39–'77, playwright (*DNB, L*).—('77) 'Lucy thinks nothing of my prologue for Kelly' (*see* Index VI) 535.

Kemble, John Philip, '57–1823, actor (*DNB, L*).—('83) 'Her (Mrs. Siddons) brother Kemble calls on me, and pleases me very well' 895.

Kennedy, John, 1698–'82, Rector of Bradley, Derbyshire; m. Catherine —, 'oo (?)– '79 (*L*, R vi, ix).—('79) 'Mrs. Kennedy, Queeny's Baucis' dead 618; ('81) 'Mr. Kennedy's daughter has married a shoemaker' 747.

Kennet, Brackley, — –'82, Lord Mayor of London '79–'80 (*GM* '82, 263).—677.

Kenneth, 'a Scottish Saint' (*L* v. 325).—322 (378).

Kilmurrey: John Needham, '11–'91, 10th Vt Kilmorey '68; of Shavington Hall, Shropshire (*L*).—('83) 'We were at his house in Cheshire' (*sic*) 900.

Kindersley: *see* Kinsderley.

King, William, 1685–'63; D.C.L. '15; Principal of St. Mary Hall '19 (*DNB, L*).—('55) K brings J the news of his Oxford M.A. 62; ('59) 'I have clapped my hands till they are sore, at Dr. King's speech' (apparently never published) 132.1.

Kinsderley (Kindersley), Mrs., author of *Letters from the Island of Teneriffe . . . and the East Indies,* 1777.—('83) J visited by her 891.

Kitty: *see* Chambers, Catherine.

Knapton: Paul K., — –12 June '55, and his b. John, — –'70, Booksellers; they were among the publishers of the Dictionary (*L*).—('47) the agreement for the Dictionary 23.1, 23.2; ('55) 'two of our partners are dead' 73.

Knight, Joseph, a negro set free by the Court of Session (*L*).—('76) J tells B of the decision in the case of James Somerset (q.v.) 493; 'is the question about the negro determined?' 505; ('77) 'I long to know how the Negro's cause will be decided' 528; ('78) 'you

have ended the negro's cause much to my mind' 568.

Knowles: Mary Morris, '33–1807; m. — Thomas K (*DNB, L*).—('76) 'there was Mrs. Knowles the Quaker that works the sutile pictures' 479.

Knox, John, 15(?)–1572 (*DNB, L*).—('73) Knox's 'reformation' 321.

Lade: Mary Thrale, '33 (?)–1802; m. Sir John Lade, — –'59, 1st Bt '58; her o. s. Sir John, 1 Aug. '59–1838, 2nd Bt (*Th, L*).—('75) 'barley enough for us and . . . Lady Lade' (i.e. to repay her loan to HT) 418; ('77) Sir J thought to be dying, pity for his mother 543, 545, 548, 550; 'I suppose Sir John is by this time recovered 560; ('80) Lady L 'called at Mrs Gardiner's' 679; J sends HLT 'a short song of congratulation' on Sir J's coming of age 691; ('81) Lady L and 'Cummins's claim' 745. See R. Thrale p. 418.

Langdon: Robert Longden, '31–1802, cheesemonger of Ashbourne (*L* iii. 505).—('76) to JT: L asked to send barley for JB 469; ('77) 'Mr. Langdon bought . . . fifteen tuns of cheese' 554.

LANGLEY, Rev. WILLIAM, '22–'95, probably M.A. Magdalen Hall, Oxford, '46; Headmaster '52 of Ashbourne Grammar School (*L* iii. 494).—('72) 'the Langleys' report on JT's health 277; ('74) J to Strahan about L's protégé Davenport 368; ('75) 'Mr. Langley of Ashbourne was here (L'd) today' 409; L and JT 'at variance . . . I therefore step over at bytimes' 418; L's 'improvements' 421; ('77) 'Mr. Langley and his Lady are well, but the Doctor and they are no friends' 541.1; 'Mr. Langley and the Doctor still live on different sides of the street' 548; ('79) to JT: 'I will . . . write to Mr. Langley' 605.1; ('82) J will show JT a letter from L 766.1; 'let him (JT) act alone' 792.1; J asks JT 'if you would have me write to Mr. Langley' about the Colliers, q.v., 806; 821 (see note); ('83) J has not consulted L (about the Colliers) 'because you dislike him' 823; (n.d.—? '83) J writes to L about the Colliers; he will send him by Davenport a set of *Lives* 841.1.

Langtons: Bennet Langton the elder, 1696–'69, of Langton near Spilsby, Lincs.; his b. Peregrine, '03–'66, of Partney (183); BL m. Diana Turnor ('Mrs. Langton'), '12–'93; their children were: BENNET LANGTON the younger, '37–1801; ELIZABETH ('Miss Langton'), d. Dec. '90; Diana, '42–1809; and Juliet, '57–'90. BL the younger m. '70 Mary, d. 1820, widow of the 9th E of Rothes (who retained the name 'Lady Rothes'); their nine children included George, '72, Mary, '73, and JANE, '76. (Lady R and children *passim* in letters to BL; his m. 'Mrs. Langton' and his ss., esp. 'Miss Langton', are also frequent.) BL was of Trinity Coll., M.A. '65, D.C.L. '90; original member of the Club (*DNB, L*).

  Letters to BL: ('55) 70; ('58) 110, 116; ('59) 117; ('60) 135; ('66) 182, 183; ('67) 192; ('70) 240.1; ('71) 246, 268; ('72) 273; ('74) 358; ('75) 388, 394; ('76) 491.1; ('77) 506.3, 525, 526.1; ('78) 581.1, 587; ('81) 732; ('82) 770; ('83) 886, 887; ('84) 945, 948, 952, 976, 999, 1039.2.
  Letter to Elizabeth L: ('71) 247.
  Letter to Jane L: ('84) 959.

  ('55) L's letters to J; J's Dictionary, 'of which I beg to know your father's judgement, and yours'; he hopes to go to Langton 70; ('58) J to T. Warton: 'Mr Langtons are well' 114, W's pupil (BL) 'will . . . be a credit to you and to the University' 115; J asks L 'what you expected, and what you have found' at O'd 110; ('59) L 'tutour to your sisters', Mrs. L 'as wise as Sibyl', 117; ('60) L's family, writings etc. 135; ('62) L in Paris with Beauclerck 147; ('63) his return 148.1; ('66) nothing heard of L since 'dear Miss Langton left us' (BL's eldest s. according to Croker, i.e. Elizabeth) 182; life and death of Peregrine L; J sends messages to 'dear Miss Langton, and Miss Di, and Miss Juliet' 183; ('67) L spends the summer in L'n 192; ('68) L 'gave me a guinea' 211.1; ('70) Lady R's 'commands' 240.1; ('71) 'the danger with which your navigation was threatened' 246; J's letter of condolence to Miss L (on an illness?) and defence against her 'censure of me as deficient in friendship'; hopes to go to Langton 'after Lady Rothes's recovery' 247; L's 'attention' to Mrs. Salusbury 249; Miss L's indignant reply to J's 'frigid' letter (247) 262, 'what to say to Miss Langton I cannot devise' 263; J's visit to Langton frustrated by L's 'design of visiting Scotland' 268; ('72) 'Poor Miss Langton' and 'her Aunt Langton' then dying 273 (see note); ('73) 'Langton left the town without taking leave of me . . . where is now my legacy?' 313; ('74) J asks L to send him a copy of J's Latin version of 'Busy, curious, thirsty fly'; 'remember me to young George and his sister. I reckon George begins to show a pair of heels' 358; ('75) 'Langton is here; we are all that ever we were. He is . . . without malice, though not without resentment' 374; L 'goes this week' 395, 'went yesterday to Lincolnshire' 398; J suggests to HLT that she send Lizard (a horse) to L 408.1, 419; ('76) 'I dined with Langton'; his lovely children; 'I know not how his money goes' 477; J hopes to visit L soon 491.1; J tells JB that he dined with L 'the other day'; a passage follows which JB did not print 494; J asks JB if he hears from L; 'I visit him sometimes, but he does not talk. I do not like his scheme of life' 502; J and L to call on Percy 503; ('77) J and L dine with Markham 505.3, 506, 506.3; 'his children are very pretty, and, I think, his lady loses her Scotch' 507; L 'has been exercising the militia' 524; J asks L to get from Markham a promise of the next vacancy at St. Cross for a poor old man 525; J asks L to come and see him 526.1; J tells JB he has dined with L; 'I do not think he goes on well. His table is rather coarse, and he has his children too much about him' 528; 'I have left Langton in London. He has been down with the militia, and is again quiet at home' 534; 'The scene at Richmond', *progenies Langtoniana*, 'the second girl is my favourite' 547;

'Master is very inconstant to Lady R—' (J's blank, i.e. Rothes) 549; J and JB encounter Mrs. L and Juliet at A'n 552; Mrs. L grows old, her 'stage' (see note), Juliet 'airy and cheerful' 553; L 'has got another wench' (Elizabeth) 565; ('78) L to fix the day for J's dining with Richard Clark 574.2; J's and JB's efforts to amend L's economy; 'he has laid down his coach'; his navigation, &c. 578; J to visit L at Warley 581.1, the visit 587, 593, L's move to Coxheath 593; ('79) L 'in camp' 628, no news of him 646; ('80) L guardian of Beauclerck's children if Lady Di B. should die 655; J to dine with L 662; Mrs. L and Knightsbridge 662 (note 6); L 'gone to be an engineer at Chatham' 675; mentioned 682; ('81) L's welcome 'account of yourself and invitation to your new house'; their friendship 'matured by time'; 'pretty Mrs. Jane' 732; ('82) J deplores the failure of their correspondence; George and his sisters 770; the 'eighth child (Isabella), all alive' 778; ('83) L 'by no means at ease'; his mortgage 835.1 (19); 'Lady Rothes's conversation'; J dines with L 839.1; L visits J 853; J visits L at Rochester 861, 863 ('eight children in a small house . . . a chorus not very diverting') 865, 869, 869.1, 886; 'my Jenny' 887(1); 'your solicitude for my recovery'887(2); ('84) Miss Langton's health, 'the two principal ladies in your house' (see note, and 976) 945; J on health of himself and 'your young Lady' (? Mary, see 952) 948; L's 'circumduction', his children, 'how does Miss Mary?', 'I owe Jenny a letter' 952 (see 959); L's neglect of his friends, his attention to his mother, his family 976; his right to recriminate (see 976), his neglect of his accounts, his 'young people, too many to enumerate' 999; (29 Nov.) J begs to see L, 'do not be hasty to leave me, I have much to say' 1039.2.

Latrobe, Rev. Benjamin, '28–'86, a Moravian (L, RES xxiv. 94, Apr. 1948, 145).—('77) L visits Dodd 524.

Laurence, Thomas, 'opposite Norfolk Street Park, Southwark', exhibited '76 at the Society of Artists 'A View of the House of H. Thrale Esq. Streatham Surry' 478.

Lawrence: LAWRENCE (often Lau-), THOMAS, '11–6 June '83; M.D. Oxon. '40; J's physician until '82; P.R.C.S. '67; of Essex St. (189.2); m. '44 Frances Chauncy (d. 2 Jan. '80); their 9 children inc. Soulden ('51–1814, judge, DNB), Rev. CHARLES (d. '91), William Chauncy (d. Madras Dec. '83), John (d. '83, see 846); ELIZABETH (d. '90); L left L'n for Canterbury '82 (DNB, L).

Letters to TL: ('67) 189.2, 189.3; ('74) 362.1; ('75) 375.1, 377; ('77) 531.2; ('78) 582.1, 595.1; ('79) 626.1; ('80) 650, 699.1; ('82) 756.2, 757, 757.1, 759.1, 766.2, 767.2, 767.5, 779.1; ('83) 833.3; (n.d.) 1134.

Letter to Charles L: ('80) 704.

Letters to Elizabeth L: ('82) 782.2, 788.1, 792.3, 794, 802; ('83) 828.

('55) 'my Physician' 77; ('55–'56) L attending Hill Boothby 78–82; ('59) mentioned 117; ('67) J describes Kitty Chambers's case for L's opinion 189.2, 189.3; L's Hydrops, Disputatio Medica, 1756, 189.2; ('73) 'Dr. Lawrence laughs at me when he sees me in a great coat' 296; L says J 'may let bark alone' 309, 310; J advises JT to consult L 312; J recommends 'young Lawrence' (Chauncy) to Chambers (both were going to India) 329.1; ('74) negotiations with Hardy and Sandwich 362.1 (see note), 365.1; J recommends to Hastings 'a young adventurer, one Chauncy Lawrence' 367; ('75) 'the account of Mr. Lawrence's conduct' 375.1 (probably Soulden, see note and 531.2); J consults L on the meaning of the terms doctor of medicine and physician 377, 378; mentioned 390; 'thinks every thing the gout' 432; ('76) AW's illness: 'Dr. Lawrence confesses that his art is at an end' 502, see 524; J sees L 504.1; ('77) J dines with L 505.3; L 'sent for a Chirurgeon' and bled J 506, 506.2; mentioned 351; J sends L 'a very handsome letter just received from Mr. Lawrence' 531.2 (probably Soulden, see note and 375.1); L does

PERSONS

not credit Akenside on ipecacuanha
538; ('78) mentioned 583, 585, 591,
595.1, ('79) mentioned 605, 608,
626.1; 'if Laurence is fit for business'
629; L 'desponded some time ago' of
AW (see '76) 633; Mrs. L 'is by the
help of frequent operations still kept
alive' 647; ('80) J's letter of condolence
(20 Jan.) on Mrs. L's death 650; J
dines with L 654, 'deafer than ever'
657; L read *Evelina* three times 657;
'Miss Laurence' 659; L's opinion on
HT's illness 672; J 'went with Dr.
Lawrence and his two Sisters in law to
dine with Mr. Gawler at Putney' 687;
J sends HLT 'our conversation' 699
(see 699.1); J writes to L 'I have read
the account and do not like it' (HT's
health) 699.1, 703.1; 'Dr. Lawrence
shewed me a letter, in which you make
mention of me'; J accordingly writes
to the writer, L's s. Charles, on reading
the liturgy and making sermons 704;
('82) Death of Levet 757; L 'more
timorsome' than Jebb 767; mentioned
756.3, 767.1; J details his symptoms
to L in Latin 756.2, 757.1, 766.2,
779.1, 780.2; 'send me your papers'
759.1, 767.2; lends him Hawkins's
'Historia Musices' 767.2, 767.5; sends
him 'Nugae anapaesticae 770.1;
mentioned 779.3; 'is very bad' 780.1,
'I have seen poor dear Lawrence . . .
without hope' 782.1; J consults him in
a letter to Elizabeth L, asks her to
'write out those short lines which I
sent to the Doctor' ('Nugae Anapaesticae', see note)782.2; 'the Doctor has
my prayers' 788.1; asks her to tell him
'from time to time the state of his
health and of his mind' 792.3; L's recovery of speech, 'Mr. John Laurence'
794; 'poor dear Dr. Lawrence is gone
to die at Canterbury' 797; 'small advances towards recovery' 802; ('83) J
asks EL for news of 'my kind Physician'
828; 'can neither speak nor write';
'totally disabled' 835.1 (18); 'in the
first rank of my friends', J recommends
Chauncy L to Chambers 835.1 (19);
mentioned 839; (13 June) 'poor Dr.
Lawrence and his youngest son (but
see note) died almost on the same day'

846; J compares his own stroke to L's
850; L said 'medical treatises should
be always in Latin' 851; mentioned
857, 892; ('84) mentioned 993; (n.d.)
1134 (? about Chauncy, see note).
Layer: presumably Christopher L, 1683–
'23 (*DNB*).—('43) 'extracted' from
the *State Trials* 16.
Lee, Arthur, '40–'92, American diplo-
mat; his b. William, '39–'95, merchant
of Tower Hill, Alderman (Aldgate
Ward) (*D Amer. B, L*).—('76) 'I dined
. . . in the poultry (*see* Dilly) with Mr.
Alderman Wilkes, and Mr. Alderman
Lee, and Counsellor Lee' 479.
Leicester or Leycester, George, *c.* '33–
1809; Trinity Coll., Cambridge '53,
Fellow '60; of Toft, Cheshire; cousin
of Beauclerk (*L* i. 517, F. W. M.
Draper in *The New Rambler*, 31 July
1948, p. 15).—655.
LELAND, THOMAS, '22–'85, Fellow
'46 of Trinity Coll., Dublin; D.D.
(*DNB, L*).— ('65) J thanks L for his
Dublin degree 178; ('75) J recommends
Twiss to L 390, 391 (lost); ('77) 'Dr.
Leland begins his history too late' 517
(*History of Ireland from the Invasion of
Henry II* 1773); ('81) L on 'the pedigree of Bingham' 712.1 (but see note).
Len(n)ox, Charlotte, '20–1804, d. of Col.
James Ramsay; m. *c.* '48 — L (*DNB,
L*).—('51) to Lord Orrery: 'our Char-
lotte's Book' (*Memoirs of Harriet
Stuart* 1750) 36; ('52) J to Orrery: 'I
congratulate myself upon the accident
by which I introduced Mrs. Lenox to
your Lordship' 42.1; ('79) 'C— L—
accuses — (Cumberland) of making a
party against her play (HLP's erasures)
640; ('80) accident to her daughter
684; ('81) 'Mrs. Lennox . . . in great
distress'; her husband's cruelty; 'she
is a great genius' 736.1.
Lester, —, HT's clerk.—('75) 426.
Lever, Ashton, '29–'88, Kt '78 (*DNB,
L*): *see* Greene, Richard.
LEVET (sometimes -ett), ROBERT,
'05–'82 (*DNB, L*).—('56) mentioned 98.1; ('62) his marriage 142;
'has married a street-walker' 147; ('73)
mentioned 330, 334, 340.1, 354.1;
('74) J's letter from Wales 359; ('75)

J's letters from France **436**, **437**; (′76)
L's accident **489**, **498.1**, 'sound, wind
and limb' 502, cf. 578, 640.1, 687, 692;
(′77) helps J to bleed himself 506; J
asks HLT to 'invite Mr. Levet to
dinner and make enquiry what family
he has' 548, 550; 'the Levet that has
been found in the register must be
some other Levet' 551; (′78) 'the habitation is all concord and Harmony;
only Mr. Levet harbours discontent'
583; 'stands at bay, *fierce as ten furies*'
590; 'Levet hates Desmoulins, and
does not love Williams' 591; (′79) L
'wants me to turn her out' (Desmoulins) 633; 'rather a friend to
Williams, because he hates Desmoulins
more' 644; (′80) 'just come in at fourscore from a walk to Hampstead, eight
miles in August' 692; (′82) L's death
(17 Jan.) 757, 758, 835.1 (18), J's
obituary of him 758.1; J applies to
the Recorder of Hull for information
760, 'a faithful adherent for thirty
years' 765; L's brothers in Yorkshire
found 768; 'very useful to the poor'
770; (′82–′83) J misses him 834, 839,
857 ('a man who took interest in everything and therefore was very ready at
conversation'), 862, 875, 921.
LEVETT (sometimes -et), THEO-
PHILUS, 1693–May ′46; his son
JOHN, ′21–′99; of Lichfield (*L*, R;
see note on 19 for the question to
whom certain letters are addressed,
and other matters).—(′43) J thanks
TL for his 'forbearance with respect
to the interest' on his mortgage **19**;
(′44) J asks for TL's help on another
matter of business **20**; (after May ′46)
to JL about the interest **21**, **22**, **26**;
'Levett's affair' **25**; (′51?) to JL on
the same subject **32.1**; (′52) to JL;
'I have sold a property principally to
satisfy you' **40**, 'ashamed to have disappointed you' **42.2**.
Levy, —, (?) a S'k politician.—(′80)
664.
Lewis, Erasmus, 1670–′54 (*DNB*; *Life of
Swift* ¶ 65 'a conversation which I
once heard between the Earl of Orrery
and old Mr. Lewis').—(′80) 'When
Lord Orrery was in an office, Lewis

was his Secretary . . . I knew him'
694–5 (see note).
Lewis, Dr.: probably William L, ′14–′81,
M.D. Oxon. ′45 (*DNB*).—(′77–′79) L
attends AW 548, 633.
Lewis, John and Charlotte: *see* Cottrell.
Lisgow, Thomas, a S'k elector (*Tb*).—
294.
Littleton, Edward, c. ′25–1812, 4th Bt
′42 of Pillaton Hall, Staffs. (*L*).—(′80)
'Sir Edward Littleton's business with
me' about 'a School at Brewood' 672.
Lizard, a horse (*L* ii. 528).—408.1, 419.
Lloyd (Loyd), Sampson, ′28–1807,
Banker of B'm (*L* ii. 535, R).—(′76) 'I
dined with some Quaker Friends'
464.1; (′82) J asks Hector to make his
compliments to L 771.
Longden: *see* Langdon.
LONGMAN, THOMAS, the elder,
1699–18 June ′55, bookseller; one of
the publishers of the Dictionary
(*DNB*, *L*).—(′46) the agreement for
the Dictionary **23.1**, 23.2; (′55) 'two
of our partners are dead' 73.
Lord Chief Baron: *see* Ord.
Loudon: Hugh Campbell, — ′31, 3rd
E of Loudoun; m. ′00 Margaret Dal-
rymple, 1684–′79; their children: John
C, 4th E of L, ′05–′82; Elizabeth
(*L*).—(′73) J's visit 337 (388).
Louis XIV.—'Lewis le Grand' 7; 'Lewis
. . . as a patron of Learning' 204.1.
Louis XVI and his Queen (*L*).—(′75)
'We went to see the King and Queen
at dinner, and the Queen was so im-
pressed by Miss . . .' 437, 441.
LOWE, —, not identified.—**740**, (?)
755.
LOWE, MAURITIUS, ′46–′93, painter
(*L*).—(? ′78) J pleads for L with JR
and Garrick; G's present to L **577**;
(′80) J asks Lady Southwell to continue
Lord S's pension to 'Mr. Mauritius
Lowe, a son of your late lord's father'
705; (′82) J congratulates L on the
receipt of money (probably from Lord
Southwell) **811**; (′83) J's exertions on
behalf of L at the R. Academy's exhibition: to JR: 'cut off from all . . .
hope, by the rejection of his picture'
832; to Barry 833; 'I interposed for
him, and prevailed' 837; J too ill 'to

wait on Mr. Barry '852; J recommends L to Tomkeson 890.

LOWTH, ROBERT, '10–'87; M.A. New Coll. '37, D.D. '53; Bp of London '77 (*DNB, L*).—('80) J writes to L on behalf of Stockdale 686.1, 687; ('82) J suggests Compton's dedicating to L 811.1.

Lucan: see Bingham.

Lucas, Henry, *c.* '40– — (*DNB, L* iii. 531).—*Poems to Her Majesty; to which is added a new Tragedy. . . . The Earl of Somerset* 1779: 516.

Lucy, Thomas.—('51) 33 (see on 32).

Lunardi, Vincenzo, '59–1806, balloonist (*DNB, L*).—('84) 'forgot his barometer' 1014.

LYE, EDWARD, 1694–'67, Saxonist; of Hertford Coll.; Vicar of Yardley Hastings, Northants. (*DNB, L, Nichols, LA* ix. 751).—('65) J advises L 'to open your subscription', and about the printing of his *Dictionarium Saxonico- et Gothico-Latinum* (posthumously 1772) 174, 174.1; ('66) 'all the Club subscribes' 182.

Lysons, Samuel, '63–1819, Antiquary (*DNB, L, Tb*).—('84) 'I saw Mr. Lysons: he is an agreeable young man' 969.

LYTTELTON (Littylton, Littleton): George L., '09–'73, 'the good Lord L'; of Christ Church; 1st Baron L of Frankley, '56; of Hagley, Worcestershire; his s. Thomas, '44–'79, 'the wicked Lord L'; his b. WILLIAM HENRY, '24–1808, 1st B Westcote '76; of Little Hagley, Worcestershire (*DNB, L, Tb*).—('71) 'I would have been glad to go to Hagley in compliance with Mr. Littylton's (i.e. WHL) kind invitation' 257; ('73) Lord L's death, 'hastened by the vexation which his son had given him' 337 (385); ('77) 'You (HLT) have Lord Westcote and every body' 537; ('80) J asks Lord W to help him with the Life of his brother 688, 689; Lord W 'knows not whom to employ' 690; J asks Nichols for 'Lyttelton's Works' (the collection, 1774) 696; 'is there not one (a *Life*) before the quarto Edition'? 698; 'what shall I do with Lyttelton's Life?' 699.

Macartney, George, '37–1806, Diplomatist; of Trin. Coll., Dublin; 1st Baron M '76; member of the Club (*DNB, L*).—M gave JB a copy of 145; ('79) J meets 'Lord Maccartney' at the Veseys' 645.1.

Macaulay, Kenneth, '23–'79, Minister of Cawdor; m. '58 Penelope Macleod, — –'99; their s. Aulay, '62–1842, Lieutenant of Marines '79 (*L* v. 505). —('75) J recalls his promise (see *L* ii. 380) to 'Mrs. Macaulay that I would try to serve her son at Oxford' 398.

Macbean, Alexander, — –'84, J's amanuensis; 'a very learned Highlander'; a poor brother of the Charterhouse '80 (*DNB, L*).—(? '38) his materials for a military dictionary 11; ('52) M's wager with Hamilton on progress of Dictionary 44; ('75) 'Peyton and Macbean are both starving' 393; ('77) M 'examined and approved' Shaw's Erse Grammar 510; ('78) M 'has no business' 591; 'desires a weekly payment of sixteen shillings' (on account of the index to 'Johnson's Poets') 595; ('81) 'the Bearer is one of my old Friends, a man of great Learning, whom the Chancellor has been pleased to nominate to the Chartreux' 720; ('84) 'Macbean . . . is dead' 969.

Macbeth, King of Scotland.—323 (349).

Macclesfield: presumably Thomas Parker, 1666 (?)–'32, 1st E of M (*DNB*).— ('43) 'extracted' from the *State Trials* 16.

Macdonald, Alexander, *c.* '45–'95, 9th Bt of Sleat '66, 1st Baron M '76; m. '68 Elizabeth Diana Bosville, '48–'89 (*L*). —('73) 'A house of Sir Alexander Macdonald in the Isle of Skie' (Armadale) 323; M 'kept up but ill the reputation of Highland hospitality' 324; 'Sir Alexander and Lady Macdonald, she (Mrs. Boswell) said, came back from Skie, so scratching themselves'; JB 'reproached him with his improper parsimony' 326 (358); 'Sir Sawney . . . has disgusted all mankind. . . Boswel has some thought of . . . making a novel of his life' 337 (387).

Macdonald, Allan, '26–'92, of Kingsburgh, Skye; m. '50 Flora Macdonald, '22–'90 (*DNB*); emigrated to North Carolina '74, but returned later; his mother Mrs. Alexander M (*L*, v. 529, 545).—('73) at Kingsburgh 'I had the honour of saluting the far famed Flora Macdonald. . . . She and her husband are poor, and are going to try their fortune in America'; J slept in the Prince's bed 329 (367).

Mackinnon, Lachlan, — –'89, of Corrichatachin, Skye; one of his sons (*L* v. 520).—('73) 'at night we came to a tenant's house . . . where we were entertained better than at the landlord's' 326 (360); ('82) 'I entertained lately a young gentleman from Corrichatachin' 803.

Maclaurin, John, '34–'96, Advocate (*DNB*, *L*).— ('76) 'Mr. Maclaurin's plea' (for a negro) 494.

Maclean, Allan, *c.* '10–'83, 6th Bt '51 of Brolas, Mull; m. Una Maclean of Coll, — –'60 (*L* v. 556).—('73) 'Sir Allan, a Chieftain, a Baronet, and a soldier, inhabits . . . a thatched hut'; 'his daughters . . . who in their cottage neither forgot their dignity, nor affected to remember it'; 'Sir Allan's affairs are in disorder, by the fault of his ancestors'; 'one of the Ladies read . . . the Evening services—And Paradise was open'd in the wild'; M shows J and JB Icolmkil 332; ('75–'77) M's lawsuit with the Duke of Argyle 398, 505, 524, 'I am more afraid of the debts than of the House of Lords' 528.

Maclean, Donald, — –25 Sept. '74, of Coll; his y. b. Alexander, — –1835 (*L* v. 543).—('73) 'the young Laird of *Col*. . . . He has first studied at Aberdeen, and afterwards gone to Hertfordshire to learn agriculture' 329 (370), 331; 'the young Laird entertained us very liberally' 331; 'Coll made every Maclean open his house' 332 (378); ('74) J wants to send 'a cask of porter to . . . Col' 348; Col's death by drowning 362; ('75) 'lamentation' for his death, at L'd 406; 'Young Col' (Alexander) dines with J at the Mitre 443, 446.

MACLEOD of Macleod; Norman M,

'54– —, 20th Chief; o. s. of John M (s. of Norman M, '06–'72, 'the old Laird' 326), — –'67, who m. Emilia Brodie; of St. Andrews and University Coll., '69–'71 (*L* v. 527).—('73) 'a fine young Gentleman, and fine ladies' (at Dunvegan); 'I . . . am miserably deaf, and am troublesome to Lady Macleod' 324; 'Lady Macleod is very kind to me'; 'Macleod has offered me an Island' 326 (cf. 337); 'the old Laird of Macleod' (i.e. Norman) 326 (356); 'I sat . . . at the left hand of Lady Raarsa, and young Macleod of Skie, the chieftain of the clan sat on the right'; 'Macleod the chieftain, and Boswel, and I, had all single chambers' 327; J returns M's horses; he remembers 'Lady Macleod and the young Ladies . . . with great tenderness and great respect' **328**; M 'very distinguishable' at Raasay; of St. Andrews and Oxford; 'the full spirit of a Feudal Chief'; his invitation to Dunvegan; 'left by his Grandfather overwhelmed with debts'; his sisters 329 (365, 368); 'Miss Macleod made me a great flannel nightcap' 337 (387); ('74) Dunvegan 'a good house' 342; J wants to send 'a cask of porter' to Dunvegan 348.

MACLEOD of Raasay: John M, — –'86, 9th Chief; s. of Malcolm M, —; m. Jane Macqueen; their 13 children included Flora, — –'80, who '77 m. the 5th E of Loudoun (*L* v. 523).—('73) 'Raarsa is . . . under the dominion of one Gentleman, who has 3 sons and 10 daughters' 324; his estates and rental 326 (361); his house and manners; 'Lady Raarsa makes no very sublime appearance for a Sovereign'; 'Miss Flora Macleod is a celebrated beauty . . . dresses her head very high'; M's father 'joined some prudence with his zeal' and in '45 handed over his estate to his son 327; M's beautiful children 329 (365); 'the princesses of Raarsa' 337 (387); ('74) J wants to send 'a cask of porter to . . . Rasay' 348; ('75) M's complaint (to JB) of an 'erroneous' passage in J's *Journey*; J apologizes, and has asked JB to 'anticipate the correction in the Edinburgh papers' 389; 'I have offended . . . the Nation of Rasay'; 'it will be thirteen days . . . before my recantation can reach him. Many a dirk will imagination . . . fix in my heart' 390; (to JB) 'let me know the answer of Rasay' 398; JB 'has established Rasa's Chieftainship in the Edinburgh papers' 408; 'very much pleased that he is no longer uneasy' 431; M's letter 446; ('77) 'I rejoice at Miss Rasay's advancement' 524, 528; ('82) 'Rasay has been here; we dined cheerfully together' 803.

Macleod of Talisker: John M, '18–'98, a Colonel in the Scots Brigade in Holland; m. Florence Maclean of Coll (*L* v. 524).—('73) 'We are now with Colonel Macleod in a more pleasant place than I thought Skie able to afford' 327, 328; Mrs. M 'having travelled with her husband . . . speaks four languages' 329 (369).

Macleod, Malcolm, *c.* '11–'77 or later, cousin to M of Raasay (*L* v. 523).—('73) 'we went to Raarsa, under the conduct of Mr. Malcolm Macleod, a Gentleman who conducted Prince Charles through the mountains' 326 (360); 'old Malcolm in his Fillibeg, was as nimble (in dancing) as when he led the prince over the mountains' 327 (363); mentioned 329 (365); in London with Flora Macdonald 329 (367); ('75) mentioned 389.

M'Lure, captain of the Bonnetta (*L* v. 319).—'the Captain of a sloop . . . sent his boat' 332 (378).

MACPHERSON, JAMES, '36–'96, translator. *See also* Ossian, Index III (*DNB*, *L*).—('75) J's letter of defiance 373; M 'is very furious' 374; 'I hear no more of Macpherson' 375; M 'never in his life offered me the sight of any original' 378; 'is said to have made some translations himself', (i.e. into Gaelic) 380.

Macpherson, Isabel, sister of the Minister of Slate (*L* v. 519).—326 (360).

MacQuarry, Lauchlan, *c.* '15–1818, of Ulva, his estate sold '77 (*L* v. 556).—('73) 'The head of a small Clan . . . his negligence and folly' 332 (378); ('76)

'What is become of poor Macquarry?' 505; 'Every eye must look with pain on a *Campbell* turning the *Macquarries* at will out of their *sedes avitae*' 528.

Macqueen, Donald, *c.* '16–'85, Minister of Kilmuir-in-Trotternish, Skye, '40 (*L* v. 522).—('73) 'One of the Ministers who has adhered to us almost all the time is an excellent Scholar' 329 (370); ('75) mentioned 389; his adherence to Macpherson 431.

Macqueen, innkeeper at Anoch, and his daughter (*L* v. 514).—323, 326 (354).

Macqueen, —, not identified.—814.2.

Macraes, the, of Auchnashiel. (*L*)—('73) 'a very coarse tribe' 326 (355).

Madden (Madan), Samuel, 1686–'65, of Dublin; D.D. '23 (*DNB*, *L*).—('81) 'my friends Madan and Leland' 712.1 (but see note).

Madox, — (a lawyer known to JT?).—807.

MALONE, EDMOND, '41–1812; member of the Club '82 (*DNB*, *L*).—('82) J's apologies for not being 'with you and Dr. Farmer' 764; writes to him about Chatterton 766.

Mansfield: William Murray, '05–'93, 1st Baron M '56, 1st E of M '76; of Bloomsbury and 'Caen Wood'; a Clarendon Trustee (*DNB*, *L*).—('75) 'We must find some way of applying to Lord Mansfield' (about Carter, q.v.); 'ask Murphy the way to Lord Mansfield' 386; (n.d., about this time) 1136; ('76) M's decision in the negro's case 493; ('80) M made light of the Gordon riots, but had his house in L'n destroyed 677.

Manucci, Count, —, of Florence (*L*, *Th*).—('76) M's visit to the Thrales at Bath 476–9.

Mara, a would-be sailor.—787.4, 792.2.

Markham, William, '19–1807, of Christ Church; a Clarendon Trustee; Bp of Chester '71, Preceptor to the Princes '71–'76; Archbp of York Dec. '77 (*DNB*, *L*).—('75–'76) application to M about Carter (q.v.) 386, 399, 459, 461.1; ('76) M's part in the 'Revolution in the Prince's Household' 492; ('77) J dines 'with Mr. Langton and the Bishop of Chester' 505.3, 506.3, asks BL to ask M for the next vacancy at St. Cross (for De Groot) 525; ('78) M tells CB of MSS. at Christ Church 588 (see note); ('80) at the Academy 'I sat over against the Archbishop of York' 663.

Markland, Jeremiah, 1693–'76 (*DNB, L*).—812.

Marsigli (-ili), Dr., of Padua, Physician (*L*).—('57) J introduces to T. Warton 'Dr. Marsili of Padua, a learned Gentleman, and good Latin Poet' 109; ('62) J tells Baretti to remember him to M 142; ('79) M's recovery from a stroke; 'is now a professor at Padua' 617.

Martin, Saint 692.

Martinelli, Vincenzo, '02–'85 (*L*).—('53) J recommends M, author of 'a large Edition of Machiavel which he published in Holland', 200 sets of which he wants to sell, to Richardson 49.

Mary, Queen of Scotland, 1542–87.— 320, 972.

Mathias, James, '12–'82, Hamburg merchant; friend of Joseph Porter (R, *Reades* 240, FB's *Diaries*).—229, 656, 723.

Maurice, Rev. Thomas, '54–1824, of University Coll. (*L*).—('79) J asks Wetherell to nominate M or another as curate of Bosworth 618.1.

Mawbey, Joseph, '30–'98, distiller, of Vauxhall; Kt. —; M.P. S'k '61–'74, Surrey '75–'90, of Grosvenor Street, and Botleys, Surrey (*L*, *Tb*).—('75) 'Will Sir Joseph succeed this time?' 397.1; glad 'that Norton opposes him' 407; 'I was afraid Mawbey would succeed' 408.

Maxwell (-el); presumably William M '32–1818, assistant preacher at the Temple church, Rector of Mount Temple, Westminster, '75; moved to Bath, '80; m. '77 Anne Massingbird (4 children) (*DNB, L*).—('83) his wife in Bath with her babies 845.

Mayne, Sir William, Beattie's host in '73, 316.1.

Mayo, Henry, '33–'93, dissenting minister, 'the literary anvil' (*L* ii. 252) (*DNB, L*).—('73) 'I dined . . . at a dissenting Bookseller's . . . and disputed against toleration, with one Doctor Mayo' (date and name doubtful, see note) 393.

Mazarin, Cardinal, 1602–61, 206 (218).

Melmoth, William ('Pliny'), '10–'99, author '42–'49 of *Letters of Sir Thomas Fitzosborne* (*DNB, L*).—('80) J had 'about thirty years ago . . . reduced him to whistle' 663.

Memis, John, physician of Aberdeen (*L*). —('75–'76) J consults Lawrence on M's complaint of the title 'Doctor of Medicine' 377, 378, 505.

MERCERS' COMPANY.—('83) J's application for Compton 835.

METCALFE, PHILIP, '33–1818, M.P., brewer; of Savile Row and the Steyne, Brighton (*L*).—('82) J thanks M for offering his carriage 806.1; J's tour with M 812.1; ('83) 'The Doctor and Mr. Metcalf have taken me out' 895; ('84) M elected for Horsham 953.

Meyer: *see* Mayo.

Middleton: Lady Diana Grey, — –'80, d. of E of Stamford; m. '36 George M of Seaton, '14–'72 (*L, Scots Mag.* 1780; *Scots Peerage* vi (1909) 178).—('73) 322 (346).

MILLAR, ANDREW, '06–'68, bookseller (*DNB, L*).—('51–'56) J's paymaster, &c., for the Dictionary: 38, 52, 94; J writes to M about a wager on the progress of the Dictionary; borrows books from him 44; mentioned 49.1; J asks Richardson to introduce an author to M 58.1; ('60) M's offer for Percy's *Reliques* 136; (n.d.) J asks M to lend a book 1135.

Miller: Anna Riggs, '41–'81; m. '65 JOHN MILLER, — –'98, of Batheaston, 1st Bt '78 (*DNB, L, Tb*).—('80) 'Do you go to the House where they write for the myrtle?' 657; ('83) J's application, presumably to Sir John, on behalf of Carter 1136.

Mills, Sir Thomas: Shaw, *Knights of England* 1906, ii. 293 records that Thomas Mills, town major of Quebec, was a knight bachelor '72 (*Tb*).—('79) 'civil and officious' 645.

Mitchell, John Henry, of King's Coll., Cambridge, 'the Boy who won the Prize at Cambridge by his Greek Verses on Capt. Cook' (*Tb* 447).—('80) author of verses to HLT which J quotes 703.

Moisy or Moysey, Abel, '16–'80, M.D.; physician of Bath.—('80) M attends HT 654, 657, 675.

Monboddo: James Burnett, '14–'99, Lord of Session '67, styled Lord M (the pron. is Munbúddo) (*DNB, L*).— ('73) 'We . . . dined at Lord Monbodo's . . . who has lately written a strange book about the origin of Language' (*Of the Origin and Progress of Language*, vol. i, 1773), shopkeeper and savage 321 (344); ('75) M on Ossian; 'if there are men with tails, catch an *homo caudatus*' 431; ('77) J asks JB what M thinks of the negro's cause 528; ('80) J meets M at Ramsay's 663.

Monckton (Monk-), Mary, '46–1840, d. of 1st Vt Galway; of Charles St., Berkeley Square; m. '86 the 7th E of Cork (*DNB, L*).—('80) 'Tonight I go to Miss Monkton's' 664; 'I was last night at Miss Monkton's' 669; ('82) 'I have an appointment to Miss Monkton' 779.

MONTAGUE, Mrs.: Elizabeth Robinson, '20–1800; m. '42 Edward Montague, — –'75 (*DNB, L*).—('59) J thanks her for getting subscribers for AW **132**, asks her to help Mrs. Ogle **133**; ('74) her 'eminence' **341** (cf. other letters to her for J's flattery); ('75) J dines with her 386.1; 'Mr. Montague is so ill that the Lady is not visible' **390**; her illness **442**; asks J to dinner **443, 445**; ('76) her condolence with HLT on Harry's death 466, 467, 474; ('77) intends to visit HLT 505.3; mentioned 539; ('78) her invitation, her subscription for T. Davies **573, 574**; J hopes she will give him her print 583 (cf. 608); 'I am sorry for Mrs. Montague' (who did not like *Evelina*) . . . 'Montague has got some vanity in her head' 585; ('79) J meets her at Mrs. Vesey's, 'I called for the print (583), and got good words' 608; ('80) letters to HLT at Bath *passim*; 'having mentioned Shakespeare and Nature does not the name of Montague force itself upon me?' (her *Essay on Shakspeare* 1769) . . . 'I wish her name

had connected itself with friendship' 657; '*par pluribus*' 663; J suggests her as HT's 'governess' if HLT goes to S'k 664; inferior to HLT in 'wit' and 'literature' 666; 'now Montague (*om.* 1788) is gone, you have the sole and undivided empire of Bath' 669; J 'hears nothing from her' 690; 'has been very ill' 700; ('83) the Circus (Bath) too narrow for her 839; mentioned 839.1; J reports to her the death of 'your Pensioner Anna Williams' 884; her reply 'not only civil but tender. So I hope, peace is proclaimed' 891.

Moore, Edward, '12–'57, playwright and fabulist (*DNB, L*).—('80) 'Poor Moore the fabulist' had been in J's company 'about thirty years ago' 663.

Moore, William, 'publisher of a seditious paper' (*L* iii. 537).—678.

MORE (usually Moore), HANNAH, '45–1833, authoress (*DNB, L*).—('82) 'a letter from Miss Moore to engage me for the evening' 779; 'here is Miss Moore at Dr. Adams's' (at O'd) 789; 'I dined at Dr. Adams's with Miss Moore, and other personages of eminence' 791; 'Dr. Edwards has invited Miss Adams and Miss More' 792; ('84) J hopes to wait on Mrs. Garrick 'and to tell Miss Moor all that *envy* will sufer him to say of her last poem' **940.1**; 'Miss Moore has written a poem called Le Bas blue which is in my opinion, a very great performance. It wanders about in manuscript' 954 (*The Bas Bleu* was first published, with *Florio*, 1786); for his letter to her on the subject see iii. 337); 'Miss Adams, and Miss Moore are not yet come' (to O'd) 965.2; J sends 'my compliments to dear Miss Moore' 1018.1; (n.d.) J promises to wait on her, **1137, 1138**; a missing letter **1139**.

Morrison, Rev. Thomas, '05–'78, Rector of Langtree near Great Torrington, Devon; (*teste* his descendant J. T. Kirkwood); New Coll., M.A. 1731 (*not* D.D.).—('62) J tells FR that he will send 'Dr.' M 'Idlers' 'with my sincere acknowledgements of all his civilities' 146.

Moser, George Michael, '04–'83, first

Keeper of the R. Academy (*DNB, L*).
—('83) mentioned 842.

Mountstuart: see Bute.

Mouseley, —, of Ashbourne.—('56)
JT's 'reconciliation' with M 98, 106.

MUDGE, JOHN, '21–'93, physician of
Plymouth; F.R.S. '77 (*DNB, L*).—
('62) J tells FR that if M asks him to
stand godfather (his son William born
('62) he will consent; 'I am much
pleased to find myself so much esteemed by a man whom I so much
esteem' 146; ('64) J sends 'compliments to Mr. Mudge' by JR 166; ('83)
J consults M about his sarcocele 874,
884.2, and quotes his opinion *passim*
in letters Sept.–Oct.; 'my godson
called on me' 874: his s., J's godson,
William, '62–1820 (*L* i. 378, *DNB*)
146, 874 (1).

Mulso: see Chapone.

Murchison, John, '31–1811, of Glenelg,
factor '64–'78 to the Laird of Macleod
(*L* v. 517).—('73) 'a Gentleman in the
Neighbourhood sent us rum' 326 (357).

Murphy, Arthur, '27–1805, barrister,
actor, and playwright (*DNB, L, Tb*).
—('58) J attributes to 'Mr. Murphy,
who formerly wrote the Gray's Inn
Journal' (1753–4) the 'splendid en-
comium' prefixed to his Shakespeare
Proposals in *London Chronicle* Apr. '57,
113; (Jan. '59) 'Murphy is to have his
Orphan of China acted next month'
(Drury Lane Apr. '59) 117; ('65) M
'brought back' J to the Thrales 173;
('73) 'Murphy is preparing a whole
pamphlet against Garrick' 304 (and
see 303.2); ('74) M undertakes 'Miss
Carmichael's cause' 343.1; 'Murphy
drew up the Appellants' case' against
perpetual copyright 344; ('75) J asks
HLT to ask M 'the way to Lord Mansfield' 386; 'Tell him (Harry Thrale)
that Mr. Murphy does not love him
better than I do' 415; ('76) HLT
sends a servant 'to her friend Murphy's
play' 474 (see note); ('77) M ought to
write Foote's life, 'at least to give the
world a Footeana' 561; ('78) M had
told J that HLT 'wrote to him about
Evelina' 591; ('83) M 'visits me very
kindly' 859.

Musgrave, Richard, '46–1818, M.P.
for Lismore '78; 1st Bt '82 of Tourin,
co. Waterford (*DNB, L, Tb,* FB's
Diary).—('76) 'this new friend of
mine' 482, 483; ('83) J's 'charitable
office to propose to him' 839, his
present to HLT 846; ('84) J asks for
his direction 925.

Myddleton, John, '24–'92, of Gwayny-
nog (*L* iv. 421, *Tb*).—('77) 'Mr. —'s
erection of an urn looks like an intention to bury me alive' 548 (see note);
('80) 'Mr. Middleton' 684 (perhaps not
the same).

Nesbitt, Arnold, — –'79; m. '58 Anne,
d. of Ralph Thrale, q.v.; merchant;
M.P. for Cricklade, Wilts.; of West
Wickham, Kent (*Tb*).—('73) 'What
poor Nesbitt said, is worthy of the
greatest mind' 310, 311; 'was Fanny
(Rice) dressed à la Nesbitienne?' 311;
('77) J sends 'compliments . . . to be
kept as rarities, to . . . Mrs. Nesbit'
556; 'I am sorry for poor Nezzy' 562;
('80) 'a vial, like Mrs. Nesbit's vial, of
essence of roses' 672; ('81) 'Nesbit
(HLP; suppressed in 1788) needed not
have died if he had tried to live' 748.

NEWBERY (-berry), JOHN, '13–'67,
bookseller; publisher of *The Idler*
(*DNB, L*).—('51) J asks N for loans,
or money on account **32, 33, 34;** ('56)
J 'engaged Mr. Newberry' in Paul's
affair 104; ('58) N and Chambers
115.1.

Newdigate, Roger, '19–1806, 5th Bt '34;
M.P. for Oxford University '50–'80
(*DNB*).—('68) N heads the poll 201;
('80) the election on his retirement
666.

Newton, Andrew, '29–1806, b. of
Thomas N; wine-merchant of L'd
(*L* v. 428, *Letters* 1788, ii. 218, R,
Reades 200).—('77) mentioned 537.

Newton, Thomas, '04–'82, of Lichfield
and Westminster Schools; Bp of Bristol
'61 (*DNB, L*).—('62) J promises to
'apply . . . to the Bishop of Bristol' for
a widow 146; ('73) J asks HLT to lend
FR 'Newton on the Prophecies'
(*Dissertation on the Prophecies* 1754–58,
'Tom's great work' *L* iv. 286) 294.

Nicholls, Frank, 1699–'78, physician;

death of the unfortunate man, I believe Europe thinks as you (Joseph Fowke) think' 834.

Nurse, at the Thrales'.—('75) 393.

O'CONNOR or O'Conor, CHARLES, '10–'91, Irish antiquary (*DNB, L*).—('57) 'I have lately . . . seen your account of Ireland' (*Dissertations on the Ancient History of Ireland* 1753) 107; ('77) J urges O'C to write more on the same subject 517.

Ogle, Mrs.—('59) J appeals to Mrs. Montague for 'Mrs. Ogle, who kept the music-room in Soho Square' and hoped for a benefit concert 133.

Oglethorpe, James Edward, 1696–'85, soldier and philanthropist (*DNB, L*). —('74) 'Mr. Oglethorpe was with me this morning' 344; ('76) J dines with O 476.

Okeover, Edward Walhouse, c. '52–'93, of O. Hall, Staffs. (*L* v. 580).—418.

Oldys, William, 1696–'61 (*DNB, L*).— ('74) J's Latin version of his 'Busy, curious, thirsty fly' 1732 (*Poems* 171) 358.

Opie (Opey), John, '61–1807, painter (*DNB, L* iv. 455).—('83) 'I sat to Opey . . . I think the head is finished, but it is not much admired' 879.

Ord, Robert, — –'78, Chief Baron of the Scottish Exchequer (*DNB, L*).—('73) O dines with JB to meet J 320.

Ord, William, '37–'89, of Fenham, Northumberland; m. Anna Dillingham, — –1808; of Queen Anne St. ('85) (*L, Tb*).—('80) J goes to 'Mrs. Ord's', or meets her, 660.1, 661, 662, 663, 681, 685.

Osborne, Thomas, — –'67, bookseller (*DNB, L*).—('43) J gives his address as 'At Mr. Osborne's, bookseller, in Gray's Inn' 19.

Otho, Roman Emperor.—His death by suicide 427.

O'Toole, Arthur 292.

Otway, 'young'.—('73) put to school 304 (a Mrs. O is mentioned *Tb* 66).

Oughton, James Adolphus Dickenson, '20–'80, soldier; KB '68; commander-in-chief in North Britain (*DNB, L*).— ('73) O dines with JB to meet J 320.

Owen, Henry, '16–'95, of Jesus Coll.

(*DNB, L*).—–('84) O's editorship of Edwards's posthumous Xenophon 946.1.

OWEN, MARGARET, '43–1816, distant cousin to HLT (*L, Tb*).—('77) 'Thus . . . am I hindred from being with you (HLT) and Miss Owen' 505.3; 'Miss Owen had a sight' (of famous people, at JR's) 512; J sends compliments to her 556, 558; ('80) '—'s case', possibly MO's, see note; HLT's 'melancholy account' of Scrase and MO; 'I wish them both their proper relief' 685; 'poor Miss Owen called on me . . . with that fond and tender application which is natural to misery' 686; 'your letter about Mr. Scrase and Miss Owen' 690; ('81) J's letter of condolence on 'the disgrace of your family' 714.1.

Page, Francis, — –1801, of New Coll., D.C.L. '49; M.P. for the University '68–1801.—('68) 'an Oxfordshire gentleman, of no name'; his election 201.

Page, Miss, of Abingdon; see Bright.— ('63) 148, 160.

PALMER: Mary Reynolds, '16–'94, s. of Sir Joshua; m. '40 John Palmer of Torrington, Devon (who d. '70): their children, JOSEPH, '49–1829, Dean of Cashel; Mary, '50–1820, Theophila, '57– —; the girls lived with JR from c. '70 (*DNB* s.v. Mary Palmer, *L*).— ('75) J's letter to JP about a prologue 380.1; ('79) 'your (FR) nieces will tell you how rarely they have seen me' 602.

Palmerston: Henry Temple, '39–1802, 2nd Vt P '57; member of the Club '84 (*DNB, L*).—('83) 'I . . . dined with the Club, when Lord Palmerston . . . against my opinion, was rejected' 861.

Paoli, Pascal, '25–1807, Corsican patriot; in England from '69; of Edgeware Road 1807 (*DNB, L*).—('75) J dines with P; JB 'lives much with his friend Paoli who says a man must see Wales to enjoy England' 390; ('76 to '79) J dines with P 476, 576, 633; ('77) 'Paoli I never see' 507; ('78) 'came to the (Warley) camp and commended the soldiers' 593; ('83) 'where I love to dine' 837, 839; (n.d.) mentioned 1139.

PARADISE, JOHN, '43–'95; M.A. Oxon. '69, D.C.L. '76, F.R.S. '71; of the Essex Head Club; m. Mary Moser, 'a beautiful American' (*DNB, L*).— ('75–'84) J dines with P 386, 505.3, 506, 778, 840, 875, 960; ('80) meets him at Burney's 685; ('83) 'Nobody has shown more affection than Paradise' (by his visits in J's illness) 853; ('84) his great and constant kindness; 'your Lady and the young Charmers' **1025.**

Parker, Sackville, bookseller at Oxford (*L* iv. 308).—('81) 'Mr. Parker the Bookseller sends his respects to you' (HLT) 741; ('82) 'write to me at Mr. Parker's, bookseller' 789, 789.1.

Parr, Samuel, '47–1825; D.D. '81 (*DNB, L*).—('77) J writes 'for Mr. Parr' 506.3.

PATERSON, SAMUEL, '28–1802, bookseller and auctioneer in Essex St.; his s. Charles, J's godson (*DNB, L*).— ('72) J recommends two translators **274.1**; ('76) Young P, 'the son of a man for whom I have long had a kindness, and who is now abroad in distress' 496; ('83) 'I have sent you (JR) some of my god-son's performances' 842; ('84) J's letters to Humphry, who allowed young P to watch him paint 947, 949, 962.

PATRICK, CHARLES, of Hull.—('82) J's letter about R. Levet **760.**

PATTEN, THOMAS, '14–'90, Rector of Childrey, Berks. (Hill on 739; *L* iv. 507–8).—('81) J writes to P, who had asked him to accept the dedication of Thomas Wilson's (q.v.) Dictionary **739**; ('82) 'my excellent friend, Dr. Patten' 820.

PAUL, LEWIS, — –'59, inventor of spinning machinery; of Brook Green, Hammersmith, and later (see on 77) of Kensington (*DNB*).—J's letters to P about his invention and his financial relations with the Caves and Henry: ('41) **13** (see note), **14**; ('55) **77**; ('56) **83, 86, 91, 92, 99, 100, 101, 102, 104, 105**; ('65) Warren's 'friend Paul has been long dead' 179; (n.d.) J's letter for P to the D of Bedford, Appendix A, i. **441.**

Pauson, Charlotte Lennox's landlord.— ('81) 736.1.

Payne, John, — –'87, bookseller and banker; publisher of *Rambler* and *Adventurer*; member of the Ivy Lane Club; accountant-general of the Bank of England '80 (*DNB, L*).—('84) J's invitation to P and Ryland to dine 923.3; P sends money to Bagshaw for J's wife's tombstone 977; 'poor Payne's illness' 1003.1, 1016, 'poor dear Payne' 1021.

Pearson (Pier- 656), John Batteridge, '49–1808; Perpetual Curate of St. Michael's L'd '74–'82; V of Croxall, Derbyshire, '79; Prebendary of L'd '90; LP's heir (*L* ii. 541, R).—('79) J 'pleased to find that he has got a living' (Croxall, Derbyshire) 605; ('80) 'Compliments to Mr. Pierson' 656; ('81) 'respects to Mr. Pearson' 714.2; ('82) 'compliments to . . . Mr. Pearson' 765; ('83) 'Return my thanks to . . . Mr. Pearson' for his attention 862; 'let Mr. Pearson write for you' (LP) 914; ('84) 'Make my compliments to . . . all my friends, particularly to Mr. Pearson' 939; LP's amanuensis 983.1.

Pellé, Mrs., an object of charity.—('83) 844 (?); ('84) J's letters to Anthony Hamilton 933, 934.1, 965.

PENNECK, RICHARD, c. '27–1803, Rector of St. John's, Horsley-down, S'k; Keeper of the Reading Room, British Museum (FB's *Early Diary*). —('68) 'Mr. Pennick I have seen, but with . . . little approach to intimacy' 195; J's letter to him on HT's behalf as candidate for S'k **196.**

Pepys, Lucas, '42–1830, of Eton and Christ Church; M.D. '74; Bt '84; y. b. of WWP, q.v. (*DNB, L, Tb*).—('79) 'the advice given by Dr. Pepys' in HT's case 633; ('80) P attends HT at B'n 686; ('83) 'my compliance with Dr. Pepys's directions' 825.1; P discourages bleeding 848; P offended because J did not call him in 863.

Pepys, William Weller, '40–1825, Master in Chancery; Bt 1801; of Wimpole St. ('85) (*L, Tb*).—('75) P as dramatic critic 376.2; ('79) 'I dined at Mr. Vesey's with Lord Lucan and Mr.

Pepys' 645.1; ('80) J meets P at Mrs.
Vesey's 657; 'I am to be at Mr. Pepys's
669; J meets him at CB's 685; ('81)
'P— whom you pressed into the service' (as executor to HLT) 727 (see
note); ('83) J has a message 'from Mr.
Pepys . . . enquiring in your (HLT)
name after my health' 853.

PERCY, THOMAS, '29–1811, M.A.
Christ Church '53; D.D. Emmanuel
Coll., Cambridge, '70; Vicar of
Easton-Maudit, Northants., '53; m.
'59 Anne Gutteridge or Goodriche
(d. 1806); 6 children (of whom Anne
d. '70, a son d. '83); Chaplain to the
D of Northumberland; Dean of Carlisle '78, Bp of Dromore '82; member
of the Club 15 Feb. '68 (DNB, L).—
('60) Terms offered by Dodsley for
Reliques of Antient English Poetry
(1765) 134.2, Millar agrees to 100
guineas 136; ('61) J offers to visit P
after the coronation 139; ('63) the
projected visit, 'I purpose to bring
Shakespeare with me' 159.1; ('64) J
and AW propose to start 25 June
165.1, J's letter of thanks 166.1; ('65)
AW asks Lye to thank Mrs. P for a
letter 174.1; ('69) J asks P for a
'Charity Sermon' 224; ('70) death of
'poor little Miss Anne' 240.2; ('71)
P's 'long ballad in many fits' (The Her-
mit of Warkworth 1771) 246; acquaintance with AW and Mrs. Rolt 247.1;
('72) P's contempt for cascades 288;
('73) J hopes to see P at Alnwick 316.2,
'Dr. Percy is not there' 318 (340); ('76)
P to give dates for Goldsmith's epitaph
480, J asks P to get from the Duke admission to the Middlesex Hospital of
Thomas Coxeter 503, sends him facts
about the Coxeters 504, 504.1; ('77)
Mrs. P mentioned 549 (see note); ('78)
J writes to JB about his 'foolish
controversy' with P; praise of P, whose
'attention to poetry has given grace
and splendour to his studies of antiquity' 575; 'Dr. Percy is now Dean of
Carlisle. . . . He is provided for' 587;
('79) P 'may be very happy'; livings
in his gift 646; ('80) P's loss by a fire
at Northumberland House 655; P on
the influence of clergy on parish-

ioners 704; ('83) P 'is now Bishop of
Dromore, but has I believe lost his
only son' 835.1 (18; see note); (n.d.)
J asks P to lend Amadis 1145.

PERKINS, JOHN, '29 or '30–1812,
HT's manager at the brewery and
after his death part-owner (with Barclay, q.v.); m. c. '74 Amelia, sister
of Edward Moseley and widow of
Timothy Bevan; she d. 1830; their
children included a John and a Harry,
Tb 407, 636 (L, Tb).

Letters to: ('74) 361; ('77) 512.1;
('81) 730, 735, 738.1, 739.2; ('82)
758.2, 779.4, 796, 814.2; ('83) 821.2,
916.1; ('84) 923.2, 924.1, 927, 927.1,
952.2, 965.5, 1019, 1029.1; (n.y.)
1146–8.

('73) P 'always a credible witness'
301.3; 'sent to Ireland' 321 (345);
('74) J asks P to do him a favour 361;
('76) P 'crows and triumphs' 482; ('77)
see end of article; ('79) 'let Mr.
Perkins go to Ireland' 623; HLT's
'treatment of little (Harry) Perkins'
636; ('80) P's criticism of HLT's
letter to the electors 662; urges her
to come to S'k 664, 665; his conduct
during the Gordon riots 681; mentioned 690; 'cannot be discharged,
and will never suffer a superior' 702;
('81) Cator offers P money (after HT's
death) 718; P complains of HLT's
absence, his 'appetite for partnership'
721; mentioned 724; his proposals for
his remuneration as manager 725, 727,
729.3; J sends P 'good wishes for the
prosperity of you and your partner'
(Barclay) 730; P's difficulties about
raising the purchase-money 735; J
borrows £30 'of your house' 738.1;
J hopes 'you found all your family
well, and particularly my little Boy'
(presumably his godson: perhaps the
second s. Harry (Tb 636) who was
HLT's godson) 739.2; P's illness 748,
750; ('82) J offers to visit P 'for a little
private conversation' 758.2; P's voyage
in search of health; J prescribes 'rules'
796; ('83) robbery at the brewhouse
897; P sends J 'a pig' 901; ('82–'84) J's
letters to P of these years, not described
here, and the undated letters 1146,

1147, 1148, mainly concern friendly messages, domestic matters (money, coals), and invitations to P and his family to visit him; ('77) a newspaper report of HT's health, J asks P for news **512.1**.

Perks, 'an attorney of Birmingham', — –'45 (*L*).—('44) 20.

Peter the Great 331, 585.1.

Peyton, V. J., — –'76, J's amanuensis; his wife (*L* i. 187, 536. Dr. Powell hesitated to identify our P with V. J. P., believing the latter's *Elements of the English Language* to have been first published 1779. But the Yale Univ. Library has a second edition 1776, with a dedication (not by J) to the 'Countess of Guerchy', to whom V. J. P. had taught English).—('75) 'Peyton and Macbean are both starving' 393; ('76) 'Peyton was not worse this morning' 463.1, (1 Apr.) 'Poor Payton expired this morning' (before his wife 'was buried') 467.

Philipps, John, *c*. '01–'64, of Pembroke Coll., 6th Bt '43 of Picton, Pembrokeshire; M.P. '54–'64; m. '25 Elizabeth Shepperd, 'oo–'88 (*L* v. 550).—('58) J's letter 113.1 is franked 'J. Philipps'; ('60) 'Sir John Philips . . . is . . . ill . . . at Oxford. He is the chief friend of Miss Williams' 136.1.

Phillips, Peregrine, d. 1801, attorney; his d. Anna Maria, '63–1805, singer and actress, 'the celebrated Mrs. Crouch' (Boswell) (*DNB* s.v. Crouch, *L* iv. 521).—('83) 'The bringer of this letter is the father of Miss Philips, a singer . . . Mr. Philips is one of my old friends' 841.

Phipps, Constantine John, '44–'92, Capt. R.N.; 2nd B Mulgrave '75 (*DNB*, *L*).—('73) 'Two ships . . . are under the command of Captain Constantine Phipps to explore the Northern Ocean' 299; 'they congratulate our return (from the Hebrides) as if we had been with Phipps or Banks' 338.

Piozzi, Gabriele Mario, '40–1809, singer; m. Hester Lynch Thrale, q.v. (*DNB*, *L*, *Tb*).—(24 Nov. '81) 'Piozzi, I find, is coming in spite of Miss Harriet's prediction' 750; (3 Dec. '81) 'You

have got Piozzi again' 752; (Apr. '82) 'Do not let Mr. Piozzi nor any body else put me quite out of your head' 778; (8 July '84) 'Prevail upon Mr. Piozzi to settle in England' 972.

Pitches, —, one of the 5 dd. of Sir Abraham P, Kt, of Streatham (*Tb*).—('77) J warns HLT lest 'your hearers should tell you, like Miss Pitches, "You never saw a Fête" ' 518.

Pitt (Pit), William, 'o8–'78, 1st E of Chatham '66 (*DNB*, *L*).—('66) commended Burke's maiden speech 182.

Pitt, William, '59–1806, Prime Minister 19 Dec. '83 (*DNB*, *L*).—(18 Mar. '84) 'Mr. Pitt will have great power' 942.

Polhill, Nathaniel, — –'82, M.P. for S'k; re-elected Sept. '80 (*L*, *Tb*).— (May '80) 'Mr. Polhil . . . has refused to join with Hotham, and is thought to be in more danger than Mr. Thrale' 666.

Pompey 585.1.

Plumb(e), Samuel, — –'84; m. Frances, — –1811, d. of Ralph Thrale, q.v. Their s. Ralph, '54 (?)–'76. Their d. Fanny, '58–'90, m. May '73 John, '52– —, s. of — Rice (*Tb*, Clifford 99).—('70) J asks Bright of Abingdon to take 'Mr. Alderman Plumbe's' son in his school 226, 226.2; Mrs. P takes the boy there 228.1; ('72) 'Do the Plumbes take her (Mrs. Salusbury's) house furnished?' 285; ('73) 'Your declaration to Miss Fanny' on the right of a parent to veto a child's marriage; Plumbe's stipulation 308; 'Fanny's flight with her lover'; Rice's consent to his son's marriage 309; Plumbe can be bullied into acquiescence 310; 'I suppose they go to Scotland. Was Fanny dressed à la Nesbitienne?' 311;' What should Rice and his Wife do at the wrong end of the town . . . ? his Genius . . . will bid him live in Lothbury, and measure brandy' 337 (385); ('75) 'So you left out the . . . s' from the regatta (*sic* 1788, original not seen; 'Rices' HLP) 411; 'Of Mrs. Fanny I have no knowledge' (reference doubtful) 422.

Poole, Sir Ferdinando, — –1804, of the Hooke near Lewes, Sussex; 4th Bt '67;

m. '73 — White of Horsham (*Tb*).— 556.

Porter, Jervis Henry, '18–'63, Capt. R.N., of Spring Gardens; e. b. of Lucy P, q.v. (*L*, R vi, 19).—('63) His death and his will 150.

Porter, Joseph, *c*. '24–'83, merchant of Leghorn; y. b. of Lucy P, q.v. (*L*, R vi).—('68) When JP comes to L'd J will write to him 202; ('70) 'he says that he often calls and never finds me' 228, 229; ('75) is he at L'd? 444; ('80) J has bought 'about one hundred and fifty Sermons, which I will put in a Box, and get Mr. Mathias to send him' 656; ('81) J regrets the miscarriage of the box 723; ('83) his death 898, 900, 914.

PORTER, LUCY, '15–'86, of L'd, o. d. of Harry P of B'm (1691–'34) and Elizabeth Jervis (1689–'52, m. '35 SJ); heiress '63 of her b. Jervis Henry P, q.v.; lived with J's mother till her death '59; his hostess at L'd '67, '69, '70, '71, '72, '75, '76, '77, '79, '81, '84. She is addressed in terms varying from 'Dear Madam' to 'My Dearest Love' (154); never as 'Lucy', though in letters to others she is called that as well as 'Miss' or Miss Porter or Mrs. Porter (*L*, R vi).—('40) 'Lucy always sends her Duty' to J's wife 12; ('42) J thanks JT for what he has done for 'Miss' 17; ('44) mentioned 20; ('49) J writes to her about 'Levett's affair'; 'you little Gipsy' 25; (? '51) she pays a debt for J 32.1; ('52) J on his wife's death intends to buy 'mourning for Miss Porter' 42; ('59) *passim* in letters to his mother and to LP during his mother's last illness or about subsequent arrangements; 'you are wiser and better than I' 126; 'I have nobody but you' 127, 119, 122, 125, 126.1, 128, 129, 130, 131, 132.2; ('61) 'I wish you long life, and happiness always encreasing' 137; ('62) 'my daughter-in-law, from whom I expected most, and whom I met with sincere benevolence, has lost the beauty and gaiety of youth, without having gained much of the wisdom of age' 142; J sends news of his pension 144; ('63) Capt.

P's death; hopes he has left her well off; if not, he will try to have 'sufficient for us both' 150; congratulates her on 'so large a fortune' and offers to visit L'd 153, deplores her ambition to build 154; ('64) sends her books and a diamond ring 164; ('66) his reluctance to sell his house at L'd; 'cannot well come during the Session' 180, plans 'to repair the poor old house' 187; ('67) 'Miss Lucy is more kind and civil than I expected', her virtues 'a little discoloured by hoary virginity' 190; her loss in Kitty Chambers's death 194; ('68) condoles with her on Kitty's death, 'will take care of your reading glass', 'the punctuality of your correspondence' 202; has sent her books and reading glass, 'make your letters as long as you can' 207.1; 'I love to think on you, but do not know when I shall see you' 209; 'do not you owe me a Letter?' 209.1; ('69) visits her 220; ('70) consults her about 'giving away the money'; 'do not learn of me to neglect writing' 228; the money 229; ('71) 'very kind to me' 252; she is pleased with HLT's mention of her, thinks J 'much improved' 255; 'Lucy is a Philosopher' 260; 'a very peremptory maiden' and insists on his staying longer 266; 'my Lucy' 267; ('72) J tells JT that LP will not keep him long 278; her cat 282.1; 'Lucy . . . wheedling for another week' 289.2; ('73) his visit 296; her feeble hearing 311.2; ('75) mentioned 379, 398.1; her gout 404, 405, 406, 407, 408, 411, 425; HLT's present of a work-bag 407; 'very good humoured, while I do just as she would have me' 408; mentioned 409; commends his behaviour 413; mentioned 424; reads Hammond on the Psalms 425; 'a little paroxysm' of 'tenderness' 427; sends her books and glasses 433, 444; sends her 'a little box' bought in Paris 439; ('77) mentioned 509, 511, 535; 'Lucy says "When I read Dod's Sermon . . . I said, Dr. Johnson could not make a better" ' 536; Queeney's remembrance of her 538; does not attend the races or the ball 539; her health 558; sends her a cast of his

'head' by Nollekens 564; ('78) her dislike of the Nollekens 'Bust' 572; ('79)
no visit in '78; offers her books 600;
has sent her 'a little print' and oysters,
and will soon send 'some little books'
(i.e. *Lives* i–iv) 605; the books sent
614; lame and deaf 616.1; 'Lucy shows
some tenderness' 623.1; writes to her
of the threatened French invasion
627.1; his letter to her of 19 Oct. not
published 635.1; sends her letter about
Miss Doxy to JB 646; sends her JB's
reply 649; ('80) has sent her 'a little
stuff gown' bought for him by
Queeney; hopes to visit L'd 656; sends
her letter to HLT 660.1; hopes to
come in May (year doubtful) 661.1;
mentioned 686; ('81) hopes to visit her
714.2, 723; will send his *Lives*, and
hopes to visit her 730.2, 740.1; 'I
think Lucy is kinder than ever' 742;
'deaf and inarticulate' 744, 745, 'but
she will have *Watts's Improvement of the
Mind*. Her mental powers are not
impaired, and her social virtues seem
to encrease' 745; her recent 'dreadful
ilness' 746; mentioned 748; ('82)
apologies for silence; his melancholy
state; 'Let me have your prayers' 765,
768; ('83) intends a visit 833.1; tells
her of his stroke 856; visit doubtful
862; death of 'poor Mr. Porter'
(Joseph P), preparation for death 898;
her infirmities 914, 'if I come to you
(JT), I must go to Lichfield' 913; ('84)
preparation for death 935; his visit
972.1; 'Mrs. Porter much mended'
1018.1; mentioned 1016, 1040; other
letters to her of this year (939, 957,
983.1, 991.1, 1010.1) deal with his
health and hers, and the imminence of
death; the last is 2 Dec., 'may God
pardon and bless us' 1041.
Porter, Mary, d. '65 (*fl.* '05–'43), actress
(*DNB*, *Tb*, *L* i. 369).—('55) J mentions her in letter to Miss Cottrell 74;
('62) 'Miss Cotterel still continues to
cling to Mrs. Porter' 142; ('83) 'Mrs.
Porter the tragedian, with whom
— (*sic* 1788, original not seen,
'Mrs. Cottrell' HLP) spent part of
his (*sic* 1788, 'her' HLP) earlier life'
894.

Porteus, Beilby, '31–1808, of Christ's
Coll., Cambridge; Chaplain '62 to
Abp Secker; Bp of Chester '76, of
London '87; m. Margaret, 2nd d. of
Brian Hodgson of Ashbourne, q.v.
(*DNB*, *L*).—('81) 'The Bishop of
Chester is here (A'n) now with his
Father in law' 747; ('82) J dines with
P in London 778.
PORTMORE: Charles Colyear, '00–'85,
2nd E of P '30 (*L*).—('84) P's note
'desiring that I would give you (BL)
an account of my health' 952; J's ac-
knowledgement 952.1.
Pott (Pot), Percivall, '14–'88, Surgeon to
St. Bartholomew's; hero of 'Pott's
fracture' (*DNB*, *L*).—(9 Sept.–1 Nov.
'83) *passim* in letters about J's sarco-
cele; his *mot* in 892, 'fire and sword',
deserves honourable mention.
Povilleri (Povoleri), Giovanni, teacher of
Italian (*Tb*).—('82) 'That Povilleri
should write these verses is impossible'
767.
Powell (-l), William, '35–'69, actor
(*DNB*).—('69) 212 (see note).
Price, John, '34–1813, Bodley's Librarian
'68–1813 (*DNB*).—403.1.
Prince of Wales: *see* George IV.
Prince, Daniel, — –'96, bookseller of
O'd (*L*).—('55) 'Mr. Prince the bookseller' 75.
Proby, Baptist, '26–1807, Dean of L'd
'76; m. Mary Susannah, d. of Sir Nigel
Gresley, 6th Bt.—('77) 'We have a
new Dean whose name is Proby, he
has the manner of a Gentleman. . . .
He has a lady that talks about Mrs.
Montague and Mrs. Carter' 539.
Prowse, Elizabeth,' 12–'80, of Berkeley
near Frome; her d. MARY m. the
Rev. John Methuen Rogers; benefac-
tresses of Elizabeth Herne, q.v. (Hill on
693, 934, *L* iv. 441).—('80) J condoles
with Miss P on the death of her mother,
'a very bright and eminent example';
her allowance to EH 693, 710; ('81)
J thinks he has been overpaid; offers
his *Lives* 729; ('82) acknowledges her
'letter and bill' 787; ('84) J offers to
leave Mrs. Rogers £100 for the benefit
of EH 934.
Prujean, William, d. '90 or later; m. '55

Sophia, '13–before '90, 7th d. of Sir Thomas Aston, q.v. (R v).—('79) 'Mr. Prujean called' with news of Elizabeth Aston's health 599.

Prussia: *see* Frederick.

R—, Mr., presumably the Rushworth of 702a.—('80) His 'nice discernment of loss and gain' 702 (see note).

Ramsay, Allan, '13–'84, painter; of 67 Harley Street (*DNB, L*).— J dines with R ('78–'80) 576, 610, 632, 633, 662, 663; ('83) in Italy 836.1; 'is now walking the streets of Naples in full possession of his locomotive powers' 876.1, cf. 932; ('84) his death 995.

Ranby, John, '03–'73, Surgeon to George II; F.R.S. '24 (*DNB*).—('40) J urges his wife to call in 'Ranby or Shipton' 12.

Rann, Joseph, '33 (?)–1811, V of Holy Trinity, Coventry '73.—('77) 'Our good friend Mr. Rann' intercedes with J for his cousin Tom J 565.1; ('79) 'We dined with Mr. Rann at Coventry' 616; J's application to Burke for 'the Vicar of Coventry' 610.1 (ii. 529).

Ray, presumably a S'k tradesman.—303.2.

Reed, Isaac, '42–1807, scholar (*DNB, L*).—(n.d.) J asks Nichols 'to procure the dates of Pope's Works upon the Dunciads. Mr. Reed can probably supply them' 1143.

Reid, John, — –'74, convict (*L*).—JB's efforts to save him 360.

REPINGTON, GILBERT, '12– —, of Christ Church; his b. John, '11– —, of Exeter Coll.; ss. of Gilbert R of Tamworth, Warwickshire (R iii).—('35) J writes to GR about 'the kind offer' (of JR) 'that you would take some care about my Books'; he hopes R will excuse 'this trouble from a former Schoolfellow' 3.1; his 'obligation' 3.2.

REYNOLDS, FRANCES, '29–1807, s. of Sir JR; of Dover Street ('Renny' 264.2, 644, 681; in direct address she is usually 'My dearest' or the like) (*DNB, L*).—('59) 'much employed in miniatures' 117; ('62) welcomes her letters 146; ('64) Her 'sudden folly', 'the grossness of a ship' 162; J hopes to hear from JR 'or from dear Miss

Reynolds' 166; ('69) Louise Flint's conquest of her 213; ('71) message to her 261; affair of an undergraduate 264.1, 264.2; ('73) asks HLT to lend her 'Newton on the Prophecies' 294; ('74) their mutual regard 356.1; ('75) mentioned 442; ('76) her intimacy with the Thrales 471, 474; 'pray tell Sir Joshua . . .' 474; 'your dear little production' 489.1; 'Mrs. Thrale has a great regard for Miss Reynolds' 490; FR wants to send Goldsmith's epitaph to Beattie 491; her impracticable request 497; ('77) FR, the Thrales, etc., at JR's 512; ('78) Nollekens's bust of J condemned by FR 572; ('79) she 'employs' J 602; J sends money for 'your German friend' 624; J asks her to buy him prints 634; offers to visit her 636.1; 'I am to dine with Renny to morrow' 637; 'I dined on Tuesday with — (erased by HLP) and hope her little head begins to settle'; her scruples 640; 'on Saturday I dined with Renny' 644; ('80) 'Renny's conversatione'; she is going to Ramsgate 681; 'Do not burn your papers. I have mended little but some bad rhymes' 682; mentioned 700; 'Renny goes to Richmond' 703; ('81) 'you may give the books (i.e. *Lives?*) to Mrs. Horneck, and I will give you another for yourself'; HLT's 'custom for your pictures' 734; J's praise and criticism of her manuscript 738 (see ii. 530); ('82) 'your work is full of very penetrating meditation' 777; J meets her at Hoole's 779, visits her 782.1, 793.2; ('83) hopes to visit her 875.1; her journey 876.2; 'it is a comfort to me to have you near me' 889; asks her to dine 894.1, 910.1, 916.2, 919; looks forward to her return 896; ('84) 'I think very well of your dinner' 931.1; FR shows him Hannah More's poem 940.1; asks her to come to tea and bring 'the copy to show the printer' 951.1; procures her an estimate for printing 958; his failure as intermediary between FR and JR, is glad she gave up the idea of printing 961; (n.d.) his draft of a letter from FR to JR 1149; visits 1150, 1151.

REYNOLDS, JOSHUA, '23–'92, Kt and P.R.A. '69; of Leicester Fields and Richmond, Surrey; founder of the Club '63–'64 (*DNB, L, Tb*). (*See also* Reynolds, F., Palmer, and Johnson, William.)—('59) 'twenty guineas a head' 117; ('61) 'without a rival', adds 'thousands to thousands' 138; 'six thousand a year' 142; ('62) 'business' with him 146; increases 'in reputation and in riches' 147; ('64) 'almost the only man whom I call a friend' 166; ('66) 'very constant' at the Club 182; ('71) his portrait of J at L'd 261; J asks him for money for a charity 264.1; J asks him to forward the motto for Banks's goat 271; ('73) J dines with him 294; ('74) on Goldsmith's debts 357; ('75) 'has taken too much to strong liquor, and seems to delight in his new character' 374; J recommends E. Allen to R 407.1, 408.2; mention 435; ('76) mention 474; Goldsmith's epitaph 480, 491; 'I dined at Sir Joshua's house on the hill' (Richmond) 483; J sent R two copies of Goldsmith's epitaph 490; J asks him to help Paterson 496; Baretti's translation of the *Discourses* 505; ('77) J dines with R 505.3, 506; 'Did you [HLT] stay all night at Sir Joshua's?' 512; ('78) J dines with R 576, pleads with him for Lowe 577, 'I have sat twice to Sir Joshua . . . he has projected another' 584, picture finished 586; ('79) J dines with R 637, gets him to help 'my poor neighbours' 640; ('80) 'much company at Reynolds's' 662; J meets R at Ramsay's 663; J dines with R 687; J let a volume of the *Lives* 'get to the Reynolds's, and could never get it again' 690; mention 700; 'goes to Devonshire' 703; ('81) Thrale's death 716; 'your splendid benefaction' 733 (see note); ('82) 'your country has been in danger of losing one of its brightest ornaments, and I of losing one of my oldest and kindest friends' 813; his recovery 815; his speech at the Painters' distribution of prizes, 'the King is not heard with more attention' 817.1; J declines an invitation 819; ('83) 'As I suspect you to have lost

your Lives' J sends R another edition 829, Crabbe's *Village* 830, J pleads for Lowe 832; R 'continues to rise in reputation and in riches' 835.1 (18); Barry's 'satirical pictures' of R and others 837, J recommends Cruikshank 838; R's estimate of the profits of the exhibition 839, J dines with R 840, 875; J recommends Paterson 842; 'your kind attention' 879.2; the Essex-Head Club 916; R visits J 922; ('84) J intercedes with R for FR 961, asks him 'for some relief for a poor man' 964, application to Thurlow 971 (see 1008), R's 'tenderness' 980; calls on him to remember 'that we must all die' 995; R's 'furious purposes' (see note), retrospect of their friendship, 'perhaps few people have lived so much and so long together, with less cause of complaint on either side' 1002; R's application to Thurlow 1007, 1008, 'Do not write about the ballon' 1013, R's copy of J's letter to Thurlow 1018; 'Sir Joshua told me long ago that my vocation was to publick life' 1029 (see note); (n.d.) J's letter to R written for FR 1149; J sends R a book to read and return 1152.

Rhudde (Rudd) or Wood, Mary, JT's (q.v.) opponent in his lawsuit of '76; *see also* Wood, Ralph (*L*, Taylor, *Life of Taylor*, 64).—('76) 461, 478; ('77) 541.1.

Rice: *see* Plumbe.

Richard III 257.

RICHARDSON, SAMUEL, (?) 1689–4 July '61 (*DNB, L,* W. M. Sale's *Bibliography*).—(Mar. '51) 'though Clarissa wants no help from external Splendour I was glad to see her improved in her appearance' (by publication Apr. '51 of the 'fourth' ed. in 8° simultaneously with the 'third' 12°) 'but more glad to find that she was now . . . confident enough of success, to supply whatever had been hitherto suppressed' (the suppressions were made good in the editions of '51); 'I wish you would add an *Index Rerum*' (see below) 31; (Apr. '53) J sends R a pamphlet 'with a few little notes' (see note); 'I hope your new book is printing. Macte novâ virtute' (*Sir Charles Grandison*; 2 volumes were circulated privately in July) **48**; (Sept. '53) J thanks R for 'the volumes of your new work' (Vols. 1–4 published Nov. '53); criticizes the preface; recommends Martinelli; 'cannot I prevail this time for an Index; such as I wished and shall wish, to Clarissa'; 'I am not cool about this piracy'; suggests an edition in brevier **49**; (? Dec. '53) 'I hear you take subscriptions' (J seems to have been misinformed) **49.1**; 'I have almost a mind to retain these till you send me the next volume'; R's 'art of improving on yourself' **49.2**; (Mar. '54) J sends R thanks from AW for his present; her projected dictionary; 'I am extremely obliged by the seventh volume' (published Mar. '54); 'I wish . . . Sir Charles had not compromised in matters of religion' (see note); introduces Adams of Pembroke Coll.; asks R to send 'Mr. Falkner's letter to me' (see note) to Lord Corke; recommends 'Miss Williams's little business' **51.1**; (Feb. '55) J recommends an author for 'the universal History' if any part is 'yet unengaged' (see note); 'pray favour me with an account of the translations of Clarissa' (see note) **58.1**; ('56) J thanks R for a kindness and sends him 'this little book' (Browne's *Christian Morals*) **90**; J 'obliged to entreat your assistance; I am now under an arrest for five pounds eighteen shillings' **94**; ('59) 'the pheasant (sent by BL) I gave to Mr. Richardson' **117**; ('62) R's death **142, 147**; ('76) *Clarissa* quoted **478**; ('77) *Grandison* quoted **553**; ('78) *Clarissa* quoted **590**; ('80) R's quarrel with Hester Mulso **659**; ('83) J misses R **839, 857**.

Richardson, William, '01–'88, printer, nephew and successor of Samuel R.—('56) **94** is endorsed 'Sent Six Guineas, Witness Wm. Richardson'.

Ritter, Joseph, — JB's Bohemian servant (*L*).—('75) 'He is a fine fellow, and one of the best travellers in the world' **446**; ('78) 'my service to my fellow-traveller, Joseph' **658**.

RIVINGTON, JOHN, '20–'92, bookseller; one of the publishers of J's Shakespeare (*DNB*).—('71) J writes to R about 'the new impression of Shakespeare' **243**.

Rizzio, David, 1533 (?)–1566, secretary to Mary Queen of Scots, **320**.

Robert of Doncaster: see Byrkes.

Roberts, James, *c.* 1669–'54, bookseller; publisher of J's *Life of Savage* (*L*).—('43) **23**.

Roberts, Miss, BL's first cousin (*L* i. 430).—('58) 'Miss Roberts, whom I have at last brought to speak, upon the information which you (T. Warton) gave me, that she had something to say' **114**.

Robertson, William, '21–'93, historian; D.D. Edinburgh '58, Principal of the University '62 (*DNB*, *L*).—('67) 'Dr. Robertson, to whom I am a little known' **189**; J's reliance on his judgement **193**; ('73) 'Dr. Robertson came in and promised to show me' Edinburgh **320**; ('74) R's 'censure of my negligence' **348**; ('76) J's offer to help Watson 'as formerly in Dr. Robertson's publication' **499**.

Robson, Bateman, *c.* '19–'91, attorney; see Norris (*Th*).—('73) R's advice to HLT on tithes **321**; ('80) R gave J 'the character' of 'one Mr. Jones, a Shoemaker' **707.1**; ('81) R's 'oration flaming with the terrifick'; J asks him for HT's will **725**; 'Mr. Norris (Mr. Robson's partner)' promises to send the will **727**.

Rockingham : Charles Watson-Wentworth, '30–'82, 2nd M of R (*DNB*, *L*).—(July '82) 'I did not think Rockingham of such importance as that his death should have had such extensive consequences' **793**.

Roebuck, Mrs., *née* Cambden, '15–'77 (*L* iii. 492, R v. 265).—('77) 'at Birmingham I heard of the death of an old friend' **535**.

Rogers, Mary: see Prowse.

ROLT, Mrs. not identified, **247.1**.

Rose, William, '19–'86, of Chiswick; a schoolmaster and editor of the *Monthly Review*; his d. Sarah m. '83 Charles Burney jun. (*L* iv. 509, FB's *Early*

SCOTT (-t), WILLIAM, '45–1836, Fellow of Univ. Coll. '65, Camden Reader in Ancient History '73–'85, D.C.L. '79; 1st B Stowell 1821; member of the Club Dec. '78 and of the Essex-Head Club; m. '81 Anna Maria Bagnall; their d. Marianne, c. '83–1842 (*DNB, L*).—('75) 'Mr. Scot . . . says, that rather than the Scheme (for Carter, q.v.) should miscarry he will ride himself' 384.2, 432; ('80) S's abortive candidature for the University 666; 'I walked with Dr. Scot to look at Newgate' 677; ('83) J asks S to employ a young man 831; S 'prospers exceedingly in the commons' 835.1 (18); ('84) J reports on his health 1021.1.

Scot, —: perhaps the neighbour of the Thrales mentioned in *Th*, 814.2 (see note).

Scrase, Charles, '09–'92, 'many years partner with the late Mr. Robson (q.v.) of Lincoln's Inn' *GM* 1792; later of the Steyne, B'n (*L, Th*).—('71) 'I suppose, like Scrace, that you (HLT) are thinking how to reduce me' 267; ('75) J advises HLT to consult S about settling her estate 415; his loan to HT 418, 426; ('76) 'a solicitor, another Scrase' 478 (see note), 479; ('77) 'the rejuvenescency' of S 562; ('78) 'his knowledge of business, and of the law' 591; ('79) HT and HLT 'may both be the better for his conversation' 633; 'a friend upon all occasions' 636; consulted by HT and J about HT's will 640, 642; his mental obtuseness in old age 645; mentioned 647, 648; ('80) 'Scrase is doubtless pleased with the payment of your debts' 659 (passage suppressed by HLP); mentioned 679; his illness 685, 686; mentioned 690; ('81) S's advice about the brewery at HT's death 725, 727.

Scrimshaw, Charles: Charles Skrymsher, 1688–'62, probably J's first cousin (R iii. 21).—(Nov. '84) J asks Vyse for information about S, 'he being very nearly related to me' 1039.

Secker, Thomas, 1693–'68, Abp of Canterbury '58–'68 (*DNB, L*).—('62) 'a great man to whom I never spoke'

141; ('65) S's patronage of Lye 174.

Sedgwick, of L'd, probably Joseph, who is named in Court Leet Records '69.—('76) 'had a dropsy' 455.

Selwyn (-in) presumably Charles S, banker, '15–'94 (*L*, FB's *Diary, Th*).—('83) 'Mr. Selwin sent me two partridges' 893.1.

Seward (Sh-), 'Mrs.' an acquaintance of HLT.—('83) 'Mrs. Sheward is an old maid . . . yet *sur le pavé*' 857, 'glad that Mrs. Sheward . . . loves me' 860, 'Sheward was with me this morning, just such as Sheward uses to be' 888.1 (see note).

Seward, Thomas (the traditional pron. is See-ward; in *BP* xiii. 22 it is spelled Seyward), '08–'90, of St. John's Coll., Cambridge; Rector of Eyam, Derbyshire, and of Kingsley, Staffs., Prebendary of L'd; m. Elizabeth Hunter; their e. d. Anna, 'the Swan of Lichfield', '42–1809 (*DNB, L,* R).—('42) his 'treaty' with JT about a living 17; ('68) 'the Sewards, and all my friends' 202; Miss S's kindness 209; ('71) S's intention of visiting HLT 266; ('81) 'Miss Seward has been enquiring after Susan Thrale' 745; ('84) 'Mr. Seward is very lame, but his daughter flourishes in poetical reputation' 1018.1.

Seward, William, '47–'99, of Oriel Coll.; F.R.S. and F.S.A. '79; member of the Essex-Head Club. (The pron. is shown by the spelling Su-, see Hill's note on 346; in *French Journals* 45 the name is spelled Sheward) (*DNB, L, Th*).—('75) 'Poor dear — (HLP's erasure)! He only grows dull because he is sickly' 417 (doubtful; see note); ('76) S visits J 482; ('77) J asks JB to do the honours for S, 'a great favourite at Streatham' 522, 524; 'sorry for poor Sewards pain' 548; 'Boswell liked Seward better as he knew him more' 549; ('79) J hopes HLT has S's comfort 617; ('80) S visits J 564, 703.1; ('83) S's journey 'to contemplate the pictures of Claude Loraine' 846; J sees him 901; ('84) 'I ought to write to him' 1027.

Shakespeare, — –'77, a horse.—('75)

superannuated 408.1, 413; ('77) 'Old Shakespeare is dead' 553.

Sharp, James, 1613–1679, Abp of St. Andrews (*DNB, L*).—972.

Sharp, Samuel, 1700(?)–78, surgeon and writer (*L*).—His view of cataract 135.

SHARP, WILLIAM (*L*).—('77) J's letter to S about Watts **526.**

Sharpe, Mary, 'a single lady of large fortune, who afterwards married the Rev. Osmund Beauvoir' (Carter, *Memoirs* 1807, i. 457; FB's *Diary*).—('82) 'Mrs. Carter's Miss Sharpe is going to marry a schoolmaster sixty-two years old' 778.

Shaw, Rev. William, '49–1813, M.A. Glasgow '72; Celtic scholar (*DNB, L*). —('77) J's patronage of S's 'Erse Grammar' (*Analysis of the Galick Language* 1778) 510 (and ? 499); S asks J to interest Lord Eglintoune on his behalf 567; ('80) J introduces S, 'a studious and literary man', to Charles Allen 711.1.

Shaw, —, apparently of S'k; perhaps a physician or apothecary (but not in *Tb*).—('76) mentioned 479, perhaps the same as ('80) 692 (his claim to have 'saved my Master').

Shebbeare (-b-), John, '09–'88, political writer (*DNB, L*).—(n.d.) mentioned 1111.

Sheffield: John Baker-Holroyd, c. '35–1821, 1st Baron S '81; m. '67 Abigail Way, d. '93 (*DNB, L*).—('82) J meets Lady S 779; mentioned with Mrs. Way, after 779.3 (see iii. 388); ('83) Lady S mentioned 891.

Shelburne: see Fitzmaurice.

Shelley (Shelly), Sir John, — –'83, M.P., 5th Bt '71 of Michelgrove, Sussex; m. (1) Wilhelmina Newnham, who d. '72 (her o. s. John became 6th Bt), (2) Elizabeth Woodcock (3 dd.) (*L, Tb*).—('77) 'you will see the Shellys, and perhaps hear something about the Cottons' 553; ('78) 'long live Sir John Shelly, that lures my Master to hunt' 586; ('80) 'the S—y scheme' 702, 'the expedition to Sir John Shelly's' 703.

Shepherd, father and son, of Bath: the father perhaps the Methodist S. of *Tb* 580.—('83) 892, 893.1.

Sheridan, Thomas, 'Old Sherry', '19–'88, actor and elocutionist; m. '47 Frances Chamberlaine, '24–'66 (*DNB, L*).—('60) J criticizes S's acting; 'however, I wish him well among other reasons because I like his wife' 135.

Sheridan, Elizabeth Ann, *née* Linley, '54–'92, singer; m. '73 Richard Brinsley S (*DNB, L*).—('80) 'Mrs. Sheridan refused to sing . . . a song to the Prince of Wales' 779.

Sheward: see Seward.

Shipley, Jonathan, '14–'88, M.A. Oxon. '38; Canon of Christ Church '48; Bp of St. Asaph '69; member of the Club '80 (*DNB, L*).—('76) J meets S, 'knowing and conversible', at dinner at JR's 483; ('80) J dines with S 662; 'comes to every place' 663; 'a Bishop little better than *your* Bishop' 669; ('82) J dines with S 778, at the Club 817.1.

Shipton, John, 1680–'48, surgeon (*DNB*). —('40) 12.

Siddons, Sarah, '55–1831, e. d. of Roger Kemble; m. '73 William S (*DNB, L*). —('82) at the Club 'the talk was of Mrs. Siddons. . . . I had nothing to say' 817.1; ('83) 'yesterday I gave tea to Mrs. Siddons' 893.1; she 'behaved with great modesty and propriety' 895.

SIMPSON, JOSEPH, '21–'68, e. s. of Stephen S and Jane Adey, of L'd; of the Inner Temple '43; m. c. '54 Elizabeth, d. of Edward Gravenor, silk merchant of Coventry (*L, Tb, R* iv, viii).—('52) J suggests to Levett that he 'terminate the affair with Mr. J. Sympson' 40; ('59 or later) J writes to S of his father's 'inexorability' in resenting his marriage and refusing him financial help **134** (see i. 430); ('68) 'poor Jos: Simpson is dead at last' 207.1.

Simpson, Mrs., of Oxford.—('55) 75.1.

Simpson, Mr., of Lincoln, an acquaintance of the Langtons (*L*).—('66) 182.

Sinclair, John, '54–1835, M.P. for Caithness '80; 1st Bt '86 (*DNB, L*).—('82) introduced by JB to J 756.

Skrymsher: see Scrimshaw.

Smalbroke (Smalbrook), Richard, '16 (?)–1805, s. of Richard S, Bp of Lichfield;

D.C.L. Oxon. '45; of Doctors' Commons (*L*, R vi. 116).—('63) J advises JT to consult S 159.

SMART, Anna Maria *née* Carnan, '32–1809, wife of the poet (*L*).—(n.y.) J's letter 1154.

Smelt, Leonard, '19 (?)–1800, deputy-governor to the Prince of Wales and D of York '71–'81 (*DNB, L,* FB's *Diary*).—('80) J meets S at Ramsay's 663.

Smith, Henry, '56 (?) – '89, HT's first cousin and one of his executors (*L, Tb*).—('80) 707.1 (doubtful identification); ('81) 'Smith (suppressed in 1788, but the initial S is legible in original) appears a very modest inoffensive man' 727.

SMITH, JOSEPH, ironmonger, of Bishop's Stortford, Herts. (R ii. 23).—('70) The 'Mr. Smith', to whom J sends his compliments, writing to Frank at Bishop's Stortford, 238, 241, is doubtless the Joseph S of that place whom ('71) he asks to pay Mrs. Clap (q.v.) what he owes her 269.1, and see 242.

Smith, Lady: Catherine, '38–'86, y. d. of Rev. William Vyse, q.v.; m. '68 Sir George S, 1st Bt of Stoke, Notts. (who d. '69); of the Close, L'd (R v. 211).—('75) 'Lady Smith is settled at last here, and sees company at her new house' 405; 'Lady Smith has got a new postchaise' 408; 'Lady Smith took her tea before her Mother' 409; ('79) J finds 'Lady Smith and Miss Vyse' (her s.) at LP's 616.

Smith, Mrs.: not identified; perhaps the Mrs. Ralph S of *Tb* 299.—('74) 'I hope to be your (HLT) slave in the morning, and Mrs. Smith's in the Evening' 350.

Smith, Richard, General, M.P. for Wendover.—('82) 'General Smith . . . understood . . . that it was not the sense of the House that that Judge [Chambers] should be recalled.' *Parl. Register* vii, debate of 27 June. 793.1.

'Smith, S', to whom Cave is asked to address a reply to J's letter 3.

Smollett, James, — –'75, a Commissary of Edinburgh; of Cameron, Loch Lomond, '63; m. Jean Clerk of Pennicuik (*L* v. 564).—('73) 'Mr. Smollet's, a relation of Dr. Smollet' 336; ('75) 'Mr. Smollet of Loch Lomond and his Lady have been here' (O'd) 399.

Solander, Daniel Charles, '36–'82, Swedish botanist; came to England '60; official in British Museum '63; F.R.S. '64, D.C.L. Oxon. '71 (*DNB, L*).—('72) J thanks Banks and S for the pleasure of their conversation 272.

Somerset, James, negro (*see also* Knight, Joseph) (*L*).—('76) Mansfield's decision 'that a negro cannot be taken out of the kingdom without his own consent' 493.

Southwell, Edward, Baretti's pupil (*L*). There is no reason to connect him with Lord S's family; he cannot be the 1st Vt's e. b., who predeceased his father, for his name was Thomas (*GEC* vii. 210 note). Dr. Powell suggests Edward S, '38–'77, Baron Clifford '76 (*GEC* 1913, iii. 298).—('61) With Baretti in Venice 138.

SOUTHWELL: Thomas S, 1698–'66, 2nd Baron S; m. '19 Mary Coke (d. '66); father of Mauritius Lowe; succeeded by his 2nd but e. surviving s. Thomas George, '21–29 Aug. '80, 3rd Baron and 1st Vt '66, m. '41 MARGARET HAMILTON, '22–1802. The Misses S, Lucy and Frances, were presumably sisters of the first Vt, 'Mr. Southwell' perhaps their brother (*L*).—('73) J meets Lucy S 'at Mr Southwell's'; 'Miss Frances is not well' 294; ('75) J dines with 'Mrs Southwells' 390 (see note for an attempt to explain the phrase); ('80) J dines with 'Mrs. Southwell' 664, 665; J's letter to Lady S on behalf of Lowe 705.

Spence, Joseph, 1699–'68, Professor of Poetry at O'd '28–'38; compiler of the *Anecdotes* published 1820 but used by J and others in MS.; 'a weak, conceited man' (*DNB, L, Tb*).—('80) J used S's *Anecdotes* 654, 668.

Spencer: *see* Bingham.

Spicer, John, *c.* '14– —, of Christ Church (R v. 28).—('35) J's books in S's hands 3.1.

Stanhope, James, 1673–'21, 1st E S '18;

soldier and statesman (*DNB*).—('43) 18.

STAUNTON, GEORGE LEONARD, '37–1801, M.D. Montpellier '58; medical writer and diplomatist; 1st Bt '85 (*DNB, L*).—('62) J answers his letter written on departure for the W. Indies, and exhorts him to study 'natural curiosities' 140.

STEEVENS, GEORGE, '36–1800, of King's Coll., Cambridge; of the Temple, later at Upper Flask, Hampstead; member of the Club Feb. '74, of the Essex-Head Club '83 (*DNB, L*). —('65) J to meet Tonson 'at Mr. Steevens's' 176.1; ('70) J asks Farmer to help S in an account of translations used by Shakespeare 227; S 'helps me in this edition' 230; S 'treated with you (Rivington) about the new impression' 243; ('71) J asks Farmer to return S's 'catalogue' (see 227); his diligence in collecting authorities 244; ('73) S shows mercy to Jennens 304; ('74) J asks S to lend books on Scotland 345; J offers to nominate S for the Club, reports him elected 346, 347, 348; ('76) S on Chatterton 479; ('77) J reports Mrs. Goldsmith's letter 508; ('81) J sends S his *Lives* 731; ('82) S visits J 758; ('83) S on the value of Croft's books 839; S fails to 'hunt out' the author of a parody of J 863; (n.d.) mentioned 1111.

Stevenson, —, of Abingdon Grammar School.—('63) mentioned 160.

Stewart or Stuart, Francis, s. of an Edinburgh bookseller; one of J's amanuenses; his sister 'Mrs.' S (*L* i. 536).—('51) Strahan's message to J 'by Mr. Stuart' 35; (? '52) 'since poor Stuart's time' 39; ('80) 'Your (JB) transaction with Mrs. Stewart gave me great satisfaction . . . her brother . . . was an ingenious and worthy man' 655; ('84) J asks JB to recover from 'Mrs. Stewart' 'a letter relating to me' 936, 942.

Steyning 707.1 (possibly a place).

Stockdale, Percival, '36–1811, writer; in holy orders '59 (*DNB, L*).—('76) J recommends (? to Cadell) S's projected history of Spain 497.1; (? '78) recommends S to Burke 598.1; ('80) J

recommends S to Lowth for ordination 686.1; 'Something was to be done by the Bishop of London which has been refused' 687.

Stockton, —. ('46) 'Mr. Stockton who writes for me' 23.3.

Stormont: David Murray, '27–'96, Vt S '48; 2nd E of Mansfield '93, Ambassador in Paris '72–'78 (*DNB, L*).—436 (see note).

STRAHAN, GEORGE, '44–1824, 2nd s. of William S (q.v.); of Abingdon Grammar School; M.A. University Coll. '71, Fellow '67; Vicar of St. Mary's Islington '73; m. '78 Margaret Robertson (*DNB, L*).—('62) J recommends S to Henry Bright (q.v.) as a pupil 144.1; ('63) J's advice on S's studies at school 148, 149, 151, 160, on his views of friendship 155; ('64) J reports to WS that GS is entered at Univ. Coll. and will be elected a scholar 167; ('65) 'if you be diligent you will be a scholar' 170; ('70) mentioned 226; ('73) tutor to Macleod of Skye 329 (365); ('78) his marriage 592; ('79) J dines with S and 'his new wife' 608; ('82–'83) J attempts to reconcile S to his father 800, 809, 824, 825; cost of his cloaths 817; ('84) J's health 1023.

STRAHAN, WILLIAM, '15–'85, printer and publisher; partner of Millar and of Cadell; of New Street, Fetter Lane; M.P. for Malmesbury '74, for Wootton Bassett '80; m. '38 MARGARET PENELOPE ELPHINSTON, d. of William E; his sons William, '40–'81; GEORGE, q.v.; Andrew, '50–1831, his father's successor; his granddaughter — Johnson (*DNB, L*).—('50) Elphinston's letters to Mrs. S 30; ('51) J's ultimatum to S about the Dictionary 35; (?) J promises a sheet a day 37; 'the point is to get two Guineas' 38; difficulties of preparing copy 39; (? '52) Mrs. S mentioned 44; (? '53) J explains Bathurst's scheme 47; (? '54) J asks S to supply AW with money 52; ('56) J mentions S as his regular paymaster 94; ('58) S mentioned 112.1; ('59) J writes about terms for *Rasselas* 124; ('64) J tells S about GS's expenses at O'd 167; ('69) S's efforts in securing a benefit for AW 212; ('72) J asks S to advance money 278.1; ('74) J on the question of Copyright 349; J sends Levet 'a bill upon Mr. Strahan' 359; S as publisher of the *Journey* 363; J asks S to cancel a leaf 364; S 'does not publish till after the Holidays' 365.2; J asks him to take Davenport as apprentice 368; ('75) S will send JB copies of *Journey* 380; 'alterations proposed' in *Taxation No Tyranny* 381, 382; S to send copies 384; 'the greatest printing house in London' 387; ('76) S inexorable against Calder 456; J sends 'some copy' (? for Shaw's Proposals, see 510); offers help with Watson's *Philip II* 499; J's approbation of Blair's Sermons 505.1; J's letter of reconciliation 579; J asks S for £100 for a friend 589.2; WS and GS choose the same wife for GS 592; ('79) J dines with S 632; S's charity to J's 'poor neighbours' 640; J dines with S 641; ('80) Mrs. S ill at Bath 654, J asks HLT to 'be civil to her' 666; S insulted by the Gordon rioters 677; J asks HLT to 'take a little notice of' S's grand-daughter at B'n 686; S 'got a garrison into his house' 701; J asks S if a seat can be found for HT 706; asks him for payment for *Lives* 713; ('81) J condoles with Mrs. S on 'the death of an amiable son' (William) 728, her letter to AW 759; ('82) S mentioned 786; J writes to GS (q.v.) about the quarrel 800, 809; S franks letters 810; J reports on his health, sends a message to 'dear Mrs. Strahan' 811.2, 814; expenses of GS and his wife 817; ('83) J to GS about the quarrel 824, 825; Mrs. S mentioned 867; S's frank 876.1, 877, 879; ('84) S resigns from the Essex-Head Club 972.2; Heely told to apply for money to 'Mr. Strahan, or in his absence Mr. Andrew Strahan' 988; J hopes 'we shall all have a little more enjoyment of each other' 992.1; J's letter about the Polyglot Bible, and returning thanks for a 'generous offer' 1006.1 (ascription conjectural, see note); J asks S for £20 1016.1; (29 Nov.) 'I am very weak', asks about

his pension 1039.1; (7 Dec.) 'I was not sure that I read your figures right' 1042.1; (10 Dec., the last extant letter) J by an amanuensis asks for as much of his pension as 'you can spare with prudence and propriety' 1042.2; (n.y.) J to Mrs. S putting off a meeting 1043a.

Stratico, Simone, '33–1824, Professor at Padua (*L*).—('62) J meets him 142.

Streatfeild (Stratfield), Anne, '32–1812, widow '62 of Henry S of Chiddingstone, Kent; lived with her d. Sophia, '54–1835, at Mt. Ephraim, Tunbridge Wells (*Th*, FB's *Diary*).—('78) 'You (HLT) may set the Streatfields at defiance'; Sophia's book 'too fine for a scholar's talons' 583; 'if Streatfield has a little kindness for me, I am glad' 585; 'Miss Burney is just gone from me, I told her how you took to them all, but told her likewise how you took to Miss —' (so 1788; erased in original, but initial S legible; 'Streatfield' HLP) 586; ('79) 'I find that Dr. Vyse talks here (L'd) of Miss Stratfield' 616.

Strickland, Cecilia, '41–1814, widow '70 of Charles S of Sizergh Castle, Westmorland (*L*, *Th*).—('76) Mrs. S at Paris 483.

Stuart, James, '00–'89, minister of Killin, Perthshire; translator of the New Testament into Erse (*L*).— ('66– '67) 184, 189, 193.

Sunderland: Charles Spencer, 1674–'22, 3rd E of S '02; statesman (*DNB*).— ('43) 18 (the context suggests that the third Earl not the second is meant).

Sutton, —, a physician.—('67) 189.1.

Swinburne, Henry, '43–1803, 'the Spanish traveller' (*DNB*).—('79) 'he did not speak or I did not hear him' 645.1.

Swinfen or Swynfen, Samuel, 1679–'36, of L'd and B'm, physician; J's godfather (*DNB*, *L*, R iii).—('80) 'Mrs. Desmoulins, a daughter of the late Dr. Swinfen' 711.

Swinton, John, '03–'77, M.A. Wadham Coll. '26; Keeper of the Archives at Oxford '67 (*DNB*, *L*).—('84) 'the late learned Mr. Swinton of Oxford' 1042 (the authors named in the enclosure are not indexed).

Swynfen, —, and his wife 86 (to Paul; the connexion if any with Swinfen has not been made out).

Talbot, Thomas, ——'88, of Exeter Coll.; B.A. '32, D.D. Cambridge '64.—('75) 395 (see note); ('84) 'Dr. Talbot's book' 923.1.

Tamerlane 585.1.

TAYLOR, JOHN, '11–'88, of Lichfield Grammar School and Christ Church; M.A. '42, LL.D. '52; Rector of Market Bosworth, Leicestershire '40, Prebendary of Westminster '46; R of St. Margaret's Westminster '84; of The Mansion, Ashbourne, Derbyshire; m. (2) Mary Tuckfield of Fulford, Devon (*DNB*, *L*, R, *Life* by Thomas Taylor 1910). Since J and T, whose 'talk was of bullocks', had little in common, the burden of these letters is T's health and his own. These topics are hardly touched in this article; much that J writes of his health will be found in other indexes, s.v. For T's friends and enemies in the Midlands *see* Barker, Butter, Cavendish, Collier, Davenport, Flint, Gell, Hodgson, Langdon, Langley, Mouseley, Rudd, Scarsdale, Tuckfield, Wood, Woodcock; for his colleagues at Westminster and other clerical acquaintances Ballard, Bell, Thomas, Wilson—('32) J asks T for his interest at A'n 2; ('35) J's books 'were left with Mr Taylor, from whom I had reason to expect a regard to my Affairs' 3.1; ('42) J's wife's health 14.1; T's 'treaty' with Seward, his hopes from the Duke of Devonshire; J urges him to buy 'Thurloe's papers' 17; ('52) J's lost letter on his wife's death 41; 'let me have your Company and your Instruction'; Mrs. T to advise about mourning 42; ('53 or '55) 'one never sees you' 68; ('56) T's quarrel with Mouseley 98, 106; his estrangement from his sister; hopes to see T 'at least once a week' when in London 106 (endorsed by T 'the best Letter in the World'); ('63) T's matrimonial troubles; J's letters of advice: 'contribute nothing to the publication of your own misfortune' 156; 'do not nurse vexation in solitude' 157; leave

Ashbourne 158; take legal advice 159, 161; ('64) 'the happy end of so vexatious an affair'; T's house at Westminster 165; ('65) T's 'building and feasting'; J threatens a visit 171; let us 'spend a little of our short life together' 175; ('69) complains of T's silence 223; ('70) T's invitation 229, his illness 230.1, 231, his delay 'to come or send' (to L'd for J) 233, his 'very pleasant house' 236; ('71) 'every thing is done here to please me' 257; a man who said 'he had seen a bigger' bull 258; T's deer 259; his health 260, 264; 'weary of my stay, and grieved at my departure' 266; ('72) J to dine with T 275; their failure to write 275.1; T's ill health and gloom 277; J hopes 'you will fetch me' from L'd 278, 278.2, 279.1; 'I know not how to get away' 285.1, 291.1; ('73) failure to write 296; 'we... should care a little for one another' 303.1; 'do not lye down and suffer without struggle' 312; 'your solicitude for me' 316; ('74) T 'informed that I was in the Sky' 342; T's political 'advertisements' 360.1; 'in many respects we bear time better than most of our friends' 369; ('75) J asks how he shall send T his *Journey* 372; T's trouble with 'that wild woman' 378.1; J will send *Taxation No Tyranny* 384.4; J offers a visit 387; T's wish 'to buy a Governours staff' 387.2; J's visit 398.1; T 'wants to be gardening' 417; 'my company would not any longer make the Doctor happy' 424, 425; 'our Friendship... is valuable for its antiquity' 440; ('75–6) T's 'cause' 446.1, 449; J perplexed by 'the case which you sent me' 455; J advises T to come to L'n for consultation 461; J and JB at L'd, waiting for T to fetch them 464; they regret they were 'summoned away so soon' 469; T to consult the Attorney-General 473; an untraced letter 475.1; J dines with T 476; T's 'business' keeps J in town 477, 478; 'Livings and preferments... run in his head' 479; 'D Taylor's business stagnates' 482; he is 'resolved not to stay much longer...'; he is hurt only in his vanity' 483; 'M

Thrale would gladly have seen you at his house' **492**; ('77) AW's thanks to T for a turkey and hare; J hopes to see T in L'n in February **506.2**; J offers a visit **516**; J asks T to get HLT a ticket for Devonshire House **518, 519**; J tells JB 'I purpose to make Dr Taylor invite you' **528**; 'Dr Taylor will probably take me away' **538**; 'Dr Taylor says you (JB) shall be welcome' **540**; T's garden, his musical instruments, his sale of cattle, his hopes of his lawsuit **541.1**; JB 'very brisk and lively, and laughs a little at' (a blank 1788, original not seen; HLP fills the blank with Taylor's name) **547**; 'Dr Taylor has another Buck' **548**; 'he is in his usual way very busy,—getting a Bull to his cows' **553**; ('79) 'what have two sick old Friends to say to one another?' **614.1**; T at L'd **616**; in L'n **616.1**; T 'one of the people that are growing old' **617**; wants a curate for Market Bosworth **618.1**; has a stroke of paralysis **620**; 'well enough content to see me go' **623.1**; 'let us do our duty, and be cheerful' **627**; 'you have enough, if you are satisfied' **635**; ('80) 'keep yourself totally quiet' **660**; J sends T's letter to HLT **660.1**; T coming to L'n to 'drive his lawsuit forward' **669**; 'nothing in all life can now be more *profligater* than what he is' (and more in T's manner) **672**; T 'is gone away brisk and jolly' **684**; his 'claim upon the Abby' **675**; 'bustle about your hay and your cattle' **676**; T 'has written to me without a syllable of his lawsuit' **691**; ('81) 'Write to me immediately. Neither you nor I can now afford to lose time' **729.1**; T's hopes from the Cavendishes **739.1**; T 'not wholly without hope of Lincoln' **747**; his 'resolute adherence to bread and milk' and hopes of the deanery **749**; ('82) J to see T in L'n **766.1**; their scruples about a silver coffee-pot **767.1, 773, 793**; the question of the Collier girls and Flint **791.1, 793, 795, 797, 806, 807, 815.1, 816, 821**; T's hopes of an 'exchange' from the Cavendish interest **795, 797**; J warns T against 'useless and unnecessary vexation' **798, 799**;

'join your prayers with mine, that the next (year) may be more happy' **821**; ('83) the Collier–Flint question **823**; T's political 'friends' **827**; J's paralytic stroke; begs T to come to him **848, 850**; 'the time will come when one of us shall lose the other' **871**; J did not understand that T expected him at A'n **879**; J's sarcocele **885, 893**; 'the Doctor and Mr Metcalf have taken me out' **895**; T's complaint of J's letter **898.1**; 'you desire me to write often' **904**; 'poor Dr. Taylor' **906**; 'let us do what we can to comfort one another' **907**; 'make your mind easy, and trust God' **913**; 'we are almost left alone' **918**; ('84) 'write soon, and often' **923**; 'one of my amusements is to write letters' **928**; all the friends of J's youth dead except T and Hector **951**; J dines with T **960**; 'let nothing vex you' **965.4**; J advises moderation in bleeding **967**; Hawkins reports that T 'preached with great vigour' **968**; T will fetch J from L'd **972.1**; T's half-built house; 'we seem formed for different elements' **981**; 'Dr Taylor is at his farm, and I sit at home' **991.1**; 'you would surely have written' **1027.1**; 'you . . . charge me with neglecting . . . my own health' **1028** (endorsed by T 'last letter'); (n.d.) **1155, 1156.**

Taylor, John, '11–'75, inventor of Birmingham (*L* i. 86).—('65) 'my old friend' 179.

Thomas, John, '12–'93, Dean of Westminster '68, Bp of Rochester '74 (*DNB*).—('84) 'your (JT) Dean' 923.

Thomas, Rev. Dr., a schoolmaster at Streatham (C 97, 100).—('73) 'I am glad Dr. — (so 1788, original not legible) goes with them' (Rice and Fanny Plumbe, q.v.) 311.

Thomas, —, bookseller at Brighthelmstone (FB's *Diary*).—('79) 633, 636.

THRALES (*DNB, L, Th,* C; unpublished letters and other documents, esp. HLT's 'Children's Book', quoted by C and by K. C. Balderston in her edition of *Th*). For the Thrales' kinsfolk see the references below; for their acquaintance *see* Index I FRIENDS

§ ix. A full index to J's letters to the Thrales would contain at least 500 entries. Assuming that any intensive student of their relation will read all letters to or from any Thrale, I have indexed these letters lightly. References to them in letters to other correspondents I have indexed more fully.

Thrale, Ralph, the elder, 1698 (?)– '58, brewer; M.P. '41; His children: Henry, q.v.; Anne, m. '58 Arnold Nesbitt, q.v.; Mary, m. '55 Sir John Lade, q.v.; Frances, — –1811, m. Samuel Plumbe, q.v.

THRALE, HENRY, (prob.) '28 or '29–4 Apr. '81; m. 11 Oct. '63 Hester Lynch Salusbury; brewer; M.P. for Southwark 23 Dec. '65 – Mar. '68, 23 Mar. '68–Sept. '74, 18 Oct. '74– 1 Sept. '80; of Southwark, and Streatham, Surrey, and (from '67) West St., Brighthelmstone. His widow lived in Harley St. in the early part of '82, at 37 Argyle St. winter of '82–'83. He is addressed as 'Dear (My dear) Sir'. He is named to outsiders as 'Mr. Thrale', occasionally (628, 660, 723, 770) as 'Thrale'; to his wife as 'Mr. Thrale', in less serious contexts as '(my) Master'; to his children as 'Mr. Thrale', 'Master', or 'papa'. It should be noted that most of J's letters to HLT were directed to HT (who as M.P. received them free) and were often read, and meant to be read, by him; see iii. 297.

The Thrale Children: HESTER MARIA, '64, q.v.; Frances, 27 Sept.– 7 Oct. '65; Henry, '67, q.v.; Anna Maria, '68, q.v.; Lucy Elizabeth, '69, q.v.; SUSANNAH ARABELLA, '70, q.v.; SOPHIA, '71, q.v.; Penelope, b. and d. 15 Sept. '72; Ralph, '73, q.v.; Frances Ann, '75, q.v.; Cecilia Margaretta, '77, q.v.; Henrietta Sophia, 'Harriet', '78, q.v.

The Correspondence. Letters not to HLT are distinguished by initials, letters to J by italic and *a*, &c.

'65: 172, 173 (lost); '67: 189.1, 190, 191, 192.1; '68: 194.1, 195, 197, 199, 201, 203, 204, 205, 208, 210, 211.1; '69: 214, 216, 217, 218 HT, 219, 220; '70: 226.1, 227.2, *229a*, 232, 233, 234, *234a*, 235, 236, 237, 237.1, 240 (? date); '71: 245 HT, 249, 251, 252, 253, *253a*, 254, 255, 256, 257, 258, 259, 260, *260a*, 262, 263, *263a*, 264, 264.3 HMT, *264.3a*, *3b*, 265 HT, 266, 267; '72: 278.3, 279, 280, 281, 282, 282.1 HMT, 283, *283a*, 284, *284a*, 285, 285.1, 286, 286.1, 287, *287a* HMT, 288, 288.1 HMT, *288.1a*, *1b*, 289, 289.2; '73: 293, 294, *294a*, 300, *300a*, *b*, *c*, 301, 301.1, .2, .3, 302, 302.1, *302.1a*, 303, 303.2, 304, *304a*, *b*, 304.1, *304.1a*, *b*, *c*, *d*, 306, *306a*, 306.1, 306.2, *307a*, *b*, 307.1, 308, *308a*, 309, 310, 311, *311a*, *b*, 311.1, 311.2, *311.1a*, *b*, *313a*, 318, 320, 321, 322, 323, 324, 326, 327, 329, 330 HT, 331, 332, 333 HT, 334 HT, 336, *336a*, 337, 338, 339; '74: 350, *360a*, 365.2, 369.2, *369.2a*; '75: 370 HT, 376, *376a*, 376.2, 379 HT, *379a*, 383, 384.1, *384.1a*, *b*, 384.2, 386, *386a*, 386.1, 389.1 HT, 389.2, 390, 393, *393a*, 395, 396, 397, 397.1, 399, 400, 401, 402, 403, *403a*, 404, 405, 406, *406a*, 407, 408, 408.1, 409, 410, 411, *411a*, 413, *413a*, 414, 415, *415a*, 416, *416a*, 417, *417a*, 418, 419, *419a*, 420, 421, *421a*, 422, *422a*, 423, 424, 425, 426, 427, 428, 429, 432; '76: 463.1, 464.1, 465, 466, 467, *467a*, 468, 470, *470a*, 476, *476a*, 477, 478, 479, 482, *482a*, 483, 483.1, *484a*, 485 HT, 486, 487, 488, *488a*, *b*, 489, *489a*, *493a*; '77: 505.3, *505.3a*, 506, 351, *506a*, *506.2a*, 512, *512a*, 513 HT, 518, *519a*, 519.1, 519.2, 532 HT, *532a*, 533, 535, 536, 537, *537a*, 538, 539, *539a* HMT, *539b*, 541.1 HMT, 542, *542a*, 543, 545, 547, *547a*, 548, *548a*, 549, *549a*, 550, 551, *551a*, 552, 553, *553a*, *b*, 554, *554a*, 555, 556, *556a*, *b*, 557, 558, 559, 560, 561, 561.1, *561a*, 562; '78: *572a*, *b*, 575a, 576, 577a, 583, 583a, 584a, 585, 585.1 HMT, *585.1a*, 586, 589.1a, 590, 591, 592, *592a*; '79: 606, *606a*, 608, *608a*, 608.1, 615, *615a*, 616, 616.1, 617, 618, 619 HT, 620, *620a*, 621, 622 HT, 623, *623a*, 623.1, *623.1a*, *627a*, 629, 630, 631, 632, 633, 636, 637, 640, 641, 642, 644, 645, 645.1 HMT, 647, 648, 649.1, 649.2 HMT, 649.3 HMT; '80

will with J and Scrase 640; 'he is columen domus' 642; ('80) 'poor Mr. Thrale . . . recovered, beyond the expectation of his physicians' 655; 'I believe, under the protection of a glass of water drank at the pump, he may venture once a week upon a stew'd lamprey' 658; 'Mr. Thrale never will live abstinently, till he can persuade himself to abstain by rule' 663; 'Mr. Thrale certainly shall not come' (to S'k to face the electors) 665; 'to sit in Parliament for Southwark is the highest honour that his (HT) station permits him to attain' 672; 'you always used to tell me, that We could never eat too little . . . your position is verified' 674; 'his illwillers are very unwilling to think that he can ever sit more in parliament' 684; Lawrence quoted: 'he who in that case should once eat too much, might eat no more' 690; 'did Master read my Books?' (the Lives) 691; 'Mr. Thrale . . . has withdrawn himself from business' 700; 'having lost our election at Southwark we are looking for a Borough less uncertain'; HT wants a seat that can be 'had without natural interest' 706; (? Sept. '80) a letter to Lord North written for Thrale, who asks for a 'recommendation to some Borough' and an interview 706.1; ('81) (4 Apr.) J knows that members of the Club 'will excuse his incompliance with the Call, when they are told that Mr. Thrale died this morning' 716; their happiness in marriage (see s.v. HLT); the will 717; 'I have lost a friend of boundless kindness' 718; (11 Apr.) 'I had interwoven myself with my dear friend' 721; ('82) 'Thrale, a man whose eye for fifteen years had scarcely been turned upon me but with respect or tenderness'; 'I passed the summer at Streatham, but there was no Thrale' 770; ('83) 'One great abatement of all miseries was the attention of Mr. Thrale' 835.1 (17); HLT not to 'sit forming comparisons between Sophy and her poor father' 910.

SALUSBURY, HESTER MARIA (Cotton), HLT's mother, c. '09–

18 June '73; of Dean St. and, from '72, at S'k or S'm (Th.).—('67) (14 Feb.) J asks her for news of HLT 188; ('68) 'I hope that Mrs. Salusbury will favour me now and then with an account of you' (HLT) 199; 'I cannot but think the life of Mrs. Salusbury some addition to the happiness of all that know her' 210; ('69) 'Tell Mrs. Salusbury that I beg her to stay at Streatham, for little Lucy's sake' 220; ('70) her house robbed 234; ('71) offers to 'attend her, if she will accept of my company' on a journey (to Malvern?) 249; (to Q) 'tell dear Grandmama that I am very sorry for her pain' 264.3; ('72) her present to J of a chair 278.3; (Oct. '72–May '73): her illness and death, passim in letters to HLT and Q; ('75) J's epitaph 403.

THRALE, HESTER LYNCH, 7 Jan. '41–22 May 1821, only child of John Salusbury, '07–'62, of Bachygraig, Flintshire, who m. '39 Hester Maria Cotton, sister of Sir Robert Cotton of Lleweney, Denbighshire; see above, Mrs. Salusbury. HLT m. (1) 11 Oct. '63 Henry Thrale; (2) 23 July '84 in London by a Roman Catholic chaplain, 25 July at St. James's, Bath, Gabriel Piozzi, q.v. For J's multifarious forms of address to HLT see the letters, or R. W. C. in Essays on the Eighteenth Century, Oxford 1945; she is named to outsiders as 'Mrs. Thrale', once (? only, see 978) as 'Thrale'; in the family as 'Mrs. Thrale', '(my) Mistress', or (to the children) 'Mama'. For her kinsfolk see Mrs. Salusbury in this article, and Cotton, Lynch, Salusbury.—('65) (13 Aug.) Work prevents J's going to B'n with HT; he hopes to follow them there 172; his lost letter (to HT or HLT) from there, 'disappointed and enraged' (HLP) to find them gone 173; ('67) his longing to 'repose' at 'home' 190; 'I shall see Streatham with great delight' 192.1; ('68) birth of 'little Miss Nanny' 203; 'gratitude and respect' 208; ('69) J to stand godfather 218; ('70) 'though you do not know it, three groats make a shilling' 232; 'if you were lost, hope would be lost with you' 236; ('71) 'the little Stranger safe in the cradle'? 253; 'once more I sit down to write, and hope you will once more be willing to read' 256 (year doubtful); 'indifference is indeed a strange word in a Letter from me to you' 257; 'the Queen and Mrs. Thrale, both ladies of experience, yet both missed their reckoning this summer' 268; sends Beattie 'an invitation from a very valuable family' 268.1; ('72) 'Mrs. Thrale loves you' (JB) 274; 'the Brewhouse must be the scene of action' 280; they write with nothing to say 283; 'in great matters you are hardly ever mistaken' 284; 'I entreat I may not be flattered' 287; ('73) JB stands 'very high in the favour of Mrs. Thrale' 295; (9 Mar.) 'my heart is with you in your whole System of Life' 300; 'you have made this year a great progress in reformation' 303.2; (? May) an enigmatic letter in French, see note, 307.1; 'never imagine that your letters are long'; always reads them twice 308; 'still Flatter flatter?' 310; 'why should you vitiate my mind with a false opinion of its own merit?' 311; 'I long to be in my own room. Have you got (? yet) your key?' 311.1; 'I hope my mistress keeps all my very long letters' 330; ('74) J takes her to Amwell 355.1, 355.2; going to Wales with the Thrales 'to take possession' of her new estate 358; 'a fall from her horse . . . but she has not miscarried' 360.1; sends her an early copy of the *Journey* 365.2; tells her the secret of the King and Queen and the *Journey* 369.2; ('75) 'my wicked mistress' 370; his Oxford diploma, containing praises 'very like your praises' 386; in French: 'point de nouvelles' 400; 'you connect us, and rule us, and vex us, and please us' 401; 'you left a good impression behind you' at L'd; 'you never told me . . . how you were entertained by Boswell's Journal' 405; 'Do you read Boswell's Journals?' 408; (n.d.; ? part of 414) 'your dissertation upon Queeney is very deep' 408.1; 'I am

glad that you are to be at the regatta. You know how little I love to have you left out of any shining part of life' 409; 'I love the Thrales and the Thralites' 410; 'talk not of the Punick war . . . but talk, and talk, and talk of the regatta' 414; 'I am glad you have read Boswel's Journal' 415; Ralph's death: 'think now only on those which are left you'; 'be copious and distinct, and tell me a great deal of your mind; a dear little mind it is' 422; 'do you keep my letters?' why 'not desirous hereafter to read the history of your own mind?' 428 ;'Mrs. Thrale was so entertained with your (JB) *Journal*, that she almost read herself blind' 431; ('76) Harry Thrale's death; J's condolence 465, 466; the abandoned Italian tour 467; 'Mr. Thrale's behaviour has united you to him by additional endearments' 468; 'I am sorry not to owe so much, but to repay so little' 470; 'I think, his grief is deepest' 473; her 'great regard for Miss Reynolds' 490; ('77) her 'conquest of the Prince of Castiglione' 513; 'Mrs. Thrale has but four out of eleven' 515; 'such tattle as filled your last sweet Letter' 537; (23 Aug., L'd) 'I suppose you are pretty diligent at the Thraliana'; his advice about this collection 542; 'I do love to hear the sea roar (at B'n) and my Mistress talk'; 'I am to be very busy about my Lives. Could not you do some of them for me?' 554; 'you may well dance these dozen years, if you keep your looks as you have yet kept them' 556; 'how small a part of our minds have we written'; 'be pleased by pleasing' 558; (27 Oct., L'd) 'if our Correspondence were printed I am sure Posterity . . . would say that I am a good writer too'; 'I have indeed concealed nothing from you' 559; 'our letters will pass and repass like shuttlecocks' 561.1; 'every body was an enemy to that wig' 562; ('78) the bust of J 'condemned by Mrs. Thrale' 572; 'a letter which when you know the hand you will perhaps lay aside' till tomorrow 583; his picture by JR 'seems to please every body, but

I shall wait to see how it pleases You' 586; ('79) 'it is good to wander a little, lest one should dream that all the world was Streatham' 616; 'there is nobody left for me to care about but you and my Master'; 'keep yourself airy and be a *funny little thing*' (see note) 623; 'if such Letters as this were to cost you any thing, I should hardly write them' 644; HLT and Q negligent in dating letters 645.1; 'your despicable dread of living in the borough' 647; ('8o) 'my mistress . . . never thinks of poor Colin'; 'you do not date your letters' 657; (15 Apr.) 'the Wits court you, and the Methodists love you . . . and so, go thy ways, poor Jack' 658; she must show herself to the electors 665; HLT and Mrs. Montagu: 'I said you had most wit and most literature'; she must come to S'k 666; HLT 'has run about the Borough like a Tigress' 667.1; (23 May) 'now Montague is gone, you have the sole and undivided empire of Bath' 669; 'Congreve . . . is one of the best of the little lives; but then I had your conversation' 672; 'your letter of battle and conflagration . . . the commotions at Bath' (they had fled to B'n) 679; 'do not let separation make us forget one another' 684; 'Pray do you never add to the other vexations any diminution of your kindness' 687; Sulpitius 'above your reading' 692; 'you write of late very seldom' 699; ('81) (5 Apr.) Death of HT: her 'injunctions, to pray for you and write to you'; her 'happiness in marriage to a degree of which . . . I should have thought the description fabulous' 717; 'I hope to be always ready at your call'; he applauds her 'design to return so soon to your business and your duty'; shall he be at S'm to receive her? 719; 'when we meet, we may try what fidelity and tenderness will do for us' 722; 'If you apply to business perhaps half the mind which you have exercised upon knowledge and elegance, you will need little help' 725; J hopes she recovers her 'plumpness and complexion' 741; 'the dear home

which I have left' 746; when Piozzi comes, 'you will have two about you that love you' 750; 'do not neglect me, nor relinquish me' 753; ('82) 'do not add to my other distresses any diminution of kindness' 758; 'admiration of excellence and gratitude for kindness' 761; 'such letters would make any man well' 762; 'your kind attention is a great part of what life affords' 763; J during his illness 'lived much with Mrs. Thrale' 776; 'do not let Mr. Piozzi nor any body else put me quite out of your head' 778; J is going to O'd 'not to frisk as you express it with very unfeeling irony' 788; his letter (788) 'perhaps peevish, but not unkind' 790; 'on Thursday you . . . will fetch me . . . When I come back to retirement, it will be great charity in you to let me come back to something else' 792; 'it remains to dream if I can of Argyle Street' 817.2; ('83) Harriet's death: 'I loved her, for She was Thrale's and your's' 837; 'why do you write so seldom? . . . do not please yourself with showing me that you forget me' 845; (13 June) 'your last letter was very pleasing' 846; 'a narrative which would once have affected you . . ., but which you will perhaps pass over now with the careless glance of frigid indifference . . . let not all our endearment be forgotten . . . I am almost ashamed of this querulous letter' 850; 'your kind letter' . . . her offer to come to him 'charmingly kind' 854; 'think on me, as a man who . . . has done You all the good he could' 858; 'How lov'd how honour'd once avails thee not 876; 'consider ⟨me⟩ as one that has loved you much' 884.1; she should reform her 'instability of attention 894; 'that kindness which you could not throw away if you tried' 895; 'you have written to me with the attention and tenderness of ancient time'; 'let not your loss be added to the mournful catalogue' 900; 'such society I had with Levet and Williams, such I had where—I am never likely to have i more' 921; ('84) 'let your Children b

... your pleasure; close your thoughts upon them' 926; 'Shall we ever exchange confidence by the fireside again?' 938; 'your last letter had something of tenderness' 943; 'settle your thoughts and controul your imagination, and think no more of Hesperian felicity . . . your kind letter' 956; 'think on me, if You can, with tenderness' (some words suppressed) 963; 'I read your (Q) letter with anguish and astonishment, such as I never felt before. I had fondly flattered myself that time had produced better thoughts' 969.1; 'If I interpret your letter right, you are ignominiously married, if it is yet undone, let us once talk together . . . I who long thought you the first of human kind, entreat that . . . I may once more see you . . . I will come down if you permit it' 970; 'what I think of your (Q) mother's conduct I cannot express but by words which I cannot prevail upon myself to use' 970.1; 'I . . . breathe out one sigh more of tenderness . . . that kindness which soothed twenty years of a life radically wretched . . . the tears stand in my eyes' 972; to Hawkins: 'Poor Thrale! I thought that either her virtue or her vice would have restrained her from such a marriage' 978; 'I loved your (Q) Mother as long as I could' 988.1.

Letters not dated, or with no year, not conjecturally placed: (27 Mar.) 'you have now been at court' 1103; (n.d.) notes in French 1108, 1109.

THRALE, HESTER MARIA, 17 Sept. '64–1857; m. 1808 Admiral Viscount Keith. She is addressed by various terms of endearment, but also (and as early as '79) as 'Madam'. She is named as 'Miss Thrale', 'Miss', 'Hetty' (195, 556); most frequently as 'Queen(e)y'. J never uses her mother's nicknames for her, 'Tit' and 'Niggey'. —('68) 'Compliments to . . . Miss Hetty' 195; ('71) 'what is the matter that Queeny uses me no better?' 260; 'perhaps she designs that I should love Harry best' 263; J's first (extant) letter to his 'dearest Miss' 264.3; ('72) 'I

have got nothing yet for Queeny's Cabinet' 282; (2 Nov., A'n) 'your pretty letter was too short' 282.1; 'Queeny is a naughty Puss' 286.1; (28 Nov., A'n) 'Mamma . . . dos not know how much I should love to read your letters, if they were a little longer' 288.1; ('73) 'Miss will want him (Harry) for all her vapouring' 304; 'dear Queeney's day (birthday) is next' 326; thanks 'dear Queeney for her letter' and wishes he 'had been able to collect more for her Cabinet' 337, 338; ('74) 'your (JT) little Friend Miss is hard at her Italian' 360.1; ('75) 'Queeny perhaps is a little lovesick, you will see how she recovers when I come home' 384.2; are Baretti 'and Queeney plague and darling as they are used to be?' 401; 'Queeney revenges her long tasks upon Mr. Baretti's hen' 408; (n.d., part of 414?) 'your dissertation upon Queeney is very deep' 408.1; (Paris) 'the Queen was so impressed by Miss, that she sent one of the gentlemen to enquire who she was' 437; ('76) 'don't let me be defrauded of Queeney's letter' 482; JT's orphaned fawn; 'I wish Miss Thrale had it to nurse' 555; 'Miss may change her mind . . . I am glad that Hetty has no design to dance you down' 556; 'Miss has a mind to be womanly, and her womanhood does not sit well on her' 564; ('78) 'Return my thanks . . . to Queeney for her letter. I do not yet design to leave her for Susy . . . Queeny, whom you (HLT) watched while I held her, will soon think our care of her very superfluous' 592; ('79) 'Mrs. Kennedy, Queeny's Baucis' 618; 'I begin now to let loose my mind after Queeney and Burney' 621; 'the young ones (Q and FB) are very good in minding their book' 636; 'Queeney sent me a pretty letter, to which ⟨Burney⟩ added a silly short note' 642; 'glad that Queeny danced . . . the Sultaness of the evening' 647; 'tell my Queeney how I love her for her letters' 648; ('80) 'enjoy as much of the intellectual world as you can' 656.1; Lady Lucan 'hears Queeney is wonderfully accomplished' 666; 'if she does not write oftener, I will try to forget her. There are other pretty girls' 679; Miss Owen's 'very honourable account of' Q 686; 'Queeney and I . . . are none of the giddy gabblers, we think before we speak' 687; 'when we meet again, we will have . . . two lessons in a day' 690; 'what a hussey she is to write so seldom . . . let her write sentiment' 692; a letter of advice; 'I have been very grave, but you are a very thinking Lady'; 'now am I turning to the second leaf just as if I was writing to your Mamma' 703.1; ('81) 'the world is all before us' 727.2; 'if my dear little Perversity continues to be cross, Susy may be my Girl too, but I had rather have them both' 745; ('82) 'if I had Queeney here (O'd), how would I shew her all the places' 789; 'never omit those little ceremonial notices' 818.1; ('83) 'arithmetick' 836.1; 'crescent illae crescetis amores' 839.1; legibility 843.1; 'to the Girls . . . I earnestly recommend as their Guardian and Friend, that They remember their Creator in the days of their Youth' 850; 'snatch the broom from the maid' 869.1; asks her to read the story of the *Grosvenor* 893.1; ('84) 'Miss Thrale rather neglects me, suppose she should try to write me a little Latin letter' 941; 'I read your letter with anguish' 969.1; 'I sincerely pity you and . . . approve your conduct' 970.1; 'you will soon be mistress of yourself' 970.2; 'Obey God. Reverence Fame' 988.1; 'I hope I am sometimes remembered in your prayers' 1003.2.

Thrale, Henry, the younger, 15 Feb. '67–23 Apr. '76.—('71) 'Queeney . . . perhaps designs that I should love Harry best' 263; 'tell Harry that you (Q) have got my heart' 264.3; ('73) 'Harry will be happier now he goes to school and reads Milton' 304; 'Harry you know is so rational' 339; ('75) 'tell him that Mr. Murphy does not love him better than I do' 415; ('76) 'poor dear sweet little Boy . . . yet I could not love him as you loved him, nor reckon on him for a future comfort, as you and his Father reckoned upon him' 465; 'I loved him as I never expect to love any other little boy' 466.

Thrale, Anna Maria, 1 Apr. '68–20 Mar. '70.—('68) 'I design to love little Miss Nanny very well' 203.

Thrale, Lucy Elizabeth, 22 June '69 (Streatham Register; the family Bible, erroneously, July)–22 Nov. '73; J's god-daughter, named Elizabeth after his wife (J 'insisted on her being Elizabeth': 'Children's Book', C. 81).— ('69) 'very much honoured by the choice . . . of me to become related to the little Maiden . . . I will very punctually wait on her' 218; 'I took care to tell Miss Porter, that I have got another Lucy' 220; ('72) 'Doctor Taylor asked . . . on what I was thinking, and I was thinking on Lucy' 282; 'I suppose she is grown a pretty good scholar, and a very good playfellow' 288.1.

THRALE, SUSANNAH ARABELLA, 23 May '70–1858.—('75) 'if Susy had been at all disposed to the horrid malady' she would have had it earlier 419; J 'was always on her side' 422; ('77) 'I was always a Susey, when nobody else was a Susy' 554; ('80) Susy and Sophy 'make verses, and act plays' 690; ('81) 'Miss Seward . . . has heard much' of her; she 'may be my Girl too' 745; ('83) 'Susy is, I believe at a loss for matter' 863; fill 'your mind with genuine scenes of nature' 880; 'do you read the Tatlers?' 901; ('84) 'cultivate an acquaintance' with Herschel 944; 'I send my kindest respects to your (Q) sisters' 969.1.

THRALE, SOPHIA, 22 July '71–1824; m. 1807 Henry Merrick Hoare.—('76) 'I went this afternoon to visit the two Babies at Kensington'; 'Sophy sends her duty to you (HLT), and her love to Queeney and Papa' 477; ('79) 'take care that Susy sees all that Sophy has seen' 615; ('80) (1 Aug.) 'Susy and Sophy . . . make verses, and act plays' 690; ('83) (5 July) 'I shall be glad to see pretty Sophy's production' 863; 'why you should think yourself not a favourite, I cannot guess'; 'arithmetick' 870.

Thrale, Ralph, the younger, 8 Nov. '73–13 (?) July '75.—('75) 'Ralph like other young Gentlemen will travel for improvement' 393; (June–July) illness and death *passim*.

Thrale, Frances Ann, 4 May–9 Dec. '75.—('75) 'you never so much as told me the name of the little one' 413; 'the two small ladies' (Sophia and Frances) 419; 'of Mrs. Fanny I have no knowledge' 422 (doubtful).

Thrale, Cecilia Margaretta, 8 Feb. '77–1857; m. '95 John Meredith Mostyn.—('83) Cator's 'affectionate attention to Miss Cecy' 859; ('84) Cator's account of her 'such as you must delight to hear' 926.

Thrale, Henrietta Sophia, 21 June '78–18 Apr. '83.—('81) 'Miss Harriet's prediction, or second sight' 750, 752; ('83) 'you could not save the dear, pretty, little girl' 837.

THURLOW, EDWARD, '31–1806, Attorney-General '71, Lord Chancellor and 1st Baron T '78 (*DNB, L*).—('76) JT consults him 473, 475; ('81) T nominates Macbean to the Chartreux 720; ('84) JB's 'pious negociation' to enable J to go to Italy: 'I am very desirous to avoid the appearance of asking money upon false pretences' 971, 981; 'the Chancellor's liberality and your (JR) kind offices' 1007, J's letter of thanks to T sent through JR; 'I shall now live *mihi carior*' 1008; 'I was much pleased that you (JR) liked my letter' 1018.

Tigh 376.2 (see note).

Tolcher, Henry, Alderman of Plymouth (*L* i. 152).—('62) T 'a brisk young fellow of seventy-four' 146.

TOMKESON, —, of Southampton St.; possibly Charles or William Tomkins, both of whom exhibited pictures in the period; Southampton St. was in the artists' quarter.—('83) J recommends Mauritius Lowe to T **890**.

TONSON, JACOB, d. '67, bookseller (*DNB, L*).—('58) J asks T for a loan of £40 **112.1**; ('65) receipts for *Shakespeare* **176.1**; J complains that the book is being sold by booksellers below the subscription price **178.1**; 'the

receipts and second payment' to be sent to T **179**; ('66) J tells Garrick 'that there is an hundred pounds of yours in Mr. Tonson's hands' 186.

Tooke, William, '44–1820, Chaplain to the Factory at St. Petersburg '74–'92 (*DNB*).—('84) his information about a Russian translation of the *Rambler* 931 (see note).

Tuckfield, John or Henry, half-brother of John Taylor's wife.—('63) 156, 157.

Turton, Catherine, — –'77, of Lichfield (*L, R* v. 265).—('67) J sends 'compliments to Miss Turton' 194; ('71) 'Miss T— (so 1788, original not seen) wears spectacles' 252; ('75) 'grows old' 408; ('77) 'Miss Turton and Harry Jackson are dead' 537.

Turton, John, '35–1806, grandson of Gregory Hickman (q.v.); physician in London (*DNB, L, R* v. 66).—('80) 'Mrs. Desmoulins had a mind of Dr. Turton' 691, 692.

Twiss, Richard, '47–1821 (*DNB, L*).— *Travels through Portugal and Spain* 1775: ('75) T sends HLT a copy of the print from the book; J gives him letters of introduction to Ireland 390; Chandler's travels 'duller than Twiss's' 395; ('76) *A Tour in Ireland in 1775* 1776: T's letter to J and copy of this book 482.

Tyrwhitt (-it), Thomas, '30–'86; Fellow of Merton Coll. '55; F.R.S. '71; editor of Chatterton's 'Rowley' Poems '77, '78 (*DNB, L* iii. 478).—('76) 'Stevens seems to be connected with Tyrwhit in publishing Chatterton's poems; he . . . is not well pleased to find us so fully convinced' 479; 'Calcot . . . has written his recantation to Tyrwhitt, who . . . perhaps is not much pleased to find himself mistaken' 485.

Tyson, Master of the Ceremonies at Bath (FB's *Diary* June '80).—('80) 677.

Vaillant, Paul, '16–1802, bookseller of 87 Strand; 'my good friend' 99.1 (V was not a publisher of J's Shakespeare; he was no doubt J's correspondent's bookseller).

Vansittart, Robert, '28–'89, Fellow of All Souls Coll.; D.C.L. '57, Regius

Prof. of Civil Law '67 (*DNB*, *L*).—
('59) '— is now making tea for me'
('perhaps Vansittart' Hill, *L* i. 347)
132.1; ('73) 'poor Vansittart'; his virtues and parts 337 (386).

Vass, Lauchlan, one of J's Highland
guides (*L* v. 131).—323 (350).

Vernon: probably George Venables V,
'08–'80, of Sudbury, Derbyshire; 1st
Baron V '62 (R v. 81).—('32) 2.

Vesey, Elizabeth, '15 (?)–'91; m. before
'46 Agmondesham V (— –'85), M.P.
for Kinsale, Ireland, member '73 of
the Club; of Bolton Row and Clarges
St. (*DNB*, *L*, R. Blunt, *Mrs Montagu*
1923, ii. 59).— (? '77) 'at Mrs. Vesey's
last night', his prologue commended
519.1; ('79) 'came late to Mrs. Vesey'
608; 'invited twice to Mrs. Vesey's
Conversation, but have not gone' 632;
'invited by the Veseys . . . a large company . . . to dine and spend the evening. Too much at a time' 644; 'dined
at Mr. Vesey's with Lord Lucan and
Mr. Pepys' 645.1; ('80) 'at night go to
Mrs. Vesey' 654, 'we made a noise all
the evening' 657; 'Mrs. Vesey suspects
still that I do not love them since that
skrimage' 675; sent 'an excuse to
Vesey' 681.

Vespucci, 'Americo'.—929.1.

Victor of Sardinia 206 (217).

Villette, John, d. '99, Ordinary of Newgate (*L*).—('77) 'I have just seen the
Ordinary that attended him' (Dodd,
q.v.) 524.

Viri: presumably Comte de Viry, '37–
1810, Sardinian minister in London,
who '61 m. Gray's friend Henrietta
Speed (Gray's Letters ed. Toynbee–
Whibley 1935, ii. 770).—('54) Croker's
application to 'the Sardinian Envoy'
53.1 (i. 443); ('77) 'I hope Master will
soon put Viri's money into the Funds'
560.

Vise: *see* Vyse.

VYSE (Vise), William, '09–'70, of Stan-
don, Staffs.; of Pembroke Coll. '29;
Treasurer of Lichfield Cathedral '34;
m. '33 Catherine Smalbroke of L'd,
— –'92; his e. s. WILLIAM, '42–
1816, R of Lambeth '77, Chancellor
of L'd '98; his y. d. Catherine, Lady

Smith (q.v.) (*L*, R v. 210).—('68)
'Miss Vise' must not think J has forgotten her; he hopes 'Mr. Vise' is
better 209; ('76) 'Miss Vyse has been
ill' 408; ('77) J writes to William V
the younger about De Groot **527, 531,
531.1**; ('79) at LP's J finds 'Lady
Smith and Miss Vyse' 616; ('80) J
writes to William V the younger on
behalf of Mrs. Desmoulins, 'who was
well known to your father' **711**; ('81)
J sends him a letter introducing Macbean **720**; ('82) J sends 'Dr. Vyse's
letter' to Compton 808; suggests to C
that he dedicate his book 'to the Bishop
of London or to Dr. Vyse' 811.1; ('84)
'Dr. Vyse has been with me this evening'
957; J asks V about Scrimshaw **1039**.

Wade, —, presumably the man who
later was 'hooted out of Bath for
shewing a lady's love letters' (*Piozzi
Letters*, ii. 134, Hayward 1861[2], ii. 83).
—('79) 'I am glad that Queeny
danced with Mr. Wade' (at B'n) 647.

Walker, John, '32–1807, orthoepist; 'the
celebrated master of elocution' (*DNB*,
L iv, 519).—('82) W visits J 819.1.

Wall, John, '08–'76, Fellow of Merton
Coll. '35, M.D. '59, physician at Wor-
cester '36–'76 (*DNB*).—('71) W's view
of the efficacy of 'water' 249, 258.

Walmesley, Magdalen, '09–'86, 3rd d. of
Sir Thomas Aston (q.v.); widow '51 of
Gilbert W of Lichfield; of Bath, later
of L'd (*L*, R v. 251).—('77) 'Mrs.
Aston paralytick, Mrs. Walmsley lame,
Mrs. Hervey blind' 557; her invitation
to J to stay with her at Bath 560; ('80)
'she and her husband exhibited two
very different appearances of human
Nature' 659.

Walpole, Horatio, '17–'97, y. s. of Sir
Robert W (*DNB*, *L*; it is remarkable,
in view of the number of their common acquaintances, that—as HW
recorded—they never spoke).—('80)
the stolen MS. of W's tragedy 650.1.

Walpole, Sir Robert, 1676–'45 (*DNB*).—
496.

Warburton, William, 1698–'79; Bp of
Gloucester '59 (*DNB*, *L*).—('55) 'Mr.
Warburton's phrase' 58; his view of
Pope's collaborators in the Odyssey 668.

Ward, William, mercer in Birmingham (R v. 106).—('44) 20.

Warren, Thomas, — –'67, printer of Birmingham; publisher of J's *Lobo* (*L*, R v. 93).—('41) W's connexion with Paul's affair 13, 14; ('55) J reminds Hector of 'evenings . . . at Warren's and the Swan' 69; ('65) 'What is become of Mr. Warren?' 179.

Warren, —, a maid at Thrales'.—('70) one of 'my countrywomen' 235.

Warter, Thomas, matric. Oriel Coll. '46; M.A. Christ Church '52; seems not to have taken the B.D.—('63) 148.1.

WARTON, JOSEPH, '22–1800; of Oriel Coll., M.A. '59; D.D. '68; Second Master '55, Headmaster '66, of Winchester; member of the Club '77; m. (1) '48 — Daman (d. '72); (2) '73 — Nicholas (*DNB*, *L*).—('53) J invites W to contribute to *The Adventurer*; his *Virgil* (*The Works in Latin and English* 1753) 46; ('54) J congratulates W on the conclusion of *Adventurer*, asks about Collins 51; W's letter to J about Collins 56, 57; ('55) mentioned 58, 60; J hopes W will contribute to his Bibliotheque 65; mentioned 72; ('56) W's failure to visit J; 'I have lately seen an octavo book which I suspect to be yours' (*Essay on the Genius and Writings of Pope* 1756, anon.); 'your new situation. You have now a kind of royalty' 96; ('58) J wishes W would help him with Shakespeare 114; 'the two Wartons just looked into the town' 117; ('65) Mrs. W's 'kindness and civility . . . at Winchester'; W a subscriber to J's *Shakespeare* 176; ('70) W's 'opinion of Lear'; J hopes to visit Winchester 239; ('77) J dines with JR and W 505.3; J's efforts to get an old man into St. Cross; 'Dr. Warton has promised to favour him with his notice' 525; ('80) W tells J about 'Collins's first piece' 652; J thanks W for help in his *Lives*; hopes to revisit Winchester; 'the ladies of your house' 668; (n.d.) mentioned 1157.1.

WARTON, THOMAS, '28–'90, y. b. of Joseph W; of Trinity Coll., M.A. '50; Prof. of Poetry '57–'67; Laureate '85;

member of the Club '82 (*DNB*, *L*).—('54) J thanks W for his book (*Observations on the Faerie Queene of Spenser* 1754), praising it as a pioneer work; hopes to visit Oxford 'in about a fortnight' 53; J asks Chambers to inquire of W about Bodleian MSS. for Zon 54; J thanks W and Wise 'for the uncommon care which you have taken of my interest'; can he 'do anything to promoting the diploma' (of M.A.)? If the design succeeds, he will come to Oxford; 'hindrance in your Spenserian design' (the second edition published 1762) 55; the Dictionary is not quite printed, 'and I will keep back the title-page for such an insertion as you seem to promise me' (i.e. 'M.A.'); recommends Barclay's 'Eglogues' 56; ('55) J asks W to lend Baretti Crescembeni 58; thanks W and Wise (as before); 'where hangs the new volume' (of Spenser)? 59; J ignorant 'in what state my little affair stands' 60; Dr. King brought him news of the degree 'a few Minutes before your Letter'; J sends a letter for the Vice-Chancellor for W's approval 62; 'I have a great mind to come to Oxford at Easter, but you will not invite me'; quotes W's *Progress of Discontent* (1750, 1755) 64; W has promised to contribute to J's Bibliotheque 65; 'how goes Apollonius? . . . I think to com to Kettle hall' 71; J will come next week to Kettle Hall; 'I shall expect to see Spenser finished' 72; another postponement 73; J inquires about Bodleian MSS. of Sir Thomas More 75; ('56) mentioned 96; ('57) J introduces 'Dr. Marsili of Padua'; W never writes, 'Professors forget their friends' 109; J tells W of plans for 'some literary business' that might be done at Oxford 111; ('58) J thanks W for help with Shakespeare 114; introduces Baretti; praise of Langton 115; mentioned 110, 117; ('62) W introduces J to Bright of Abingdon 144.1; ('69) J sends W a Baskerville Virgil for the college library 215; ('70) J invites W to contribute to the revised edition of Shakespeare 230; ('74) J wishes more men in

the Brewhouse 386, J hopes HT will invite him 386.1; J and W see the Vice-Chancellor 399; HT or HLT should write to W 410, 'Dr. Wetherel is in earnest' 419; ('76) J's application to W for Carter 459, 461.1, 463.1; J's letter to him about the Clarendon Press 463; ('77) W not at O'd 533; ('79) J suggests to W that Maurice become JT's curate 618.1; ('80) W visits J 685; ('82) J dines with W 790, 791; (n.d.) mentioned 1102.

WHEELER, BENJAMIN, c. '33–22 July '83, Fellow of Magdalen '61; Professor of Poetry '66–'76; D.D. '70; Reg. Prof. of Divinity and Canon of Christ Church '76 (L; for his claim to be called 'learned', Macray, *Magdalen College Register* v (1906), 102).— ('75) J consults W about an inscription at Genoa 385.1, 387.3; ('78) J asks W to show Christ Church MSS. to CB 588; ('80) 'my learned friend, Dr. Wheeler of Oxford' 704; ('82) J dines with W 792; ('83) 'I have just lost Wheeler' 876; ('84) 'I much regret the loss of Dr. Wheeler' 946.1; 'my learned friend' 963.

Whitbread, Samuel, '20' (?)–'96, brewer (*DNB*, *L*, *Tb*).—('77) 'Would you for the other thousand (pounds) have my master such a man as —?' (so 1788, original not seen; 'Whitbread' HLP) 538; ('78) 'the ambition of *outbrewing Whitbread*' 585; ('83) 'I dine with Mr. Whitebread' (presumed the same) 839.1.

Whitby, Thomas, 1672 (?)–'47, 'of Great Haywood near Lichfield' (R v).—('35) J's letter from his house 3.2.

WHITE, WILLIAM, '48–1836, Bp of Pennsylvania (*DAmerB*, *L* ii. 499).— ('73) J thanks W for a copy of the American edition of *Rasselas* 298.

WILKES, JOHN, '27–'97; m. Mary Mead; his d. Mary, '50–1802; M.P. Aylesbury '57, Middlesex '68; Alderman for Farringdon Without '69; attacked by J in *The False Alarm* '70; Lord Mayor '74 (*DNB*, *L*).—('59) W procures Frank Barber's discharge from the navy 132.3; ('76) 'I dined in the poultry (see Dilly) with Mr. Alder-

man Wilkes' 479; 'Wilkes is two hundred behind' Hopkins 492; ('80) The Gordon riots: W seizes 'the publisher of a seditious paper' 678; 'Jack, who was always zealous for order and decency, declares . . . he will not leave a rioter alive' 679; ('83) J thanks 'Mr. and Miss Wilkes for their kind invitation' 840.

Wilk(e)s, Father, Benedictine of Paris (L).—('75) 'I am very kindly used by the English Benedictine friars' (in Paris) 437 (see note); ('76) J has a visit from 'Father Wilks the Benedictine, and Father Brewer, a Doctor of the Sorbon . . . Father Cowley is well' 483; 'Father Wilkes . . . and another of the same monastery dined with me' 483.1; J's letter to Adams introducing W 484; 'I furnished Wilkes with letter' 489, 551; ('84) the Prior's (Cowley) letter about MSS. in Paris 946.1.

WILLIAMS, ANNA, 'the blind lady', '06–6 Sept. '83, d. of Zachariah W of Haverfordwest, Pembrokeshire, physician and inventor, J's friend; AW lived with J from '52. In early letters (from '54) she is sometimes styled 'Miss Williams' ('Miss' alone 91); from '59 she is promoted to 'Mrs. Williams', but in letters to HLT is often 'Williams'. Routine references to her health are not indexed (*DNB*, *L* i. 232 and *passim*).—('50) 'a blind person' (presumably AW) 28; ('54) J sends Richardson W's thanks for a present, and asks him to help her with a projected dictionary; 'a being more pure from anything vicious I have never known 51.1; J asks Strahan to supply W with money in his absence 52; ('56) her benefit (Garrick's; see also 212), J's application for support, &c. 85, 87, 88, 89, 91 ('Miss'); 'Miss W— sends her compliments' to Hawkesworth 93; ('59) receipts for 'subscribers' (? to W's *Miscellanies* 1766) procured by Mrs. Montagu 132; ('60) W inquires about Sir John Philipps, her 'chief friend' 136.1; ('62) 'your (Baretti) old friends. Miss Williams and I live much as we did' 142; 'compliments' to Chambers 144.2, to FR

146; thinks well of a candidate 'for the school' 146 (cf. 224); 'very much loves you' (Baretti) 147; ('63) 'compliments to all our friends' at Abingdon 151; ('64) J and W visit Percy 165.1; ('65) J sends Lye W's 'compliments' to Mrs. Calvert 174; thanks to Mrs. Percy for letter 174.1; ('67) 'subscription' 187.4 (iii. 431); J asks BL to 'communicate this to Mrs. Williams' 192; ('69) her benefit (Colman's; see also s.a. '56) 212; J asks Percy to preach for 'a Charity School on Snow hill' (cf. 146), 'please to send your answer to Mrs. Williams' 224; ('70) J and W condole with Percy 240.2; ('71) 'Irish Cloath' for W 242; W and Mrs. Rolt 247.1; her letter to J 263; ('72) 'Mrs. Thrale loves you, and Mrs. Williams loves you' (JB) 274; ('73) Sir Alexander Gordon's letter to her 340; J takes her to the Southwells', borrows a book for her 294; J asks HT to send her money 330, 334; ('74) W, 'who has good judgement', sends advice to Cumins 354.1; W 'a petitioner for Mr. Hetherington's Charity' 361; ('75) W 'at Mr. Strahan's table' 380; 'very bad, worse than I ever saw her' 386, recurrent pimples 390; Mrs. Chambers's letter to J sent to W 418; 'has been very ill' 419; W reports that HLT visited her and 'behaved lovely' 427; ('76) 'I have written to Mrs. Williams' 500; her illness hopeless; 'Death is, however, at a distance' 502, 505; ('77) W thanks JT for turkey and hare 506.2; offers JB accommodation, asks about her book for Sir A. Gordon 507; 'is, I fear, declining' 524; 'age, and sickness, and pride, have made her so peevish that I was forced to bribe the maid to stay with her' 528; 'very ill of a pituitous defluxion' 541; writes to J 548; W and Desmoulins: 'without any great dearness in the comparison, Williams is I think, the dearer of the two' 553; ('78) 'Mrs. Williams is come home better' 583; 'Mrs. Williams and Mrs. Desmoulins had a scold, and Williams was going away, but I bid her *not turn tail*' 586; 'growls and scolds, but Poll (Carmichael) does not much flinch' 590,

'Williams hates every body' 591; ('79) 'Mrs. Williams talks of coming home from Kingston . . . there will be *merry* doings' 640; 'Levet is rather a friend to Williams, because he hates Desmoulins more' 644; ('80) W at Kingston, 'she is right to pick a little variety as she can' 686.2; 'frighted from London' by the riots 687; ('83) 'much broken' 834, 835.1 (18); 'When I first settled in this neighbourhood . . . I had Mrs. Williams then no bad companion' 839, 'Mrs. Desmoulins left us last week, so that I have only one sick woman to fight or play with' 839.1; W 'so weak that she can be a companion no longer' 857, 862; J's letter to her 867, **868** (?); 'poor Williams is making haste to die' 875; 'a day of great emotion; the office of the Communion of the Sick . . . in poor Mrs. Williams's chamber . . . I hope . . . that I shall learn to die as dear Williams is dying' 876, cf. 951; 'I doubt she gave perverse answers to my enquiries, because she saw that my tenderness put it in her power to give me pain' 876.1; her decline 877, 878; Brocklesby's letter reporting her death 'from mere inanition' 880; 'Mrs. Davis that was about Mrs. Williams' 881; 'her acquisitions were many, and her curiosity universal' 882; 'a companion to whom I have had recourse for domestick amusement for thirty years' 886, cf. 879.2, 883, 884, 887 (2), 889, 898 ('in the place of a sister'), 921, 1003.1; 'had she had good humour and prompt elocution, her universal curiosity and comprehensive knowledge would have made her the delight of all that knew her' 883; J reports to Mrs. Montagu 'your pensioner . . . she sustained forty years of misery with steady fortitude' 884.

Williams, Zachariah, 1673 (?)–'55, father of Anna W (*L*).—For letters written for him by J *see* Appendix A, i. 433.

Williams-Wynn, Sir Watkin, '49–'89, 4th Bt '49; matric. Oriel Coll. '66.—('68) 198 (*see* Apperley).

WILSON, THOMAS, '03–'84, son of Bp Thomas W (*see* Index III); pre-

AUTHORS (NOT IN INDEX II) AND BOOKS

See note on p. 341. For untraced quotations see p. 441.

A. ANCIENT

Aelian 3.3.

'Anacreon' (i.e. the spurious poems now called *Anacreontea*). Baxter's (q.v. in Index III B) edition 1695: 827.2, 888, 942. See note on 827.2, and *L* iv. 163. The Foulis (q.v. in Index II) edition 1751: 276.

Anthologia Graeca. J's translations ('84) into Latin 954 (see note, or *Poems* 208).

Apollonius Rhodius. T. Warton's projected translation 71.

Aristophanes studied by BL 999.

Aristotle. *Metaphysics* quoted 580.

Ausonius. *De XII Caesaribus* quoted 427 (tantum for solum).

Bible in ancient languages: 'the Codex 1458'. Hill quotes Maittaire's *Annales Typographici* 1719, p. 35, where the first printed book is said to be '*Psalmorum Codex* . . . 1457' 206 (218); 'the edition of 1462' of the Bible: 'a vague opinion' of three earlier printed editions 206 (218); Brian Walton's *Biblia Sacra Polyglotta* 1657: 1006.1 (see note).

Caesar mentioned 3.3.

Cebes mentioned 3.3.

Celsus quoted 310. See i. 429.

Cicero (Tully). Editions of *De Officiis* 206 (216); *De Officiis* a schoolbook 151; Quotations: *De Senectute* 260; *Brutus* 451, 608; *De Officiis* 703; *Epp. ad Atticum* 982.1 (see note). Mentioned 3.3; Cicero's 'character' 979.

Epici Graeci, Neander's edition, 347.

Euripides. Quoted 56 (the lost *Bellerophon*), 982.1 (the lost *Telephus*, see note). Mentioned 3.3.

Galen. *Comment. in Hippocratis Aphorismos* quoted 692.

Hadrian quoted 655.

Hesiod quoted 217.

Homer. *Iliad* quoted 282.1, 1144 (vii. 220); *Hymns* quoted 835.1 (19). Mentioned 3.3.

Horace. Quotations: *Odes* 201, 233, 235, 250, 267, 298, 331, 591, 592, 633 (a possible echo), 786, 1001, 1144 (*Odes* i. 26). *Satires* 294 (?), 568. *Epistles* 246.1, 326 (354), 535, 568, 640, 646, 973, 992. *Ars Poetica* 256. Mentioned 3.3.

Juvenal quoted 117, 983, 1010; misquoted by Brocklesby 851; 'Juvenals Sentiments' adapted in *London* 7.

Liturgy quoted 358.

Lucan quoted 203.1.

Lucian mentioned 3.3.

Lucretius quoted 65.

Manilius quoted 947.1.

Martial quoted 561.

Nepos. A school book 3.3, 148.

Oppian. A MS. to be collated 974.

Ovid. Quotations: *Amores* 875; *Ars Amatoria* 548, 684; *Heroides* 147.1, 592; *Metamorphoses* 284, 318, 388, 556, 877, 921, 1008 (see note); *Tristia* 191; *Tristia* and *Epistulae ex Ponto* alluded to 1010.2.

Persius quoted 97, 739.

Phaedrus mentioned 3.3.

Pindar. The Foulis (q.v. in Index II) edition 1751 276, 295. Quoted 712.1 (see note).

Plato 'a multitude' 451, 608.

Pliny quoted (?) 259.

Plutarch. *Life of Cicero* quoted (in Latin) 686.

Sallust mentioned 3.3.

Sappho quoted (in Latin, and at second hand at best) 507 (see note).

Seneca. *Hercules Furens* quoted 622; *De Tranquillitate* quoted 736.1.

Sulpitius Severus quoted 692.

B. MODERN

Beach or Beech, Thomas, d. '37: *Eugenio: or, Virtue and Happy Life. A Poem. Inscrib'd to Mr. Pope.* Dodsley 1737 (*L* ii. 240) 7.

Beattie: see Index II.

Bembo, Pietro, 1470–1547: his ascription to Virgil of minor poems 1003.

Bentham, Edward: see Index II.

Bentham, Jeremy, '48–1832. His Ode on the accession of George III 136.2.

Berkeley, George, 1685–'53. *Siris* 1744 quoted 656.1.

Bible (in modern languages).—('59 to his mother) 'I would have Miss (LP) read to you from time to time the Passion of our Saviour' 118; quoted 419; J sends LP a 'Commentary on the New Testament', probably Hammond's, q.v., 444; 'the Jewish law' 454; 'the Hebrew part' of a Lexicon of Antiquities, might become a concomitant to the Family Bible' 739. Psalms quoted 42, 465 (see note); quoted 835.1 (19), P.B. version. Ecclesiastes quoted 850. St. Mark quoted 1029. St. Matthew quoted 466. St. Paul quoted 580 (see note). ('82) J's 'another perusal' 807 (see note). The Erse translation 1767, 184, 360 (*L* ii. 29, 508).

'Bibliographia' Britannica: see Biographia.

Bibliotheca Graeca: J. A. Fabricius 206 (218); Hill quotes ed. 1726, xiii. 606.

Bibliotheca Thuaneana: see De Thou.

Biographia Britannica 1747–66, new ed. 1778–93.—('77) J borrows it from S'm 551 ('Bibliographia' is his slip), 561.1.

Birch: see Index II.

Blacklock: see Index II.

Blackmore, Sir Richard, d. '29. For J's *Life see* Index VI. *Essays upon Several Subjects* 1716. 671.

Blair: see Index II.

Blount, Sir Thomas Pope, 1649–1697. *Censura Celebriorum Authorum* 1690 (and later).—('53) J asks Birch to lend 45.

Boece, Hector, 1465 (?)–1536. *Scotorum Historiae* 1526.—('74) 345 'Boetius'; J asks JB to get him his 'head' 942.

Boileau-Despréaux, Nicholas, 1636–'11. *L'Art Poétique* quoted 61, 976. *See also* Racine.

Boswell: see Index II.

Boyle, John: see Index II.

Boyle, Robert, 1627–1691. His *Usefulness of Experimental Natural Philosophy* 1664 is perhaps the book which HLT ordered from Davies 791 (*Th* 830).

Broome, William, 1689–'45. For J's *Life see* Index VI.

Browne, Sir Thomas 1605–1682.—('56) J sends Birch his edition of *Christian Morals* (1716) 1756. 95.

Buchanan, George, 1506–1582. *Rerum Scoticarum Historia* 1582. 345; an epigram quoted 702.

Burke: see Index II.

Burnet, Gilbert, 1643–'15. *History of his Own Time* 1724–34 (2 vols.), 1753 (4 vols.) 814.2.

Burney, Charles and Frances: see Index II.

Burton, Robert, 1577–1640. *Anatomy of Melancholy* 1621 and later: quoted 338, 466, 639.

'Burton's Books': *see* Crouch.

Calder: *see* Index II.

Callender, James Thomson, d. 1803. *Deformities of Dr. Samuel Johnson* 1782. 775 (*L* iv. 499).

Calmet, Augustin, 1672–'57. *Dictionnaire historique . . . de la Bible* 1722, trans. D'Oyly and Colson 1732. C on the Bible of 1462. 206 (218); 954.

Camden, William, 1531–1623. *Britannia* 1586 and later: quoted on Stonehenge 892.

Campbell, Archibald, *The Doctrines of a Middle State* 1721 (*L* v. 356) 335.

Carlisle: *see* Index II.

Carter, Elizabeth: *see* Index II.

Catalogus librorum MSS. in bibliothecis Angliae et Hiberniae. Oxon. 1697, Fᵒ (Lot 340 in J's Sale Catalogue) 54, 75.

Catholicon, the: 426 (see note).

Cervantes, Miguel de, 1547–1616, *Don Quixote* quoted (?) 109.

Chamberlayne, Edward, 1616–'03. *Angliae Notitiae, or the Present State of England* 1669 and later. J borrows 44.

Chambers, Ephraim, d. 1740. *Cyclopaedia, or an Universal Dictionary of Arts and Sciences* 1728, 1738. Calder's

Lancastre and York 1548. ('52) Shakespeare's use 42.1.

Hammond, Henry, 1605–1660. *Paraphrase and Annotations upon* . . . *the Psalms* 1659: LP 'had Hammond's Commentary on the Psalms before her . . . she says, there is enough that any body may understand' 425, 739; the 'Commentary on the New Testament' which J sent LP was no doubt H's (1653 and later) 444.

Hardy, Samuel: *see* Index II.

Hawkesworth: *see* Index II.

Hawkins: *see* Index II.

Helsham, Richard, 1682 (?)–'38. *Course of Lectures on Natural Philosophy* 1739: (? '52) J borrows 'Helsham's Philosophy' 44.

Hénault, Charles Jean François, 1685–1770 (*L* ii. 383). *Nouvel Abrégé chronologique de l'histoire de France* 1744 and often reprinted and continued. His inferiority to Lord Hailes 431, 447, 454.

Hill, Aaron, 1685–'50. *The Plain-Dealer* 1724–5: J borrows 15.

Hoadly, Benjamin, '06–'57. *The Suspicious Husband* 1747 dedicated to the King 1004.

Hodder, James, Arithmetic (1661) 839.1.

Hollingshead (Hollinshed), Raphael, d. (?) 1580: *Chronicles* 1577+, 1722. ('52) Shakespeare's use 42.1.

Home, Henry, Lord Kames, 1696–'82. J borrows his *Elements of Criticism* (1762) 1135.

Hoole: *see* Index II.

Howard, John: *see* Index II.

Howell, James, 1594 (?)–1666. *Epistolae Ho-elianae* 1645–55 and later: quoted 549.

Hughes, John, 1677–'20. For J's *Life see* Index VI. Spenser's *Works* ed. by H 1715, 1750. 53. *Letters . . . including the Correspondence of John Hughes* 1772 (2 vols.), 1773 (vol. iii), 1773 (incorporating vol. iii): ('79) 'the last edition of Hughes's Letters' 611.

Hume, David, '11–'76. *Philosophical Essays* 1748: ('54) Adams's 'confutation of Hume on Miracles' 51.1.

Jack the Giant-Killer (?) 1711 (*CBEL*): 197 (*L* iv. 8).

Jennens, Charles, 1700–'73. His edition of *Hamlet* 1773: ('73) 304.

Jephson, Robert, '36–1803. *Braganza* 'liked' by J 376.2 (a guess, see note).

Johnston, Arthur, 1587–1641. *Poemata Omnia* Middelburg 1642: 507 (*L* v. 95); J asks JB to get him Johnston's 'head' 942.

Jones, William: *see* Index II.

Jortin, John, 1698–'70. Coupled with Markland and Thirlby, 'three contemporaries of great eminence' 812.

Kelly: *see* Index II.

Kinsderley: *see* Index II.

La Bruyère, Jean de, 1645–1696. Untraced quotation 266.

Law, William, 1686–1761. *An Appeal to All that Doubt* 1740 is probably the book lent to J by Miss Boothby 84.

Lawrence, Thomas: *see* Index II.

Le Courayer: *see* Paul.

Lee, Nathaniel, 1649 (?)–1693. *The Rival Queens* 1677: adapted 294, 554 (also in *Spectator* 39).

Leedes, Edward, 1627–1707. His edition of Lucian 1743. 3.3.

Leibnitz, Gottfried Wilhelm, 1646–1716: *see* Crousaz.

Leland: *see* Index II.

Lennox: *see* Index II.

Lesley or Leslie, John, 1527–1596. *De Origine Moribus et Rebus Gestis Scotorum* 1578, 1675. ('74) J asks Steevens to lend 345.

Literary Magazine see Index VI s.a. 1757.

Liturgy, Western (Roman): Κύριε, ἐλέησον, Kyrie eléison, 'Lord, have mercy' 358.

Locke, John, 1632– '04. Coupled with Pascal 738. Quoted 194.

London Chronicle 113.

Louis XIV, 1638–1715. His motto, 'Nec pluribus impar', might suggest 'par pluribus' 663.

Lucas: *see* Index II.

Lye: *see* Index II.

Lyttelton: *see* Index II.

Macbean: *see* Index II.

Machiavelli, Nicolò: *see* Martinelli in Index II.

Macpherson, James: *see* Index II.

Maintenon, Mme de, 1635–'19: quoted 681.

Mallet (Malloch), David, '05 (?)-'65. *William and Margaret* n.d., ? 1723; reprinted in Percy's *Reliques* 1765: quoted 876.

Markland, Jeremiah, 1693–1776: *see* Jortin.

Mason, William, '24–'97. His edition of the Letters, &c., of Gray (q.v.) 1775. 390; Du Fresnoy's *Art of Painting* trans. by M 1783. 829.

Melmoth: *see* Index II.

Milbourne, Luke, 1649–'20. His 'Invocation to the Georgicks' appended to J's *Life of Dryden* 582.

Milton, John, 1608–1674. For J's *Life* *see* Index VI. ('50) 'our incomparable Milton'; J's Prologue for *Comus* 27; M read by Harry Thrale *aet.* seven 304; quotations: Sonnet 22, 746; *Comus* 871.1 (?); *L'Allegro* 871.1; *Paradise Lost* 578, 590, 647 (parody), 727.2, 836.1, 877; A parody of Milton 895 (?).

Molière, Jean Baptiste Poquelin de, 1622–73. *L'École des Femmes*: 'do not play Agnes' 558; 'the season for Agnes is now over' 725.

Monboddo: *see* Index II.

Montague: *see* Index II.

Moore, Edward: *see* Index II.

More, Hannah: *see* Index II.

More, Sir Thomas, 1478–1535. Bodleian MSS. 75.

Murphy: *see* Index II.

Naudeus: Gabriel Naudé, 1600–1653 206 (218).

Neander, Michael, *Opus Aureum* 1577. 347 (see note).

Nelson, Robert, 1656–1715. *Festivals and Fasts* 1704. 609, 1121.

Newton, Thomas: *see* Index II.

Nichols: *see* Index II.

Nursery Rhymes 561, 592, 839.

O'Conor: *see* Index II.

Oldys, William: *see* Index II.

Orrery: *see* Boyle in Index II.

'Ossian'. *See also* Macpherson, James, in Index II. Monboddo's and Macqueen's credulity; 'if there are men with tails, catch an *homo caudatus*' 431; 'this wild adherence to Chatterton more unaccountable than the obstinate defence of Ossian' 766.

Owen, Henry: *see* Index II.

Parliamentary History used in *Life of Waller* § 26. 580.1.

Parnell, Thomas, 1679–'18: 'Hymn to Contentment' quoted 326 (355).

Pascal, Blaise, 1623–1662. Coupled with Locke 738.

Paul, Father (Paolo Sarpi, 1552–1623): *see* Index VI.

Pennant, Thomas, '26–'98. His *Tours*, 'a very intelligent traveller' 575; 'seems to have seen a great deal which we did not see' 528.

Percy: *see* Index II.

Perrault, Charles, 1621–'03 *Charactères* trans. Ozell 1704. Quoted 542.

Petrarch, Francis, 1304–1374. J's reading P with Sastres 1003; Susannah Dobson's *Life of Petrarch collected from Mémoires pour la Vie de Pétrarch* 1775 (by De Sade 1764–7) 846.

Peyton: *see* Index II.

Philips or Phillips, Ambrose, 1674–'49. For J's *Life see* Index VI.

Politian, Angelus, 1454–1494. J's Proposals ('34) for an edition of his Latin poems 2.1.

Polydore Vergil, *fl. c.* 1540. Quoted (?) 109.

Pompadour: 'little Pompadour', i.e. *The History of the Marchioness de Pompadour* 1758, 1759. 124 (see note).

Pope, Alexander, 1688–'44. For J's *Life see* Index VI. Crousaz (q.v.) on *Essay on Man* 10; P's *Miscellanies* 694–5; his Epitaphs 697; Ruffhead's *Life* 696; 'un politique aux choux et aux raves' 721.1. Quotations: *Eloisa to Abelard* 332 (380); *Essay on Criticism* 1144 (' 'Twere well might critics still this freedom take, But Appius', &c.); *Dunciad* 616, 1143; *Epistle to Arbuthnot* (*Prologue to Satires*) 669; *Essay on Man* 749, 761; in French (by Du Resnel, q.v.) 869.1; *Characters of Men* (*Moral Essays, Ep.* 1) 850; *The Rape of the Lock* 633; *The Basset-Table* 259; *To the Memory of an Unfortunate Lady* 876; *One Thousand Seven Hundred and Thirty Eight* (*Epilogue to Satires*) 1024.

Prayer Book, see *Common Prayer*.

Preces in Usum Sarum 277.

Prideaux, Humphrey, 1648–'24. *The*

Tatler 1709–11: 'the sources of conversation' 901; an untraced quotation 220; S's dedication to Addison's *Drummer* 1142 (1716, 1722; 'original preface' refers to the former).

Steevens: *see* Index II.

Stewart, James: *see* Index II.

Stockdale: *see* Index II.

Stuart, James, the first translator of the New Testament into Gaelic, Edinburgh 1767 (*L* ii. 28, 508) 184, 189, 193.

Swan, John, *fl.* '42. *Works of Dr. Thomas Sydenham newly made English from the original Latin* 1742. 652 (*see* Index VI).

Swift, Jonathan, 1667–'45. For J's *Life see* Index VI. Orrery's *Remarks* (*see* Boyle, Index II) 42.1; 'Presto' 214; Hawkesworth's *Life* 514; S's 'works' 689.1 (see note). Quotations: *On the Death of Dr. Swift* 560 (see note), 662, 692, 850, 969, 1016.

Sydenham, Thomas, 1624–1689. *Observationes Medicae* 1676, trans. John Swan (q.v.) 1742. 652.

Talbot: *see* Index II.

Tasso, Torquato, 1544–1595. Hoole's translation 712. *See also* Fairfax.

Tatler, The: *see* Steele.

Temple, Sir William, 1628–1699. *Introd. to Hist. of England* 1695 quoted 107; *Popular Discontents* 1701 quoted 454; *Heroic Virtue* 1690 quoted 647; *United Provinces* 1673 quoted 982.1.

Theobald, Lewis, 1688–'44 *Double Falsehood* 1728 quoted 616.

Thirlby, Styan, 1692–1753: *see* Jortin 812.

Thomson, James, 1700–'48. For J's *Life see* Index VI. ('56) 'a man of genius, but not very skilful in the art of composition' 106.1; song 'For ever, Fortune' quoted 659.

Thurloe, John, 1616–1688. *State Papers of John Thurloe* ed. T. Birch 1742. 17.

Topsell, Edward, d. (?) 1638. *The Historie of Fourefooted Beastes* 1607: J asks Cave to 'lend me Topsel on Animals' 11.

Trissino: *Sophinisba* (1524) quoted 752.

Turner, William, *c.* 1658–'26. 148 (see note).

Twiss: *see* Index II.

Tyrwhitt: *see* Index II.

Universal History 58.1 (see note).

Voltaire, François Marie Arouet de, 1694–'78. *Siècle de Louis XV* 7, 639; *Siècle de Louis XIV* quoted 681.

Walker, William, 1623–1684. *Treatise of English Particles shewing how to render them according to the proprietie and elegance of the Latine* 1655 (?) and often reprinted; 15th ed. 1720. 151.

Waller, Edmund, 1606–1687. For J's *Life see* Index VI.

Walpole, Horace: *see* Index II (where I have placed him; though not an acquaintance he moved in a circle that included J).

Walsh, William, 1663–'08. 'The sublime and pathetick Mr. Walsh' 681.

Walton, Izaak, 1593–1683. *Lives of Dr. John Donne* (and others) 1670 (and earlier in part) and later, no 18th-century edition before 1796: projected editions by Hailes and Horne (qq.v. in Index II) 353.2, 357, 360; Hawkins's 'materials for the completion of Walton's lives' 947.1; Hawkins's edition of *The Compleat Angler* 353.2.

Warburton: *see* Index II.

Warton, Joseph and Thomas: *see* Index II.

Watson: *see* Index II.

Watts, Isaac, 1674–'48. For J's *Life see* Index VI. 'To the collection of . . . Poets, I have recommended the volume of Dr. Watts to be added' 526; *Improvement of the Mind* 1741. 745.

Welsh Grammar: 206 (216; see note).

Wesley: *see* Index II.

Wilkins, John, 1614–1672. *An Essay towards a Real Character and a Philosophical Language* 1668. 870.

Williams, Anna: *see* Index II.

Wilson, Bishop Thomas, 1663–1755. ('82) J's veneration for his works 821.1.

Wilson (of Clitheroe): *see* Index II.

Wingate, Edmund, *Arithmetic* (1650) 839.1.

Wood, Anthony à, 1632–1695. *Athenae Oxonienses* 1691–2: ('55) J borrows 'Wood's Ath: Ox:' 76; ('82) urges Nichols to 'undertake the Supplement to Wood' 810.

World, The: *see* Chesterfield and Moore, Edward, in Index II.

Wraxall: *see* Index II.

Young, Edward, 1683–'65. For J's *Life* *see* Index VI. *See also* Index II.

Young, George. *A Treatise on Opium* (Millar) 1753; (? '53) '*Young upon Opium*, which I had from Mrs. Strahan' 44.

Young, John, '50 (?)–1820, Prof. of Greek, Glasgow. *A Criticism on the Elegy written in a Country Churchyard: being a Continuation of Dr. J—n's Criticism on the Poems of Gray* 1783 (anon.): 'I suspect the writer to be wrong-headed' 863.

UNTRACED QUOTATIONS

The following list is of quotations, or phrases that may probably be quotations, that are of unknown authorship and are untraced. If a phrase is only suspected of being a quotation, it is followed by a mark of interrogation. For untraced quotations of known authorship see above, under the author's name.

Vol. I

Letter 1.1 vitam continet una dies.

294 the rest that dwell in darker fame (?).

329 (369) If thou likest her opinions thou wilt praise her virtue.

353.2 . . . times when writers of value emerge from oblivion by general consent.

Vol. II

386 sic nunquam rediturus labitur annus (?).

408 We deal in nicer things Than routing armies etc. I fear not you, nor yet a better man.

485 Johnny Wilcocks.

505.3 Tempora mutantur, et nos mutamur in illis. Perhaps the earliest source is Harrison's *Description of Britain* 1577, III. iii. 99, 'the saying of the Poet'. Harrison gives it in the unmetrical form (mutantūr et nos). The corrected form (mutantur nos et) is found in the poems of Matthias Borbonius, *c.* 1612.

552 Take heed, my dear, youth flies apace.

561 will Genius change his sex to weep? (?)

576 She's gone, and never knew how much I lov'd her.

592 will neither grant the question nor deny.

623 be a funny (? sunny) little thing (?).

632 outrun time and outface misfortune (?).

636 provoke a bugle (perhaps not a literary quotation; a family joke or the like?).

640, 744 merry doings (? like 636).

642 neither D— . . . nor B— have given occasion to his loss (?).

647 Living on God, and on thyself rely.

666 Cette Anne si belle . . . (Mr. Austin Gill suspects this of being English French).

672 What wouldst thou more of man? (?)

685 l'Enfant toûjours est homme.

690 what avails it to be wise? (?—see note).

744 See 640.

751.1 Thus we sigh on from day to day etc.

752 hold all together (?—see note).

Vol. III

817.2 to have heard, Ye Gods! and to have seen.

876 the patience of *Mortal born to bear.*

892 ended . . . joy and woe.

894 The wheel of life is daily turning round, And nothing in this world of certainty is found.

984 who can run the race with death? (?)

PLACES

References are to the numbers of the letters (page-numbers occasionally added in brackets). Places that Johnson is known or believed to have visited are distinguished by CAPITALS. Names of persons connected with places are often added in brackets.

beach 332 (380); 'a bath in the morning and an assembly at night' 424; 'Air, and Vacancy, and novelty' 426; 'very dull' 502; HLT 'left alone (Nov. '78) to wander over the Steene' 592; HT's hunting 628; 'a dangerous place, we were told, for children' 633; postal delays 647; 'the commotion' (the riots of '80), B'n 'will soon begin to be peopled' (12 June) 679.

BRISTOL: Savage's death 23; his 'Defence', whether there 15 (Bagshaw).

BROMLEY, Kent: J's wife's grave 975, 1012, 1041.

BUCHAN, Aberdeenshire 322.

Cairo 417.

CALAIS 436.

Calcutta 351, 413.

CAMBRIDGE: King's College 227; 'the civilities of Cambridge' ('65) 530; Burney's discoveries 636; 'college or university registers' 673, 683; booksellers 888.

Cannae 672.

CANTERBURY (Lawrence) 779.1, 797.

Capua 672.

Carlisle 524, 528, 544.

CARNARVONSHIRE 360.1.

Caspian 641.

CASTLE ASHBY, Northants. 134.2, 139.

CAWDOR, Nairn 323.

Chatham, Kent (BL) 675.

CHATSWORTH, Derbyshire: see Cavendish in Index II: house and cascade 288, 291, 553, 1009, 1011, 1015.

CHESHIRE: Beauclerk (? his cousin Leicester) 135; Sir R. Cotton 585.1.

CHESTER: J's visit 360.1, JB's 639.

COL (Coll): see Maclean in Index II: 329 (370), 331.

Coleshill (Colshil), Warwickshire 290.

Cornwall (-al): Elliot 637.

Corsica: JB's visit 181, 185, 200.

COVENTRY, Warwickshire: a 'Chirurgeon' 135; J's night there '69, 220; J's visit there '79, 616 (Rann, Tom Johnson).

Coxheath, Kent 587

Cranbroke, Kent 871.1.

CUBLEY, Derbyshire 711.3.

Cumae 117.

CUPAR (Coupar, Cowpar), Fife: education 116.1; J passes through 321.

DARLINGTON, Durham: fine spire 318.

DAVENTRY, Northants.: J sleeps there '79, 616.

DENBIGH: 'not a mean town' 359.

DERBY and DERBYSHIRE (abbr. Derbys 387): see also Ashbourne, Chatsworth, Dovedale, Kedleston, Matlock, Peak: 'feracissima metallorum regio' 259; 'not the place that cures coughs' 296; HT's visit 420, 422, 423; a rainy county 548; Derby china and silk 549.

DONCASTER, Yorkshire: church and monument 318.

DOVEDALE, Derbyshire 237.

Dublin: the University (Leland, Andrews) 178; Eblana (Goldsmith) 539.1; inferior to London, better than Iceland (Mrs. Smart) 1154.

DUNBUY, Aberdeenshire 322.

DUNDEE, Angus, 'a dirty, despicable town' 321 (344).

DUNVEGAN, Skye 326 (353), 348.

DURHAM: the cathedral, 'rocky solidity and indeterminate duration', the castle, the library 'mean and scanty' 318 (339, see note).

EDINBURGH 318, 319, 320, 338.

ELGIN: cathedral, piazzas 323 (349).

ELSFIELD, near Oxford 72 (Wise).

Eton (Eaton), Berks. 657 (E. Barnard).

Falmouth, Cornwall 138.

FONTAINEBLEAU 437.

Forney, co. Longford 539.1 (Goldsmith).

FORRES (Foris), Nairn 323 (349).

FORT AUGUSTUS, Inverness-shire 323 (350), 326 (356); J's sound sleep 593.

FORT GEORGE, Inverness-shire 323 (349).

FORTH, Firth of 321 (342).

FOYERS (Fiers), Falls of, Inverness-shire 323 (350).

FRANCE. See also Calais, Fontainebleau, Paris, Rouen, Versailles: financial crisis '42, 17; 'the way through France is now open' '62, 147; J advises FR 'to go through France' (? to Italy) 162; 'cour de l'amour' 262; for J's visit see letters from Sept. '75 to Jan. '76, and 460.

Frome, Somerset 693, 710 (Prowse, Nathaniel Johnson).

445

Denbigh, Llewenny, Penmanmaur, Snowdon, Swansea, Wrexham. 'Not afraid of a Welch journey' 337 (387); the tour '74, 357–360.1; 'a man must see Wales to enjoy England' 390 (Paoli); 'what is there in Wales?' 545.

WARE, Hertfordshire 355.2 (John Scott); 'Wear' 1012.1 (Barclay).

WARLEY, Essex 581.1, 587, 593 (BL's camp).

Weymouth, Dorset, 860, 865 ('a new nothing'), 875 (HLT and girls).

Wight, Isle of 684 (Thrales).

WINCHESTER, Hants: J's visit to JW 176; hope of another 239; St. Cross hospital 525 (De Groot); hope of another visit; Huntingford 668.

Windsor, Berkshire 884.1, 983 (Heberden).

Woodsease, Staffordshire 1039 (Scrimshaw).

WREXHAM, Denbighshire 360.1.

Yardley, Northants. 174.1 (Lye).

Yarmouth, Norfolk 132.3 (Barber).

YORK 227.1 (Chambers), 318 (338, the Minster compared to St. Paul's).

Youngsbury, Hertfordshire 1012.1 (Barclay).

INDEX V

SUBJECTS

See also Index I. Johnson's opinions on general topics are here grouped under the headings Americans, Architecture, Balloons, Building, Clubs, Death and Immortality, Economics, Education, the English, Food and Drink, Friendship, Gardens, Health and Disease, History, Languages, Law and Lawyers, Letters, Libraries, Literature, Mind, Morals and the Emotions, Mythology, Natural Science, Nature, Newspapers and Rumour, Painting and Sculpture, Politics, Post, Poverty, Quarrels, Record and Retrospect, Religion, Scots, Sea and Ships, Theatre, Things, Transport, Travel, Youth.

Hill appended to his *Life*, and to the *Miscellanies*, *Dicta Philosophi*; but he appended no *Scripta Philosophi* to the *Letters*. This index is in part an attempt to fill that gap. But it is fuller than Hill's anthologies, and evades the tyranny of the alphabet.

AMERICANS, the. *See also* POLITICS, and for J's 'American friends' Index I Friends VIII. ('66) J denounces 'the practice of the planters of America' 184; (Aug. '75) J predicts American victory 427; (Feb. '76) Wesley's approval of *Taxation No Tyranny* 451; (Jan. '84) loss of 'even the titular dominion of America' 928.

ARCHITECTURE. Aberbrothick: the abbey 'once of stupendous magnificence' 321 (344); Durham Cathedral: 'rocky solidity and indeterminate duration' 318 (339); Lincoln Cathedral: the chapter-house superior to York 318 (338); St. Andrews 321 (343); St. Paul's Cathedral: 'the middle walk' compared to Durham 318 (338); Salisbury Cathedral 'the last perfection in architecture' 892; Stonehenge 892; Blackfriars Bridge i. 446.

BALLOONS (usually ballon). 883 (description, see note), 891.1, 897, 917, 925 ('iron wings'), 929.1 (J subscribes), 929.2, and *passim* in letters from Aug. '84, see especially 989. 'to pay for seats...is not very necessary', 997, 1013 (a prayer for mercy), 1020 (of no scientific value).

BUILDING. 'That mode of ostentatious waste' condemned in LP 154, in the Davenants 900, in JT 981, condoned in HT 417.

CLUBS

(1) *The Ivy-Lane Club* (*L* i. 190). Reunion of survivors in '83–'84, 908, 915, 917, 953, 954.

(2) *The Literary Club*. For its members *see* in Index I J's Friends § x. 9.

(3) *The Essex-Head Club* (*L* iv. 253, 436). *passim* in letters from L'n in Dec. '83, frequent in '84.

('65) 174; ('66) 'all the Club subscribes' to Lye's Dictionary 182 (see note 6); 'holds very well together' 183; ('68) 211.1; ('71) 246; ('73) 304.1; apology for absence, proposes JB 305; ('74) proposes Steevens 346, 347; Gibbon rejected 347; Fox, Bunbury, and Fordyce elected 348, 363; ('75) 386.1; ('76) Goldsmith's epitaph shown to the Club 480, 506.1; ('77) proposed increase of numbers; 'I am for reducing it to a mere miscellaneous collection of conspicuous men' 510; Dunning elected 528, 565; ('78) 576; Banks proposed 587, 593; ('82) 779; ('83) 859, 860; Palmerston rejected 861, 862; ('84) 968.

DEATH and IMMORTALITY. 'a holy death'; have the dead knowledge of the living? 30 (34); preparation for death 87 (Cave 'died I am afraid unexpectedly to

450

himself') 116, 519.3 (Dodd; a full discussion, cf. 523); J's mother 'not unfit to face death' 120, cf. 935 (nothing else worth our care), 970.2, 983, 995 (J 'calls on' JR 'to remember that we must all die'); death in battle not more terrible than natural death 116; 'hope that a good life might end . . . in a contented death' 138 (135); 'on death we cannot always be thinking' 197; death of children 240.2 (consolation from survivors); 'the next to translation' (Miss Aston on Harry Thrale), 'remember . . . that your child is happy' 465; 'we shall soon be where our doom will be fixed for ever' 147; 'there is surely something beyond' 565; 'reasonable hope of a happy futurity' 578; 'a time . . . when we shall not borrow all our happiness from hope' 142 (140); 'we forget that death is hovering over us' 618; 'where there is neither want, nor darkness, nor sorrow' 887 (2); 'a sinner approaching the grave is not likely to be very cheerful' 935.1; 'confidence with respect to futurity' no part of wisdom 938; 'who can run the race with death?' 984; on every side 'mortality presents its formidable frown' 995.

ECONOMICS. For the economics of authorship, publishing, &c., see LITERA-TURE. See also Scotland in Index IV.

(1) General: debts 134 (great and small); 'three groats make a shilling' 232; bills (negotiable) 242; 'rise upon stock' 253; bankruptcy of Fordice, its consequences 275.1; 'scarcity produces plenty' 289; objections to 'tying up money in trade' illusory 308; 'plenty and splendour' on a capital of £10,000 'diligently occupied' 308, cf. 417; Tom Johnson's expenditure of £40 in 16 months 'very strange' 365; visitors 'no expence' to a rich host 528, contrast 538 'the cost of entertaining company'; financial crisis of '79, 606, 624, 643, 649.1; 'trade could not be managed by those who manage it, if it had much difficulty' 647; fluctuations in the Stocks 891; 'tax on servants' 952.2.

(2) Prices, &c. barley, malt, 253, 279, 280, 337 (388), 482; beer 538; board 153, 8s. a week 934; books, see literature; building 154, 303.2; cattle 237, 541.1; cloth 242, 572; coal 779.4, 791; doctors' fees 12; education, q.v.; malt, see barley; money 154, 286, 835.1; musk 582.1; 'pot', a, 767.1 (a silver coffee-pot, 793); rents, Highland 326 (361), 329 (368); salmon 146; statues 572; table cloath £25, 572; transport, q.v.; travel 329 (371); turnpike 3s. 6d., 583; wheat 407.

EDUCATION. For the study of Greek and Latin see 3.3 and the early letters to G. Strahan (Index II). School and university 144.1; Education should follow inclination: 'it is very dangerous to cross the stream of curiosity' 116.1, cf. 148, 149 ('any method will do, if there be but diligence'), 170 (read 'remisso animo'), 477 (very young children should not be harassed 'with the violence of painful attention'); cost: at O'd 167, good and cheap schools in the north of England 398, see also Scotland in Index IV; 'take in a literary journal once a month' 170; 'innocent amusements' needed 'to keep the young men from pernicious pleasures' 405; versification in English recommended 151; self-education and its limit of age 428, 429; 'schemes of study and improvement' 912; arithmetick 'a species of knowledge perpetually useful and indubitably certain' 836.1, 839.1, 843.1, 870, 912; handwriting 843.1, 918.1.

ENGLISH, THE. It is characteristic of his race that a great Englishman hardly mentions the subject. The 'English school' of painting and sculpture 138; 'the English keep no secret' 571.

FOOD and DRINK. See also HEALTH.
    Alphabetical list: asparagus 488; barley, Siberian, 421, 469; cabbage 321 (345, the Highlands); marmalade (Mrs. Boswell's) 529, 533 ('orange Marmalade'), 607; oats, Polish or Poland, 421, 422; oysters sent to LP 592 ('a barrel'), 604 ('two barels'), 605; pineapples 547; porter 348; sugar animals 477 (Thrale children); venison 547.

FRIENDSHIP. See also Index I, Friends. Friendship considered 3.2; we must 'take

SUBJECTS

friends such as we can find them' 155; few temporal goods equal to 'the familiarity of worthy men' 29; friends of youth (and their retention later) 69, 75.2 ('a kind of restoration to youth'), 105.1, 106, 455; 'the form and exercise of friendship varies' 103; 'every heart must lean to somebody' 127; not many friends are to be expected 181; new friends 'at our age' (his own and JT's in '73) 'uncommon instances of happiness' 312; duties of 'a common friend' to 'two adversaries' 495; friendships by birth superior to 'fortuitous' friendships 837; old friends 900.

GARDENS. John Scott's 'Dryads and Fairies' 355.1; Langley's 'improvements' 421; LP's garden 425; HT's improvements at S'm 425, his pool 427, cf. 551, 554, 'the eighth wonder of the world' 558; JT's pool, &c. 541.1; Myddelton's urn 548.

HEALTH and DISEASE; MEDICINE. For J's own health *see also* Index I.

(1) *General*: 'Health is the basis of all social virtues' 247; 'physicians do not love intruders' 79; 'wild nations trust to simples' 140; sickness kindles the affections 204; causes selfishness 213; self-indulgence 460; 'my opinion of alterative medicine is not high' 388; 'physicians, be their power less or more, are the only refuge that we have' 629; 'Health is the basis of all happiness' 806; 'the first talk of the sick is commonly of themselves' 925; 'a sick man is almost as impatient as a lover' 926; a sick man 'impossible to please' 966.

(2) *Diseases and Symptoms*: apoplexy and hysteria 617, 618; cancer 281, 291, and letters '73 to HLT about her mother; 591; cataract 135; consumption 545; defluxion, pituitous 541; dropsy 189.2, 189.3, 354.1, and J's letters of '84 *passim*; dysenteries suspected 'to be produced by animalcula' 748; fever 310, 312; gout 432 ('Dr. Lawrence thinks every thing the gout'), 492 ('of my own acquisition'), 494 ('has not alleviated my other disorders'), 635 ('no great opinion of the benefits which it is supposed to convey'), cf. 766.2; 891, 893 (thought by Mudge 'a security against the palsy'); grumous and serous disorders 630; headach 419; hydrops pectoris 918.1; hystericks and apoplexies 910; indigestion 79; influenza 789; paralysis not necessarily recurrent 621, 623; rheumatism 388; scorbutick humour 504; spitting blood 534; strangury 969; taenia 536, 560; ulcer 354.1.

(3) *Remedies, Drugs, &c.*: aloes 1029; antimonial wine 687; balsam of Peru 82; bark 79, 118, 140, 309, 967; barley sugar 779.5; blister 850; bleeding 312, 351, 423, 506, 630, 660, 702, 'only for exigences' 703, 967; calomel 676, 687, 839; cantharides 851, 860, 992; carrots 301.2; castor oil 1020, 1027.2; compounded medicines 993; diacodium *see* opium; electricity 802; emetick tartar 993; fontanel 627; gum ammoniacum 993; hartshorn 850; ipecacuanha 359, 506, 528; jalap 687; Knightsbridge powders 536, 543; laurel 253, 258; lovage 388; mercury 291, 407, 627, 635, 676; musk 582.1, 583; mustard 388; oil and sugar 82; ol. ter. (terebinth) 1000; opium 258 (HLT), 266 (Seward), 762 (J, cf. 786, 848, 921, J's 'horrour of' opiates, 925.1, 931 'I had the same terrour' (as HLT), 941 (reducing the dose), 944, 1003.1 (Ryland's 'jealousy of opium'); orange 79 (see note); physick (*see* purge, and physick in Index VII); pix Burgundica 933.1; purge *passim*, e.g. 312 'about thirteen purges in fifteen days' 616, 630, 798; quince 79; Rhenish and water 82; rhubarb 937; sloes 79; son (bran) 1109; squills 937 vinegar preferred to powder, 993 dosage, *passim* in letters to physicians in '84; sulphur 388; Thebaick tincture 993; valerian 591; vesicatories, -ations, 851, 854; vomit 848.

(4) *Regimen*: 'It is neither necessary nor prudent to be nice in regimen' 637; see especially the 'rules' for a sea voyage 796; bathing 189.1, 645.1, 914.1; diet: fasting *passim*, e.g. 311, 608 ('the teapot', see note), 631, 647, 656, 659 ('alternate diet', cf. 654, 662), 684 ('semivegetable diet'); drinking (i.e. liquid): 316, 492 (gout ascribed to insufficient drink), 605, 616.1, 798; exercise 312, 614.1, defined 622, 627, 904.

(5) *Health and Cheerfulness*: 277 no ordinary ailment 'on which the mind has not some influence'; 546 Elizabeth Aston's reluctance 'to use any means' for recovery,

452

563 her 'resolute inactivity'; 605.1 ('attention should be something less than anxiety'); 620, 622 ('Vivite laeti is one of the great rules of health'); 799 ('suffer nothing disagreeable to approach you after dinner'); 806 ('open no letter of business but in the morning').

HISTORY. 'the Spirit of History contrary to minute exactness' 15; 'Talk not of the Punick war' 414; 'the feudal establishment . . . very important' 276, cf. 639; 'all histories a narrative of misery' 999.

LANGUAGES. *See also* EDUCATION, and for J's knowledge of languages that article in Index I.

(1) *General*: 'To use two languages . . . without contaminating . . . very difficult 138; 'my zeal for languages' 184; 'Languages are the pedigree of nations' (*L* v. 225): 184 (188–9).

(2) *Single Languages*: Arabic MSS. 591; Asiatick Literature 835.1 (19); Basque *see* Irish; Erse 184, 324, 326 (360), 327 (363), 343, 360 (books for Bodleian), 378; Frisick 163 (166); German 274.1; Gothic and Saxon 174.1; Greek 236 (nouns in -ω); Irish, its relation to Welsh and to the language of Biscay 107; Italian proverbs 515, 559; Latin: Inscription at Genoa 385.1, 387.3; Q's Latin letter 941, 953; Persian 353 (Hastings); Saxon 174.1; Spanish proverb 549; Welsh *see* Irish; Welsh MSS. 431, 589, 591.

LAW and LAWYERS. *See in* Index II Boswell (J's letters on legal points), Chambers. The civil law 163; J approves JB's description of legal study as 'copious and generous' 185; 'I know very few attorneys' 292.1; Scots lawyers 'great masters of the law of nations' 374; law of inheritance 450, 452.

LETTERS. For J's remarks on his own habits, &c., *see* CORRESPONDENCE in Index I; *see also* POST below.

(1) *Literary Aspect*: 'the great epistolick art' humorously described 559; 'the most useless letter . . . shows one not to be forgotten' 98; 'a short letter to a distant friend . . . an insult' 138 (132); 'ceremony' condemned 183.1, cf. 262 and 553 ('Madam' and 'Dear Madam') 739; unauthorized publication 200; lack of matter 414, cf. 559 (letters written 'with nothing to say'), 614.1, 657 ('a letter about nothing . . . the pure voice of nature'), 692 ('then let her write sentiment'); 'no man is always in a disposition to write' 544, cf. 578; jocular description of the ethics of letter-writing 549; 'how small a part of our minds have we written' 558; concluding formula 640 (see note); 'I wish you (HLT) would write upon *subjects*' 699.

(2) *Formal aspects; see also* POST, and Appendix F. Paper: 119 and 120 on one sheet to avoid double postage, cf. 64 'a double letter'; 211 ruled paper, 549 'mourning paper'; 583 'the paper will not hold much more'; seal: 271, 549 'black wax', 25 'black wafer'; franks: 232 'I have taken the liberty to enclose a letter', cf. 265, 379 ('free'), 315, 536.

(3) *Dates*. Many of J's early letters are undated or incompletely dated. Later he usually gives the day of month (seldom of week) and year, often the place. He exhorts HLT to greater exactitude (see e.g. 645.1, 660.1, 663, 675). Some of his own letters are (certainly or probably) misdated, e.g. 166, 256, 402, 562, 619, 627.1, 660, 660.1, 788, 807, 947.1, 989. I note that three letters (402, 619, 788) are dated July.for June; and in J's unpublished diary for 1732 is a corrigendum: 'hac pag: Jul: pro Jun: habeo' (possibly 'haec . . . habet'). The reverse mistake may occur in 973. The year is wrong in 627.1, 660, 660.1, 894.2, 923.1. '1748' for 1784 is probably a unique aberration.

LIBRARIES. The Royal Library 206 *passim*; Durham: 'mean and scanty' 318 (339, see note); Edinburgh: the Advocates' and the College 320; Oxford: 'the Libraries of Oxford' 53; Paris: the King's 206; St. Andrews: 'luminousness and elegance', compared to the 'new edifice at Streatham' 321 (344).

SUBJECTS

LITERATURE

(1) The book-trade

Printing: 134.2, 958 (cost), 174, 174.1 (speed), 206 (antiquarian, &c.), 387 (a guinea a week a compositor's wage), 709 ('revises'), 1006.1 (the Polyglot Bible).

Bookselling: 5 'a mercenary bookseller'; 6 author to pay any loss; 17 Irish reprints, 49 'I am not cool about this piracy', cf. 51.1 and note, 615; 106.1 'season of publication . . . beginning' (Nov. '56); 178.1 prices, cf. 463 (a full and important discussion of trade discounts, &c.), 510; 363 author's copies (*and see* Index VII, 'book').

(2) Authorship as profession

'Literary property': 'the schemes of a writer are his revenue' 111, cf. 3; J's doctrine of copyright 344, 349; retention of rights 498; patronage 58.1, 61 (both Feb. '55); dedication 58.1, 296, 712, 739, 811.1, 829.

Subscription: 49.1 (Richardson), 132 (AW), 174 and 174.1 (Lye), 178.1 and 179 (J's Shakespeare).

Payment of authors (for payments to J *see* Index VI): 11 (12s. a sheet), 47 (31s. 6d. a sheet), 134.2 (see note), 136 (Percy's *Reliques*; a hundred guineas for three volumes), 514 (Hawkesworth; £100 a volume), 779 (Cumberland's 'third night', £5 net), 811.1 (a hundred guineas for a large octavo), 950 (half-profits after expense of printing recovered).

Anonymity (for J's *see* Index VI): reduces pecuniary value 777.

(3) Composition

'versifying against inclination', 'build without materials' 1; 'daily imitation of the best authours' 3.3.

(4) Kinds

fugitive pieces 3; 'a novel' (i.e. a fictional biography) 23, cf. 326 (353) 'Gothick romances'; epitaphs 269 (Hogarth), 399 (Mrs. Salusbury, cf. 405); books of travel 222 (Boswell), 236 (Baretti), 318 (340, disappointing); books of occasional use 494; juvenilia (J deprecates publication) 514; composition of sermons 704; dramatic dialogue: 'quickness of reciprocation' 911; 'dictionaries are like watches' 998.

(5) Scholarship

'learning' *not* distinguished from literature 6; 'the study of our ancient authours' 53; 'index rerum' 31 and 49 (Richardson); Irish literature 107, 517; 'commentary must arise from . . . fortuitous discoveries' 114; 'he who calls much for information will advance his work but slowly' 348; chronological arrangement recommended in collected works 514; 'lay the foundation, and leave the superstructure to posterity' 517, cf. 453 'superfluous diligence'.

(6) Criticism

'invective' by 'scribblers', its motives 42.1; authors' susceptibility or otherwise to criticism 58, 65; 'the Criticks of the coffeehouse' 70; gallicism 93; 'shorter paragraphs' advised in a poem 106.1; 'we must confess the faults of our favourite' (Shakespeare) 177; a phrase in a poem condemned as 'quite prose', faulty rhymes 269; old writers 'emerge from oblivion by general consent' 353.2; 'a mere antiquarian is a rugged being' 575; few attacks on authors 'make much noise, but by the help of those that they provoke' 863; 'sincere criticism' and 'involuntary criticism' distinguished 911.

(7) Book-collecting

206 *passim*; J's interest in 'large paper' 1006.1.

(8) General

'They who do not read can have nothing to think, and little to say' 686.2.

MIND. *See also* EDUCATION, RECORD. Scepticism: 'Trust as little as you can to report' 140; curiosity: JB's 'wise and noble curiosity' 181; 'curiosity, both rational and fanciful' 276; genius: 'a man of genius seldom ruined but by himself'

147; 'the efficacy of ignorance' 184; omne ignotum: 'things that are at hand are always slighted' 258; intellect: 'intellectual nature abhors a vacuum' 250; common sense: 'in the highest and the lowest things we are all equal' 310; 'mind not at all times equally ready to be put in motion' 326 (355); mental development: the mind after a certain age 'commonly attains its stationary point' 428; 'the greater part of human minds never endeavour their own improvement' 429; chronological arrangement of an author's works 'shows the progress of his mind' 514; history of a man's mind can be written only by himself 519.3; controversy: 'vanity with which every man resists confutation' 575; 'attention should be something less than anxiety' 605.1; mind 'seldom sufficient for its own amusement' 865.1; mind is 'elevated by mere purposes' 912; 'all truth is valuable' 944.

MORALS, the EMOTIONS, &c. Despairing of the alphabet in a region where synonyms abound, and doubtful of my powers of logical classification, I collect here a number of judgements on human nature, partly in the order of their occurrence. This arrangement may illustrate the development of J's thought. For J's own Character see also Index I, and in this Index MIND, RELIGION. The headings below are (with page numbers): Anger (457), Benevolence (456), Bereavement (457), Captiousness (457), Caution (457), Conformity (457), Cunning (457), Discipline (456), Envy (457), Family (456), Faultfinding (456), Favours (455), Flattery (456), Friendship (457), Futurity (455), Gaiety (457), Gluttony (457), Gossip (456), Grief (455), Habit (456), Heroism (457), Idleness (456), Leisure (456), Life seen steadily (456), Local attachment (456), Love, &c. (456), Method (457), Old Age (456), Pleasure (457), Power (457), Principle (457), Prosperity (455), Public Opinion (456), Quarrels (455), Self (456), Sickness (456), Social Intercourse (456), Solitude (455), Stoicism (457), Trifles (456), Veracity (457), Vexation (457), Virtue, Exercise of (456), Vows (456).

Solitude (*see also* Index I, Loneliness): an 'obstacle to pleasure and improvement', contrasted with friendship 3.2; rural innocence 3.2 (ironical, cf. 58 'we are not perhaps as innocent as villagers'); see 326 (359) 'pastoral felicity', 329 (365–6) for J's rejection of the 'philosophers' ' doctrine that the simplest life is the happiest; monastic life attractive but fallacious 138; 'solitude excludes pleasure and does not always secure peace' 194; 'one of the old man's miseries' lack of 'a companion able to partake with him of the past' 571; 'moral suicide' 571.1; folly of 'retiring into Wales' 888.1.

Quarrels: see also QUARRELS in this index: pleasure of 'reconciling variances' 14.

Grief: 'the business of life summons us away from useless grief' 30; 'there is some pleasure in being able to give pain' 204; 'grief is a species of idleness' 302; 'it is not prudent, perhaps not lawful, to indulge it' 338; 'do not indulge your sorrow' 466; 'all sorrow that lasts longer than its cause is morbid' 583; 'sadness only multiplies self' 627.

Favours: 'He that desires only to do right . . . must offend every man that expects favours' 13, cf. 26 (how favours are rated).

Futurity; hope and disappointment: 'next week is but another name for tomorrow' 73, cf. 311; 'fallaciousness of hope and uncertainty of schemes' 78; value of comparing 'experience with expectation' 110, cf. 117; hope 'a species of happiness' 141; 'fallacy of our self-love' 147; 'to prefer one future mode of life to another' requires superhuman faculties 185; 'expectation and disappointment' 266, cf. 190; 'hope was left in the box of Prometheus' 289; 'hope more pleasing than fear' 306; 'at sixty four what promises . . . can Futurity . . . make?' 326 (357); 'all pleasure . . . preconcerted ends in disappointment' 411.

Prosperity: 'success always produces either love or hatred' 51.

SUBJECTS

Idleness: discussed 106 (the 'busy mortal' who 'engages himself in trifles' is excusing himself for neglect of 'more important duties'); excessive idleness 'must end in slavery' 159, cf. 483 (temptation to 'inactivity and delitescence'); 'universal negligence' supposed characteristic of genius 163; 'the incessant cravings of vacancy' 185; 'resolute inactivity' 563; 'sors de l'enchantement' 869.1.

Habit: 'affectation in time improves to habit' 163 (165).

Old Age: 'spiritual ideas' can hardly be acquired in old age 645.

Virtue, Exercise of: a frequent topic, e.g. 106 'an opportunity to exercise the virtue of forgiveness'; see also 724, 785 a rich man 'has it always in his power to benefit others'.

Life seen steadily: 'let us endeavour to see things as they are' 116; 'the common course of life' discussed 864.

Family: 'good brothers make good sisters' 117, cf. J's envy of the Burneys' 'consanguineous unanimity' 749; limits of parental authority 134 (father and son), 308 (father and daughter); 'parents we can have but once' 181; 'I could not love him (Harry Thrale) as a parent' 466; family discord 505.

Love, Marriage, Women: 'you, Madam, whose heart cannot yet dance to such musick' 74; life has nothing better than 'a prudent and virtuous marriage' 147; 'unhappy marriage happens every day to multitudes' 156; 'Nature has given women so much power that the law has very wisely given them little' 157; women 'timorous and yet not cautious' 162; results of happy marriage 222; children should be free from parental authority in marriage 308.

Benevolence: 'men have commonly benevolence in proportion to their capacities' 132.3 (a letter asking a favour); 'stagnation of unactive kindness' 280; 'kindness . . . commonly the exuberance of content' 724; 'kindness . . . is in our power, but fondness is not' 803; man is 'capable of benevolence' 1016.

Leisure: few fit for it; 'the greater part would prey upon the quiet of each other' 140.

Local attachment: 'there is a pleasure in being considerable at home' 138 (133), cf. 233, 261 (J and L'd).

Trifles: 'to rid us of our time' (pictures) 138 (134); small things 'make up the general mass of life' 142; 'sands form the mountain . . . and trifles life' (Young) 252, cf. 537.

Public opinion: 'the world has always a right to be regarded' 159, cf. 988.1.

Self: we can all find time to do what we want 49.3; 'every man's affairs important to himself' 145; 'sordid self-indulgence' produced by disease 369; 'we are seldom sure that we sincerely meant what we omitted to do' 422; 'incommunicative taciturnity' 906.

Gossip: 'every human being a spy' in a small town 159.

Vows: 'do not . . . enchain your volatility by vows' (to JB) 185; 'all unnecessary vows folly' 308.

Fault-finding: 'men do not suspect faults which they do not commit' 70; 'men should not be told of the faults which they have mended' 193.

Social intercourse (see also *solitude* above in this article): 'communication of sentiments . . . necessary, to give vent to the imagination' 194; masquerades condoned 295; 'company better than solitude' 409, cf. 888.1; 'publick life supplies agreeable topics' 414.

Sickness: kindles the natural affections 204; produces selfishness 213, self-indulgence 460.

Discipline: 'the art of government is learned by obedience' 255.

Flattery: 'heroes and princes ruined by flattery' 287; cf. 310 ('why should the poor be flattered?'), 311 (compared to hospitality that 'forces a guest to be drunk'); 'unusual compliments . . . embarrass the feeble . . . and disgust the wise' 405;

'hyperbolical praise corrupts' 855; praise and money 'the two great corrupters' 895.

Envy: neither J nor an old acquaintance 'had risen to the other's envy' 321 (346).

Cunning: of clowns 326 (356).

Principle: 'Principles can only be strong, by the strength of understanding, or the cogency of religion' 337 (386).

Conformity: 'love and reverence . . . produce conformity' 401.

Scruples deprecated 454, 458.

Vexation: aggravated by darkness; 'light your candle and read' 455.

Veracity: 'the Denial ('not at home' to a caller), if it had been feigned, would not have pleased me' 474.

Method: J recommends JB to 'throw life into a method' (a 'prudence' he 'had not practised' himself) 502.

Bereavement: 'to lose three out of four (children) is more than your share' 515; 'a laceration of the mind' 466, cf. 580 (the same phrase), 650 'the continuity of being is lacerated'.

Anger: 'useless resentment' and 'stubborn malignity' 502; family discord 505.

Gaiety 'a duty when health requires it' 511.

Pleasure must be known 'before we can rationally despise' 518; 'every body has some desire . . . to look for pleasure in a bye-path' 647.

Caution: JB's 'cowardly caution' 565.

Stoicism 578.

Servants: 'servants never tell their Masters' 629.

Power: 'few minds to which tyranny is not delightful' 636; ' desire of fame not regulated' dangerous 640; 'ambition in little things better than cowardice in little things' 647; the power of giving pain 876.1.

Heroism: 'the heroick virtues' 647.

Captiousness discussed 746.1.

Friendship: importance of keeping it, as J once said, in repair, 770.

Gluttony described 872.

MYTHOLOGY: an alphabetical list. Baucis 618 (Ovid's); Calypso 58; Chloris 326 (359); Daedalus 925; Dryads 355.1; Ganymede 576; Hercules 233; Hesperian felicity 956; Janus 505; Juno 260; Polyphemus 58; Prometheus 289 (see note); Styx 191; Tantalus 752.

NATURAL SCIENCE: Fauna and Flora of the New World 140; Growth of walnut-tree 194; 'chimistry or experimental philosophy' recommended to JT 277; 'natural curiosities' for Q's cabinet 286.1, 289.2; J 'as Zoologist' 326 (359); J's box filled in Scotland 340; the Burning Glass 858; shells 'have a claim to curiosity' 875; 'genuine scenes of nature' 880; 'the Speaking Image' 965.1.

NATURE. *See also* NATURAL SCIENCE, GARDENS. 'I shall delight to . . . see the stars twinkle in the company of men to whom nature does not spread her volumes . . . in vain' 70; 'the breeze whistling, and the birds singing, and her own heart dancing' 74; 'the beauties of my native plains' 254 (ironical); the waterfall at A'n 282; 'delight in the survey of a Caledonian loch' 313; 'the fall of Fiers' 323 (350); 'Nature's magnificence . . . her minuter beauties'; 'barren desolation' 326 (359), and *passim* in letters from the Hebrides; Talisker: 'a place where the imagination is more amused cannot easily be found' 329 (369); 'the silent solemnity of faint moonshine' 332 (381); 'the rougher powers of Nature . . . in motion . . . crowded the scene' 333; Ignorance of the 'natural productions' of India 353.

NEWSPAPERS ('papers') 362, 524, 649; 'the paper' 279; 'publick papers' 98.1), RUMOUR, &c. Politics 98.1; Illness of Sir J. Philips 136.1; death of Capt. Porter 150; J 'maintains' them 182; Publick transactions in 298; Death of Col (J and JB 'were once drowned') 362; the Edinburgh papers 389; JB's 'paper for the Chronicle'

SUBJECTS

447; a 'saying ... given me in the papers' 524; Foreign newspapers, 'the English keep no secret' ('78) 571; 'Do not pay any regard to the newspapers' 627.1, 'Do not let the papers fright you' 649; J's unwillingness to credit 'report' 329 (365), 362, 645, 645.1; gossip in 'a small country town ... every human being ... is a spy' 159; 'all the noise of the newspapers' 655; 'I am accustomed to think little of newspapers' 781; J's communication to the *London Chronicle* 781, 783; '... privacy, that I may elude the vigilance of the papers' 977.

PAINTING and SCULPTURE. For J's acquaintance among artists *see in* Index I Friends, § x 8; for portraits of himself, Index I Portraits. The English school, 'trifles to rid us of our time' 138, cf. Seward's journey 'to contemplate the pictures of Claude Loraine' 846.

POLITICS. *See also* Politics in Index I.

(1) *General*: 'Publick affairs vex no man' (*L* iv. 220), cf. 98.1, 147, 835.1 (17); private people 'have nothing to do but to serve God' 643; 'who can tell where changes will stop?' 827; 'to a sick man what is the publick?' 922; the profits of office a danger to the national interest 928.

(2) *Events*: a chronological list. ('42) affairs in Europe 17; ('56) 'marches and countermarches in America' 98.1; ('61) 'a new king', 'long in the hands of the Scots' 138; ('63) tumults and distress of the Court 159.1; ('68) the O'd election: principle prevails over interest 201; ('69) 'these times are not much to my mind' 217; ('73) 'faction fills the town with pamphlets' 298; J expects 'violence and outrage' at the next election 299; 'these (Macdonalds of Kingsburgh) are not Whigs' 329 (367); ('74) 'the struggles of a feeble ministry' 353; ('75) 'confidence in Government diminished' 382; 'I have little confidence in our present statesmen' 415; 'I do not much like the news' from America; 'we shall teach them our own knowledge' 427; ('77) regard due to public petitions 522.1, 'the voice of the publick ought to be heard' 524; the militia 534; futility of 'political controversy' 549; ('78) the militia camps 583, 585.1, 587; ('79) 'is any King a Whig?' 606; the threat of invasion 627.1, 629, 635, 638, 'has vanished as I expected' 643; 'the nation full of distress' 638, 'all trade is dead' 643; ('80) the contractor's bill 659; ('82) 'The Men are got in, whom I have endeavoured to keep out' 776 (30 March); 'we have taken seventeen French transports' 778 (see note); 'these are not pleasant times' 793, 'we seem to be sinking' 797; ('83) 'Equal representation' condemned, 'I am afraid of a civil war' 827; 'foreign miscarriages' and 'intestine discontents' 835.1 (17); the East India company 907, cf. 928; 'the times are dismal and gloomy' 922; ('84) party-strife, when the 'real power of Government' is lost 928; 'corrupt ... atmosphere of the house of commons' 935.1; affairs in India 928; 'the indecency with which the King is ... treated' 936, 942; limits of a minister's power 942.

POST. *See* Appendix F. The L'n penny post used occasionally by J, e.g. 6; none on Sunday 497; express 679; by-post 427; cost: 'a double letter' (i.e. two sheets) 64; 'double postage' (on a forwarded letter) 106; money sent by post 119; post to and from places: A'n (miscarriage or delay) 285, 417, 543; B'n 'awkward' 709; Hebrides: Skye once a week 324, Mull none 332 (378), 'insular posts uncertain' 334; L'd: post-night 425 (Wed.), 427 (Mon.); O'd: daily 201; 'so ill-regulated that we cannot receive letters and answer them the same day' 401, cf. 382, 383; Spilsby, Lincolnshire (?) 268.

POVERTY. *See in* Index II J's admonitions to JB to live within his means.

QUARRELS. *See in* Index II: Carmichael, Desmoulins, Levet, Williams. The polish of eighteenth-century society was often scratched by noisy altercation. Baretti and an abbot 142, and Davies 295, and Huggins 147; Colman and Goldsmith 304; Colson and J 401, 403; Davies and Baretti 295; Dodsley and Garrick 117; Garrick and Dodsley 117, and Murphy 303.2, 304; Goldsmith and Colman 304; Huggins and Baretti 147; J and Colson 401, 403, and Percy 575, and TW 215 (see note);

Langley and JT 418; Murphy and Garrick 303.2, 304; Percy and J 575; JT and Langley 418; Warton, T, and Johnson 215 (see note).

RECORD and RETROSPECT. These are some of the places in which J urges his favourite theme of the value of recording events and thoughts, and of the danger of delaying to do so, or discusses the pains and pleasures of recollection. To Elphinston; 'write down minutely what you remember of her' (his mother) 30; to Hector 71.1, 105.1; to BL 110 ('while the first impression remains fresh'), 183 ('if you neglect to write, information will be vain'); to Baretti: 'keep an exact journal' 138; to JB: 'I hope you continue your journal' 163; to HLT: 'proper memorials of all that happens' 329 (371); 'the history of your own mind' 428; 'the Thraliana . . . a very curious collection posterity will find it' (it was first published in full in 1942) 542; of Dodd: 'the history of his own mind' can be written only by himself 519.3; to Welch: full directions for his daughter's journal in Italy 571; 'do not imagine that you shall always remember even what perhaps you now think it impossible to forget' 704; *See also* 326 (356, birthday thoughts), 338 (vain regrets).

RELIGION and RELIGIOUS OBSERVANCE. See Religion in Index I and DEATH above. Grandison's 'compromise in religion' (mixed marriages) 51.1; 'contemplation on the great event which (Christmas) commemorates' 57; prayer 'for any thing temporal' must be conditional 79; 'prayers can pass the line, and the Tropics' 834; study of theology every man's duty 163; 'Christianity the highest perfection of humanity' 184; limited denial, by the Roman Church, of 'the use of the bible' 184; Italy said to be 'divided between bigotry and atheism' 206 (219); immunities claimed by dissenters 298; Edinburgh: 'the Cathedral . . . once a church' 320; chapels in the Hebrides, created by 'the superstitious votaries of the Romish Church' and demolished by 'the active zeal of Protestant devotion' 329 (366), cf. 332 (379 'presbyterian bigotry', 381 'the venerable seat of ancient sanctity'); place of fancy in religion 352; toleration deprecated 393; J's 'Quaker friends' (Lloyd) at B'm 464.1; resignation in bereavement 465 (*see also* Bereavement p. 457); 'enemies to the clergy' likely to be encouraged by Dodd's execution 520; 'the blindness of Mahometans' 598; ('79) stipend of a curate £50, 618.1; pluralism 646; clergy as civilizers 704.

SCOTS, the. *See also* Scotland in Index IV. J's observations on Scotland and the Scots are almost confined to the letters from Sc. of '73 and those written early in '74, so that a full index seems not necessary. Much the same ground is covered by the indexes to my edition of the *Journey* and *Tour*, and by the relevant articles in the index to the *Life*.

(1) *General*: Speech: 'broad Scotch' (Duchess of Douglas) 320, 'loses her Scotch' (Lady Rothes) 507, 'not much' (Mrs. Boswell), 'very little' (JB) 510; 'Scotch conspiracy in national falsehood' 378; cf. ('61) 138, George III 'long in the hands of the Scots'; J's praise of '. . . every thing Scotch but . . .' 398 (if any reader is inclined to resent J's (almost invariable) use of this form, I remind him that JB himself is described, in an Edinburgh title-page of 1760, as one of a number of 'Scotch Gentlemen'); Inferiority of education in Scotland 398; 'jokes with Jack Wilkes upon the Scots' 479; Trees or their absence; though the references in the letters, see below, are almost all to the Highlands, J extends his censure to all Scotland; 'The Scotch write English wonderfully well' 515.

(2) *Highlands and Islands*: A selection. Beggars 323 (349); Cleanliness 329 (372); Climate *passim*, especially 326 (360, 'almost every Breath of air . . . a storm'), 329 (374), 331 ('wind and rain . . . our weather'), 336 ('cataracts'), 342 (storms almost continuous for five months); the travellers chose a very bad year; Dress: *see also* THINGS in this index; 321 (345, women in plaids); 327 (362 'headdress'); 329 (373, Highland dress 'forbidden by law'); Earse: *see* LANGUAGES; Emigration 326 (354), 329 (366); Fees 322 'no officer gaping for a fee' (Aberdeen); Feudalism

528 (approaching end of 'the feudal modes of life'); Food and Drink *passim*; 329 (373) the dram; 'Forty-five', the 326 (360 Malcolm Macleod and the Prince); 'no foolish healths' 327; 327 (362 Macleod of Raasay), 329 (367 Flora Macdonald), 639 ('History of the late insurrection'); Hospitality *passim*; 329 (368 'the golden age', 373), 398; Improvements: 323 (349, 'for immediate profit'), 329 (372, 'not arrived at delicate discriminations'), 331 (Col); Islands: 'Our ramble hangs upon my imagination' 528; 'Laxity of Highland conversation' (*Journey* ed. 1924, 45) 380; Rents: *See* ECONOMICS in this index; Scenery: *See also* NATURE in this index. 332 (381 'silent solemnity of faint moonshine'), 333 ('the rougher powers of Nature'), 337 ('that wild recess of life'); Second Sight, 'some talk of the' 326 (360); Highland Susceptibility 390 ('many a dirk'); Travel dearer in proportion than in England 329 (371); Trees or Absence of Trees 323 (348 'not . . . five trees fit for the Carpenter, 349 fruit trees), 329 (369 'a garden . . . shaded by trees'), 331 (Mull, 'literally no tree'), 528 (Dick 'not angry that I could not find trees, where trees were not').

The SEA and SHIPS. For Sea-bathing *see* HEALTH. 'the grossness of a ship' unsuitable for a lady (FR) 162; 'the Shrewsbury an Eastindia Ship' 245; ('73) J and JB 'imagined that the sea was an open road' 329 (364).

THEATRE. *See also in* Index II Abington, Chetwood, Colman, Fletewood, Foote, Garrick, Kemble, Porter (M.), Powell, Sheridan, Siddons. J's theatre-going 138.

THINGS, HOUSEHOLD CONCERNS, &c. *See also* FOOD, and for prices ECONOMICS, for Highland dress SCOTS. China: Derby china pretty, 'contagion of Chinafancy' 549; cloath: Irish 242; coaldust (fuel) 321 (343); dress: mourning 42, 393, 395; Highland 329 (373); 'dress and feathers' 539; HLT's wig 562; granite (Aberdeen, London pavements) 321 (345); musical instruments 541.1 (JT); plaid 321 (345); prints 634; reading-glass 207.1 (LP); sanitation: 'the garden' 979; shoes 321 (345), 323 (349, Highlanders); 'silk mils' 549 (Derby); silver preferred to fine china 549; snuff 326 (356, Highlanders); sugar animals 477; table cloaths 572 (HLT); tipping 322 ('no officer gaping for a fee' at Aberdeen); refused by a keeper 326 (Loch Lomond); tobacco 326 (356, Highlanders); turf (fuel) 321 (343); turnips 331 (Col); washing week 538; watch 649.2.

TRANSPORT. *See also* TRAVEL.

(1) *Of persons*: Public coaches (usu. 'coach', sometimes 'carriage'; 'stage' 251, 278.2; 'stage coach' 279; 'Berlin' 165.1): 'not the worst bed' 279; L'n and A'n 237.1; and Bath 476; and B'n 220; and Edinburgh 339; and L'd 192, 192.1, 220, 251 (Frank 'rather upon' than 'in' it), 265, 278.2, 279; and O'd 340.1, 397.1, 401, 402; ('82) 789.1 'without fatigue in the . . . coach', cf. 891; B'm and O'd 289.2, 290; Post-chaises: J goes from L'd to B'm by chaise 193.1, 289.2; from L'n to Edinburgh (with Chambers as far as Newcastle) and from Edinburgh to Inverness (with JB) 318 (339), 323 (350) (but from Edinburgh to L'n by coach, *L* v. 401); 'les chaises de poste me couteront beaucoup' 400, 401, 'I grudge the cost' 403, 'I took a post-chaise' 404 ('75, O'd to L'd); J offers to 'take a chaise' L'd to A'n 464; 'to go down' (L'n to L'd) 'cost me seven guineas' 623; Private carriages: Miss Aston's chaise 616; By water: 20 miles for a shilling, Gravesend to Billingsgate 869.

(2) *Of goods*: carrier weekly, O'd to B'm 3.1; J sends books to B'm 'by the carrier' 69, to L'd 164, cf. 433, 536, 564 ('I will pay the carriage when we meet'); J asks JB if he can send 'porter into the Hebrides' and asks him to send documents, if bulky, 'by the carrier. I do not like trusting winds and waves' 343; sends JB the *Journey* by post; this very unusual 371 (see note); offer to send a book to A'n 'in any parcel which is sent weekly to the tradesmen' 372; inquires if the Knightsbridge powder can be franked 536.

TRAVEL. *See also* TRANSPORT. travellers 'see mores hominum multorum' 256; 'he that wanders . . . sees new forms of human misery', travel, like books of travel, 'ends in disappointment', travellers see 'minute discriminations of places and manners' 318 (340); 'the use of travelling is to regulate imagination by reality' 326 (359); J's humorous notion to 'take a ramble in India' 417; foreign travel: 'vast accession of images and observations' 571; highwaymen 583.

YOUTH. 'every new action a kind of experiment' 103; 'towering in the confidence of twenty one' 117; 'apt to be too rigorous in our expectations' 155; choice of profession 185; 'transition from the protection of others to our own conduct is a very awful point of human existence' 387.2.

JOHNSON'S WORKS

This index lists, in the order of first publication, all J's own books, and his contributions to periodicals or to books by others, that are mentioned in his letters. His projected works are given under the year. Works written or projected by others with his advice, encouragement, &c., are given in square brackets under the year of mention.

References are not ordinarily given to the Bibliography (Courtney–Smith) or its Supplement (Chapman–Hazen), since these works follow the same plan as mine. The symbol + after the date of first publication indicates that there were later editions in J's lifetime, not here specified. The format is presumed to be octavo unless it is stated.

J's reluctance to put his name to a book seems to be mere 'anfractuosity'. As early as 1759 he writes 'I will not print my name,'—to *Rasselas*—'but expect it to be known' (124). But earlier still, 1756, he warned Chambers not to betray him: 'though it is known conjecturally, I would not have it made certain' (98.1). Yet earlier still, perhaps in 1753, he had offered to write a preface for Bathurst 'and put my name to it' (47). I believe that he put his name only to *Irene*, the *Dictionary*, and *The Lives of the Poets*. In 1756 he criticized JW for publishing his *Essay* on Pope 'without acquainting your friends' (96).

1734. 'Proposals' for an edition of the Latin Poems of Politian. These were abortive 2.1.

1738. 'On a Riddle by Eliza', in Greek and Latin. *GM* Mar. '38, 210. ('38) J writes to Cave 'I have compos'd a Greek Epigram to Eliza' 7; 'Chinese Stories' 9 (see note); 'Ad Urbanum'. *GM* Mar. '38, 156; ('38) 'your (Cave's) commendation of my trifle' 5.

1738 (June)–43 (Feb.). Debates in the senate of Magna Lilliputia. *GM* '38–'43. Collected as *Debates in Parliament by Samuel Johnson* 1787, 2 vols., Stockdale. *L* i. 115, 501. ('38) 'fewer alterations than usual in the debates' 9; ('43) 'With the debates shall I not have business enough?' 15.

1738 (Sept.). 'To Lady F—ce at Bury Assizes'. *GM* Sept. '38, 486. ('38) 'The verses on Lady Firebrace' 9.

1738 (Oct.). 'Proposals for printing the History of the Council of Trent, translated from the Italian of Father Paul Sarpi; with the Authour's Life, and Notes . . . from the French edition of

Dr. Le Courayer. . . . By S. Johnson'. *Weekly Miscellany* 21 Oct. '38 (*L* i. 107, 135). Dodsley, Rivington, Cave. The translation though partly printed and paid for was not published. ('38) J proposes 'a new translation' 4, 'impediments . . . a negligent Translator' 9, asks Cave for 'a dozen Proposals' 10 (but see note).

1738+. London: A Poem, in Imitation of the Third Satire of Juvenal. Dodsley, 1s. Fo. *Poems* p. 1. ('38) Sends Cave 'the inclosed poem in my hands to dispose of for the benefit of the author' who is in difficulties, offers to 'alter any stroke of satire which you may dislike' 5, discusses terms, proposes to 'read the lines' to Dodsley and secure 'his name in the Title-page' 6, has taken 'the Copy to Dodsley's', the quotations from Juvenal 'must be subjoined', 'beauty of the performance' 7, Dodsley's concurrence 8.

1739. *A Commentary on Mr. Pope's Principles of Morality, or Essay on Man. By Mons*^r *Crousaz*. Dodd, 1739. Cave,

1742. (*L* iv. 494, where the translation of the French original (for which *see* Index III) was first attributed to J by Dr. Powell. *See also* Chapman–Hazen 124 for the edition of 1739, which was unknown to Dr. P., and i. 429.) ('38) 'the Commentary cannot be prosecuted with any appearance of success' 10.

1742. 'Charles of Sweden', a projected drama, an early form of *The Vanity of Human Wishes*. (Aug. '42) 'I propose to get Charles of Sweden ready for this winter' 17.

1743. 'Historical Design', a projected work the plan of which J submitted to Cave, two guineas a sheet 15; 'the Inscription' 15 (see note); 'at a loss for the Lives and Characters' of four politicians, presumably wanted for this project 18.

1743–4. *Catalogus Bibliothecae Harleianae.* Osborne. 206 (215).

1744+ (Feb.). An Account of the Life of Mr. Richard Savage. Roberts, 2*s.* 6*d.* ('43) Tells Cave he is ready to start, and do half a sheet daily, suggests types to be used, asks for printed materials 15, letter to 'Mr. Urban', the Life will depend on personal knowledge and authentic documents 23.

[1747. A work by Richard Bathurst, q.v. in Index II. (? '53) 47.]

1749+. Irene: a Tragedy. . . . By Mr. Samuel Johnson. Dodsley and Cooper, 1*s.* 6*d. Poems* 233. ('38) 'Irene looks upon you (Cave) as one of her best friends' 8; ('40) Garrick reports that *I.* 'is at last become a kind of Favourite among the Players', Fletewood promises to produce this or next season, Chetwood offers 50 guineas for the copy 12; ('42) tells Taylor to 'keep Irene close' 17; ('50) prologue to *Comus* 'by the author of *Irene*' 27; ('84) J hopes to send a copy to Adams 1038.

1750 (20 Mar.)–52 (14 Mar.)+. The Rambler. Payne and Bouquet, 2*d.* each number, F°.

The Rambler. Edinburgh, Gordon Wright and others, 1750–2, 1*d.* each number, small 8° ('duodecimo'). ('51 or '52) J asks Elphinston to send him 'six more volumes' of the Edinb. ed. and to send a set to Ruddiman, thanks E for his translations of mottoes 29.

Other References (general, or to later edd.). ('83) given to 'the bearer' 843; 'the boy that likes Rambler better than apples' 897; ('84) a Russian translation promised (it did not appear), J's prayer for 'all who shall read my pages' 931; sends two sets to Adams 1038.

1750–1. The Student, or the Oxford and Cambridge Monthly Miscellany. Oxford, Newbery (London), and J. Barrett (Oxford). ('51) J asks Newbery for £2, presumably in connexion with his contribution to this periodical, of which N was the London publisher 32.

1751. 'my Book', not identified 36.

1752 (7 Nov.)–54 (9 Mar.)+. The Adventurer. Payne, 2*d.* each number, F°. ('53) J 'as one of the fraternity', though not (yet, 8 Mar.) a contributor 'beyond now and then a motto', invites J. Warton to 'furnish one paper a month, at two guineas', literary or critical, two of the writers (i.e. Hawkesworth and ? Bathurst) 'my particular friends' 46 (see note); ('54) congratulates JW on his share 51, will send Wise 'a set of my own Books (i.e. author's copies) of the new edition' (in 4 vols. 8° '54) 55.

[? 1753. Richard Bathurst (q.v. in Index II): A Geographical Dictionary. J recommends the work to Strahan and offers a preface 47.]

1755 (15 Apr.). A Dictionary of the English Language. . . . By Samuel Johnson, A.M. In Two Volumes. Printed by Strahan for the Knaptons, the Longmans, Hitch and Hawes, Millar, and the Dodsleys. F°, 90*s.*

Composition and Printing. ('46) J invites 'the Gentlemen' to breakfast 'that we may sign' 23.1; ('47) The agreement 'fairly engrossed', the 'Partners' 23.2; ('51) J refuses to see the Partners till Vol. I is in the press 35, undertakes to furnish a sheet daily 37, has little assistance from his assistants 38, difficulties of preparing copy 39; ('52) Macbean and Hamilton, their wager, J asks Millar to lend books 44; ('53) printing far advanced 48; ('54) asks Birch to lend Clarendon 50; ('54) 'cannot finish to my mind without visiting the Libraries of Oxford' 53, finds little there 52; ('55) will keep back the title-page for insertion of his Oxford M.A. 56, begins 'to see land' after 'this vast sea of words', speculates on the reception of the book 58, 65, hopes (20 Mar.) to see it bound next week, 'vasta mole superbus' 64, now coming 'in luminis oras' 65, (29 Mar.) sends parts for Birch's inspection 66.

Publication and Reception. ('55) Refers Burney (8 Apr.) to Dodsley 67, intends to send to Hector 69 but 'all my Books were got from me' 71.1, dictionary-making 'not so very unpleasant' 69, 'criticks of the coffeehouse' 70, 'sells well' 72, confusion caused by death of Knapton and Longman 73; ('57) CB's 'commendation' 112.

Other References. Borowcop hill 232; ('73) 'found it full as often better, as worse, than I expected' 295.

Later Editions. The 8vo Abridgement 1756 (Jan.). The same booksellers, 10*s*.; ('56) 94 may refer to advance payments on this; ('84) sends copies of both books to Adams 1038.

The Fourth Edition, revised by the Author, 1773 (early). ('71) 'A very great work, the revision of my Dictionary', asks BL for corrections 268; ('72) work will keep him in L'n till end of Sept. 275.1, hopes to finish 277, (8 Oct.) finished 278, 278.1, 'not much delighted' 278; ('73) 'the main fabrick ... remains as it was' 295, 'added little to its usefulness' 298, Bagshaw's additions too late 307, before May '74 tells Governor Johnstone he was satisfied with his treatment by the booksellers 1132.

1755. 'I intend in the winter to open a Bibliotheque' 65. The scheme was abortive. In the same year J asks T. Warton for information about MSS.

of Sir Thomas More in Bodley 'that I may know whether they are yet unpublished' 75. Perhaps he contemplated an account or an edition of these works.

1756. 'A Dissertation on the Epitaphs written by Pope': in *The Universal Visiter.* Reprinted in the Life of Pope.

1756 (Mar. or earlier). Christian Morals: by Sir Thomas Brown, of Norwich.... The Second Edition, With a life of the author, by Samuel Johnson. Payne, 2*s*. 6*d*. ('56) Sends Richardson (Feb.) 'this little book, which is all that I have published this winter' 90, sends Birch 'the Life of Sir Thomas Browne' 95; ('58) mentioned 113.

1756 (June). For the Shakespeare Proposals see below s.a. 1765.

1756-7. The Literary Magazine: or Universal Review (monthly May '56 to July '58). J. Richardson. (31 July '56) Thanks Chambers for his 'Life' and invites further contributions; his own share in the Mag. 'known conjecturally' 98.1 (see note); (Mar. '58) 'Since the Life of Brown ('56) I have been a little engaged from time to time in the *Literary Magazine*, but not very lately', will send Mrs. Burney the numbers to which he contributed 113.

1758-60+. The Idler: in *The Universal Chronicle*; R. Stevens and/or J. Payne; weekly 15 Apr. '58-5 Apr. '60, F°; republished Oct. '61 as The Idler, 2 vols. 12°, Newbery, 5*s*. sewed. ('62) the 12° ed. sent to Baretti 142, to Morison 146; ('84) sends a copy to Adams 1038.

1759 Letters for John Gwynn. *See* App. A in Vol. I.

1759 (19 Apr.)+. (Rasselas:) The Prince of Abissinia. A Tale. The Dodsleys and Johnston. 5*s*. ('59) J tells Strahan (20 Jan.) of 'a thing which I was preparing', 'The choice of Life or The History of ... Prince of Abissinia', its bulk, choice of bookseller, and terms of publication, 'I will not print my name, but expect it to be known' 124; (23 Mar.) 'I am going to publish a little story book' 130; (10 May) 'I sent, last week, some of my works' ('books' conj. R. W. C.; see note) for L. Porter and others 131; ('73) 'The little Book has been well received, and is translated into Italian, French, German, and Dutch' 298, 'I have got an Italian Rasselas' 338.

The History of Rasselas, Prince of Abissinia. An Asiatic Tale. . . . America: Printed for every purchaser. Philadelphia 1768. ('73) 'it flatters an Authour, because the Printer seems to have expected that it would be scattered among the People' 298.

Later Reference. ('84) sends a copy to Adams 1038.

1756–65. Shakespeare.

1756. 1 June. Proposals for printing, by Subscription, the Dramatick Works of William Shakespeare, Corrected and Illustrated by Samuel Johnson (Tonson and others). ('56, '57) Proposals or Receipts for 'a work which requires the concurrence of my friends' sent to Birch 97, to an anon. corresp. 99.1, to Hector 103, 105.1, 108, to Burney 112 (subscription 'not very successful'), 113, to T. Warton and Allen 114, to Chambers 114.1; ('65) J. Warton's receipt(s) 176; some receipts for two guineas, of which J entitled to one only 176.1; receipts must be sent to a bookseller 179.— Proposals printed in *London Chronicle* 12–14 April '57, 113.

1765 Oct. + The Plays of William Shakespeare, in eight volumes, with . . . Notes by Sam. Johnson (Tonson and others; 2 guineas unbound). Mr. Johnson's Preface to his Edition of Shakespear's Plays (1s.).

(1) *Progress of the Work.* ('56) asks Birch to lend 'any of the contemporaries or ancestors' of Sh. 97; ('57) printing began (June) 109, hopes (Dec.) to publish 'about March' 112; ('58) asks Tonson to lend £40 (? on the Sh.) 112.1, (March) 'will be published before summer' 113, 'where I am quite at a loss, I confess my ignorance' 113, welcomes T. Warton's contributions, intends an Appendix, 'so that nothing comes too late' 114, wishes JW would join 114, hopes for more from TW

115; ('62) hopes soon to send to Baretti 142; ('63) intends to take Sh. with him on a visit to Percy 159.1; (? '64) 'I must finish my book' 162; ('65) offers to submit plays to Garrick 168, hopes to finish in Aug. 172, 'out of my hands' (1 Oct.) 175; (? '65) asks Dodsley to send a Sh. 'though in sheets' 179.1; (n.d.) asks Garrick to return plays 1127.1.

(2) *Publication and Reception.* ('65) 'as I felt no solicitude about this work, I receive no great comfort from its conclusion' 176, Burney's approbation and J's defence, 'we must confess the faults of our favourite, to gain credit to our praise of his excellencies' 177, sold by booksellers for 40s. contrary to agreement, demand brisk 178.1, Jenkinson's approbation 178.2; ('66) has 'maintained the newspapers these many weeks' 182.

(3) *Later Edition.*

1773. . . . Notes by Samuel Johnson and George Steevens. With an Appendix. ('70) asks Farmer to perfect Steevens's catalogue of translations which Sh. might have used 227 (L ii. 489), St. 'helps me in this edition', T. Warton asked for notes, no appendix this time (but see L ii. 490) 230, asks J. Warton to rewrite the account of his opinion of *Lear* 239 (L ii. 115), reminds Rivington of an agreement that the additions be printed separately for former purchasers 243; ('71) 'I have done very little', but Steevens has plundered Farmer's pamphlet and has diligently collected authorities, he 'undertakes the whole care of this impression'; can Farmer now send the catalogue of translations? 244.

1770 (Jan.). The False Alarm. Cadell, 1s. ('70) 'the papers' to be sent to HLT 226.1; ('71) J has 2 copies bound 270.

1771 (Mar.). Thoughts on the late Transactions respecting Falkland's Islands. Cadell, 1s. 6d. [(2 Oct., n.y.) J sends HLT 'a pamphlet' 240 (but see note)]; (24 Oct. '70) 'I have now so far done my work, that . . .' probably refers to this pamphlet, 240.1; (20 Mar. '71) 'after much lingering of my own, and much of the Ministry, I have at length got out my paper', but Lord North 'ordered the sale to stop', though not in time 246, mentioned 268, J has 2 copies bound 270.

Garrick's Epitaph on Hogarth, Johnson's suggestions for its improvement (*Poems* 154). ('71) 'Suppose you worked upon something like this' (8 lines follow) 269.

1772. 'Motto' (a Latin couplet) for Banks's goat 271, 272.

1773 (Dec.). Latin verses on Inchkenneth. For the date see *Poems* 169. ('75) J sends them to JB 374.

1774 (Dec. or later). The Patriot. Cadell. 6d. ('74) 'called for by my political friends on Friday ⟨18 Nov.⟩' and 'written on Saturday' 363.

Greek Epitaph on Goldsmith. ('74) J sends Langton his 'tetrastick on poor Goldsmith' 358.

1774 or earlier. Translation of Oldys's verses 'Busy, curious, thirsty Fly' (*Poems* 171). ('74) J asks Langton to transcribe, if he has it, J's Latin version 358.

1775 (end of Dec. '74). A Journey to the Western Islands of Scotland. Strahan and Cadell. 5s.

Composition and Printing. ('73) For J's probable use of his letters to HLT see 321 note; 'I keep a book of remarks (lost) and Boswell writes a regular journal' 329 (370), asks JB to 'enquire the order of the Clans' and to 'quicken Dr. Webster' 340; ('74) nothing from JB or Dr. W 343, asks Steevens to lend Lesley's *History* or any book on Scotland except Boetius and Buchanan 345, Dr. W's help disappointing 348, hopes to be diligent 'next week' (March) 352, 'first sheets' of MS. put to press June, JB praised in first paragraph, 'one volume in octavo, not thick' 356, impracticable to entrust MS. to JB 357, 360, expects some mistakes, but 'I deal more in notions than in facts' 357, tells BL printing begun 358, (1 Oct.) regrets interruption by Welsh tour 360 (but all 'except two sheets' written previously, i.e. by 4 July, 363), (20 Oct.) 240 pages

printed, 'a pretty book, I hope, it will be' 360.1, 362; (25 Nov.) last page corrected, 'I have mentioned all that you (JB) recommended' 363, 374, asks JB to report what he and others think 363, asks Strahan to cancel a page, the cancelled passage due to 'zeal or wantonness' 364, (17 Dec.) Strahan does not publish till after the holidays, only the King and HLT to have early copies, HLT to mark the Errata 365.2.

Publication and Reception. ('73) Presentation copies: JB to have 25 356, ('74) J will follow JB's advice 360, cannot send before publication, 'trade is as diligent as courtesy' 363, HLT's copy and the King's 365.2, Warren Hastings's 367, the King's sent through Hunter 369.1, Hunter's own 369.1, King's and Queen's avidity, the Q borrows Hunter's 369.2; ('75) JB's sent by post, J will send a parcel, JB had not included his father, 371, Taylor's, how to be sent 372, will send JB's parcel as soon as possible 374, 375, Hector's 376.1, Strahan promises to send 24 to JB, 4 are for himself the rest to distribute 380, cf. 505; J refuses to retract about Macpherson 373, Macph. furious, J asks JB for help, the book 'much liked' in L'n 374, JB's praise and Macph.'s silence 375, 'the Scotch are angry', King says J must not go there again 376.1, J discusses Ossian with JB 378+ (*see also* Index II, Macpherson), asks JB to note errors, sale 'sufficiently quick', 'they printed four thousand' 380, apologies to Macleod of Raasa for a mistake, will correct when reprinted, and JB shall advertise correction in Edinburgh papers 389, 'I have offended . . . the Nation of Rasay . . . many a dirk will imagination . . . fix in my heart' 390; ('78) 'my old reckoning with Mr Cadell' probably refers to money due for the *Journey* 589.2; ('79) 'an hundred pounds', possibly a payment for the *Journey* 622 (see note); ('81) money still due 713.

Later Editions: [Second edition] 1775. ('75) This no doubt formed part of the 4,000 printed 380; *A New*

Edition. 1785. This includes the Edinburgh advertisement (above, 389); ('84) J sends a copy to Adams 1038.

1775 (8 Mar.). Taxation No Tyranny; an Answer to the Resolution and Address of the American Congress. Cadell. 1s. 6d. ('75) 'Going (21 Jan.) to write against the Americans', can JB help? it is a secret 374, (3 Feb.) progress slow 376, (end of Feb.) going to Oxford, 'shall leave the pamflet to shift for itself' 379, (1 Mar.) ministerial changes 'evidence of timidity' but J acquiesces, asks Strahan to print 6 without change, to send a copy to Miss Aston, 'the last paragraph was indeed rather contemptuous' [L ii. 314, its original state] 381, (3 Mar.) reasons of acquiescence, send presentation copies to AW, lay by the 6, send to Cooper, &c. 382, will send to Hector 384.3, 'again gotten into politicks', will send to Taylor 384.4, 'the patriots pelt me with answers' [Courtney 126, a list] 387, Edward Bentham's approval 387.1 (?), sends to Miss Aston 405; ('76) Wesley's approval 451.

1776 (May). Political Tracts (the 4 pamphlets). Strahan and Cadell, 4s. ('76) 'a man who has had the honour of vindicating his Majesty's government' (in reference to his political writings in general) 472, 'my political tracts' printed, a copy for HT 476, copies for the Benedictines 489; ('79) 'an hundred pounds', possibly a payment for the Tracts 622 (see note); ('81) payment still due 713; ('84) sends a copy to Adams 1038.

Dedication for Burney, see below s.a. 1784.

Latin Epitaph on Goldsmith in Westminster Abbey. ('76) 'the poor dear Doctor's epitaph', JR to show it to Club 480, two copies 490, 491.

[Percival Stockdale's projected History of Spain in 3 vols. 8vo proposed (? to Cadell). ('76) not published 497.1.]

1777 (Jan.) J's charade on Barnard 506.1.

(March) J's Proposals for Shaw's *Analysis of the Galic Language* 510.

1777 (May). Prologue to Hugh Kelly's A Word to the Wise, revived at Covent Garden 13 and 29 May. *Public Advertiser* 31 May, &c., &c. *Poems* 60. 'Commended by fine (?) Ladies' 1 June 519.1, 'disowned' by Lucy Porter 535.

1777 (May–June). The Convict's Address to his Unhappy Brethren and other pieces written for William Dodd. See, in addition to the usual sources, R. W. C., *Papers Written by Dr. Johnson and Dr. Dodd*, Oxford 1926. This conjectural reconstruction was in some particulars rectified by the discovery 1929 of a copy of *Occasional Papers by the late William Dodd* 1777, and other evidence; see Chapman–Hazen. See also Dodd in Index II. J enjoins secrecy about 'this letter' (to the King) 521; 'Many of his petitions and some of his letters' written by J 524, a false attribution 524; his Sermon (i.e. the *Address*) to be sent 'to the King if it can be done' and to Ministers 521.1; JB's request for information 528; 'Dr. J could not make a better' sermon (Lucy Porter, not in the secret) 536.

1777 (July). J submits two epitaphs to Lawrence 531.2.

1779. Baretti's *Carmen Seculare* (n.d.). See *Poems* 187. ('79) 592 (see note).

1779–81. 'The Lives of the Poets.'
(1) The 'Poets'.
(2) The 'Prefaces'.
(3) Later Editions.
(4) Later References, to no specified edition.
(5) Alphabetical List of the Lives.

(1) The Works of the English Poets. With Prefaces, Biographical and Critical, by Samuel Johnson. 1779 (? June), 56 vols. Many Booksellers. Often lettered 'Johnson's Poets'. The price of the first instalment, '79, 56 vols. of *Poets* and 4 of *Prefaces*, was £7. 10s.; in '81 were added 2 vols. of *Index* (dated 1780) and Vols. 5–10 of *Prefaces*, £1. The *Prefaces* were not sold separately. Index to the English Poets, 1780. 2 vols. (The physical relation of the *Poets* to the *Prefaces* is discussed in Chapman–Hazen. Both series are in the very small 8° which was often called 12°; so the ed. in 4 vols. 1781 (see below) was distinguished

467

as 'the octavo edition'.) ('77) 'I think I have persuaded the booksellers to insert something of Thomson' 515 (May), 'I have recommended the volume of Dr. Watts to be added' 526 (July), drama excluded 530; ('78) the index 594, 595; ('79) a set for Mrs. Boswell 607, 714, 'our edition' 611; sales by Bowen of B'n (his '4 shares' = 60 sets, which may suggest that 1,500 were printed) 636, 637; ('80) J complains of an obscene piece by Rowe in 'your Edition, which is very impudently called mine' 670.

(2) The 'Lives'. Prefaces, Biographical and Critical, to the Works of the English Poets. By Samuel Johnson. The same Booksellers. Vols. 1–4 (? June) 1779, vols. 5–10 (? May) 1781. ('77) 'I am engaged (May) to write little Lives, and little Prefaces, to a little edition of the English Poets' 515, asks Sharp for information about Watts 526, Farmer for Cambridge materials 530, picks up information in Bodleian 532, 533, asks HLT to lend *Biographia Britannica* 551, 561.1, 'I am to be very busy about my Lives' 554, 'you know, I have some work to do' 555, 556, 'little lives and little criticisms may serve' 561; ('78) 'languid neglect of my affairs' (Jan.) 568, asks Nichols for Denham, Butler, and Waller in half-binding to show to friends, and hopes 'the press shall stand no more' 581, apologies to Cadell for delay 584, hopes (Nov.) to send JB 'a few lives to read' 593, asks Nichols for revises 597; ('79) a week's work left 602, 'some little books to send soon' to LP 605, (10 Mar.) Lives 'not yet quite printed, put neatly together' for the King 606, copies for Mrs. Boswell 607, 625, for Hailes 607, for Auchinleck (?) 607, for HLT, 'I have sent you the books' 608.1, Cadell's complaint that presentation copies were 'lent about', the original plan to 'unite every writer's life to his works' 609, copies for LP 614, for Miss Aston 613, 'an hundred pounds' entrusted to HT, possibly a payment for the Lives 622 (but see note), Lord Hailes's

'description of Dryden' commended and his views on the chronology of D solicited 628; ('80) work resumed 651, (Apr.) 'I have not quite neglected my Lives' 654, they 'will take some time' 656, his ignorance of some of his poets, and even of their verses, Nichols's liking for *Addison* 657, hopes to 'despatch four or five of them' in one week 658, 'no great progress' 662, 'my Lives creep on' (May) 666, information from JW 668, applies to Farmer about Cambridge poets 673, 683, 'I wish they were well done' 679, 'I stay at home to work, and yet do not work diligently' (July); what can anyone 'hope I shall do better? yet I wish the work was over' 686, 686.2; 'the number of my lives now grows less', two volumes for HLT in a few days 687, 690, 691; the Reynoldses' failure to return the first 690; fails to persuade Lord Westcote to take charge of the Life of Lyttelton 688, 689 (and see 698); 'I have a great mind to end my work under the Virgin' (1 Aug.) 690, borrows books from Nichols, 'and with these he hopes to have done' 696, asks him to 'save the proof sheets of Pope' for FB 697, 'I still think to do the rest', will send the remaining vols. to Mrs. Boswell 701, 714, lonely 'but not diligent' 703, 'burthening the luggage cart' with books for his use at B'n 707.1, 'staid in town to work, without working much' (Oct.) 708, revises need not be sent (to B'n) 'unless something important occurs' 709, sends Nichols Croft's Life of Young 711.2; ('81) 'having now done my lives I shall have money to receive' (5 Mar.) 713, copies (perhaps) for Lord Auchinleck 714, JB to have the MS. 715 ('what did you make of all your copy?' 815), J asks for 'a set of the last lives' (i.e. vols. 5–10) 726, writes to F. A. Barnard about completing his and the King's sets, the booksellers have been penurious with author's copies 730.1, will send to LP 730.2, asks Nichols to exchange superfluous copies of 1–4 for copies of 5–10, and to send Steevens a complete set 'of the lives in 12mo' 731, offers a set to BL 732, HLT may give 'the books' (presumably the *Lives*) to Mrs. Horneck, 'I will give you another' 734, sends 5–10 to FB to be 'sent after the former to the gentleman whose name I do not know' 736.

(3) *Later Editions*. The Lives of the most Eminent English Poets; with Critical Observations on their Works. By Samuel Johnson. 16 June 1781. 4 vols. 8°. The same booksellers. One guinea. ('81) J asks Nichols 'how the octavo edition goes forward' 726, offers a set to Mary Prowse 729, sends Nichols draft title-pages 729.2.

The Lives, &c. A new Edition, corrected. 1783. 21*s*. ('82) J consults Malone about Pope's *Iliad* 798.1, 'my 'Lives' are reprinting' (Aug.), asks JB for 'the authour of Gray's character' 801, 'the advertisement for the new Edition', 'what will the Booksellers give me?', asks for 24 sets 'in plain calf', 'for the rest they may please themselves' 812, 'this is all that I can think on' (i.e. for the Advertisement) 812 (but perhaps a distinct letter from the preceding 812), 3,000 printed, had Lord Hailes a set? (see 607) 815, offers a copy to Thomas Wilson 820; ('83) sends JR a set 'as I suspect you to have lost your Lives' 829 (he had not), orders sets to be sent to Hastings, Chambers, and Joseph Fowke in India 833.2, 834, 835.1 (16), sends to Cruikshank 873 (2); ('84) offers Miss Langton a set 945, sends a set to Adams 1038.

Later Reference, to no specified edition. None of his writings 'more generally commended' 771.

(4) *Alphabetical List of the 'Lives'* mentioned in the Letters.

Addison: ('79) asks Nichols for 'Dennis upon Cato' 611; ('80) 654, Nichols thinks it 'the most *taking* of all that I have done' 657, 666. *Akenside:* ('80) admired by HLT 699. *Blackmore:* ('79) 611, ('80) 671, 686, 699. *Broome:* ('80) his share in Pope's *Odyssey* 668, 683. *Butler:* ('78) 581. *Collins:* ('80) 652, 666, 699. *Congreve:* ('80) 666, 'one of the best of the little lives' 672. *Cowley:* ('78) 'never had

any critical examination before' 581. *Denham:* ('78) 581. *Dryden:* ('78) 578.1, 581, 'very long' 582, 584; ('79) 'Lord Hailes's description' 628. *Duke:* ('78) 597. *Fenton:* ('80) 666, his share in Pope's *Odyssey* 668, on the Gout 694–5. *Gay:* ('80) 699. *Granville:* ('80) *British Enchanters*, &c. 653, 666, 691. *Gray:* ('80) Asks Farmer's help 673, ('82) asks JB for 'the authour of Gray's character' (W. J. Temple) 801, ('83) John Young's 'imitation of my stile' 863. *Hammond:* ('80) 671. *Hughes:* ('79) 611. *Lyttelton:* ('80) Asks Lord Westcote to nominate a biographer 688, his refusal 689, 'an ingenious scheme to save a day's work . . . defeated' 690, borrows his Works 696, asks Nichols if there is a Life prefixed to the Works 698, consults HLT 699. *Milton:* ('78) 'the next great life' 581, ('79) 603, hostile criticism 637. *Philips, Ambrose:* ('80) Asks Farmer for help 673, asks Nichols 683, ('83) mention of 'Mr. Ing' 875. *Philips, John:* ('79) 603. *Pitt:* ('80) 666. *Pope:* ('79–'80) Asks Nichols for Dennis against P 611, for Ruffhead's *Life* 696; ('80) collaborators in the *Odyssey* 668, his Epitaphs 697, proof sheets kept for F. Burney 697, borrows P's Works 696, ('82) 'the publication of the English Iliad' 798.1. *Prior:* ('80) 'The turtle and sparrow', 'the Conversation' 651, 654, 666. *Rowe:* ('80) 'cannot fill much paper' 654, 658, 666. *Sheffield:* ('80) 666. *Smith:* ('79) 603. *Stepney:* ('78) 597. *Swift:* ('80) asks Nichols for 'Swift's Works with Dr. Hawkesworths life' 696. *Thomson:* ('77) 515 ('80) 652. *Waller:* ('78) 580.1, 'never had any critical examination before' 581, ('79) 'professed to have imitated Fairfax' 611. *West:* ('80) Asks Lord Westcote for information 689. *Young:* ('80) 'I think I have got a life of Dr Young' 690, 'given me' 691, sends it to Nichols 711.2.

1780 (Aug.). 'One-and-Twenty'. J sends HLT (for her eye only) 'a short song of congratulation. . . . a beginner is always to be treated with tenderness' 691. *Poems* 196.

1781–2 (Nov. '81). The Beauties of Johnson. G. Kearsly, 3s. Rapidly reprinted; (? Nov. '82) Part II. G. Kearsly, 2s. 6d. ('82) 'said to have got money to the collector' 775, 'the production of I know not whom' 781, asks Kearsley to bring him the last edition 782.

1782. [J. Thomson Callendar] Deformities of Dr. Samuel Johnson. Edinburgh, for the Author, 1s. L iv. 499. ('82) If it has the success of *The Beauties* 'I shall be still a more extensive benefactor' 775.

Epitaph on Henry Thrale in Streatham Church. See *Th* 542, *Anecd.* 238 (*JM* i. 237–9), H. W. Bromhead, *Heritage of St. Leonard's* 1932, 24. ('83)

'left me to write his epitaph' 835.1 (17).

1784. Translation from the Greek Anthology. Published by Bennet Langton in Vol. xi of *Works* 1787. *Poems* 208. J beguiled sleepless nights 'by turning Greek epigrams into Latin. I know not if I have not turned a hundred' 954 (see note). J's offer to write a preface, not written, to a posthumous collection of the works of John Scott. (16 Sept.) 1012.1.

Dedication for Burney. The publication of 998.1 and of the full text of 984 and 1004 reveals J's authorship of the dedication of CB's *History of Music* 1776 and *Commemoration of Handel* 1785.

JOHNSON'S ENGLISH

I offer a somewhat casual collection of obsolete words and senses, of words or senses noted by J as innovations or deprecated by him, or uses otherwise of possible interest. I have not indexed the words pilloried in 549, where J parodies current journalese.

I. Vocabulary

admission. 'to prejudices' 159.

advertisement. 194.1, a letter (for HT) to the electors of S'k.

age. 691 'Sir John Lade is come to a.'

airy. 80 'a. civilities'. 640 'I take physick . . . and fancy that I grow light and a.'

almost. 643 'nothing a. is purchased' except necessities. See *L* ii. 446, 530, for the use by J and others of 'a. nothing', sometimes regarded as a Scotticism.

alternate. 662, 'a. diet', see note; 675.

amuse. 329 (p. 369) 'a place where the imagination is more amused cannot easily be found'. 333 he describes a journey in a storm as 'uncommonly amusing'. 722 'I give it (his 'uneasiness') little vent, and a. it as I can'. 1029.2 he asks his correspondent not to impute his silence 'to idleness, or amusement of any other kind'.

ancient. 53 'our a. authours' (English authors before Spenser).

apology. 472 'I have only this a. to make for presuming to trouble you . . . — that a stranger's petition . . . can be easily refused'.

appendage = appendix (in a book). 691.

at. 'at London' 1028.

Atlantick. 206, Dr. Onions suggests that this may be a gallicism; the present passage is the only one quoted in *OED*. The *format atlantique* as defined by Littré is not what we commonly call folio, but is made up of unfolded sheets. The largest sheet of hand-made paper, if folded to form two leaves, would not be as large as some atlases.

attractive. 1017 'a very powerful a.'

bedrider (?). See note on 556.

berlin. 165.1 'the Berlin in which we could not get places last week'.

big. 282 'a bigger bull'. 322 'a bigger egg'. For J's use of the word see *L* iii. 348, v. 425, and my note on 322.

bill. 143 'the bills were yesterday delivered to me by Mr. Wedderburne'.

blackmore 550.1.

bolt. 654 'I think to b. upon you at Bath'.

book, where we usually say *copy*; frequent, especially of author's or presentation copies. 382 'send me one . . . of the corrected books'. 369.2 George III read J's *Journey* 'aloud to the Queen, and the Queen could not stay to get the King's book, but borrowed Dr. Hunter's'. A minute of the Delegates of the Oxford Press, 25 July 1711, has '200 books of any book printed by the University'. See my notes on 131, 176.

box-club. 406 'Lichfield is full of Box clubs'.

bring. 357 'Mrs. Thrale brought . . . five girls running', 217.

bringer. 640.1 'the b. of this letter'.

broken. 658 'b. is a very bad word in the city'.

*canal = '*ornamental water' 591. A c. in the modern sense is *navigation*, q.v.

candour. 194.1 'a man . . . acquainted with the c. of those who must be judges of his conduct'.

catarrhous. 785 'a c. cough'.

character almost always means *repute* or the like. 115.1 'c. makes opposition hopeless'. 318 'the only one of my relations who ever rose in fortune above penury, or in c. above neglect'. 524 (Dodd's) 'moral c. is very bad: I hope all is not true that is charged upon him'. 936 'Your paper . . . will certainly raise your c.'

chirurgeon 684, 756.3, 938; the form *surgeon* also occurs.

chief. 144 'I was sent for by the c. Minister the Earl of Bute'.

circumduction. 952 'an account of my health. You might have had it with less c.' (Langton instead of writing direct had asked Lord Portmore to inquire.)

close. 926 (Cecilia Thrale was on a visit to Cator) 'I think well of her for pleasing him, and of him for being pleased; and at the close am delighted to find him delighted'. Hill explains this as = *in fine.* I have not found it elsewhere.

clown. 326 (p. 356) 'the cunning that clowns never can be without' (the Macraes).

comatous. 1033.1.

come on. 183 'I hope something will yet c. on it'.

comfortable. 925.1 'a Friends letter is always c.'

companiable. 862 Levett 'was useful and c.' (*companionable* 1791).

conduct. 387.2 'the transition from the protection of others to our own c. is a very awful point of human existence'.

congratulate. 338 'they c. our return'.

contemplation. 537 'a workhouse which they have in *contemplation*—there's the word now'.

conversation(e). 632 'Mrs. Vesey's c.', 681.

cross (prep.). 298 'c. the Atlantick'.

danger. 418 'as the doctors say, out of d.'

darkling. 311.1 'My eye is yet so dark . . . I have had a poor d. week'.

daughter-in-law = step-d. 142.

delitescence. 483.

difficultly. 329 (p. 372).

direction. 508 'her letter is not at hand, and I know not the d.'

discontented. of a temporary emotion. 'I was . . . d. that I heard nothing yesterday'. 553 'she was d. that I wrote only Madam to her, and dear Madam to Mrs. Williams'. 1142.

discover = *show.* 875 'I discovered no reliques of disease'.

discuss = *disperse.* 303.2.

disentanglement (dramatic). 366, see note.

disgust. 132.3 Frank Barber 'being disgusted in the house . . . ran away to sea'. Jane Austen describes Jane Fairfax in *Emma* as 'disgustingly reserved'. When J condemned *Lycidas* as pastoral, and as 'easy, vulgar, and therefore disgusting' he meant much less than would be meant today.

dismission. 793.

drank (p. part.). 658.

dry. 855 'the journal now . . . grows very dry'.

easy. 699 'any good of myself I am not very e. to believe'.

enthusiastically. 853 'a letter of consolation . . . piously, though not e. written'.

fancied. 409 'a f. dress'.

fee. 322 'there was no officer gaping for a f.'

feel. 269 '*Feeling* for tenderness or sensibility is a word merely colloquial of late introduction'. 647 'poor Mrs. Byron is a feeler' (see L iv. 503).

feudist. 206 (p. 217) 'the collection (i.e. library) of an eminent Civilian, F., or Mathematician'. Not in J's Dictionary.

fire room. 327 (p. 362) 'the house . . . we were told . . . had eleven fire rooms'.

flesh. 279 'f. is very dear'. 386.1 'you must have something not f.' (for dinner).

Frenchman. 1003, see note.

fume. 406 'a lady in a f. withdraws her name' (from the Amicable Society of Lichfield).

genius. 686 'my g. is always in extremes'. 736.1 Mrs. Lennox 'is a great g.'

give over. 362.1 'I do not intend to g. it over' (= *up*).

go to. 686 'I will end my letter and go to Blackmore's life'. *go to tea* (1141), *cards, prayers* does not necessarily imply going into another room.

gotten. 413, 693.

government. 367 'There is . . . within your g. . . . one Chauncy Lawrence' (to Warren Hastings).

great. 295 'a new edition of my g. Dictionary' (i.e. the folio not the 8vo abridgement); cf. 209 'my large Dictionary'. 581 'the next g. life I purpose to be Milton's'.

habitation. 551 'send the *Bibliographia Britannica* to my h.' See note.

heartless = in low spirits 1029.2.

here is, &c. 'You are not to suppose that h. are to be any more towns' 323.

hospital. 116.1 'a public h. and public lectures'. The reference is to the University of Edinburgh.

house = *college* (Oxford). 114.1 'few men stay in the houses who are qualified to live elsewhere'. 167 'a scholar of the H.' (University Coll.). 274.2 'University college, or any other h.' 533 (Gwynn) 'is still in the best houses, and at the best tables' (not a certain example of this sense). In 468 'the h.' seems to be the H. of Commons.

however. 223 'Write to me h.' (= 'in any case'), and so 405, 566.

humm = *hoax.* 590. Not in J's Dictionary.

huspelled. 554, see note.

illwiller. 684.

immediate = *direct.* J 178 distinguishes his 'particular and i. acknowledgements' to his correspondent from his 'general thanks' communicated through another.

immediately. 54, J asks Chambers to give a message to Warton, 'to whom I should have written i. but that I know not if he be yet come back'. 486, see note. 739.1.

independently on. 321 (p. 345).

indolence. 976 'that voluntary debility, which modern language is content to term i.' J in his Dictionary gives the Ciceronian sense 'freedom from pain' and also 'laziness, inattention, listlessness'.

inimical. 860 'the winter has been, in modern phrase, very i. to' (himself).

initials for Christian names: 'who is bound to recollect initials?' 895. When few people had more than one Christian name initials were not much used.

interview, of a prolonged sojourn of two persons in the same house. 541, 544 'I shall not love you less after our i.';

J and Boswell were to spend some time together at Ashbourne.

irremeable. 191, 972 (Virgil's irremeabilis unda).

lag. 558 'How long do you stay ...? why should you be the l.?' J in his Dictionary had quoted Pope and Dryden for this.

large. 4 'large Notes'.

lecture-room. 1003.2 'our little pretty l. at Streatham'.

less = *smaller.* 259; 659 'I think I grow rather l.'

lesson. 405 'Did I think ... that I should write a l. to my mistress?'

let ... to. 449 'do not let an event to disturb you'.

like. J seldom uses the verb, being content to *love* without too nice discrimination. See, however, 105.1, 'shall we like each other ... as we liked once?'; 135 'I like his wife'; 313 'caressed, and invited, and treated, and liked'; 703.1 'you love a book ... that you have had a great part of your life. ... You can never say that your [J has omitted part of his sentence] a very late acquaintance; you can only like, or only admire'.

like. 478 'there is in the exhibition ... a picture of the house at Streatham. ... This is something, or something l.'

lilly, lolly. 553, see note.

literary property. 349 'Copyright or l. P.' This is the general term for what we now call copyright; in J's time *copyright* (far oftener, *copy*) is usually the right in a particular piece of work; 'he sold the copy for £10'.

look (up) on. 75 'pass an hour in looking on them' (certain MSS.). 201 'I like it (a book) the more, as I look more upon it.'

loss. 657 'I have no l. of my mistress', see note.

lunes. 591, see note.

Mass house. 677.

mean. For 'in the mean' see on 874 (2), iii. 86. But 'in the mean' I have noted, in an unpublished letter in the collection of Col. Parker of Browsholme (T. Shaw to G. Holme 7 June 1722) 'In the mean I am, dear Sir', &c.

mediterranean. 322 (the Buller of Buchan) 'of height not stupendous, but to a m. visiter uncommon'.

memento. 605.1 'if any Mementos of mine could do you good'.

middle. 381 'the m. counties'.

mind. 387 J hopes to visit Taylor, 'if you have any m. of me'.

miss. 583 'Miss (i.e. Queeney) has seen the camp'. 217 'you . . . have brought a little Miss'.

moral. 286 'a m. certainty'.

mortality. 585 'I call . . . on the Burneys, where you are at the top of m.'

moss. 326 (p. 355) 'Moss in Scotland, is Bog in Ireland'.

mould. 482 (Boswell) 'carries with him two or three good resolutions; I hope they will not m. upon the road'.

move. 834 'it was not fit for me to m. a question in public, which I was not qualified to discuss'.

Mrs. of spinsters 956, see note.

mum. 292 'but m., it is a secret', 944 'you are resolved to keep m.'

mumm. 606 'it is a m. to see who will speak first'.

my. 49.1, 51.1 'My Lord Corke'. This use never, I think, appears in later letters.

navigation. 246, 578. *See canal.*

need. 399 'he needed have no scruples'; 490.

nerve, nervous. 329 (p. 373) 'my nerves (i.e. muscles) seem to grow weaker', 622 'weariness is a temporary resolution of the nerves'; 859 'the nervous system . . . somewhat enfeebled'; 909 'as it is not very properly called, a nervous constitution'. This sense is in J's Dictionary called 'medical cant'.

nice. 207.1, see note.

occur. 709 (to Nichols) 'you need never send back the revises unless something important occurs'—that is, occurs to you, comes into your mind? In 542 'occurrences' probably means 'happenings' not 'thoughts'; see the context. J defines the word as *incident.*

officious. 906 'that social officiousness by which we are . . . endeared to one another'. 1003 'a very kind and o. neighbour'.

one another. 184, see note.

part. 1006.1 'when I parted from London'.

passion. 888.1 'if pity be a p. ever to come in use'.

perequitate. 681 'perambulate or p. High street'.

phenomena. 1017 'the *phaenomena* of sickness'.

philosophy. 258 'p. will not warrant much hope in a lotion'. 259 'philosophical lectures'. 277 'chimistry or experimental p.', see note.

physical. 945 'the p. race' (physicians).

physick. 'in common phrase, a purge': J's Dictionary, and that is the regular meaning in the letters, e.g. 663. In 904 it is opposed to regimen, and means drugs in general.

piazza 322.

practice. 617 'Bromfield . . . by his p. appears not to suspect an apoplexy'.

presently. 937 'p. after I had sent away my last letter, I received your . . . packet'.

preserved. 911 'the characters (in a tragedy) . . . as conceived or p.' (sustained).

presume. 'hopes of excellence which I once presumed' 686.

pretender. 672 'a candidate for a school . . . to which . . . there are seventeen pretenders'.

probable. 79 'an easy and I think a very p. remedy for indigestion'. Here, and when J said to Lowe 'Your picture is noble and p.' (*L* iv. 203), I think he meant 'deserving approbation'. Cf. Ker's Dryden i. 123 'means . . . which I thought p. for the attaining of that end'; *Treasure Island* c. xii: 'casting about . . . to find some p. excuse'. The title of a book on distemper in cattle, 1753, is 'a Probable Scheme'.

problematical. 562 'our success is yet as the French call it, p.'

prognostick = *prognosis* 749.

publick. In J 'the p.' usually means the p. interest, the common weal, or the government; a clear example is 891, 'when . . . the ministry gave so high a price for money, all the money that could be disengaged from trade was lent to the p.' Other examples: 680 'now you are at ease about the p.' (when the Gordon Riots had subsided); 799 'of the p. I have nothing to say'; 920 'the present dreadful confusion of the p.'; 922 'to a sick man what is the p.?' Cf. *L* iv. 335: 'He wished Lord Orford's pictures . . . might be purchased by the publick.' The modern sense is seen in 176 'the p. has no further claim upon me', 438, 524 'the voice of the p.' (asking that Dodd might be reprieved).

push. 583 'I never could get anything from her (Mrs. Montagu) but by pushing a face.'

quiet. 414 'people go into the country to be at q.'; so 679.

race. 945 'the physical r.' (physicians).

relation = relationship. 705 'his want, his relation, and his merit, which excited his lordship's charity'; 760.

repellent = repulse. 549 'forty such repellents from Mrs. P——'.

reverberation not of noise. 323 (350), see note.

review = revise. 269 'When you have reviewed it (a poem), let me see it again'. 748 'I would never r. the work of an anonymous authour'.

rout. 564 'Let me know what the ladies of your (Lucy Porter's) r. say to it' (his head by Nollekens).

rucks. 554, see note.

run out, exceed one's income. 743 'I . . . applaud your resolution not to r. o.'

rustication. 869 'whether this short r. has done me any good I cannot tell'. Not in J's Dictionary.

salute = kiss (?). 329 (p. 367), see note.

Scotch. J like Boswell often used this word, the rejection of which is modern. 320, 378, 398, 510. I think *Scottish* occurs in the letters once only, 344 'my S. friends'. *Scotsman* 528.

scrupulosity. 660 'the s. of his physicians, who never bled him copiously'. See *L* iv. 5 for J's fondness for the word.

sculpture = engraving. 206 (p. 217).

security. 657 's. will produce danger'.

sick. 955 'the taylor . . . brought me a s. dress'.

solicitate (?) 736.1. J often uses *solicit(e)*.

solicitor. 103 'the activity of a few solicitors may produce great advantages' (in getting subscribers for his Shakespeare).

speak to. 657 'Pray s. to Queeney to write again'.

state. 13 'each party should draw up . . . his own s. of the case'.

stay. 264.1 'if you write on Saturday direct to . . . if you s. longer, to . . .'; 410. 565 'I did not s. to add my voice to that of the publick'.

strike = bushel. 279.

sure. 547 'pine-apples it is s. we have none'; so 575. We say 'I am sure', but usually 'it is certain'.

survivance. 306.

taking. 657 'Mr. Nicols holds that Addison is the most *taking* of all that I have done'.

tea-board. 193.1.

the. 637 'some old gentlewomen at the next door'. 14 'by the return of the post'. 643 'the Parliament'. Contrast 839.1 'at club'.

thee occurs in 12, our only letter to J's wife. I have not noticed it elsewhere.

think of. 898. Hill suspected the text, the original is untraced. J usually, perhaps always, wrote *think on*.

timorsome. 767 'Dr. Lawrence who is ten times more *timorsome* than is your Jebb'.

touch. 857 'I must t. my journal'.

trace = trait. 645.1 'traces of character'.

truce. 538 'take t. with ipecacuanha'.

try. 883 'the gout is now trying at my feet'.

tumour = tumidity. 935.1, 1022.

Turkish. 284 'Never a letter! . . . This is T. usage'.

unroosted. 679 'I am sorry that you should be so outrageously u.' (the riots of 1780 had driven the Thrales from Bath).

use. 888.1 'as Sheward uses to be'.

vacancy. J suggests that one of Thrale's clerks be sent to Brighton, where he would benefit from 'air, and v., and novelty' 426.

valuable. 268.1 'a very v. family' (the Thrales). Boswell writes of 'my v. wife'.

vellication. 917 'these vellications of my breast'.

vex. 479 'I shall v., unless it does you good'.

want. 304 'if my letters can do you any good, it is not fit that you should w. them'.

way. 386 'ask Murphy the w. to Lord Mansfield'. 1104 'if I could know when the cart would come I would take care to have somebody in the w.'

well. 679 'my Lives go on but slowly. . . . I wish they were well done'. 340 'I know Mrs. Boswell wished me well to go'.

will. 343 'gather me all you can, and do it quickly, or I w. and shall do without

it'. See note. (Nelson wrote to Lady Hamilton 24 Oct. 1778 'I shall and will know everything as soon as the Marquis is gone'.) 589.2 'I will be glad if you will find me the bill' is surprising.

work = *needle-work*, &c. 864 'Your (Susannah Thrale's) time passes . . . in Devotion, reading, w., and Company'; so 872.

would. 461 'I would (should 1788) be glad to take my usual round'. 708 'I would be glad to love all that love you'.

yester night. 427.

youngling. 478 'my visit to the younglings' (Thrale children).

II. Spelling

J's spelling, except of proper names, is fairly uniform, and the differences from modern use are relatively few. He often ends a word with a single consonant which modern use doubles, e.g. 822 *ilness*, 549 *mil*, 825 *recal*, 763 *caled* (157 *butt* is perhaps a slip). This is noticeable in proper names, e.g. *Boswel, Pot, Dod.* Final *-ck* in words like *almanack* and *musick* is almost universal, as is *-our* in *authour*, &c., *-ye* is common, e.g. *lye, dye*; so *-red* for *-ered* as in *hindred*, and plural *-ies* as *journies*.

Miscellaneous: *abby* 675, *ashma* 946.1 (*bis*), *cloaths* 710, *Council* (for *-sel*) 461, *diner* 1007, *dos* 455, 636, *eugh* 336, *enervaiting* 934, *flower* (i.e. *flour*) 327, *gayety* 511, *gypsey* 657, *happyest* 638, *oister* 649, *peny* 518, *persue* 332 and elsewhere, *pouns* 12, *skrimage* 675, *solicite* 519, *spritely* 550, *stuborn* 659, *unkle* 280.

III. Grammar, Etc.

Such archaic flavour as J's letters have is almost entirely a matter of style; it is little due to vocabulary, and hardly at all due to construction or idiom. Apart from a more liberal use of the subjunctive, and a few uses like 'I know not' or 'is become', I find little that in this kind is at variance with modern custom.

am, &c., *to* of a right or obligation: 871 (J had expected a letter) 'he that goes away, you know, is to write'. Cf. his remark to Percy: 'we are to be as rude as we please'.

was = *were*: 895 'the letter that you was answering'. This is the only example I have noted.

being+another participle: 531 'being going soon to Lichfield'.

Plural of surnames with Mr., &c., prefixed: 114 'Mr Langtons are well'. 1148 'Mr Johnson expected Master Perkins's yesterday'. 793, 816 '(the) Miss Colliers'.

me, &c., without *-self*: 183 'Has Mr. Langton got him the little horse?' 1022 'I could not without great difficulty button me at my knees'.

PUNCTUATION

IV. Punctuation

J's punctuation though not always careful has little to mislead even a careless reader. I have occasionally written a cautionary note.

An interesting specimen of the emphatic comma is 396 'Do, send the cloaths'. Cole wrote to Walpole 30 Sept. 1780 'Do, be so kind to gratify . . .'; cf. 15 'I thought my Letter would be long but it is now, ended'.

Two obsolete uses are seen in 9 'a backwardness to determine their degrees of merit, is nothing peculiar to me, you may, if you please still have what I can say'.